Life Studies

AN ANALYTIC READER

Life Studies

AN ANALYTIC READER

SEVENTH EDITION

EDITED BY

David Cavitch

Tufts University

Bedford/St. Martin's

BOSTON ♦ NEW YORK

For Bedford / St. Martin's

Developmental Editor: Joanne Diaz
Production Editor: Karen S. Baart
Production Supervisor: Joe Ford
Director of Marketing: Karen Melton
Marketing Manager: Brian Wheel
Editorial Assistant: Caroline Thompson
Copyeditor: Nancy Bell Scott
Text Design: Anna George
Cover Design: Donna Lee Dennison
Cover Art: Info Transfer by Barry Waldman
Composition: Stratford Publishing Services, Inc.
Printing and Binding: Haddon Craftsmen, an R. R. Donnelley & Sons Company

President: Charles H. Christensen
Editorial Director: Joan E. Feinberg
Director of Editing, Design, and Production: Marcia Cohen
Managing Editor: Elizabeth M. Schaaf

Library of Congress Control Number: 00–106437

For information, write: Bedford / St. Martin's, 75 Arlington Street, Boston, MA 02116
(617-399-4000)

ISBN: 0–312–25818–6

Acknowledgments

Diane Ackerman, "The Chemistry of Love." From *A Natural History of Love* by Diane Ackerman. Copyright © 1992 by Diane Ackerman. Reprinted by permission of Random House, Inc.

Kurt Andersen, "Animation Nation," *The New Yorker,* June 16, 1997. Reprinted by permission; ©1997 The New Yorker Magazine, Inc. All rights reserved.

Ian Angell, "Winners and Losers in the Information Age." *Society,* November/December, 1996. Copyright © 1996 by Transaction Publishers; all rights reserved.

TO INSTRUCTORS

Teachers of composition know that good writing emerges from strong responses to good reading. *Life Studies* has been a popular reader chiefly because the selections truly matter to students. They think about the readings and are moved by them. They try to attain in their writing the convincing views and stimulating effects of the essays they have read. The seventh edition strengthens the analytic approach to each author's purpose and method by including illuminating questions and challenging writing topics that prompt critical comprehension and well-reasoned responses. In addition, a new feature called *Forum* encourages students to think independently and argue their point about controversial issues raised in grouped selections. The Forums offer contrasting views on "Work and Power" and "Guns and Aims." Forum writing topics ask students to focus on privilege and powerlessness in the workplace, and on the pros and cons of gun control, among other issues. The introduction, newly revised around a brief essay by Bernard Cooper, gives practical advice for reading and writing analytically. An added appendix offers guidelines and examples for using sources in writing.

A new part titled "Learning Curves" examines our schooling both in and out of the classroom. The selections balance the aims of educators and the tribulations of students. All chapters have been updated to renew their relevance. "Media Images" adds a movie review of *Titanic* as well as critical assessments of film production and Internet sites. Each part adds major new essays. *Life Studies* continues to introduce fresh voices. Of the eighty selections, twenty-five are new to this edition, and seventeen of these new pieces have never appeared in a composition reader.

With these revisions, each thematic part now progresses from personal to general awareness. The selections begin with self-knowledge and lead into considerations of the larger world. The topics address our self-images; our family relationships; our love for people and creatures outside the family; our identification with religious, ethnic, or racial groups; our fateful schools; our compromising or fulfilling work roles; our connection to valued possessions; our cultural images reflected by films, magazines, and computer screens; and our dilemmas over moral issues that cannot be sidestepped. In addition to the essays, each part contains one short story that develops the theme imaginatively. Each part opens with a number of

Insights—succinct, often controversial statements by well-known writers whose colloquy of opinions and poems offers a lively introduction to the theme. Next, each part offers Focusing by Writing: warm-up questions that can be used for in-class writing exercises or to generate class discussion. The Focusing topics are framed to show students that they—like the authors of the Insights—possess knowledge and opinions about the topics in the chapter. The questions raise students' awareness of the issues and underscore the significance of their own experience. Instructors may wish to use some Focusing topics for longer writing assignments as well.

Preceding each selection is a biographical and introductory headnote. Each selection is then followed by three categories of questions that promote analytic reading and writing. Analyzing This Selection encourages students to consider the reading's content and meaning as well as the writer's methods and approaches. A question called The Writer's Method asks students to focus on effective writing strategies. Next, the Analyzing Connections questions ask students to connect, integrate, and analyze the reading with earlier material. (Because many instructors flexibly assign their own order of readings, other links are suggested in the instructor's manual, *Resources for Teaching LIFE STUDIES*, by Debra Spark. But as a model for students, a pattern of progressive, expansive reflection is built into the book itself.) Finally, Analyzing by Writing offers a topic and suggests possible approaches to developing clear and convincing views.

To help students acquire composition techniques, the book opens with an introduction that stresses attentive, critical reading as a means to improving writing. "Finding a Trail: An Introduction to Reading and Writing Analytically" offers guidelines and methods for improving reading comprehension. This revised introduction is built around an entertaining essay, Bernard Cooper's "The Fine Art of Sighing," which is annotated to suggest how a student might respond to it during a close reading. A brief discussion of Cooper's essay shows students how to pursue their observations and develop them into insightful viewpoints. The introduction also identifies and illustrates common writing problems.

Advice on using sources, presented in a new appendix, follows MLA guidelines. Examples illustrating the differences between quoting, paraphrasing, and summarizing draw on the selections in *Life Studies*. A rhetorical index to the selections appears in the back of the book, and Debra Spark's *Resources for Teaching LIFE STUDIES* offers suggestions for dealing with each piece in class. The instructor's manual also offers further writing suggestions.

Many instructors helped improve this book by responding to a questionnaire about the sixth edition. I am grateful for the careful consideration given by Anne Beaufort, American University; Susan A. Borden, University of Minnesota; Jane Elizabeth Dougherty, Bentley College; Diane H. Feigenson, Fairfield University; S. Rosemary Kolich, Saint Mary College; Loren P. Quiring, University of Wisconsin; Beverly Richardson, Porterville

College; Rita W. Tesler, New Jersey City University; James S. Torrence, Bellevue Community College; and Gregory A. Wilson, Brandeis University.

The exceptionally capable people at Bedford/St. Martin's provided much assistance. Joanne Diaz, the developmental editor of the previous edition, returned as a freelance editor to renew a fruitful collaboration. Many fresh selections and helpful features in the apparatus reflect her unstinting resourcefulness, discriminating judgment, and excellent sense of the class-room. Christopher Stripinis cleared permissions, and Nancy Bell Scott copyedited the manuscript with a light yet sure touch. Karen Baart imagi-natively and skillfully guided the production of this edition, and Elizabeth Schaaf carefully managed the production process. Once again, Charles Christensen and Joan Feinberg gave their vision and high standards to the entire endeavor.

CONTENTS

1. SELF-IMAGES   11

3. SIGNIFICANT OTHERS   125

5. LEARNING CURVES   253

8. MEDIA IMAGES   457

9. DILEMMAS 521

A critic of medical ethics examines the justifications for cloning and provides his own argument against this "pollution and perversion" of human procreation.

A journalist remembers his life as a young door-to-door salesman and his response to an episode of police brutality.

A world-renowned pediatrician meditates on the pros and cons of children playing with toy guns.

Though the Second Amendment possesses significant historical and ideological importance, it is a premodern law that does not help us with today's gun control debate.

Life Studies

AN ANALYTIC READER

FINDING A TRAIL

*An Introduction to Reading
and Writing Analytically*

For the Good of It   Good readers become good writers. And every attentive response to good reading stimulates new possibilities of improvement in our writing.

Reading is the most important, and the most pleasurable, training for writers. From essays, fiction, and poetry we acquire a vastly increased vocabulary of knowledge and an array of models for more expressive, analytical ways of thinking about our world and ourselves. From reading we take in special verbal tools and methods that we use in writing. But we can't just swallow words and digest the meanings and uses of them. We have to become active intellectually and imaginatively in order to read with clear perception and firm emotional response. This introduction offers some practical advice on how to read and write more *analytically*, an approach explained in the next paragraph. The particular suggestions will prove effective as you practice them again and again. Like playing the piano, reading and writing are acquired abilities that no one is born with. But as we become good at what we're doing, the pleasure of doing it grows deeper and richer.

Analysis Defined   The literary meaning of *analysis* is to examine the parts and details of a piece of writing in order to explain their function and effects when all the parts work together. The basic premise of analysis is that style and form work together with ideas and emotions. The analytic reader clarifies what an author says by taking note of matters such as particular words, figures of speech, sentence structures, and links between sentences, paragraph development, the order of paragraphs, the structure of the piece as a whole, and the author's explicit and implicit attitudes — called *tone* — toward the subject and toward the reader.

That's a lot of parts and details to analyze. To keep track of them, a reader has to be systematic, and the full analysis must accumulate step by step. For instance, an observation about a writer's colloquial use of the word *colossal* may lead to another observation about her chummy tone toward the reader, and discovering that attitude may further illuminate how she controls the flow of ideas from one paragraph to the next. Good writers are always in control of their writing, even when they sound casual and spontaneous. They want readers to grasp their intended meaning. They lay out as clear a path as they can to define their exact meaning, which is often not simple or easy to arrive at. This introduction demonstrates ways to pick up and follow the trail of the author's intentions.

Focus Your Attention   When you read, give an essay your undivided attention. It is probably a good idea to turn off the radio or stereo or television. You need to be able to hear how an essay sounds in your head. Read one or two paragraphs aloud to help you discover and express spoken inflections to the writing. Then return to reading silently, and listen for the tones of the written voice. "Heard melodies are sweet," wrote John Keats, "but those unheard are sweeter." The poet was not urging students to turn off the stereo, but nevertheless follow his suggestion to open your mind to the vibrations of silent things.

Approach a selection with an intention to read it word by word. Don't skim, and don't skip over details. At least once through the whole essay, take it all in, so that its full meaning will be accessible in your mind for you to consider. There is nothing in this anthology that takes very long to read. You are reading not for the broad outline or vague gist of what is said, but to grasp the full substance, both explicit and implicit, and to see how an essay is developed.

Read Actively   Begin with the title because the title is part of an essay. Paying attention to the title is a good first step in analytic reading. Be aware of what the title tells you or leads you to expect. For example, from the title of Nora Ephron's essay, "Shaping Up Absurd," you can foresee the author's critical attitude toward her subject, an attitude that comes across throughout the essay. The title of Raymond Carver's essay, "My Father's Life," defines the subject matter but does not hint at the author's attitude. Carver's title fittingly withholds that suggestion because the essay explores his ambivalent, hard-to-define attitudes about his father. Some titles intrigue us with their ambiguity. Wendy Lesser's title, "The Conversion," cleverly suggests a weightier subject than the author presents. Susan Allen Toth's title, "Boyfriends," is deliberately general. Such titles acquire their specific meaning only after you plunge into the essay. Some titles reveal their appropriateness, or lack of it, only after you have reached the conclusion. All titles are worth reconsidering after you know where the whole essay leads.

Continue your analytic methods as you move through the essay. Give close attention to details by making observations as you read. Read with a pencil in hand, and use the pages of your anthology (only in your own copy, please!) to jot down your responses. Underline or circle whatever sounds important as you read. Words, phrases, and suggestions of meaning that seem prominent as you read are reliable indicators of what is important in the essay. Circle words you don't understand, and try to figure out what they mean from the context. The circles will remind you to look them up later. When you compare the dictionary definition with your initial sense of the word, you will discover the precise shade of meaning that the author attains in that particular word choice. Write comments in the margins. You will come back to them too. Some of your comments will refer directly to the essay's contents, and some will record your own associations or reactions.

Readers and writers learn a great deal from using a dictionary constantly. This anthology encourages you to look up words; glosses are provided only for words that do not appear in a good American dictionary. For convincing testimony about the importance of dictionaries, you might want to read Ha Jin's story about his army service in China, "Ocean of Words."

Read in Person   If you begin with good intentions to read analytically but find that your attention is waning and your mind wandering, perhaps the selection itself is at fault. When you are too bored to read well, ask yourself, Why is this writing so uninteresting? What is the author doing here that makes it harder to pay attention? Whether the fault is in the essay or in your reading of it, don't succumb to passivity, reading pages without noting or remembering what they are about. Like half-conscious driving, half-conscious reading can lead to no good end.

As you read, reformulate in your mind what the author is saying. Try to put the author's point into your words, even if you doubt or don't like what is said. Get the ideas up off the page and into your head. The more conscious you are of the author's thoughts, the more energized you will be to respond with thoughts of your own, in either agreement or disagreement. Be sure to record in the margin wherever you balk over an assertion or concept. Are you disagreeing? Are you puzzled? Take your mental pulse and note it. The good thing about questions is that they provoke response. Perhaps your question can be dealt with in class discussion. Sometimes you will want to answer your own question later — perhaps by writing on the topic.

Don't hesitate to include personal associations in your margin comments. Does a passage remind you of something that once happened to you? something you read or heard? something you learned in another class? Make a note of it. If the connection can be expressed briefly, your margin note will suffice. But sometimes the connections that occur as you read are worth pursuing later with a more lengthy response in a notebook or journal. The mark or note in your margin will lead you back to the thought for further development. Connections you make while reading help you to assimilate and thoroughly comprehend new material. They also frequently lead to terrific writing topics.

Paragraph Development   A good way to proceed analytically is to note how each paragraph serves the writer's purpose. Writers shape their thoughts into paragraphs in order to focus concentrated attention (theirs and yours). Identify what seems to be the main substance of important paragraphs, even when you are unsure that you grasp the point. You will later return to the paragraph to understand its purpose better. Of course, you know the usefulness of locating a topic sentence in a paragraph, when you can find one. A topic sentence states the main substance, and other sentences help make it convincing by arguing or illustrating the point. The topic often appears in the first or second sentence or in the final sentence. Note where the paragraph's strongest emphasis occurs. Does the paragraph lead off with an emphatic assertion followed by sentences supporting it, or does the paragraph progressively build up to a conclusive statement at the end? Either pattern can give effective *development* to the main point.

Identifying the substance and development of each paragraph helps you to notice also how the paragraphs fit together — that is, how the essay is organized. Look for the connecting link, or *transition*, which is usually but not always in the first sentence and which echoes or refers to the preceding paragraph. What is added to the subject as the author proceeds? Now you need to note the new paragraph's purpose.

The sequence, or order, of paragraphs establishes the author's path or direction of thought. Paragraphs cannot be jumbled into another sequence and still work effectively in an essay. They are not in random order like items on a list; they are more like chapters in a novel. They make full sense only in their intended sequence.

As you observe an author's paragraph development and organization, you will acquire a sense of the author's goal in writing the essay. You will begin to say, "I see what this is getting at." Or, if the essay is a narration of events, "I see what's shaping up here." This impression of the essay's overall coherence may build up clearly during your first careful reading. But often it comes after repeated study. In this book the questions on Analyzing This Selection that appear at the end of each essay can help you reconsider its content and approach.

Tone   One constant guide to the author's intended meaning is his or her tone. In the margin, try to describe the writer's voice that is heard silently inside your head. Any voice includes tones that convey more than the words themselves mean — that impart the speaker's attitudes and implications. The tones of voice in written language are more subtle than in spoken language, but they are nevertheless essential to the meaning. You can begin to identify the writer's tone of voice if you first approach it as a more general quality, one of *manner*. Is the writer formal? humorous? solemn? earnest? casual? authoritative? ironic? straightforward? playful? argumentative? Come up with two or three adjectives that best describe the writer's general manner and jot them down in the margin. Then closely examine the passage that prompted your observation, and find the specific words and phrases that fit your description of the writer. Underline those words. Try to hear them as spoken words in order to check the accuracy of your description. Do they illustrate the manner you noted? Perhaps you will need to adjust your initial description of the writer's manner as you recognize the nuances of the language that express the tone of voice.

A writer's word choice expresses a particular slant, or viewpoint, toward the subject. A specialized or technical vocabulary establishes the tone of an expert authority, such as a sportswriter who addresses an audience of fans who understand the jargon of baseball or horse racing. Sportswriters also use many figures of speech to suggest the excitement of the game. The statement "Rice exploded the horsehide into the stands" doesn't make much sense to an ordinary reader or even to any too literal-minded fan. The selections in this anthology seldom use such jargon. But even common diction and more comprehensible figures of speech indicate the writer's attitude toward the subject. Look at the first paragraph of Maya Angelou's "Graduation" (on p. 258). Words and phrases like "glorious release," "nobility," "exotic destinations," and "rites" indicate Angelou's — and the African American community's — feelings about the school graduation.

Keep noticing the tone to see where and how it changes within a selection. Sometimes it is possible to underline the sentence or circle a pivotal word or phrase where the tone shifts to express a different attitude. For example, in "Graduation" the intense, poetic language continues until the entrance of the white man who gives the speech at the ceremony. Now the language changes to officialese — boring generalities and flat clichés — revealing the white speaker's attitude toward the event. Angelou is making a point about race relations by this change in the essay's tone.

Endings It is especially important to identify the tone at the conclusion of a selection because you want to recognize the writer's final attitude. On what note does the essay end? How does the ending affect you? Has the writer been building up to this effect all along? Or is it a slight surprise? Even a relatively short essay such as Brent Staples's "Black Men and Public Space" can achieve a shift in tone from beginning to end. Carver's essay "My Father's Life" includes several changes of tone and ends on a note that is still unexpected. The concluding paragraph of Terry Galloway's "I'm Listening as Hard as I Can" introduces a new tone to the essay that suggests another dimension of the subject.

Paying close attention to the conclusion's tone gives you a way to pull together your observations about the entire essay. Your reconsideration of the whole is the most fruitful step in making sense of your reading. It is often an exciting synthesis of the material that leads to discoveries and fresh insights. From your overview of *all* the material, you can determine what the whole essay conveys through its ideas and techniques. Reaching that kind of comprehensive viewpoint about an essay is what you want to achieve from your analytic examination.

To demonstrate these reading suggestions, we have annotated an essay as you might do when reading it on your own. Important points and connotative words are underlined, and varied comments or questions are noted in the margins. Puzzling words are circled, as are clues to vague or puzzling matters. As you read the following essay, you may find that your reactions differ from what you see in the margins. Freely add your own.

Bernard Cooper

THE FINE ART OF SIGHING

BERNARD COOPER (b. 1951) studied visual arts at the California Institute of the Arts, where he took both his undergraduate and master's degrees. His essays, initially published in magazines such as *Grand Street, Georgia Review, Harper's,* and *Kenyon Review,* have been collected in *Maps to Anywhere* (1990) and *Truth Serum* (1996).

Me?

What burden?

You feel a gradual welling up of pleasure, or boredom, or melancholy. Whatever the emotion, it's more abundant than you ever dreamed. You can no more contain it than your hands can cup a lake. And so you surrender and suck the air. Your esophagus opens, diaphragm expands. Poised at the crest of an exhalation, your body is about to be unburdened, second by second, cell by cell. A kettle hisses. A balloon deflates. Your shoulders fall like two ripe pears, muscles slack at last.

Grim view

Neglected child?

Unhappy scene

Does he know now what she was?

My mother stared out the kitchen window, ashes from her cigarette dribbling into the sink. She'd turned her back on the rest of the house, guarding her own solitude. I'd tiptoe across the linoleum and fix my lunch without making a sound. Sometimes I saw her back expand, then heard her let loose one plummeting note, a sigh so long and weary it might have been her last. Beyond our backyard, above telephone poles and apartment buildings, rose the brown horizon of the city; across it glided an occasional bird, or the blimp that advertised Goodyear tires. She might have been drifting into the distance, or lamenting her separation from it. She might have been wishing she were somewhere else, or wishing she could be happy where she was, a middle-aged housewife dreaming at her sink.

Father's are happy

My father's sighs were more melodic. What began as a somber sigh could abruptly change pitch, turn gusty and loose, and suggest by its very transformation that what begins in sorrow might end in relief. He could prolong the rounded vowel of *oy*, or let it ricochet like an echo, as if he were shouting in a tunnel or a cave. Where my mother sighed from ineffable sadness, my father sighed at simple things: the coldness of a drink, the softness of a pillow, or an itch that my mother, following the frantic map of his words, finally found on his back and scratched.

He has both

He's very unhappy

A friend of mine once mentioned that I was given to long and ponderous sighs. Once I became aware of this habit, I heard my father's sighs in my own and knew for a moment his small satisfactions. At other times, I felt my mother's restlessness and wished I could leave my body with my breath, or be happy in the body my breath left behind.

Yes!

It's a reflex and a legacy, this soulful species of breathing. Listen closely: My ancestors' lungs are pumping like bellows, men towing boats along the banks of the (Volga,) women lugging baskets of rye bread and pike. At the end of each day, they lift their weary arms in a toast; as thanks for the heat and sting of vodka, their aahs condense in the cold (Russian) air.

Why Russia?

At any given moment, there must be thousands of people sighing. A man in Milwaukee heaves and shivers and blesses the head of his second wife, who's not too shy to lick his toes. A judge in Munich groans with pleasure after tasting again the silky bratwurst she ate as a child. Every day, meaningful sighs are expelled from schoolchildren, driving instructors, forensic experts, certified public accountants, and dental hygienists, just to name a few. The sighs of widows and widowers alone must account for a significant portion of the carbon dioxide released into the atmosphere. Every time a girdle is removed, a foot is submerged in a tub of warm water, or a restroom is reached on a desolate road...you'd think the sheer velocity of it would create (mistrals, siroccos,) hurricanes; arrows should be swarming over satellite maps, weathermen talking a mile a minute, ties flapping from their necks like flags.

!

The pace gets wild here

6

Before I learned that Venetian prisoners were led across it to their execution, I imagined that the (Bridge of Sighs) was a feat of invisible engineering, a structure vaulting above the earth, the girders and trusses, the stay ropes and cables, the counterweights and safety rails, connecting one human breath to the next.

What is it?

Ahh!
Sigh, sigh

7

Pick Up a Fresh Trail   Think about an essay as soon as you finish reading; don't put it aside for later. You will think of more concrete details and your thought-associations will be faster when the essay is fresh. In thinking about "The Fine Art of Sighing" there is no difficulty in formulating the main subject. The title announces the subject and the short essay focuses on it. But even after reading longer, multilayered essays you can begin to pull your thoughts together by forming simple, fundamental observations like "This essay is mainly about such and such" or "This essay asserts this and that." A matter-of-fact observation gives you a foundation on which to build other observations and connections.

Cooper's essay does not develop a logical argument or present a thesis. The author's memories and reflections, however, lead him into specific themes. The essay develops those themes in a logically ordered, assertive way. It builds a point — and Cooper leaves a trail.

In paragraph 1 Cooper evokes the immediately recognizable sensations of sighing. The precise feelings and sharp images are meant to raise your awareness of ordinary experience. The paragraph is even addressed to "you," the "you" that is everyone. Cooper quickly redirects the general interest onto a specific person and a particular moment. In paragraph 2 the evocation of his mother introduces wistfulness and melancholy. The paragraph stirs our concern over issues in her life and her son's upbringing. We begin to explore particular, sad dimensions of sighing.

Those dimensions are not dropped by the contrasting next paragraph: they are further expanded to include sighs of pleasure as well. The father's sighs are more variable. By turning from mother to father Cooper is also expanding the family context that allows unguarded expressions of feelings. We see sighs come out in deeply personal situations. Cooper combines both his parents' sighs in his own. Paragraph 4 indicates his identification with their complete emotional range. The family context receives a surprisingly vast extension in paragraph 5 to include his Old World ancestors at their toil and their pleasures. Sighing links Cooper to unknown forebears across many generations and lost worlds.

In the next paragraph, sighing also links him to all humanity. Cooper imagines the intensities of feelings everywhere that can't be otherwise expressed. Only sighs get at true and universal realities. This fanciful, humorous expansion toward a whole world of people sighing concludes with a paragraph focusing on a single image of childlike, naive wonder. Cooper dwells on a childish misunderstanding about the name of the prisoners' bridge in Venice. His mistake now seems true, symbolically. Indeed, his essay has made it memorably true.

As you retrace Cooper's trail of themes you see that the essay has a steadily expanding viewpoint and a rational structure, a carefully sequential organization. It develops a convincing viewpoint, which is an implicit thesis. The essay has a purpose, which is to change our perceptions and understanding of something we ordinarily dismiss as meaningless or regard as trivial.

Write to Find Thoughts   You cannot expect to make this much sense of an essay by just mulling it over in your mind. Your responses and observations have to be articulated in words in order to become coherent ideas. Writing in the margins and taking notes as you read start this process of finding what you mean. Participating in class discussions will take your understanding further. But the process of making sense is not complete until you write out your views in a fully developed essay of your own. You never really know what you think until you see what you say.

If you have been given a topic to write on, write on the assigned topic. It has probably been carefully phrased to direct your thoughts and to identify a subject that you can handle in a few pages. If you have to find your own topic after reading an essay, rely on your responses to the reading. After concentrating on "The Fine Art of Sighing," for instance, you should have plenty of personal associations that suggest something to write about, such as mannerisms or odd expressions of family members, or other customary signals of melancholy, tension, relief, or pleasure. You may have already found traces of those expressions in yourself at similar moments. Do you welcome or resist those incursions by other personalities? The mixing of identities across generations is something you can discover in your own experience. You may not have thought about this aspect of your life, but writing about it is an opportunity to examine it closely and freely.

Don't trap yourself into feeling blocked about writing. You can always begin to write by jotting down fleeting phrases. Don't worry about connecting up the jumble of thoughts that may cover your sheet of paper. Keep writing even if you are formulating only fragments. As you continue to energize your mind into forming phrases and sentences, you will soon begin to write longer passages and more cohesive thoughts. The important activity is to make your mind use words that you write down. The object of writing at any stage of preparation or revision is to get thoughts out of your head and onto paper. To achieve this goal you must work on the page. If you have trouble focusing your attention and getting started, push yourself to articulate one thought and then another. (It also helps to have privacy and silence where you write.)

What you get down onto paper during your first hour or two of effort will be patchy and often vague. Don't be disheartened. You can't construct the complicated network of ideas in an essay as easily and methodically as you knit a scarf or add a column of figures.

Revise to Develop Thoughts   To turn your rough material into a well-formed draft, think of yourself laying out a trail that your reader must be able to follow. You are in charge of the meaning now, and you want to make yourself fully understood.

Try to establish a purpose or central idea for each paragraph. Explain your idea so that your thoughts expand into a developed paragraph with a main point and supporting discussion. Often you will have to pull together a couple of brief, fragmentary paragraphs in your rough material and synthesize them into a longer paragraph that contributes a substantive point. Do not hesitate to write paragraphs that are longer than what you find in newspapers and most magazines. You want to learn to sustain and control extended thought processes. Add concrete details and illustrations that make your writing more convincing. Paragraph by paragraph, spell out what you mean.

And emphasize what *you* mean. Don't just repeat the author. Present your ideas. Students tend to summarize what is written without adding much personal comment on it, instead of forming an idea or attitude about the selection. For example, the following sentence merely reports what happened:

> Whenever the mother gazed out the kitchen window and sighed, the boy didn't dare disturb her.

Turn this kind of sentence into one that includes more of your own interpretation:

> His mother's melancholy sighs roused young Cooper's anxiety over her distracted gazing out the window.

The revised sentence still summarizes the event but includes an explanation of its significance. The sentence is more analytic in its purpose. The following sentence does not summarize at all. It refers to the event but does not recount it.

> The depth of his mother's sighs worried the boy because they suggested her inaccessible, private dimensions that baffled and distanced him.

That sentence is fully analytic because it explains how Cooper achieves his purpose and effect.

You can make your sentences more analytic by revising parts that begin with *when* and *after*; use words that show causes or consequences like *because* and *since*. Such words help build supporting clauses that assert your point.

Your sentences are the very flesh and muscle of your writing. Making them strong and energetic is probably the semester goal of classroom instruction. Commonly, sentences are too inactive and do not convey specific information. Using active instead of passive verbs can galvanize lazy sentences. As you shape up your sentences, listen critically for the dull sound of flab that arises from using vague words and too many words.

Remember that your intended meaning is expressed by both what you say and how you say it. Your own tone of voice should be faintly audible in your head as you write. Is it a voice that sounds worth listening to on this particular topic? Is it a voice with a purpose?

Writers share one basic intention — that is, to be *convincing*. Whatever their subject, method, or tone, writers try to build confidence in the reader that the essay merits attention. Even humorous writing must be reliably funny. Whether it is a personal narrative, a logical argument, an explanation, or an analysis, all writing has to validate what it says. The full context gives a good essay credibility. Careful revising increases your essay's credibility.

When you think that you are finished, muster up the energy and courage to take one more critical look at your introduction and conclusion. These paragraphs have special functions that cannot be achieved until you have fully understood the point of your essay and your purpose in writing. You should make last-minute adjustments to your introduction and conclusion so that they serve your intentions. Remember from your readings that there is a rich variety of ways to begin and end an essay. Don't be humdrum in your introduction and conclusion. You owe it to yourself to win some attention to your fully developed views.

Your Turn   This brief bit of advice about writing should remind you that readers and writers confront much the same problems. But writing is more difficult. Writing is difficult for everyone, so you should never lose your nerve. The frustrations you face are the same frustrations that experienced writers face in their work. The standards you strive to attain are the same goals set by authors in this anthology. The work of writing is very democratic work: students, teachers, authors — we are all on this path together. If it is your turn to blaze a trail, take us to see something interesting.

PART 1

SELF-IMAGES

INSIGHTS

We enter the world as purely physical beings and leave it in the same way. In between, through our lifetimes, we labor pridefully to establish *identities, selves* distinct from our bodies. Not *what* we are but *who* we are. This is the crux of our humanity.

—JOYCE CAROL OATES

I conceive a man's body as a kind of flame, like a candle flame, forever upright and yet flowing: and the intellect is just the light that is shed on to the things around. And I am not so much concerned with the things around — which is really mind — but with the mystery of the flame forever flowing, coming God knows how from out of practically nowhere, and being *itself*, whatever there is around it, that it lights up. We have got so ridiculously mindful that we never know that we ourselves are anything — we think there are only the objects we shine upon. And there the poor flame goes on burning ignored, to produce this light. And instead of chasing the mystery in the fugitive, half-lighted things outside us, we ought to look at ourselves, and say "My God, I am myself!"

—D. H. LAWRENCE

We are creatures of *outside influences* — we originate *nothing* within. Whenever we take a new line of thought and drift into a new line of belief and action, the impulse is *always* suggested from the *outside*.

—MARK TWAIN

The Eagle-Feather Fan

The eagle is my power,
And my fan is an eagle.
It is strong and beautiful

In my hand. And it is real.
My fingers hold upon it
As if the beaded handle
Were the twist of bristlecone.
The bones of my hands are fine
And hollow; the fan bears them.
My hand veers in the thin air
Of the summits. All morning
It scuds on the cold currents;
All afternoon it circles
To the singing, to the drums.
—N. SCOTT MOMADAY

The nicknames children bestow on one another can confer power. Like ancient Rome, the playground republic marks off the inner core of citizens from barbarians. Those who have no nicknames have no social existence; they are the nonpeople....To be nicknamed is to be seen as having an attribute that entitles one to social attention, even if that attention is unpleasant. Thus, it may be better to be called "Sewage" than merely John.
—ROM HARRÉ

My advice to everyone is to change their name at once if they're the least unhappy with their lives. In [my] Utopia everyone will choose a new name at seven, at eleven, at sixteen, and at twenty-four. And naturally women at forty-five, or when the last child has grown up and left home, whichever is the earliest....Then life will be seen to start over, not finish. It is a perfectly legal thing to do....So long as there is no intent to defraud....But so many of us, either feeling our identities to be fragile, or out of misplaced loyalty to our parents, feel we must stick with the names we start out with. The given name is a dead giveaway of our parents' ambition for us — whether to diminish or enhance, ignore us as much as possible or control us forever....No, it will not do. It will have to change.
—FAY WELDON

All memories — personal, societal, cultural — are a construct. Neither a single individual nor a single institution can remember everything or provide for total recall. Individuals, institutions, academics: all choose what is worth remembering and on the basis of their choices construct their personal or cultural memories and identities. But they can do so only from among the materials made available to them by circumstances and opportunities for choice that are only partially under their own control. Those materials are the result, that is, of a construction — of many constructions — made prior to the individual's, the institution's, or the academic's.

—DANIEL TRAISTER

Show me a sensible person who likes himself or herself! I know myself too well to like what I see. I know but too well that I'm not what I'd like to be.

—GOLDA MEIR

FOCUSING BY WRITING

1. People are apt to think of their personal identities as resembling either an *artichoke* or an *onion*. The outer leaves of an artichoke are inedible; they shield and nurture the vegetable but are easily peeled away. The essence of the vegetable appears closer to the innermost core, the heart of the artichoke. An onion, by contrast, has concentric layers of homogenous identity. It extends uniformly from its inner rings to its outermost. Which are you like? Explain why one metaphor reflects your sense of self better than the other.

2. If you were going to write an autobiography, where would you start — at some point in your own experience, or in someone else's experience? or with some place, such as a town, a house, or a country? Explain your reason for deciding on a particular beginning. Do not write it; merely explain why you would start your life story at that point.

3. As a child, did you ever create an imaginary name for yourself? Could you create one for yourself as you are at present? Recalling or inventing an imaginary name, explain its attractions and advantages over your given name.

4. Write about the pleasures and other possible effects of looking at old photographs, as in leafing through an album including pictures of yourself among those of other people. Do the photographic images evoke special reactions?

Nora Ephron

SHAPING UP ABSURD[1]

NORA EPHRON (b. 1941) grew up in the adult world of Hollywood screen-writers, entertainers, and celebrities. After graduating from Wellesley College she began a career as a journalist in New York by writing for *Newsweek* and contributing articles to entertainment magazines, eventually joining the staff of *New York* and *Esquire* magazines. Her essays have been collected in *Wallflower at the Orgy* (1970), *Crazy Salad* (1975), and *Nora Ephron Collected* (1991). She has also written a comic novel, *Heartburn* (1983), and several screenplays. Ephron directed the films *Sleepless in Seattle* (1992) and *You've Got Mail* (1998). "Shaping Up Absurd" considers a troubling self-image in her early life.

I have to begin with a few words about androgyny. In grammar school, 1
in the fifth and sixth grades, we were all tyrannized by a rigid set of rules
that supposedly determined whether we were boys or girls. The episode in
Huckleberry Finn where Huck is disguised as a girl and gives himself away
by the way he threads a needle and catches a ball — that kind of thing. We
learned that the way you sat, crossed your legs, held a cigarette and looked
at your nails, your wristwatch, the way you did these things instinctively was
absolute proof of your sex. Now obviously most children did not take this
literally, but I did. I thought that just one slip, just one incorrect cross of
my legs or flick of an imaginary cigarette ash would turn me from whatever
I was into the other thing; that would be all it took, really. Even though I
was outwardly a girl and had many of the trappings generally associated
with the field of girldom — a girl's name, for example, and dresses, my own
telephone, an autograph book — I spent the early years of my adolescence
absolutely certain that I might at any point gum it up. I did not feel at all
like a girl. I was boyish. I was athletic, ambitious, outspoken, competitive,
noisy, rambunctious. I had scabs on my knees and my socks slid into my
loafers and I could throw a football. I wanted desperately not to be that
way, not to be a mixture of both things but instead just one, a girl, a definite indisputable girl. As soft and as pink as a nursery. And nothing would
do that for me, I felt, but breasts.

[1]Editor's title.

I was about six months younger than everyone in my class, and so for ₂
about six months after it began, for six months after my friends had begun
to develop — that was the word we used, develop — I was not particularly
worried. I would sit in the bathtub and look down at my breasts and know
that any day now, any second now, they would start growing like everyone
else's. They didn't. "I want to buy a bra," I said to my mother one night.
"What for?" she said. My mother was really hateful about bras, and by the
time my third sister had gotten to that point where she was ready to want
one, my mother had worked the whole business into a comedy routine.
"Why not use a Band-Aid instead?" she would say. It was a source of great
pride to my mother that she had never even had to wear a brassiere until
she had her fourth child, and then only because her gynecologist made
her. It was incomprehensible to me that anyone would ever be proud of
something like that. It was the 1950s, for God's sake. Jane Russell. Cash-
mere sweaters. Couldn't my mother see that? *"I am too old to wear an
undershirt."* Screaming. Weeping. Shouting. "Then don't wear an undershirt," said my mother. "But I want to buy a bra." "What for?"

I suppose that for most girls, breasts, brassieres, that entire thing, has ₃
more trauma, more to do with the coming of adolescence, of becoming a
woman, than anything else. Certainly more than getting your period,
although that too was traumatic, symbolic. But you could *see* breasts; they
were there; they were visible. Whereas a girl could claim to have her
period for months before she actually got it and nobody would ever know
the difference. Which is exactly what I did. All you had to do was make a
great fuss over having enough nickels for the Kotex machine and walk
around clutching your stomach and moaning for three to five days a month
about The Curse and you could convince anybody. There is a school of
thought somewhere in the women's lib/women's mag/gynecology establishment that claims that menstrual cramps are purely psychological, and I lean
toward it. Not that I didn't have them finally. Agonizing cramps, heating-
pad cramps, go-down-to-the-school-nurse-and-lie-on-the-cot cramps. But
unlike any pain I had ever suffered, I adored the pain of cramps, welcomed
it, wallowed in it, bragged about it. "I can't go. I have cramps." "I can't do
that. I have cramps." And most of all, gigglingly, blushingly: "I can't swim.
I have cramps." Nobody ever used the hard-core word. Menstruation. God,
what an awful word. Never that. "I have cramps."

The morning I first got my period, I went into my mother's bedroom to ₄
tell her. And my mother, my utterly-hateful-about-bras mother, burst into
tears. It was really a lovely moment, and I remember it so clearly not just
because it was one of the two times I ever saw my mother cry on my
account (the other was when I was caught being a six-year-old kleptoma-
niac), but also because the incident did not mean to me what it meant to
her. Her little girl, her firstborn, had finally become a woman. That was
what she was crying about. My reaction to the event, however, was that I
might well be a woman in some scientific, textbook sense (and could at

least stop faking every month and stop wasting all those nickels). But in another sense — in a visible sense — I was as androgynous and as liable to tip over into boyhood as ever.

I started with a 28AA bra. I don't think they made them any smaller in those days, although I gather that now you can buy bras for five year olds that don't have any cups whatsoever in them; trainer bras they are called. My first brassiere came from Robinson's Department Store in Beverly Hills. I went there alone, shaking, positive they would look me over and smile and tell me to come back next year. An actual fitter took me into the dressing room and stood over me while I took off my blouse and tried the first one on. The little puffs stood out on my chest. "Lean over," said the fitter (to this day I am not sure what fitters in bra departments do except to tell you to lean over). I leaned over, with the fleeting hope that my breasts would miraculously fall out of my body and into the puffs. Nothing.

"Don't worry about it," said my friend Libby some months later, when things had not improved. "You'll get them after you're married."

"What are you talking about?" I said.

"When you get married," Libby explained, "your husband will touch your breasts and rub them and kiss them and they'll grow."

That was the killer. Necking I could deal with. Intercourse I could deal with. But it had never crossed my mind that a man was going to touch my breasts, that breasts had something to do with all that, petting, my God they never mentioned petting in my little sex manual about the fertilization of the ovum. I became dizzy. For I knew instantly — as naive as I had been only a moment before — that only part of what she was saying was true: the touching, rubbing, kissing part, not the growing part. And I knew that no one would ever want to marry me. I had no breasts. I would never have breasts.

My best friend in school was Diana Raskob. She lived a block from me in a house full of wonders. English muffins, for instance. The Raskobs were the first people in Beverly Hills to have English muffins for breakfast. They also had an apricot tree in the back, and a badminton court, and a subscription to *Seventeen* magazine, and hundreds of games like Sorry and Parcheesi and Treasure Hunt and Anagrams. Diana and I spent three or four afternoons a week in their den reading and playing and eating. Diana's mother's kitchen was full of the most colossal assortment of junk food I have ever been exposed to. My house was full of apples and peaches and milk and homemade chocolate-chip cookies — which were nice, and good for you, but-not-right-before-dinner-or-you'll-spoil-your-appetite. Diana's house had nothing in it that was good for you, and what's more, you could stuff it in right up until dinner and nobody cared. Bar-B-Q potato chips (they were the first in them, too), giant bottles of ginger ale, fresh popcorn with melted butter, hot fudge sauce on Baskin-Robbins jamoca ice cream, powdered-sugar doughnuts from Van de Kamps. Diana and I had been best friends since we were seven; we were about equally popular in school (which is to say, not particularly), we had about the same success with boys (extremely intermittent), and we looked much the same. Dark. Tall. Gangly.

It is September, just before school begins. I am eleven years old, about 11 to enter the seventh grade, and Diana and I have not seen each other all summer. I have been to camp and she has been somewhere like Banff with her parents. We are meeting, as we often do, on the street midway between our two houses and we will walk back to Diana's and eat junk and talk about what has happened to each of us that summer. I am walking down Walden Drive in my jeans and my father's shirt hanging out and my old red loafers with the socks falling into them and coming toward me is...I take a deep breath...a young woman. Diana. Her hair is curled and she has a waist and hips and a bust and she is wearing a straight skirt, an article of clothing I have been repeatedly told I will be unable to wear until I have the hips to hold it up. My jaw drops, and suddenly I am crying, crying hysterically, can't catch my breath sobbing. My best friend has betrayed me. She has gone ahead without me and done it. She has shaped up.

Here are some things I did to help: 12
Bought a Mark Eden Bust Developer. 13
Slept on my back for four years. 14
Splashed cold water on them every night because some French actress 15
said in *Life* magazine that that was what *she* did for her perfect bustline.

Ultimately, I resigned myself to a bad toss and began to wear padded 16 bras. I think about them now, think about all those years in high school I went around in them, my three padded bras, every single one of them with different sized breasts. Each time I changed bras I changed sizes: one week nice perky but not too obtrusive breasts, the next medium-sized slightly pointed ones, the next week knockers, true knockers; all the time, whatever size I was, carrying around this rubberized appendage on my chest that occasionally crashed into a wall and was poked inward and had to be poked outward — I think about all that and wonder how anyone kept a straight face through it. My parents, who normally had no restraints about needling me — why did they say nothing as they watched my chest go up and down? My friends, who would periodically inspect my breasts for signs of growth and reassure me — why didn't they at least counsel consistency?

And the bathing suits. I die when I think about the bathing suits. That 17 was the era when you could lay an uninhabited bathing suit on the beach and someone would make a pass at it. I would put one on, an absurd swimsuit with its enormous bust built into it, the bones from the suit stabbing me in the rib cage and leaving little red welts on my body, and there I would be, my chest plunging straight downward absolutely vertically from my collarbone to the top of my suit and then suddenly, wham, out came all that padding and material and wiring absolutely horizontally.

Buster Klepper was the first boy who ever touched them. He was my boyfriend my senior year of high school. There is a picture of him in my high-school yearbook that makes him look quite attractive in a Jewish, horn-rimmed glasses sort of way, but the picture does not show the pimples, which were air-brushed out, or the dumbness. Well, that isn't really fair. He wasn't dumb. He just wasn't terribly bright. His mother refused to accept it, refused to accept the relentlessly average report cards, refused to deal with her son's inevitable destiny in some junior college or other. "He was tested," she would say to me, apropos of nothing, "and it came out 145. That's near-genius." Had the word underachiever been coined, she probably would have lobbed that one at me, too. Anyway, Buster was really very sweet — which is, I know, damning with faint praise, but there it is. I was the editor of the front page of the high-school newspaper and he was editor of the back page; we had to work together, side by side, in the print shop, and that was how it started. On our first date, we went to see *April Love* starring Pat Boone. Then we started going together. Buster had a green coupe, a 1950 Ford with an engine he had handchromed until it shone, dazzled, reflected the image of anyone who looked into it, anyone usually being Buster polishing it or the gas-station attendants he constantly asked to check the oil in order for them to be overwhelmed by the sparkle on the valves. The car also had a boot stretched over the back seat for reasons I never understood; hanging from the rearview mirror, as was the custom, was a pair of angora dice. A previous girlfriend named Solange who was famous throughout Beverly Hills High School for having no pigment in her right eyebrow had knitted them for him. Buster and I would ride around town, the two of us seated to the left of the steering wheel. I would shift gears. It was nice.

There was necking. Terrific necking. First in the car, overlooking Los Angeles from what is now the Trousdale Estates. Then on the bed of his parents' cabana at Ocean House. Incredibly wonderful, frustrating necking, I loved it, really, but no further than necking, please don't, please, because there I was absolutely terrified of the general implications of going-a-step-further with a near-dummy and also terrified of his finding out there was next to nothing there (which he knew, of course; he wasn't that dumb).

I broke up with him at one point. I think we were apart for about two weeks. At the end of that time I drove down to see a friend at a boarding school in Palos Verdes Estates and a disc jockey played *April Love* on the radio four times during the trip. I took it as a sign. I drove straight back to Griffith Park to a golf tournament Buster was playing in (he was the sixth-seeded teenage golf player in Southern California) and presented myself back to him on the green of the 18th hole. It was all very dramatic. That night we went to a drive-in and I let him get his hand under my protuberances and onto my breasts. He really didn't seem to mind at all.

"Do you want to marry my son?" the woman asked me.

"Yes," I said.

I was nineteen years old, a virgin, going with this woman's son, this big strange woman who was married to a Lutheran minister in New Hampshire and pretended she was Gentile and had this son, by her first husband, this total fool of a son who ran the hero-sandwich concession at Harvard Business School and whom for one moment one December in New Hampshire I said — as much out of politeness as anything else — that I wanted to marry.

"Fine," she said. "Now, here's what you do. Always make sure you're on top of him so you won't seem so small. My bust is very large, you see, so I always lie on my back to make it look smaller, but you'll have to be on top most of the time."

I nodded. "Thank you," I said.

"I have a book for you to read," she went on. "Take it with you when you leave. Keep it." She went to the bookshelf, found it, and gave it to me. It was a book on frigidity.

"Thank you," I said.

That is a true story. Everything in this article is a true story, but I feel I have to point out that that story in particular is true. It happened on December 30, 1960. I think about it often. When it first happened, I naturally assumed that the woman's son, my boyfriend, was responsible. I invented a scenario where he had had a little heart-to-heart with his mother and confessed that his only objection to me was that my breasts were small; his mother then took it upon herself to help out. Now I think I was wrong about the incident. The mother was acting on her own, I think: That was her way of being cruel and competitive under the guise of being helpful and maternal. You have small breasts, she was saying; therefore you will never make him as happy as I have. Or you have small breasts; therefore you will doubtless have sexual problems. Or you have small breasts; therefore you are less woman than I am. She was, as it happens, only the first of what seems to me to be a never-ending string of women who have made competitive remarks to me about breast size. "I would love to wear a dress like that," my friend Emily says to me, "but my bust is too big." Like that. Why do women say these things to me? Do I attract these remarks the way other women attract married men or alcoholics or homosexuals? This summer, for example, I am at a party in East Hampton and I am introduced to a woman from Washington. She is a minor celebrity, very pretty and Southern and blonde and outspoken and I am flattered because she has read something I have written. We are talking animatedly, we have been talking no more than five minutes, when a man comes up to join us. "Look at the two of us," the woman says to the man, indicating me and her. "The two of us together couldn't fill an A cup." Why does she say that? It isn't even true, dammit, so why? Is she even more addled than I am on this subject? Does she honestly believe there is something wrong with her size breasts, which, it seems to me, now that I look hard at them, are just right? Do I unconsciously bring out competitiveness in women? In that form? What did I do to deserve it?

As for men.   29

There were men who minded and let me know they minded. There   30 were men who did not mind. In any case, I always minded.

And even now, now that I have been countlessly reassured that my fig-   31 ure is a good one, now that I am grown up enough to understand that most of my feelings have very little to do with the reality of my shape, I am nonetheless obsessed by breasts. I cannot help it. I grew up in the terrible Fifties — with rigid stereotypical sex roles, the insistence that men be men and dress like men and women be women and dress like women, the intolerance of androgyny — and I cannot shake it, cannot shake my feelings of inadequacy. Well, that time is gone, right? All those exaggerated examples of breast worship are gone, right? Those women were freaks, right? I know all that. And yet, here I am, stuck with the psychological remains of it all, stuck with my own peculiar version of breast worship. You probably think I am crazy to go on like this: Here I have set out to write a confession that is meant to hit you with the shock of recognition and instead you are sitting there thinking I am thoroughly warped. Well, what can I tell you? If I had had them, I would have been a completely different person. I honestly believe that.

After I went into therapy, a process that made it possible for me to tell   32 total strangers at cocktail parties that breasts were the hang-up of my life, I was often told that I was insane to have been bothered by my condition. I was also frequently told, by close friends, that I was extremely boring on the subject. And my girlfriends, the ones with nice big breasts, would go on endlessly about how their lives had been far more miserable than mine. Their bra straps were snapped in class. They couldn't sleep on their stomachs. They were stared at whenever the word "mountain" cropped up in geography. And *Evangeline,* good God what they went through every time someone had to stand up and recite the Prologue to Longfellow's *Evangeline:* "...*stand like druids of eld.../With beards that rest on their bosoms.*" It was much worse for them, they tell me. They had a terrible time of it, they assure me. I don't know how lucky I was, they say.

I have thought about their remarks, tried to put myself in their place,   33 considered their point of view. I think they are full of shit.

Analyzing This Selection

1. **THE WRITER'S METHOD**   Ephron establishes an informal, colloquial tone right from the start. Underline the key words and phrases in the opening paragraph that help set this tone. What is the correlation between this tone and the subject of her essay?

2. As a child, Ephron felt sure that fateful disaster lurked around every corner. In addition to her flat-chestedness, what does she worry about? How does she express these worries?

3. What is the point of the section about her friend Diana? Does her name fit the effect that she has on Ephron? Similarly, what is the point of the section about Buster Klepper? And what are the connotations of his name? Do they fit his effect on her?

Analyzing Connections

4. Two contrasting metaphors for personal identity are mentioned in the first topic of Focusing by Writing (see p. 15). Which metaphor suggests Ephron's image of herself?

Analyzing by Writing

5. Being unusually tall or short, thin or fat, red-haired, freckled, pretty, or thoroughly average can seem to be the most important fact in your existence. Write an essay explaining how one trait came to have exaggerated importance for some period of your life. Be sure to examine the reasons for their importance at that time.

Anthony Walton

HAMBURGER

ANTHONY WALTON (b. 1960) was raised in the industrial belt surrounding Chicago, a society that influenced his development in ways this essay explores. In his memoir *Mississippi: An American Journey* (1996), Walton traced the effects of the rural South on his parents, who had worked in cotton fields before moving north. This memoir connects the state's history and the experience of many families like his. Walton graduated from Notre Dame University and earned an M.F.A. from Brown University, where he studied with the poet Michael Harper. Walton lives in Maine and writes frequently for the *New York Times* and other publications. His recent book *Go and Tell the Pharaoh: The Autobiography of Reverend Al Sharpton* is a collaboration similar to Alex Haley's with Malcolm X. "Hamburger" appeared in a volume of essays on sport, *Body Language: Writers on Sport* (1998).

1   Most of my adolescence was spent wondering — worrying, really — if I was ever going to be able to measure up to the considerable challenge, as I perceived it, of "being a man." My worry didn't have much to do with the typical concerns about women and sex — how to impress the former in pursuit of the latter — though that was a small part of it. It had to do rather with something both more innocent and much darker: I would lie awake nights at the age of eleven or twelve wondering how a man went to work every day, how he paid a mortgage, how he kept control of the complex and crazy variables that came with a wife and children. I didn't see how it could be done.

2   I don't know why I worried about these things. It was odd, to say the least. I think it may have been because my father worked his way up from nothing; because in that peculiar way of children I was aware of more things than I could consciously *know*, and sensed beneath the placid surface of suburban life the fragility of what we had.

3   In any case, my fretting set me apart a little from the rest of my peers. I don't think they wasted too much time worrying about the distant and unforeseeable future, a future several of them, I'm sorry to say, would not live to see. I don't, of course, know for certain that they didn't worry; this was not the sort of topic discussed by boys of that age in that time and place. But I felt lonely, and deeply insecure. How could I ever know for sure that I could handle the everyday pressures of being a man? What I

decided to do, living there in the Midwest in the mid-seventies, was to prove myself (*to* myself) in the way that boys and young men seemed to do then — I decided to play football.

There was more to it than this, of course, and some of it a good deal more innocent. In one sense, I simply wanted to be a part of the unselfconscious and uncynical spectacle that was sports at that time. The mid-sixties through the mid-seventies were a theater of many dark dramas in the country's life, but that time was also a golden age for the sport of football, an age when the spectacle of twenty-two men wrestling and thrusting for turf on a fall afternoon still had a feel of dignified authenticity, of enormous integrity. This was before the entertainment aspect had overrun the game; even the professionals then seemed to be playing for pride and honor.... Football seemed to be something that men *did*, not just a marketing vehicle for caps and jackets, not just a way for loudmouths and reprobates to become multimillionaires. I wanted to be a part of it. I wanted to be like them.

I first played tackle football in the seventh grade, suffering a serious knee injury when I was clipped (blocked from behind and below the waist, an illegal move) in the last game of the season. Short, slow, and fat, I played noseguard that year, my chief responsibility to clog up the middle so that other boys could remain unblocked and make tackles. My injury was severe enough that I missed several weeks of school, limped through the winter, and was tentative and handicapped as a player the next year. But I enjoyed the attention, the solicitude of the coaches and other kids, and the status I seemed magically to possess as the survivor of such a calamity. I can still remember the pleasure of having girls who would not otherwise have known I existed signing my cast and helping with my cane and books.

Football was a serious affair where I grew up, in the Fox River Valley of northern Illinois; if not quite the life-and-death cosmic undertaking that was basketball, then a very close second. The valley is lined with towns and cities — Elgin, St. Charles, Geneva, Batavia, Aurora — that are now considered suburbs of Chicago; but at that time, twenty years ago, they were principally prairie towns whose inhabitants tended to work in the factories and foundries of the two largest municipalities: Elgin, home of Elgin watches and Borden's Dairy, and Aurora, which boasted Caterpillar Tractor, Lyon Metal, Richards-Wilcox, and my father's plant, All-Steel, among many others. Most of these plants have since closed, leaving behind demoralization and economic dislocation.

There was a good chance if you were a young man living in the valley that your father did something to earn his family's way that was physically demanding, if not dangerous — another reason why it was so important to be "tough" in those towns, why a little boy might spend hours wondering if he measured up. Those factories were places where men lost fingers and arms and eyes, and in one particularly horrific accident, a man had been crushed and burned to death by molten steel in a foundry. I used to listen to my father get ready for work every morning and wonder how he found the strength.

My own football life became fixed — something I could no longer turn away from — my freshman year in high school. I was attending, for academic and avoidance-of-trouble reasons, Aurora Central Catholic, a medium-sized diocesan high school. Catholic's Chargers were the most consistently successful team in that part of the state, due largely to the genius of head coach Michael Dunn. Coach Dunn — handsome, black-haired, stocky, and willful — saw the entire field at once, whole, rather than in segments, and had a gift for talking, cheering, and flogging pre-MTV adolescents into decisively accomplishing tasks they might not otherwise have thought possible. In the fall of 1974 I became one of those adolescents, suiting up for the freshman squad.   8

A lot had changed for me since the seventh grade. I had grown nearly a foot, and somehow the baby fat had melted away. I was still a bit gawky and uncoordinated, but I *looked* like an athlete, and when I joined my new teammates for fall practice, I said I was a receiver and defensive back — two positions I had never played, but which I considered to be far superior to blocking on the line.   9

I didn't immediately thrive, footballwise, at Aurora Central. I wasn't in shape, and I wasn't used to the tempo and intensity of those boys, some of whom had been playing full-contact football since the fourth grade. I wanted to quit in the beginning and would have but for several long conversations I had with Pat Langan (like Coach Dunn, an Irishman), one of the freshman coaches who gave me advice that was a revelation to me then but that basically boiled down to "one day at a time." I walked to school in the morning sometimes with Coach Langan, and we would discuss things like mortgage down payments and car loans — which also weighed heavily on his mind, though he had the excuse of having a young wife and new baby. I wouldn't have dreamed of talking to my father about those things: When I asked him what he thought about my leaving the team, he just rolled his eyes and snapped, "Quit if you want, but not until the season's over. We Waltons stick things out."   10

High school athletic coaches are often portrayed in the media as near-misfits who couldn't quite cut it anywhere else — "those who can't do, teach, those who can't teach, teach gym" — but as I get older I am more and more amazed by the job they do as quasi-shamans, initiating young people into the world. Though he probably wouldn't remember them, my whining talks with Coach Langan were crucial to me because I was able to talk things out with a man who had my best interests at heart *at a time when I could not talk to my father*. We now have a joking, familiar, and easy relationship; but in my teens I think my father, who had left home at thirteen and who, with the exception of five years in the military, has worked brutal low-echelon jobs ever since, saw through my gallant facade to the soft, dissembling skirt-hugger I was, and couldn't understand how we were   11 related. And, tough as he was, he wasn't crazy about football, except as an occupier of male teenage energy and time. Football, in his mind, was a luxury, an abstraction; he believed in toughness in the real world. He thought I could be out making money, or better, studying, preparing myself to be chairman of Caterpillar or president of Continental Illinois Bank. He thought the coaches were giving me a big head that I couldn't live up to in life.

I didn't have much to do with Coach Dunn on the football field the first   12 year. In fact, I didn't even realize that my freshman history teacher was the legendary coach until, while I was trudging to the practice field one day after school, he came sprinting up behind me, clapped me hard on the shoulder pads, and yelled "Walton!" Continuing on, he looked back over his shoulder and smiled, "How you like school? I hear you got a pretty good history teacher," then bolted over to the varsity field. All that school year, though, he paid very special attention to me, giving me his *Chicago Tribunes* and *Time* magazines to read when he was finished with them, and assigning several special projects in class that allowed (or forced) me to do research on arcane (to a ninth grader) subjects like Frederick Douglass and the Abraham Lincoln–Stephen Douglas debates.

The freshman season was one of the enduring triumphs of my life. We   13 rolled through the fall, thrashing all of our opponents, including such bigger schools as Batavia and Aurora West Blue (Aurora West was such a big school, over 4,000 students, that they had two freshmen teams). The season was delicious for me; I started at defensive back, leading the team in interceptions, and got in a lot of work on offense (though mostly as a decoy and blocker). Getting on the yellow school buses to ride to away games brought to my romantic and overly imaginative mind the thought of warriors sailing for Troy.

The crowning glory of that season for me was that the boys I had known   14 around town and up and down the valley, my childhood friends and cousins — most of whom had dismissed me as an egghead — were forced to acknowledge me as an athlete. I had been fighting with some of these guys since Little League, and had almost always been on the losing end.

In fact, football became the largest part of my life outside of school,   15 more important to me than anything else. I began lifting weights and doing serious workouts three or four days a week, and the other sports I pursued, basketball and track, I rationalized as being de facto training modes for football. I began to buy sports magazines in earnest, especially those that focused on football, and mailed away to college sports information offices for the media guides of my favorite teams. In 1975, before cable and satellite television, before the World Wide Web and homesites, I could tell you, in detail, about the offensive-line needs at Texas A&M, the quarterback situation at Mississippi State, whether that sophomore flanker at Nebraska was living up to his high school billing or was only a pale imitation of Johnny Rodgers.

I don't know what I hoped to accomplish by all this. I suppose I thought   16
that all this information would somehow make me a better player. I was too
inexperienced to know that the vast majority of the guys who became great
college football players — as I had secretly started hoping I would — didn't
read enough material to serve as sports editors at the Associated Press. I didn't
know that, for the most part, they rarely read anything at all. What I had
found in football, in being one of the fifty or so boys who got to wear the
blue-and-gold "Charger Football" jackets that we so prized, was a way of
being in the world, an identity. I was a football player.

Sophomore year I was ready. As we entered two-a-days, the brutal pre-   17
season rites of August, with ninety-five- and one-hundred-degree practices
meant to winnow down the team and condition the survivors, I felt the
equal of any boy my age (I reiterate, *my* age), and was scraping to take
them all on. Then, one afternoon about a week in, something happened
that I've since come to see as one of the two or three most significant
events in my life.

We were engaged in "hamburger" drills — one of the harshest rituals of   18
the game, one-on-one tackling maneuvers in which two players lie on the
ground, one with the ball, then hop up on the whistle and sprint for the
space between two cones, where a tremendous collision occurs. The team
had been divided into two circling lines, and we all clapped rhythmically
and chanted inanities like "He's a beast!" after particularly stirring smashups.

Standing in line, I had been careful to keep count and make sure that   19
my tackling partner would be Matt Patterson, a fellow sophomore and good
friend. We would run the drill as hard as we could and deliver solid licks,
but with each other as partners we could also be reasonably sure of surviving the occasion. When my time to step up came, however, the opponent
who stood before me was not Matt, but Walt Rodriguez, a senior tight end,
two-year starter and universally respected tough guy. He bore me no special
animus, and unlike most of the upperclassmen had even deigned to
acknowledge my existence a few times. But what could I do? I couldn't just
run and let him hit me, because *he* had the ball. *I* had to tackle *him*. How
had Matt messed up? Had I lost count? I pondered the psychic costs of
sprinting off the field and transferring to another school.

Coach Dunn blew the whistle. "Come on, Tony," he said. "Show him   20
what you got." I lay down on the hot grass, sweat drenching my face, closed
my eyes, and waited. And waited. With the whistle I vaulted to my feet,
sighted the cones, slammed my eyes shut and threw every single thing I
had at that space, praying primarily that I wouldn't miss him completely,
that I would bounce off, that he would run over me, but that I would at
least have had the honor of sacrificing my body without fear. I could live
with being humiliated, even with being brutalized, but not with being seen
as the coward, in truth, that I was.

I wasn't humiliated. Eyes still shut, I ran full force into Walt, hit him   21
with my left shoulder square in the solar plexus, followed through by lowering my helmet and, *shazaam!*, popped the ball loose from his grip as I
strained to wrap my arm around him. I was expecting to be dragged on the
ground and laughed at, but instead I felt him yield, stumble backward, and
collapse, taking me down with him. We lay there tangled for several seconds until Coach Dunn ran up screaming, "Did you see that! Did you see
that!" and pulled me — in a daze — to my feet, with my teammates cheering and seeing me, I think, for the first time as a serious person. I could hit.

And that became my reputation, the most cherished reputation of foot-   22
ball players everywhere, *a hitter.* My fellow sophomores looked at me with
something approaching awe the next few days (I omitted telling them how
terrified I had been). The thing snowballed. That moment somehow
became a model for manly conduct on the field, and I had to live up to it,
though I didn't always want to.

During a practice before a big game a couple of weeks later when the   23
regular punt returners were having a bad day, fumbling the ball several
times, Coach Dunn yelled out, "Put that Walton kid back there, he'll catch
it!" I remember, to this day, looking around for another guy named Walton,
the one he was referring to. But I did it, I went and caught punts, including many fair catches in one critical and close game, and including running two back for touchdowns in other games (but only because I'd had no
choice after mishandling fair catches; when a player signals for a fair catch
he must be allowed to catch the ball unmolested; if he drops it, it's a free
ball, precipitating a free-for-all. I had no choice after missing the catch but
to scoop the ball up and run for my life.) After one of the runbacks, one of
our coaches ran onto the field and congratulated me by screaming, "You've
got cast-iron balls!" I still didn't understand what was going on, only that I
was more afraid of looking foolish from failure than I was of whatever pain
or punishment would come from not living up to expectations.

But that was a life lesson I learned in football — if you can just hang on,   24
things have a way of working out. Half of being pretty good was in understanding the flow of a play or a game, knowing that this or that *tended* to
happen; the other half was, as Woody Allen says, just being there, just
showing up. Punt coverage by your opponents was planned based on the
ball being in the air for a certain length of time, but if you dropped it
and then picked it up and ran, or caught it cleanly, counted to two, and
sprinted in the opposite direction, often the first wave of defenders would
overrun you — as you would take longer to start moving than they'd
counted on — and as if by magic you would have open field.

Coach Dunn showed me a similar trick for the classic counterplay   25
(which is run to the opposite guard-center hole from the hand off). He
said, emphatically, "Hit the hole, keep your head down, count three steps,
then break against the grain. It'll be wide open." The first few times I blew

it badly, then he smacked me on the helmet and said very evenly, *"Don't look, don't think, just do it."* I did, and that play began to feel like the parting of the Red Sea.

I slowly came to understand why Coach Dunn won all the time. He practiced and prepared constantly and was a disciple of, among others, Vince Lombardi, who said, "Winning isn't everything, it's the only thing." Coach Dunn was a rationalist; he believed that you could analyze situations, draw parameters, assess your capabilities against your opponents', and implement plans. There was no excuse for losing; you just had to plan. We watched hours of film on our opponents each week, spending much of practice running their plays, learning their identifying ticks and tendencies. We studied them so fully that when it came to the actual game we would often know what they were going to do before they did it. This sort of intensity may be routine today in prep sports, but it wasn't in 1976; it gave us an almost supernatural advantage.

And I needed it, I needed any kind of edge I could get as I was still something of an impostor in my new incarnation as tough guy and enforcer. I was also beginning to learn that no matter how well I did, no matter how skilled I became, there were levels of players above me, guys who were born for the contained violence and mayhem of the football field. I wasn't one of those guys; I was a half-step slow and ten pounds too light.

As I see it now, my sin as a football player was that I thought too much, I wasn't what I would call a meat eater, a psycho. I could hit and liked it, but I wasn't like the guys I would later know at Notre Dame who routinely beat each other bloody, smashed their fists through windows, smashed lightbulbs with their teeth (a friend of mine who was All-American and All-Pro did this as a party trick), and other assorted kinds of mayhem. Another friend of mine at Notre Dame told me that the way to imagine what college ball was like was to think of the absolute hardest hit you had suffered in high school, from a guy like DeKalb's Mel Owens (later a Michigan and then L.A. Rams star) or Elgin's Mel Cole (later an Iowa star), and imagine that level of violence on every play. I couldn't. I cringed thinking about it. Taking a hit from one of those guys was enough to make me start considering what else I might be good at.

I had a headache during much of my sophomore year from being hit so much and I sometimes wondered whether it was worth it. But I admit it, I liked being seen, in that small circle, as a man among men; I liked being feted with the candy-bar signs the cheerleaders and poms made for us every Friday; I even liked being teased, as happened one day when I was limping up the stairs between classes, and a wiseass classmate called out, "Walton, you're even slower here than you are out on the field!" The way everybody laughed, with pleasure, told me that this wasn't an insult.

Junior year, I played "The Victor," a position on our defense that was roughly analogous to the University of Michigan's "Wolfman," which is to say, a position of honor. The Victor was a kind of floating safety whose job it was to line up into the opposition's strength, read the play as it developed, and get to the ball with decisive force. The Victor was also supposed to be able to defend the run or the pass with equal skill and ferocity; and when the coaches counted blue helmets around the ball at the close of a play in the game-film frame, the Victor's head had better have been there, preferably planted firmly in the middle of the ball carrier's chest.

I was doing quite well, the team, surprisingly, less so, when the unimaginable happened. I suffered a separated shoulder, an extremely painful injury (the arm bone tears out of the shoulder socket) that was to occur to me twice more. But adhering to the cult of toughness, I missed only a week of practice, though I moved for a while to less demanding positions. I felt driven to prove to the coaches and my teammates that I could cut it. Signs were posted in our training room and over the last door we walked through on the way to the field: "Pain is a badge of courage, wear it with pride," and "Those who stay will be champions." I believed both. . . .

But the dreams of glory were not to be fulfilled, not for me or for the team. I was having trouble with my shoulder, and, calamity of calamities, contracted pneumonia after several days of practice in rain and mud. I missed the last game of the regular season. I couldn't help wondering, what *was* the point? I made it back for the play-offs as a backup, only to participate in a decisive loss at home to Benet Academy, an upscale Catholic school from nearby Lisle, in the first round. We collapsed in that game and gave up, the one thing we were not *ever* supposed to do, and I have since wondered whether it happened because we were tired physically and mentally from the long season, or whether we, all of us, were simply tired of football and saw a way out. We were supposed to hate Benet, "rich" boys from Naperville and Wheaton and Hinsdale, and were supposed to teach them a thing or two about intensity and tempo.

But we were the ones who were schooled. We were pitiful. During that year, unlike the previous season, we had maintained the fiction that we were warriors and heroes throughout the regular season; but we folded in the most humiliating fashion, 27–6, when it mattered. And I think Coach Dunn saw something, too, saw that his beloved Catholic boys were succumbing to the culture at large and would no longer believe what they needed to believe — study, contemplation, violence — to be great. He resigned from our school a few weeks later, accepting a job as head coach at a huge public school in a northern Chicago suburb.

We betrayed that man, and I think we broke his heart, but how could we have known? We were supposed to be hitters, but were, in fact, phonies. We were sixteen- and seventeen-year-old boys living in a culture that was loosening up; we wanted to sample slack. Had the rest of my teammates been perpetrating the same masquerade I had?

In the locker room after the play-off loss, I remember sitting on the floor and crying, more from relief, I think, than sadness. Coach walked up to me, knelt before me, lifted my chin up, and said, "One thing: You can be as good as you want to be at anything you want." After a moment he stood up, bent over, and kissed the top of my head; then he straightened, turned, and walked away. I was stunned by this show of tenderness from a man whom, for all his kindness to me, I had always seen as remote, and I didn't understand what he meant. But then I realized (I thought) that he didn't know I had no intention of playing football in college, that I had begun to get recognition for my schoolwork and writing and had begun to meet the kind of girl who thought football was stupid, but that knowing about poetry and jazz was very, very cool. I had started to think football was stupid as well, and I was tired of the pain, of being sore and battered from the middle of August until Thanksgiving.

Years later, however, I don't see any of it as that simple, and I think that Coach Dunn might have known exactly what I was thinking. He was, after all, the man who had taken me, on his own time, to visit various colleges, including Northwestern (where he also arranged for me to meet their coaches and to spend some time with their then-star, Pete Shaw), which was decidedly "up" in our neck of the woods. He was also the one who had told me, when I expressed interest in attending a small local college, "I'm sure _____ is a fine school with a lot of fine Christian folks, in fact the coach is a good friend of mine, but around here we don't think about _____, we think about Southern Cal and Notre Dame." That was the first time I had thought about Notre Dame as a possibility for me. How had this Irishman from Chicago's rough-and-tumble West Side come to see so much in me, a secretive, suburban black kid, a would-be poet pretending to be a football hero, scheming to get out of what he considered to be nowhere? How had he known? Had this been what he meant that afternoon in sophomore practice, "Come on, Tony, show him what you got"? 36

The tackling drill that afternoon lingers; I have replayed it a thousand times. Something happened to me that day, and in the movie of my life that plays through my mind it is the proverbial first turning point, when the hero, in ignorance and valor, embarks upon the dark road of sorrow that will lead to his redemption. *I was so afraid*, and would remain so for some time. I would be into my late twenties before I was truly sure of myself, partially from implementing lessons — don't look, don't think, just do it, plan, practice, *and don't give up* — that I learned from Coach Dunn and from playing football, lessons I learned before I knew there was a life for men beyond sports and work. 37

Later in my life I've probably gone too far the other way, away from the timidity I had then and toward a certain ruthlessness — I have often thought that if I had possessed the mental ferocity when I was playing that I have now, bred from surviving long stretches of unemployment without money in hostile New York City and cold, cold Maine, I *would* have been All-American. But on that hot day in August I learned the sort of lesson that is crucial to becoming what we in our culture call "a man," something you must figure out for yourself because no one, not your coach, not your 38 brother, not even, perhaps especially not, your father, will ever tell you: The first step in a man's learning not to be afraid lies in hanging in there, hanging on, not under any circumstances giving up, and, most of all, not under any circumstances giving any hint, clue, or acknowledgment that he is, or might be, afraid.

Analyzing This Selection

1. How did the author's worries about "being a man" change during adolescence? Do these worries continue to affect the writer as an adult?

2. How did the father's attitude toward the boy's potential differ from his coach's? Did the boy live up to the expectations of either his father or his coach? Explain how.

3. **THE WRITER'S METHOD**   Walton does not indicate until paragraph 36 that he was a "black kid." How does that detail contribute to our understanding of his experience? For what effect does he withhold this detail until his concluding section?

Analyzing Connections

4. Explain how Walton's experience confirms or contradicts Mark Twain's view in the Insights on page 12. What motivation, if any, came to the boy from the *inside?*

Analyzing by Writing

5. Do you think people can best overcome worries by not showing them or by acknowledging them? Examine the concept of *being an adult* that the essay suggests, and explain your reasons for agreeing or disagreeing with the lessons Walton learned.

Terry Galloway

I'M LISTENING AS HARD AS I CAN

TERRY GALLOWAY (b. 1950) was born in Stuttgart, Germany, and grew up in Berlin and Austin, Texas. She graduated from the University of Texas. As a writer, director, and performer of one-woman performance pieces, Galloway has toured the United States, Canada, and the United Kingdom. Her first full-length play, *In the House of Moles*, was recently produced in Austin, Texas (2000). She has written for a public television series about disabled children. For the following essay about her own disability, Galloway always liked the title "Huh?" — but no editor has yet agreed with her.

At the age of twelve I won the swimming award at the Lions Camp for Crippled Children. When my name echoed over the PA system the girl in the wheelchair next to me grabbed the box speaker of my hearing aid and shouted, "You won!" My ear quaking, I took the cue. I stood up straight — the only physically unencumbered child in a sea of braces and canes — affixed a pained but brave grin to my face, then limped all the way to the stage.

Later, after the spotlight had dimmed, I was overcome with remorse, but not because I'd played the crippled heroine. The truth was that I was ashamed of my handicap. I wanted to have something more visibly wrong with me. I wanted to be in the same league as the girl who'd lost her right leg in a car accident; her artificial leg attracted a bevy of awestruck campers. I, on the other hand, wore an unwieldy box hearing aid buckled to my body like a dog halter. It attracted no one. Deafness wasn't, in my eyes, a blue-ribbon handicap. Mixed in with my envy, though, was an overwhelming sense of guilt; at camp I was free to splash in the swimming pool, while most of the other children were stranded at the shallow end, where lifeguards floated them in lazy circles. But seventeen years of living in the "normal" world has diminished my guilt considerably, and I've learned that every handicap has its own particular hell.

I'm something of an anomaly in the deaf world. Unlike most deaf people, who were either born deaf or went deaf in infancy, I lost my hearing in chunks over a period of twelve years. Fortunately I learned to speak before my loss grew too profound, and that ability freed me from the most severe problem facing the deaf — the terrible difficulty of making themselves understood. My opinion of deafness was just as biased as that of a person who can hear. I had never met a deaf child in my life, and I didn't know how to sign. I imagined deaf people to be like creatures from beyond: animal-like because their language was so physical, threatening because they were unable to express themselves with sophistication — that is, through speech. I *could* make myself understood, and because I had a talent for lipreading it was easy for me to pass in the wider world. And for most of my life that is exactly what I did — like a black woman playing white, I passed for something other than what I was. But in doing so I was avoiding some very painful facts. And for many years I was inhibited not only by my deafness but my own idea of what it meant to be deaf.

My problems all started when my mother, seven months pregnant with   4 me, developed a serious kidney infection. Her doctors pumped her full of antibiotics. Two months later I was born, with nothing to suggest that I was anything more or less than a normal child. For years nobody knew that the antibiotics had played havoc with my fetal nervous system. I grew up bright, happy, and energetic.

But by the time I was ten I knew, if nobody else did, that something   5 somewhere had gone wrong. The people around me had gradually developed fuzzy profiles, and their speech had taken on a blurred and foreign character. But I was such a secure and happy child that it didn't enter my mind to question my new perspective or mention the changes to anyone else. Finally, my behavior became noticeably erratic — I would make nonsensical replies to ordinary questions or simply fail to reply at all. My teachers, deciding that I was neither a particularly creative child nor an especially troublesome one, looked for a physical cause. They found two: I wasn't quite as blind as a bat, but I was almost as deaf as a doornail.

My parents took me to Wilford Hall Air Force Hospital in San Antonio,   6 where I was examined from ear to ear. My tonsils were removed and studied, ice water was injected into my inner ear, and I underwent a series of inexplicable and at times painful exploratory tests. I would forever after associate deafness with kind attention and unusual punishment. Finally a verdict was delivered: "Congenital interference has resulted in a neural disorder for which there is no known medical or surgical treatment." My hearing loss was severe and would grow progressively worse.

I was fitted with my first hearing aid and sent back home to resume my   7 childhood. I never did. I had just turned twelve, and my body was undergoing enormous changes. I had baby fat, baby breasts, hairy legs, and thick pink cat-eye glasses. My hearing aid was about the size of a small transistor radio and rode in a white linen pouch that hit exactly at breast level. It was not a welcome addition to my pubescent woe.

As a vain child trapped in a monster's body, I was frantic for a way to survive the next few years. Glimpsing my reflection in mirrors became such   8 agony that I acquired a habit of brushing my teeth and hair with my eyes closed. Everything I did was geared to making my body more inhabitable, but I only succeeded in making it less so. I kept my glasses in my pocket and developed an unbecoming squint; I devised a smile that hid two broken front teeth, but it looked disturbingly like the grin of a piranha; I kept my arms folded over my would-be breasts. But the hearing aid was a different story. There was no way to disguise it. I could tuck it under my blouse, but then all I could hear was the static of cotton. Besides, whenever I took a step the box bounced around like a third breast. So I resigned myself: A monster I was, a monster I would be.

I became more withdrawn, more suspicious of other people's intentions.   9
I imagined that I was being deliberately excluded from school-yard talk because the other children didn't make much of an effort to involve me — they simply didn't have the time or patience to repeat snatches of gossip ten times and slowly. Conversation always reached the point of ridiculousness before I could understand something as simple as "The movie starts at five." (The groovy shark's alive? The moving stars that thrive?) I didn't make it to many movies. I cultivated a lofty sense of superiority, and I was often brutal with people who offered the "wrong" kind of help at the "wrong" time. Right after my thirteenth birthday some well-meaning neighbors took me to a revivalist faith healing. I already had doubts about exuberant religions, and the knee-deep hysteria of the preacher simply confirmed them. He bounded to my side and put his hands on my head. "O Lord," he cried, "heal this poor little lamb!"

I leaped up as if transported and shouted, "I can walk!"   10

For the first few years my parents were as bewildered as I was. Nothing   11
had prepared them for a handicapped child on the brink of adolescence. They sensed a whole other world of problems, but in those early stages I still seemed so normal that they just couldn't see me in a school for the deaf. They felt that although such schools were there to help, they also served to isolate. I have always been grateful for their decision. Because of it, I had to contend with public schools, and in doing so I developed two methods of survival: I learned to read not just lips but the whole person, and I learned the habit of clear speech by taking every speech and drama course I could.

That is not to say my adolescent years were easygoing — they were mis-   12
ery. The lack of sound cast a pall on everything. Life seemed less fun than it had been before. I didn't associate that lack of fun with the lack of sound. I didn't begin to make the connection between the failings of my body and the failings of the world until I was well out of college. I simply did not admit to myself that deafness caused certain problems — or even that I was deaf.

From the time I was twelve until I was twenty-four, the loss of my hear-   13
ing was erratic. I would lose a decibel or two of sound and then my hearing would stabilize. A week or a year later there would be another slip and then I'd have to adjust all over again. I never knew when I would hit bottom. I remember going to bed one night still being able to make out the

reassuring purr of the refrigerator and the late-night conversation of my parents, then waking the next morning to nothing — even my own voice was gone. These fits and starts continued until my hearing finally dropped to the last rung of amplifiable sound. I was a college student at the time, and whenever anyone asked about my hearing aid, I admitted to being only slightly hard of hearing.

My professors were frequently alarmed by my almost maniacal intensity 14 in class. I was petrified that I'd have to ask for special privileges just to achieve marginal understanding. My pride was in flames. I became increasingly bitter and isolated. I was terrified of being marked a deaf woman, a label that made me sound dumb and cowlike, enveloped in a protective silence that denied me my complexity. I did everything I could to hide my handicap. I wore my hair long and never wore earrings, thus keeping attention away from my ears and their riders. I monopolized conversations so that I wouldn't slip up and reveal what I was or wasn't hearing; I took on a disdainful air at large parties, hoping that no one would ask me something I couldn't instantly reply to. I lied about the extent of my deafness so I could avoid the stigma of being thought "different" in a pathetic way.

It was not surprising that in my senior year I suffered a nervous collapse 15 and spent three days in the hospital crying like a baby. When I stopped crying I knew it was time to face a few things — I had to start asking for help when I needed it because I couldn't handle my deafness alone, and I had to quit being ashamed of my handicap so I could begin to live with its consequences and discover what (if any) were its rewards.

When I began telling people that I was *really* deaf, I did so with grim 16 determination. Some were afraid to talk to me at any length, fearing perhaps that they were talking into a void; others assumed that I was somehow an unsullied innocent and always inquired in carefully enunciated sentences: "Doooooooo youuuuuuuu driiinnk liquor?" But most people were surprisingly sympathetic — they wanted to know the best way to be understood, they took great pains to talk directly to my face, and they didn't insult me by using only words of one syllable.

It was, in part, that gentle acceptance that made me more curious about 17 my own deafness. Always before it had been an affliction to wrestle with as one would with angels, but when I finally accepted it as an inevitable part of my life, I relaxed enough to do some exploring. I would take off my hearing aid and go through a day, a night, an hour or two — as long as I could take it — in absolute silence. I felt as if I were indulging in a secret vice because I was perceiving the world in a new way — stripped of sound.

Of course I had always known that sound is vibration, but I didn't know, 18 until I stopped straining to hear, how truly sound is a refinement of feeling. Conversations at parties might elude me, but I seldom fail to pick up on moods. I enjoy watching people talk. When I am too far away to read lips I try reading postures and imagining conversations. Sometimes, to everyone's horror, I respond to things better left unsaid when I'm trying to find out what's going on around me. I want to see, touch, taste, and smell everything within reach; I especially have to curb a tendency to judge things by their smell — not just potato salad but people as well — a habit that seems to some people entirely too barbaric for comfort. I am not claiming that my other senses stepped up their work to compensate for the loss, but the absence of one does allow me to concentrate on the others. Deafness has left me acutely aware of both the duplicity that language is capable of and the many expressions the body cannot hide.

Nine years ago I spent the summer at the University of Texas's experimental Shakespeare workshop at Winedale, and I went back each year for eight years, first as a student and then as a staff associate. Off and on for the last four years I have written and performed for Esther's Follies, a cabaret theater group in Austin. Some people think it's odd that, as deaf as I am, I've spent so much of my life working in the theater, but I find it to be a natural consequence of my particular circumstance. The loss of sound has enhanced my fascination with language and the way meaning is conveyed. I love to perform. Exactly the same processes occur onstage as off — except that onstage, once I've memorized the script, I know what everybody is saying as they say it. I am delighted to be so immediately in the know. It has provided a direct way to keep in touch with the rest of the world despite the imposed isolation. 19

Silence is not empty; it is simply more sobering than sound. At times I prefer the sobriety. I can still "hear" with a hearing aid — that is, I can discern noise, but I can't tell you where it's coming from or if it is laughter or a faulty drain. When there are many people talking together I hear a strange music, a distant rumbling in my consciousness. But when I take off my hearing aid at night and lie in bed surrounded by my fate, I wonder, "What is this — a foul subtraction or a blessing in disguise?" For despite my fears there is a kind of peace in the silence — albeit an uneasy one. There is, after all, less to distract me from my thoughts. 20

But I know what I've lost. The process of becoming deaf has at times been frightening, akin perhaps to dying, and early in life it took away my happy confidence in the image of a world where things always work right. When I first came back from the Lions Camp that summer I cursed heaven and earth for doing such terrible wrong to me and to my friends. My grandmother tried to comfort me by promising, "Honey, God's got something special planned for you." 21

But I thought, "Yes. He plans to make me deaf." 22

Analyzing This Selection

1. How does the author's deafness differ from that of most other deaf people? In what ways has this difference made her problems both easier and more burdensome?

2. **THE WRITER'S METHOD**   At the end of paragraph 5, the author uses two clichés about herself. What emotions in the twelve-year-old child do the clichés suggest? How does her use of cliché affect the reader?

3. In high school and college, why did Galloway refuse to acknowledge the serious consequences of her deafness? What other important considerations were at stake for her? Do you think that her denials were wise or immature for her age?

4. How has deafness influenced the author's adult awareness of the world? How has it influenced her self-awareness?

5. In paragraphs 21 and 22, is the interchange between the author and her grandmother an appropriate or disappointing conclusion to the essay? What attitudes and feelings does it suggest the author has found beneficial?

Analyzing Connections

6. Both Galloway and Ephron (see "Shaping Up Absurd," p. 16) suffer mortifications. Compare the kinds of humiliation they endure. What similarities and differences do you find in their self-images?

Analyzing by Writing

7. Helen Keller, who became deaf and blind when she was nineteen months old, said that deafness was the more difficult of her two misfortunes. Which deprivation would be more threatening to you? Are you primarily visually or aurally oriented? Write an essay explaining how the complete loss of sight or hearing would disconnect you from what you now value most in the world and in yourself.

Brent Staples

BLACK MEN AND PUBLIC SPACE

BRENT STAPLES (b. 1951) was born in Chester, Pennsylvania. He earned
his undergraduate degree at Widener University and a Ph.D. in psychology
from the University of Chicago. After working at the *Chicago Sun-Times*
and several Chicago periodicals, he became an assistant metropolitan
editor at the *New York Times* in 1985. He is now on the editorial board of
that newspaper. Staples has published a memoir, *Parallel Time: Growing
Up in Black and White* (1994). The following essay, which appeared first
in *Ms.* magazine, describes his experience of "being ever the suspect" in
urban America.

My first victim was a woman — white, well dressed, probably in her early 1
twenties. I came upon her late one evening on a deserted street in Hyde
Park, a relatively affluent neighborhood in an otherwise mean, impover-
ished section of Chicago. As I swung onto the avenue behind her, there
seemed to be a discreet, uninflammatory distance between us. Not so. She
cast back a worried glance. To her, the youngish black man — a broad six
feet two inches with a beard and billowing hair, both hands shoved into the
pockets of a bulky military jacket — seemed menacingly close. After a few
more quick glimpses, she picked up her pace and was soon running in
earnest. Within seconds she disappeared into a cross street.

That was more than a decade ago. I was twenty-two years old, a gradu- 2
ate student newly arrived at the University of Chicago. It was in the echo
of that terrified woman's footfalls that I first began to know the unwieldy
inheritance I'd come into — the ability to alter public space in ugly ways.
It was clear that she thought herself the quarry of a mugger, a rapist, or
worse. Suffering a bout of insomnia, however, I was stalking sleep, not
defenseless wayfarers. As a softy who is scarcely able to take a knife to a raw
chicken — let alone hold one to a person's throat — I was surprised, embarrassed, and dismayed all at once. Her flight made me feel like an accom-
plice in tyranny. It also made it clear that I was indistinguishable from the
muggers who occasionally seeped into the area from the surrounding
ghetto. That first encounter, and those that followed, signified that a vast,
unnerving gulf lay between nighttime pedestrians — particularly women —
and me. And I soon gathered that being perceived as dangerous is a hazard
in itself. I only needed to turn a corner into a dicey situation, or crowd

some frightened, armed person in a foyer somewhere, or make an errant move after being pulled over by a policeman. Where fear and weapons meet — and they often do in urban America — there is always the possibility of death.

In that first year, my first away from my hometown, I was to become thoroughly familiar with the language of fear. At dark, shadowy intersections, I could cross in front of a car stopped at a traffic light and elicit the *thunk, thunk, thunk, thunk* of the driver — black, white, male, or female —hammering down the door locks. On less traveled streets after dark, I grew accustomed to but never comfortable with people crossing to the other side of the street rather than pass me. Then there were the standard unpleasantries with policemen, doormen, bouncers, cabdrivers, and others whose business it is to screen out troublesome individuals *before* there is any nastiness.

I moved to New York nearly two years ago and I have remained an avid night walker. In central Manhattan, the near-constant crowd cover minimizes tense one-on-one street encounters. Elsewhere — in SoHo, for example, where sidewalks are narrow and tightly spaced buildings shut out the sky — things can get very taut indeed.

After dark, on the warrenlike streets of Brooklyn where I live, I often see women who fear the worst from me. They seem to have set their faces on neutral, and with their purse straps strung across their chests bandolier-style, they forge ahead as though bracing themselves against being tackled. I understand, of course, that the danger they perceive is not a hallucination. Women are particularly vulnerable to street violence, and young black males are drastically overrepresented among the perpetrators of that violence. Yet these truths are no solace against the kind of alienation that comes of being ever the suspect, a fearsome entity with whom pedestrians avoid making eye contact.

It is not altogether clear to me how I reached the ripe old age of twenty-two without being conscious of the lethality nighttime pedestrians attributed to me. Perhaps it was because in Chester, Pennsylvania, the small, angry industrial town where I came of age in the 1960s, I was scarcely noticeable against a backdrop of gang warfare, street knifings, and murders. I grew up one of the good boys, had perhaps a half-dozen fistfights. In retrospect, my shyness of combat has clear sources.

As a boy, I saw countless tough guys locked away; I have since buried several, too. They were babies, really — a teenage cousin, a brother of twenty-two, a childhood friend in his mid-twenties — all gone down in episodes of bravado played out in the streets. I came to doubt the virtues of intimidation early on. I chose, perhaps unconsciously, to remain a shadow — timid, but a survivor.

The fearsomeness mistakenly attributed to me in public places often has a perilous flavor. The most frightening of these confusions occurred in the late 1970s and early 1980s, when I worked as a journalist in Chicago. One day, rushing into the office of a magazine I was writing for with a deadline story in hand, I was mistaken for a burglar. The office manager called security and, with an ad hoc posse, pursued me through the labyrinthine halls, nearly to my editor's door. I had no way of proving who I was. I could only move briskly toward the company of someone who knew me.

Another time I was on assignment for a local paper and killing time   9
before an interview. I entered a jewelry store on the city's affluent Near North Side. The proprietor excused herself and returned with an enormous red Doberman pinscher straining at the end of a leash. She stood, the dog extended toward me, silent to my questions, her eyes bulging nearly out of her head. I took a cursory look around, nodded, and bade her good night.

Relatively speaking, however, I never fared as badly as another black   10
male journalist. He went to nearby Waukegan, Illinois, a couple of summers ago to work on a story about a murderer who was born there. Mistaking the reporter for the killer, police officers hauled him from his car at gunpoint and but for his press credentials would probably have tried to book him. Such episodes are not uncommon. Black men trade tales like this all the time.

Over the years, I learned to smother the rage I felt at so often being   11
taken for a criminal. Not to do so would surely have led to madness. I now take precautions to make myself less threatening. I move about with care, particularly late in the evening. I give a wide berth to nervous people on subway platforms during the wee hours, particularly when I have exchanged business clothes for jeans. If I happen to be entering a building behind some people who appear skittish, I may walk by, letting them clear the lobby before I return, so as not to seem to be following them. I have been calm and extremely congenial on those rare occasions when I've been pulled over by the police.

And on late-evening constitutionals I employ what has proved to be an   12
excellent tension-reducing measure: I whistle melodies from Beethoven and Vivaldi and the more popular classical composers. Even steely New Yorkers hunching toward nighttime destinations seem to relax, and occasionally they even join in the tune. Virtually everybody seems to sense that a mugger wouldn't be warbling bright, sunny selections from Vivaldi's *Four Seasons*. It is my equivalent of the cowbell that hikers wear when they know they are in bear country.

Analyzing This Selection

1. **THE WRITER'S METHOD**   What is the effect of the opening paragraph?

2. How does the author's presence "alter public space in ugly ways"? Describe the difference between Staples's image of himself and how he is perceived by others.

3. Why doesn't Staples see the suspicion he elicits from being a young black man on the street as solely the result of racial attitudes?

4. How does the author defuse the explosive tensions his presence produces in other people? Do his methods compromise his own self-image and integrity?

5. What is the essay's overall purpose? Does Staples propose any remedies for the unjust assumptions he describes?

Analyzing Connections

6. Staples and Galloway (see "I'm Listening as Hard as I Can," p. 34) each relate a brief incident in their opening paragraphs. Compare the themes and tones they introduce within these anecdotal openings. Both essays conclude by echoing the opening anecdotes. What is the effect of such endings?

Analyzing by Writing

7. In what way have you been stereotyped? Perhaps as "a brain" or "a jock"; or as a black, a Jew, an Italian; or as someone who is always "good-natured" or always "responsible." In an essay, examine the stereotype that falsifies and denigrates something that is true in your nature.

Nan Levinson

THE SAD PLEASURES OF TRAVEL

NAN LEVINSON (b. 1950) writes about human rights concerns such as
free expression by artists in various parts of the world. She graduated
from the University of Rochester and earned a master's degree in international administration. Her essays and reviews have appeared in the
Chicago Tribune, the *Christian Science Monitor,* the *Boston Globe,* and
other publications. Levinson teaches writing at Tufts University. This
essay was printed in the issue "In Praise of Pleasure" in the *Women's
Review of Books* (1998).

"For my part, I travel not to go anywhere, but to go," wrote Robert Louis 1
Stevenson. "The great affair is to move." To move, to go, to travel; the need
can be so great as to be almost a sickness, away-sickness, maybe, an untam-
ably sweet longing to go somewhere that will never be your home among
people you'll never know well enough to belong to.

When I was little, my uncle gave me storybooks with pictures of kids 2
around the world: a Dutch girl surrounded by tulips and wearing a
starched white cap with wings; a Chinese boy with a pigtail who slept on a
brick bed heated by coals. They were clichés so bald it's embarrassing to
think about, but I loved those books and wanted to be everywhere those
children were. More than that, I wanted to be those children, each of them
in turn. I think maybe the first real sadness of my life came when I realized
that I couldn't.

Later on, I pinned a map to a wall and drew a red line along the routes 3
I had traveled: Europe, the Andes, India and Nepal; for some reason, not
the U.S. or Canada. Then I realized that all I had seen was what was on
either side of that line, and that made me too sad to continue.

One night in the seventies, friends and I, probably stoned, created a 4
travel agency of the mind. We'd offer package deals to tiny countries
(Andorra, San Marino, Fiji), or to countries colored green on the globe, or
we'd organize terrorism tours to the sites of bombings, kidnappings and
assassinations. (I used to walk a version of that in Washington on my way to
work.) We would call our agency Book in Haste, Repent at Leisure.

And why not, really? Once you eliminate travel for work or family oblig- 5
ation, you have tourism, and tourists usually have more pretexts than reasons

for choosing one place over another. But once you do choose, the world becomes full of reasons: the tart crunch of the apples the Buddhist monk pulled like a magic trick from his maroon-and-saffron robe when we shared a bus seat on the world's highest highway; the Andean air that's ripe as cheese and thin as gauze (music and smells are most evocative of place and time); the moment the lights come on in Florence's Brancacci Chapel and you see the Masaccios for the first — or tenth — time. I have no words for that.

In Venice late one afternoon, as I put my camera to my eye to shoot a narrow canal with laundry flapping overhead like Chinese kites, a man came out of his house right in front of my lens. He looked at me as if I were nuts, photographing his underwear, and all I could do was point at the sky and say, "La luce." The light. "Ah," he said, nodding gravely, and walked on. 6

So there's that too in the mix: those giddy moments when you connect across language and custom and all the ways that we divide the world into pieces. And we do divide. Every culture I know of has a word that means "not-us." 7

With luck and time, you make deeper connections, too, but the odd convergences are particularly seductive because they can't last, would turn into something else if they did. Travel, too, by definition moves and changes. Travelers arrive with such expectation, peer into a landscape and leave. They're always passers-through, outsiders. They try to hold onto a place with travelogues and photos, but even the teller tires of twelfth-told tales, and snapshots begin to seem like the blur of calendar pages that movies use to signify the passing of time. Travel is sweet because it doesn't wear out its welcome, bittersweet because it puts time and place in perspective and reminds us how small we are. 8

I went through a sixties graduate program in which one of our "learning modules" (we had nothing so pedestrian as courses) was Cross Cultural Training. We studied a seven-step acculturation process, which began with establishing communication and ended somewhere around Nirvana. In between were all the clumsiness and victories people go through when they try to navigate a place they don't know very well. 9

One assignment was a Peace Corps exercise called the drop-off. With one dollar and whatever fit in a small backpack, you were left in an unfamiliar town for 24 hours to fend for yourself. I ended up in Zoar, Massachusetts, which, as far as I could tell, was home to three workers building a nuclear power plant, ten snarling dogs and one whorehouse. I immediately hitched to the next town. There, embarrassed by the preciousness of my situation, I told people I was researching the psychology of humor, whereupon they invited me in, answered my impromptu questions and fed me cookies. It wasn't the last time I traveled on prevarication, little money and the kindness — and strangeness — of strangers. 10

When I was 33, dissatisfied at work, bored at play and living as if busy- 11
ness were the moral dimension of my days, I decided to move to Portugal.
Why Portugal? everyone asked, right after they said, You're so, lucky; I wish
I could do that, which I knew they didn't mean because I'd learned that
Americans view anyone who chooses to live somewhere else with suspi-
cion. Besides, most of them could have done it if they had really wanted to.

I suppose I was working on the assumption that if you can't change who 12
you are, at least you can change where you are, but I still don't know why
I chose Portugal. I told people it was because it was cheap, until my
mother told me to cut it out, but when it came time to go somewhere —
anywhere (and what a dizzying freedom that is) — Portugal was it. I broke
my lease, threw out what I couldn't pack and stored the rest in a friend's
attic. I bought a map of Portugal, an international driver's license, and a
plane ticket to Lisbon and left before I could chicken out. More busyness,
but it worked.

The woman at the *pensão* where I stayed made me speak Portuguese. "A 13
practicar," she said. When I could bear to practice no longer, I fled to the
streets, getting happily lost for hours. Lisbon is a wonderful city, full of half-
seens and dead ends, and I'd find triumph one minute in mastering the
ticket machines for the subway, despair the next when I couldn't understand directions back to my hotel. Being a tourist must be the single most
disconcerting occupation in the world.

How I reveled in anonymity those first days! I could be anyone I wanted, 14
could make myself up out of whole cloth in the good American traditions
of lying and rebirth. I imagined disappearing, simply slipping away — easy
enough, since no one knew me there and the people who knew me elsewhere didn't know where I was. (If a tourist falls in a strange city, does she
make a sound?)

I headed to the Algarve, the south coast, to live by the sea out of season, 15
as I had promised myself I would, then did everything in reverse: place to
live, clothes in closets, calls to contacts of the contacts I had called in
the States. I had arrived with only two suitcases, English and Portuguese
dictionaries and baggies of the five spices I had determined I couldn't
do without. I had nowhere to be for the rest of my life. But soon enough,
other things found their way into this new life of mine and they, too, had
to be hauled around whenever I moved. You can run under Moorish arches
and down to the sea's edge every day, but you're still running on your own
feet.

Sometime around then it occurred to me that the only way to avoid 16
being a culture cliché is to live in someone else's culture. It may be also
the only way to live outside history. When you travel, it's easy to avoid your
own history in the making; you just don't buy a *Herald Tribune* or watch
CNN. As for the history of another country, you escape that without trying
too hard to translate the rapid-fire newscasts, too complicated to unravel

the allegiances of power. After a while, it comes to seem no more conse-
quential than a children's story: Once upon a time in a far-off land called
Portugal, the escudo was devalued for the third time in a year, so one day
when little José and Maria went to the store, they found that the price of
bread had risen once again.

We travel to look at people who have stayed put. We'd rather their cul-   17
tures stayed put too, stalled in some moment we think of as genuine. The
Guambiano Indians, who live on a high plain in the Colombian Andes,
used to hand-dye the deep blue fabric from which they made their clothing, but by the time I lived there, RIT and polyester had taken over. When
I bemoaned this — what — impurity? — to an anthropologist (the place was
lousy with anthropologists), she scolded me: insisting the Guambianos stop
at the plant-dye stage, she said, was like insisting that American culture be
Elvis Presley.

I think about that often, and not just because some people do think   18
American culture is Elvis Presley. The commercial dyes were crummier
than the natural ones, but they seemed to come along with the paved road
and potable water that our town was lucky to have in this poor region. The
changes made life easier and safer for the Guambianos at the same time
that they undermined what I — and probably they — thought of as their culture. So I'm not sure where I stand. Predictability is the enemy, inimical to
travel, but no matter how lightly they tread, travelers leave footprints. I
travel to find what I don't already know, and the more I and everyone else
aims for that, the less possible it becomes.

After nine months in Portugal, I returned to London, where I had   19
worked two years before. I'd sit in pubs for hours, nursing a whiskey and
reading, while the other patrons watched me with suspicion since pubs
aren't libraries. I gloried in hearing my language spoken all around me,
though, if pressed, I'd have to admit that I'm most at home when I'm out
of place. It was probably the first time in my life that being taken for a
tourist didn't seem like a mortal sin.

Then I walked. At Parliament Hill, I imagined taking a little house fur-   20
nished with a desk and a daybed pushed in front of the window to look out
over London's rooftops. I'd live there from April to October, when it wasn't
perpetually damp, and I'd read and write and take a lover who was married
and lived a little ways off. (Oxford sounded right.) He'd visit me a few afternoons a week when we'd make vigorous love, and after, we'd wrap ourselves in robes and drink whiskey or tea, whatever the weather demanded.
Then he'd go back to his town and his wife and not bother me. Laws of
travel: To know how a society functions, transact business at the post office.
To know how a society falls apart, fall in love.

Expatriates tend to be great monologuists, as if they are renting space in   21
their adopted country and using words to form the walls and ceilings and
floors. They strike up conversations easily (people on the move recognize
each other by their lack of belongings and their shoes), but all they really
share is the knowledge that they don't fit and the itch to move on. So many
ways to be out of place, all these refugees fleeing nothing and playing at
exile because, unlike real exiles, they can go home again. Travel is the rare
situation in which you can change and be yourself at the same time.

Travelers also like to talk, and have a penchant for sweeping statements   22
like the ones in this essay. The best of them are able to sum up whole con-
tinents in a single adjective. They're notorious plagiarizers, too, forever
quoting opinions and seldom giving more credit than "someone said" or "I
hear." *I hear Indian men are the most sexist in the world. My friend says Portugal is a cold country with a warm sun. Someone told me Parisians are less
rude these days.* Oh no, please not that last one. Insult is part of travel, and
one of its many mixed blessings.

Travelers collect things — factoids, addresses, train routes, totemic cloth-   23
ing. I collect words about states of travel.

Querencia (Spanish): A sense of belonging intensely to a place, which   24
can be as big as a country or as small as a room. You don't have to know
you're looking, but when you find it, you feel as if the only time you're
whole is when you're there.

Saudade (Portuguese): Inchoate longing, fond remembrance, the almost   25
but not quite, the satisfaction just beyond reach. It's the kind of voluptuous
yearning that infects travelers, expatriates, refugees, exiles, all the people
out of place by choice or circumstance. But these definitions miss the delicious languor of its melancholy. They miss, too, the understanding of how
futile it is to try to tame sadness (some cultures embrace it, others deny
it) — which is just as well, because if you could say the ineffable, it would
be just one more thing with a name.

Two final stories. The first takes place at a casino on Portugal's south   26
coast where a bunch of us who were living nearby went to hear a friend
sing. She sent over bottles of wine and joined us between sets as we jab-
bered about all the places we had been and liked best; but after a while,
our talk lessened. "It is well known," wrote Neruda, "that he who returns
never really left." But that's true only sometimes. Love for a place is like
love for a person, and remembering from a distance is really very lonely.
Then, as she was going back on stage, the singer threw her arms wide to
encompass us all and with a cackle proclaimed, "You know, for people
who've never had any money, we certainly have had a good time."

The second story takes place in Lisbon. Two old women are taking pho-   27
tos of each other in front of a looming statue, and I stop to watch for several minutes as one takes a picture, then walks carefully across the plaza to
hand the other the camera before arranging herself — a little to the left, the

right, smile. Then, their task complete, they help each other down the subway stairs and disappear. That will be me too someday, I think (do I laugh or mourn?), a traveling companion to some equally lost old woman, taking pictures to prove we were there, so light and dry that we rustle.

Ah yes — but having a very good time.   28

Analyzing This Selection

1. Is there a central, consistent impulse in the author's lifelong reasons for travel?

2. What "disconcerting" dissatisfactions arise in Levinson's travels?

3. **THE WRITER'S METHOD** The essay jumps through different times and places; it doesn't follow a narrative or logical progression. How does Levinson build, expand, and move her points forward?

Analyzing Connections

4. Relate Levinson's desire for change to Fay Weldon's advice in the Insights on page 13. Do the writers agree about the makeup of identity? Before jumping to conclusions, reconsider paragraphs 24 and 25 of Levinson's essay.

Analyzing by Writing

5. Analyze the real and fantasy elements in an early travel impulse. What distant place did you powerfully want to go to? How much did you know about the place? What were some of your reasons for wanting to go there? What aspects of your desire and expectations did you keep partly or wholly private? If you ultimately went, then or later, how did the place fulfill, or not fulfill, your anticipations?

Garry Trudeau

MY INNER SHRIMP

GARRY TRUDEAU (b. 1948) produces the celebrated comic strip *Doonesbury*. Growing up in upstate New York, he was absorbed by the fantasies of A. A. Milne, author of *Winnie-the-Pooh* and other children's books. Trudeau graduated from Yale University, where he began a college satirical comic strip, later transformed and syndicated as *Doonesbury*. Trudeau's work has won a Pulitzer Prize (1975) and other awards.

For the rest of my days, I shall be a recovering short person. Even from my lofty perch of something over six feet (as if I don't know within a micron), I have the soul of a shrimp. I feel the pain of the diminutive, irrespective of whether they feel it themselves, because my visit to the planet of the teenage midgets was harrowing, humiliating, and extended. I even perceive my last-minute escape to have been flukish, somehow unearned — as if the Commissioner of Growth Spurts had been an old classmate of my father.

My most recent reminder of all this came the afternoon I went hunting for a new office. I had noticed a building under construction in my neighborhood — a brick warren of duplexes, with wide, westerly-facing windows, promising ideal light for a working studio. When I was ushered into the model unit, my pulse quickened: The soaring, twenty-two-foot living room walls were gloriously aglow with the remains of the day. I bonded immediately.

Almost as an afterthought, I ascended the staircase to inspect the loft, ducking as I entered the bedroom. To my great surprise, I stayed ducked: The room was a little more than six feet in height. While my head technically cleared the ceiling, the effect was excruciatingly oppressive. This certainly wasn't a space I wanted to spend any time in, much less take out a mortgage on.

Puzzled, I wandered down to the sales office and asked if there were any other units to look at. No, replied a resolutely unpleasant receptionist, it was the last one. Besides, they were all exactly alike.

"Are you aware of how low the bedroom ceilings are?" I asked.

She shot me an evil look. "Of course we are," she snapped. "There were some problems with the building codes. The architect knows all about the ceilings.

"He's not an idiot, you know," she added, perfectly anticipating my next 7 question.

She abruptly turned away, but it was too late. She'd just confirmed that 8 a major New York developer, working with a fully licensed architect, had knowingly created an entire twelve-story apartment building virtually uninhabitable by anyone of even average height. It was an exclusive high-rise for shorties.

Once I knew that, of course, I couldn't stay away. For days thereafter, as 9 I walked to work, some perverse, unreasoning force would draw me back to the building. But it wasn't just the absurdity, the stone silliness of its design that had me in its grip; it was something far more compelling. Like some haunted veteran come again to an ancient battlefield, I was revisiting my perilous past.

When I was fourteen, I was the third-smallest in a high school class of 10 one hundred boys, routinely mistaken for a sixth grader. My first week of school, I was drafted into a contingent of students ignominiously dubbed the "Midgets," so grouped by taller boys presumably so they could taunt us with more perfect efficiency. Inexplicably, some of my fellow Midgets refused to be diminished by the experience, but I retreated into self-pity. I sent away for a book on how to grow tall, and committed to memory its tips on overcoming one's genetic destiny — or at least making the most of a regrettable situation. The book cited historical figures who had gone the latter route — Alexander the Great, Caesar, Napoleon (the mind involuntarily added Hitler). Strategies for stretching the limbs were suggested — hanging from door frames, sleeping on your back, doing assorted floor exercises — all of which I incorporated into my daily routine (get up, brush teeth, hang from door frame). I also learned the importance of meeting girls early in the day, when, the book assured me, my rested spine rendered me perceptibly taller.

For six years, my condition persisted; I grew, but at nowhere near the 11 rate of my peers. I perceived other problems as ancillary, and loaded up the stature issue with freight shipped in daily from every corner of my life. Lack of athletic success, all absence of a social life, the inevitable run-ins with bullies — all could be attributed to the missing inches. The night I found myself sobbing in my father's arms was the low point; we both knew it was one problem he couldn't fix.

Of course what we couldn't have known was that he and my mother 12 already had. They had given me a delayed developmental timetable. In my seventeenth year, I miraculously shot up six inches, just in time for graduation and a fresh start. I was, in the space of a few months, reborn — and I made the most of it. Which is to say that thereafter, all of life's disappointments, reversals, and calamities still arrived on schedule — but blissfully free of subtext.

Once you stop being the butt, of course, any problem recedes, if only to 13 give way to a new one. And yet the impact of being literally looked down on, of being *made* to feel small, is forever. It teaches you how to stretch, how to survive the scorn of others for things that are beyond your control. Not growing forces you to grow up fast.

Sometimes I think I'd like to return to a high-school reunion to surprise   14 my classmates. Not that they didn't know me when I finally started catching up. They did, but I doubt they'd remember. Adolescent hierarchies have a way of enduring; I'm sure I am still recalled as the Midget I myself have never really left behind.

Of course, if I'm going to show up, it'll have to be soon. I'm starting to   15 shrink.

Analyzing This Selection

1. **THE WRITER'S METHOD**   Identify exaggerated phrases and terms that contribute to Trudeau's tone. Explain how these overstatements strengthen or weaken his point.

2. Trudeau claims that "adolescent hierarchies" endure (para. 14). If true, what causes or motivates this inflexibility? Support or refute Trudeau's contention.

Analyzing Connections

3. If Trudeau had remained short, how would his recollections and attitude resemble or differ from Ephron's in "Shaping Up Absurd" (p. 16)?

Analyzing by Writing

4. Unlike Trudeau's, our secret body image can be more versatile or more perfect than our everyday form. Our ideal or imagined body image can include the effects of achievements and exhilarations, whether temporary or permanent. Athletics, survival skills (as in those achieved by taking part in Outward Bound), acting, dance, horseback riding, perhaps music, can increase our sense of our body's potential. Analyze the origins and dimensions of your inner best body image.

Jamaica Kincaid

GIRL

JAMAICA KINCAID (b. 1949) was born in Antigua in the West Indies, and much of her work draws on her early life on the island. She came to the United States at seventeen and soon began writing fiction and essays. From 1974 to 1995 Kincaid was a staff writer at the *New Yorker* and wrote fiction at the same time, producing a collection of stories, *At the Bottom of the River* (1983), and three novels, *Annie John* (1985), *Lucy* (1990), and *The Autobiography of My Mother* (1996). Kincaid's reflections about gardening in *My Garden Book* (1999) range from her garden in Vermont to her Caribbean memories to colonial history. The very short story "Girl" is her first published piece of fiction.

Wash the white clothes on Monday and put them on the stone heap; wash the color clothes on Tuesday and put them on the clothesline to dry; don't walk barehead in the hot sun; cook pumpkin fritters in very hot sweet oil; soak your little cloths right after you take them off; when buying cotton to make yourself a nice blouse, be sure that it doesn't have gum on it, because that way it won't hold up well after a wash; soak salt fish overnight before you cook it; is it true that you sing benna[1] in Sunday school?; always eat your food in such a way that it won't turn someone else's stomach; on Sundays try to walk like a lady and not like the slut you are so bent on becoming; don't sing benna in Sunday school; you mustn't speak to wharf-rat boys, not even to give directions; don't eat fruits on the street — flies will follow you; *but I don't sing benna on Sundays at all and never in Sunday school*; this is how to sew on a button; this is how to make a buttonhole for the button you have just sewed on; this is how to hem a dress when you see the hem coming down and so to prevent yourself from looking like the slut I know you are so bent on becoming; this is how you iron your father's khaki shirt so that it doesn't have a crease; this is how you iron your father's khaki pants so that they don't have a crease; this is how you grow okra — far from the house, because okra tree harbors red ants; when you are growing dasheen,[2] make sure it gets plenty of water or else it makes your throat itch when you are eating it; this is how you sweep a corner; this is how you sweep a whole house; this is how you sweep a yard; this is how you smile to someone you don't like too much; this is how you smile to someone you

1

[1] *benna* Calypso music. [All notes are the editor's.]
[2] *dasheen* Tropical plant with an edible root.

don't like at all; this is how you smile to someone you like completely; this is how you set a table for tea; this is how you set a table for dinner; this is how you set a table for dinner with an important guest; this is how you set a table for lunch; this is how you set a table for breakfast; this is how to behave in the presence of men who don't know you very well, and this way they won't recognize immediately the slut I have warned you against becoming; be sure to wash every day, even if it is with your own spit; don't squat down to play marbles — you are not a boy, you know; don't pick people's flowers — you might catch something; don't throw stones at black-birds, because it might not be a blackbird at all; this is how to make a bread pudding; this is how to make doukona;[3] this is how to make pepper pot; this is how to make a good medicine for a cold; this is how to make a good medicine to throw away a child before it even becomes a child; this is how to catch a fish; this is how to throw back a fish you don't like, and that way something bad won't fall on you; this is how to bully a man; this is how a man bullies you; this is how to love a man, and if this doesn't work there are other ways, and if they don't work don't feel too bad about giving up; this is how to spit up in the air if you feel like it, and this is how to move quick so that it doesn't fall on you; this is how to make ends meet; always squeeze bread to make sure it's fresh; *but what if the baker won't let me feel the bread?*; you mean to say that after all you are really going to be the kind of woman who the baker won't let near the bread?

[3]*doukona* Spicy pudding made from plantains.

Analyzing This Selection

1. **THE WRITER'S METHOD**   "Girl" is a running monologue with no interrupting explanations. Explain who the speakers are and their relationship. How do you know?

2. What kind of warnings and instructions are repeated? What do they tell you about the other speaker? How does the girl answer? Find specific instances of her responses.

3. What sort of adult do you think this girl will become? Support your answer by referring to details in the story that indicate her probable, or possible, future.

Analyzing Connections

4. This girl and Galloway (see "I'm Listening as Hard as I Can," p. 34) both react to humiliating situations. How does each adolescent try to protect her self-image?

Analyzing by Writing

5. Write a brief script of voices inside your head this semester — parents, professors, friends. Include your own voice and responses. Try to vary the voices and attitudes without breaking the monologue.

Andrew Sullivan

WHAT IS A HOMOSEXUAL?

ANDREW SULLIVAN (b. 1963) graduated from Oxford University and received a Ph.D. in political science from Harvard University. His writing about American politics and social issues has appeared in the *New York Times*, the *Wall Street Journal*, *Esquire*, and the *New Republic*, where he is a senior editor. Sullivan's concerns over HIV stir his assessment of personal values and health-care attitudes in *Love Undetectable: Notes on Friendship, Sex, and Survival* (1998). The following selection is excerpted from his book about gay identity, *Virtually Normal* (1995).

Gay adolescents are offered what every heterosexual teenager longs for: 1 to be invisible in the girls' locker room. But you are invisible in the boys' locker room, your desire as unavoidable as its object. In that moment, you learn the first homosexual lesson: that your survival depends upon self-concealment. I remember specifically coming back to high school after a long summer when I was fifteen and getting changed in the locker room for the first time again with a guy I had long had a crush on. But since the vacation, he had developed enormously: suddenly he had hair on his chest, his body had grown and strengthened, he was — clearly — no longer a boy. In front of me, he took off his shirt, and unknowingly, slowly, erotically stripped. I became literally breathless, overcome by the proximity of my desire. The gay teenager learns in that kind of event a form of control and sublimation, of deception and self-contempt, that never leaves his consciousness. He learns that that which would most give him meaning is most likely to destroy him in the eyes of others; that the condition of his friendships is the subjugation of himself.

In the development of any human being, these are powerful emotions. 2 They form a person. The homosexual learns to make distinctions between his sexual desire and his emotional longings — not because he is particularly prone to objectification of the flesh, but because he needs to survive as a social and sexual being. The society separates these two entities, and for a long time the homosexual has no option but to keep them separate. He learns certain rules; and, as with a child learning grammar, they are hard, later on in life, to unlearn.

It's possible, I think, that whatever society teaches or doesn't teach 3 about homosexuality, this fact will always be the case. No homosexual child, surrounded overwhelmingly by heterosexuals, will feel at home in his sexual and emotional world, even in the most tolerant of cultures. And every homosexual child will learn the rituals of deceit, impersonation, and appearance. Anyone who believes political, social, or even cultural revolution will change this fundamentally is denying reality. This isolation will always hold. It is definitional of homosexual development. And children are particularly cruel. At the age of eleven, no one wants to be the odd one out; and in the arena of dating and hormones, the exclusion is inevitably a traumatic one.

It's also likely to be forlorn. Most people are liable to meet emotional 4 rejection by sheer force of circumstance; but for a homosexual, the odds are simply far, far higher. My own experience suggests that somewhere between two and five percent of the population have involuntarily strong emotional and sexual attractions to the same sex. Which means that the pool of possible partners *starts* at one in twenty to one in fifty. It's no wonder, perhaps, that male homosexual culture has developed an ethic more of anonymous or promiscuous sex than of committed relationships. It's as if the hard lessons of adolescence lower permanently — by the sheer dint of the odds — the aspiration for anything more.

Did I know what I was? Somewhere, maybe. But it was much easier to 5 know what I wasn't. I wasn't going to be able to enter into the world of dating girls; I wasn't going to be able to feel fully comfortable among the heterosexual climate of the male teenager. So I decided, consciously or subconsciously, to construct a trajectory of my life that would remove me from their company; give me an excuse, provide a dignified way out. In Anglo-Saxon culture, the wonk has such an option: he's too nerdy or intellectual to be absorbed by girls. And there is something masculine and respected in the discipline of the arts and especially the sciences. You can gain respect and still be different.

So I threw myself into my schoolwork, into (more dubiously) plays, into 6 creative writing, into science fiction. Other homosexuals I have subsequently met pursued other strategies: some paradoxically threw themselves into sports, outjocking the jocks, gaining ever greater proximity, seeking respect, while knowing all the time that they were doomed to rejection. Others withdrew into isolation and despair. Others still, sensing their difference, flaunted it. At my high school, an older boy insisted on wearing full makeup to class; and he was accepted in a patronizing kind of way, his brazen otherness putting others at ease. They knew where they were with him; and he felt at least comfortable with their stable contempt. The rest of us who lived in a netherworld of sexual insecurity were not so lucky.

Most by then had a far more acute sense of appearances than those who 7 did not need to hide anything; and our sense of irony, and of aesthetics, assumed a precociously arch form, and drew us subtly together. Looking back, I realize that many of my best friends in my teen years were probably homosexual; and that somewhere in our coded, embarrassed dialogue we admitted it. Many of us also embraced those ideologies that seemed most alien to what we feared we might be: of the sports jock, of the altar boy, of the young conservative. They were the ultimate disguises. And our recognition of ourselves in the other only confirmed our desire to keep it quiet.

I should add that many young lesbians and homosexuals seem to have   8 had a much easier time of it. For many, the question of sexual identity was not a critical factor in their life choices or vocation, or even a factor at all. Perhaps because of a less repressive upbringing or because of some natural ease in the world, they affected a simple comfort with their fate, and a desire to embrace it. These people alarmed me: their very ease was the sternest rebuke to my own anxiety, because it rendered it irrelevant. But later in life, I came to marvel at the naturalness of their self-confidence, in the face of such concerted communal pressure, and to envy it. I had the more common self-dramatizing urge of the tortured homosexual, trapped between feeling wicked and feeling ridiculous. It's shameful to admit it, but I was more traumatized by the latter than by the former: my pride was more formidable a force than my guilt.

When people ask the simple question, *What is a homosexual?* I can only   9 answer with stories like these. I could go on, but too many stories have already been told. Ask any lesbian or homosexual, and they will often provide a similar account. I was once asked at a conservative think tank what evidence I had that homosexuality was far more of an orientation than a choice, and I was forced to reply quite simply: my life. It's true that I have met a handful of lesbians and gay men over the years who have honestly told me that they genuinely had a choice in the matter (and a few heterosexuals who claim they too chose their orientation). I believe them; but they are the exception and not the rule. As homosexual lives go, my own was somewhat banal and typical.

This is not, of course, the end of the matter. Human experience begins   10 with such facts, it doesn't end with them. There's a lamentable tendency to try to find some definitive solution to permanent human predicaments — in a string of DNA, in a conclusive psychological survey, in an analysis of hypothalami, in a verse of the Bible — in order to cut the argument short. Or to insist on the emotional veracity of a certain experience and expect it to trump any other argument on the table. But none of these things can replace the political and moral argument about how a society should deal with the presence of homosexuals in its midst. I relate my experience here not to impress or to shock or to gain sympathy, but merely to convey what the homosexual experience is actually like. You cannot discuss something until you know roughly what it is....

In a society more and more aware of its manifold cultures and subcul-   11 tures, we have been educated to be familiar and comfortable with what has been called "diversity": the diversity of perspective, culture, meaning. And this diversity is usually associated with what are described as cultural constructs: race, gender, sexuality, and so on. But as the obsession with diversity intensifies, the possibility of real difference alarms and terrifies all the more. The notion of collective characteristics — of attributes more associated with blacks than with whites, with Asians than with Latinos, with gay men than with straight men, with men than with women — has become anathema. They are marginalized as "stereotypes." The acceptance of diversity has come to mean the acceptance of the essential sameness of all types of people, and the danger of generalizing among them at all. In fact, it has become virtually a definition of "racist" to make any substantive generalizations about a particular ethnicity, and a definition of "homophobic" to make any generalizations about homosexuals.

What follows, then, is likely to be understood as "homophobic." But I 12 think it's true that certain necessary features of homosexual life lead to certain unavoidable features of homosexual character. This is not to say that they define any random homosexual: they do not. As with any group or way of life, there are many, many exceptions. Nor is it to say that they define the homosexual life: it should be clear by now that I believe that the needs and feelings of homosexual children and adolescents are largely interchangeable with those of their heterosexual peers. But there are certain generalizations that can be made about adult homosexuals and lesbians that have the ring of truth.

Of course, in a culture where homosexuals remain hidden and wrapped 13 in self-contempt, in which their emotional development is often stunted and late, in which the closet protects all sorts of self-destructive behavior that a more open society would not, it is still very hard to tell what is inherent in a homosexual life that makes it different, and what is simply imposed upon it. Nevertheless, it seems to me that even in the most tolerant societies, some of the differences that I have just described would inhere.

The experience of growing up profoundly different in emotional and 14 psychological makeup inevitably alters a person's self-perception, tends to make him or her more wary and distant, more attuned to appearance and its foibles, more self-conscious and perhaps more reflective. The presence of homosexuals in the arts, in literature, in architecture, in design, in fashion could be understood, as some have, as a simple response to oppression. Homosexuals have created safe professions within which to hide and protect each other. But why these professions? Maybe it's also that these are professions of appearance. Many homosexual children, feeling distant from their peers become experts at trying to figure out how to disguise their inner feelings, to "pass." They notice the signs and signals of social interaction, because they do not come instinctively. They develop skills early on that help them notice the inflections of a voice, the quirks of a particular movement, and the ways in which meaning can be conveyed in code. They have an ear for irony and for double meanings. Sometimes, by virtue of having to suppress their natural emotions, they find formal outlets to express themselves: music, theater, art. And so their lives become set on a trajectory which reinforces these trends.

As a child, I remember, as I suppressed the natural emotions of an ado-   15 lescent, how I naturally turned in on myself — writing, painting, and participating in amateur drama. Or I devised fantasies of future exploits — war leader, parliamentarian, famous actor — that could absorb those emotions that were being diverted from meeting other boys and developing natural emotional relationships with them. And I developed mannerisms, small ways in which I could express myself, tiny revolts of personal space — a speech affectation, a ridiculous piece of clothing — that were, in retrospect, attempts to communicate something in code which could not be communicated in language. In this homosexual archness there was, of course, much pain. And it came as no surprise that once I had become more open about my homosexuality, these mannerisms declined. Once I found the strength to be myself, I had no need to act myself. So my clothes became progressively more regular and slovenly; I lost interest in drama; my writing moved from fiction to journalism; my speech actually became less affected.

This of course, is not a universal homosexual experience. Many homo-   16 sexuals never become more open, and the skills required to survive the closet remain skills by which to earn a living. And many homosexuals, even once they no longer need those skills, retain them. My point is simply that the universal experience of self-conscious difference in childhood and adolescence — common, but not exclusive, to homosexuals — develops identifiable skills. They are the skills of mimesis; and one of the goods that homosexuals bring to society is undoubtedly a more highly developed sense of form, of style. Even in the most open of societies, I think, this will continue to be the case. It is not something genetically homosexual; it is something environmentally homosexual. And it begins young.

Analyzing This Selection

1. **THE WRITER'S METHOD**   In paragraphs 1 to 3 the author argues that a gay adolescent learns a lesson true only for gays and lesbians. How does Sullivan use personal experience to support that generalization?

2. What protective strategies did Sullivan adopt as a teenager? Which did he reject?

3. According to Sullivan, what is flawed about current attitudes supporting "diversity"? In view of the risks involved in stereotyping, how do you deal with this dilemma? Does Sullivan solve the problem?

4. What are the positive adult traits that usually develop in homosexuals? Since there is no way to validate or challenge Sullivan's assertion, what makes it convincing in the essay?

Analyzing Connections

5. Did Sullivan and Staples (see "Black Men and Public Space," p. 40) become similar in their "collective characteristics," or do their adult types contrast? Does considering race weaken or strengthen Sullivan's point about his development?

Analyzing by Writing

6. This essay defines *homosexuality*, while carefully avoiding the pitfalls of either reductiveness or overgeneralization. Write an essay that defines your dominant self-image. Are you primarily an intellectual? an explorer? a competitor? an outsider? an organizer? Write concretely about the abstraction, giving examples from your experience and analyzing their formative influences.

PART 2

FAMILY TIES

INSIGHTS

The family, not the individual, is the real molecule of society, the key link in the social chain of being.

—ROBERT NISBET

The family is a subversive organization. In fact, it is the ultimate and only consistently subversive organization. Only the family has continued throughout history and still continues to undermine the State. The family is the enduring permanent enemy of all hierarchies, churches, and ideologies. Not only dictators, bishops, and commissars, but also humble parish priests and café intellectuals find themselves repeatedly coming up against the stony hostility of the family and its determination to resist interference to the last.

—FERDINAND MOUNT

No people are ever as divided as those of the same blood.

—MAVIS GALLANT

But what we think of as a social crisis of this generation — the rapid growth of divorce, the emancipation of women and adolescents, the sexual and educational revolutions, even the revolution in eating which is undermining the family as the basis of nourishment, for over a hundred years ago the majority of Europeans never ate in public in their lives — all of these things, which are steadily making the family weaker and weaker, are the inexorable result of the changes in society itself. The family as a unit of social organization was remarkably appropriate for a less complex world of agriculture and craftsmanship, a world which stretches back some seven thousand years, but ever since industry and highly urbanized societies began to take its place, the social functions of the family have steadily weakened — and this is a process that is unlikely to be halted. And there is no historical reason to believe that human beings could be less or more happy, less or more stable.

—J. H. PLUMB

The family is the basic cell of government: it is where we are trained to believe that we are human beings or that we are chattel, it is where we are trained to see the sex and race divisions and become callous to injustice even if it is done to ourselves, to accept as biological a full system of authoritarian government.

—GLORIA STEINEM

Those Winter Sundays

Sundays too my father got up early
and put his clothes on in the blueblack cold,
then with cracked hands that ached
from labor in the weekday weather made
banked fires blaze. No one ever thanked him.

I'd wake and hear the cold splintering, breaking.
When the rooms were warm, he'd call,
and slowly I would rise and dress,
fearing the chronic angers of that house,

Speaking indifferently to him,
who had driven out the cold
and polished my good shoes as well.
What did I know, what did I know
of love's austere and lonely offices?

—ROBERT HAYDEN

Children become attached to parents whatever the parents' characteristics, so long as the parents are adequately accessible and attentive. It does not matter to the intensity of the children's attachment, though it may matter greatly in the development of their personalities, whether their parents are reliable, consistently loving, or considerate of the children's health and welfare. Nor does it matter whether the children admire their parents or even whether they feel friendly toward them. Children who are battered and bruised by parents will continue to feel attached to them. Attachment, like walking or talking, is an intrinsic capacity that is developed under appropriate circumstances; it is not willed into being after a calculation of its advantages.

—ROBERT WEISS

FOCUSING BY WRITING

1. Do you have too many brothers and sisters or too few? Almost everyone sometimes wishes for a few changes in that area of fate. Explain one way your life might have been improved by changing the number, sex, or ages of your siblings.

2. It usually requires more than one person's adverse behavior to produce a black sheep in any family. A child or adult who is consistently a maverick or a delinquent may be relegated to that role by other family members who maintain stereotypical attitudes and expectations. Examine an example of family stereotyping that contributed to the formation of a black sheep you know.

3. Does family life encourage independence or dependence? Does it promote liberty or authority? Present at least two good reasons why in your view the effects of family life support mainly a free individual or mainly a cohesive society.

4. Adolescents and their parents customarily go through a period of sustained bickering, which may last a few years, over simple issues such as household cleanliness, going out, studying, or spending money. In your family, what were the recurrent themes or persistent issues during this period of mutual irritation? Were the differences ever resolved? In a brief essay, clarify both sides of the key issue in your own passage through the valley of family harassment.

Thomas Simmons

MOTORCYCLE TALK

THOMAS SIMMONS (b. 1956) lived his first thirteen years in West Chester, Pennsylvania, where he developed an enduring passion for motorcycles. Simmons graduated from Stanford University and received a Ph.D. in English at the University of California at Berkeley. He has taught writing at the Massachusetts Institute of Technology and at the University of Iowa. "Motorcycle Talk" is taken from *The Unseen Shore: Memories of a Christian Science Childhood* (1991), his memoir about struggling with his religious upbringing. His autobiography continues in his book about learning how to fly, *A Season in the Air* (1993). Simmons is currently writing about tribal customs, including American Indian traditions, and the return of shamanism in modern culture.

My father, who suffered from so many private griefs, was not an easy 1 man to get along with, but in one respect he was magnificent: he was unfailing in his devotion to machines of almost any variety. When he chose to, he could talk to me at length on the virtues of, say, the 1966 Chevrolet four-barrel carburetor or the drawbacks of the Wankel rotary engine. Talking, however, was not his strongest suit: he was a man of action. As he liked to point out, talking would never make an engine run more smoothly.

On weekends sometimes, or on his rare summer days of vacation, he 2 would encourage me in my first and last steps toward automotive literacy. He would allow me to stand beside him as he worked on the car, and when he needed a simple tool — a crescent wrench or needlenose pliers — I would be allowed to hand them to him. And when I was twelve, he and my daring mother bought me a motorcycle.

It was a 50cc Benelli motocross bike — neither new, nor large, nor pow- 3 erful, nor expensive. But it gave form and life to my imaginings. No longer did I have to confine myself wistfully to magazine photos of high-speed turns and hair-raising rides through rough country. I had the thing itself — the device that would make these experiences possible, at least to some degree.

And, although I did not know it at the time, I also had a new kind of lex- 4 icon. The motorcycle was a compendium of gears and springs and sprockets and cylinder heads and piston rings, which between my father and me acquired the force of more affectionate words that we could never seem to use in each other's presence.

Almost immediately the Benelli became a meeting ground, a magnet for   5
the two of us. We would come down to look at it — even if it was too late in the day for a good ride — and my father would check the tension of the chain, or examine the spark plug for carbon, or simply bounce the shock absorbers a few times as he talked. He'd tell me about compression ratios and ways of down-shifting smoothly through a turn; I'd tell him about my latest ride, when I leaped two small hummocks or took a spill on a tight curve.

More rarely, he'd tell the stories of his youth. His favorite, which he   6
recounted in slightly different versions about four times a year, had to do with the go-kart he built from scrap parts in his father's basement during the Depression. It was by any account a masterful performance: he managed to pick up a small, broken gasoline engine for free, and tinkered with it until it came back to life. The wheels, steering gear, axles, chassis — all were scrounged for a few cents, or for free, from junkyards and vacant lots in and around Philadelphia.

Winter was in full swing when my father had his go-kart ready for a test-   7
drive; snow lay thick on the ground. But he'd built the go-kart in his father's large basement, and given the weather he felt it made sense to make the trial run indoors. His engineering skills were topnotch. Assembled from orphaned parts, the go-kart performed like a well-tuned race car. My father did what any good thirteen-year-old would have done: he got carried away. He laid on the power coming around the corner of the basement, lost control, and smashed head-on into the furnace. It was a great loss for him. The jagged wood and metal cut and bruised him; he had destroyed his brand-new car. Far worse was the damage to the furnace. In 1933 such damage was almost more than the family finances could sustain. Furious, my father's father called him names, upbraided him for his stupidity and irresponsibility, and made him feel worthless. Years later, as he would tell this story to me, my father would linger over those words — "stupid," "irresponsible" — as if the pain had never gone away.

In these moments he and I had a common stake in something. Though   8
he might not know whether I was reading at the eighth-grade level or the twelfth-grade level — or whether my math scores lagged behind those of the rest of the class — he was delighted to see that I knew how to adjust a clutch cable or stop after a low-speed, controlled skid. These skills were a source of genuine adventure for me, and I came to life when he observed my progress.

But this was only part of our rapport with the motorcycle. My father   9
found few occasions to be overtly tender with the family, but he could be tender with a machine. I began to notice this in the countless small adjustments he regularly made. His touch on the cranky carburetor settings for gas and air was gentle, even soothing; at least it seemed to soothe the motorcycle, which ran smoothly under his touch but not under mine.

I found that, from time to time, this tenderness buoyed me up in its   10 wake. If my father was, in his dreams, a flat-track mechanic, then I was his driver: he owed me the best he could give me; that was his job. This dream of his bound us in a metaphor which, at its heart, was not so different from the kind of straightforward love another child might have received from a more accessible father. I did not know this then, not exactly. But I knew, when we both hovered over the Benelli's cylinder head or gearbox, adjusting a cam or replacing a gasket, that he would not have worked on this machine for himself alone.

Yet there was a secret to our new language, a secret that only slowly 11 revealed itself. What we shared through the motorcycle contradicted most of our other encounters in the family. It was almost as if we lived in another world when we came together over this machine, and for a time I hoped that that world might be the new one, the ideal on the horizon. I was wrong. The bands of our words were strong, but too narrow to encompass the worlds rising before me.

Almost without knowing it I began to acquire other vocabularies — the 12 tough, subtle speech of girls, the staccato syllables of independence, the wrenching words of love and emptiness. In this I began to leave him behind. He could not talk of these things with me. He remained with his engines; and long after I had ceased to ride it, he would occasionally open the gas jets, prime the carburetor, and take my motorcycle for a spin around the block.

But as it seems that nothing is ever wholly lost, this vocabulary of the 13 garage and the flat-track speed-way has a kind of potency, a place in the scheme of things. When, recently, I had dinner with my father, after not having seen him for nearly a year, we greeted each other with the awkwardness of child cousins: we hardly knew what to say. I had almost given up on the possibility of a prolonged conversation until I happened to mention that my car needed a new clutch. Suddenly we were safe again, as we moved from the clutch to the valves on his souped-up VW and the four-barrel carburetor on the '66 Chevrolet Malibu, still pouring on the power after all these years. We had moved back to the language of our old country. And though one of us had journeyed far and had almost forgotten the idioms, the rusty speech still held, for a time, the words of love.

Analyzing This Selection

1. **THE WRITER'S METHOD**   The first sentence carries many implications about the author and his family. Which suggestions are fully considered in the rest of the essay? Which remain implied?

2. How does the motorcycle change the son's and father's perceptions of each other?

3. How does the father appear different from the adult writer? What resemblances are visible?

Analyzing Connections

4. In the Insights on page 63, psychologist Robert Weiss theorizes about the development of a child's attachment to his or her parents. Test out the strengths and weaknesses of the theory by applying it to Simmons's relationship with his father.

Analyzing by Writing

5. In many families, a sport or hobby provides the vocabulary for talk between the generations. Baseball, basketball, tennis, hockey, skiing, photography, camping: each can become the medium for relationships that do not flow as smoothly without this shared interest. Examine a shared interest that bridges the generation gap in your family (or in another family you know well). As if you were examining the dialect of another tribe, clarify the vocabulary that the family uses to discuss the interest. For instance, does custom allow for praise and criticism from young to old and not just from old to young? Explain the forms and limits of expressiveness in this family idiom.

Raymond Carver

MY FATHER'S LIFE

RAYMOND CARVER (1938–1988), acclaimed for his poetry and for his short stories about hardscrabble contemporary lives, was born in a logging town in Oregon. He graduated from California State University at Humboldt and spent a year at the Writers' Workshop at the University of Iowa. He taught writing at the University of California at Santa Cruz and at Syracuse University. His poetry and short stories appeared in magazines such as *Esquire, Harper's,* the *Atlantic,* and the *New Yorker.* His fiction has been collected in *What We Talk About When We Talk About Love* (1981) (see the story on page 182), *Cathedral* (1984), and *Where I'm Calling From* (1988). His verse is collected in three books — *Where Water Comes Together with Other Water* (1985), *Ultramarine* (1986), and the posthumously published *A New Path to the Waterfall* (1989). In this memoir of his father, which first appeared in *Esquire* in 1984, Carver emphasizes the hardships that his father faced as a laborer during the Great Depression of the 1930s and later during the years of his psychological depression.

My dad's name was Clevie Raymond Carver. His family called him Raymond and friends called him C.R. I was named Raymond Clevie Carver, Jr. I hated the "Junior" part. When I was little my dad called me Frog, which was okay. But later, like everybody else in the family, he began calling me Junior. He went on calling me this until I was thirteen or fourteen and announced that I wouldn't answer to that name any longer. So he began calling me Doc. From then until his death, on June 17, 1967, he called me Doc, or else Son.

When he died, my mother telephoned my wife with the news. I was away from my family at the time, between lives, trying to enroll in the School of Library Science at the University of Iowa. When my wife answered the phone, my mother blurted out, "Raymond's dead!" For a moment, my wife thought my mother was telling her that I was dead. Then my mother made it clear *which* Raymond she was talking about and my wife said, "Thank God. I thought you meant *my* Raymond."

My dad walked, hitched rides, and rode in empty boxcars when he went from Arkansas to Washington State in 1934, looking for work. I don't know whether he was pursuing a dream when he went out to Washington. I doubt it. I don't think he dreamed much. I believe he was simply looking for steady work at decent pay. Steady work was meaningful work. He picked apples for a time and then landed a construction laborer's job on the Grand Coulee Dam. After he'd put aside a little money, he bought a car and drove back to Arkansas to help his folks, my grandparents, pack up for the move west. He said later that they were about to starve down there, and this wasn't meant as a figure of speech. It was during that short while in Arkansas, in a town called Leola, that my mother met my dad on the sidewalk as he came out of a tavern.

"He was drunk," she said. "I don't know why I let him talk to me. His   4
eyes were glittery. I wish I'd had a crystal ball." They'd met once, a year or so before, at a dance. He'd had girlfriends before her, my mother told me. "Your dad always had a girlfriend, even after we married. He was my first and last. I never had another man. But I didn't miss anything."

They were married by a justice of the peace on the day they left for   5
Washington, this big, tall country girl and a farmhand-turned-construction worker. My mother spent her wedding night with my dad and his folks, all of them camped beside the road in Arkansas.

In Omak, Washington, my dad and mother lived in a little place not   6
much bigger than a cabin. My grandparents lived next door. My dad was still working on the dam, and later, with the huge turbines producing electricity and the water backed up for a hundred miles into Canada, he stood in the crowd and heard Franklin D. Roosevelt when he spoke at the construction site. "He never mentioned those guys who died building that dam," my dad said. Some of his friends had died there, men from Arkansas, Oklahoma, and Missouri.

He then took a job in a sawmill in Clatskanie, Oregon, a little town   7
alongside the Columbia River. I was born there, and my mother has a picture of my dad standing in front of the gate to the mill, proudly holding me up to face the camera. My bonnet is on crooked and about to come untied. His hat is pushed back on his forehead, and he's wearing a big grin. Was he going in to work or just finishing his shift? It doesn't matter. In either case, he had a job and a family. These were his salad days.

In 1941 we moved to Yakima, Washington, where my dad went to work   8
as a saw filer, a skilled trade he'd learned in Clatskanie. When war broke out, he was given a deferment because his work was considered necessary to the war effort. Finished lumber was in demand by the armed services, and he kept his saws so sharp they could shave the hair off your arm.

After my dad had moved us to Yakima, he moved his folks into the same   9
neighborhood. By the mid-1940s the rest of my dad's family — his brother, his sister, and her husband, as well as uncles, cousins, nephews, and most of their extended family and friends — had come out from Arkansas. All because my dad came out first. The men went to work at Boise Cascade, where my dad worked, and the women packed apples in the canneries. And in just a little while, it seemed — according to my mother — everybody was better off than my dad. "Your dad couldn't keep money," my

mother said. "Money burned a hole in his pocket. He was always doing for others."

The first house I clearly remember living in, at 1515 South Fifteenth Street, in Yakima, had an outdoor toilet. On Halloween night, or just any night, for the hell of it, neighbor kids, kids in their early teens, would carry our toilet away and leave it next to the road. My dad would have to get somebody to help him bring it home. Or these kids would take the toilet and stand it in somebody else's backyard. Once they actually set it on fire. But ours wasn't the only house that had an outdoor toilet. When I was old enough to know what I was doing, I threw rocks at the other toilets when I'd see someone go inside. This was called bombing the toilets. After a while, though, everyone went to indoor plumbing until, suddenly, our toilet was the last outdoor one in the neighborhood. I remember the shame I felt when my third-grade teacher, Mr. Wise, drove me home from school one day. I asked him to stop at the house just before ours, claiming I lived there.

I can recall what happened one night when my dad came home late to find that my mother had locked all the doors on him from the inside. He was drunk, and we could feel the house shudder as he rattled the door. When he'd managed to force open a window, she hit him between the eyes with a colander and knocked him out. We could see him down there on the grass. For years afterward, I used to pick up this colander — it was as heavy as a rolling pin — and imagine what it would feel like to be hit in the head with something like that.

It was during this period that I remember my dad taking me into the bedroom, sitting me down on the bed, and telling me that I might have to go live with my Aunt LaVon for a while. I couldn't understand what I'd done that meant I'd have to go away from home to live. But this, too — whatever prompted it — must have blown over, more or less, anyway, because we stayed together, and I didn't have to go live with her or anyone else.

I remember my mother pouring his whiskey down the sink. Sometimes she'd pour it all out and sometimes, if she was afraid of getting caught, she'd only pour half of it out and then add water to the rest. I tasted some of his whiskey once myself. It was terrible stuff, and I don't see how anybody could drink it.

After a long time without one, we finally got a car, in 1949 or 1950, a 1938 Ford. But it threw a rod the first week we had it, and my dad had to have the motor rebuilt.

"We drove the oldest car in town," my mother said. "We could have had a Cadillac for all he spent on car repairs." One time she found someone else's tube of lipstick on the floorboard, along with a lacy handkerchief. "See this?" she said to me. "Some floozy left this in the car."

Once I saw her take a pan of warm water into the bedroom where my dad was sleeping. She took his hand from under the covers and held it in the water. I stood in the doorway and watched. I wanted to know what was going on. This would make him talk in his sleep, she told me. There were things she needed to know, things she was sure he was keeping from her.

Every year or so, when I was little, we would take the North Coast Lim- 17
ited across the Cascade Range from Yakima to Seattle and stay in the Vance Hotel and eat, I remember, at a place called the Dinner Bell Cafe. Once we went to Ivar's Acres of Clams and drank glasses of warm clam broth.

In 1956, the year I was to graduate from high school, my dad quit his 18
job at the mill in Yakima and took a job in Chester, a little sawmill town in northern California. The reasons given at the time for his taking the job had to do with a higher hourly wage and the vague promise that he might, in a few years' time, succeed to the job of head filer in this new mill. But I think, in the main, that my dad had grown restless and simply wanted to try his luck elsewhere. Things had gotten a little too predictable for him in Yakima. Also, the year before, there had been the deaths, within six months of each other, of both his parents.

But just a few days after graduation, when my mother and I were packed 19
to move to Chester, my dad penciled a letter to say he'd been sick for a while. He didn't want us to worry, he said, but he'd cut himself on a saw. Maybe he'd got a tiny sliver of steel in his blood. Anyway, something had happened and he'd had to miss work, he said. In the same mail was an unsigned postcard from somebody down there telling my mother that my dad was about to die and that he was drinking "raw whiskey."

When we arrived in Chester, my dad was living in a trailer that 20
belonged to the company. I didn't recognize him immediately. I guess for a moment I didn't want to recognize him. He was skinny and pale and looked bewildered. His pants wouldn't stay up. He didn't look like my dad. My mother began to cry. My dad put his arm around her and patted her shoulder vaguely, like he didn't know what this was all about, either. The three of us took up life together in the trailer, and we looked after him as best we could. But my dad was sick, and he couldn't get any better. I worked with him in the mill that summer and part of the fall. We'd get up in the mornings and eat eggs and toast while we listened to the radio, and then go out the door with our lunch pails. We'd pass through the gate together at eight in the morning, and I wouldn't see him again until quitting time. In November I went back to Yakima to be closer to my girlfriend, the girl I'd made up my mind I was going to marry.

He worked at the mill in Chester until the following February, when he 21
collapsed on the job and was taken to the hospital. My mother asked if I would come down there and help. I caught a bus from Yakima to Chester, intending to drive them back to Yakima. But now, in addition to being physically sick, my dad was in the midst of a nervous breakdown, though none of us knew to call it that at the time. During the entire trip back to Yakima, he didn't speak, not even when asked a direct question. ("How do

you feel, Raymond?" "You okay, Dad?") He'd communicate, if he communicated at all, by moving his head or by turning his palms up as if to say he didn't know or care. The only time he said anything on the trip, and for nearly a month afterward, was when I was speeding down a gravel road in Oregon and the car muffler came loose. "You were going too fast," he said.

Back in Yakima a doctor saw to it that my dad went to a psychiatrist. My mother and dad had to go on relief, as it was called, and the county paid for the psychiatrist. The psychiatrist asked my dad, "Who is the President?" He'd had a question put to him that he could answer. "Ike," my dad said. Nevertheless, they put him on the fifth floor of Valley Memorial Hospital and began giving him electroshock treatments. I was married by then and about to start my own family. My dad was still locked up when my wife went into this same hospital, just one floor down, to have our first baby. After she had delivered, I went upstairs to give my dad the news. They let me in through a steel door and showed me where I could find him. He was sitting on a couch with a blanket over his lap. *Hey,* I thought. *What in hell is happening to my dad?* I sat down next to him and told him he was a grandfather. He waited a minute and then he said, "I feel like a grandfather." That's all he said. He didn't smile or move. He was in a big room with a lot of other people. Then I hugged him, and he began to cry.

Somehow he got out of there. But now came the years when he couldn't work and just sat around the house trying to figure what next and what he'd done wrong in his life that he'd wound up like this. My mother went from job to crummy job. Much later she referred to that time he was in the hospital, and those years just afterward, as "when Raymond was sick." The word *sick* was never the same for me again.

In 1964, through the help of a friend, he was lucky enough to be hired on at a mill in Klamath, California. He moved down there by himself to see if he could hack it. He lived not far from the mill, in a one-room cabin not much different from the place he and my mother had started out living in when they went west. He scrawled letters to my mother, and if I called she'd read them aloud to me over the phone. In the letters, he said it was touch and go. Every day that he went to work, he felt like it was the most important day of his life. But every day, he told her, made the next day that much easier. He said for her to tell me he said hello. If he couldn't sleep at night, he said, he thought about me and the good times we used to have. Finally, after a couple of months, he regained some of his confidence. He could do the work and didn't think he had to worry that he'd let anybody down ever again. When he was sure, he sent for my mother.

He'd been off from work for six years and had lost everything in that time — home, car, furniture, and appliances, including the big freezer that had been my mother's pride and joy. He'd lost his good name too — Raymond Carver was someone who couldn't pay his bills — and his self-respect was gone. He'd even lost his virility. My mother told my wife, "All during that time Raymond was sick we slept together in the same bed, but we didn't have relations. He wanted to a few times, but nothing happened. I didn't miss it, but I think he wanted to, you know."

During those years I was trying to raise my own family and earn a living. 26 But, one thing and another, we found ourselves having to move a lot. I couldn't keep track of what was going down in my dad's life. But I did have a chance one Christmas to tell him I wanted to be a writer. I might as well have told him I wanted to become a plastic surgeon. "What are you going to write about?" he wanted to know. Then, as if to help me out, he said, "Write about stuff you know about. Write about some of those fishing trips we took." I said I would, but I knew I wouldn't. "Send me what you write," he said. I said I'd do that, but then I didn't. I wasn't writing anything about fishing, and I didn't think he'd particularly care about, or even necessarily understand, what I was writing in those days. Besides, he wasn't a reader. Not the sort, anyway, I imagined I was writing for.

Then he died. I was a long way off, in Iowa City, with things still to say 27 to him. I didn't have the chance to tell him goodbye, or that I thought he was doing great at his new job. That I was proud of him for making a comeback.

My mother said he came in from work that night and ate a big supper. 28 Then he sat at the table by himself and finished what was left of a bottle of whiskey, a bottle she found hidden in the bottom of the garbage under some coffee grounds a day or so later. Then he got up and went to bed, where my mother joined him a little later. But in the night she had to get up and make a bed for herself on the couch. "He was snoring so loud I couldn't sleep," she said. The next morning when she looked in on him, he was on his back with his mouth open, his cheeks caved in. *Graylooking,* she said. She knew he was dead — she didn't need a doctor to tell her that. But she called one anyway, and then she called my wife.

Among the pictures my mother kept of my dad and herself during those 29 early days in Washington was a photograph of him standing in front of a car, holding a beer and a stringer of fish. In the photograph he is wearing his hat back on his forehead and has this awkward grin on his face. I asked her for it and she gave it to me, along with some others. I put it up on my wall, and each time we moved, I took the picture along and put it up on another wall. I looked at it carefully from time to time, trying to figure out some things about my dad, and maybe myself in the process. But I couldn't. My dad just kept moving further and further away from me and back into time. Finally, in the course of another move, I lost the photograph. It was then that I tried to recall it, and at the same time make an attempt to say something about my dad, and how I thought that in some important ways we might be alike. I wrote the poem when I was living in an apartment house in an urban area south of San Francisco, at a time when I found myself, like my dad, having trouble with alcohol. The poem was a way of trying to connect up with him.

Photograph of My Father in His Twenty-Second Year

October. Here in this dank, unfamiliar kitchen
I study my father's embarrassed young man's face.
Sheepish grin, he holds in one hand a string
of spiny yellow perch, in the other
a bottle of Carlsberg beer.

In jeans and flannel shirt, he leans
against the front fender of a 1934 Ford.
He would like to pose brave and hearty for his posterity,
wear his old hat cocked over his ear.
All his life my father wanted to be bold.

But the eyes gave him away, and the hands
that limply offer the string of dead perch
and the bottle of beer. Father, I love you,
yet how can I say thank you, I who can't hold my liquor either
and don't even know the places to fish.

The poem is true in its particulars, except that my dad died in June and not October, as the first word of the poem says. I wanted a word with more than one syllable to it to make it linger a little. But more than that, I wanted a month appropriate to what I felt at the time I wrote the poem — a month of short days and failing light, smoke in the air, things perishing. June was summer nights and days, graduations, my wedding anniversary, the birthday of one of my children. June wasn't a month your father died in.

After the service at the funeral home, after we had moved outside, a woman I didn't know came over to me and said, "He's happier where he is now." I stared at this woman until she moved away. I still remember the little knob of a hat she was wearing. Then one of my dad's cousins — I didn't know the man's name — reached out and took my hand, "We all miss him," he said, and I knew he wasn't saying it just to be polite.

I began to weep for the first time since receiving the news. I hadn't been able to before. I hadn't had the time, for one thing. Now, suddenly, I couldn't stop. I held my wife and wept while she said and did what she could do to comfort me there in the middle of that summer afternoon.

I listened to people say consoling things to my mother, and I was glad that my dad's family had turned up, had come to where he was. I thought I'd remember everything that was said and done that day and maybe find a way to tell it sometime. But I didn't. I forgot it all, or nearly. What I do remember is that I heard our name used a lot that afternoon, my dad's name and mine. But I knew they were talking about my dad. *Raymond,* these people kept saying in their beautiful voices out of my childhood. *Raymond.*

Analyzing This Selection

1. In paragraphs 1 and 2, the author implicitly suggests some of the effects of having a name similar to his father's. What were these effects? Define his reaction explicitly.

2. **THE WRITER'S METHOD**   Carver includes his mother's remarks and her other direct views about his father. How do we know whether the author's attitude differs from the mother's? Why does Carver merely imply agreement and disagreement?

3. What episodes and details in Carver's early life indicate that he and his father felt closely connected?

4. In Carver's poem about his father he writes, "All his life my father wanted to be bold." Do you think that line sums up the father fairly accurately? Does the essay indicate other things that the father also wanted to be? Was he more successful or less successful in those other aspirations?

5. In the final paragraph, Carver again notes the similarity of their names. How has his attitude toward this similarity changed from his attitude at the beginning of the essay?

Analyzing Connections

6. Both Carver and Simmons (see "Motorcycle Talk," p. 65) express mixed attitudes toward their difficult fathers. Compare their mixture of admiration and blame. Compare Carver and Robert Hayden in the Insights on page 63. Which writer identifies more closely with his father?

Analyzing by Writing

7. Write an extended description of the person in your family whom you most closely resemble in physical appearance. Be precise and detailed about his or her features that are like your own. If it is useful, include matters such as the person's tone of voice, way of walking, gestures and mannerisms, or other physical characteristics. Be sure to differentiate yourself at some point or at various points in your essay. In what ways do the similarities please or disturb you?

bell hooks

INSPIRED ECCENTRICITY

BELL HOOKS (b. 1952), who explains her choice of a pen name in the following essay, writes about constraints of race, sex, and class on American black women. Raised in the South, she graduated from Stanford University and earned a Ph.D. at the University of California at Santa Cruz. Her provocative cultural studies include *Ain't I a Woman: Black Women and Feminism* (1981), *Yearning: Race, Gender, and Cultural Politics* (1990), and other books and essays. She taught at Oberlin College and currently teaches at City College of New York.

There are family members you try to forget and ones that you always 1 remember, that you can't stop talking about. They may be dead — long gone — but their presence lingers and you have to share who they were and who they still are with the world. You want everyone to know them as you did, to love them as you did.

All my life I have remained enchanted by the presence of my mother's 2 parents, Sarah and Gus Oldham. When I was a child they were already old. I did not see that then, though. They were Baba and Daddy Gus, together for more than seventy years at the time of his death. Their marriage fascinated me. They were strangers and lovers — two eccentrics who created their own world.

More than any other family members, together they gave me a world- 3 view that sustained me during a difficult and painful childhood. Reflecting on the eclectic writer I have become, I see in myself a mixture of these two very different but equally powerful figures from my childhood. Baba was tall, her skin so white and her hair so jet black and straight that she could have easily "passed" denying all traces of blackness. Yet the man she married was short and dark, and sometimes his skin looked like the color of soot from burning coal. In our childhood the fireplaces burned coal. It was bright heat, luminous and fierce. If you got too close it could burn you.

Together Baba and Daddy Gus generated a hot heat. He was a man of 4 few words, deeply committed to silence — so much so that it was like a religion to him. When he spoke you could hardly hear what he said. Baba was just the opposite. Smoking an abundance of cigarettes a day, she talked endlessly. She preached. She yelled. She fussed. Often her vitriolic rage would heap itself on Daddy Gus, who would sit calmly in his chair by the

77

stove, as calm and still as the Buddha sits. And when he had enough of her words, he would reach for his hat and walk.

Neither Baba nor Daddy Gus drove cars. Rarely did they ride in them. They preferred walking. And even then their styles were different. He moved slow, as though carrying a great weight; she with her tall, lean, boyish frame moved swiftly, as though there was never time to waste. Their one agreed-upon passion was fishing. Though they did not do even that together. They lived close but they created separate worlds.

In a big two-story wood frame house with lots of rooms they constructed a world that could contain their separate and distinct personalities. As children one of the first things we noticed about our grandparents was that they did not sleep in the same room. This arrangement was contrary to everything we understood about marriage. While Mama never wanted to talk about their separate worlds, Baba would tell you in a minute that Daddy Gus was nasty, that he smelled like tobacco juice, that he did not wash enough, that there was no way she would want him in her bed. And while he would say nothing nasty about her, he would merely say why would he want to share somebody else's bed when he could have his own bed to himself, with no one to complain about anything.

I loved my granddaddy's smells. Always, they filled my nostrils with the scent of happiness. It was sheer ecstasy for me to be allowed into his inner sanctum. His room was a small Van Gogh–like space off from the living room. There was no door. Old-fashioned curtains were the only attempt at privacy. Usually the curtains were closed. His room reeked of tobacco. There were treasures everywhere in that small room. As a younger man Daddy Gus did odd jobs, and sometimes even in his old age he would do a chore for some needy lady. As he went about his work, he would pick up found objects, scraps. All these objects would lie about his room, on the dresser, on the table near his bed. Unlike all other grown-ups he never cared about children looking through his things. Anything we wanted he gave to us.

Daddy Gus collected beautiful wooden cigar boxes. They held lots of the important stuff — the treasures. He had tons of little diaries that he made notes in. He gave me my first wallet, my first teeny little book to write in, my first beautiful pen, which did not write for long, but it was still a found and shared treasure. When I would lie on his bed or sit close to him, sometimes just standing near, I would feel all the pain and anxiety of my troubled childhood leave me. His spirit was calm. He gave me the unconditional love I longed for.

"Too calm," his grown-up children thought. That's why he had let this old woman rule him, my cousin BoBo would say. Even as children we knew that grown-ups felt sorry for Daddy Gus. At times his sons seemed to look upon him as not a "real man." His refusal to fight in wars was another sign to them of weakness. It was my grandfather who taught me to oppose war. They saw him as a man controlled by the whims of others, by this tall, strident, demanding woman he had married. I saw him as a man of profound beliefs, a man of integrity. When he heard their put-downs — for they talked on and on about his laziness — he merely muttered that he had no use for them. He was not gonna let anybody tell him what to do with his life.

Daddy Gus was a devout believer, a deacon at his church; he was one of the right-hand men of God. At church, everyone admired his calmness. Baba had no use for church. She liked nothing better than to tell us all the ways it was one big hypocritical place: "Why, I can find God anywhere I want to — I do not need a church." Indeed, when my grandmother died, her funeral could not take place in a church, for she had never belonged. Her refusal to attend church bothered some of her daughters, for they thought she was sinning against God, setting a bad example for the children. We were not supposed to listen when she began to damn the church and everybody in it.

Baba loved to "cuss." There was no bad word she was not willing to say. The improvisational manner in which she would string those words together was awesome. It was the goddamn sons of bitches who thought that they could fuck with her when they could just kiss her black ass. A woman of strong words and powerful metaphors, she could not read or write. She lived in the power of language. Her favorite sayings were a prelude for storytelling. It was she who told me, "Play with a puppy, he'll lick you in the mouth." When I heard this saying, I knew what was coming — a long polemic about not letting folks get too close, 'cause they will mess with you.

Baba loved to tell her stories. And I loved to hear them. She called me Glory. And in the midst of her storytelling she would pause to say, "Glory, are ya listenin'. Do you understand what I'm telling ya." Sometimes I would have to repeat the lessons I had learned. Sometimes I was not able to get it right and she would start again. When Mama felt I was learning too much craziness "over home" (that is what we called Baba's house), my visits were curtailed. As I moved into my teens I learned to keep to myself all the wisdom of the old ways I picked up over home.

Baba was an incredible quilt maker, but by the time I was old enough to really understand her work, to see its beauty, she was already having difficulty with her eyesight. She could not sew as much as in the old days, when her work was on everybody's bed. Unwilling to throw anything away, she loved to make crazy quilts, 'cause they allowed every scrap to be used. Although she would one day order patterns and make perfect quilts with colors that went together, she always collected scraps.

Long before I read Virginia Woolf's *A Room of One's Own* I learned from Baba that a woman needed her own space to work. She had a huge room for her quilting. Like every other space in the private world she created upstairs, it had her treasures, an endless array of hatboxes, feathers, and trunks filled with old clothes she had held on to. In room after room there were feather tick mattresses; when they were pulled back, the wooden slats of the bed were revealed, lined with exquisite hand-sewn quilts.

In all these trunks, in crevices and drawers were braided tobacco leaves   15 to keep away moths and other insects. A really hot summer could make cloth sweat, and stains from tobacco juice would end up on quilts no one had ever used. When I was a young child, a quilt my grandmother had made kept me warm, was my solace and comfort. Even though Mama protested when I dragged that old raggedy quilt from Kentucky to Stanford, I knew I needed that bit of the South, of Baba's world, to sustain me.

Like Daddy Gus, she was a woman of her word. She liked to declare   16 with pride, "I mean what I say and I say what I mean." "Glory," she would tell me, "nobody is better than their word — if you can't keep ya word you ain't worth nothin' in this world." She would stop speaking to folk over the breaking of their word, over lies. Our mama was not given to loud speech or confrontation. I learned all those things from Baba — "to stand up and speak up" and not to "give a good goddamn" what folk who "ain't got a pot to pee in" think. My parents were concerned with their image in the world. It was pure blasphemy for Baba to teach that it did not matter what other folks thought — "Ya have to be right with yaself in ya own heart — that's all that matters." Baba taught me to listen to my heart — to follow it. From her we learned as small children to remember our dreams in the night and to share them when we awakened. They would be interpreted by her. She taught us to listen to the knowledge in dreams. Mama would say this was all nonsense, but she too was known to ask the meaning of a dream.

In their own way my grandparents were rebels, deeply committed to rad-   17 ical individualism. I learned how to be myself from them. Mama hated this. She thought it was important to be liked, to conform. She had hated growing up in such an eccentric, otherworldly household. This world where folks made their own wine, their own butter, their own soap; where chickens were raised, and huge gardens were grown for canning everything. This was the world Mama wanted to leave behind. She wanted store-bought things.

Baba lived in another time, a time when all things were produced in the   18 individual household. Everything the family needed was made at home. She loved to tell me stories about learning to trap animals, to skin, to soak possum and coon in brine, to fry up a fresh rabbit. Though a total woman of the outdoors who could shoot and trap as good as any man, she still believed every woman should sew — she made her first quilt as a girl. In her world, women were as strong as men because they had to be. She had grown up in the country and knew that country ways were the best ways to live. Boasting about being able to do anything that a man could do and better, this woman who could not read or write was confident about her place in the universe.

My sense of aesthetics came from her. She taught me to really look at   19 things, to see underneath the surface, to see the different shades of red in the peppers she had dried and hung in the kitchen sunlight. The beauty of the ordinary, the everyday, was her feast of light. While she had no use for the treasures in my granddaddy's world, he too taught me to look for the living spirit in things — the things that are cast away but still need to be touched and cared for. Picking up a found object he would tell me its story or tell me how he was planning to give it life again.

Connected in spirit but so far apart in the life of everydayness, Baba and Daddy Gus were rarely civil to each other. Every shared talk begun with goodwill ended in disagreement and contestation. Everyone knew Baba just loved to fuss. She liked a good war of words. And she was comfortable using words to sting and hurt, to punish. When words would not do the job, she could reach for the strap, a long piece of black leather that would leave tiny imprints on the flesh.

There was no violence in Daddy Gus. Mama shared that he had always been that way, a calm and gentle man, full of tenderness. I remember clinging to his tenderness when nothing I did was right in my mother's eyes, when I was constantly punished. Baba was not an ally. She advocated harsh punishment. She had no use for children who would not obey. She was never ever affectionate. When we entered her house, we gave her a kiss in greeting and that was it. With Daddy Gus we could cuddle, linger in his arms, give as many kisses as desired. His arms and heart were always open.

In the back of their house were fruit trees, chicken coops, and gardens, and in the front were flowers. Baba could make anything grow. And she knew all about herbs and roots. Her home remedies healed our childhood sicknesses. Of course she thought it crazy for anyone to go to a doctor when she could tell them just what they needed. All these things she had learned from her mother, Bell Blair Hooks, whose name I would choose as my pen name. Everyone agreed that I had the temperament of this great-grandmother I would not remember. She was a sharp-tongued woman. Or so they said. And it was believed I had inherited my way with words from her.

Families do that. They chart psychic genealogies that often overlook what is right before our eyes. I may have inherited my great-grandmother Bell Hooks's way with words, but I learned to use those words listening to my grandmother. I learned to be courageous by seeing her act without fear. I learned to risk because she was daring. Home and family were her world. While my grandfather journeyed downtown, visited at other folks' houses, went to church, and conducted affairs in the world, Baba rarely left home. There was nothing in the world she needed. Things out there violated her spirit.

As a child I had no sense of what it would mean to live a life, spanning so many generations, unable to read or write. To me Baba was a woman of power. That she would have been extraordinarily powerless in a world beyond 1200 Broad Street was a thought that never entered my mind. I believed that she stayed home because it was the place she liked best. Just as Daddy Gus seemed to need to walk — to roam.

After his death it was easier to see the ways that they complemented and   25
completed each other. For suddenly, without him as a silent backdrop,
Baba's spirit was diminished. Something in her was forever lonely and
could not find solace. When she died, tulips, her favorite flower, surrounded
her. The preacher told us that her death was not an occasion for grief, for
"it is hard to live in a world where your choicest friends are gone." Daddy
Gus was the companion she missed most. His presence had always been
the mirror of memory. Without it there was so much that could not be
shared. There was no witness.

Seeing their life together, I learned that it was possible for women and   26
men to fashion households, arranged around their own needs. Power was
shared. When there was an imbalance, Baba ruled the day. It seemed
utterly alien to me to learn about black women and men not making families and homes together. I had not been raised in a world of absent men.
One day I knew I would fashion a life using the patterns I inherited from
Baba and Daddy Gus. I keep treasures in my cigar box, which still smells
after all these years. The quilt that covered me as a child remains, full of
ink stains and faded colors. In my trunks are braided tobacco leaves, taken
from over home. They keep evil away — keep bad spirits from crossing the
threshold, like the ancestors they guard and protect.

Analyzing This Selection

1. Find indications of role reversal in the grandparents' marriage. In your opinion, is their amount of reversal a good thing for them? for the author? for
   you?

2. **THE WRITER'S METHOD** How does bell hooks express the sense of
   enchantment, of living under the spell of the grandparents' powers?

Analyzing Connections

3. Generalizations about family such as the Insights by Robert Nisbet, Ferdinand Mount, J. H. Plumb, and Gloria Steinem (pp. 62–63) do not differentiate between generations. How is each of those contrasting views
   strengthened or weakened by bell hooks's analysis of her family generations?

Analyzing by Writing

4. Grandparents often transmit the values we accept and try to live by. Even
   children who have no living grandparents usually find someone in the grandparents' generation to fulfill that role. Analyze the role of a grandparent (or
   a similar figure) in your moral and emotional development.

Calvin Trillin

IT'S JUST TOO LATE

CALVIN TRILLIN (b. 1935) grew up in Kansas City, Missouri, and attended Yale University. He worked as a reporter for *Time* magazine, and from 1963 to 1982 he was a staff writer for the *New Yorker*. His regular reports of his travels around the United States focused on daily life, including where and how Americans eat. His widely syndicated humorous columns are collected in *If You Can't Say Something Nice* (1987) and *Enough's Enough* (1990). On the darker side, Trillin wrote a memoir of a Yale classmate who committed suicide, *Remembering Denny* (1993). Believing that the way people die can illuminate the way they lived, Trillin reported about deadly crimes and accidents in *Killings* (1984), which included the following account of the death of a teenage girl. Much fonder accounts of family life appear in *Family Man* (1998).

Knoxville, Tennessee
March 1979

Until she was sixteen, FaNee Cooper was what her parents sometimes 1 called an ideal child. "You'd never have to correct her," FaNee's mother has said. In sixth grade, FaNee won a spelling contest. She played the piano and the flute. She seemed to believe what she heard every Sunday at the Beaver Dam Baptist Church about good and evil and the hereafter. FaNee was not an outgoing child. Even as a baby, she was uncomfortable when she was held and cuddled. She found it easy to tell her parents she loved them but difficult to confide in them. Particularly compared to her sister, Kristy, a cheerful, open little girl two and a half years younger, she was reserved and introspective. The thoughts she kept to herself, though, were apparently happy thoughts. Her eighth-grade essay on Christmas — written in a remarkably neat hand — talked of the joys of helping put together toys for her little brother, Leo, Jr., and the importance of her parents' reminder that Christmas is the birthday of Jesus. Her parents were the sort of people who might have been expected to have an ideal child. As a boy, Leo Cooper had been called "one of the greatest high-school basketball players ever developed in Knox County." He went on to play basketball at East Tennessee State, and he married the homecoming queen, JoAnn Henson. After college, Cooper became a high-school basketball coach and teacher and, eventually, an administrator. By the time FaNee turned thirteen, in 1973, he was in his third year as the principal of Gresham Junior High School, in Fountain City — a small Knox County town that had been swallowed up by Knoxville when the suburbs began to move north. A tall man, with curly black hair going on gray, Leo Cooper has an elaborate way of talking ("Unless I'm very badly mistaken, he has never related to me totally the content of his conversation") and a manner that may come from years of trying to leave errant junior-high-school students with the impression that a responsible adult is magnanimous, even humble, about invariably being in the right. His wife, a high-school art teacher, paints and does batik, and created the name FaNee because she liked the way it looked and sounded — it sounds like "Fawn*ee*" when the Coopers say it — but the impression she gives is not of artiness but of soft-spoken small-town gentility. When she found, in the course of cleaning up FaNee's room, that her ideal thirteen-year-old had been smoking cigarettes, she was, in her words, crushed. "FaNee was such a perfect child before that," JoAnn Cooper said some time later. "She was angry that we found out. She knew we knew that she had done something we didn't approve of, and then the rebellion started. I was hurt. I was very hurt. I guess it came through as disappointment."

Several months later, FaNee's grandmother died. FaNee had been 2 devoted to her grandmother. She wrote a poem in her memory — an almost joyous poem, filled with Christian faith in the afterlife ("Please don't grieve over my happiness / Rejoice with me in the presence of the Angels of Heaven"). She also took some keepsakes from her grandmother's house, and was apparently mortified when her parents found them and explained that they would have to be returned. By then, the Coopers were aware that FaNee was going to have a difficult time as a teenager. They thought she might be self-conscious about the double affliction of glasses and braces. They thought she might be uncomfortable in the role of the principal's daughter at Gresham. In ninth grade, she entered Halls High School, where JoAnn Cooper was teaching art. FaNee was a loner at first. Then she fell in with what could only be considered a bad crowd.

Halls, a few miles to the north of Fountain City, used to be known as 3 Halls Crossroads. It is what Knoxville people call "over the ridge" — on the side of Black Oak Ridge that has always been thought of as rural. When FaNee entered Halls High, the Coopers were already in the process of building a house on several acres of land they had bought in Halls, in a sparsely settled area along Brown Gap Road. Like two or three other houses along the road, it was to be constructed basically of huge logs taken from old buildings — a house that Leo Cooper describes as being, like the name FaNee, "just a little bit different." Ten years ago, Halls Crossroads was literally a crossroads. Then some of the Knoxville expansion that had swollen Fountain City spilled over the ridge, planting subdivisions here and there on roads that still went for long stretches with nothing but an occasional house with a cow or two next to it. The increase in population did not create a town. Halls has no center. Its commercial area is a series of two or three shopping centers strung together on the Maynardville Highway, the four-lane that leads north into Union County — a place almost synonymous in east Tennessee with mountain poverty. Its restaurant is the Halls Freezo Drive-In. The gathering place for the group FaNee Cooper eventually found herself in was the Maynardville Highway Exxon station.

At Halls High School, the social poles were represented by the Jocks and the Freaks. FaNee found her friends among the Freaks. "I am truly enlighted upon irregular trains of thought aimed at strange depots of mental wards," she wrote when she was fifteen. "Yes! Crazed farms for the mental off — Oh! I walked through the halls screams & loud laughter fill my ears — Orderlys try to reason with me — but I am unreasonable! The joys of being a FREAK in a circus of imagination." The little crowd of eight or ten young people that FaNee joined has been referred to by her mother as "the Union County group." A couple of the girls were from backgrounds similar to FaNee's, but all the boys had the characteristics, if not the precise address, that Knoxville people associate with the poor whites of Union County. They were the sort of boys who didn't bother to finish high school, or finished it in a special program for slow learners, or got ejected from it for taking a swing at the principal. 4

"I guess you can say they more or less dragged us down to their level with the drugs," a girl who was in the group — a girl who can be called Marcia — said recently. "And somehow we settled for it. It seems like we had to get ourselves in the pit before we could look out." People in the group used marijuana and Valium and LSD. They sneered at the Jocks and the "prim and proper little ladies" who went with Jocks. "We set ourselves aside," Marcia now says. "We put ourselves above everyone. How we did that I don't know." In a Knox County high school, teenagers who want to get themselves in the pit need not mainline heroin. The Jocks they mean to be compared to do not merely show up regularly for classes and practice football and wear clean clothes; they watch their language and preach temperance and go to prayer meetings on Wednesday nights and talk about having a real good Christian witness. Around Knoxville, people who speak of well-behaved high-school kids often seem to use words like "perfect," or even "angels." For FaNee's group, the opposite was not difficult to figure out. "We were into wicked things, strange things," Marcia says. "It was like we were on some kind of devil trip." FaNee wrote about demons and vultures and rats. "Slithering serpents eat my sanity and bite my ass," she wrote in an essay called "The Lovely Road of Life," just after she turned sixteen, "while tornadoes derail and ever so swiftly destroy every car in my train of thought." She wrote a lot about death. 5

FaNee's girlfriends spoke of her as "super-intelligent." Her English teacher found some of her writing profound — and disturbing. She was thought to be not just super-intelligent but super-mysterious, and even, at times, super-weird — an introverted girl who stared straight ahead with deep-brown, 6 nearly black eyes and seemed to have thoughts she couldn't share. Nobody really knew why she had chosen to run with the Freaks —whether it was loneliness or rebellion or simple boredom. Marcia thought it might have had something to do with a feeling that her parents had settled on Kristy as their perfect child. "I guess she figured she couldn't be the best," Marcia said recently. "So she decided she might as well be the worst."

Toward the spring of FaNee's junior year at Halls, her problems seemed   7
to deepen. Despite her intelligence, her grades were sliding. She was what her mother called "a mental dropout." Leo Cooper had to visit Halls twice because of minor suspensions. Once, FaNee had been caught smoking. Once, having ducked out of a required assembly, she was spotted by a favorite teacher, who turned her in. At home, she exchanged little more than short, strained formalities with Kristy, who shared their parents' opinion of FaNee's choice of friends. The Coopers had finished their house — a large house, its size accentuated by the huge old logs and a great stone fireplace and outsize "Paul Bunyan"–style furniture — but FaNee spent most of her time there in her own room, sleeping or listening to rock music through earphones. One night, there was a terrible scene when FaNee returned from a concert in a condition that Leo Cooper knew had to be the result of marijuana. JoAnn Cooper, who ordinarily strikes people as too gentle to raise her voice, found herself losing her temper regularly. Finally, Leo Cooper asked a counselor he knew, Jim Griffin, to stop in at Halls High School and have a talk with FaNee — unofficially.

Griffin — a young man with a warm, informal manner — worked for the   8
Juvenile Court of Knox County. He had a reputation for being able to reach teenagers who wouldn't talk to their parents or to school administrators. One Friday in March of 1977, he spent an hour and a half talking to FaNee Cooper. As Griffin recalls the interview, FaNee didn't seem alarmed by his presence. She seemed to him calm and controlled — Griffin thought it was something like talking to another adult — and, unlike most of the teenagers he dealt with, she looked him in the eye the entire time. Griffin, like some of FaNee's friends, found her eyes unsettling — "the coldest, most distant, but, at the same time, the most knowing eyes I'd ever seen." She expressed affection for her parents, but she didn't seem interested in exploring ways of getting along better with them. The impression she gave Griffin was that they were who they were, and she was who she was, and there didn't happen to be any connection. Several times, she made the same response to Griffin's suggestions: "It's too late."

That weekend, neither FaNee nor her parents brought up the subject of   9
Griffin's visit. Leo Cooper has spoken of the weekend as being particularly happy; a friend of FaNee's who stayed over remembers it as particularly strained. FaNee stayed home from school on Monday because of a bad headache — she often had bad headaches — but felt well enough on Monday evening to drive to the library. She was to be home at nine. When she wasn't, Mrs. Cooper began to phone her friends. Finally, around ten, Leo

Cooper got into his other car and took a swing around Halls — past the teenage hangouts like the Exxon station and the Pizza Hut and the Smoky Mountain Market. Then he took a second swing. At eleven, FaNee was still not home.

She hadn't gone to the library. She had picked up two girlfriends and   10 driven to the home of a third, where everyone took five Valium tablets. Then the four girls drove over to the Exxon station, where they met four boys from their crowd. After a while, the group bought some beer and some marijuana and reassembled at Charlie Stevens's trailer. Charlie Stevens was five or six years older than everyone else in the group — a skinny, slow-thinking young man with long black hair and a sparse beard. He was married and had a child, but he and his wife had separated; she was back in Union County with the baby. Stevens had remained in their trailer — parked in the yard near his mother's house, in a back-road area of Knox County dominated by decrepit, unpainted sheds and run-down trailers and rusted-out automobiles. Stevens had picked up FaNee at home once or twice — apparently, more as a driver for the group than as a date — and the Coopers, having learned that his unsuitability extended to being married, had asked her not to see him.

In Charlie's trailer, which had no heat or electricity, the group drank   11 beer and passed around joints, keeping warm with blankets. By eleven or so, FaNee was what one of her friends has called "super-messed-up." Her speech was slurred. She was having trouble keeping her balance. She had decided not to go home. She had apparently persuaded herself that her parents intended to send her away to some sort of home for incorrigibles. "It's too late," she said to one of her friends. "It's just too late." It was decided that one of the boys, David Munsey, who was more or less the leader of the group, would drive the Coopers' car to FaNee's house, where FaNee and Charlie Stevens would pick him up in Steven's car — a worn Pinto with four bald tires, one light, and a dragging muffler. FaNee wrote a note to her parents, and then, perhaps because her handwriting was suffering the effects of beer and marijuana and Valium, asked Stevens to rewrite it on a large piece of paper, which would be left on the seat of the Coopers' car. The Stevens version was just about the same as FaNee's, except that Stevens left out a couple of sentences about trying to work things out ("I'm willing to try") and, not having won any spelling championship himself, he misspelled a few words, like "tomorrow." The note said, "Dear Mom and Dad. Sorry I'm late. Very late. I left your car because I thought you might need it tomorrow. I love you all, but this is something I just had to do. The man talked to me privately for one and a half hours and I was really scared, so this is something I just had to do, but don't worry. I'm with a very good friend. Love you all. FaNee. P.S. Please try to understand I love you all very much, really I do. Love me if you have a chance."

At eleven-thirty or so, Leo Cooper was sitting in his living room, looking   12 out the window at his driveway — a long gravel road that runs almost four hundred feet from the house to Brown Gap Road. He saw the car that

FaNee had been driving pull into the driveway. "She's home," he called to his wife, who had just left the room. Cooper walked out on the deck over the garage. The car had stopped at the end of the driveway, and the lights had gone out. He got into his other car and drove to the end of the driveway. David Munsey had already joined Charlie Stevens and FaNee, and the Pinto was just leaving, traveling at a normal rate of speed. Leo Cooper pulled out on the road behind them.

Stevens turned left on Crippen Road, a road that has a field on one side   13 and two or three small houses on the other, and there Cooper pulled his car in front of the Pinto and stopped, blocking the way. He got out and walked toward the Pinto. Suddenly, Stevens put the car in reverse, backed into a driveway a hundred yards behind him, and sped off. Cooper jumped in his car and gave chase. Stevens raced back to Brown Gap Road, ran a stop sign there, ran another stop sign at Maynardville Highway, turned north, veered off onto the old Andersonville Pike, a nearly abandoned road that runs parallel to the highway, and then crossed back over the highway to the narrow, dark country roads on the other side. Stevens sometimes drove with his lights out. He took some of the corners by suddenly applying his hand brake to make the car swerve around in a ninety-degree turn. He was in familiar territory — he actually passed his trailer — and Cooper had difficulty keeping up. Past the trailer, Stevens swept down a hill into a sharp left turn that took him onto Foust Hollow Road, a winding, hilly road not much wider than one car.

At a fork, Cooper thought he had lost the Pinto. He started to go right   14 and then saw what seemed to be a spark from Stevens's dragging muffler off to the left, in the darkness. Cooper took the left fork, down Salem Church Road. He went down a hill and then up a long, curving hill to a crest, where he saw the Stevens car ahead. "I saw the car airborne. Up in the air," he later testified. "It was up in the air. And then it completely rolled over one more time. It started to make another flip forward, and just as it started to flip to the other side it flipped back this way, and my daughter's body came out."

Cooper slammed on his brakes and skidded to a stop up against the   15 Pinto. "Book!" Stevens shouted — the group's equivalent of "Scram!" Stevens and Munsey disappeared into the darkness. "It was dark, no one around, and so I started yelling for FaNee," Cooper had testified. "I thought it was an eternity before I could find her body, wedged under the back end of that car....I tried everything I could, and saw that I couldn't get her loose. So I ran to a trailer back up to the top of the hill back up there to try to get that lady to call to get me some help, and then apparently she didn't think that I was serious....I took the jack out of my car and got under, and it was dark, still couldn't see too much what was going on...and started prying and got her loose, and I don't know how. And then I dragged her over to the side, and, of course, at the time I felt reasonably assured that she was gone, because her head was completely —on one side just as if you had taken a sledgehammer and just hit it and bashed it in. And I did have the pleasure of one thing. I had the pleasure of listening to her breathe about the last three times she ever breathed in her life."

David Munsey did not return to the wreck that night, but Charlie 16 Stevens did. Leo Cooper was kneeling next to his daughter's body. Cooper insisted that Stevens come close enough to see FaNee. "He was kneeling down next to her," Stevens later testified. "And he said, 'Do you know what you've done? Do you really know what you've done?' Like that. And I just looked at her, and I said, 'Yes,' and just stood there. Because I couldn't say nothing." There was, of course, a legal decision to be made about who was responsible for FaNee Cooper's death. In a deposition, Stevens said he had been fleeing for his life. He testified that when Leo Cooper blocked Crippen Road, FaNee had said that her father had a gun and intended to hurt them. Stevens was bound over and eventually indicted for involuntary manslaughter. Leo Cooper testified that when he approached the Pinto on Crippen Road, FaNee had a strange expression that he had never seen before. "It wasn't like FaNee, and I knew something was wrong," he said. "My concern was to get FaNee out of the car." The district attorney's office asked that Cooper be bound over for reckless driving, but the judge declined to do so. "Any father would have done what he did," the judge said. "I can see no criminal act on the part of Mr. Cooper."

Almost two years passed before Charlie Stevens was brought to trial. Part 17 of the problem was assuring the presence of David Munsey, who had joined the Navy but seemed inclined to assign his own leaves. In the meantime, the Coopers went to court with a civil suit — they had "uninsured-motorist coverage," which requires their insurance company to cover any defendant who has no insurance of his own — and they won a judgment. There were ways of assigning responsibility, of course, which had nothing to do with the law, civil or criminal. A lot of people in Knoxville thought that Leo Cooper had, in the words of his lawyer, "done what any daddy worth his salt would have done." There were others who believed that FaNee Cooper had lost her life because Leo Cooper had lost his temper. Leo Cooper was not among those who expressed any doubts about his actions. Unlike his wife, whose eyes filled with tears at almost any mention of FaNee, Cooper seemed able, even eager to go over the details of the accident again and again. With the help of a school-board security man, he conducted his own investigation. He drove over the route dozens of times. "I've thought about it every day, and I guess I will the rest of my life," he said as he and his lawyer and the prosecuting attorney went over the route again the day before Charlie Stevens's trial finally began. "But I can't tell any alternative for a father. I simply wanted her out of that car. I'd have done the same thing again, even at the risk of losing her."

Tennessee law permits the family of a victim to hire a special prosecutor   18
to assist the district attorney. The lawyer who acted for the Coopers in the
civil case helped prosecute Charlie Stevens. Both he and the district attorney assured the jurors that the presence of a special prosecutor was not to
be construed to mean that the Coopers were vindictive. Outside the courtroom, Leo Cooper said that the verdict was of no importance to him — that
he felt sorry, in a way, for Charlie Stevens. But there were people in
Knoxville who thought Cooper had a lot riding on the prosecution of Charlie Stevens. If Stevens was not guilty of FaNee Cooper's death — found so
by twelve of his peers — who was?

At the trial, Cooper testified emotionally and remarkably graphically   19
about pulling FaNee out from under the car and watching her die in his
arms. Charlie Stevens had shaved his beard and cut his hair, but the effort
did not transform him into an impressive witness. His lawyer — trying to
argue that it would have been impossible for Stevens to concoct the story
about FaNee's having mentioned a gun, as the prosecution strongly
implied — said, "His mind is such that if you ask him a question you can
hear his mind go around, like an old mill creaking." Stevens did not deny
the recklessness of his driving or the sorry condition of his car. It happened
to be the only car he had available to flee in, he said, and he had fled in
fear for his life.

The prosecution said that Stevens could have let FaNee out of the car   20
when her father stopped them, or could have gone to the commercial strip
on the Maynardville Highway for protection. The prosecution said that Leo
Cooper had done what he might have been expected to do under the circumstances — alone, late at night, his daughter in danger. The defense said
precisely the same about Stevens: He had done what he might have been
expected to do when being pursued by a man he had reason to be afraid of.
"I don't fault Mr. Cooper for what he did, but I'm sorry he did it," the
defense attorney said. "I'm sorry the girl said what she said." The jury delib-
erated for eighteen minutes. Charlie Stevens was found guilty. The jury
recommended a sentence of from two to five years in the state penitentiary.
At the announcement, Leo Cooper broke down and cried, JoAnn Cooper's
eyes filled with tears; she blinked them back and continued to stare straight
ahead.

In a way, the Coopers might still strike a casual visitor as an ideal fam-   21
ily — handsome parents, a bright and bubbly teenage daughter, a little boy
learning the hook shot from his father, a warm house with some land
around it. FaNee's presence is there, of course. A picture of her, with a
small bouquet of flowers over it, hangs in the living room. One of her
poems is displayed in a frame on a table. Even if Leo Cooper continues to
think about that night for the rest of his life, there are questions he can
never answer. Was there a way that Leo and JoAnn Cooper could have prevented FaNee from choosing the path she chose? Would she still be alive
if Leo Cooper had not jumped into his car and driven to the end of the

driveway to investigate? Did she in fact tell Charlie Stevens that her father would hurt them — or even that her father had a gun? Did she want to get away from her family even at the risk of tearing around dark country roads in Charlie Stevens's dismal Pinto? Or did she welcome the risk? The poem of FaNee's that the Coopers have displayed is one she wrote a week before her death:

> I think I'm going to die
> And I really don't know why.
> But look in my eye
> When I tell you good-bye.
> I think I'm going to die.

Analyzing This Selection

1. **THE WRITER'S METHOD** What is the author's purpose in giving detailed descriptions, as in paragraph 3 and other places, of the setting and the local conditions of life?

2. What is the effect of the two full paragraphs that recount the car chase? What would be lost by condensing paragraphs 13 and 14 into a short statement that reports what happened?

3. FaNee's own writings, including her farewell note, show sharp contrasts between her different outlooks on life. Does this contrast make her any more sympathetic as a person? Or does it turn her into more of a freak?

4. If Mr. Cooper had been able to stop Charlie Stevens's car (immediately after para. 12), what might have happened? Use your insight into the characters and your sense of the situation to explain the most likely reactions of each of the main characters.

Analyzing Connections

5. In Focusing by Writing (see p. 64), the second topic suggests that families sometimes play an unwitting role in the formation of a "black sheep." Considering FaNee as a "black sheep," do you think this role was partly created by her family? Why or why not?

Analyzing by Writing

6. The essay presents the difficulties of assigning legal and moral blame for the death of FaNee. Do you think the author is too harsh or too soft in his judgment of who is guilty? who is responsible? who is victimized? In a short essay, explain the author's implied judgment in this accidental death. Include at least one point on which your judgment differs from the author's viewpoint.

7. The only viewpoint missing from Trillin's account is, of course, FaNee's. Offer some possible explanations for FaNee's withdrawal from her family. You might want to draw on insights from the other daughters and sons described in this chapter.

Tillie Olsen

I STAND HERE IRONING

TILLIE OLSEN (b. 1913) dropped out of high school in Nebraska at fifteen in order to help support her family during the Depression. She held jobs as a factory worker or secretary while she organized labor unions, married, raised four children, and continued to read prodigiously. "Public libraries were my college," she has said. When she was forty, she resumed her early efforts to write fiction. Her volume of stories, *Tell Me a Riddle* (1961), established her as a champion of the poor and overburdened. In *Silences* (1978), a collection of essays, Olsen examines the injustices of social class, racism, and sexism that hinder creativity, particularly in women. The cruelty of harmful social conditions is a theme in all her work, including the following story.

I stand here ironing, and what you asked me moves tormented back and 1 forth with the iron.

"I wish you would manage the time to come in and talk with me about 2 your daughter. I'm sure you can help me understand her. She's a youngster who needs help and whom I'm deeply interested in helping."

"Who needs help."... Even if I came, what good would it do? You think 3 because I am her mother I have a key, or that in some way you could use me as a key? She has lived for nineteen years. There is all that life that has happened outside of me, beyond me.

And when is there time to remember, to sift, to weigh, to estimate, to 4 total? I will start and there will be an interruption and I will have to gather it all together again. Or I will become engulfed with all I did or did not do, with what should have been and what cannot be helped.

She was a beautiful baby. The first and only one of our five that was 5 beautiful at birth. You do not guess how new and uneasy her tenancy in her now-loveliness. You did not know her all those years she was thought homely, or see her poring over her baby pictures, making me tell her over and over how beautiful she had been — and would be, I would tell her — and was now, to the seeing eye. But the seeing eyes were few or nonexistent. Including mine.

I nursed her. They feel that's important nowadays. I nursed all the chil- 6 dren, but with her, with all the fierce rigidity of first motherhood, I did like the books then said. Though her cries battered me to trembling and my breasts ached with swollenness, I waited till the clock decreed.

Why do I put that first? I do not even know if it matters, or if it explains 7 anything.

She was a beautiful baby. She blew shining bubbles of sound. She loved 8 motion, loved light, loved color and music and textures. She would lie on the floor in her blue overalls patting the surface so hard in ecstasy her hands and feet would blur. She was a miracle to me, but when she was eight months old I had to leave her daytimes with the woman downstairs to whom she was no miracle at all, for I worked or looked for work and for Emily's father, who "could no longer endure" (he wrote in his good-bye note) "sharing want with us."

I was nineteen. It was the pre-relief, pre-WPA world of the depression. I 9 would start running as soon as I got off the streetcar, running up the stairs, the place smelling sour, and awake or asleep to startle awake, when she saw me she would break into a clogged weeping that could not be comforted, a weeping I can hear yet.

After a while I found a job hashing at night so I could be with her days, 10 and it was better. But it came to where I had to bring her to his family and leave her.

It took a long time to raise the money for her fare back. Then she got 11 chicken pox and I had to wait longer. When she finally came, I hardly knew her, walking quick and nervous like her father, looking like her father, thin, and dressed in a shoddy red that yellowed her skin and glared at the pockmarks. All the baby loveliness gone.

She was two. Old enough for nursery school they said, and I did not 12 know then what I know now — the fatigue of the long day, and the lacerations of group life in the kinds of nurseries that are only parking places for children.

Except that it would have made no difference if I had known. It was the 13 only place there was. It was the only way we could be together, the only way I could hold a job.

And even without knowing, I knew. I knew the teacher that was evil 14 because all these years it has curdled into my memory, the little boy hunched in the corner, her rasp, "why aren't you outside, because Alvin hits you? that's no reason, go out, scaredy." I knew Emily hated it even if she did not clutch and implore "don't go Mommy" like the other children, mornings.

She always had a reason why we should stay home. Momma, you look 15 sick. Momma, I feel sick. Momma, the teachers aren't there today, they're sick. Momma, we can't go, there was a fire there last night. Momma, it's a holiday today, no school, they told me.

But never a direct protest, never rebellion. I think of our others in their 16 three-, four-year-oldness — the explosions, the tempers, the denunciations, the demands — and I feel suddenly ill. I put the iron down. What in me demanded that goodness in her? And what was the cost, the cost to her of such goodness?

The old man living in the back once said in his gentle way: "You should 17 smile at Emily more when you look at her." What *was* in my face when I looked at her? I loved her. There were all the acts of love.

It was only with the others I remembered what he said, and it was the 18 face of joy, and not of care or tightness or worry I turned to them — too late for Emily. She does not smile easily, let alone almost always as her brothers and sisters do. Her face is closed and somber, but when she wants, how fluid. You must have seen it in her pantomimes, you spoke of her rare gift for comedy on the stage that rouses a laughter out of the audience so dear they applaud and applaud and do not want to let her go.

Where does it come from, that comedy? There was none of it in her 19 when she came back to me that second time, after I had had to send her away again. She had a new daddy now to learn to love, and I think perhaps it was a better time.

Except when we left her alone nights, telling ourselves she was old 20 enough.

"Can't you go some other time, Mommy, like tomorrow?" she would 21 ask. "Will it be just a little while you'll be gone? Do you promise?"

The time we came back, the front door open, the clock on the floor in 22 the hall. She rigid awake. "It wasn't just a little while. I didn't cry. Three times I called you, just three times, and then I ran downstairs to open the door so you could come faster. The clock talked loud. I threw it away, it scared me what it talked."

She said the clock talked loud again that night I went to the hospital to 23 have Susan. She was delirious with the fever that comes before red measles, but she was fully conscious all the week I was gone and the week after we were home when she could not come near the new baby or me.

She did not get well. She stayed skeleton thin, not wanting to eat, and 24 night after night she had nightmares. She would call for me, and I would rouse from exhaustion to sleepily call back: "You're all right, darling, go to sleep, it's just a dream," and if she still called, in a sterner voice, "now go to sleep, Emily, there's nothing to hurt you." Twice, only twice, when I had to get up for Susan anyhow, I went in to sit with her.

Now when it is too late (as if she would let me hold and comfort her like 25 I do the others) I get up and go to her at once at her moan or restless stirring. "Are you awake, Emily? Can I get you something?" And the answer is always the same: "No, I'm all right, go back to sleep, Mother."

They persuaded me at the clinic to send her away to a convalescent 26 home in the country where "she can have the kind of food and care you can't manage for her, and you'll be free to concentrate on the new baby." They still send children to that place. I see pictures on the society page of sleek young women planning affairs to raise money for it, or dancing at the affairs, or decorating Easter eggs or filling Christmas stockings for the children.

They never have a picture of the children so I do not know if the girls 27 still wear those gigantic red bows and the ravaged looks on the every other Sunday when parents can come to visit "unless otherwise notified" — as we were notified the first six weeks.

Oh it is a handsome place, green lawns and tall trees and fluted flower 28 beds. High up on the balconies of each cottage the children stand, the girls in their red bows and white dresses, the boys in white suits and giant red ties. The parents stand below shrieking up to be heard and the children shriek down to be heard, and between them the invisible wall "Not To Be Contaminated by Parental Germs or Physical Affection."

There was a tiny girl who always stood hand in hand with Emily. Her 29 parents never came. One visit she was gone. "They moved her to Rose Cottage," Emily shouted in explanation. "They don't like you to love anybody here."

She wrote once a week, the labored writing of a seven-year-old. "I am 30 fine. How is the baby. If I write my leter nicly I will have a star. Love." There never was a star. We wrote every other day, letters she could never hold or keep but only hear read — once. "We simply do not have room for children to keep any personal possessions," they patiently explained when we pieced one Sunday's shrieking together to plead how much it would mean to Emily, who loved so to keep things, to be allowed to keep her letters and cards.

Each visit she looked frailer. "She isn't eating," they told us. 31

(They had runny eggs for breakfast or mush with lumps, Emily said 32 later, I'd hold it in my mouth and not swallow. Nothing ever tasted good, just when they had chicken.)

It took us eight months to get her released home, and only the fact that 33 she gained back so little of her seven lost pounds convinced the social worker.

I used to try to hold and love her after she came back, but her body 34 would stay stiff, and after a while she'd push away. She ate little. Food sickened her, and I think much of life too. Oh she had physical lightness and brightness, twinkling by on skates, bouncing like a ball up and down up and down over the jump rope, skimming over the hill; but these were momentary.

She fretted about her appearance, thin and dark and foreign-looking at a 35 time when every little girl was supposed to look or thought she should look a chubby blonde replica of Shirley Temple. The doorbell sometimes rang for her, but no one seemed to come and play in the house or be a best friend. Maybe because we moved so much.

There was a boy she loved painfully through two school semesters. 36 Months later she told me how she had taken pennies from my purse to buy him candy. "Licorice was his favorite and I brought him some every day, but he still liked Jennifer better'n me. Why, Mommy?" The kind of question for which there is no answer.

School was a worry to her. She was not glib or quick in a world where 37
glibness and quickness were easily confused with ability to learn. To her
overworked and exasperated teachers she was an overconscientious "slow
learner" who kept trying to catch up and was absent entirely too often.

I let her be absent, though sometimes the illness was imaginary. How 38
different from my now-strictness about attendance with the others. I wasn't
working. We had a new baby, I was home anyhow. Sometimes, after Susan
grew old enough, I would keep her home from school, too, to have them
all together.

Mostly Emily had asthma, and her breathing, harsh and labored, would 39
fill the house with a curiously tranquil sound. I would bring the two old
dresser mirrors and her boxes of collections to her bed. She would select
beads and single earrings, bottle tops and shells, dried flowers and pebbles,
old postcards and scraps, all sorts of oddments; then she and Susan would
play Kingdom, setting up landscapes and furniture, peopling them with
action.

Those were the only times of peaceful companionship between her and 40
Susan. I have edged away from it, that poisonous feeling between them,
that terrible balancing of hurts and needs I had to do between the two, and
did so badly, those earlier years.

Oh there are conflicts between the others too, each one human, need- 41
ing, demanding, hurting, taking — but only between Emily and Susan, no,
Emily toward Susan that corroding resentment. It seems so obvious on the
surface, yet it is not obvious. Susan, the second child, Susan, golden- and
curly-haired and chubby, quick and articulate and assured, everything in
appearance and manner Emily was not; Susan, not able to resist Emily's
precious things, losing or sometimes clumsily breaking them; Susan telling
jokes and riddles to company for applause while Emily sat silent (to say to
me later: That was *my* riddle, Mother, I told it to Susan); Susan, who for
all the five years' difference in age was just a year behind Emily in developing physically.

I am glad for that slow physical development that widened the differ- 42
ence between her and her contemporaries, though she suffered over it. She
was too vulnerable for that terrible world of youthful competition, of preen-
ing and parading, of constant measuring of yourself against every other, of
envy, "If I had that copper hair," "If I had that skin...." She tormented herself enough about not looking like the others, there was enough of the
unsureness, the having to be conscious of words before you speak, the constant caring — what are they thinking of me? without having it all magnified by the merciless physical drives.

Ronnie is calling. He is wet and I change him. It is rare there is such a 43
cry now. That time of motherhood is almost behind me when the ear is not
one's own but must always be racked and listening for the child cry, the

child call. We sit for a while and I hold him, looking out over the city spread in charcoal with its soft aisles of light. "*Shoogily,*" he breathes and curls closer. I carry him back to bed, asleep. *Shoogily.* A funny word, a family word, inherited from Emily, invented by her to say: *comfort.*

In this and other ways she leaves her seal, I say aloud. And startle at my 44 saying it. What do I mean? What did I start to gather together, to try and make coherent? I was at the terrible, growing years. War years. I do not remember them well. I was working, there were four smaller ones now, there was not time for her. She had to help be a mother, and housekeeper, and shopper. She had to set her seal. Mornings of crisis and near hysteria trying to get lunches packed, hair combed, coats and shoes found, everyone to school or Child Care on time, the baby ready for transportation. And always the paper scribbled on by a smaller one, the book looked at by Susan then mislaid, the homework not done. Running out to that huge school where she was one, she was lost, she was a drop; suffering over the unpreparedness, stammering and unsure in her classes.

There was so little time left at night after the kids were bedded down. 45 She would struggle over books, always eating (it was in those years she developed her enormous appetite that is legendary in our family) and I would be ironing, or preparing food for the next day, or writing V-mail[1] to Bill, or tending the baby. Sometimes, to make me laugh, or out of her despair, she would imitate happenings or types at school.

I think I said once: "Why don't you do something like this in the school 46 amateur show?" One morning she phoned me at work, hardly understandable through the weeping: "Mother, I did it. I won, I won; they gave me first prize; they clapped and clapped and wouldn't let me go."

Now suddenly she was Somebody, and as imprisoned in her difference 47 as she had been in her anonymity.

She began to be asked to perform at other high schools, even in col- 48 leges, then at city and statewide affairs. The first one we went to, I only recognized her that first moment when thin, shy, she almost drowned herself into the curtains. Then: Was this Emily? The control, the command, the convulsing and deadly clowning, the spell, then the roaring, stamping audience, unwilling to let this rare and precious laughter out of their lives.

Afterwards: You ought to do something about her with a gift like that — 49 but without money or knowing how, what does one do? We have left it all to her, and the gift has as often eddied inside, clogged and clotted, as been used and growing.

She is coming. She runs up the stairs two at a time with her light grace- 50 ful step, and I know she is happy tonight. Whatever it was that occasioned your call did not happen today.

---

[1]**V-mail** Postal forms for microfilming mail to servicemen during World War II. [Editor's note.]

"Aren't you ever going to finish the ironing, Mother? Whistler painted   51
his mother in a rocker. I'd have to paint mine standing over an ironing
board." This is one of her communicative nights and she tells me everything and nothing as she fixes herself a plate of food out of the icebox.

She is so lovely. Why did you want me to come in at all? Why were you   52
concerned? She will find her way.

She starts up the stairs to bed. "Don't get *me* up with the rest in the   53
morning." "But I thought you were having midterms." "Oh, those," she
comes back in, kisses me, and says quite lightly, "in a couple of years when
we'll be all atom-dead they won't matter a bit."

She has said it before. She *believes* it. But because I have been dredging   54
the past, and all that compounds a human being is so heavy and meaningful in me, I cannot endure it tonight.

I will never total it all. I will never come in to say: She was a child sel-   55
dom smiled at. Her father left me before she was a year old. I had to work
her first six years when there was work, or I sent her home and to his relatives. There were years she had care she hated. She was dark and thin and
foreign-looking in a world where the prestige went to blondeness and curly
hair and dimples, she was slow where glibness was prized. She was a child
of anxious, not proud, love. We were poor and could not afford for her the
soil of easy growth. I was a younger mother, I was a distracted mother.
There were the other children pushing up, demanding. Her younger sister
seemed all that she was not. There were years she did not let me touch her.
She kept too much in herself, her life was such she had to keep too much
in herself. My wisdom came too late. She has much to her and probably
little will come of it. She is a child of her age, of depression, of war, of fear.

Let her be. So all that is in her will not bloom — but in how many does   56
it? There is still enough left to live by. Only help her to know — help make
it so there is cause for her to know — that she is more than this dress on the
ironing board, helpless before the iron.

Analyzing This Selection

1. **THE WRITER'S METHOD**   Who has phoned Emily's mother? How has
   the caller's request affected the mother?

2. Does the mother blame herself too much or too little for causing Emily's
   hardships? At which points do you disagree with the mother's judgment of
   her own actions?

3. How did Emily differ from her brothers and sisters? What explanations does
   the mother have for Emily's difference? Which of her explanations do you
   think are most valid and important?

4. In the final two paragraphs, why does the mother refuse to consult about
   Emily?

5. Does the story reflect specific political views toward particular social conditions and historical events? What attitudes toward government assistance does the story stimulate in the reader?

6. To what extent do the mother's aspirations for Emily reflect her own?

Analyzing Connections

7. Emily and FaNee (see "It's Just Too Late," p. 83) both cause problems for their parents. What lessons have the parents learned?

Analyzing by Writing

8. How would a child like Emily perceive her mother's conflict of responsibilities? What problems do you think the child faced? Adopt Emily's viewpoint in a monologue (like this story) that explores Emily's thoughts during any one incident or situation suggested in the fiction.

Debra Spark

LAST THINGS

DEBRA SPARK (b. 1962), fiction writer and essayist, was raised in Boston, the main site in the following essay. She graduated from Yale University and earned an M.F.A. at the University of Iowa Writers' Workshop. Her work includes the novels *Coconuts for the Saint* (1994) and *The Ghost of Bridgetown* (2001). Spark directs the creative writing program at Colby College.

My sister and I step briskly out of the greengrocer to get away from the men behind us in line who have told us, in great detail, what they'd like to do to us, where they intend to put certain parts of their bodies. The clerk, kindly, rings their purchases up slowly, so Cyndy and I have a chance to hurry across the street, almost bumping into two men who are breaking raw eggs in their hands and leaning over to slip the viscous mess into their mouths.

One of those Manhattan nights, I think.

Earlier today, as Cyndy and I were taxiing away from Grand Central to her apartment in Chelsea, we were thrilled, saying: "New York. It's so great. Look at the dirt! Look at the guy peeing in the alley! I love it!" A joke, sure, but only partially. We'd just spent a claustrophobic weekend with our parents and other two siblings in the Berkshires. The occasion, I guess, was Cyndy's mastectomy last week.

Cyndy's nerves are pretty much gone in the right side of her body, so the operation didn't hurt as much as the lumpectomy she had two years ago, when she was twenty-one. Still, I can't help thinking, Wound, especially now that we're out with the crazies. And also, I'm thinking of my own toes, which are so black-and-blue with cold (a circulatory problem I will learn later in the month) that I am having trouble walking. Indeed, at the moment, I feel more damaged than Cyndy appears to. We shuffle by the guys with the eggs, and I put my right arm around Cyndy's back — companionably, I think, because I want to restore the playful order that has reigned most of today, that was operative when we were at the New York City Opera, and I was meeting Cyndy's coworkers and admiring the Mr. Potato Head doll she had placed over her desk, presumably to supervise her efforts as rehearsals coordinator. My arm has barely touched Cyndy's black coat (the coat I will someday wear) when she says, vicious as possible, "Don't you *dare* try to protect me."

I am quiet. My throat, for a minute, as pained as my toes, and then I say, my voice strangulated, half the words swallowed, "...not trying...protect you."

Cyndy is dead, of course. That is why I wear her black coat now. She died of breast cancer at age twenty-six, a fact I find unbelievable, a fact that is (virtually) statistically impossible. When she was twenty-one, she was in the shower in her dorm room at the University of Pennsylvania. She was washing under her arm when she found the lump. She was not checking for breast cancer. What college girl does monthly exams on her own breasts? Laura, my twin sister, says that I was the first person Cyndy called about the cancer. I don't think this is true, though Laura insists. I'm certain Cyndy called my father, the doctor, and that he told her to fly home to Boston. He demanded her return even though the doctors at Penn's health service pooh-poohed her concern. Finally, after a long conversation, I realize why Laura thinks Cyndy called me first and I tell her: "I think you're thinking about the rape."

"Oh, yeah," Laura says. "That's probably right."

When my father called me in Wisconsin to tell me about Cyndy, I said, "Oh, well, I'm sure, she's okay. Lots of women have fibrous breasts."

"No, Debra," my father said sternly. "That's not what this is about."

"Do you think she'll have to have a biopsy?"

He was quiet.

"A mastectomy?"

"That's the least of my concerns."

I guess I wasn't quite able to hear him right then. I hung up the phone and pulled out my copy of *Our Bodies, Ourselves*, to look at that book's photograph of a jubilant naked woman — out in the sun, with one breast gone, the stitches running up her chest like a sideway zipper. I remember wailing, literally wailing, at the image and at the prospect of my sister losing her breast.

I didn't know yet that my father had examined my sister when she came home from college. My father is an endocrinologist, a fertility specialist. He examines women every day in his office, but to feel your adult daughter's breast — breaking *that* taboo, because medical care is shoddy and you *do* love your daughter desperately and *appropriately* — and to know, right away, what it is you are feeling...I have to stop myself from imagining it. And I think my father has to disremember it too, because even though he knew, right then, she had cancer, he tells this story about himself. When the X ray of Cyndy's chest was up on the lightboard, my father pulled the X ray off the board and turned it over to look at the name. "Spark, C." He looked back at the picture. Turned the X ray over again to check the name. "Spark, C." He did the whole thing again. And again.

Later, two weeks before she died, I remember seeing her X ray up on a   16
lightboard. Not something I was supposed to see, I know, but Cyndy's treatment all took place at the same hospital my father has worked in for
twenty-five years. I knew my way about and I knew how to take silent
advantage when I needed to. I looked, but from a distance. I was out in the
hall, standing over Cyndy in her gurney, as orderlies were about to move
her out of the emergency ward and up to a floor. My view was oblique and
once I knew there was nothing happy to see there, I said, Don't look.
Though later, all I would do was say, Look, Debra. Look, this is a person
dying. Look, this is Cyndy going away.

My mother was always the most pessimistic of all of us, and I used to   17
hate her for it. "She'll be okay," I'd say. And, "We can't read the future."
My mother said we were lucky we *couldn't* read the future or we'd never
get through it. Which is probably true. That night in Manhattan, things
seemed tragic but manageable. In the past was the lumpectomy and the
radiation. Now the mastectomy was completed. The chemo was to come.
Cyndy had cut her hair short so the loss of it wouldn't be too upsetting.
Back in Boston, she'd gone with my mother to buy a wig. Now she was trying to wear it over her hair. That was the advice she had been given: to
start wearing it so it would be like a new haircut and no one would notice.
I thought, Who cares who notices? I was for announcing the illness as just
another fact, among many, about Cyndy. To keep it secret was to imply that
it was either shameful, like a sin, or special, like a surprise gift, and it was
neither.
    The wig bothered Cyndy. It was itchy and, though we'd tell her other-   18
wise, it had a dowdy look, a look that owed nothing to the haircuts Cyndy
had always had — the funky asymmetrical do she'd sported when she'd
gone to London for a year or the long red mane she'd had as a child. One
day, while I was still visiting with her in New York, we went out to lunch
with some friends of mine who had never met Cyndy. In the middle of
lunch, Cyndy, impatient and in the midst of a story (she was a magnificent
and voluble talker), pulled off her hair — to my friends' surprise, especially
since there was another head of hair under the one she pulled off.
    After all the preparation for baldness, however, Cyndy's hair didn't fall   19
out. At least, not that year. The first round of chemo was bad, but, again,
in the realm of the get-overable. Every three or four weekends, my mother
would come into New York and take Cyndy to the hospital and then out to
my grandmother's house for a weekend of puking. Cyndy handled it well.
The biggest long-term effect was that she wouldn't let anyone say "pot
roast" when they were around her. And she couldn't stand the smell of
toast for years to come.
    Some time later, after Cyndy had finished up the chemo, she decided to   20
go to business school, to get a degree in arts administration at UCLA. She
loved school. She had never been too happy as an undergraduate, but

UCLA was right for her. Her goal had been to make opera, which she adored, accessible to people who ordinarily wouldn't go. She had a special column in the school newspaper called "Kulture, Kulture, Kulture"; she was proud of her ability to drag business students (a surprise! stiff business students!) to the opera. I imagine Cyndy as the life of the party in those days. Cyndy going to the graduate student "beer bashes"; Cyndy leading the talk at the business school study sessions; Cyndy still earning her nickname "Symphony."

I know she slimmed down in those years, too. She had an intermittent   21
problem with her weight, and it was probably the real clue that Cyndy — handle-everything Cyndy — sometimes had her unhealthy way of handling things. When I visited Cyndy in Chelsea, after her mastectomy, we were toying with the idea of living together. At the time, I was profoundly (read "clinically") depressed. I had left the man I had been living with for four years and had been unenthusiastically debating what I should do next. Cyndy was moving up to Inwood, and we had found a small apartment that would accommodate the two of us should I decide to move with her. I remember that one of her real enthusiasms about the two of us living together had to do with food. She was convinced that I'd have her eating large green salads for dinner, that my own good habits would rub off on her, and she would no longer find herself in the middle of secret, ruinously upsetting food binges.

Cyndy had been a chubby kid, but never really fat, even when she   22
weighed a lot. When she was older, her figure was sensual if robust. Still her weight was an occasional issue: my father telling her, at dinner, not to be a *chazar*;[1] my mother spinning her own anxiety about weight onto Cyndy. At Cyndy's college graduation, Cyndy said "No, thank you" to the dessert tray that a waiter was offering our table. We were all too full. My mother said, "Oh, I'm so proud of you" to Cyndy. Cyndy said, "I'll have that chocolate cake" to the waiter. And the rest of the children — Laura, David, and I — hooted with laughter. It was our turn to be proud. After all, the request for cake was her version of "Oh, stop it, Mom."

Still, toward the end of Cyndy's stay in Chelsea, I got my first glimpse of   23
how painful the problem with food could be. Like many women, I had my own issues, and Cyndy and I would often have long talks about what all this meant. Once, she told me about how she used to have a secret way of slipping cookies silently out of the cookie jar and hiding under a dining room table to eat. This might have struck me as funny — so often our childhood stories charmed me — but I wanted to sob when she told me. I felt stricken by our — her, my, everybody's — desires. How easily they became desperate or grotesque or hateful, especially to the person who did all that desiring.

---

[1] *chazar* Pig. [Editor's note.]

Her desires must have been met in L.A., however, because she looked so 24 good. At the end of her first year there, she organized a student show, a big campy celebration that everyone dressed for. She brought a videotape of the show back to Boston for the rest of us to see. Now we fast-forward through the tape so we can see the intermission. Someone has filmed her — happy her — backstage exuberantly organizing things. Then we fast-forward again and there is Cyndy in a gorgeous, retro, off-the-shoulder dress. Her hair is long, just above her shoulders. She needs to flip it out of her eyes. She has long dangling earrings. She is glamorous by anyone's account and quite sexy. By this point, she's had reconstructive surgery. The new breast is lumpy and disappointing — not that anyone says this. It's just clear that when my uncle, the surgeon, said, "Sometimes they do such a good job you can't tell the difference," he wasn't 100 percent correct. Part of the problem is that Cyndy, like all the women in the family, has large breasts. They couldn't reconstruct her breast so it would be as big as the original one, so she had a smaller breast made, and she wore a partial prosthesis. The doctors had asked her if she wanted the other breast reduced — for balance's sake. But she decided no. After all, she didn't want to run the risk of not having feeling in either breast.

In the videotape, when Cyndy starts to sing, the audience is clearly 25 amazed. And they should be: her voice is stunning. She could have had an operatic career if she had wanted it. Months before her death, a singing instructor made it clear to Cyndy that she not only could, but she had to, have a singing career. Her voice was that beautiful.

Now when I listen to the tape, I watch Cyndy's mannerisms. Each time, 26 I am surprised by the fact that she seems a little nervous about performing. Cyndy nervous? Cyndy is never nervous, as she herself will admit. (Except about men. That's the one exception.) But she gets comfortable as she proceeds, as the audience's approval is clear. She sings, beautifully, the Carole King song "Way Over Yonder." *Way over yonder, that's where I'm bound.*

Even before she died, I knew the irony would always break my heart, 27 once she was gone.

In the summer after Cyndy's first two semesters in L.A., I was living in 28 Lincoln, Nebraska. I was teaching a summer class, and late at night, I'd get tearful calls from Cyndy. Mostly about men, for I was, in many things, Cyndy's confidante. Sometimes, now, I think that I am wrong about this. I *was* Cyndy's confidante, wasn't I? She *was* the person I was closest to, wasn't she? When we were young, I always thought that Cyndy and I belonged together, and David and Laura belonged together. Laura always had a special way with David. Laura and I were close (the twins, after all), and Cyndy and David (the youngest) were playmates. Still, I felt Cyndy and I were a pair. When they met Cyndy, people used to say, "Oh, so she's your twin?" And I'd shake my head no. "Your older sister?" No, I'd say again.

Cyndy loved being mistaken for my older sister. "I really am the smartest one in the family," she'd say, even when she was in her twenties. I'd have to disagree; it was a distinction I thought I deserved if by smart you meant (and Cyndy did) commonsensical.

Our closeness was somewhat competitive. We delighted in being competent — more competent than the one in the family who was spacy, the one who was overemotional. We just had things together, and we understood the world. The one fight I remember us having (I'm sure we had many when we were young, but I can't remember them) is about driving the car. She snapped at me for correcting her driving. She hated it when I played older sister. 29

When Cyndy first started making her tearful phone calls to me, I was proud. I took a secret pleasure in the fact that she confided in me, that she came to me first. I'd even felt a slight pleasure — mixed with my horror — when she called to tell me, and, at first, only me, that she'd been raped. It was during her first year at college. I was in my senior year at Yale. It was a date rape, I suppose, although that term doesn't fit exactly. The man was someone she met in a bar — a sailor, good God — and Cyndy got drunk and later, after some flirting, he didn't understand that no meant no. I honestly don't think he knew he raped her. I think for a while Cyndy was bewildered too. Her previous sexual encounters had not amounted to much, and, later in college, her experiences remained disappointing. 30

Given her history, Cyndy's tears on the phone made sense to me. I thought she was finally addressing the issue that had always so frightened her. She spoke, with uncharacteristic frustration, of the way her women friends were always talking about *their* relationships, and she didn't have any relationships and how upset it made her. With the encouragement of the family, Cyndy started talking to a therapist. I was all for this, I would tell Cyndy, as I sat late at night in my small rental in Nebraska. After all, I had been helped, enormously, by a psychiatrist. My parents agreed with my assessment, I think, although Cyndy spent less of her time on the phone with them talking about men and more time talking about her headaches, her terrible headaches, that stopped her from getting any work done. 31

So, it's clear where this goes, no? We hope it's not, we hope it's not — as with each test or checkup we have hoped — but it is. Cyndy has cancer in her brain. When they do the initial radiation on her brain, and later when they do an experimental treatment that *does* shrink the tumor, it becomes clear that all that crying had a physiological base. Her tumor shrunk, her headaches go away. She stops crying or talking about men. 32

But, of course, she does cry, though only once, when she learns about the brain tumor. When I find out, I am standing in my kitchen and kneading bread. I get the call, and then I phone MIT to tell a friend of Laura's not to let her go to lunch. I want to come get her and take her to the hospital. I feel like a rock when I do all this, like a cold rock. I throw the 33 dough in the trash and hear the *thump-swish* of it hitting the plastic bag. Then I go and get Laura, who screams — as in bad movies, screams — and I drive to the hospital. Laura, instantly feeling everything, spins out of control with grief. She's sharp with nurses who seem to be blocking her way to Cyndy. She won't allow what my father says when he says it. She just tells him, No, no, you're wrong. She turns to me and says, Why aren't you acting like anything? And I think, because I am so very competent.

In the fall, Cyndy comes and lives with me in my big apartment in   34 North Cambridge. This is so clearly better than staying with my parents in their suburban home. She is immensely disappointed about having to take time off from UCLA. But it is only time off, we reassure her. She will get back there. And she does. After a year with me, she goes back for a semester. But she is too sick and has to come back to live with me for good. She lives with me for two years. This is the part that I'm glad I didn't get to see when I was in my Wisconsin apartment, worrying about the possibility of my sister having a mastectomy. I think now, A mastectomy! A lousy mastectomy! Who cares? I remember once, not long after I'd moved to Cambridge and before Cyndy moved in with me, I was in bed with a temporary lover. He was an old college friend, a doctor, in town to do some work for the year. Cyndy and I had been talking, earlier that day, over the phone, about men. I was encouraging her to approach a young man she was interested in in L.A. She'd said, "But it's so complicated. Like at what point do I say, 'Hey, buddy. One of these isn't real.'" I knew she'd be gesturing, even though we were on the phone, to her chest, pointing to first one, then the other. ("I can always tell," she'd said, "when someone knows and they're trying to figure out which one it is.") That night, in bed, I'd said to my friend, "Well, if you loved someone, it wouldn't make a difference... say, before you were involved...if you found out they had a mastectomy, would it?"

He looked at me. "Yeah," he said. "I don't mean to be horrible, but of   35 course it would."

"But," I said, as if he'd change his mind because I needed him to, "I said   36 it wouldn't. That's what *I* said."

Cyndy and I had fun in the apartment where we lived. My boyfriend   37 Jim would come by in the evenings, and they would talk music or we'd go out for dinner. Nights when Jim was working, we'd get George, a musician friend from around the corner, to come over. Cyndy took classes at Boston University. She worked for the Boston Opera Theater. She got involved with a project involving musicians in Prague. Related to that, Vaclav Havel's press secretary and her son came to live with us for a while. And during all this, cancer would pop up in one place or another — her knees, the back of her tongue. Still, it always honestly seemed to me that we could make her better. Healthy denial, I suppose. Certainly, Cyndy had a lot of it. She was always willing to be cheered up, to imagine her future.

Some things stand out, but I can't (I won't) put them in order. Like: the 38
number of times I would be in bed, making love with Jim, and hear Cyndy
hacking away in the next room. That would be the cancer in her lungs.

Or the way she would call out to me each morning that Jim wasn't 39
there: "Derba, Derba, Derba," she'd say, in a high-pitched silly voice. And
I'd call back, "Der-ba Bird," because that was what she was, chirping out
the family nickname for me. Then I'd go crawl into her bed and rub her
back. There was cancer in the spine by then, and she could never get comfortable. Sometimes she'd wail at her pillows. She couldn't get them in the
right position.

Or the way, one night, when I was making dinner, she said, "Oh, God," 40
and I said, "What is it?" and she snapped, angry as could be, "You *know*
what it is!"

There was an odd stretch when I felt her oncologist was trying to con- 41
vince her that her symptoms were psychosomatic. Like when she couldn't
get enough energy to move, and we'd spend days inside, only making an
occasional trek to the back porch. Perhaps, he seemed to be suggesting, she
was only depressed?

The few times Cyndy did snap at me, I felt like I would dissolve. My 42
mother said, "Well, I guess you're getting a sense, before your time, of what
it's like to have an adolescent." In truth, my mother got the brunt of it.
When Cyndy was in the most pain, she would leave the apartment for a
stay with my parents. When she was well enough, she would come back to
stay with me. Wherever she was, though — my house, my parents' house —
we were all there, all the time.

And even when she was doing relatively well, there were lots of visits 43
back and forth. One day, in the beginning of her stay with me, Cyndy and
I were driving out to our parents' house for dinner. We were talking about
death, and Cyndy said, "Oh, well, you know, sometimes I think about
death. And I try to force myself to imagine what it would be like but then
I'm like...whoa...you know, I just can't do it."

"Yes," I said, for I knew exactly what she meant. "I'm like that too." 44

Now I'm even more "like that." For if a parent's job is to protect his or 45
her child, a sister's is to identify with her sibling. Which means, of course,
that the whole family gets, in the case of a terminal illness, to fail in what
they most want to do for one another. So I push my imagination to death,
make myself think "no consciousness." I have, regretfully, no belief in
heaven, an afterlife, reincarnation. I believe in nothingness. I try not to let
myself pull back, try not to say, "Whoa, that's too much." But my brain —
its gift to me — is that it won't let me do what I want.

I think, in this regard, of the time ten-year-old Cyndy came home from 46
school in a snit. She'd learned about black holes in science class. She'd
stomped up to her room and flopped on her bed. As she went, she ordered
the family to never talk to her about black holes. I thought she was joking.
So, I opened the door to her bedroom, stuck my head in — cartoon-fashion,

the accordion player poking his head through the stage curtain to get a peek at the crowd — and I said rapidly, "Black hole, black hole, black hole." Cyndy, already lying on her bed, threw herself against the mattress so that she bounced on it like a just-captured fish hitting land. She started to sob. "I'm sorry," I said. "I was kidding. I thought *you* were kidding." But why should she have been? What's more terrible than everything going out?

Once, during one of her final stays in the hospital, Cyndy said to my mother, "I'm going to be good now," as if that would make her healthy, as if a planet could blame itself for being in the wrong part of the universe. 47

"Oh, honey," my mother had said. "You *are* good. You are so *good*." 48

One trip out to my parents that stands in my mind: Cyndy had the shingles, an enormously painful viral infection that runs along the nerve path on one side of the body. Just getting her down the staircase into my car was horrible. Cyndy was sobbing and sobbing, and ordinarily she didn't cry. I put her in the passenger's seat and cursed myself for having the kind of life that made me buy such an inexpensive and uncomfortable car. The requirement of bending was too much, and Cyndy wept and wept. I drove as fast as I could and neither of us talked. I thought, "I'll just get her home and it will be all right." My father, the doctor, would know what to do. My mother would be, as she could be, the most comforting person in the world. When we got there, I said, "It's okay, it's going to be okay," as Cyndy walked with tiny paces from the car to the front steps. My parents were at the front door and it was night. My mother brought a kitchen chair to the front hall so as soon as Cyndy got up the stairs, she could sit down. I stood behind her and my parents stood at the top of the six stairs that led to our front door: my mother (blue turtleneck and jeans), my father (stooped). Both of them had their hands out and were reaching for Cyndy but they couldn't get her up the stairs. She had to do that herself. And I thought, looking at them in the light, and Cyndy still forcing herself up through the night — *Oh, my God. All this love, all this love can't do a thing.* 49

But that wasn't completely true. The love did do something. It just didn't save her. 50

Laura, my twin sister, gave Cyndy foot rubs and Cyndy loved them. Laura would give foot rubs, literally for hours. I gave back rubs but I never liked giving them, would wait for Cyndy to say I could stop. When Cyndy told Laura she could stop if she wanted to, Laura would ask for permission to keep going — as if Cyndy were doing her a favor by putting her feet in the vicinity of Laura's hands. One day, Cyndy was lying on her bed in our apartment and Laura was on a chair at the end of the bed and she was rubbing Cyndy's feet. I was "spooning" Cyndy and occasionally rubbing up and down her spine where the cancer was. We were talking about masturbation. "I can't believe you guys," Laura was saying, telling us again about how amazing it was that, of the three of us, she had discovered masturbation first. We were giggling. This conversation wasn't unfamiliar. We'd had it before, but we could always find something new to tell each other. 51

"What was that bathtub thing you were talking about?" Cyndy said.   52

Years earlier, I'd instructed both of my sisters about the virtues of mas-   53
turbating in the bathtub. Something I'd learned from my freshman year
roommate at college. "Got to try it," I said now.

"Exactly how do you do it again?" asked Cyndy.   54

"Lie in the tub. Scoot your butt under the waterspout and put your legs   55
up on the wall and let the water run into you. Guaranteed orgasm."

"De-bra," Cyndy said, hitting me, as if I'd gone too far in this being-   56
open-with-sisters conversation.

"Sor-ry," I said. "Still, you've got to try it, but wait till this thing gets bet-   57
ter." I pointed at her head. There was a new problem these days, something
that caused Cyndy to get, on occasions, dizzy. She had some new medicine, so I talked as if the problem would be solved in a matter of weeks.
(Aside from the dizziness, Cyndy had occasional aphasia. One night when
I was on the phone, Cyndy screamed from her bedroom. I ran in. She'd
forgotten a word, couldn't produce it and felt her head go weirdly blank.
The word, she realized, five minutes later, was *cancer*.)

We decided to leave the topic of sex behind for something else. But not   58
before I insisted, once again, that Cyndy try this bathtub thing. I was rubbing her back and Laura was still rubbing her feet, and I was thinking, as I
stroked her skin, Yes, an orgasm. Let this body give her some pleasure.

You *do* get inappropriately intimate with a body when the body is ill.   59
Sometimes there's something nice about it. Cyndy used to sit on the toilet
in our bathroom and I'd take a soapy washcloth and wash her bald head.
I'd say, "Stamp out dry scalpy skin." This struck us, for some reason, as terribly funny. We'd soak our feet in the bathtub and talk about our favorite
Gogol stories. We'd walk arm in arm. Say: "This is what we'll be like when
we are old ladies."

When Cyndy's symptoms were at their worst, my own body struck me,   60
especially my legs, which stretched — it seemed amazing — from my torso
to the ground. The miracle of walking. I still feel it. The air behind my legs
is creepily light as I move. Who would have ever suspected that you can
feel grief behind your kneecaps?

One very bad night: Cyndy was upset about everything, but especially   61
men, relationships, never having had a boyfriend. According to her, I didn't,
couldn't understand because I had had a boyfriend. This was a point of
connection between Cyndy and a few of her intimates, an absence they
could discuss and from which I was excluded. It didn't matter that I felt, for
the sadness of my own relationships, included. I had had sex. Many times
even — enough to have had a sexually transmitted disease which I (paranoid, irrational) thought I could pass on to Cyndy through ordinary contact. It didn't matter that I was cured of the problem. Her immune system
was down. Anything I did might hurt her. My own desires might kill her.

This one night, Cyndy was crying, so I went into her room to put my   62
arm around her, and she said, "Don't. Don't you touch me." Fierce, again.

Vicious. I retreated to my bedroom. Cried softly, but still felt I had to do something. I stepped back to her bedroom, and she started to scream, waving me away, but saying, "It's just that I realize that nobody but my family or a doctor has touched me in the past five years."

It'll change, it'll change, it'll change. That was always my mantra for these   63
relationship conversations. But it didn't. She died before it could change.

After that terrible night when Cyndy had the shingles and had to struggle   64
out of our apartment to the car, she spent six weeks at my parents' house. Those were miserable times. She couldn't move from her bed. We'd all climb onto the double bed, a ship in the ocean of her room, and play word games or watch TV or be quiet because a lot of the time she couldn't stand for anything to be going on. As she started to feel a bit better, she worked on the course that she was going to teach in January of 1992. It was going to be called "Opera — What's All the Screaming About?" and it was going to be for high school girls, for kids who, presumably, could care less about opera. We rented opera videos and watched them with her. Then she decided she was ready to come back to our apartment to work on her course syllabus. I cleaned the kitchen while she worked. At one point, she started to faint, but she grabbed the doorjamb, and I came in and caught her, wrapped my arms around her waist — big now, she was bloated with steroids — and set her down on the ground. She was okay, so she started to work at her computer, and I made us some cocoa. She handed me her syllabus to proofread. She sipped while I read it, and she said, in a sort of campy voice, "Mmmm... this is love-ly." I laughed, still reading. She made a funny gurgling noise. I thought it was a joke but when I looked up from the syllabus, Cyndy was slipping out of her chair. I ran the few feet to her. She was crumpled on the ground. I rolled her onto her back and saw blood. There was water on the floor — her urine. "Are you okay? Are you okay?" I screamed. Her wig had rolled off her head and she looked like a gigantic toppled mannequin. She was gasping, breathing oddly. A seizure, I knew. I am, after all, a doctor's daughter. When the convulsive breathing stopped, she said, "What happened? What just happened?" She was as purely frightened as I'd ever seen her.

"Close your eyes," I said. "You just fainted. Close your eyes." I didn't   65
want her to see her own blood. I thought that would scare her. I ran to the bathroom to get a towel and wipe her up. I tried to see where the blood was coming from.

"It's okay, you bit your tongue."   66

I felt — I have to say this, only because it's so horrible — a slight pleasure.   67
It was the old thing: I would be competent, take care of this trouble. I was good in an emergency. But there was also part of me — small, I promise myself now, very small — that thought, with some relief, "It's over."

The ambulance came. We rode over to the hospital. My parents were   68
there before us. When they rolled Cyndy away, I cried to my mother, "Oh, Mommy. I thought she was dying. I thought she was dying."

Inside, Cyndy was saying the same to my father, "I thought I was dying. 69
I thought I was going to die."

And about two weeks later she did. But not before her body put her 70
through enormous suffering. Not before she had a little more fun with the
family. So, last things. The last thing she ever produced was a picture from
a coloring book. She had asked for the book and some crayons, and we all
earnestly filled in Mickey Mouse's ears and then signed our names and
ages. Debra, 29. Laura, 29. David, 24. Mommy, 53. Daddy, 55. Cyndy
signed hers, "The Queen." (A joke from our two years together. When she
was queen, Boston drivers were not going to be allowed to be obnoxious.)
Under "age," Cyndy wrote, "None of your damn business." Last meal: gray
fish from the kosher kitchen, but she didn't eat it. Last thing she *did* eat:
Jell-O. I know, I spooned it into her mouth. Last thing I said to her: I told
her that the man she was interested in was in love with her, that I knew
because of what he'd said when I called to tell him she was in the hospital.
(I was making this up, but who cares?) Last thing Cyndy ever said to me:
"Oh, good. Well, tell him we'll get together when I get out of here." Last
thing she ever said: I didn't hear this because I wasn't in the room, but she
woke up, delusional and panicked and worried because she was going on a
long trip and she hadn't packed her suitcase.

As my fiction writer friends always say, You can't make this stuff up. No 71
one would believe you if you tried.

And I have to agree: real life is just too heavy-handed. 72

Very last thing: her body still desiring life, she takes every third breath, 73
though her fingers are dusky, though her kidneys have already shut down.
We give the funeral director the pretty purple dress she bought for special
occasions. We put her in the ground.

Our desires, I sometimes think now, as I'm walking down the street. 74

Today, outside a bakery, I stop myself and say, "Yes, Debra? What about 75
them?" And I realize I don't know. "What? What?" I stand for a while feeling disgusted with the world — those horrible leering men in the green-
grocers; that stupid sailor in the bar; foolish me, making love with my sister
dying in the next room. *Our desires, our desires, our desires.* I know what the
refrain is; I just don't know what to do about it. It's a reproach for me, an
always unfulfilled wish for my family, and a sad song — it's a dirge — for
Cyndy. Still, since I am here, stuck among the living, I have to remind
myself that the song owes nothing to the beautiful ones that Cyndy sang.
So I go into the bakery and get a shortbread cookie dipped in chocolate. It
is so delicious I start to cry.

Analyzing This Selection

1. Paragraphs 1 to 16 mix various times during Cyndy's illness and after her
   death. How does this mix emphasize the author's point about the events?

2. What details convey Cyndy's personality to the reader? What qualities do Cyndy and Debra believe they share? What disturbances occur in their sisterly bond?

3. How does the family respond to the futility of their efforts? Despite Cyndy's death, what do their efforts achieve?

4. **THE WRITER'S METHOD**   The author speaks directly to the reader in paragraphs 32, 38, 67, and 71. Do these comments enhance or undermine her tone toward the reader in the rest of the essay?

5. The essay's "last thing" is Debra weeping over a cookie. What issues and events are reflected in her reaction? How has the essay as a whole developed significance in that incident?

Analyzing Connections

6. Spark and Olsen (see "I Stand Here Ironing," p. 92) each write about helplessness over family distresses. In what ways does Cyndy's family differ from Emily's? In your opinion, how would Emily fit into Cyndy's family?

Analyzing by Writing

7. Families are where we first learn not only how to love but also how to face loss and death. Even much less tragic situations than Cyndy's death reveal attitudes and values of various family members. Analyze a loss that you and at least one other person in your family faced. Were differences evident between generations? between siblings? Were the differences divisive or unifying?

Barbara Dafoe Whitehead

WOMEN AND THE FUTURE
OF FATHERHOOD

BARBARA DAFOE WHITEHEAD (b. 1944), a social historian, earned her
B.A. at the University of Wisconsin and a Ph.D. in American social history from the University of Chicago. Her essays on parenting and family
life have appeared in magazines such as the *Atlantic Monthly, Common-
weal,* and the *Wilson Quarterly,* where "Women and the Future of
Fatherhood" first appeared. Her book *Goodbye to Girlhood: What's Troubling Girls and What We Can Do About It* (1999) examines the problem
of teen pregnancy.

Much of our contemporary debate over fatherhood is governed by the 1
assumption that men can solve the fatherhood problem on their own.
Organizers of the Million Man March asked women to stay home, and the
leaders of Promise Keepers and other grass-roots fatherhood movements
whose members gather with considerably less fanfare simply do not admit
women.

There is a cultural rationale for the exclusion of women. The father- 2
hood movement sees the task of reinstating responsible fatherhood as an
effort to alter today's norms of masculinity and correctly believes that such
an effort cannot succeed unless it is voluntarily undertaken and supported
by men. There is also a political rationale in defining fatherlessness as a
men's issue. In the debate about marriage and parenthood, which women
have dominated for at least thirty years, the fatherhood movement gives
men a powerful collective voice and presence.

Yet however effective the grass-roots movement is at stirring men's con- 3
sciences and raising their consciousness, the fatherhood problem will not
be solved by men alone. To be sure, by signaling their commitment to
accepting responsibility for the rearing of their children, men have taken
the essential first step. But what has not yet been acknowledged is that the
success of any effort to renew fatherhood as a social fact and a cultural
norm also hinges on the attitudes and behavior of women. Men can't be
fathers unless the mothers of their children allow it.

Merely to say this is to point to how thoroughly marital disruption has 4
weakened the bond between fathers and children. More than half of all

American children are likely to spend at least part of their lives in one-parent homes. Since the vast majority of children in disrupted families live with their mothers, fathers do not share a home or a daily life with their children. It is much more difficult for men to make the kinds of small, routine, instrumental investments in their children that help forge a good relationship. It is hard to fix a flat bike tire or run a bath when you live in another neighborhood or another town. Many a father's instrumental contribution is reduced to the postal or electronic transmission of money, or, all too commonly, to nothing at all. Without regular contact with their children, men often make reduced emotional contributions as well. Fathers must struggle to sustain close emotional ties across time and space, to "be there" emotionally without being there physically. Some may pick up the phone, send a birthday card, or buy a present, but for many fathers, physical absence also becomes emotional absence.

Without marriage, men also lose access to the social and emotional 5 intelligence of women in building relationships. Wives teach men how to care for young children, and they also encourage children to love their fathers. Mothers who do not live with the father of their children are not as likely as married mothers to represent him in positive ways to the children; nor are the relatives who are most likely to have greatest contact with the children — the mother's parents, brothers, and sisters — likely to have a high opinion of the children's father. Many men are able to overcome such obstacles, but only with difficulty. In general, men need marriage in order to be good fathers.

If the future of fatherhood depends on marriage, however, its future is 6 uncertain. Marriage depends on women as well as men, and women are less committed to marriage than ever before in the nation's history. In the past, women were economically dependent on marriage and assumed a disproportionately heavy responsibility for maintaining the bond, even if the underlying relationship was seriously or irretrievably damaged. In the last third of the twentieth century, however, as women have gained more opportunities for paid work and the availability of child care has increased, they have become less dependent on marriage as an economic arrangement. Though it is not easy, it is possible for women to raise children on their own. This has made divorce far more attractive as a remedy for an unsatisfying marriage, and a growing number of women have availed themselves of the option.

Today, marriage and motherhood are coming apart. Remarriage and 7 marriage rates are declining even as the rates of divorce remain stuck at historic highs and childbearing outside marriage becomes more common. Many women see single motherhood as a choice and a right to be exercised if a suitable husband does not come along in time.

The vision of the "first stage" feminism of the 1960s and '70s, which held 8 out the model of the career woman unfettered by husband or children, has been accepted by women only in part. Women want to be fettered by children, even to the point of going through grueling infertility treatments or artificial insemination to achieve motherhood. But they are increasingly ambivalent about the ties that bind them to a husband and about the necessity of marriage as a condition of parenthood. In 1994, a National Opinion Research survey asked a group of Americans, "Do you agree or disagree: One parent can bring up a child as well as two parents together." Women split 50/50 on the question; men disagreed by more than two to one.

And indeed, women enjoy certain advantages over men in a society   9
marked by high and sustained levels of family breakup. Women do not need marriage to maintain a close bond to their children, and thus to experience the larger sense of social and moral purpose that comes with raising children. As the bearers and nurturers of children and (increasingly) as the sole breadwinners for families, women continue to be engaged in personally rewarding and socially valuable pursuits. They are able to demonstrate their feminine virtues outside marriage.

Men, by contrast, have no positive identity as fathers outside marriage.   10
Indeed, the emblematic absent father today is the infamous "deadbeat dad." In part, this is the result of efforts to stigmatize irresponsible fathers who fail to pay alimony and child support. But this image also reflects the fact that men are heavily dependent on the marriage partnership to fulfill their role as fathers. Even those who keep up their child support payments are deprived of the social importance and sense of larger purpose that comes from providing for children and raising a family. And it is the rare father who can develop the qualities needed to meet the new cultural ideal of the involved and "nurturing" father without the help of a spouse.

These differences are reflected in a growing virtue gap. American popu-   11
lar culture today routinely recognizes and praises the achievements of single motherhood, while the widespread failure of men as fathers has resulted in a growing sense of cynicism and despair about men's capacity for virtuous conduct in family life. The enormously popular movie *Waiting to Exhale* captures the essence of this virtue gap with its portrait of steadfast mothers and deadbeat fathers, morally sleazy men and morally unassailable women. And women feel free to vent their anger and frustration with men in ways that would seem outrageous to women if the shoe were on the other foot. In *Operating Instructions* (1993), her memoir of single motherhood, Ann LaMott mordantly observes, "On bad days, I think straight white men are so poorly wired, so emotionally unenlightened and unconscious that you must approach each one as if he were some weird cross between a white supremacist and an incredibly depressing T. S. Eliot poem."

Women's weakening attachment to marriage should not be taken as a   12
lack of interest in marriage or in a husband-wife partnership in child rearing. Rather, it is a sign of women's more exacting emotional standards for husbands and their growing insistence that men play a bigger part in caring

for children and the household. Given their double responsibilities as breadwinners and mothers, many working wives find men's need for ego reinforcement and other forms of emotional and physical upkeep irksome and their failure to share housework and child care absolutely infuriating. (Surveys show that husbands perform only one-third of all household tasks even if their wives are working full-time.) Why should men be treated like babies? women complain. If men fail to meet their standards, many women are willing to do without them. Poet and polemicist Katha Pollitt captures the prevailing sentiment: "If single women can have sex, their own homes, the respect of friends, and interesting work, they don't need to tell themselves that any marriage is better than none. Why not have a child on one's own? Children are a joy. Many men are not."

For all these reasons, it is important to see the fatherhood problem as   13
part of the larger cultural problem of the decline of marriage as a lasting relationship between men and women. The traditional bargain between men and women has broken down, and a new bargain has not yet been struck. It is impossible to predict what that bargain will look like — or whether there will even be one. However, it is possible to speculate about the talking points that might bring women to the bargaining table. First, a crucial proviso: There must be recognition of the changed social and eco-nomic status of women. Rightly or wrongly, many women fear that the fatherhood movement represents an effort to reinstate the status quo ante, to repeal the gains and achievements women have made over the past thirty years and return to the "separate spheres" domestic ideology that put men in the workplace and women in the home. Any effort to rethink marriage must accept the fact that women will continue to work outside the home.

Therefore, a new bargain must be struck over the division of paid work   14
and family work. This does not necessarily mean a 50/50 split in the work load every single day, but it does mean that men must make a more deter-mined and conscientious effort to do more than one-third of the household chores. How each couple arrives at a sense of what is fair will vary, of course, but the goal is to establish some mutual understanding and com-mitment to an equitable division of tasks.

Another talking point may focus on the differences in the expectations   15
men and women have for marriage and intimacy. Americans have a "best friends" ideal for marriage that includes some desires that might in fact be more easily met by a best friend — someone who doesn't come with all the complicated entanglements of sharing a bed, a bank account, and a bath-room. Nonetheless, high expectations for emotional intimacy in marriage often are confounded by the very different understandings men and women have of intimacy. Much more than men, women seek intimacy and affec-tion through talking and emotional disclosure. Men often prefer sex to talk-ing, and physical disrobing to emotional disclosing. They tend to be less than fully committed to (their own) sexual fidelity, while women view

fidelity as a crucial sign of commitment. These are differences that the sexes need to engage with mutual recognition and tolerance.

In renegotiating the marital bargain, it may also be useful to acknowl-   16
edge the biosocial differences between mothers and fathers rather than to assume an androgynous model for the parental partnership. There can be a high degree of flexibility in parental roles, but men and women are not interchangeable "parental units," particularly in their children's early years. Rather than struggle to establish identical tracks in career and family lives, it may be more realistic to consider how children's needs and well-being might require patterns of paid work and child rearing that are differ-ent for mothers and fathers but are nevertheless equitable over the course of a lifetime.

Finally, it may be important to think and talk about marriage in another   17
kind of language than the one that suffuses our current discourse on rela-tionships. The secular language of "intimate relationships" is the language of politics and psychotherapy, and it focuses on individual rights and indi-vidual needs. It can be heard most clearly in the personal-ad columns, a kind of masked ball where optimists go in search of partners who respect their rights and meet their emotional needs. These are not unimportant in the achievement of the contemporary ideal of marriage, which emphasizes egalitarianism and emotional fulfillment. But this notion of marriage as a union of two sovereign selves may be inadequate to define a relationship that carries with it the obligations, duties, and sacrifices of parenthood. There has always been tension between marriage as an intimate relation-ship between a man and a woman and marriage as an institutional arrange-ment for raising children, and though the language of individual rights plays a part in defining the former, it cannot fully describe the latter. The parental partnership requires some language that acknowledges differences, mutuality, complementarity, and, more than anything else, altruism.

There is a potentially powerful incentive for women to respond to an   18
effort to renegotiate the marriage bargain, and that has to do with their children. Women can be good mothers without being married. But espe-cially with weakened communities that provide little support, children need levels of parental investment that cannot be supplied solely by a good mother, even if she has the best resources at her disposal. These needs are more likely to be met if the child has a father as well as a mother under the same roof. Simply put, even the best mothers cannot be good fathers.

Analyzing This Selection

1. **THE WRITER'S METHOD** According to Whitehead, why were women more committed to marriage in the past than they are today? Does she rec-ommend that families return to that situation?

2. What is the "growing virtue gap" that Whitehead observes in contemporary culture?

3. In what ways have women raised the standards for husbands? Do you think there has been a comparable change in men's standards for wives?

Analyzing Connections

4. Do men need women *or* marriage? Do Whitehead's observations strengthen or weaken Jonathan Rauch's views about gay marriage (see "For Better or Worse?" p. 173)?

Analyzing by Writing

5. Whitehead cites some writers who question whether men are even desirable in a family. Do you think fathers provide advantages that financially self-reliant, emotionally responsive women do not? Explain your views on this issue.

Amitai Etzioni

THE VALUE OF FAMILIES[1]

AMITAI ETZIONI (b. 1929) is a noted social policy advisor and a leader of the Communitarian movement to improve society. He emigrated from Germany and fought in the Israeli army before graduating from Hebrew University in Jerusalem. He received a Ph.D. in sociology from the University of California at Berkeley. Formerly a professor at Columbia University, Etzioni currently teaches at George Washington University. His books include *The Spirit of Community: The Reinvention of American Society* (1993), from which the following selection is excerpted. His most recent book is *The Limits of Privacy* (1999).

Consider for a moment parenting as an industry. As farming declined, most fathers left to work away from home. Over the past twenty years millions of American mothers have sharply curtailed their work in the "parenting industry" by moving to work outside the home. By 1991 two-thirds (66.7 percent) of all mothers with children under eighteen were in the labor force and more than half (55.4 percent) of women with children under the age of three. At the same time a much smaller number of child care personnel moved into the parenting industry.[2]

If this were any other business, say, shoemaking, and more than half of the labor force had been lost and replaced with fewer, less-qualified hands and still we asked the shoemakers to produce the same number of shoes of the same quality (with basically no changes in technology), we would be considered crazy. But this is what happened to parenting. As first men and then women left to work outside the home, they were replaced by some child care services, a relatively small increase in baby-sitters and nannies, and some additional service by grandparents — leaving parenting woefully shorthanded. The millions of latchkey children, who are left alone for long stretches of time, are but the most visible result of the parenting deficit.

Is this the "fault" of the women's movement, feminism, or mothers per se? Obviously not. All women did was demand for themselves what men

---

[1]Editor's title.

[2]Two-thirds of mothers with children under eighteen are in the labor force: *Current Population Survey.* Bureau of Labor Statistics, unpublished tabulations, 1991. [This and all subsequent notes are Etzioni's.]

had long possessed, working outside the home not only for their own personal satisfaction, but because of what they often perceived as the economic necessity. Whatever the cause, the result is an empty nest. Only it isn't the small fry who grew up and took off: it is the parents who flew the coop. Those who did not leave altogether increased their investment of time, energy, involvement, and commitment outside the home.

Although parenting is the responsibility of both parents — and may well 4
be discharged most effectively in two-parent families immersed in a community context of kin and neighbors — *most important is the scope of commitment.* Single parents may do better than two-career absentee parents. Children require attention, as Robert Beliah and the other authors of *The Good Society* declared. Kids also require a commitment of time, energy, and, above all, of self.

The prevalent situation is well captured by a public service commercial 5
in which a mother calls her child and reassures him that she has left money for him next to the phone. "Honey, have some dinner," she mutters as the child takes the twenty-dollar bill she left behind, rolls it up, and snorts cocaine. One might add that the father didn't even call.

The fact is that parenting cannot be carried out over the phone, however 6
well meaning and loving the calls may be. It requires physical presence. The notion of "quality time" (not to mention "quality phone calls") is a lame excuse for parental absence; it presupposes that bonding and education can take place in brief time bursts, on the run. *Quality time occurs within quantity time.* As you spend time with your children — fishing, gardening, camping, or "just" eating a meal — there are unpredictable moments when an opening occurs and education takes hold. As family expert Barbara Dafoe Whitehead puts it: "Maybe there is indeed such a thing as a one-minute manager, but there is no such thing as a one-minute parent."[3] . . .

Is the answer to the parenting deficit building more child care centers? 7
After all, other societies have delegated the upbringing of their children, from black nannies in the antebellum South to Greek slaves in ancient Rome. True enough. But in these historical situations the person who attended to the children was an adjunct to the parents rather than a replacement for them and an accessory reserved mostly for upper-class families with leisure. A caregiver remained with the family throughout the children's formative years and often beyond; she was, to varying degrees, integrated into the family. The caregiver, in turn, reflected, at least in part, the family's values and educational posture. Some children may have been isolated from their parents, but as a rule there was a warm, committed figure dedicated to them, one who bonded and stayed with them.

---

[3]Barbara Dafoe Whitehead says there's no such thing as a one-minute parent: Barbara Whitehead, "The New Politics in Action — Fortifying the Family," presentation at the conference "Left and Right: The Emergence of a New Politics in the 1990s?" sponsored by the Heritage Foundation and the Progressive Foundation, October 30, 1991, Washington, D.C. (see transcript, 25).

Today most child care centers are woefully understaffed with poorly paid   8
and underqualified personnel. Child care workers are in the lowest tenth of
all wage earners (with an average salary of $5.35 per hour in 1988), well
below janitors.[4] They frequently receive no health insurance or other benefits, which makes child care an even less attractive job. As Edward Zigler,
a professor of child development at Yale, put it: "We pay these people less
than we do zoo keepers — and then we expect them to do wonders."[5] The
personnel come and go, at a rate of 41 percent per year at an average day
care center.

Bonding between children and caregivers under these circumstances is   9
very difficult to achieve. Moreover, children suffer a loss every time their
surrogate parents leave. It would be far from inaccurate to call the worst of
these facilities "kennels for kids." Sure, there are exceptions. There are a few
fine, high-quality child care centers, but they are as rare and almost as expensive as the nannies that some truly affluent households can command.
These exceptions should not distract us from the basically dismal picture:
substandard care and all-too-frequent warehousing of children, with overworked parents trying frantically to make up the deficit in their free time.

Government or social supervision of the numerous small institutions and   10
home facilities in which child care takes place to ensure proper sanitation
and care, even to screen out child abusers, is difficult and is often completely neglected or only nominally carried out. We should not be surprised to encounter abuses such as the case of the child care home in
which fifty-four children were left in the care of a sixteen-year-old and were
found strapped into child car seats for the entire day.[6]

Certainly many low-income couples and single parents have little or no   11
choice except to use the minimum that such centers provide. All we can
offer here is to urge that before parents put their children in such institutions, they should check them out as extensively as possible (including surprise visits in the middle of the day). Moreover, we should all support these
parents' quest for additional support from corporations and government if
they cannot themselves spend more on child care.

Particularly effective are cooperative arrangements that require each par-   12
ent to contribute some time — four hours a week? — to serve at his or her
child's center. Not only do such arrangements reduce the center's costs,
they also allow parents to see firsthand what actually goes on, ensuring
some measure of *built-in accountability*. It provides for continuity — while
staff come and go, parents stay. (Even if they divorce, they may still participate in their child care center.) And as parents get to know other parents

[4]Child care workers in the lowest tenth percentile for income: Richard T. Gill, Nathan
Glazer, Stephen A. Thernstrom, *Our Changing Population* (Englewood Cliffs, N.J.:
Prentice-Hall, 1992), 278. Child care workers' average salary: *Who Cares? Child Care and
the Quality of Care in America* (Oakland, CA: Child Care Employee Project, 1989), 49.
[5]Zigler says child care workers are treated like zoo keepers: Kenneth Labich, "Can Your
Career Hurt Your Kids?" *Fortune*, May 20, 1991, 49.
[6]Children strapped into car seats all day: ibid., 49.

of children in the same stage of development, they form social bonds, which can be drawn upon to work together to make these centers more responsive to children's needs.

Above all, age matters. Infants under two years old are particularly vul- 13
nerable to separation anxiety. Several bodies of data strongly indicate that infants who are institutionalized at a young age will not mature into well-adjusted adults.[7] As Edward Zigler puts it: "We are cannibalizing children. Children are dying in the system, never mind achieving optimum development."[8] A study of third-graders by two University of Texas researchers compared children who returned home after school to their mothers with children who remained in day care centers:

> children who stayed at the day care centers after school were having problems. They received more negative peer nominations, and their negative nominations outweighed their positive nominations. In addition, the day care third-graders made lower academic grades on their report card and scored lower on standardized tests. There was some evidence of poor conduct grades.[9]

Unless the parents are absent or abusive, infants are better off at home. 14
Older children, between two and four, may be able to handle some measure of institutionalization in child care centers, but their personalities often seem too unformed to be able to cope well with a nine-to-five separation from a parent.

---

[7]Several bodies of data showing that institutionalized children become maladjusted adults: N. Baydar and Jeanne Brooks-Gunn, "Effects of Maternal Employment and Child Care Arrangements on Preschoolers' Cognitive and Behavioral Outcomes: Evidence from the Children of the National Longitudinal Survey of Youth," *Developmental Psychology* 27 (November 1991): 932–46; J. Belsky and Michael J. Rovine, "Nonmaternal Care in the First Year of Life and the Security of Infant-Parent Attachment," *Child Development* 59 (February 1988): 157–67; T. B. Brazelton, "Issues for Working Parents," *American Journal of Orthopsychiatry* 56 (1986): 14–25; J. Belsky and D. Eggebeen, "Early and Extensive Maternal Employment in Young Children's Socioemotional Development: Children of the National Longitudinal Survey of Youth," *Journal of Marriage and Family* 53 (November 1991): 1083–1110; B. E. Vaughn, K. E. Deane, and E. Waters, "The Impact of Out-of-Home Care on Child-Mother Attachment Quality: Another Look at Some Enduring Questions," 1–2, in I. Bretherton and E. Water, eds., *Growing Points of Attachment Theory and Research. Monographs for the Society for Research in Child Development*, 50 (1985): 1–2, serial no. 209.

Some studies have found that the effects of child care are not different from parental care. For example, see K. A. Clarke-Stewart and G. G. Fein, "Early Childhood Programs," 917–99, in P. H. Mussen, ed., *Handbook of Child Psychology*, Vol. 2 (New York: Wiley, 1983). And a few studies show that child care rather than parental care is more effective for the intellectual development of poor children. For example, see Jay Belsky, "Two Waves of Day Care Research: Development Effects and Conditions of Quality," 1–34, in R. C. Ainslie, ed., *The Child and the Day Care Setting: Qualitative Variations and Development* (New York: Praeger, 1984).

[8]Zigler says we are cannibalizing children: Kenneth Labich, "Can Your Career Hurt Your Kids?" *Fortune*, May 20, 1991, 38.

[9]University of Texas study: Deborah Lowe Vandell and Mary Anne Corasaniti, "The Relationship Between Third-Graders' After-School Care and Social, Academic, and Emotional Functioning," *Child Development* 59 (August 1988): 874.

As a person who grew up in Israel, I am sometimes asked whether it is   15
true that kibbutzim succeed in bringing up toddlers in child care centers. I
need to note first that unlike the personnel in most American child care
centers, the people who care for children in kibbutzim are some of the
most dedicated members of the work force because these communities
consider child care to be a very high priority. As a result, child care positions are highly sought after and there is little turnover, which allows for
essential bonding to take place. In addition, both parents are intimately
involved in bringing up their children, and they frequently visit the child
care centers, which are placed very close to where they live and work. Even
so, Israeli kibbutzim are rapidly dismantling their collective child care centers and returning children to live with their families — because both the
families and the community established that even a limited disassociation
of children from their parents at a tender age is unacceptable.

There is no sense looking back and beating our breasts over how we got   16
ourselves into the present situation. But we must acknowledge that as a
matter of social policy (as distinct from some individual situations) we have
made a mistake in assuming that strangers can be entrusted with the effective personality formation of infants and toddlers. Over the last twenty-five
years we have seen the future, and it is not a wholesome one. With poor
and ineffective community child care, and with ever more harried parents,
it will not suffice to tell their graduates to "just say no" and expect them to
resist all temptations, to forgo illegal drugs and alcohol, and to postpone
sexual activity. If we fervently wish them to grow up in a civilized society,
and if we seek to live in one, let's face facts: it will not happen unless we
dedicate more of ourselves to our children and their care and education....

Nobody likes to admit it, but between 1960 and 1990 American society   17
allowed children to be devalued, while the golden call of "making it" was
put on a high pedestal. Recently, college freshmen listed "being well off
financially" as more important than "raising a family." (In 1990 the figures
were 74 percent versus 70 percent, respectively, and in 1991 they were 74
percent versus 68 percent.)[10]...

Some blame this development on the women's rights movement, others   18
on the elevation of materialism and greed to new historical heights. These
and other factors may have all combined to devalue children. However,
women are obviously entitled to all the same rights men are, including the
pursuit of greed.

But few people who advocated equal rights for women favored a society   19
in which sexual equality would mean a society in which all adults would
act like men, who in the past were relatively inattentive to children. The
new gender-equalized world was supposed to be a combination of all that
was sound and ennobling in the traditional roles of women and men.
Women were to be free to work any place they wanted, and men would be

---

[10]Poll on college freshmen's views on being well off, raising a family: American Enterprise
Institute, 1990.

free to show emotion, care, and domestic commitment. For children this was not supposed to mean, as it too often has, that they would be bereft of dedicated parenting. Now that we have seen the result of decades of widespread neglect of children, the time has come for both parents to revalue children and for the community to support and recognize their efforts....

We return then to the value we as a community put on having and 20 bringing up children. In a society that places more value on Armani suits, winter skiing, and summer houses than on education, parents are under pressure to earn more, whatever their income. They feel that it is important to work overtime and to dedicate themselves to enhancing their incomes and advancing their careers. We must recognize now, after two decades of celebrating greed and in the face of a generation of neglected children, the importance of educating one's children.

Analyzing This Selection

1. **THE WRITER'S METHOD**   The essay begins with a comparison between parenting and another "industry." What point does the analogy illustrate? Is the analogy fully valid, or do you see ways it doesn't solidly hold?

2. What does the author recommend for short-term improvement of day care centers? for their permanent remedy?

3. According to Etzioni, what reasons explain our neglect of child raising? Do you think his explanation faults men and women equally?

Analyzing Connections

4. Etzioni and Whitehead (see "Women and the Future of Fatherhood," p. 113) each find family life currently failing its purpose. How do they agree or disagree in their suggestions for strengthening its purpose?

Analyzing by Writing

5. Examine one practical way in which society can raise the perceived value of child raising. Explain how your measure would affect fathers and mothers.

PART 3

SIGNIFICANT OTHERS

Susan Allen Toth, *Boyfriends*
Stephen Dunn, *Locker Room Talk*
Diane Ackerman, *The Chemistry of Love*
Meghan Daum, *On the Fringes of the Physical World*
Steve Tesich, *Focusing on Friends*
Patricia J. Williams, *My Best White Friend*
Leslie Lawrence, *Propelled by Love*
Jonathan Rauch, *For Better or Worse?*
Raymond Carver, *What We Talk About
When We Talk About Love* (fiction)

INSIGHTS

All love is self-love.

—FRANÇOIS DE LA ROCHEFOUCAULD

The word love has by no means the same sense for both sexes, and this is one of the serious misunderstandings that divide them.

—SIMONE DE BEAUVOIR

Christ here's my discovery. You have got hold of the wrong absolutes and infinities. God as absolute? God as infinity? I don't even understand the words. I'll tell you what's absolute and infinite. Loving a woman. But how would you know? You see, your church knows what it's doing: Rule out one absolute so you have to look for another.

Do you know what it's like to be a self-centered not unhappy man who leads a tolerable finite life, works, eats, drinks, hunts, sleeps, then one fine day discovers that the great starry heavens have opened to him and that his heart is bursting with it. It? She. Her. Woman. Not a category, not a sex, not one of two sexes, a human female creature, but an infinity. $♀ = ∞$. What else is infinity but a woman become meat and drink to you, life and your heart's own music, the air you breathe? Just to be near her is to live and have your soul's own self. Just to open your mouth on the skin of her back. What joy just to wake up with her beside you in the morning. I didn't know there was such happiness.

But there is the dark converse: Not having her is not breathing. I'm not kidding: I couldn't get my breath without her.

What else is man made for but this? I can see you agree about love but you look somewhat ironic. Are we talking about two different things? In any case, there's a catch. Love is infinite happiness. Losing it is infinite unhappiness.

—WALKER PERCY

During the first six months, the baby has the rudiments of a love language available to him. There is the language of the embrace, the language of the eyes, the language of the smile, vocal communications of pleasure and distress. It is the essential vocabulary of love before we can speak of love. Eighteen years later, when this baby is full grown and "falls in love" for the first time, he will woo his partner through the language of the eyes, the language of the smile, through the utterance of endearments, and the joy of the embrace. In his declarations of love he will use such phrases as "When I first looked into your eyes," "When you smiled at me," "When I held you in my arms." And naturally, in his exalted state, he will believe that he invented this love song.

—SELMA FRAIBERG

No one can fall in love if he is even partially satisfied with what he has or who he is. The experience of falling in love originates in an extreme depression, an inability to find something that has value in everyday life. The "symptom" of the predisposition to fall in love is not the conscious desire to do so, the intense desire to enrich our lives; it is the profound sense of being worthless and of having nothing that is valuable and the shame of not having it. This is the first sign that we are prepared for the experience — the feeling of nothingness and shame over our own nothingness. For this reason, falling in love occurs more frequently among young people, since they are profoundly uncertain, unsure of their worth, and often ashamed of themselves. The same thing applies to people of other ages when they lose something in their lives — when their youth ends or when they start to grow old. There is an irreparable loss of something in the self, a feeling that we will inevitably become devoid of value or degraded, compared with what we have been. It isn't the longing for an affair that makes us fall in love, but the conviction that we have nothing to lose by becoming whatever we will become; it is the prospect of nothingness stretching before us. Only then do we develop the inclination for the different and the risky, that propensity to hurl ourselves into all or nothing which those who are in any way satisfied with their lives cannot feel.

—FRANCESCO ALBERONI

Sex Without Love

How do they do it, the ones who make love
without love? Beautiful as dancers,

gliding over each other like ice skaters
over the ice, fingers hooked
inside each other's bodies, faces
red as steak, wine, wet as the
children at birth whose mothers are going to
give them away. How do they come to the
come to the   come to the   God   come to the
still waters, and not love
the one who came there with them, light
rising slowly as steam off their joined
skin? These are the true religious,
the purists, the pros, the ones who will not
accept a false Messiah, love the
priest instead of the God. They do not
mistake the lover for their own pleasure,
they are like great runners: they know they are alone
with the road surface, the cold, the wind,
the fit of their shoes, their over-all cardiovascular health — just factors, like the partner
in the bed, and not the truth, which is the
single body alone in the universe
against its own best time.

— SHARON OLDS

We are too ego-centered. The ego-shell in which we live is the hardest thing to outgrow. We seem to carry it all the time from childhood up to the time we finally pass away. We are, however, given many chances to break through this shell, and the first and greatest of them is when we reach adolescence. This is the first time the ego really comes to recognize the "other." I mean the awakening of sexual love. An ego, entire and undivided, now begins to feel a sort of split in itself. Love hitherto dormant deep in his heart lifts its head and causes a great commotion in it. For the love now stirred demands at once the assertion of the ego and its annihilation. Love makes the ego lose itself in the object it loves, and yet at the same time it wants to have the object as its own. This is a contradiction, and a great tragedy of life.

— D. T. SUZUKI

FOCUSING BY WRITING

1. Is your campus preparing you for equality or for war between the sexes? How were sex roles and sexual expectations discussed by college officials during your freshman orientation program? What possible positive or negative results do you foresee from the presentation of the issues?

2. Children of early elementary school age often develop a crush on somebody — frequently a teacher, sometimes another child two or three years older. Characterize the person you had a crush on. How did the object of your crush resemble or differ from your family members? Examine the wishes and ideas that your crush expressed to you.

3. A fan is usually involved in an imaginary romantic relationship. A fan cherishes the star's face and image, delights in knowing details of the star's life, identifies with the star's successes and tribulations, and often fantasizes reciprocated attention and affection. Define one specific imaginary relationship that you have had as a fan. Do not just reminisce; keep your attention on examining the behavior and responses of a fan.

4. What is your favorite song that deals with love? Write down the lyrics you can remember, and examine the attitude about love that the song expresses both explicitly and implicitly.

Susan Allen Toth

BOYFRIENDS

SUSAN ALLEN TOTH (b. 1940) grew up in Ames, Iowa, and graduated from Smith College before she returned to the Midwest for a Ph.D. in English and a college teaching career. She describes her college years in *Ivy Days: Making My Way Out East* (1984). Toth writes for magazines such as *Redbook* and *Harper's*, and she has written travel books about England, including *England for All Seasons* (1997). She recounts her precollege years in *Blooming: A Small Town Girlhood* (1981), from which this excerpt is taken. In regard to boyfriends generally, she writes, "I can't remember when I didn't want one."

Just when I was approaching sixteen, I found Peter Stone. Or did he find me? Perhaps I magicked him into existence out of sheer need. I was spooked by the boys who teased us nice girls about being sweet-sixteen-and-never-been-kissed. I felt that next to being an old maid forever, it probably was most demeaning to reach sixteen and not to have experienced the kind of ardent embrace Gordon MacRae periodically bestowed on Kathryn Grayson between choruses of "Desert Song." I was afraid I would never have a real boyfriend, never go parking, never know true love. So when Peter Stone asked his friend Ted to ask Ted's girlfriend Emily who asked me if I would ever neck with anyone, I held my breath until Emily told me she had said to Ted to tell Peter that maybe I would.

Not that Peter Stone had ever necked with anyone either. But I didn't realize that for a long time. High-school courtship usually was meticulously slow, progressing through inquiry, phone calls, planned encounters in public places, double or triple dates, single dates, handholding, and finally a goodnight kiss. I assumed it probably stopped there, but I didn't know. I had never gotten that far. I had lots of time to learn about Peter Stone. What I knew at the beginning already attracted me. He was a year ahead of me, vice-president of Hi-Y, a shot-putter who had just managed to earn a letter sweater. An older man, *and* an athlete. Tall, heavy, and broad-shouldered, Peter had a sweet slow smile. Even at a distance there was something endearing about the way he would blink nearsightedly through his glasses and light up with pleased recognition when he saw me coming toward him down the hall.

For a long while I didn't come too close. Whenever I saw Peter he was 3
in the midst of his gang, a group of five boys as close and as self-protective
as any clique we girls had. They were an odd mixture: Jim, an introspective
son of a lawyer; Brad, a sullen hot-rodder; Ted, an unambitious and gentle
boy from a poor family; Andy, a chubby comedian; and Peter. I was a little
afraid of all of them, and they scrutinized me carefully before opening their
circle to admit me, tentatively, as I held tight to Peter's hand. The lawyer's
son had a steady girl, a fast number who was only in eighth grade but
looked eighteen; the hot-rodder was reputed to have "gone all the way"
with his adoring girl, a coarse brunette with plucked eyebrows; gentle Ted
pursued my friend Emily with hangdog tenacity; but Peter had never
shown real interest in a girlfriend before.

Although I had decided to go after Peter, I was hesitant about how to 4
plot my way into the interior of his world. It was a thicket of strange shrubs
and tangled branches. Perhaps I see it that way because I remember the
day Peter took me to a wild ravine to shoot his gun. Girls who went with
one of "the guys" commiserated with each other that their boyfriends all
preferred two other things to them: their cars and their guns. Although
Peter didn't hunt and seldom went to practice at the target range, still he
valued his gun. Without permits, "the guys" drove outside of town to fire
their guns illegally. I had read enough in my *Seventeen* about how to attract
boys to know I needed to show enthusiasm about Peter's hobbies, so I asked
him if someday he would take me someplace and teach me how to shoot.

One sunny fall afternoon he did. I remember rattling over gravel roads 5
into a rambling countryside that had surprising valleys and woods around
cultivated farmland. Eventually we stopped before a barred gate that led to
an abandoned bridge, once a railroad trestle, now a splintering wreck. We
had to push our way through knee-high weeds to get past the gate. I was
afraid of snakes. Peter took my hand; it was the first time he had ever held
it, and my knees weakened a little. I was also scared of walking onto the
bridge, which had broken boards and sudden gaps that let you look some
fifty feet down into the golden and rust-colored brush below. But I didn't
mind being a little scared as long as Peter was there to take care of me.

I don't think I had ever held a gun until Peter handed me his pistol, a 6
heavy metal weapon that looked something like the ones movie sheriffs carried in their holsters. I was impressed by its weight and power. Peter fired it
twice to show me how and then stood close to me, watching carefully,
while I aimed at an empty beer can he tossed into the air. I didn't hit it.
The noise of the gun going off was terrifying. I hoped nobody was walking
in the woods where I had aimed. Peter said nobody was, nobody ever came
here. When I put the gun down, he put his arm around me, very carefully.
He had never done that before, either. We both just stood there, looking off
into the distance, staring at the glowing maples and elms, dark red patches
of sumac, brown heaps of leaves. The late afternoon sun beat down on us.

It was hot, and after a few minutes Peter shifted uncomfortably. I moved away, laughing nervously, and we walked back to the car, watching the gaping boards at our feet.

What Peter and I did with our time together is a mystery. I try to picture 7 us at movies or parties or somebody's house, but all I can see is the two of us in Peter's car. "Going for a drive!" I'd fling at my mother as I rushed out of the house; "rinking" was our high-school term for it, drawn from someone's contempt for the greasy "hoods" who hung out around the roller-skating rink and skidded around corners on two wheels of their souped-up cars. Peter's car barely made it around a corner on all four wheels. Though he had learned something about how to keep his huge square Ford running, he wasn't much of a mechanic. He could make jokes about the Ford, but he didn't like anyone else, including me, to say it looked like an old black hearse or remind him it could scarcely do forty miles an hour on an open stretch of highway. Highways were not where we drove, anyway, nor was speed a necessity unless you were trying to catch up with someone who hadn't seen you. "Rinking" meant cruising aimlessly around town, looking for friends in *their* cars, stopping for conversations shouted out of windows, maybe parking somewhere for a while, ending up at the A&W Root Beer Stand or the pizza parlor or the Rainbow Cafe.

Our parents were often puzzled about why we didn't spend time in each 8 other's homes. "Why don't you invite Peter in?" my mother would ask a little wistfully, as I grabbed my billfold and cardigan and headed toward the door. Sometimes Peter would just pause in front of the house and honk; if I didn't come out quickly, he assumed I wasn't home and drove away. Mother finally made me tell him at least to come to the door and knock. I couldn't explain to her why we didn't want to sit in the living room, or go down to the pine-paneled basement at the Harbingers', or swing on the Harrises' front porch. We might not have been bothered at any of those places, but we really wouldn't have been alone. Cars were our private space, a rolling parlor, the only place we could relax and be ourselves. We could talk, fiddle with the radio if we didn't have much to say, look out the window, watch for friends passing by. Driving gave us a feeling of freedom.

Most of my memories of important moments with Peter center in that 9 old black Ford. One balmy summer evening I remember particularly because my friend Emily said I would. Emily and Ted were out cruising in his rusty two-tone Chevy, the lawyer's son Jim and his girl had his father's shiny Buick, and Peter and I were out driving in the Ford. As we rumbled slowly down the Main Street, quiet and dark at night, Peter saw Ted's car approaching. We stopped in the middle of the street so the boys could exchange a few laconic grunts while Emily and I smiled confidentially at each other. We were all in a holiday mood, lazy and happy in the warm breezes that swept through the open windows. One of us suggested that we all meet later at Camp Canwita, a wooded park a few miles north of town. Whoever saw Jim would tell him to join us too. We weren't sure what we would do there, but it sounded like an adventure. An hour or so later, Peter and I bumped over the potholes in the road that twisted through the woods to the parking lot. We were the first ones there. When Peter turned off the motor, we could hear grasshoppers thrumming on all sides of us and leaves rustling in the dark. It was so quiet, so remote, I was a little frightened, remembering one of my mother's unnerving warnings about the dangerous men who sometimes preyed upon couples who parked in secluded places. We didn't have long to wait, though, before Ted's car coughed and sputtered down the drive. Soon Jim arrived too, and then we all pulled our cars close together in a kind of circle so we could talk easily out the windows. Someone's radio was turned on, and Frank Sinatra's mournful voice began to sing softly of passing days and lost love. Someone suggested that we get out of the cars and dance. It wouldn't have been Peter, who was seldom romantic. Ted opened his door so the overhead light cast a dim glow over the tiny area between the cars. Solemnly, a little self-consciously, we began the shuffling steps that were all we knew of what we called "slow dancing." Peter was not a good dancer, nor was I, though I liked putting my head on his bulky shoulder. But he moved me around the small lighted area as best he could, trying not to bump into Ted and Emily or Jim and his girl. I tried not to step on his toes. While Sinatra, Patti Page, and the Four Freshmen sang to us about moments to remember and Cape Cod, we all danced, one-two back, one-two back. Finally Emily, who was passing by my elbow, looked significantly at me and said, "This is something we'll be able to tell our grandchildren." Yes, I nodded, but I wasn't so sure. The mosquitoes were biting my legs and arms, my toes hurt, and I was getting a little bored. I think the others were too, because before long we all got into our cars and drove away.

Not all the time we spent in Peter's car was in motion. After several 10 months, we did begin parking on deserted country roads, side streets, even sometimes my driveway, if my mother had heeded my fierce instructions to leave the light turned off. For a while we simply sat and talked with Peter's arm draped casually on the back of the seat. Gradually I moved a little closer. Soon he had his arm around me, but even then it was a long time before he managed to kiss me good-night. Boys must have been as scared as we girls were, though we always thought of them as having much more experience. We all compared notes, shyly, about how far our boyfriends had gone; was he holding your hand yet, or taking you parking, or...? When a girl finally got kissed, telephone lines burned with the news next day. I was getting a little embarrassed about how long it was taking Peter to get around to it. My sixteenth birthday was only a few weeks away, and so far I had nothing substantial to report. I was increasingly nervous too because I still didn't know quite how I was going to behave. We girls joked about wondering where your teeth went and did glasses get in the way, but no one could give a convincing description. For many years I never told anyone about what *did* happen to me that first time. I was too ashamed.

Peter and I were parked down the street from my house, talking, snuggling, listening to the radio. During a silence I turned my face toward him, and then he kissed me, tentatively and quickly. I was exhilarated but frightened. I wanted to respond in an adequate way but my instincts did not entirely cooperate. I leaned towards Peter, but at the last moment I panicked. Instead of kissing him, I gave him a sudden lick on the cheek. He didn't know what to say. Neither did I.

Next morning I was relieved that it was all over. I dutifully reported my news to a few key girlfriends who could pass it on to others. I left out the part about the lick. That was my last bulletin. After a first kiss, we girls also respected each other's privacy. What more was there to know? We assumed that couples sat in their cars and necked, but nice girls, we also assumed, went no farther. We knew the girls who did. Their names got around. We marveled at them, uncomprehending as much as disapproving. Usually they talked about getting married to their boyfriends, and eventually some of them did. A lot of "nice" girls suffered under this distinction. One of them told me years later how she and her steady boyfriend had yearned and held back, stopped just short, petted and clutched and gritted their teeth. "When we went together to see the movie *Splendor in the Grass*, we had to leave the theater," she said ruefully. "The part about how Natalie Wood and Warren Beatty wanted to make love so desperately and couldn't.... Well, that was just how we felt."

My mother worried about what was going on in the car during those long evenings when Peter and I went "out driving." She needn't have. Amazing as it seems now, when courting has speeded up to a freeway pace, when I wonder if a man who doesn't try to get me to bed immediately might possibly be gay, Peter and I gave each other hours of affection without ever crossing the invisible line. We sat in his car and necked, a word that was anatomically correct. We hugged and kissed, nuzzling ears and noses and hairlines. But Peter never put a hand on my breast, and I wouldn't have known whether Peter had an erection if it had risen up and thwapped me in the face. I never got that close. Although we probably should have perished from frustration, in fact I reveled in all that holding and touching. Peter seemed pleased too, and he never demanded more. Later, I suppose, he learned quickly with someone else about what he had been missing. But I remember with gratitude Peter's awkward tenderness and the absolute faith I had in his inability to hurt me.

After Peter graduated and entered the university, our relationship changed. Few high-school girls I knew went out with college men; it was considered risky, like dating someone not quite in your social set or from another town. You were cut off. At the few fraternity functions Peter took me to, I didn't know anyone there. I had no idea what to talk about or how to act. So I refused to go, and I stopped asking Peter to come with me to parties or dances at the high school. I thought he didn't fit in there either. When I was honest with myself, I admitted that romance had gone. Already planning to go away to college, I could sense new vistas opening before me, glowing horizons whose light completely eclipsed a boyfriend like Peter. When I got on the Chicago & Northwestern train to go east to Smith, I felt with relief that the train trip was erasing one problem for me. I simply rode away from Peter.

On my sixteenth birthday, Peter gave me a small cross on a chain. All 14 the guys had decided that year to give their girlfriends crosses on chains, even though none of them was especially religious. It was a perfect gift, they thought, intimate without being soppy. Everyone's cross cost ten dollars, a lot of money, because it was real sterling silver. Long after Peter and I stopped seeing each other, I kept my cross around my neck, not taking it off even when I was in the bathtub. Like my two wooden dolls from years before, I clung to that cross as a superstitious token. It meant that someone I had once cared for had cared for me in return. Once I had had a boyfriend.

Analyzing This Selection

1. What moved Toth into her first romance? What was apparently *not* part of the impetus?

2. Where did Toth learn how to interest Peter? What indicates her present attitude toward the episode with the gun?

3. **THE WRITER'S METHOD**   Is there any part of this account that strikes you as probably oversimplified or idealized? What additions might make it more true to life without changing the main points of her memoir?

4. What was the lasting effect of this romance after it ended? Was it different from what she sought or expected?

Analyzing Connections

5. Toth, born in 1940, and Nora Ephron, born in 1941, grew up during the same period, the 1950s (see "Shaping Up Absurd," p. 16). What are some similarities in their adolescent experiences? What differences arise in the authors' tones and attitudes toward their adolescence?

Analyzing by Writing

6. Many high schools distribute condoms in order to reduce the likelihood of teenage pregnancies and sexually transmitted diseases. How would, or did, this sort of prevention program affect student attitudes in the school you attended? Explain the impact on high school attitudes toward romance and sexuality.

Stephen Dunn

LOCKER ROOM TALK

STEPHEN DUNN (b. 1939), a poet and essayist, graduated from Hofstra University. His ten collections of poetry include *New and Selected Poems* (1994) and *Different Hours* (2000). Dunn has received a Guggenheim Fellowship and other major awards. His essays are collected in *Walking Light: Essays and Memoirs* (1993). The following piece was included in an anthology of brief nonfiction, *In Short* (1996).

Having been athletic most of my life, I've spent a fair amount of time in 1
locker rooms and have overheard my share of "locker room talk." For reasons I couldn't understand for many years, I rarely participated in it and certainly never felt smug or superior about my lack of participation. In fact, I felt quite the opposite; I thought something was wrong with me. As a teenager and well into my twenties I'd hear someone recount his latest real or wishful conquest, there'd be a kind of general congratulatory laughter, tacit envy, but what I remember feeling most was wonderment and then embarrassment.

There was of course little or no public information about sex when I was 2
growing up in the forties and fifties. The first time I heard someone talk about having sex was in the school yard (the locker room without walls) when I was twelve or thirteen. Frankie Salvo, a big boy of sixteen. Frankie made it sound dirty, something great you do with a bad girl. It was my first real experience with pornography and it was thrilling, a little terrifying too. My mind conjured its pictures. Wonderment. Not wonderful.

Some years later, after experience, wonderment gave way to embarrass- 3
ment. I wasn't sure for whom I was embarrassed, the girl spoken about, the story teller, or myself. Nevertheless, I understood the need to tell. I, too, wanted to tell my good friend, Alan, but for some reason I never told him very much. In retrospect, it was my first test with what Robert Frost calls knowing "the delicacy of when to stop short," a delicacy I took no pride in. I felt excessively private, cut off.

I began thinking about all of this recently because in the locker room at 4
college a young man was telling his friend — loud enough for all of us to hear — what he did to this particular young woman the night before, and

136

what she did to him. It was clear how important it was for him to impress his friend, far more important than the intimacy itself, as if the sexual act weren't complete until he had completed it among other men.

This time I knew something about the nature of my embarrassment. It wasn't just that he had cheapened himself in the telling, but like all things which embarrass us it had struck some part of me that was complicitous, to a degree guilty, the kind of guilt you feel every time there's a discrepancy between what you know you're supposed to feel (correct feelings) and what in fact you've thought of, if not done. But more than that, I was embarrassed by the young man's assumption — culturally correct for the most part — that we other men in the locker room were his natural audience. There were five or six of us, and we certainly didn't boo or hiss. Those of us who were silent (all of us except his friend) had given our quiet sanctions.

What did it all mean? That men, more often than not, in a very fundamental way prefer other men? Or was it all about power, an old story, success with women as a kind of badge, an accoutrement of power? Was the young man saying to the rest of us, "I'm powerful"? I thought so for a while, but then I thought that he seemed to be saying something different. He was saying out loud to himself and to the rest of us that he hadn't succumbed to the greatest loss of power, yielding to the attractiveness and power of women, which could mean admitting he felt something or, at the furthest extreme, had fallen in love.

From Samson, to the knight in Keats' poem "La Belle Dame Sans Merci," to countless examples in world literature, the warning is clear: women take away your power. To fall in love with one is to be distracted from the world of accomplishment and acquisitiveness. But to have sex and then to talk about it publicly is a kind of final protection, the ultimate prophylactic against the dangers of feeling.

"Love means always having to say you're sorry," a friend once said to me. The joke had its truth, and it implied — among other things — a mature love, a presumption of mutual respect and equality. On some level the young man in the locker room sensed and feared such a relationship. He had ventured into the dark and strange world of women and had come out unscathed, literally untouched. He was back with us, in the locker room which was the country he understood and lived in, with immunity. He thought we'd be happy for him.

Analyzing This Selection

1. **THE WRITER'S METHOD**   The author makes a strong point in a very brief essay. What makes his presentation convincing? Find details that illustrate Dunn's method.

2. Dunn acquired an older man's understanding of his lifelong embarrassment. Why is he still embarrassed by locker room talk? How does his analysis of embarrassment hold up when applied to nonsexual topics?

Analyzing Connections

3. Compare Dunn's worries about locker room talk with Anthony Walton's worries about being a man (see "Hamburger," p. 24). In your opinion, which author explains more fundamental reasons for men's anxieties?

Analyzing by Writing

4. What might have happened in this locker room situation if one or more men had reacted differently to the storyteller? Would the embarrassment have persisted or even increased? Explain your views about how to deal with conversations about sex that overstep the limits of some but not all members of the group. Use Dunn's methods to help make your point.

Diane Ackerman

THE CHEMISTRY OF LOVE

DIANE ACKERMAN (b. 1948), a poet and natural history writer, earned a doctorate in English from Cornell University. Her collections of verse include *Jaguar of Sweet Laughter* (1991). As a staff contributor to the *New Yorker*, Ackerman writes about various roles of nature in human experience. Her *Natural History of the Senses* (1990) examines each of the five senses. The following essay is excerpted from A *Natural History of Love* (1994). Recently, Ackerman wrote about states of heightened, revelatory experience in *Deep Play* (1999).

Oxytocin, a hormone that encourages labor and the contractions during childbirth, seems to play an important role in mother love. The sound of a crying baby makes its mother's body secrete more oxytocin, which in turn erects her nipples and helps the milk to flow. As the baby nurses, even more oxytocin is released, making the mother want to nuzzle and hug it. It's been called the "cuddle chemical" by zoologists who have artificially raised the oxytocin level in goats and other animals and produced similar behavior. Oxytocin has many functions, some of them beneficial for the mother. The baby feels warm and safe as it nurses, and its digestive and respiratory systems run smoothly. The baby's nursing, which also coaxes the oxytocin level to rise in the mother, results, too, in contractions of the uterus that stop bleeding and detach the placenta. So mother and baby find themselves swept away in a chemical dance of love, interdependency, and survival.

Later in life, oxytocin seems to play an equally important role in romantic love, as a hormone that encourages cuddling between lovers and increases pleasure during lovemaking. The hormone stimulates the smooth muscles and sensitizes the nerves, and snowballs during sexual arousal — the more intense the arousal, the more oxytocin is produced. As arousal builds, oxytocin is thought to cause the nerves in the genitals to fire spontaneously, bringing on orgasm. Unlike other hormones, oxytocin arousal can be generated both by physical and emotional cues — a certain look, voice, or gesture is enough — and can become conditioned to one's personal love history. The lover's smell or touch may trigger the production of oxytocin. So might a richly woven and redolent sexual fantasy. Women are more responsive to oxytocin's emotional effects, probably because of the important role it plays in mothering. Indeed, women who have gone through natural childbirth sometimes report that they felt an orgasmic sense of pleasure during delivery. Some nonorgasmic women have found it easier to achieve orgasm after they've been through childbirth; the secretion of oxytocin during delivery and nursing melts their sexual blockage. This hormonal outpouring may help explain why women more than men prefer to continue embracing after sex. A woman may yearn to feel close and connected, tightly coiled around the mainspring of the man's heart. In evolutionary terms, she hopes the man will be staying around for a while, long enough to protect her and the child he just fathered.

Men's oxytocin levels quintuple during orgasm. But a Stanford University study showed that women have even higher levels of oxytocin than men do during sex, and that it takes more oxytocin for women to achieve orgasm. Drenched in this spa of the chemical, women are able to have more multiple orgasms than men, as well as full body orgasms. Mothers have told me during their baby's first year or so they were surprised to find themselves "in love" with it, "turned on" by it, involved with it in "the best romance ever." Because the same hormone controls a woman's pleasure during orgasm, childbirth, cuddling, and nursing her baby, it makes perfect sense that she should feel this way. The brain may have an excess of gray matter, but in some things it's economical. It likes to reuse convenient pathways and chemicals for many purposes. Why plow fresh paths through the snow of existence when old paths already lead part of the way there?

"The meeting of two personalities is like the contact of two chemical substances," Carl Jung wrote, "if there is any reaction, both are transformed." When two people find each other attractive, their bodies quiver with a gush of PEA (phenylethylamine), a molecule that speeds up the flow of information between nerve cells. An amphetaminelike chemical, PEA whips the brain into a frenzy of excitement, which is why lovers feel euphoric, rejuvenated, optimistic, and energized, happy to sit up talking all night or making love for hours on end. Because "speed" is addictive, even the body's naturally made speed, some people become what Michael Liebowitz and Donald Klein of the New York State Psychiatric Institute refer to as "attraction junkies," needing a romantic relationship to feel excited by life. The craving catapults them from high to low in an exhilarating, exhausting cycle of thrill and depression. Driven by a chemical hunger, they choose unsuitable partners, or quickly misconstrue a potential partner's feelings. Sliding down the slippery chute of their longing, they fall head over heels into a sea of all-consuming, passionate love. Soon the relationship crumbles, or they find themselves rejected. In either case, tortured by lovesick despair, they plummet into a savage depression, which they try to cure by falling in love again. Liebowitz and Klein think that this roller coaster is fueled by a chemical imbalance in the brain, a craving for PEA.

When they gave some attraction junkies MAO inhibitors — antidepressants that work by disabling certain enzymes that can subdue PEA and other neurotransmitters — they were amazed to find how quickly the therapy worked. No longer craving PEA, the patients were able to choose partners more calmly and realistically. Other studies with humans seem to confirm these findings. Researchers have also found that injecting mice, rhesus monkeys, and other animals with PEA produces noises of pleasure, courting behavior, and addiction (they keep pressing a lever to get more PEA). All this strongly suggests that when we fall in love the brain drenches itself in PEA, a chemical that makes us feel pleasure, rampant excitement, and well-being. A sweet fix, love.

The body uses PEA for more than infatuation. The same chemical soars 5 in thrill-seeking of any kind, because it keeps one alert, confident, and ready to try something new. That may help explain a fascinating phenomenon: People are more likely to fall in love when they're in danger. Wartime romances are legendary. I am part of a "baby boom" produced by such an event. Love thrives especially well in exotic locales. When the senses are heightened because of stress, novelty, or fear, it's much easier to become a mystic or feel ecstasy or fall in love. Danger makes one receptive to romance. Danger is an aphrodisiac. To test this, researchers asked single men to cross a suspension bridge. The bridge was safe, but frightening. Some men met women on the bridge. Other men encountered the same women — but not on the bridge — in a safer setting such as a campus or an office.

The men who met the women on the trembling bridge were much 6 more likely to ask them out on dates.

While the chemical sleigh ride of infatuation carries one at a fast clip 7 over uneven terrain, lives become blended, people mate and genes mix, and babies are born. Then the infatuation subsides and a new group of chemicals takes over, the morphinelike opiates of the mind, which calm and reassure. The sweet blistering rage of infatuation gives way to a narcotic peacefulness, a sense of security and belonging. Being in love is a state of chaotic equilibrium. Its rewards of intimacy, warmth, empathy, dependability, and shared experiences trigger the production of that mental comfort food, the endorphins. The feeling is less steep than falling in love, but it's steadier and more addictive. The longer two people have been married, the more likely it is they'll stay married. And couples who have three or more children tend to be lifelong spouses. Stability, friendship, familiarity, and affection are rewards the body clings to. As much as we love being happily unsettled, not to mention dizzied by infatuation, such a state is stressful. On the other hand, it also feels magnificent to rest, to be free of anxiety or fretting, and to enjoy one's life with a devoted companion who is as comfortable as a childhood playmate, as predictable if at times irksome as a sibling, as attentive as a parent, and also affectionate and loving: a longtime spouse. This is a tonic that is hard to give up, even if the relationship isn't perfect, and one is tempted by rejuvenating affairs. Shared events, including shared stresses and crises, are rivets that draw couples closer together. Soon they are fastened by so many it becomes difficult to pull free. It takes a vast amount of courage to leap off a slowly moving ship and grab a lifebuoy drifting past, not knowing exactly where it's headed or if it will keep one afloat. As the "other women" embroiled with long-married men discover, the men are unlikely to divorce, no matter how mundane their marriages, what they may promise, or how passionately in love they genuinely feel.

Analyzing This Selection

1. Ackerman lists several functions researchers have noted for oxytocin. How does she explain its many unrelated or contradictory functions?

2. Ackerman says, "When the senses are heightened…it's much easier to… fall in love" (para. 5). Do you agree? Some might argue that novelty, fear, and danger can also deaden the senses — that fear, for example, retards love. Explain where you stand on this question and whether Ackerman's arguments about PEA ring true.

3. **THE WRITER'S METHOD**   Find phrases and sentences that help you recognize Ackerman's purpose in identifying love chemicals. Does she achieve this purpose?

Analyzing Connections

4. Ackerman and Francesco Alberoni in the Insights on page 127 explain chemical or psychological mechanisms to account for love. Does either scientific view allow for free choice? Do you think a free choice can occur?

Analyzing by Writing

5. Since the love chemicals affect our good feelings, should we sometimes use supplemental doses? For instance, in recent years the hormone melatonin has been widely sold to help people fall asleep. How do the love chemicals differ, if at all, from taking vitamins or antidepressants, which also supply the body's natural chemicals? Explain what you would consider and decide if given the choice.

Meghan Daum

ON THE FRINGES OF THE PHYSICAL WORLD

MEGHAN DAUM (b. 1970) contributes essays and articles to magazines such as *Harper's Bazaar,* the *New Yorker, Vogue, GQ,* and the *New York Times Book Review.* Daum graduated from Vassar College and earned an M.F.A. at Columbia University. Her essays are collected in *Let the Trinkets Do the Talking* (2000).

It started in cold weather; fall was drifting away into an intolerable chill. I was on the tail end of twenty-six, living in New York City and taking part in the kind of urban life that might be construed as glamorous were it to appear in a memoir in the distant future. At the time, however, my days felt more like a grind than an adventure: hours of work strung between the motions of waking up, getting the mail, watching TV with my roommates, and going to bed. One morning I logged on to my America Online account to find a message under the heading "is this the real meghan daum?" It came from someone with the screen name PFSlider. The body of the message consisted of five sentences, entirely in lowercase letters, of perfectly turned flattery, something about PFSlider's admiration of some newspaper and magazine articles I had published over the last year and a half, something else about his resulting infatuation with me, and something about his being a sportswriter in California.

I was charmed for a moment or so, engaged for the thirty seconds it took me to read the message and fashion a reply. Though it felt strange to be in the position of confirming that I was indeed "the real meghan daum," I managed to say "Yes, it's me. Thank you for writing." I clicked the Send Now icon and shot my words into the void, where I forgot about PFSlider until the next day, when I received another message, this one labeled "eureka." "wow, it is you," he wrote, still in lowercase. He chronicled the various conditions under which he'd read my few and far between articles: a boardwalk in Laguna Beach, the spring training press room for the baseball team he covered for a Los Angeles newspaper. He confessed to having a "crazy crush" on me. He referred to me as "princess daum." He said he wanted to propose marriage or at least have lunch with me during one of his two annual trips to New York. He managed to do all of this without sounding like a schmuck. As I read the note I smiled the kind of smile one tries to suppress, the kind of smile that arises during a sappy movie one never even admits to seeing. The letter was outrageous and endearingly pathetic, possibly the practical joke of a friend trying to rouse me out of a temporary writer's block. But the kindness pouring forth from my computer screen was unprecedented, bizarrely exhilarating, and I logged off and thought about it for a few hours before writing back to express how flattered and touched — it was probably the first time I had ever used "touched" in earnest — I was by his message.

I had received e-mail messages from strangers before, most of them kind   3 and friendly and courteous, all of those qualities that generally get checked with the coats at the cocktail parties that comprise what the information age has now forced us to call the "three-dimensional world." I am always warmed by an unsolicited gesture of admiration or encouragement, amazed that anyone would bother, shocked that communication from a stranger could be fueled by anything other than an attempt to get a job or make what the professional world has come to call "a connection."

I am not what most people would call a "computer person." I have   4 utterly no interest in chat rooms, news groups, or most Web sites. I derive a palpable thrill from sticking an actual letter in the U.S. mail. But e-mail, though I generally only send and receive a few messages a week, proves a useful form for my particular communication anxieties. I have a constant, low-grade fear of the telephone. I often call people with the intention of getting their answering machines. There is something about a real voice that has become startling, unnervingly organic, as volatile as live television.

PFSlider and I tossed a few innocuous, smart-assed notes back and forth   5 over the week following his first message. His name was Pete. He was twenty-nine and single. I revealed very little about myself, relying instead on the ironic commentary and forced witticisms that are the conceit of most e-mail messages. But I quickly developed an oblique affection for PFSlider. I was excited when there was a message from him, mildly depressed when there wasn't. After a few weeks he gave me his phone number. I did not give him mine, but he looked me up anyway and called me one Friday night. I was home. I picked up the phone. His voice was jarring yet not unpleasant. He held up more than his end of the conversation for an hour, and when he asked permission to call me again, I accepted as though we were in a previous century.

Pete, as I was forced to call him on the phone — I never could wrap   6 my mind around his actual name, privately referring to him as PFSlider, "e-mail guy," or even "baseball boy" — began calling me two or three times a week. He asked if he could meet me in person and I said that would be okay. Christmas was a few weeks away, and he would be returning east to see his family. From there, he would take the short flight to New York and have lunch with me. "It is my off-season mission to meet you," he said. "There will probably be a snowstorm," I said. "I'll bring a team of sled dogs," he answered. We talked about our work and our families, about baseball and Bill Clinton and Howard Stern and sex, about his hatred for Los Angeles and how much he wanted a new job. Other times we would find each other logged on to America Online at the same time and type back and forth for hours. For me, this was far superior to the phone. Through typos and misspellings, he flirted maniacally. "I have an absurd crush on you," he said. "If I like you in person you must promise to marry me." I was coy and conceited, telling him to get a life, baiting him into complimenting me further, teasing him in a way I would never have dared in the real world or even on the phone. I would stay up until 3:00 A.M. typing with him, smiling at the screen, getting so giddy that I couldn't fall asleep. I was having difficulty recalling what I used to do at night. My phone was tied up for hours at a time. No one in the real world could reach me, and I didn't really care.

In off moments I heard echoes of things I'd said just weeks earlier: "The   7 Internet is destroying the world. Human communication will be rendered obsolete. We will all develop carpal tunnel syndrome and die." But curiously the Internet, at least in the limited form in which I was using it, was having the opposite effect. My interaction with PFSlider was more human than much of what I experienced in the daylight realm of live beings. I was certainly putting more energy into the relationship than I had put into any before, giving him attention that was by definition undivided, relishing the safety of the distance by opting to be truthful rather than doling out the white lies that have become the staple of real life. The outside world, the place where I walked around on the concrete, avoiding people I didn't want to deal with, peppering the ground with half-truths, and applying my motto of "let the machine take it" to almost any scenario, was sliding into the periphery of my mind. I was a better person with PFSlider. I was someone I could live with.

This borrowed identity is, of course, the primary convention of Internet   8 relationships. The false comfort of the cyberspace persona has been identified as one of the maladies of our time, another avenue for the remoteness that so famously plagues contemporary life. But the better person that I was to PFSlider was not a result of being a different person to him. It was simply that I was a desired person, the object of a blind man's gaze. I may not have known my suitor, but for the first time in my life I knew the deal. I knew when I'd hear from him and how I'd hear from him. I knew he wanted me because he said he wanted me, because the distance and facelessness and lack of gravity of it all allowed him to be sweeter to me than most real-life people had ever managed. For the first time in my life, I was involved in an actual courtship ritual. Never before had I realized how much that kind of structure was missing from my everyday life.

And so PFSlider became my everyday life. All the tangible stuff — the   9 trees outside, my friends, the weather — fell away. I could physically feel my brain. My body did not exist. I had no skin, no hair, no bones; all desire had converted itself into a cerebral current that reached nothing but my frontal lobe. Lust was something not felt but thought. My brain was devouring all of my other organs and gaining speed with each swallow. There was no outdoors, the sky and wind were irrelevant. There was only the computer screen and the phone, my chair, and maybe a glass of water. Pete started calling every day, sometimes twice, a few times three times. Most mornings I would wake up to find a message from PFSlider, composed in Pacific time while I slept in the wee hours. "I had a date last night," he wrote. "And I am not ashamed to say it was doomed from the start because I couldn't stop thinking about you." Then, a few days later, "If you stood before me now I would plant the warmest kiss on your cheek that I could muster."

I fired back a message slapping his hand. "We must be careful where we   10 tread," I said. This was true but not sincere. I wanted it, all of it. I wanted the deepest bow before me. I wanted my ego not merely massaged but kneaded. I wanted unfettered affection, soulmating, true romance. In the weeks that had elapsed since I picked up "is this the real meghan daum?" the real me underwent some kind of meltdown, a systemic rejection of all the savvy and independence I had worn for years like a grownup Girl Scout badge. Since graduating from college, I had spent three years in a serious relationship and two years in a state of neither looking for a boyfriend nor particularly avoiding one. I had had the requisite number of false starts and five-night stands, dates that I wasn't sure were dates, emphatically casual affairs that buckled under their own inertia even before dawn broke through the iron-guarded windows of stale, one-room city apartments. Even though I was heading into my late twenties I was still a child, ignorant of dance steps or health insurance, a prisoner of credit card debt and student loans and the nagging feeling that I didn't want anyone to find me until I had pulled myself into some semblance of a grownup. I was a true believer in the urban dream, in years of struggle succumbing to brilliant success, in getting a break, in making it. Like most of my friends, I was selfish by design. To want was more virtuous than to need. I wanted someone to love me, but I certainly didn't need it. I didn't want to be alone, but as long as I was I had no choice but to wear my solitude as though it were haute couture. The worst sin imaginable was not cruelty or bitchiness or even professional failure but vulnerability. To admit to loneliness was to slap the face of progress. It was to betray the times in which we lived.

But PFSlider derailed me. He gave me all of what I'd never even real-   11 ized I wanted. He called not only when he said he would but unexpectedly, just to say hello. His guard was not merely down but nonexistent. He let his phone bill grow to towering proportions. He thought about me all the time and admitted it. He talked about me with his friends and admitted it. He arranged his holiday schedule around our impending date. He managed to charm me with sports analogies. He courted and wooed and romanced me. He didn't hesitate. He was unblinking and unapologetic, all nerviness and balls to the wall. He wasn't cheap. He went out of his way. I'd never seen anything like it.

Of all the troubling details of this story, the one that bothers me the most is the way I slurped up his attention like some kind of dying animal. My addiction to PFSlider's messages indicated a monstrous narcissism. But it also revealed a subtler desire that I didn't fully understand at the time. My need to experience an old-fashioned kind of courtship was stronger than I had ever imagined. The epistolary quality of our relationship put our communication closer to the eighteenth century than the uncertain millennium. For the first time in my life, I was not involved in a protracted "hang out" that would lead to a quasi-romance. I was involved in a well-defined structure, a neat little space in which we were both safe to express the panic and intrigue of our mutual affection. Our interaction was refreshingly orderly, noble in its vigor, dignified despite its shamelessness. We had an intimacy that seemed custom made for our strange, lonely times. It seemed custom made for me.

The day of our date was frigid and sunny. Pete was sitting at the bar of the restaurant when I arrived. We shook hands. For a split second he leaned toward me with his chin as if to kiss me. He was shorter than I had imagined, though he was not short. He registered with me as neither handsome nor unhandsome. He had very nice hands. He wore a very nice shirt. We were seated at a very nice table. I scanned the restaurant for people I knew, saw no one, and couldn't decide how I felt about that.

He talked and I heard nothing he said. He talked and talked and talked. I stared at his profile and tried to figure out if I liked him. He seemed to be saying nothing in particular, though it went on forever. Later we went to the Museum of Natural History and watched a science film about storms. We walked around looking for the dinosaurs, and he talked so much that I wanted to cry. Outside, walking along Central Park West at dusk, through the leaves, past the horse-drawn carriages and yellow cabs and splendid lights of Manhattan at Christmas, he grabbed my hand to kiss me and I didn't let him. I felt as if my brain had been stuffed with cotton. Then for some reason I invited him back to my apartment, gave him a few beers, and finally let him kiss me on the lumpy futon in my bedroom. The radiator clanked. The phone rang and the machine picked up. A car alarm blared outside. A key turned in the door as one of my roommates came home. I had no sensation at all, only the dull déjà vu of being back in some college dorm room, making out in a generic fashion on an Indian throw rug while Cat Stevens's *Greatest Hits* played on the portable stereo. I wanted Pete out of my apartment. I wanted to hand him his coat, close the door behind him, and fight the ensuing emptiness by turning on the computer and taking comfort in PFSlider.

When Pete finally did leave I sulked. The ax had fallen. He'd talked way too much. He was hyper. He hadn't let me talk, although I hadn't tried very hard. I berated myself from every angle, for not kissing him on Central Park West, for letting him kiss me at all, for not liking him, for wanting to like him more than I had wanted anything in such a long time. I was horrified by the realization that I had invested so heavily in a made-up character, a character in whose creation I'd had a greater hand than even Pete himself. How could I, a person so self-congratulatingly reasonable, have gotten sucked into a scenario that was more like a television talk show than the relatively full and sophisticated life I was so convinced I lead? How could I have received a fan letter and allowed it go this far? Then a huge bouquet of FTD flowers arrived from him. No one had ever sent me flowers before. I was sick with sadness. I hated either the world or myself, and probably both.

No one had ever forced me to forgive them before. But for some reason   16
I forgave Pete. I cut him more slack than I ever had anyone. I granted him an official pardon, excused his failure for not living up to PFSlider. Instead of blaming him I blamed the earth itself, the invasion of tangible things into the immaculate communication PFSlider and I had created. With its roommates and ringing phones and subzero temperatures, the physical world came barreling in with all the obstreperousness of a major weather system, and I ignored it. As human beings with actual flesh and hand gestures and Gap clothing, Pete and I were utterly incompatible, but I pretended otherwise. In the weeks that followed I pictured him and saw the image of a plane lifting off over an overcast city. PFSlider was otherworldly, more a concept than a person. His romance lay in the notion of flight, the physics of gravity defiance. So when he offered to send me a plane ticket to spend the weekend with him in Los Angeles, I took it as an extension of our blissful remoteness, a three-dimensional e-mail lasting an entire weekend. I pretended it was a good idea.

The temperature on the runway at JFK was seven degrees Fahrenheit.   17
We sat for three hours waiting for de-icing. Finally we took off over the frozen city, the DC-10 hurling itself against the wind. The ground below shrank into a drawing of itself. Laptop computers were plopped onto tray tables, cell phones were whipped out of pockets, the air recirculated and dried out my contact lenses. I watched movies without the sound and thought to myself that they were probably better that way. Something about the plastic interior of the fuselage and the plastic forks and the din of the air and the engines was soothing and strangely sexy, as fabricated and seductive as PFSlider. I thought about Pete and wondered if I could ever turn him into an actual human, if I could even want to. I knew so many people in real life, people to whom I spoke face to face, people who made me laugh or made me frustrated or happy or bored. But I'd never given any of them as much as I'd given PFSlider. I'd never forgiven their spasms and their speeches, never tied up my phone for hours in order to talk to them. I'd never bestowed such senseless tenderness on anyone.

We descended into LAX. We hit the tarmac and the seat belt signs   18
blinked off. I hadn't moved my body in eight hours, and now I was walking
up the jetbridge to the gate, my clothes wrinkled, my hair matted, my
hands shaking. When I saw Pete in the terminal, his face registered to me
as blank and impossible to process as the first time I'd met him. He kissed
me chastely. On the way out to the parking lot he told me that he was
being seriously considered for a job in New York. He was flying back there
next week, and if he got the job, he'd be moving within the month. I
looked at him in astonishment. Something silent and invisible seemed to
fall on us. Outside, the wind was warm, and the Avis and Hertz buses
ambled alongside the curb of Terminal 5. The palm trees shook, and the
air seemed as heavy and earthly as Pete's hand, which held mine for a few
seconds before dropping it to get his car keys out of his pocket. The leaves
on the trees were unmanageably real. He stood before me, all flesh and
preoccupation. The physical world had invaded our space. For this I could
not forgive him.

Everything now was for the touching. Everything was buildings and   19
bushes, parking meters and screen doors and sofas. Gone was the computer, the erotic darkness of the telephone, the clean, single dimension of
Pete's voice at one A.M. It was nighttime, yet the combination of sight and
sound was blinding. We went to a restaurant and ate outside on the sidewalk. We were strained for conversation and I tried not to care. We drove
to his apartment and stood under the ceiling light, not really looking at
each other. Something was happening that we needed to snap out of. Any
moment now, I thought. Any moment and we'll be all right. These
moments were crowded with elements, with carpet fibers and direct light
and the smells of everything that had a smell. They left marks as they
passed. It was all wrong. Gravity was all there was.

For three days we crawled along the ground and tried to pull ourselves   20
up. We talked about things I can no longer remember. We read the *L.A.
Times* over breakfast. We drove north past Santa Barbara to tour the wine
country. I stomped around in my clunky shoes and black leather jacket, a
killer of ants and earthworms and any hope in our abilities to speak and be
understood. Not until studying myself in the bathroom mirror of a highway
rest stop did I fully realize the preposterousness of my uniform. I felt like a
human shot put, an object that could not be lifted, something that secretly
weighed more than the world itself. We ate an expensive dinner. We
checked into a hotel and watched television. Pete talked at me and through
me and past me. I tried to listen. I tried to talk. But I bored myself and irritated him. Our conversation was a needle that could not be threaded. Still,
we played nice. We tried to care and pretended to keep trying long after we
had given up. In the car on the way home he told me I was cynical and I
didn't have the presence of mind to ask him how many cynics he had met
who would travel three thousand miles to see someone they barely knew.

Just for a chance. Just because the depths of my hope exceeded the thickness my leather jacket and the thickness of my skin and the wisdom of a million times that I had released myself into the sharp knowledge that communication had once again eliminated itself as a possibility.

Pete drove me to the airport at 7:00 A.M. so I could make my eight 21 o'clock flight home. He kissed me good-bye, another chaste peck I recognized from countless dinner parties and dud dates from real life. He said he'd call me in a few days when he got to New York for his job interview, which we had discussed only in passing and with no reference to the fact that New York was where I happened to live. I returned home to a frozen January. A few days later he came to New York and we didn't see each other. He called me from the plane back to Los Angeles to tell me, through the static, that he had gotten the job. He was moving to my city.

PFSlider was dead. Pete had killed him. I had killed him. I'd killed my 22 own persona too, the girl on the phone and on-line, the character created by some writer who'd captured him one morning long ago as he read the newspaper. There would be no meeting him in distant hotel lobbies during the baseball season. There would be no more phone calls or e-mails. In a single moment, Pete had completed his journey out of our mating dance and officially stepped into the regular world, the world that gnawed at me daily, the world that fed those five-night stands, the world where romance could not be sustained because we simply did not know how to do it. Here we were all chit-chat and leather jackets, bold proclaimers of all that we did not need. But what struck me most about this affair was the unpredictable nature of our demise. Unlike most cyber romances, which seem to come fully equipped with the inevitable set of misrepresentations and false expectations, PFSlider and I had played it fairly straight. Neither of us had lied. We'd done the best we could. We were dead from natural causes rather than virtual ones.

Within a two-week period after I returned from Los Angeles, at least 23 seven people confessed to me the vagaries of their own e-mail affairs. The topic arose, unprompted, over the course of normal conversation. Four of these people had gotten on planes and met their correspondents, traveling from New Haven to Baltimore, New York to Montana, Texas to Virginia, and New York to Johannesburg. These were normal people, writers and lawyers and scientists I knew from the real world. They were all smart, attractive, and more than a little sheepish about admitting just how deep they had been sucked in. Very few had met in chat rooms. Instead, the messages had started after chance meetings at parties and on planes; some, like me, had received notes in response to things they'd written on-line or elsewhere. Two of these people had fallen in love, the others chalked it up to strange, uniquely postmodern experience. They all did things they would never do in the real world: they sent flowers, they took chances, they forgave. I heard most of these stories in the close confines of smoky bars and crowded restaurants, and we would all shake our heads in be-wilderment as we told our tales, our eyes focused on some distant point that could never be reined in to the surface of the earth. Mostly it was the courtship ritual that had drawn us in. We had finally wooed and been wooed, given an old-fashioned structure through which to attempt the process of romance. E-mail had become an electronic epistle, a yearned-for rule book. The black and white of the type, the welcome respite from the distractions of smells and weather and other people, had in effect allowed us to be vulnerable and passionate enough to actually care about some-thing. It allowed us to do what was necessary to experience love. It was not the Internet that contributed to our remote, fragmented lives. The problem was life itself.

The story of PFSlider still makes me sad, not so much because we no 24 longer have anything to do with each other but because it forces me to grapple with all three dimensions of daily life with greater awareness than I used to. After it became clear that our relationship would never transcend the screen and the phone, after the painful realization that our face-to-face knowledge of each other had in fact permanently contaminated the screen and the phone, I hit the pavement again, went through the motions of real life, said hello and good-bye to people in the regular way. If Pete and I had met at a party, we probably wouldn't have spoken to each other for more than ten minutes, and that would have made life easier but also less inter-esting. At the same time, it terrifies me to admit a firsthand understanding of the way the heart and the ego are snarled and entwined. Like diseased trees that have folded in on one another, our need to worship fuses with our need to be worshiped. Love eventually becomes only about how much mystique can be maintained. It upsets me even more to see how this entan-glement is made so much more intense, so unhampered and intoxicating, by a remote access like e-mail. But I'm also thankful that I was forced to unpack the raw truth of my need and stare at it for a while. This was a dare I wouldn't have taken in three dimensions.

The last time I saw Pete he was in New York, three thousand miles away 25 from what had been his home and a million miles away from PFSlider. In a final gesture of decency, in what I later realized was the most ordinary kind of closure, he took me out to dinner. As the few remaining traces of affection turned into embarrassed regret, we talked about nothing. He paid the bill. He drove me home in his rental car, the smell and sound of which was as arbitrary and impersonal as what we now were to each other. Then he disappeared forever. He became part of the muddy earth, as unmysteri-ous as anything located next door. I stood on my stoop and felt that famil-iar rush of indifference. Pete had joined the angry and exhausted living. He drifted into my chaos, joined me down in reality, where even if we met on the street we'd never see each other again, our faces obscured by the branches and bodies and falling debris that make up the ether of the phys-ical world.

Analyzing This Selection

1. How did the author change during her e-mail romance? Which changes were virtual? Which, if any, were real?

2. Why does Daum continue the romance after their bad date in New York? She says, "I pretended it was a good idea" (para. 16). What possible reasons are supported by the essay?

3. **THE WRITER'S METHOD**   How does Daum turn her private, embarrassing experience into public written communication? How does her account differ from typical talk-show confessions? Examine her sentences and paragraphs.

4. The final three paragraphs are somber in tone. Is this concluding section positive or negative about Daum's future? What will she *want? need? accept?*

Analyzing Connections

5. Daum and Toth (see "Boyfriends," p. 130) each discover that courtship changes them for the better. Acknowledging their different situations, do you think their discoveries and changes are similar or contrasting?

Analyzing by Writing

6. Analyze a situation in which your crush conflicted with changes or growth. Do not merely tell the story but examine the test on affections and self-realizations. In what way, if at all, did the relationship continue? Use Daum's methods of reflection to help your analysis.

Steve Tesich

FOCUSING ON FRIENDS

STEVE TESICH (1943–1996) was a screenwriter and playwright best known for the Academy Award–winning film *Breaking Away* (1979). As a child he immigrated with his parents from Yugoslavia. Tesich graduated from Indiana University and obtained a master's degree at Columbia University.

When I think of people who were my good friends, I see them all, as I do everything else from my life, in cinematic terms. The camera work is entirely different for men and women.

I remember all the women in almost extreme close-ups. The settings are different — apartments, restaurants — but they're all interiors, as if I had never spent a single minute with a single woman outside. They're looking right at me, these women in these extreme close-ups; the lighting is exquisite, worthy of a Fellini or Fosse film, and their lips are moving. They're telling me something important or reacting to something even more important that I've told them. It's the kind of movie where you tell people to keep quiet when they chew their popcorn too loudly.

The boys and men who were my friends are in an entirely different movie. No close-ups here. No exquisite lighting. The camera work is rather shaky but the background is moving. We're going somewhere, on foot, on bicycles, in cars. The ritual of motion, or action, makes up for the inconsequential nature of the dialogue. It's a much sloppier film, this film that is not really a film but a memory of real friends: Slobo, Louie, Sam. Male friends. I've loved all three of them. I assumed they knew this, but I never told them.

Quite the contrary is true in my female films. In close-up after close-up, I am telling every woman who I ever loved that I love her, and then lingering on yet another close-up of her face for a reaction. There is a perfectly appropriate musical score playing while I wait. And if I wait long enough, I get an answer. I am loved. I am not loved. Language clears up the suspense. The emotion is nailed down.

Therein lies the difference, I think, between my friendships with men and with women. I can tell women I love them. Not only can I tell them, I am compulsive about it. I can hardly wait to tell them. But I can't tell the men. I just can't. And they can't tell me. Emotions are never nailed down. They run wild, and I and my male friends chase after them, on foot, on bicycles, in cars, keeping the quarry in sight but never catching up.

My first friend was Slobo. I was still living in Yugoslavia at the time, and   6
not far from my house there was an old German truck left abandoned after
the war. It had no wheels. No windshield. No doors. But the steering wheel
was intact. Slobo and I flew to America in that truck. It was our airplane.
Even now, I remember the background moving as we took off down the
street, across Europe, across the Atlantic. We were inseparable: the best of
friends. Naturally, not one word concerning the nature of our feelings for
one another was ever exchanged. It was all done in actions.

The inevitable would happen at least once a day. As we were flying over   7
the Atlantic, there came, out of nowhere, that wonderful moment: engine
failure! "We'll have to bail out," I shouted. "A-a-a-a-a!" Slobo made the
sound of a failing engine. Then he would turn and look me in the eye: "I
can't swim," he'd say. "Fear not." I put my hand on his shoulder. "I'll drag
you to shore." And, with that, both of us would tumble out of the truck
onto the dusty street. I swam through the dust. Slobo drowned in the dust,
coughing, gagging. "Sharks!" he cried. But I always saved him. The next
day the ritual would be repeated, only then it would be my turn to say "I
can't swim," and Slobo would save me. We saved each other from certain
death over a hundred times, until finally a day came when I really left for
America with my mother and sister. Slobo and I stood at the train station.
We were there to say goodbye, but, since we weren't that good at saying
things and since he couldn't save me, he just cried until the train started to
move.

The best friend I had in high school was Louie. It now seems to me that   8
I was totally monogamous when it came to male friends. I would have several girl friends but only one real male friend. Louis was it at that time. We
were both athletes, and one day we decided to "run till we drop." We just
wanted to know what it was like. Skinny Louie set the pace as we ran
around our high-school track. Lap after lap. Four laps to a mile. Mile after
mile we ran. I had the reputation as being a big-time jock. Louie didn't.
But this was Louie's day. There was a bounce in his step and, when he
turned back to look at me, his eyes were gleaming with the thrill of it all. I
finally dropped. Louie still looked fresh; he seemed capable, on that day, of
running forever. But we were the best of friends, and so he stopped. "That's
it," he lied. "I couldn't go another step farther." It was an act of love. Naturally, I said nothing.

Louie got killed in Vietnam. Several weeks after his funeral, I went to   9
his mother's house, and, because she was a woman, I tried to tell her how
much I had loved her son. It was not a good scene. Although I was telling
the truth, my words sounded like lies. It was all very painful and embarrassing. I kept thinking how sorry I was that I had never told Louie himself.

Sam is my best friend now, and has been for many years. A few years   10
ago, we were swimming at a beach in East Hampton. The Atlantic! The
very Atlantic I had flown over in my German truck with Slobo. We had
swum out pretty far from the shore when both of us simultaneously thought

we spotted a shark. Water is not only a good conductor of electricity but of panic as well. We began splashing like madmen toward shore. Suddenly, at the height of my panic, I realized how much I loved my friend, what an irreplaceable friend he was, and, although I was the faster swimmer, I fell back to protect him. Naturally, the shark in the end proved to be imaginary. But not my feelings for my friend. For several days after that I wanted to share my discovery with him, to tell him how much I loved him. Fortunately, I didn't.

I say fortunately because on reflection, there seems to be sufficient evidence to indicate that, if anybody was cheated and shortchanged by me, it was the women, the girls, the very recipients of my uncensored emotions. Yes, I could hardly wait to tell them I loved them. I did love them. But once I told them, something stopped. The emotion was nailed down, but, with it, the enthusiasm and the energy to prove it was nailed down, too. I can remember my voice saying to almost all of them, at one time or another: "I told you I love you. What else do you want?" I can now recoil at the impatient hostility of that voice but I can't deny it was mine. 11

The tyranny of self-censorship forced me, in my relations with male friends, to seek alternatives to language. And just because I could never be sure they understood exactly how I felt about them, I was forced to look for ways to prove it. That is, I now think, how it should be. It is time to make adjustments. It is time to pull back the camera, free the women I know, and myself, from those merciless close-ups and have the background move. 12

Analyzing This Selection

1. The author regrets not telling Louie how much he loved him. But at the end of the essay, Tesich says he is glad he did not tell his current friend about his feelings. Can you explain the difference?

2. In paragraph 12 Tesich looks forward to making "adjustments" in his relationships. What specifically does he suggest? Do you think he should make these changes?

Analyzing Connections

3. Tesich and Daum (see "On the Fringes of the Physical World," p. 143) see themselves caught in roles. Where or how did they acquire these roles? In your opinion, which person's role is more trite and clichéd? Which person is more disturbed by its triteness?

Analyzing by Writing

4. **THE WRITER'S METHOD**   Write a detailed visualization of your best male and female friendships. Try to depict the realities, not just generalities. If the cinematic technique is not adequate, add your full explanations of qualities that aren't visualized.

Patricia J. Williams

MY BEST WHITE FRIEND

PATRICIA J. WILLIAMS (b. 1951) graduated from Wellesley College and received her law degree from Harvard University. As a professor of law at Columbia University, she teaches and writes about social issues, particularly the rights of women and minorities. Her essays are published in *The Alchemy of Race and Rights* (1992) and *The Rooster's Egg* (1995). Her cautiously optimistic views about a fairer society are voiced in *Seeing a Color-Blind Future: The Paradox of Race* (1998). The following account of a friendship appeared first in the *New Yorker* in 1996.

Cinderella Revisited

My best white friend is giving me advice on how to get myself up like a trophy-wife-in-waiting. We are obliged to attend a gala fund-raiser for an organization on whose board we both sit. I'm not a wife of any sort at all, and she says she knows why: I'm prickly as all getout, I dress down instead of up, and my hair is "a complete disaster." My best white friend, who is already a trophy wife of considerable social and philanthropic standing, is pressing me to borrow one of her Real Designer gowns and a couple of those heavy gold bracelets that are definitely not something you can buy on the street.

I tell her she's missing the point. Cinderella wasn't an over-thirty black professional with an attitude. What sort of Master of the Universe is going to go for that?

"You're not a *racist*, are you?" she asks.

"How could I be?" I reply, with wounded indignation. "What, being the American Dream personified and all."

"Then let's get busy and make you *up*," she says soothingly, breaking out the little pots of powder, paint, and polish.

From the first exfoliant to the last of the cucumber rinse, we fight about my man troubles. From powder base through lip varnish, we fight about hers.

You see, part of the problem is that white knights just don't play the same part in my mythical landscape of desire. If poor Cinderella had been black, it would have been a whole different story. I tell my best white friend the kind of stories my mother raised me on: about slave girls who worked their fingers to the bone for their evil half sisters, the "legitimate" daughters of their mutual father, the master of the manse, the owner of them all; about scullery maids whose oil-and-ashes complexions would not wash clean even after multiple waves of the wand. These were the ones who harbored impossible dreams of love for lost mates who had been sold down rivers of tears into oblivion. These were the ones who became runaways.

"Just think about it," I say. "The human drama is compact enough so   8
that when my mother was little she knew women who had been slaves, including a couple of runaways. Cinderellas who had burned their masters' beds and then fled for their lives. It doesn't take too much, even across the ages, to read between those lines. Women who invented their own endings, even when they didn't get to live happily or very long thereafter."

My best white friend says, "Get a grip. It's just a party."   9

I've called my best white friend my best white friend ever since she   10
started calling me her best black friend. I am her only black friend, as far as I know, a circumstance for which she blames "the class thing." At her end of the social ladder, I am *my* only black friend — a circumstance for which I blame "the race thing."

"People should stop putting so much emphasis on color — it doesn't   11
matter whether you're black or white or blue or green," she says from beneath an avocado mask.

Lucky for you, I think, even as my own pores are expanding or contract-   12
ing — I forget which — beneath a cool neon-green sheath.

In fact, I have been looking forward to the makeover. M.B.W.F. has a   13
masseuse and a manicurist and colors in her palette like Après Sun and Burnt Straw, which she swears will match my skin tones more or less.

"Why don't they just call it Racial Envy?" I ask, holding up a tube of   14
Deep Copper Kiss.

"Now, now, we're all sisters under the makeup," she says cheerfully.   15

"When ever will we be sisters without?" I grumble.   16

I've come this far because she's convinced me that my usual slapdash   17
routine is the equivalent of being "unmade"; and being unmade, she underscores, is a most exclamatory form of unsophistication. "Even Strom Thurmond wears a little pancake when he's in public."

M.B.W.F. is somewhat given to hyperbole, but it *is* awfully hard to bear,   18
the thought of making less of a fashion statement than old Strom. I do draw the line, though. She has a long history of nips, tucks, and liposuction. Once, I tried to suggest how appalled I was, but I'm not good at being graceful when I have a really strong opinion roiling up inside. She dismissed me sweetly: "You can afford to disapprove. You are aging *so* very nicely."

There was the slightest pause as I tried to suppress the anxious rise in my   19
voice: "You think I'm aging?"

Very gently, she proceeded to point out the flawed and falling features   20
that give me away to the carefully trained eye, the insistent voyeur. There

were the pores. And those puffs beneath my eyes. No, not there — those are the bags under my eyes. The bags aren't so bad, according to her — no deep wrinkling just yet. But keep going — the puffs are just below the bags. Therein lies the facial decay that gives my age away.

I had never noticed them before, but for a while after that those puffs 21 just dominated my face. I couldn't look at myself for their explosive insolence — the body's betrayal, obscuring every other feature.

I got over it the day we were standing in line by a news rack at the Food 22 Emporium. Gazing at a photo of Princess Diana looking radiantly, elegantly melancholic on the cover of some women's magazine, M.B.W.F. snapped, "God! Bulimia must work!"

This is not the first time M.B.W.F. has shepherded me to social doom. 23 The last time, it was a very glitzy cocktail party where husband material supposedly abounded. I had a long, businesslike conversation with a man she introduced me to, who, I realized as we talked, grew more and more fascinated by me. At first, I was only conscious of winning him over; then I remember becoming aware that there was something funny about his fierce infatuation. I was *surprising* him, I slowly realized. Finally, he came clean: He said that he had never before had a conversation like this with a black person. "I think I'm in love," he blurted in a voice bubbling with fear.

"I think not," I consoled him. "It's just the power of your undone expec- 24 tations, in combination with my being a basically likable person. It's throwing you for a loop. That and the Scotch, which, as you ought to know, is inherently depoliticizing."

I remember telling M.B.W.F. about him afterward. She had always 25 thought of him as "that perfect Southern gentleman." The flip side of the Southern gentleman is the kind master, I pointed out. "Bad luck," she said. "It's true, though — he's the one man I wouldn't want to be owned by, if I were you."

My best white friend doesn't believe that race is a big social problem 26 anymore. "It's all economics," she insists. "It's how you came to be my *friend*" — for once, she does not qualify me as black — "the fact that we were both in college together." I feel compelled to remind her that affirmative action is how both of us ended up in the formerly all-male bastion we attended.

The odd thing is, we took most of the same classes. She ended up musi- 27 cally proficient, gifted in the art of interior design, fluent in the mother tongue, whatever it might be, of the honored visiting diplomat of the moment. She actively aspired, she says, to be "a cunning little meringue of a male prize."

"You," she says to me, "were always more like Gladys Knight." 28

"Come again?" I say. 29

"Ethnic woman warrior, always on that midnight train to someplace   30
else, intent on becoming the highest-paid Aunt Jemima in history."

"Ackh," I cough, a sudden strangulation of unmade thoughts fluttering   31
in my windpipe.

The night after the cocktail party, I dreamed that I was in a bedroom   32
with a tall, faceless man. I was his breeding slave. I was trying to be very,
very good, so that I might one day earn my freedom. He did not trust me.
I was always trying to hide some essential part of myself from him, which I
would preserve and take with me on that promised day when I was permitted to leave; he felt it as an innate wickedness in me, a darkness that he
could not penetrate, a dangerous secret that must be wrested from me. I
tried everything I knew to please him; I walked a tightrope of anxious servi-
tude and survivalist withholding. But it was not good enough. One morning, he just reached for a sword and sliced me in half, to see for himself
what was inside. A casual flick, and I lay dead on the floor in two dark,
unyielding halves; in exasperated disgust, he stepped over my remains and
rushed from the room, already late for other business, leaving the cleanup
for another slave.

"You didn't dream that!" M.B.W.F. says in disbelief.   33
"I did so."   34
"You're making it up," she says. "People don't really have dreams like that."   35
"*I* do. Aren't I a people, too?"   36
"That's amazing! Tell me another."   37
"O.K., here's a fairy tale for you," I say, and tell her I dreamed I was   38
being held by Sam Malone, the silly, womanizing bartender on *Cheers*. He
was tall, broad-chested, good-looking, unbelievably strong. My head, my
face were pressed against his chest. We were whispering our love for each
other. I was moved deeply, my heart was banging, he held me tight and
told me that he loved me. I told him that I loved him, too. We kissed so
that heaven and earth moved in my heart; I wanted to make love to him
fiercely. He put a simple thick gold band on my finger. I turned and, my
voice cracking with emotion and barely audible, said, "What's this?" He
asked me to marry him. I told him yes, I loved him, yes, yes, I loved him.
He told me he loved me, too. I held out my hand and admired the ring in
awe. I was the luckiest woman on earth.

Suddenly Diane Chambers, Sam's paramour on *Cheers*, burst through   39
the door. She was her perky, petulant self, bouncing blond hair and black-
green eyes like tarnished copper beads, like lumps of melted metal — eyes
that looked carved yet soft, almost brimming. She turned those soft-hard
eyes on me and said, "Oh no, Sam, not tonight — you promised!"

And with that I realized that I was to be consigned to a small room on the   40
other side of the house. Diane followed me as I left, profusely apologetic

with explanations: She was sorry, and she didn't mind him being with me once or twice a month, but this was getting ridiculous. I realized that I was Sam's part-time mistress — a member of the household somehow, but having no rights.

Then Diane went back into the master bedroom and Sam came in to   41 apologize, to say that there had been a mixup, that it was just this once, that he'd make it up to me, that he was sorry. And, of course, I forgave him, for there was nothing I wanted more than to relive the moment when he held me tightly and our love was a miracle and I was the only woman he wanted in the world, forever.

"Have you thought of going into therapy?" she jokes.   42

"As a matter of fact, I have," I say, sighing and rubbing my temples. "On   43 average, we black women have bigger, better problems than any other women alive. We bear the burden of being seen as pretenders to the thrones of both femininity and masculinity, endlessly mocked by the ambiguously gendered crown-of-thorns imagery of 'queen' — Madame Queen, snap queen, welfare queen, quota queen, Queenie Queen, *Queen* Queen Queen. We black women are figured more as stand-ins for men, sort of like reverse drag queens: women pretending to be women but more male than men — bare-breasted, sweat-glistened, plow-pulling, sole supporters of their families. Arnold Schwarzenegger and Sylvester Stallone meet Sojourner Truth, the *Real* Real Thing, the Ace-of-Spades Gender Card Herself, Thelma and Louise knocked up by Wesley Snipes, the ultimate hard-drinking, tobacco-growing-and-aspitting, nut-crushing ball-buster of all time.... I mean, think about it — how'd you like to go to the ball dressed like a walking cultural pathology? Wouldn't it make you just a wee bit tense?"

"But," she sputters, "but — you always seem so *strong!*"   44

We have just about completed our toilette. She looks at my hair as   45 though it were a rude construction of mud and twigs, bright glass beads, and flashy bits of tinfoil. I look at hers for what it is — the high-tech product of many hours of steam rollers, shine enhancers, body spritzers, perms, and about eighteen hundred watts of blow-dried effort. We gaze at each other with the deep disapproval of one gazing into a mirror. It is inconceivable to both of us that we have been friends for as long as we have. We shake our heads in sympathetic unison and sigh.

One last thing: It seems we have forgotten about shoes. It turns out that   46 my feet are much too big to fit into any of her sequined little evening slippers, so I wear my own sensible square-soled pumps. My prosaic feet, like overgrown roots, peek out from beneath the satiny folds of the perfect dress. She looks radiant; I feel dubious. Our chariot and her husband await. As we climb into the limousine, her husband lights up a cigar and holds forth on the reemerging popularity of same. My friend responds charmingly with a remarkably detailed production history of the Biedermeier humidor.

I do not envy her. I do not resent her. I do not hold my breath.   47

Analyzing This Selection

1. **THE WRITER'S METHOD**   Williams describes herself as a person "with an attitude." What is the author's tone or attitude in this essay? Choose three adjectives that fit, and explain your choice.

2. How do Williams's romantic dreams compare to the classic Cinderella fantasy?

3. What do you think are the strengths of this friendship? What might change if the friends were of the same color?

4. Do you think Williams is one of the "women who invented their own endings" (para. 8)? Using specific details from the essay to support your view, try to account for the differences between her romantic fantasies and the person she seems to be.

Analyzing Connections

5. Does friendship have different traits and meaning for men and women? Compare Williams and Tesich (see "Focusing on Friends," p. 153) for views about best friendships with their own sex. Which differences are more of personality or gender?

Analyzing by Writing

6. Parents often maintain fairy-tale expectations for their sons' and daughters' romantic lives, thinking that they will be magically awakened to adult life like Sleeping Beauty. Have you had to struggle against this or another fairy tale imposed by parents? Analyze the main features of the active myth, and explain how it is imposed on your life.

Leslie Lawrence

PROPELLED BY LOVE

LESLIE LAWRENCE (b. 1950), essayist and fiction writer, was raised in suburban Boston. She graduated from Oberlin College and obtained master's degrees in both teaching and creative writing. Her work has appeared in magazines such as the *Colorado Review*, the *Massachusetts Review*, and *Redbook*. Lawrence was awarded a National Endowment for the Arts fellowship. She has taught at Simmons College and currently teaches at Tufts University.

When I first met Corky, I had no use for him. I hated his name, which reminded me of that stocky, whistle-blowing camp counselor I had not known whether to admire or scorn; nor was I crazy about his breed. Cockers were squat, with drippy eyes and droopy lids — and this one was overweight and undertrained, an obsessive humper with a compulsion to follow his mistress everywhere. (It was she who interested me.)

They (Sandy and Cork) were living in a barn, while I and five other women were in a house a few yards away — all of us part of a mini writer's colony on the Cape.[1]... Short-haired and athletic, Sandy looked a little like that camp counselor, except for the bold hoop earrings and peppermint pink chenille bathrobe I studied from my second-story window. When she set out on a beer run, Corky made a reckless dash into her hatchback; when they returned, he careened into the kitchen, always sliding just past his bowl, an admirable move in a ballplayer, but not in someone approaching a snack.

By the following summer, Sandy and I were a couple and Corky had become tolerable to me, partly because under my influence he'd lost weight and gained manners. When I rented a place in Vermont, I was not averse to having him full-time, even though Sandy would be up only on weekends. A veterinarian's daughter, I didn't have it in me to deny any dog his summer in the country; still, I wasn't overjoyed. Instead of roaming through the woods with the doggier dogs who lived up the road, Corky would sit glumly by my feet, hour after hour, as I wrote. I was still daunted by my new computer, and every time I shifted positions, sighed, saved, or,

---

[1]Cape Cod, Massachusetts. [All notes are the editor's.]

God forbid, printed, he'd explode in anticipation of an outing. Nevertheless, I remember searching the Grand Union for the shadiest spot and feeling touched by his obvious delight when I returned with my bundles. I remember appreciating his presence during lonely nights of presidential conventions and summer Olympics. Most of all, I remember trying to train him — first to eat his biscuits in the kitchen, then to stay between me and the road's shoulder so that we could run without a leash. These were not easy tasks. No puppy, no genius, Corky had never been properly trained; nor had I ever trained an animal. I consulted no books and when, for example, I couldn't decide what the command should be ("Right," "Inside," "Shoulder"?) I felt unqualified, as if I were asking too much, not upholding my end of the bargain. His confused, pleading eyes shamed me. I became disdainful of his desire to please. Sometimes my anger frightened me; I shouted and hit him or nudged him into line with my leg, wondering if these were legitimate tactics, later suspecting I was acting out some other drama, getting just a little pleasure out of tyrannizing him. In any case, eventually he learned. We loved our runs, and the hours of training, showing us both the best and worst of each other, seemed to solidify our bond. About halfway into that summer, I noticed I began planning my afternoon outings with Corky in mind.

In truth, our tastes and inclinations were not so dissimilar; nevertheless, 4 there were days I quit work early or went one place rather than another because I knew he would enjoy it more. And when I realized this — that I had become a person capable of making sacrifices, however minor, for a dog who wasn't mine and wasn't the kind of dog I would have chosen — and later when I realized it was no longer a question of putting his desires before mine, because his pleasure had become my own — then I knew I wanted a baby.

I was thirty-three, had been feeling the urge for several years, but had 5 been plagued with doubts (not only over if/how I could manage having a baby if I lived as a lesbian but also over whether my desire was any more than some romantic notion). I knew I liked doing things I was good at and I didn't know if I'd be good at all that feeding, changing, rocking, toting, training, loving.

I had had little experience: I am a younger child, I rarely baby-sat. Mac, 6 the cairn terrier of my childhood, officially belonged to my sister — though he did provide some experience.

Once we were alone in the back patio. "I'm doing this because I love 7 you," I said as I slapped him hard. "This hurts me more than it hurts you," I added, hitting him again, my hand stinging. Had he run into the street? I believed he needed punishing. At the same time, I knew there was pleasure in the sting, in reigning over, in knowing better, in being the perpetrator instead of the child who was often victim to her parents' spanks and scoldings. Perhaps there was also a sense of loss: upbraiding another, I could no longer feel unmitigated rage when my parents did the same to me.

I also remember stroking Mac's wiry wheat-colored hair, his velvety pink   8
underbelly, perhaps venturing to his wobbly balls. My hand felt propelled
by a force outside my will and I connected this to the neighborhood girl
who "necked for hours" in her boyfriend's car. I had disapproved of her —
not because I thought necking wrong or dangerous as my parents seemed
to, but because it seemed so incredibly boring. Nevertheless, returning
again and again to Mac's body, I began to wonder if there might be something to it.

I was a freshman in college when I got the call Mac died. How I cried —   9
knowing even then that my grief wasn't only for him but for my childhood,
now over.

Parents and children, beginnings and ends, love, sex, power and respon-   10
sibility — dogs have often been the locus of these great themes for me.
Early on, I saw puppies come out of their cloudy sacs, watched my father
slice open a dog on our kitchen table; and (for some reason I can't remember) my parents and I once drove to a New Year's Eve party with a dead
dog in the trunk of our car.

The relationship I formed with Corky that first summer was unlike any   11
I'd had with a dog — or anyone. I had full responsibility, his complete devotion and obedience. Wherever I went, he went and this, especially, thrilled
me. It was like discovering masturbation — feeling forevermore freed from
getting into bad things with men just because I needed the sex. Now I no
longer needed them for protection. A woman with a dog could go places a
woman alone — or even two women could not go. So maybe a woman with
a dog could live alone, or with another woman? Maybe two women and a
dog could even raise a child together?

I'm not saying Corky was the clincher — but he did play a role.   12

My plan for my seventh month of pregnancy was to spend it in my be-   13
loved rented cabin in New Hampshire....As in previous years, Corky was
to be my daily companion, Sandy my weekend one, but because I had
some social event on the way up, we decided Cork would drive up later
with Sandy.

It was a different kind of drive without him there squashed among my   14
stuff in the back seat. Frequently, I would glance back, a reflex, surprised
not to see his beautiful muzzle on the armrest, his eyes open, bored. How
I missed his steadfast company, even in its most silent, stationary variety!
With him, a "solo" trip never felt lonely, it felt airy and grand. And when
we turned at the fire station in Dublin, to climb the winding road to Har-
risville, he would always rise, circle in his spot, then hang his head out the
window, sniffing in whatever let him know we were near. (Water, I suspect,
muddy, fishy.) Seeing him like that — his mouth open and relaxed so he
looked as if he were laughing — my own excitement would rise.

Once we arrived, he would dash to the back porch where we kept his   15 food the year before, then stick to my heels as I unloaded the car, his whole rear-half wiggling. When that task was complete, we'd walk down the mowing (the acres of downward sloping meadow in front of the cabin) and he'd run ahead just so far, disappearing in the tall grass so that I could only see him when he leaped, which he did every few seconds, looking his most graceful then, his most doggishly gorgeous. From there, we'd head down the road toward the lake. Midway, at the brook, he'd clamber down for a drink, and when we got to our beach he would sit like a statue guarding my backpack while I swam, glancing back often in search of the blue of the pack, the burnished red of his form. My beacon, my home plate, my pal.

Not that it was so bad, arriving without him. "Different," I reported to   16 Sandy on the phone that night. "More intense in a way, with nothing to keep me from my thoughts, moods, rhythms. Interesting for a day or two, but I couldn't bear it much longer."

Early the next morning, Sandy called to say that Corky was blind. Just   17 like that. He'd gone to bed fine and woken up blind.

The news was shocking, but not altogether surprising. It had been more   18 than a year since we first noticed odd symptoms — brief sudden cries, sporadic trembling, difficulty jumping onto the couch; almost exactly a year since, in this same cabin, while trying to give him his heartworm pill, I had trouble opening his jaws and finally forced them, causing a terrible, reverberating howl. During this past year we'd taken him to three vets and had as many diagnoses — Horner's syndrome, temporal mandibular joint syndrome, arthritis. Of erratic health even before the more pointed signs of trouble began, Corky's off days over the last year had greatly increased, and while he continued most of his normal activities, it was becoming clear that something was wrong.

Sandy, usually rather stoic, was crying into the phone, and while this   19 made the situation seem less remote and more awful, it caused me to remain composed, and cold-hearted enough to feel — in addition to alarmed — disappointed, even a little annoyed. I had just one month to finish a final draft of that same old novel, one month to savor what I had just begun to understand I was about to lose: time to stare at the mowing and Mount Monadnock beyond, to listen to the faint dripping off the trees, the landlord's daughter playing her flute at the bottom of the hill, time to happily disappear into the green around me — and having just unpacked my computer I was now asked to return home.

"Take him to Angell[2] and call me back," I told Sandy, hoping the vet   20 would tell her she was mistaken, or if not that, would somehow restore Corky's sight with the speed in which it had disappeared.

When Sandy called back a few hours later, Corky was still blind, so I   21 headed back to Boston. On route, I tried to prepare myself. I'd seen a few

---

[2]Angell Memorial Animal Hospital.

blind dogs, could recognize that milky blue glaze, had always been impressed by how normal they otherwise appeared.

But the next morning, what I found was far from normal. There in a   22
ward at the end of many corridors in the famous Angell Memorial was Corky, resting in his habitual position, rear legs stuck out behind him, muzzle flat on the floor; and there he stayed as I walked eagerly toward him and called his name. There he stayed, three, maybe five seconds after I was standing in the cage right next to him. Finally, he roused himself, but he did not jump up and down, wag or lick; he did not rub his flank against my legs or even position his head so that my hand would stroke and scratch it. Of course, I had never even noticed that he *always* leaned against a leg, but now that he didn't, it seemed his most essential, most defining characteristic. Though subsequently he would get much sicker, that moment was the most devastating to me. I burst into tears, sobbing loudly, unabashedly in front of the warden and the couple visiting a splinted dog in a neighboring cage. "Corky," I keened. "It's me. Me!" But still he didn't recognize my voice, my smell, my touch. I put on his leash anyway, sobbing still as we passed the now enviable couple, and I led him through the many hallways, watching helplessly as he banged into walls and corners. The second we were out the front door, he took a pee that went on and on, as if he'd been holding it in since his admission the day before. I ached for him, but was also slightly buoyed to realize perhaps all was not lost. Pride? Dignity? Slavish adherence to overtraining? Whatever it was, that pee gave me hope. And once we were safely down the stairs and in the lot for his walk, though he continued to stumble and bang his muzzle against curbs, car fenders and tree trunks, though he still did not seem to know me or enjoy the outing at all, I was somewhat comforted by the task I saw before me: I would help Corky learn to get around.

Over the next couple of days Sandy and I visited several times more,   23
sometimes separately, sometimes together. Corky had started the steroids to reduce the swelling of whatever was pressing against his optic nerve. He still seemed depressed, but at least now he'd rise when we arrived, sniff, and rub. Out in the lot, we studied his movements, taking turns playing optimist and pessimist. "Did you see that? He can see!" "What about that? Blind as a bat!" I remember once feeling certain he could see, but when the doctor shined a light in both eyes, he shook his head saying the dog was just learning to compensate.

Yet within a few more days, Corky *was* seeing, first just light and in just   24
one eye, soon much better. News from the spinal tap wasn't as good: "Abnormal fluid probably indicating a kind of encephalitis, inflamation of the lining of the brain. Three to six months." If the disease didn't kill him, the steroids would.

During these weeks, the crisis taking place outside my belly had more   25
reality than the drama inside. Corky took all our time and energy. Sandy and I both found it disconcerting — how completely absorbed we were in

our dog, how remote the impending baby felt. I worried that maybe I wasn't as ready for a child as I had presumed. And I often thought back to that moment in the animal hospital when I burst into tears. I couldn't imagine responding in any other way....

Now, when I found a moment to think about the soon-to-be baby, I had　26
new reason to be skeptical of my abilities. On the other hand, I think Sandy and I were both vaguely aware that the present ordeal might prove good training for parenting. Certainly it showed we could act as a team, gather information, make decisions, dish out money, put the rest of our lives on hold when the health of our beloved was concerned.

Within about a week, Corky recovered enough to spend a few weeks　27
with me at the cabin. I remember throwing sticks and learning to laugh as he scurried around searching for them. Also, his hearing was going and when I called him he would look everywhere but where I was. This, too, I learned to chuckle at. Our walks down the mowing, though still enjoyable, were tainted by my fear that I would lose him; for not only couldn't he see me or hear my calls, but in the tall grass, I couldn't see him, except when he leaped. Yes, he still occasionally summoned the élan to leap.

With Sam due in six weeks, Corky and I, and Sandy part-time, stayed in　28
a friend's house in Hull, a dilapidated shore town close to Boston. Hull had the scruffiest beach I'd ever seen, yet I came to love the somewhat treacherous walks my increasingly bulky body took there with Corky, now nearly blind again. The walks would have been safer and more peaceful if I'd used a leash, but I was beginning to accept the doctor's prognosis and wanted his last days to be happy and free. And so, by shouting above the surf, I, his seeing-eye woman, tried to steer him clear of the broken bottles, craggy rocks, and all manner of hazardous detritus (as well as the beckoning dead gulls and fish), tried to maintain between us the distance that he, with working eyes and ears, would have naturally kept. It was one of the things I most loved about him — that distance — never (since that first summer) too close to crowd me, nor too far to worry me. Now, he had to rely on smell, and my faintly perceived commands. It was a sport almost, one at which we both quickly improved — though not without stress. I remember once running after him, worried that perhaps I was jostling Sam too much.

It was during that month in Hull that Corky began peeing indoors.　　29

For twenty-eight hours I labored and pushed; then Sam was delivered by　30
C-section. After the initial joy of seeing him greet the world with curious eyes and a healthy wail, I felt more like sleeping than taking care of anyone else. I wished I'd known this wasn't so unusual. I felt guilty, abnormal, like maybe I wasn't cut out for this after all.

During this time, and the four-day hospital stay that followed, dog finally　31
took a back seat to baby, though I do remember asking about Corky and feeling grateful my father was around to oversee his care.

When we returned from the hospital that hot August morning with a   32
new baby, Corky was too sick to feel the full sting of jealousy. (It must have
been in one of his better periods that I looked up to find one of Sam's stray
pacifiers held firmly and correctly, glumly and defiantly, in Corky's mouth.)
He had a vestibular condition now, affecting balance which caused him to
stoop and circle so relentlessly that sometimes it looked as if his head and
tail were joined. He couldn't walk straight; he couldn't climb stairs. By day
eight, Corky was back in the hospital, and during the gala *bris*,[3] I was glad
not to have to contend with him.

Not that Sam immediately took his place in my heart. Not at all. The   33
guests came and went, as did my parents, Sandy went back to work, and I,
still post-operative, began relatively solo care of a dying dog and helpless
infant. The infant required more constant attention. So constant, that I frequently recalled the sardonic chuckle of a friend after I had confessed that
it was loving a dog that had made me want a baby. "Better stick to dogs,"
she had said. "I don't think you'll find the two at all comparable." I also
recalled my mother's skepticism when I first told her I wanted a child. She
wasn't sure I had the temperament. Too selfish, too rigid, too stuck in my
ways. She didn't say it exactly. But it was what she was thinking — I was
sure because it was what I was thinking; still I was annoyed not to have her
full endorsement. Now, while sometimes (usually when he was sleeping) I
drank in the pleasure of Sam's miraculousness, mostly I thought: that
chuckling friend was right, my mother was right.

One morning, within the first few weeks, rightly suspecting I would later   34
be unable to explain just how impossible this life was, I attempted to record
my activities. That I was able to write two pages proved it was one of the
more manageable mornings; still, even now, the document brings it all
back: the tedium and frustration, the slapstick comedy of that damn breast
pump, the way time was minced into thirty-second bits. Here's my entry
from 8:45–9:02: *Sammy fusses, pick him up while reading newspaper, I realize Corky needs heartworm pill. Call Sandy, put Sammy down, go to bathroom to write this, Sammy starts screaming before I finish my business, Corky
comes into bathroom, Sammy keeps screaming, volume increases, I leave
bathroom before finished, Corky seems disturbed by the crying.*

One beautiful fall day, after the usual grueling morning, I was to meet   35
my mother's group for a picnic. It was a short walk, maybe thirty yards,
from the parking lot to the grassy knoll where we were to gather, but I
couldn't figure out how to transport a blind/deaf/partially crippled dog, *and*
an infant, *and* my takeout lunch (a rare indulgence) without leaving anyone or thing unattended. In the end, I lost only the expendable; still, seeing that gorgeous goat cheese sandwich sprawled on the blacktop I was
reduced to tears.

---

[3]The Jewish ceremony at circumcision.

In that moment, as well as the earlier one on the beach and many sub- 36
sequent ones, Corky and Sam were in direct conflict. Yet I never resented
this. Mostly I was grateful to have both jobs — even when we began taking
Corky to a specialist in New Hampshire. It was an eighty-minute drive each
way and sometimes I went twice a week, but in truth, because Sam *always*
slept in the car and I often drove around aimlessly just so he'd sleep, I was
happy to have a more legitimate reason to spend hours there where I could
hear myself think. And there was another reason I liked having to care for
both: as Sam's mother, I was often insecure, but as Corky's I usually felt
like the vet's daughter.

We have two snapshots of Sam and Corky amidst blue-and-white striped 37
sheets. Sam asleep, intact, comfy and safe; Corky, awake, curled close to
him, looking miserable with drippy eyes and the skin on one side of his
face droopy and slack. We were touched by how Corky, perhaps in part
because he was so sick, was able to adjust to our new family, find his place
as Sam's guardian. It must have been that night, perhaps the act of taking
the photo induced the thought, it came to me in exactly these words: *This
is what it feels like to live a life propelled by love.* It was a new (and sadly,
rather fleeting) feeling and I liked it. During another moment at about this
time, one, I suspect, in which I was dealing with both dog's and child's flu-
ids, I remember a less satisfying but more amusing thought: *Look at me, the
nurse, a veritable sister of mercy!*

In January, when I daily injected Corky with gentomycin, "making a 38
tent" with the scruffy skin bordering the neck, I was no longer into the
irony. I was grave, proud, and very tender.

We lived that month in the country of illness. Gentomycin, Prednisone, 39
Baytrill, Clavimox, Tribrisson, abscess, kidney function, spinal taps, tense
waits for lab results, phone calls to doctors from restaurants and gas stations, nonstop mental gymnastics and medical detective work. Unspoken
questions about when to throw in the towel.

And eventually, spoken ones. 40

One Monday morning in late January, when he could no longer open 41
his mouth, wouldn't take the pills hidden in peanut butter, walked away
from the bowl of Campbell's soup, and we couldn't think of any way to get
his medicine down, we called the local vet and made an appointment for
three-fifteen.

I got home from work around two. Corky was lying on the blue tile of 42
the bathroom and I sat beside him, stroking him, silently saying good-bye,
until, around two-fifteen when he rose and headed into the kitchen and
began to eat. When Sandy arrived, we called the vet and canceled. Friends
were expected for dinner. Earlier, we'd thought of calling it off, but now we
were glad we hadn't. It was good to have a house full of people to celebrate
what felt like Corky's resurrection. Sandy and I kept glancing at him and
then each other — so happy we were to have him with us still!

But the next day, the babysitter said he vomited three times, and that 43
night around midnight we were awakened by his labored breathing. We
gave him some water and then he started heaving as if he were trying to
vomit but couldn't. I injected an extra dose of dex, hoping it would somehow help but it didn't. He heaved and rasped, obviously suffering, and I
thought he might die any minute and I hoped he would. But he didn't.
And when I called Angell, the only place that would be open at one A.M.,
I was told they had had a power failure. I didn't know whether emergency
lights were sufficient for euthanasia, but the image of the dark hospital was
such that I never even broached the subject. I moved into Sam's room so I
wouldn't have to hear Corky struggling, and I dreamt something about
going out in a rowboat.

In the morning, he was still alive; in fact, his breathing seemed easier. 44
But during the night, we had resolved to make the appointment first thing
in the morning and so we did. Even though he seemed to be standing a
little straighter. Even though we saw a tiny wag. And then another. That's
why we felt grateful when Sandy saw that he couldn't eat, not even a
spoonful of cottage cheese. I only wished I had seen it myself — that
moment he turned away from the bowl.

After delivering Sam to a neighbor, we took Corky to the vet and held 45
him while she shaved his leg and inserted the needle.

Then Sandy and I took a walk around Fresh Pond, his favorite local 46
spot. And I was grateful it was already happening. Instead of seeing the
stooped oozing thing I'd taken there so recently, I saw him as he'd been in
the old days — robust, shiny, darting, leaping, his red fur making the snow
whiter, everything more beautiful still.

A friend came over later, brought flowers and muffins and told me of a 47
renowned Harvard psychiatrist who led bereavement groups for people
who'd lost pets. It was a useful bit of information. I never went, found my
own satisfactory ways of grieving, yet I needed to hear that someone reputable took my pain seriously. My visitor was sympathetic, both my ex-lover
and the vet who put him down wrote beautiful letters, but there were many
people who didn't understand the magnitude of this event. My boss, for
example, mother of two children, no dogs, could only say a cheery something like, "You'll see — how pale a dog will seem in comparison to Sam as
he grows."

Pale? Not the word I'd use. Yet, many times a day, I look at Sam's open- 48
mouthed smile, those teeth with their even spaces, the furl of his visibly
thinking forehead, I hear his outbursts of delight at the smallest things, and
I listen to his marvelous grammar ("John bited me") and logic ("I can't
wear mine mittens because then they won't swing!"). Or, "You know what's
really sad Mom! When an animal dies while it's still living." I open my
arms for his amorous hugs and familiar smell, we whisper in the dark, and
I try to teach him what I know and learn what he has to teach — yes, many

times a day, I think, my boss was right: no comparison between dogs and children!

And just a few weeks ago, when Sam and I spent the day at the beach with the friend who had brought the muffins and flowers, she asked, "Is it hard, now, to imagine why you felt so devastated at the death of your dog?" "Yes," I answered, knowing I was unwilling to even imagine the loss of Sam. "And no," I added, thinking, I will not betray myself by belittling the love I felt for Corky — even if much of it was just the love I felt for myself finally learning how to love so well.

I am writing this from the cabin in New Hampshire. Sam is almost four. As with my love for Corky, my love for him was not immediate. I felt no instant bonding, railed against all the literature and oral history that taught me to expect that; was deeply grateful to those who admitted it took them some time or it didn't but they knew perfectly nice people who didn't really bond until the kid started talking. It happened sooner for me; but it took some time. Those first few months, more than once I found my arm reaching towards *his* shirt buttons when it was time to nurse. I'm still craving nurture; I still think mothering is the hardest thing. Yes, Boss: kids are infinitely more interesting and rewarding — but they're that much more demanding and infuriating. They don't get "trained" in a summer, often not in a lifetime. They rarely keep that perfect distance; more often, they're on top of you or out of sight. To carve a path to yourself (or anyone else) while in their presence is a mighty task. Sometimes I think back to the mother I once thought I wanted to be. In college, she was the bearded professor's wife. Big-boned, wearing a flour-dusted denim skirt, she appeared with fresh bread and cider, then disappeared into the eat-in kitchen where she orchestrated a stupendous arts-and-crafts project with a brood of kids. Sandy and I are both professors in need of wives. I'm just grateful we don't have that eat-in kitchen; with our small counter separating kitchen from living/dining room, I couldn't disappear even if I wanted to. And I don't. It's been a rude awakening, but I'd rather be a guest at the party than the person who makes it happen; I'd rather buy a tacky Halloween costume than give up a day to make a marvelous original; I'm still working up my resolve to bake Sam's birthday cake this year (and here we're talking mix). To my embarrassment and genuine disappointment, my mother was right: I rarely have the equanimity to ride the waves of a messy, noisy house full of kids. With Corky, I usually felt at my best. Not so, with Sam. I've thrown more than a few tantrums since his appearance. Together we struggle to grow up.

It's early July. Soon the mowing will be full of blueberries Sandy and Sam and I will gather. That will remind me of when we scattered Corky's ashes. Heavier than I had imagined, they made a long, snaky path that lasted and lasted, so that days later, they were there still and I watched with horror and satisfaction as Sam, not yet a year and already so good with his opposing thumb, picked an ash-covered berry and popped it into his mouth.

Analyzing This Selection

1. What are the early steps in Lawrence's lifelong education about love? What additional steps does Corky require of her?

2. **THE WRITER'S METHOD**   Lawrence assumes that readers instantly accept her lesbianism — or does the essay persuade us to accept it? How is the issue introduced and developed? Does the essay present an implicit thesis about lesbian love?

3. The concluding paragraph focuses on Sam while, the author says, "I watched with horror and satisfaction." Explain the complexity of Lawrence's reaction to the moment. Is this conclusion appropriate to the essay?

4. **THE WRITER'S METHOD**   Frequently, essays about dogs or babies oversentimentalize both subjects. How does Lawrence avoid sentimentalities about Corky and Sam? What aspects of love do her nonsentimentalizing methods show us?

Analyzing Connections

5. Lawrence and Daum (see "On the Fringes of the Physical World," p. 143) each write about the educating of their hearts. Though Daum does not have to deal with family responsibilities, what self-knowledge does she examine that Lawrence does not examine in this essay?

Analyzing by Writing

6. Analyze your connection to an animal that has had a lasting effect on your character. Consider either a long-term connection with a pet or horse you loved, or a brief encounter that occurred during a hunting trip or another confrontation with wildlife. Be sure to give details that establish the animal's vivid qualities. Like Lawrence, explain the animal's role in your education about important themes in your life.

Jonathan Rauch

FOR BETTER OR WORSE?

Jonathan Rauch (b. 1960) graduated from Yale University. His articles about economics and politics have appeared in the *Atlantic Monthly, Fortune, Harper's,* and the *National Journal,* where he is presently a contributing editor. He recounts his visiting-scholar's impressions of contemporary Japan in his first book, *The Outnation: A Search for the Soul of Japan* (1992). Rauch examines American economic and ideological threats to democracy in *Kindly Inquisitors: The New Attacks on Free Thought* (1993) and *Government's End: Why Washington Stopped Working* (1999). The following tightly argued selection supporting gay marriage appeared in the *New Republic.*

Whatever else marriage may or may not be, it is certainly falling apart. 1
Half of today's marriages end in divorce, and, far more costly, many never begin — leaving mothers poor, children fatherless and neighborhoods chaotic. With timing worthy of Neville Chamberlain, homosexuals have chosen this moment to press for the right to marry. What's more, Hawaii's courts are moving toward letting them do so. I'll believe in gay marriage in America when I see it, but if Hawaii legalizes it, even temporarily, the uproar over this final insult to a besieged institution will be deafening.

Whether gay marriage makes sense — and whether straight marriage 2
makes sense — depends on what marriage is actually for. Current secular thinking on this question is shockingly sketchy. Gay activists say: marriage is for love, and we love each other, therefore we should be able to marry. Traditionalists say: marriage is for children, and homosexuals do not (or should not) have children, therefore you should not be able to marry. That, unfortunately, pretty well covers the spectrum. I say "unfortunately" because both views are wrong. They misunderstand and impoverish the social meaning of marriage.

So what is marriage for? Modern marriage is, of course, based upon tra- 3
ditions that religion helped to codify and enforce. But religious doctrine has no special standing in the world of secular law and policy (the "Christian nation" crowd notwithstanding). If we want to know what and whom marriage is for in modern America, we need a sensible secular doctrine.

At one point, marriage in secular society was largely a matter of busi- 4
ness: cementing family ties, providing social status for men and economic

support for women, conferring dowries, and so on. Marriages were typically arranged, and "love" in the modern sense was no prerequisite. In Japan, remnants of this system remain, and it works surprisingly well. Couples stay together because they view their marriage as a partnership: an investment in social stability for themselves and their children. Because Japanese couples don't expect as much emotional fulfillment as we do, they are less inclined to break up. They also take a somewhat more relaxed attitude toward adultery. What's a little extracurricular love provided that each partner is fulfilling his or her many other marital duties?

In the West, of course, love is a defining element. The notion of lifelong 5 love is charming, if ambitious, and certainly love is a desirable element of marriage. In society's eyes, however, it cannot be the defining element. You may or may not love your husband, but the two of you are just as married either way. You may love your mistress, but that certainly doesn't make her your spouse. Love helps make sense of marriage emotionally, but it is not terribly important in making sense of marriage from the point of view of social policy.

If love does not define the purpose of secular marriage, what does? Nei- 6 ther the law nor secular thinking provides a clear answer. Today marriage is almost entirely a voluntary arrangement whose contents are up to the people making the deal. There are few if any behaviors that automatically end a marriage. If a man beats his wife, which is about the worst thing he can do to her, he may be convicted of assault, but his marriage is not automatically dissolved. Couples can be adulterous ("open") yet remain married. They can be celibate, too; consummation is not required. All in all, it is an impressive and also rather astonishing victory for modern individualism that so important an institution should be so bereft of formal social instruction as to what should go on inside of it.

Secular society tells us only a few things about marriage. First, marriage 7 depends on the consent of the parties. Second, the parties are not children. Third, the number of parties is two. Fourth, one is a man and the other a woman. Within those rules a marriage is whatever anyone says it is.

Perhaps it is enough simply to say that marriage is as it is and should not 8 be tampered with. This sounds like a crudely reactionary position. In fact, however, of all the arguments against reforming marriage, it is probably the most powerful.

Call it a Hayekian argument, after the great libertarian economist F. A. 9 Hayek, who developed this line of thinking in his book *The Fatal Conceit.* In a market system, the prices generated by impersonal forces may not make sense from any one person's point of view, but they encode far more information than even the cleverest person could ever gather. In a similar fashion, human societies evolve rich and complicated webs of nonlegal rules in the form of customs, traditions and institutions. Like prices, they may seem irrational or arbitrary. But the very fact that they are the customs that have evolved implies that they embody a practical logic that may not be apparent to even a sophisticated analyst. And the web of custom cannot be torn apart and reordered at will because once its internal logic is violated it falls apart. Intellectuals, such as Marxists or feminists, who seek to deconstruct and rationally rebuild social traditions, will produce not better order but chaos.

So the Hayekian view argues strongly against gay marriage. It says that 10 the current rules may not be best and may even be unfair. But they are all we have, and, once you say that marriage need not be male-female, soon marriage will stop being anything at all. You can't mess with the formula without causing unforeseen consequences, possibly including the implosion of the institution of marriage itself.

However, there are problems with the Hayekian position. It is untenable 11 in its extreme form and unhelpful in its milder version. In its extreme form, it implies that no social reforms should ever be undertaken. Indeed, no laws should be passed, because they interfere with the natural evolution of social mores. How could Hayekians abolish slavery? They would probably note that slavery violates fundamental moral principles. But in so doing they would establish a moral platform from which to judge social rules, and thus acknowledge that abstracting social debate from moral concerns is not possible.

If the ban on gay marriage were only mildly unfair, and if the costs of 12 changing it were certain to be enormous, then the ban could stand on Hayekian grounds. But, if there is any social policy today that has a fair claim to be scaldingly inhumane, it is the ban on gay marriage. As conservatives tirelessly and rightly point out, marriage is society's most fundamental institution. To bar any class of people from marrying as they choose is an extraordinary deprivation. When not so long ago it was illegal in parts of America for blacks to marry whites, no one could claim that this was a trivial disenfranchisement. Granted, gay marriage raises issues that interracial marriage does not; but no one can argue that the deprivation is a minor one.

To outweigh such a serious claim it is not enough to say that gay mar- 13 riage might lead to bad things. Bad things happened as a result of legalizing contraception, but that did not make it the wrong thing to do. Besides, it seems doubtful that extending marriage to, say, another 3 or 5 percent of the population would have anything like the effects that no-fault divorce has had, to say nothing of contraception. By now, the "traditional" understanding of marriage has been sullied in all kinds of ways. It is hard to think of a bigger affront to tradition, for instance, than allowing married women to own property independently of their husbands or allowing them to charge their husbands with rape. Surely it is unfair to say that marriage may be reformed for the sake of anyone and everyone except homosexuals, who must respect the dictates of tradition.

Faced with these problems, the milder version of the Hayekian argu- 14 ment says not that social traditions shouldn't be tampered with at all, but that they shouldn't be tampered with lightly. Fine. In this case, no one is talking about casual messing around; both sides have marshaled their arguments with deadly seriousness. Hayekians surely have to recognize that appeals to blind tradition and to the risks inherent in social change do not, a priori, settle anything in this instance. They merely warn against frivolous change.

So we turn to what has become the standard view of marriage's purpose. 15 Its proponents would probably like to call it a child-centered view, but it is actually an antigay view, as will become clear. Whatever you call it, it is the view of marriage that is heard most often, and in the context of the debate over gay marriage it is heard almost exclusively. In its most straightforward form it goes as follows (I quote from James Q. Wilson's fine book *The Moral Sense*):

> A family is not an association of independent people; it is a human commitment designed to make possible the rearing of moral and healthy children. Governments care — or ought to care — about families for this reason, and scarcely for any other.

Wilson speaks about "family" rather than "marriage" as such, but one 16 may, I think, read him as speaking of marriage without doing any injustice to his meaning. The resulting proposition — government ought to care about marriage almost entirely because of children — seems reasonable. But there are problems. The first, obviously, is that gay couples may have children, whether through adoption, prior marriage or (for lesbians) artificial insemination. Leaving aside the thorny issue of gay adoption, the point is that if the mere presence of children is the test, then homosexual relationships can certainly pass it.

You might note, correctly, that heterosexual marriages are more likely to 17 produce children than homosexual ones. When granting marriage licenses to heterosexuals, however, we do not ask how likely the couple is to have children. We assume that they are entitled to get married whether or not they end up with children. Understanding this, conservatives often make an interesting move. In seeking to justify the state's interest in marriage, they shift from the actual presence of children to the anatomical possibility of making them. Hadley Arkes, a political science professor and prominent opponent of homosexual marriage, makes the case this way:

> The traditional understanding of marriage is grounded in the "natural teleology of the body" — in the inescapable fact that only a man and a woman, and only two people, not three, can generate a child. Once marriage is detached from that natural teleology of the body, what ground of principle would thereafter confine marriage to two people rather than some larger grouping? That is, on what ground of principle would the law reject the claim of a gay couple that their love is not confined to a coupling of two, but that they are woven into a larger ensemble with yet another person or two?

What he seems to be saying is that, where the possibility of natural chil- 18 dren is nil, the meaning of marriage is nil. If marriage is allowed between members of the same sex, then the concept of marriage has been emptied of content except to ask whether the parties love each other. Then anything goes, including polygamy. This reasoning presumably is what those opposed to gay marriage have in mind when they claim that, once gay marriage is legal, marriage to pets will follow close behind.

But Arkes and his sympathizers make two mistakes. To see them, break 19 down the claim into two components: (1) Two-person marriage derives its special status from the anatomical possibility that the partners can create natural children; and (2) Apart from (1), two-person marriage has no purpose sufficiently strong to justify its special status. That is, absent justification (1), anything goes.

The first proposition is wholly at odds with the way society actually views 20 marriage. Leave aside the insistence that natural, as opposed to adopted, children define the importance of marriage. The deeper problem, apparent right away, is the issue of sterile heterosexual couples. Here the "anatomical possibility" crowd has a problem, for a homosexual union is, anatomically speaking, nothing but one variety of sterile union and no different even in principle: a woman without a uterus has no more potential for giving birth than a man without a vagina.

It may sound like carping to stress the case of barren heterosexual mar- 21 riage: the vast majority of newlywed heterosexual couples, after all, can have children and probably will. But the point here is fundamental. There are far more sterile heterosexual unions in America than homosexual ones. The "anatomical possibility" crowd cannot have it both ways. If the possibility of children is what gives meaning to marriage, then a postmenopausal woman who applies for a marriage license should be turned away at the courthouse door. What's more, she should be hooted at and condemned for stretching the meaning of marriage beyond its natural basis and so reducing the institution to frivolity. People at the Family Research Council or Concerned Women for America should point at her and say, "If she can marry, why not polygamy?"

Obviously, the "anatomical" conservatives do not say this, because they 22 are sane. They instead flail around, saying that sterile men and women were at least born with the right-shaped parts for making children, and so on. Their position is really a nonposition. It says that the "natural children" rationale defines marriage when homosexuals are involved but not when heterosexuals are involved. When the parties to union are sterile heterosexuals, the justification for marriage must be something else. But what?

Now arises the oddest part of the "anatomical" argument. Look at propo- 23 sition (2) above. It says that, absent the anatomical justification for marriage, anything goes. In other words, it dismisses the idea that there might be other good reasons for society to sanctify marriage above other kinds of relationships. Why would anybody make this move? I'll hazard a guess: to exclude homosexuals. Any rationale that justifies sterile heterosexual marriages can also apply to homosexual ones. For instance, marriage makes women more financially secure. Very nice, say the conservatives. But that rationale could be applied to lesbians, so it's definitely out.

The end result of this stratagem is perverse to the point of being funny.   24
The attempt to ground marriage in children (or the anatomical possibility thereof) falls flat. But, having lost that reason for marriage, the antigay people can offer no other. In their fixation on excluding homosexuals, they leave themselves no consistent justification for the privileged status of *het-erosexual* marriage. They thus tear away any coherent foundation that sec-ular marriage might have, which is precisely the opposite of what they claim they want to do. If they have to undercut marriage to save it from homosexuals, so be it!

For the record, I would be the last to deny that children are one central   25
reason for the privileged status of marriage. When men and women get together, children are a likely outcome; and, as we are learning in ever more unpleasant ways, when children grow up without two parents, trouble ensues. Children are not a trivial reason for marriage; they just cannot be the only reason.

What are the others? It seems to me that the two strongest candidates are   26
these: domesticating men and providing reliable caregivers. Both purposes are critical to the functioning of a humane and stable society, and both are much better served by marriage — that is, by one-to-one lifelong commit-ment — than by any other institution.

Civilizing young males is one of any society's biggest problems. Wher-   27
ever unattached males gather in packs, you see no end of trouble: wildings in Central Park, gangs in Los Angeles, soccer hooligans in Britain, skin-heads in Germany, fraternity hazings in universities, grope-lines in the mil-itary and, in a different but ultimately no less tragic way, the bathhouses and wanton sex of gay San Francisco or New York in the 1970s.

For taming men, marriage is unmatched. "Of all the institutions   28
through which men may pass — schools, factories, the military — marriage has the largest effect," Wilson writes in *The Moral Sense*. (A token of the casualness of current thinking about marriage is that the man who wrote those words could, later in the very same book, say that government should care about fostering families for "scarcely any other" reason than children.) If marriage — that is, the binding of men into couples — did nothing else, its power to settle men, to keep them at home and out of trouble, would be ample justification for its special status.

Of course, women and older men don't generally travel in marauding or   29
orgiastic packs. But in their case the second rationale comes into play. A second enormous problem for society is what to do when someone is beset by some sort of burdensome contingency. It could be cancer, a broken back, unemployment or depression; it could be exhaustion from work or stress under pressure. If marriage has any meaning at all, it is that, when

you collapse from a stroke, there will be at least one other person whose "job" is to drop everything and come to your aid; or that when you come home after being fired by the postal service there will be someone to persuade you not to kill the supervisor.

Obviously, both rationales — the need to settle males and the need to 30 have people looked after — apply to sterile people as well as fertile ones, and apply to childless couples as well as to ones with children. The first explains why everybody feels relieved when the town delinquent gets married, and the second explains why everybody feels happy when an aging widow takes a second husband. From a social point of view, it seems to me, both rationales are far more compelling as justifications of marriage's special status than, say, love. And both of them apply to homosexuals as well as to heterosexuals.

Take the matter of settling men. It is probably true that women and chil- 31 dren, more than just the fact of marriage, help civilize men. But that hardly means that the settling effect of marriage on homosexual men is negligible. To the contrary, being tied to a committed relationship plainly helps stabilize gay men. Even without marriage, coupled gay men have steady sex partners and relationships that they value and therefore tend to be less wanton. Add marriage, and you bring a further array of stabilizing influences. One of the main benefits of publicly recognized marriage is that it binds couples together not only in their own eyes but also in the eyes of society at large. Around the partners is woven a web of expectations that they will spend nights together, go to parties together, take out mortgages together, buy furniture at Ikea together, and so on — all of which helps tie them together and keep them off the streets and at home. Surely that is a very good thing, especially as compared to the closet-gay culture of furtive sex with innumerable partners in parks and bathhouses.

The other benefit of marriage — caretaking — clearly applies to homo- 32 sexuals. One of the first things many people worry about when coming to terms with their homosexuality is: Who will take care of me when I'm ailing or old? Society needs to care about this, too, as the AIDS crisis has made horribly clear. If that crisis has shown anything, it is that homosexuals can and will take care of each other, sometimes with breathtaking devotion — and that no institution can begin to match the care of a devoted partner. Legally speaking, marriage creates kin. Surely society's interest in kin-creation is strongest of all for people who are unlikely to be supported by children in old age and who may well be rejected by their own parents in youth.

Gay marriage, then, is far from being a mere exercise in political point- 33 making or rights-mongering. On the contrary, it serves two of the three social purposes that make marriage so indispensable and irreplaceable for heterosexuals. Two out of three may not be the whole ball of wax, but it is more than enough to give society a compelling interest in marrying off homosexuals.

There is no substitute. Marriage is the *only* institution that adequately 34
serves these purposes. The power of marriage is not just legal but social. It
seals its promise with the smiles and tears of family, friends and neighbors.
It shrewdly exploits ceremony (big, public weddings) and money (expensive
gifts, dowries) to deter casual commitment and to make bailing out embarrassing. Stag parties and bridal showers signal that what is beginning is not
just a legal arrangement but a whole new stage of life. "Domestic partner"
laws do none of these things.

I'll go further: far from being a substitute for the real thing, marriage-lite 35
may undermine it. Marriage is a deal between a couple and society, not just
between two people: society recognizes the sanctity and autonomy of the
pair-bond, and in exchange each spouse commits to being the other's nurse,
social worker and policeman of first resort. Each marriage is its own little
society within society. Any step that weakens the deal by granting the legal
benefits of marriage without also requiring the public commitment is begging for trouble.

So gay marriage makes sense for several of the same reasons that straight 36
marriage makes sense. That would seem a natural place to stop. But the
logic of the argument compels one to go a twist further. If it is good for society to have people attached, then it is not enough just to make marriage
available. Marriage should also be *expected*. This, too, is just as true for
homosexuals as for heterosexuals. So, if homosexuals are justified in expecting access to marriage, society is equally justified in expecting them to use
it. I'm not saying that out-of-wedlock sex should be scandalous or that
people should be coerced into marrying. The mechanisms of expectation
are more subtle. When grandma cluck-clucks over a still-unmarried young
man, or when mom says she wishes her little girl would settle down, she is
expressing a strong and well-justified preference: one that is quietly echoed
in a thousand ways throughout society and that produces subtle but important pressure to form and sustain unions. This is a good and necessary thing,
and it will be as necessary for homosexuals as heterosexuals. If gay marriage
is recognized, single gay people over a certain age should not be surprised
when they are disapproved of or pitied. That is a vital part of what makes
marriage work. It's stigma as social policy.

If marriage is to work it cannot be merely a "lifestyle option." It must be 37
privileged. That is, it must be understood to be better, on average, than
other ways of living. Not mandatory, not good where everything else is bad,
but better: a general norm, rather than a personal taste. The biggest worry
about gay marriage, I think, is that homosexuals might get it but then mostly
not use it. Gay neglect of marriage wouldn't greatly erode the bonding
power of heterosexual marriage (remember, homosexuals are only a tiny
fraction of the population) — but it would certainly not help. And heterosexual society would rightly feel betrayed if, after legalization, homosexuals
treated marriage as a minority taste rather than as a core institution of life.
It is not enough, I think, for gay people to say we want the right to marry. If
we do not use it, shame on us.

Analyzing This Selection

1. In paragraphs 1 to 6 Rauch assesses traditional social meanings of marriage. Does he value what marriage means to you? Is he accurate about what marriage currently means to society?

2. **THE WRITER'S METHOD**   By acknowledging at least two major arguments against gay marriage, does Rauch strengthen or weaken his position favoring change? Which parts of the opposing arguments does he easily refute, and which points of the opposition remain persuasive to you?

3. Rauch adds two new validations for marriage. Are both reasons compelling? That is, do they motivate marriage?

4. What new social pressures would encourage gays and lesbians to marry? How and by whom do you think these pressures would be exercised?

Analyzing Connections

5. Rauch and Barbara Dafoe Whitehead (see "Women and the Future of Fatherhood," p. 113) see a function marriage performs especially for men. Whose recommendations better serve that function?

Analyzing by Writing

6. Rauch examines the social meaning of marriage. Its meaning probably changes in different phases of life and probably differs for men and for women. Noting these fluctuations from a social norm, examine the meaning of marriage that is evident in television situation comedies.

Raymond Carver

WHAT WE TALK ABOUT
WHEN WE TALK ABOUT LOVE

See the earlier headnote about Raymond Carver on page 69. This selection is the title story of his volume *What We Talk About When We Talk About Love* (1981). The story is a contemporary symposium (Plato's *Symposium*, an after-dinner conversation about love, seems to loom in the background) in which four people half-drunkenly discuss the peculiarities of loves they have known and witnessed.

My friend Mel McGinnis was talking. Mel McGinnis is a cardiologist, 1 and sometimes that gives him the right.

The four of us were sitting around his kitchen table drinking gin. Sun- 2 light filled the kitchen from the big windows behind the sink. There were Mel and me and his second wife, Teresa — Terri, we called her — and my wife, Laura. We lived in Albuquerque then. But we were all from somewhere else.

There was an ice bucket on the table. The gin and the tonic water kept 3 going around, and we somehow got on the subject of love. Mel thought real love was nothing less than spiritual love. He said he'd spent five years in a seminary before quitting to go to medical school. He said he still looked back on those years in the seminary as the most important years in his life.

Terri said the man she lived with before she lived with Mel loved her so 4 much he tried to kill her. Then Terri said, "He beat me up one night. He dragged me around the living room by my ankles. He kept saying, 'I love you, I love you, you bitch.' He went on dragging me around the living room. My head kept knocking on things." Terri looked around the table. "What do you do with love like that?"

She was a bone-thin woman with a pretty face, dark eyes, and brown 5 hair that hung down her back. She liked necklaces made of turquoise, and long pendant earrings.

"My God, don't be silly. That's not love, and you know it," Mel said. "I 6 don't know what you'd call it, but I sure know you wouldn't call it love."

"Say what you want to, but I know it was," Terri said. "It may sound 7 crazy to you, but it's true just the same. People are different, Mel. Sure, sometimes he may have acted crazy. Okay. But he loved me. In his own way maybe, but he loved me. There was love there, Mel. Don't say there wasn't."

Mel let out his breath. He held his glass and turned to Laura and me. "The man threatened to kill me," Mel said. He finished his drink and reached for the gin bottle. "Terri's a romantic. Terri's of the kick-me-so-I'll-know-you-love-me school. Terri, hon, don't look that way." Mel reached across the table and touched Terri's cheek with his fingers. He grinned at her. 8

"Now he wants to make up," Terri said. 9

"Make up what?" Mel said. "What is there to make up? I know what I know. That's all." 10

"How'd we get started on this subject, anyway?" Terri said. She raised her glass and drank from it. "Mel always has love on his mind," she said. "Don't you, honey?" She smiled, and I thought that was the last of it. 11

"I just wouldn't call Ed's behavior love. That's all I'm saying, honey," Mel said. "What about you guys?" Mel said to Laura and me. "Does that sound like love to you?" 12

"I'm the wrong person to ask," I said. "I didn't even know the man. I've only heard his name mentioned in passing. I wouldn't know. You'd have to know the particulars. But I think what you're saying is that love is an absolute." 13

Mel said, "The kind of love I'm talking about is. The kind of love I'm talking about, you don't try to kill people." 14

Laura said, "I don't know anything about Ed, or anything about the situation. But who can judge anyone else's situation?" 15

I touched the back of Laura's hand. She gave me a quick smile. I picked up Laura's hand. It was warm, the nails polished, perfectly manicured. I encircled the broad wrist with my fingers, and I held her. 16

"When I left, he drank rat poison," Terri said. She clasped her arms with her hands. "They took him to the hospital in Santa Fe. That's where we lived then, about ten miles out. They saved his life. But his gums went crazy from it. I mean they pulled away from his teeth. After that, his teeth stood out like fangs. My God," Terri said. She waited a minute, then let go of her arms and picked up her glass. 17

"What people won't do!" Laura said. 18

"He's out of the action now," Mel said. "He's dead." 19

Mel handed me the saucer of limes. I took a section, squeezed it over my drink, and stirred the ice cubes with my finger. 20

"It gets worse," Terri said. "He shot himself in the mouth. But he bungled that too. Poor Ed," she said. Terri shook her head. 21

"Poor Ed nothing," Mel said. "He was dangerous." 22

Mel was forty-five years old. He was tall and rangy with curly soft hair. His face and arms were brown from the tennis he played. When he was sober, his gestures, all his movements, were precise, very careful. 23

"He did love me though, Mel. Grant me that," Terri said. "That's all I'm   24
asking. He didn't love me the way you love me. I'm not saying that. But he
loved me. You can grant me that, can't you?"

"What do you mean, he bungled it?" I said.   25

Laura leaned forward with her glass. She put her elbows on the table   26
and held her glass in both hands. She glanced from Mel to Terri and
waited with a look of bewilderment on her open face, as if amazed that
such things happened to people you were friendly with.

"How'd he bungle it when he killed himself?" I said.   27

"I'll tell you what happened," Mel said. "He took his twenty-two pistol   28
he'd bought to threaten Terri and me with. Oh, I'm serious, the man was
always threatening. You should have seen the way we lived in those days.
Like fugitives. I even bought a gun myself. Can you believe it? A guy like
me? But I did. I bought one for self-defense and carried it in the glove
compartment. Sometimes I'd have to leave the apartment in the middle of
the night. To go to the hospital, you know? Terri and I weren't married
then, and my first wife had the house and kids, the dog, everything, and
Terri and I were living in this apartment here. Sometimes, as I say, I'd get
a call in the middle of the night and have to go into the hospital at two or
three in the morning. It'd be dark out there in the parking lot, and I'd break
into a sweat before I could even get to my car. I never knew if he was going
to come up out of the shrubbery or from behind a car and start shooting. I
mean, the man was crazy. He was capable of wiring a bomb, anything. He
used to call my service at all hours and say he needed to talk to the doctor,
and when I'd return the call, he'd say, 'Son of a bitch, your days are numbered.' Little things like that. It was scary, I'm telling you."

"I still feel sorry for him," Terri said.   29

"It sounds like a nightmare," Laura said. "But what exactly happened   30
after he shot himself?"

Laura is a legal secretary. We'd met in a professional capacity. Before we   31
knew it, it was a courtship. She's thirty-five, three years younger than I am.
In addition to being in love, we like each other and enjoy one another's
company. She's easy to be with.

"What happened?" Laura said.   32

Mel said, "He shot himself in the mouth in his room. Someone heard   33
the shot and told the manager. They came in with a passkey, saw what had
happened, and called an ambulance. I happened to be there when they
brought him in, alive but past recall. The man lived for three days. His
head swelled up to twice the size of a normal head. I'd never seen anything
like it, and I hope I never do again. Terri wanted to go in and sit with him
when she found out about it. We had a fight over it. I didn't think she
should see him like that. I didn't think she should see him, and I still
don't."

"Who won the fight?" Laura said.   34

"I was in the room with him when he died," Terri said. "He never came   35
up out of it. But I sat with him. He didn't have anyone else."

"He was dangerous," Mel said. "If you call that love, you can have it."   36

"It was love," Terri said. "Sure, it's abnormal in most people's eyes. But   37
he was willing to die for it. He did die for it."

"I sure as hell wouldn't call it love," Mel said. "I mean, no one knows   38
what he did it for. I've seen a lot of suicides, and I couldn't say anyone ever
knew what they did it for."

Mel put his hands behind his neck and tilted his chair back. "I'm not   39
interested in that kind of love," he said. "If that's love, you can have it."

Terri said, "We were afraid. Mel even made a will out and wrote to his   40
brother in California who used to be a Green Beret. Mel told him who to
look for if something happened to him."

Terri drank from her glass. She said, "But Mel's right — we lived like   41
fugitives. We were afraid. Mel was, weren't you, honey? I even called the
police at one point, but they were no help. They said they couldn't do anything until Ed actually did something. Isn't that a laugh?" Terri said.

She poured the last of the gin into her glass and waggled the bottle. Mel   42
got up from the table and went to the cupboard. He took down another
bottle.

"Well, Nick and I know what love is," Laura said. "For us, I mean,"   43
Laura said. She bumped my knee with her knee. "You're supposed to say
something now," Laura said, and turned her smile on me.

For an answer, I took Laura's hand and raised it to my lips. I made a big   44
production out of kissing her hand. Everyone was amused.

"We're lucky," I said.   45

"You guys," Terri said. "Stop that now. You're making me sick. You're   46
still on the honeymoon, for God's sake. You're still gaga, for crying out
loud. Just wait. How long have you been together now? How long has it
been? A year? Longer than a year?"

"Going on a year and a half," Laura said, flushed and smiling.   47

"Oh, now," Terri said. "Wait awhile."   48

She held her drink and gazed at Laura.   49

"I'm only kidding," Terri said.   50

Mel opened the gin and went around the table with the bottle.   51

"Here, you guys," he said. "Let's have a toast. I want to propose a toast.   52
A toast to love. To true love," Mel said.

We touched glasses.   53

"To love," we said.   54

Outside in the backyard, one of the dogs began to bark. The leaves of   55
the aspen that leaned past the window ticked against the glass. The afternoon sun was like a presence in this room, the spacious light of ease and
generosity. We could have been anywhere, somewhere enchanted. We

raised our glasses again and grinned at each other like children who had agreed on something forbidden.

"I'll tell you what real love is," Mel said. "I mean, I'll give you a good 56 example. And then you can draw your own conclusions." He poured more gin into his glass. He added an ice cube and a sliver of lime. We waited and sipped our drinks. Laura and I touched knees again. I put a hand on her warm thigh and left it there.

"What do any of us really know about love?" Mel said. "It seems to me 57 we're just beginners at love. We say we love each other and we do, I don't doubt it. I love Terri and Terri loves me, and you guys love each other too. You know the kind of love I'm talking about now. Physical love, that impulse that drives you to someone special, as well as love of the other person's being, his or her essence, as it were. Carnal love and, well, call it sentimental love, the day-to-day caring about the other person. But sometimes I have a hard time accounting for the fact that I must have loved my first wife too. But I did, I know I did. So I suppose I am like Terri in that regard. Terri and Ed." He thought about it and then he went on. "There was a time when I thought I loved my first wife more than life itself. But now I hate her guts. I do. How do you explain that? What happened to that love? What happened to it, is what I'd like to know. I wish someone could tell me. Then there's Ed. Okay, we're back to Ed. He loves Terri so much he tries to kill her and he winds up killing himself." Mel stopped talking and swallowed from his glass. "You guys have been together eighteen months and you love each other. It shows all over you. You glow with it. But you both loved other people before you met each other. You've both been married before, just like us. And you probably loved other people before that too, even. Terri and I have been together five years, been married for four. And the terrible thing, the terrible thing is, but the good thing too, the saving grace, you might say, is that if something happened to one of us — excuse me for saying this — but if something happened to one of us tomorrow, I think the other one, the other person, would grieve for a while, you know, but then the surviving party would go out and love again, have someone else soon enough. All this, all of this love we're talking about, it would just be a memory. Maybe not even a memory. Am I wrong? Am I way off base? Because I want you to set me straight if you think I'm wrong. I want to know. I mean, I don't know anything, and I'm the first one to admit it."

"Mel, for God's sake," Terri said. She reached out and took hold of his 58 wrist. "Are you getting drunk? Honey? Are you drunk?"

"Honey, I'm just talking," Mel said. "All right? I don't have to be drunk 59 to say what I think. I mean, we're all just talking, right?" Mel said. He fixed his eyes on her.

"Sweetie, I'm not criticizing," Terri said.   60

She picked up her glass.   61

"I'm not on call today," Mel said. "Let me remind you of that. I am not 62 on call," he said.

"Mel, we love you," Laura said. 63

Mel looked at Laura. He looked at her as if he could not place her, as if 64
she was not the woman she was.

"Love you too, Laura," Mel said. "And you, Nick, love you too. You 65
know something?" Mel said. "You guys are our pals," Mel said.

He picked up his glass. 66

Mel said, "I was going to tell you about something. I mean, I was going 67
to prove a point. You see, this happened a few months ago, but it's still
going on right now, and it ought to make us feel ashamed when we talk
like we know what we're talking about when we talk about love."

"Come on now," Terri said. "Don't talk like you're drunk if you're not 68
drunk."

"Just shut up for once in your life," Mel said very quietly. "Will you do me 69
a favor and do that for a minute? So as I was saying, there's this old couple
who had this car wreck out on the interstate. A kid hit them and they were
all torn to shit and nobody was giving them much chance to pull through."

Terri looked at us and then back at Mel. She seemed anxious, or maybe 70
that's too strong a word.

Mel was handing the bottle around the table. 71

"I was on call that night," Mel said. "It was May or maybe it was June. 72
Terri and I had just sat down to dinner when the hospital called. There'd
been this thing out on the interstate. Drunk kid, teenager, plowed his dad's
pickup into this camper with this old couple in it. They were up in their
mid-seventies, that couple. The kid — eighteen, nineteen, something — he
was DOA. Taken the steering wheel through his sternum. The old couple,
they were alive, you understand. I mean, just barely. But they had everything. Multiple fractures, internal injuries, hemorrhaging, contusions, lacerations, the works, and they each of them had themselves concussions.
They were in a bad way, believe me. And, of course, their age was two
strikes against them. I'd say she was worse off than he was. Ruptured spleen
along with everything else. Both kneecaps broken. But they'd been wearing
their seatbelts and, God knows, that's what saved them for the time being."

"Folks, this is an advertisement for the National Safety Council," Terri 73
said. "This is your spokesman, Dr. Melvin R. McGinnis, talking." Terri
laughed. "Mel," she said, "sometimes you're just too much. But I love you,
hon," she said.

"Honey, I love you," Mel said. 74

He leaned across the table. Terri met him halfway. They kissed. 75

"Terri's right," Mel said as he settled himself again. "Get those seatbelts 76
on. But seriously, they were in some shape, those oldsters. By the time I got
down there, the kid was dead, as I said. He was off in a corner, laid out on
a gurney. I took one look at the old couple and told the ER nurse to get me
a neurologist and an orthopedic man and a couple of surgeons down there
right away."

He drank from his glass. "I'll try to keep this short," he said. "So we took   77
the two of them up to the OR and worked like fuck on them most of the
night. They had these incredible reserves, those two. You see that once in
a while. So we did everything that could be done, and toward morning
we're giving them a fifty-fifty chance, maybe less than that for her. So here
they are, still alive the next morning. So, okay, we move them into the
ICU, which is where they both kept plugging away at it for two weeks, hitting it better and better on all the scopes. So we transfer them out to their
own room."

Mel stopped talking. "Here," he said, "let's drink this cheapo gin the hell   78
up. Then we're going to dinner, right? Terri and I know a new place. That's
where we'll go, to this new place we know about. But we're not going until
we finish up this cut-rate, lousy gin."

Terri said, "We haven't actually eaten there yet. But it looks good. From   79
the outside, you know."

"I like food," Mel said. "If I had it to do all over again, I'd be a chef, you   80
know? Right? Terri?" Mel said.

He laughed. He fingered the ice in his glass.   81

"Terri knows," he said. "Terri can tell you. But let me say this. If I could   82
come back again in a different life, a different time and all, you know
what? I'd like to come back as a knight. You were pretty safe wearing all
that armor. It was all right being a knight until gunpowder and muskets and
pistols came along."

"Mel would like to ride a horse and carry a lance," Terri said.   83
"Carry a woman's scarf with you everywhere," Laura said.   84
"Or just a woman," Mel said.   85
"Shame on you," Laura said.   86
Terri said, "Suppose you came back as a serf. The serfs didn't have it so   87
good in those days," Terri said.

"The serfs never had it good," Mel said. "But I guess even the knights   88
were vessels to someone. Isn't that the way it worked? But then everyone is
always a vessel to someone. Isn't that right? Terri? But what I liked about
knights, besides their ladies, was that they had that suit of armor, you know,
and they couldn't get hurt very easy. No cars in those days, you know? No
drunk teenagers to tear into your ass."

"Vassals," Terri said.   89
"What?" Mel said.   90
"Vassals," Terri said. "They were called vassals, not vessels."   91
"Vassals, vessels," Mel said, "what the fuck's the difference? You knew   92
what I meant anyway. All right," Mel said. "So I'm not educated. I learned
my stuff. I'm a heart surgeon, sure, but I'm just a mechanic. I go in and
fuck around and fix things. Shit," Mel said.

"Modesty doesn't become you," Terri said.   93
"He's just a humble sawbones," I said. "But sometimes they suffocated in   94
all that armor, Mel. They'd even have heart attacks if it got too hot and

they were too tired and worn out. I read somewhere that they'd fall off their horses and not be able to get up because they were too tired to stand with all that armor on them. They got trampled by their own horses sometimes."

"That's terrible," Mel said. "That's a terrible thing, Nicky. I guess they'd   95
just lay there and wait until somebody came along and made a shish kebab out of them."

"Some other vessel," Terri said.   96

"That's right," Mel said. "Some vassal would come along and spear the   97
bastard in the name of love. Or whatever the fuck it was they fought over in those days."

"Same things we fight over these days," Terri said.   98

Laura said, "Nothing's changed."   99

The color was still high in Laura's cheeks. Her eyes were bright. She   100
brought her glass to her lips.

Mel poured himself another drink. He looked at the label closely as if   101
studying a long row of numbers. Then he slowly put the bottle down on the table and slowly reached for the tonic water.

"What about the old couple?" Laura said. "You didn't finish that story   102
you started."

Laura was having a hard time lighting her cigarette. Her matches kept   103
going out.

The sunshine inside the room was different now, changing, getting thin-   104
ner. But the leaves outside the window were still shimmering, and I stared at the pattern they made on the panes and on the Formica counter. They weren't the same patterns, of course.

"What about the old couple?" I said.   105

"Older but wiser," Terri said.   106

Mel stared at her.   107

Terri said, "Go on with your story, hon. I was only kidding. Then what   108
happened?"

"Terri, sometimes," Mel said.   109

"Please, Mel," Terri said. "Don't always be so serious, sweetie. Can't you   110
take a joke?"

"Where's the joke?" Mel said.   111

He held his glass and gazed steadily at his wife.   112

"What happened?" Laura said.   113

Mel fastened his eyes on Laura. He said, "Laura, if I didn't have Terri   114
and if I didn't love her so much, and if Nick wasn't my best friend, I'd fall in love with you. I'd carry you off, honey," he said.

"Tell your story," Terri said. "Then we'll go to that new place, okay?"   115

"Okay?" Mel said. "Where was I?" he said. He stared at the table and   116
then he began again.

"I dropped in to see each of them every day, sometimes twice a day if I   117
was up doing other calls anyway. Casts and bandages, head to foot, the both of them. You know, you've seen it in the movies. That's just the way they

looked, just like in the movies. Little eye-holes and nose-holes and mouth-holes. And she had to have her legs slung up on top of it. Well, the husband was very depressed for the longest while. Even after he found out that his wife was going to pull through, he was still very depressed. Not about the accident, though. I mean, the accident was one thing, but it wasn't everything. I'd get up to his mouth-hole, you know, and he'd say no, it wasn't the accident exactly but it was because he couldn't see her through his eye-holes. He said that was what was making him feel so bad. Can you imagine? I'm telling you, the man's heart was breaking because he couldn't turn his goddamn head and *see* his goddamn wife."

Mel looked around the table and shook his head at what he was going to say. 118

"I mean, it was killing the old fart just because he couldn't *look* at the fucking woman." 119

We all looked at Mel. 120

"Do you see what I'm saying?" he said. 121

Maybe we were a little drunk by then. I know it was hard keeping things in focus. The light was draining out of the room, going back through the window where it had come from. Yet nobody made a move to get up from the table to turn on the overhead light. 122

"Listen," Mel said. "Let's finish this fucking gin. There's about enough left here for one shooter all around. Then let's go eat. Let's go to the new place." 123

"He's depressed," Terri said. "Mel, why don't you take a pill?" 124

Mel shook his head. "I've taken everything there is." 125

"We all need a pill now and then," I said. 126

"Some people are born needing them," Terri said. 127

She was using her finger to rub at something on the table. Then she stopped rubbing. 128

"I think I want to call my kids," Mel said. "Is that all right with everybody? I'll call my kids," he said. 129

Terri said, "What if Marjorie answers the phone? You guys, you've heard us on the subject of Marjorie? Honey, you know you don't want to talk to Marjorie. It'll make you feel even worse." 130

"I don't want to talk to Marjorie," Mel said. "But I want to talk to my kids." 131

"There isn't a day goes by that Mel doesn't say he wishes she'd get married again. Or else die," Terri said. "For one thing," Terri said, "She's bankrupting us. Mel says it's just to spite him that she won't get married again. She has a boyfriend who lives with her and the kids, so Mel is supporting the boyfriend too." 132

"She's allergic to bees," Mel said. "If I'm not praying she'll get married again, I'm praying she'll get herself stung to death by a swarm of fucking bees." 133

"Shame on you," Laura said.   134

"Bzzzzzzz," Mel said, turning his fingers into bees and buzzing them at   135
Terri's throat. Then he let his hands drop all the way to his sides.

"She's vicious," Mel said. "Sometimes I think I'll go up there dressed   136
like a beekeeper. You know, that hat that's like a helmet with the plate that
comes down over your face, the big gloves, and the padded coat? I'll knock
on the door and let a loose hive of bees in the house. But first I'd make
sure the kids were out, of course."

He crossed one leg over the other. It seemed to take him a lot of time to   137
do it. Then he put both feet on the floor and leaned forward, elbows on the
table, his chin cupped in his hands.

"Maybe I won't call the kids, after all. Maybe it isn't such a hot idea.   138
Maybe we'll just go eat. How does that sound?"

"Sounds fine to me," I said. "Eat or not eat. Or keep drinking. I could   139
head right on out into the sunset."

"What does that mean, honey?" Laura said.   140

"It just means what I said," I said. "It means I could just keep going.   141
That's all it means."

"I could eat something myself," Laura said. "I don't think I've ever been   142
so hungry in my life. Is there something to nibble on?"

"I'll put out some cheese and crackers," Terri said.   143

But Terri just sat there. She did not get up to get anything.   144

Mel turned his glass over. He spilled it out on the table.   145

"Gin's gone," Mel said.   146

Terri said, "Now what?"   147

I could hear my heart beating. I could hear everyone's heart. I could   148
hear the human noise we sat there making, not one of us moving, not even
when the room went dark.

Analyzing This Selection

1. **THE WRITER'S METHOD** Think of three adjectives that together
summarize Mel's character in the first half of the story. Would you change
the adjectives to fit his character at the end of the story?

2. At what times and how do the characters express their love for their partners
and for their friends during the conversation? What motives or satisfactions
enter into their expressions of love? Examine the details closely.

3. What aspect of love is especially troubling to Mel? What bearing does it
have on his earlier intention to become a priest and his present vocation as
a cardiologist?

4. Why does Mel's language become more vulgar as he tells his story about the
old people? What is agitating him?

5. What do Nick and Laura find disturbing about Mel's story? How do we
know?

6. Mel divides love into "carnal" and "sentimental." Does his example of true love fit either category? How would you define it?

Analyzing Connections

7. Add another participant to this conversation around the kitchen table: if Simone de Beauvoir contributed her viewpoint in the Insights on page 126, how would the other characters respond?

Analyzing by Writing

8. Our commonly used expressions about love indicate that love is not just an emotion: it is also a whole set of ideas and beliefs about that emotion. Is love something to "work on"? Is it something to "share"? Is it "communication"? or a "commitment"? Is it a "feeling"? or a "trip"? Consider the assumptions and implications surrounding the concept of love that is current among a group of people you know. Examine the specific words, gestures, and reactions that indicate their assumed view of love.

PART 4

GROUP PICTURES

INSIGHTS

No man is an island, entire of itself; every man is a piece of the continent, a part of the main; if a clod be washed away by the sea, Europe is less, as well as if a promontory were, as well as if a manor of thy friends or of thine own were; any man's death diminishes me, because I am involved in mankind; and therefore never send to know for whom the bell tolls: it tolls for thee.

—JOHN DONNE

Hell is other people.

—JEAN-PAUL SARTRE

Society everywhere is in conspiracy against the manhood of every one of its members. Society is a joint-stock company, in which the members agree, for the better securing of his bread to each shareholder, to surrender the liberty and culture of the eater. The virtue in most request is conformity. Self-reliance is its aversion. It loves not realities and creators, but names and customs. Whoso would be a man must be a nonconformist.

—RALPH WALDO EMERSON

Being ashamed of one's parents is, psychologically, not identical with being ashamed of one's people. I believe every one of us will, if he but digs deeply enough into the realm of unconscious memories, remember having been ashamed of his parents. Being ashamed of our people must have another psychological meaning. It must be the expression of a tendency to disavow the most essential part of ourself. To be ashamed of being Jewish means not only to be a coward and insincere in disavowing the proud inheritance of an old people who have made an eternal contribution to the civilization of mankind. It also means to disavow the best and the most precious part we get from our parents, their parents, and their ancestors, who continue to live in us. It means, furthermore, to renounce oneself. When the Jewish proverb proclaims that he who is ashamed of his family will have no luck in life, it must mean just that: he cannot have that self-confidence which makes life worth living. Strange that the folklore of an oriental people coincides here with the viewpoint of Goethe; any life can be lived if one does not miss oneself, if one but remains oneself.

The thought that my children are sometimes ashamed of the human faults and failings of their father does not sadden me; but, for their own sake, I wish that they will never be ashamed that their father was Jewish. The one feeling concerns only the personal shortcomings of an individual who was striving, sometimes succeeding and often failing. The other shame concerns something superpersonal, something beyond the narrow realm of the individual. It concerns the community of fate, it touches the bond that ties one generation to those preceding it and those following it.

—THEODOR REIK

It is difficult to let others see the full psychological meaning of caste segregation. It is as though one, looking out from a dark cave in a side of an impending mountain, sees the world passing and speaks to it; speaks courteously and persuasively, showing them how these entombed souls are hindered in their natural movement, expression, and development; and how their loosening from prison would be a matter not simply of courtesy, sympathy, and help to them, but aid to all the world. One talks on evenly and logically in this way, but notices that the passing throng does not even turn its head, or if it does, glances curiously and walks on. It gradually penetrates the minds of the prisoners that the people passing do not hear; that some thick sheet of invisible but horribly tangible plate glass is between them and the world. They get excited; they talk louder; they gesticulate. Some of the passing world stop in curiosity; these gesticulations seem so pointless; they laugh and pass on. They still either do not hear at all, or hear but dimly, and even what they hear, they do not understand. Then the people within may become hysterical. They may scream and hurl themselves against the barriers, hardly realizing in their bewilderment that they are screaming in a vacuum unheard and that their antics may actually seem funny to those outside looking in. They may even, here and there, break through in blood and disfigurement, and find themselves faced by a horrified, implacable, and quite overwhelming mob of people frightened for their own very existence.

—W. E. B. DU BOIS

The New Colossus

Not like the brazen giant of Greek fame,
With conquering limbs astride from land to land;
Here at our sea-washed, sunset gates shall stand
A mighty woman with a torch, whose flame
Is the imprisoned lightning, and her name
Mother of Exiles. From her beacon-hand
Glows world-wide welcome; her mild eyes command
The air-bridged harbor that twin cities frame.
"Keep, ancient lands, your storied pomp!" cries she
With silent lips. "Give me your tired, your poor,
Your huddled masses yearning to breathe free,
The wretched refuse of your teeming shore.
Send these, the homeless, tempest-tost to me,
I lift my lamp beside the golden door!"

—EMMA LAZARUS

The brotherhood of man is not a mere poet's dream; it is a most depressing and humiliating reality.

—OSCAR WILDE

Among aristocratic nations families maintain the same station for centuries and often live in the same place. So there is a sense in which all the generations are contemporaneous. A man almost always knows about his ancestors and respects them; his imagination extends to his great-grandchildren, and he loves them. He freely does his duty by both ancestors and descendants and often sacrifices personal pleasures for the sake of beings who are no longer alive or are not yet born.

Moreover, aristocratic institutions have the effect of linking each man closely with several of his fellows.

Each class in an aristocratic society, being clearly and permanently limited, forms, in a sense, a little fatherland for all its members, to which they are attached by more obvious and more precious ties than those linking them to the fatherland itself.

Each citizen of an aristocratic society has his fixed station, one above another, so that there is always someone above him whose protection he needs and someone below him whose help he may require.

So people living in an aristocratic age are almost always closely involved with something outside themselves, and they are often inclined to forget about themselves. It is true that in these ages the general conception of *human fellowship* is dim and that men hardly ever think of devoting themselves to the cause of humanity, but men do often make sacrifices for the sake of certain other men.

In democratic ages, on the contrary, the duties of each to all are much clearer but devoted service to any individual much rarer. The bonds of human affection are wider but more relaxed.

Among democratic peoples new families continually rise from nothing while others fall, and nobody's position is quite stable. The woof of time is ever being broken and the track of past generations lost. Those who have gone before are easily forgotten, and no one gives a thought to those who will follow. All a man's interests are limited to those near himself.

As each class catches up with the next and gets mixed with it, its members do not care about one another and treat one another as strangers. Aristocracy links everybody, from peasant to king, in one long chain. Democracy breaks the chain and frees each link.

As social equality spreads there are more and more people who, though neither rich nor powerful enough to have much hold over others, have gained or kept enough wealth and enough understanding to look after their own needs. Such folk owe no man anything and hardly expect anything from anybody. They form the habit of thinking of themselves in isolation and imagine that their whole destiny is in their own hands.

Thus, not only does democracy make men forget their ancestors, but also clouds their view of their descendants and isolates them from their contemporaries. Each man is forever thrown back on himself alone, and there is danger that he may be shut up in the solitude of his own heart.

—ALEXIS DE TOCQUEVILLE

America has always been the most competitive of societies. It poises its citizens against one another, with the warning that they must make it on their own. Hence the stress on moving past others, driven by a fear of falling behind. No other nation so rates its residents as winners or losers.

—ANDREW HACKER

The "natural" approach to human relations presumes to know any person well enough is to love him, that the only human problem is a communication problem. This denies that people might be separated by basic, genuinely irreconcilable differences — philosophical, political, or religious — and assumes that all such differences are no more than misunderstandings.

Many forms of etiquette are employed precisely to disguise those antipathies that arise from irreconcilable differences, in order to prevent mayhem. The reason that diplomacy, for example, is so stilted is that its purpose is to head off the most natural social relation between countries in conflict, namely war.

The idea that people can behave "naturally" without resorting to an artificial code tacitly agreed upon by their society is as silly as the idea that they can communicate by using a language without commonly accepted semantic and grammatical rules. Like language, a code of manners can be used with more or less skill, for laudable or evil purposes, to express a great variety of ideas and emotions. Like language, manners continually undergo slow changes and adaptations, but these changes have to be global, not atomic. For if everyone improvises his own manners, no one will understand the meaning of anyone else's behavior, and the result will be social chaos and the end of civilization, or about what we have now.

—JUDITH MARTIN ("Miss Manners")

FOCUSING BY WRITING

1. If you had to choose among the natural dwelling places of animals, what fantasy home would be suitable for you? You might prefer to live in a robin's nest, a beaver lodge, a rabbit warren, a bear's cave, an ant colony, a beehive, an eagle's aerie, a wasp's nest, a fox's lair, a lion's den. (Do not pick manmade places such as a doghouse or fishbowl.) Describe some concrete details of your primal dwelling place. Why would it feel good to live there?

2. You must know someone you could call a "total jerk" — that is, someone who never knows the right way to act. Explain the code of behavior that this person does not follow. Do not just relate an anecdote that ridicules someone. Focus on explaining the accepted standard of behavior that this person consistently violates.

3. What particular place has made you aware of your entire country? It might be a historical site, a busy city street, or a wilderness area, a schoolyard, a stadium, a mall, or any place that at a specific moment epitomized America — for better or worse. Describe the place, giving the concrete details that affected you with their national symbolism.

4. As a tourist in a foreign country, as a visitor to a large city, or as a pre-freshman interviewee on a college campus, were you self-conscious about being an outsider? Were you embarrassed to be seen as distinguishable from the local people? What kind of exposure did you wish to cover up? Conversely, what did you try to emphasize or exaggerate about yourself?

Amy Tan

MOTHER TONGUE

AMY TAN (b. 1952), the daughter of Chinese immigrants, grew up in California and graduated from San Jose State University. She began a business career writing speeches and reports for corporate executives. She turned to fiction writing as part of her remedy for workaholism. Tan's first novel, *The Joy Luck Club* (1989), recounts interconnected stories of conflict and loyalty between Chinese mothers and their American-born daughters. The novel was made into a popular movie. The Chinese heroine in her second novel, *The Kitchen God's Wife* (1991), resembles Tan's mother as she is represented in "Mother Tongue," which first appeared in the *Threepenny Review* (1990). Tan's third novel is *The Hundred Secret Senses* (1995).

I am not a scholar of English or literature. I cannot give you much more than personal opinions on the English language and its variations in this country or others.

I am a writer. And by that definition, I am someone who has always loved language. I am fascinated by language in daily life. I spend a great deal of my time thinking about the power of language — the way it can evoke an emotion, a visual image, a complex idea, or a simple truth. Language is the tool of my trade. And I use them all — all the Englishes I grew up with.

Recently, I was made keenly aware of the different Englishes I do use. I was giving a talk to a large group of people, the same talk I had already given to half a dozen other groups. The nature of the talk was about my writing, my life, and my book, *The Joy Luck Club*. The talk was going along well enough, until I remembered one major difference that made the whole talk sound wrong. My mother was in the room. And it was perhaps the first time she had heard me give a lengthy speech, using the kind of English I have never used with her. I was saying things like, "The intersection of memory upon imagination" and "There is an aspect of my fiction that relates to thus-and-thus" — a speech filled with carefully wrought grammatical phrases, burdened, it suddenly seemed to me, with nominalized forms, past perfect tenses, conditional phrases, all the forms of standard English that I had learned in school and through books, the forms of English I did not use at home with my mother.

Just last week, I was walking down the street with my mother, and I again found myself conscious of the English I was using, the English I do use with her. We were talking about the price of new and used furniture and I heard myself saying this: "Not waste money that way." My husband was with us as well, and he didn't notice any switch in my English. And then I realized why. It's because over the twenty years we've been together I've often used that same kind of English with him, and sometimes he even uses it with me. It has become our language of intimacy, a different sort of English that relates to family talk, the language I grew up with.

So you'll have some idea of what this family talk I heard sounds like, I'll quote what my mother said during a recent conversation which I videotaped and then transcribed. During this conversation, my mother was talking about a political gangster in Shanghai who had the same last name as her family's, Du, and how the gangster in his early years wanted to be adopted by her family, which was rich by comparison. Later, the gangster became more powerful, far richer than my mother's family, and one day showed up at my mother's wedding to pay his respects. Here's what she said in part:

"Du Yusong having business like fruit stand. Like off the street kind. He is Du like Du Zong — but not Tsung-ming Island people. The local people call putong, the river east side, he belong to that side local people. That man want to ask Du Zong father take him in like become own family. Du Zong father wasn't look down on him, but didn't take seriously, until that man big like become a mafia. Now important person, very hard to inviting him. Chinese way, came only to show respect, don't stay for dinner. Respect for making big celebration, he shows up. Mean gives lots of respect. Chinese custom. Chinese social life that way. If too important won't have to stay too long. He come to my wedding. I didn't see, I heard it. I gone to boy's side, they have YMCA dinner. Chinese age I was nineteen."

You should know that my mother's expressive command of English belies how much she actually understands. She reads the *Forbes* report, listens to *Wall Street Week*, converses daily with her stockbroker, reads all of Shirley MacLaine's books with ease — all kinds of things I can't begin to understand. Yet some of my friends tell me they understand 50 percent of what my mother says. Some say they understand 80 to 90 percent. Some say they understand none of it, as if she were speaking pure Chinese. But to me, my mother's English is perfectly clear, perfectly natural. It's my mother tongue. Her language, as I hear it, is vivid, direct, full of observation and imagery. That was the language that helped shape the way I saw things, expressed things, made sense of the world.

Lately, I've been giving more thought to the kind of English my mother speaks. Like others, I have described it to people as "broken" or "fractured" English. But I wince when I say that. It has always bothered me that I can think of no way to describe it other than "broken," as if it were damaged and needed to be fixed, as if it lacked a certain wholeness and soundness.

I've heard other terms used, "limited English," for example. But they seem just as bad, as if everything is limited, including people's perceptions of the limited English speaker.

I know this for a fact, because when I was growing up, my mother's "lim-   9
ited" English limited *my* perception of her. I was ashamed of her English. I believed that her English reflected the quality of what she had to say. That is, because she expressed them imperfectly her thoughts were imperfect. And I had plenty of empirical evidence to support me: the fact that people in department stores, at banks, and at restaurants did not take her seriously, did not give her good service, pretended not to understand her, or even acted as if they did not hear her.

My mother has long realized the limitations of her English as well.   10
When I was fifteen, she used to have me call people on the phone to pretend I was she. In this guise, I was forced to ask for information or even to complain and yell at people who had been rude to her. One time it was a call to her stockbroker in New York. She had cashed out her small portfolio and it just so happened we were going to go to New York the next week, our very first trip outside California. I had to get on the phone and say in an adolescent voice that was not very convincing, "This is Mrs. Tan."

And my mother was standing in the back whispering loudly, "Why he   11
don't send me check, already two weeks late. So mad he lie to me, losing me money."

And then I said in perfect English, "Yes, I'm getting rather concerned.   12
You had agreed to send the check two weeks ago, but it hasn't arrived."

Then she began to talk more loudly. "What he want, I come to New   13
York tell him front of his boss, you cheating me?" And I was trying to calm her down, make her be quiet, while telling the stockbroker, "I can't tolerate any more excuses. If I don't receive the check immediately, I am going to have to speak to your manager when I'm in New York next week." And sure enough, the following week there we were in front of this astonished stockbroker, and I was sitting there red-faced and quiet, and my mother, the real Mrs. Tan, was shouting at his boss in her impeccable broken English.

We used a similar routine just five days ago, for a situation that was far   14
less humorous. My mother had gone to the hospital for an appointment, to find out about a benign brain tumor a CAT scan had revealed a month ago. She said she had spoken very good English, her best English, no mistakes. Still, she said, the hospital did not apologize when they said they had lost the CAT scan and she had come for nothing. She said they did not seem to have any sympathy when she told them she was anxious to know the exact diagnosis, since her husband and son had both died of brain tumors. She said they would not give her any more information until the next time and she would have to make another appointment for that. So she said she would not leave until the doctor called her daughter. She wouldn't budge. And when the doctor finally called her daughter, me, who

spoke in perfect English — lo and behold — we had assurances the CAT scan would be found, promises that a conference call on Monday would be held, and apologies for any suffering my mother had gone through for a most regrettable mistake.

I think my mother's English almost had an effect on limiting my possi- 15 bilities in life as well. Sociologists and linguists probably will tell you that a person's developing language skills are more influenced by peers. But I do think that the language spoken in the family, especially in immigrant families which are more insular, plays a large role in shaping the language of the child. And I believe that it affected my results on achievement tests, IQ tests, and the SAT. While my English skills were never judged as poor, compared to math, English could not be considered my strong suit. In grade school I did moderately well, getting perhaps B's, sometimes B-pluses, in English and scoring perhaps in the sixtieth or seventieth percentile on achievement tests. But those scores were not good enough to override the opinion that my true abilities lay in math and science, because in those areas I achieved A's and scored in the ninetieth percentile or higher.

This was understandable. Math is precise; there is only one correct 16 answer. Whereas, for me at least, the answers on English tests were always a judgment call, a matter of opinion and personal experience. Those tests were constructed around items like fill-in-the-blank sentence completion, such as, "Even though Tom was _____, Mary thought he was _____." And the correct answer always seemed to be the most bland combinations of thoughts, for example, "Even though Tom was shy, Mary thought he was charming," with the grammatical structure "even though" limiting the correct answer to some sort of semantic opposites, so you wouldn't get answers like, "Even though Tom was foolish, Mary thought he was ridiculous." Well, according to my mother, there were very few limitations as to what Tom could have been and what Mary might have thought of him. So I never did well on tests like that.

The same was true with word analogies, pairs of words in which you 17 were supposed to find some sort of logical, semantic relationship — for example, "*Sunset* is to *nightfall* as _____ is to _____." And here you would be presented with a list of four possible pairs, one of which showed the same kind of relationship: *red* is to *stoplight, bus* is to *arrival, chills* is to *fever, yawn* is to *boring.* Well, I could never think that way. I knew what the tests were asking, but I could not block out of my mind the images already created by the first pair, "*sunset* is to *nightfall*"— and I would see a burst of colors against a darkening sky, the moon rising, the lowering of a curtain of stars. And all the other pairs of words — red, bus, stoplight, boring — just threw up a mass of confusing images, making it impossible for me to sort out something as logical as saying: "A sunset precedes nightfall" is the same as "a chill precedes a fever." The only way I would have gotten that answer right would have been to imagine an associative situation, for example, my being disobedient and staying out past sunset, catching a chill at night, which turns into feverish pneumonia as punishment, which indeed did happen to me.

I have been thinking about all this lately, about my mother's English, 18 about achievement tests. Because lately I've been asked, as a writer, why there are not more Asian Americans represented in American literature. Why are there few Asian Americans enrolled in creative writing programs? Why do so many Chinese students go into engineering? Well, these are broad sociological questions I can't begin to answer. But I have noticed in surveys — in fact, just last week — that Asian students, as a whole, always do significantly better on math achievement tests than in English. And this makes me think that there are other Asian-American students whose English spoken in the home might also be described as "broken" or "limited." And perhaps they also have teachers who are steering them away from writing and into math and science, which is what happened to me.

Fortunately, I happen to be rebellious in nature and enjoy the challenge 19 of disproving assumptions made about me. I became an English major my first year in college, after being enrolled as pre-med. I started writing nonfiction as a freelancer the week after I was told by my former boss that writing was my worst skill and I should hone my talents toward account management.

But it wasn't until 1985 that I finally began to write fiction. And at first 20 I wrote using what I thought to be wittily crafted sentences, sentences that would finally prove I had mastery over the English language. Here's an example from the first draft of a story that later made its way into *The Joy Luck Club*, but without this line: "That was my mental quandary in its nascent state." A terrible line, which I can barely pronounce.

Fortunately, for reasons I won't get into today, I later decided I should 21 envision a reader for the stories I would write. And the reader I decided upon was my mother, because these were stories about mothers. So with this reader in mind — and in fact she did read my early drafts — I began to write stories using all the Englishes I grew up with: the English I spoke to my mother, which for lack of a better term might be described as "simple"; the English she used with me, which for lack of a better term might be described as "broken"; my translation of her Chinese, which could certainly be described as "watered down"; and what I imagined to be her translation of her Chinese if she could speak in perfect English, her internal language, and for that I sought to preserve the essence, but neither an English nor a Chinese structure. I wanted to capture what language ability tests can never reveal: her intent, her passion, her imagery, the rhythms of her speech and the nature of her thoughts.

Apart from what any critic had to say about my writing, I knew I had 22 succeeded where it counted when my mother finished reading my book and gave me her verdict: "So easy to read."

Analyzing This Selection

1. The author starts by emphasizing her professional viewpoint. What focus and freedoms does she claim by virtue of her profession?

2. **THE WRITER'S METHOD**   What is Tan's tone toward her mother? Find details that indicate her feelings and attitudes in their relationship. How have they changed through the years?

3. According to Tan, what is the public attitude toward people with limited English? As a child, how did she respond to this attitude?

Analyzing Connections

4. Tan says that as a writer she uses "all the Englishes I grew up with." Compare the differing styles that she and Jamaica Kincaid (see "Girl," p. 53) had to deal with. Which kind of discourse is most burdensome to either child?

Analyzing by Writing

5. The sense of inhabiting double spheres, or parallel worlds, can arise for young people in religious, ethnic, and socioeconomic groups — or in any strongly defined cultural grouping such as military families or Americans employed abroad. Analyze your own experience of participating in two groups. Explain the differing dimensions, expectations, styles, and manners of the two realms. How did you bridge them? Were you a full citizen in both groups or partly an outsider in one or both?

Henry Louis Gates Jr.

IN THE KITCHEN

Henry Louis Gates Jr. (b. 1950) was born and raised in West Virginia. He graduated from Yale University. After serving as a London correspondent for *Time* magazine, Gates earned a Ph.D. in English from Cambridge University. He has taught at Duke University and Harvard University, where he is now the chairman of Afro-American Studies. His *The Signifying Monkey: A Theory of African-American Literary Criticism* won a National Book Award in 1989. Gates writes on issues of popular culture and race relations, contributing to magazines such as *Harper's*, the *Village Voice*, and the *New Yorker*. He is the coeditor of *Africana: The Encyclopedia of the African and the African American Experience* (1999). The following essay is part of his memoir *Colored People* (1994).

We always had a gas stove in the kitchen, in our house in Piedmont, West Virginia, where I grew up. Never electric, though using electric became fashionable in Piedmont in the sixties, like using Crest toothpaste rather than Colgate, or watching Huntley and Brinkley rather than Walter Cronkite. But not us: gas, Colgate, and good ole Walter Cronkite, come what may. We used gas partly out of loyalty to Big Mom, Mama's Mama, because she was mostly blind and still loved to cook, and could feel her way more easily with gas than with electric. But the most important thing about our gas-equipped kitchen was that Mama used to do hair there. The "hot comb" was a fine-toothed iron instrument with a long wooden handle and a pair of iron curlers that opened and closed like scissors. Mama would put it in the gas fire until it glowed. You could smell those prongs heating up.

I liked that smell. Not the smell so much, I guess, as what the smell meant for the shape of my day. There was an intimate warmth in the women's tones as they talked with my Mama, doing their hair. I knew what the women had been through to get their hair ready to be "done," because I would watch Mama do it to herself. How that kink could be transformed through grease and fire into that magnificent head of wavy hair was a miracle to me, and still is.

Mama would wash her hair over the sink, a towel wrapped around her shoulders, wearing just her slip and her white bra. (We had no shower — just a galvanized tub that we stored in the kitchen — until we moved down Rat Tail Road into Doc Wolverton's house, in 1954.) After she dried it, she would grease her scalp thoroughly with blue Bergamot hair grease, which came in a short, fat jar with a picture of a beautiful colored lady on it. It's important to grease your scalp real good, my Mama would explain, to keep from burning yourself. Of course, her hair would return to its natural kink almost as soon as the hot water and shampoo hit it. To me, it was another miracle how hair so "straight" would so quickly become kinky again the second it even approached some water.

My Mama had only a few "clients" whose heads she "did" — did, I think, 4 because she enjoyed it, rather than for the few pennies it brought in. They would sit on one of our red plastic kitchen chairs, the kind with the shiny metal legs, and brace themselves for the process. Mama would stroke that red-hot iron — which by this time had been in the gas fire for half an hour or more — slowly but firmly through their hair, from scalp to strand's end. It made a scorching, crinkly sound, the hot iron did, as it burned its way through kink, leaving in its wake straight strands of hair, standing long and tall but drooping over at the ends, their shape like the top of a heavy willow tree. Slowly, steadily, Mama's hands would transform a round mound of Odetta kink into a darkened swamp of everglades. The Bergamot made the hair shiny; the heat of the hot iron gave it a brownish-red cast. Once all the hair was as straight as God allows kink to get, Mama would take the well-heated curling iron and twirl the straightened strands into more or less loosely wrapped curls. She claimed that she owed her skill as a hairdresser to the strength in her wrists, and as she worked her little finger would poke out, the way it did when she sipped tea. Mama was a southpaw, and wrote upside down and backward to produce the cleanest, roundest letters you've ever seen.

The "kitchen" she would all but remove from sight with a handheld pair 5 of shears, bought just for this purpose. Now, the kitchen was the room in which we were sitting — the room where Mama did her hair and washed clothes, and where we all took a bath in that galvanized tub. But the word has another meaning, and the kitchen that I'm speaking of is the very kinky bit of hair at the back of your head, where your neck meets your shirt collar. If there was ever a part of our African past that resisted assimilation, it was the kitchen. No matter how hot the iron, no matter how powerful the chemical, no matter how stringent the mashed-potatoes-and-lye formula of a man's "process," neither God nor woman nor Sammy Davis, Jr., could straighten the kitchen. The kitchen was permanent, irredeemable, irresistible kink. Unassimilably African. No matter what you did, no matter how hard you tried, you couldn't de-kink a person's kitchen. So you trimmed it off as best you could.

When hair had begun to "turn," as they'd say — to return to its natural 6 kinky glory — it was the kitchen that turned first (the kitchen around the back, and nappy edges at the temples). When the kitchen started creeping up the back of the neck, it was time to get your hair done again.

Sometimes, after dark, a man would come to have his hair done. It was   7
Mr. Charlie Carroll. He was very light-complected and had a ruddy nose —
it made me think of Edmund Gwenn, who played Kris Kringle in "Miracle
on 34th Street." At first, Mama did him after my brother, Rocky, and I had
gone to sleep. It was only later that we found out that he had come to our
house so Mama could iron his hair — not with a hot comb or a curling
iron but with our very own Proctor-Silex steam iron. For some reason I
never understood, Mr. Charlie could conceal his Frederick Douglass–like
mane under a big white Stetson hat. I never saw him take it off except
when he came to our house, at night, to have his hair pressed. (Later,
Daddy would tell us about Mr. Charlie's most prized piece of knowledge,
something that the man would only confide after his hair had been pressed,
as a token of intimacy. "Not many people know this," he'd say, in a tone of
circumspection, "but George Washington was Abraham Lincoln's daddy."
Nodding solemnly, he'd add the clincher: "A white man told me." Though
he was in dead earnest, this became a humorous refrain around our house —
"a white man told me" — which we used to punctuate especially preposter-
ous assertions.)

My mother examined my daughters' kitchens whenever we went home   8
to visit, in the early eighties. It became a game between us. I had told her
not to do it, because I didn't like the politics it suggested — the notion of
"good" and "bad" hair. "Good" hair was "straight," "bad" hair kinky. Even
in the late sixties, at the height of Black Power, almost nobody could bring
themselves to say "bad" for good and "good" for bad. People still said that
hair like white people's hair was "good," even if they encapsulated it in a
disclaimer, like "what we used to call 'good.'"

Maggie would be seated in her high chair, throwing food this way and   9
that, and Mama would be coming about how cute it all was, how I used to
do just like Maggie was doing, and wondering whether her flinging her
food with her left hand meant that she was going to be left-handed like
Mama. When my daughter was just about covered with Chef Boyardee
Spaghetti-O's, Mama would seize the opportunity: wiping her clean, she
would tilt Maggie's head to one side and reach down the back of her neck.
Sometimes Mama would even rub a curl between her fingers, just to make
sure that her bifocals had not deceived her. Then she'd sigh with satisfaction and relief: No kink...yet. Mama! I'd shout, pretending to be angry.
Every once in a while, if no one was looking, I'd peek, too.

I say "yet" because most black babies are born with soft, silken hair. But   10
after a few months it begins to turn, as inevitably as do the seasons or the
leaves on a tree. People once thought baby oil would stop it. They were
wrong.

Everybody I knew as a child wanted to have good hair. You could be as   11
ugly as homemade sin dipped in misery and still be thought attractive if
you had good hair. "Jesus moss," the girls at Camp Lee, Virginia, had
called Daddy's naturally "good" hair during the war. I know that he played

that thick head of hair for all it was worth, too. My own hair was "not a bad grade," as barbers would tell me when they cut it for the first time. It was like a doctor reporting the results of the first full physical he has given you. Like "You're in good shape" or "Blood pressure's kind of high — better cut down on salt."

I spent most of my childhood and adolescence messing with my hair. I definitely wanted straight hair. Like Pop's. When I was about three, I tried to stick a wad of Bazooka bubble gum to that straight hair of his. I suppose what fixed that memory for me is the spanking I got for doing so: he turned me upside down, holding me by my feet, the better to paddle my behind. Little *nigger*, he had shouted, walloping away. I started to laugh about it two days later, when my behind stopped hurting.

When black people say "straight," of course, they don't usually mean literally straight — they're not describing hair like, say, Peggy Lipton's (she was the white girl on "The Mod Squad"), or like Mary's of Peter, Paul & Mary fame; black people call that "stringy" hair. No, "straight" just means not kinky, no matter what contours the curl may take. I would have done *anything* to have straight hair — and I used to try everything, short of getting a process.

Of the wide variety of techniques and methods I came to master in the challenging prestidigitation of the follicle, almost all had two things in common: a heavy grease and the application of pressure. It's not an accident that some of the biggest black-owned companies in the fifties and sixties made hair products. And I tried them all, in search of that certain silken touch, the one that would leave neither the hand nor the pillow sullied by grease.

I always wondered what Frederick Douglass put on *his* hair, or what Phillis Wheatley put on hers. Or why Wheatley has that rag on her head in the little engraving in the frontispiece of her book. One thing is for sure: you can bet that when Phillis Wheatley went to England and saw the Countess of Huntingdon she did not stop by the Queen's coiffeur on her way there. So many black people still get their hair straightened that it's a wonder we don't have a national holiday for Madame C. J. Walker, the woman who invented the process of straightening kinky hair. Call it Jheri-Kurled or call it "relaxed," it's still fried hair.

I used all the greases, from sea-blue Bergamot and creamy vanilla Duke (in its clear jar with the orange-white-and-green label) to the godfather of grease, the formidable Murray's. Now, Murray's was some *serious* grease. Whereas Bergamot was like oily jello, and Duke was viscous and sickly sweet, Murray's was light brown and *hard*. Hard as lard and twice as greasy, Daddy used to say. Murray's came in an orange can with a press-on top. It was so hard that some people would put a match to the can, just to soften the stuff and make it more manageable. Then, in the late sixties, when Afros came into style, I used Afro Sheen. From Murray's to Duke to Afro Sheen: that was my progression in black consciousness.

We used to put hot towels or wash rags over our Murray-coated heads, in   17
order to melt the wax into the scalp and the follicles. Unfortunately, the
wax also had the habit of running down your neck, ears, and forehead. Not
to mention your pillowcase. Another problem was that if you put two palm-
fuls of Murray's on your head your hair turned white. (Duke did the same
thing.) The challenge was to get rid of that white color. Because if you got
rid of the white stuff you had a magnificent head of wavy hair. That was the
beauty of it: Murray's was so hard that it froze your hair into the wavy style
you brushed it into. It looked really good if you wore a part. A lot of guys
had parts *cut* into their hair by a barber, either with the clippers or with a
straightedge razor. Especially if you had kinky hair — then you'd generally
wear a short razor cut, or what we called a Quo Vadis.

We tried to be as innovative as possible. Everyone knew about using a   18
stocking cap, because your father or your uncle wore one whenever something really big was about to happen, whether sacred or secular: a funeral
or a dance, a wedding or a trip in which you confronted official white
people. Any time you were trying to look really sharp, you wore a stocking
cap in preparation. And if the event was really a big one, you made a new
cap. You asked your mother for a pair of her hose, and cut it with scissors
about six inches or so from the open end — the end with the elastic that
goes up to the top of the thigh. Then you knotted the cut end, and it
became a beehive-shaped hat, with an elastic band that you pulled down
low on your forehead and down around your neck in the back. To work
well, the cap had to fit tightly and snugly, like a press. And it had to fit that
tightly because it *was* a press: it pressed your hair with the force of the
hose's elastic. If you greased your hair down real good, and left the stocking
cap on long enough, voilà: you got a head of pressed-against-the-scalp
waves. (You also got a ring around your forehead when you woke up, but it
went away.) And then you could enjoy your concrete do. Swore we were
bad, too, with all that grease and those flat heads. My brother and I would
brush it out a bit in the mornings, so that it looked — well, "natural."
Grown men still wear stocking caps — especially older men, who generally
keep their stocking caps in their top drawers, along with their cufflinks and
their see-through silk socks, their "Maverick" ties, their silk handkerchiefs,
and whatever else they prize the most.

A Murrayed-down stocking cap was the respectable version of the   19
process, which, by contrast, was most definitely not a cool thing to have
unless you were an entertainer by trade. Zeke and Keith and Poochie and
a few other stars of the high-school basketball team all used to get a process
once or twice a year. It was expensive, and you had to go somewhere like
Pittsburgh or D.C. or Uniontown — somewhere where there were enough
colored people to support a trade. The guys would disappear, then reappear
a day or two later, strutting like peacocks, their hair burned slightly red
from the lye base. They'd also wear "rags" — cloths or handkerchiefs —
around their heads when they slept or played basketball. Do-rags, they were

called. But the result was straight hair, with just a hint of wave. No curl. Do-it-yourselfers took their chances at home with a concoction of mashed potatoes and lye.

The most famous process of all, however, outside of the process Malcolm X describes in his "Autobiography," and maybe the process of Sammy Davis Jr., was Nat King Cole's process. Nat King Cole had patent-leather hair. That man's got the finest process money can buy, or so Daddy said the night we saw Cole's TV show on NBC. It was November 5, 1956. I remember the date because everyone came to our house to watch it and to celebrate one of Daddy's buddies' birthdays. Yeah, Uncle Joe chimed in, they can do shit to his hair that the average Negro can't even *think* about — secret shit. 20

Nat King Cole was *clean.* I've had an ongoing argument with a Nigerian friend about Nat King Cole for twenty years now. Not about whether he could sing — any fool knows that he could — but about whether or not he was a handkerchief head for wearing that patent-leather process. 21

Sammy Davis Jr.'s process was the one I detested. It didn't look good on him. Worse still, he liked to have a fried strand dangling down the middle of his forehead, so he could shake it out from the crown when he sang. But Nat King Cole's hair was a thing unto itself, a beautifully sculpted work of art that he and he alone had the right to wear. The only difference between a process and a stocking cap, really, was taste; but Nat King Cole, unlike, say, Michael Jackson, looked *good* in his. His head looked like Valentino's head in the twenties, and some say it was Valentino the process was imitating. But Nat King Cole wore a process because it suited his face, his demeanor, his name, his style. He was as clean as he wanted to be. 22

I had forgotten all about that patent-leather look until one day in 1971, when I was sitting in an Arab restaurant on the island of Zanzibar surrounded by men in fezzes and white caftans, trying to learn how to eat curried goat and rice with the fingers of my right hand and feeling two million miles from home. All of a sudden, an old transistor radio sitting on top of a china cupboard stopped blaring out its Swahili music and started playing "Fly Me to the Moon," by Nat King Cole. The restaurant's din was not affected at all, but in my mind's eye I saw it: the King's magnificent sleek black tiara. I managed, barely, to blink back the tears. 23

Analyzing This Selection

1. **THE WRITER'S METHOD** What were Gates's boyhood attitudes toward his mother's hairstyling business? Find words and phrases that suggest the sort of child he was.

2. How does the other meaning of "kitchen" affect the essay's title?

3. Why couldn't African Americans easily switch their definitions of "good" and "bad" hair? What were the complications in using these terms?

4. When and why did Gates first accept the natural style of his hair? Why doesn't the author give more emphasis to his change in attitude?

5. What seemed so great about Nat King Cole's hair? Why does the author nearly weep when reminded of it?

Analyzing Connections

6. As children, Gates and Arthur Ashe (see "The Burden of Race," p. 239) were raised in neighboring states, Ashe only seven years older. What different forms of segregation did they encounter? Which effects did they overcome?

Analyzing by Writing

7. Men and women send messages about themselves through hairstyles. There are messages visible in the crewcut, the bouffant, the lacquered spike, the metallic dyes, shaved heads, mohawks, men's ponytails, women's butch cuts, and other styles, whether modest or outlandish. Hair can convey political, racial, ethnic, or religious meanings. Analyze the meaning of the hairstyle of your alter ego — that is, either your ideal self, a suppressed self, or some identity you would like to try out. Explain your similarities to and differences from this alter ego's appearance.

Andrew M. Greeley

WHY DO CATHOLICS STAY IN THE CHURCH? BECAUSE OF THE STORIES

ANDREW M. GREELEY (b. 1928), an authority on the sociology of religion, is an ordained Roman Catholic priest. Educated at a seminary, Greeley also earned a Ph.D. at the University of Chicago. As a scholar he often criticizes some customs and doctrines of the Church. Among his best-known work is *The Making of the Popes 1978: The Politics of Intrigue in the Vatican* (1979). Greeley also writes widely for popular audiences, as in the following essay, which appeared in the *New York Times Magazine* (1994).

You can make a persuasive case against Catholicism if you want. The 1 Church is resolutely authoritarian and often seems to be proud of the fact that it "is not a democracy." It discriminates against women and homosexuals. It tries to regulate the bedroom behavior of married men and women. It tries to impose the Catholic position regarding abortion on everyone. It represses dissent and even disagreement. The Vatican seems obsessed with sex. The Pope preaches against birth control in countries with rapidly expanding populations. Catholics often cringe when the local bishop or cardinal pontificates on social policy issues. Bishops and priests are authoritarian and insensitive. Lay people have no control of how their contributions are spent. Priests are unhappy, and many of them leave the priesthood as soon as they can to marry. The Church has covered up sexual abuse by priests for decades. Now it is paying millions of dollars to do penance for the sexual amusements of supposedly celibate priests while it seeks to minimize, if not eliminate altogether, the sexual pleasures of married lay people.

One might contend with such arguments. Research indicates that priests 2 are among the happiest men in America. The Church was organized in a democratic structure for the first thousand years and could be so organized again. But let the charges stand for the sake of the argument. They represent the way many of those who are not Catholic see the Catholic Church, and with some nuances and qualifications the way many of those inside the church see the Catholic institution. Nonetheless this case against Catholicism simply does not compute for most Catholics when they decide whether to leave or stay.

Do they in fact remain? Are not Catholics leaving the church in droves?   3
Prof. Michael Hout of the Survey Research Center at the University of California at Berkeley has demonstrated that the Catholic defection rate has
remained constant over 30 years. It was 15 percent in 1960 and it is 15 percent today. Half of those who leave the Church do so when they marry a
non-Catholic with stronger religious commitment. The other half leave for
reasons of anger, authority and sex — the reasons cited above.

How can this be, the outsider wonders. For one thing, as the general   4
population has increased, the number of Catholics has increased propor-
tionately. Still, how can 85 percent of those who are born Catholic remain,
one way or another, in the church? Has Catholicism so brainwashed them
that they are unable to leave?

The answer is that Catholics like being Catholic. For the last 30 years   5
the hierarchy and the clergy have done just about everything they could to
drive the laity out of the church and have not succeeded. It seems unlikely
that they will ever drive the stubborn lay folk out of the Church because
the lay folk like being Catholic.

But why do they like being Catholic?   6

First, it must be noted that Americans show remarkable loyalty to their   7
religious heritages. As difficult as it is for members of the academic and
media elites to comprehend the fact, religion is important to most Americans. There is no sign that this importance has declined in the last half
century (as measured by survey data from the 1940s). Skepticism, agnosti-
cism, atheism are not increasing in America, as disturbing as this truth
might be to the denizens of midtown Manhattan.

Moreover, while institutional authority, doctrinal propositions and ethi-   8
cal norms are components of a religious heritage — and important components — they do not exhaust the heritage. Religion is experience, image and
story before it is anything else and after it is everything else. Catholics like
their heritage because it has great stories.

If one considers that for much of Christian history the population was   9
illiterate and the clergy semiliterate and that authority was far away, one
begins to understand that the heritage for most people most of the time was
almost entirely story, ritual, ceremony and eventually art. So it has been for
most of human history. So it is, I suggest (and my data back me up), even
today.

Roger C. Schank, a professor of psychology at Northwestern University   10
who specializes in the study of artificial intelligence, argues in his book *Tell
Me a Story* that stories are the way humans explain reality to themselves.
The more and better our stories, Schank says, the better our intelligence.

Catholicism has great stories because at the center of its heritage is   11
"sacramentalism," the conviction that God discloses Himself in the objects
and events and persons of ordinary life. Hence Catholicism is willing to risk
stories about angels and saints and souls in purgatory and Mary the Mother
of Jesus and stained-glass windows and statues and stations of the cross and
rosaries and medals and the whole panoply of images and devotions that

were so offensive to the austere leaders of the Reformation. Moreover, the Catholic heritage also has the elaborate ceremonial rituals that mark the passing of the year — Midnight Mass, the Easter Vigil, First Communion, May Crowning, Lent, Advent, grammar-school graduation and the festivals of the saints.

Catholicism has also embraced the whole of the human life cycle in 12
Sacraments (with a capital S), which provide rich ceremonial settings, even when indifferently administered for the critical landmarks of life. The Sacrament of Reconciliation (confession that was) and the Sacrament of the Anointing of the Sick (extreme unction that was) embed in ritual and mystery the deeply held Catholic story of second chances.

The "sacramentalism" of the Catholic heritage has also led it to absorb 13
as much as it thinks it can from what it finds to be good, true and beautiful in pagan religions: Brigid is converted from the pagan goddess to the Christian patron of spring, poetry and new life in Ireland; Guadalupe is first a pagan and then a Christian shrine in Spain and then our Lady of Guadalupe becomes the patron of poor Mexicans. This "baptism" of pagan metaphors (sometimes done more wisely than at other times) adds yet another overlay of stories to the Catholic heritage.

The sometimes inaccurate dictum "once a Catholic, always a Catholic," 14
is based on the fact that the religious images of Catholicism are acquired early in life and are tenacious. You may break with the institution, you may reject the propositions, but you cannot escape the images.

The Eucharist (as purists insist we must now call the Mass) is a particu- 15
larly powerful and appealing Catholic ritual, even when it is done badly (as it often is) and especially when it is done well (which it sometimes is). In the Mass we join a community meal of celebration with our neighbors, our family, our friends, those we love. Such an awareness may not be explicitly on the minds of Catholics when they go to Church on Saturday afternoon or Sunday morning, but is the nature of metaphor that those who are influenced by it need not be consciously aware of the influence. In a *New York Times*–CBS News Poll last April, 69 percent of Catholics responding said they attend Mass for reasons of meaning rather than obligation.

Another important Catholic story is that of the neighborhood parish. 16
Because of the tradition of village parishes with which Catholics came to America, the dense concentration of Catholics in many cities and the small geographical size of the parish, parishes can and often do become intense communities for many Catholics. They actuate what a University of Chicago sociologist, James S. Coleman, calls "social capital," the extra resources of energy, commitment and intelligence that overlapping structures produce. This social capital, this story of a sacred place in the heart of urban America, becomes even stronger when the parish contains that brilliant American Catholic innovation — the parochial school.

Perhaps the Catholic religious sensibility all begins with the Christmas 17
crib. A mother shows her child (perhaps age three) the crib scene. The child loves it (of course) because it has everything she likes — a mommy, a

daddy, a baby, animals, shepherds, shepherd children, angels and men in funny clothes — and with token integration! Who is the baby? the little girl asks. That's Jesus. Who's Jesus? The mother hesitates, not sure of exactly how you explain the communication of idioms to a three-year-old. Jesus is God. That doesn't bother the little girl at all. Everyone was a baby once. Why not God? Who's the lady holding Jesus? That's Mary. Oh! Who's Mary? The mother throws theological caution to the winds. She's God's mommy. Again the kid has no problem. Everyone has a mommy, why not God?

It's a hard story to beat. Later in life the little girl may come to under- 18
stand that God loves us so much that He takes on human form to be able to walk with us even into the valley of death and that God also loves us the way a mother loves a newborn babe — which is the function of the Mary metaphor in the Catholic tradition.

It may seem that I am reducing religion to childishness — to stories and 19
images and rituals and communities. In fact, it is in the poetic, the metaphorical, the experiential dimension of personality that religion finds both its origins and raw power. Because we are reflective creatures we must also reflect on our religious experiences and stories; it is in the (lifelong) interlude of reflection that propositional religion and religious authority become important, indeed indispensable. But then the religiously mature person returns to the imagery, having criticized it, analyzed it, questioned it, to commit the self once more in sophisticated and reflective maturity to the story....

When I was in grammar school in the mid-1930s, the nuns told a story 20
that sums up why people stay Catholic. One day Jesus went on a tour of the heavenly city and noted that there were certain new residents who ought not to be there, not until they had put in a long time in purgatory and some of them only on a last-minute appeal. He stormed out to the gate where Peter was checking the day's intake on his Compaq 486DX Deskpro computer (I have edited the nuns' story) — next to which, on his work station, was a fishing pole and a papal crown.

"You've failed again, Simon Peter," said the Lord.   21
"What have I done now?"   22
"You let a lot of people in that don't belong."   23
"I didn't do it."   24
"Well, who did?"   25
"You won't like it."   26
"Tell me anyway."   27
"I turn them away from the front gate and then they go around to the 28
back door and your mother lets them in!"

It is the religious sensibility behind that fanciful story that explains why 29
Catholics remain Catholic. It might not be your religious sensibility. But if you want to understand Catholics — and if Catholics want to understand themselves — the starting point is to comprehend the enormous appeal of that sensibility. It's the stories.

Analyzing This Selection

1. **THE WRITER'S METHOD** The author summarizes criticisms of the Catholic Church and doesn't refute them. Does he accept them? How does Greeley use them to advance his own argument?

2. Greeley includes two stories that are important to Catholics. What is your reaction to his stories? How do they affect your attitude about the religion?

Analyzing Connections

3. Greeley, and Tocqueville in the Insights on page 197, explain what holds people together in social cohesion. Can "stories" accomplish what "aristocracy" provided? In your opinion, which of aristocracy's functions is best served by stories?

Analyzing by Writing

4. Analyze a great story that has been meaningful to you as a member of a group. It may be the Exodus, Paul Revere's ride, the immigration story as in Emma Lazarus's poem in the Insights on page 196, the Easter story, or any comparable narrative. Examine the ideas, values, and personal qualities it illustrates, and try to explain the story's lasting appeal.

Michael Dorris

LIFE STORIES

MICHAEL DORRIS (1945–1997) was a leading writer of fiction and essays about American Indian life and social issues. Educated at Georgetown University and Yale University, Dorris was a professor of Native American studies at Dartmouth College. In *The Broken Cord* (1990) he recounts the circumstances surrounding his adopted son's struggle with fetal alcohol syndrome. His essays, from which this selection is drawn, were collected in *Paper Trail* (1994). *Cloud Chamber* (1997) is his last novel.

In most cultures, adulthood is equated with self-reliance and responsibility, yet often Americans do not achieve this status until we are in our late twenties or early thirties — virtually the entire average lifespan of a person in a traditional non-Western society. We tend to treat prolonged adolescence as a warm-up for real life, as a wobbly suspension bridge between childhood and legal maturity. Whereas a nineteenth-century Cheyenne or Lakota teenager was expected to alter self-conception in a split-second vision, we often meander through an analogous rite of passage for more than a decade — through high school, college, graduate school. 1

Though he had never before traveled alone outside his village, the Plains Indian male was expected at puberty to venture solo into the wilderness. There he had to fend for and sustain himself while avoiding the menace of unknown dangers, and there he had absolutely to remain until something happened that would transform him. Every human being, these tribes believed, was entitled to at least one moment of personal, enabling insight. 2

Anthropology proposes feasible psychological explanations for why this flash was eventually triggered: Fear, fatigue, reliance on strange foods, the anguish of loneliness, stress, and the expectation of ultimate success all contributed to a state of receptivity. Every sense was quickened, alerted to perceive deep meaning, until at last the interpretation of an unusual event — a dream, a chance encounter, or an unexpected vista — reverberated with metaphor. Through this unique prism, abstractly preserved in a vivid memory or song, a boy caught foresight of both his adult persona and of his vocation, the two inextricably entwined. 3

Today the best approximations that many of us get to such a heady sense of eventuality come in the performance of our school vacation jobs. Sum- 4 mers are intermissions, and once we hit our teens it is during these breaks in our structured regimen that we initially taste the satisfaction of remuneration that is earned, not merely doled. Tasks defined as *work* are not only graded, they are compensated; they have a worth that is unarguable because it translates into hard currency. Wage labor — and in the beginning, this generally means a confining, repetitive chore for which we are quickly over-qualified — paradoxically brings a sense of blooming freedom. At the outset, the complaint to a peer that business supersedes fun is oddly liberating — no matter what drudgery requires your attention, it is by its very required nature serious and adult.

At least that's how it seemed to me. I come from a line of people hard   5 hit by the Great Depression. My mother and her sisters went to work early in their teens — my mother operated a kind of calculator known as a comptometer while her sisters spent their days, respectively, at a peanut factory and at Western Union. My grandmother did piecework sewing. Their efforts, and the Democratic Party, saw them through, and to this day they never look back without appreciation for their later solvency. They take nothing for granted. Accomplishments are celebrated, possessions are valuable, in direct proportion to the labor entailed to acquire them; anything easily won or bought on credit is suspect. When I was growing up we were far from wealthy, but what money we had was correlated to the hours some one of us had logged. My eagerness to contribute to, or at least not diminish, the coffer was countered by the arguments of those whose salaries kept me in school: My higher education was a sound group investment. The whole family was adamant that I have the opportunities they had missed and, no matter how much I objected, they stinted themselves to provide for me.

Summer jobs were therefore a relief, an opportunity to pull a share of   6 the load. As soon as the days turned warm I began to peruse the classifieds, and when the spring semester was done, I was ready to punch a clock. It even felt right. Work in June, July, and August had an almost Biblical aspect: In the hot, canicular weather your brow sweated, just as God had ordained. Moreover, summer jobs had the luxury of being temporary. No matter how bizarre, how onerous, how off my supposed track, employment terminated with the falling leaves and I was back on neutral ground. So, during each annual three-month leave from secondary school and later from the university, I compiled an eclectic résumé: lawn cutter, hair sweeper in a barber shop, lifeguard, delivery boy, temporary mail carrier, file clerk, youth program coordinator on my Montana reservation, ballroom dance instructor, theater party promoter, night-shift hospital records keeper, human adding machine in a Paris bank, encyclopedia salesman, newspaper stringer, recreation bus manager, salmon fisherman.

The reasonable titles disguise the madness of some of these occupations.   7 For instance, I seemed inevitably to be hired to trim the yards of the unconventional. One woman followed beside me, step by step, as I traversed her yard in ever tighter squares, and called my attention to each missed blade of grass. Another client never had the "change" to pay me, and so reimbursed my weekly pruning with an offering culled from his library. I could have done without the *Guide to Artificial Respiration* (1942) or the many well-worn copies of Reader's Digest Condensed Books, but sometimes the selection merited the wait. Like a rat lured repeatedly back to the danger of mild electric shock by the mystique of intermittent reenforcement, I kept mowing by day in hopes of turning pages all night.

The summer I was eighteen a possibility arose for a rotation at the post   8 office, and I grabbed it. There was something casually sophisticated about work that required a uniform, about having a federal ranking, even if it was GS-1 (Temp/Sub), and it was flattering to be entrusted with a leather bag containing who knew what important correspondence. Every day I was assigned a new beat, usually in a rough neighborhood avoided whenever possible by regular carriers, and I proved quite capable of complicating what would normally be fairly routine missions. The low point came on the first of August when I diligently delivered four blocks' worth of welfare checks to the right numbers on the wrong streets. It is no fun to snatch unexpected wealth from the hands of those who have but moments previously opened their mailboxes and received a bonus.

After my first year of college, I lived with relatives on an Indian reserva-   9 tion in eastern Montana and filled the only post available: Coordinator of Tribal Youth Programs. I was seduced by the language of the announcement into assuming that there existed Youth Programs to be coordinated. In fact, the Youth consisted of a dozen bored, disgruntled kids — most of them my cousins — who had nothing better to do each day than to show up at what was euphemistically called "the gym" and hate whatever Program I had planned for them. The Youth ranged in age from fifteen to five and seemed to have as their sole common ambition the determination to smoke cigarettes. This put them at immediate and on-going odds with the Coordinator, who on his first day naively encouraged them to sing the "Doe, a deer, a female deer" song from *The Sound of Music*. They looked at me, that bleak morning, and I looked at them, each boy and girl equipped with a Pall Mall behind an ear, and we all knew it would be a long, struggle-charged battle. It was to be a contest of wills, the hearty and wholesome vs. prohibited vice. I stood for dodge ball, for collecting bugs in glass jars, for arts and crafts; they had pledged a preternatural allegiance to sloth. The odds were not in my favor and each waking dawn I experienced the light-headedness of anticipated exhaustion, that thrill of giddy dissociation in which nothing seems real or of great significance. I went with the flow and learned to inhale.

The next summer, I decided to find work in an urban setting for a   10 change, and was hired as a general office assistant in the Elsa Hoppenfeld Theatre Party Agency, located above Sardi's restaurant in New York City. The Agency consisted of Elsa Hoppenfeld herself, Rita Frank, her regular deputy, and me. Elsa was a gregarious Viennese woman who established contacts through personal charm, and she spent much of the time courting trade away from the building. Rita was therefore both my immediate supervisor and constant companion; she had the most incredible fingernails I had ever seen — long, carefully shaped pegs lacquered in cruel primary colors and hard as stone — and an attitude about her that could only be described as zeal.

The goal of a theater party agent is to sell blocks of tickets to imminent   11
Broadway productions, and the likely buyers are charities, B'nai Briths, Hadassahs, and assorted other fund-raising organizations. We received commissions on volume, and so it was necessary to convince a prospect that a play — preferably an expensive musical — for which we had reserved the rights to seats would be a boffo smash hit.

The object of our greatest expectation that season was an extravaganza   12
called *Chu Chem*, a saga that aspired to ride the coattails of *Fiddler on the Roof* into entertainment history. It starred the estimable Molly Picon and told the story of a family who had centuries ago gone from Israel to China during the diaspora, yet had, despite isolation in an alien environment, retained orthodox culture and habits. The crux of the plot revolved around a man with several marriageable daughters and nary a kosher suitor within 5,000 miles. For three months Rita and I waxed eloquent in singing the show's praises. We sat in our little office, behind facing desks, and every noon while she redid her nails I ordered out from a deli that offered such exotic (to me) delicacies as fried egg sandwiches, lox and cream cheese, pastrami, *tongue*. I developed of necessity and habit a telephone voice laced with a distinctly Yiddish accent. It could have been a great career. However, come November, *Chu Chem* bombed. Its closing was such a financial catastrophe for all concerned that when the following January one Monsieur Dupont advertised on the Placement Board at my college, I decided to put an ocean between me and my former trusting clientele.

M. Dupont came to campus with the stated purpose of interviewing   13
candidates for teller positions in a French bank. Successful applicants, required to be fluent in *français*, would be rewarded with three well-paid months and a rent-free apartment in Paris. I headed for the language lab and registered for an appointment.

The only French in the interview was *Bonjour, ça va?*, after which   14
M. Dupont switched into English and described the wonderful deal on charter air flights that would be available to those who got the nod. Round-trip to Amsterdam, via Reykjavik, leaving the day after exams and returning in mid-September, no changes or substitutions. I signed up on the spot. I was to be a *banquier*, with *pied-à-terre* in Montparnasse!

Unfortunately, when I arrived with only $50 in travelers checks in my   15
pocket — the flight had cleaned me out, but who needed money since my paycheck started right away — no one in Paris had ever heard of M. Dupont.

Alors.   16

I stood in the Gare du Nord and considered my options. There weren't 17
any. I scanned a listing of Paris hotels and headed for the cheapest one: the
Hotel Villedo, $10 a night. The place had an ambiance that I persuaded
myself was antique, despite the red light above the sign. The only accommodation available was "the bridal suite," a steal at $20. The glass door to
my room didn't lock and there was a rather continual floor show, but at
some point I must have dozed off. When I awoke the church bells were
ringing, the sky was pink, and I felt renewed. No little setback was going to
spoil my adventure. I stood and stretched, then walked to a mirror that
hung above the sink next to the bed. I leaned forward to punctuate my
resolve with a confident look in the eye.

The sink disengaged and fell to the floor. Water gushed. In panic I rum- 18
maged through my open suitcase, stuffed two pair of underwear into the
pipe to quell the flow, and before the dam broke, I was out the door. I barreled through the lobby of the first bank I passed, asked to see the director,
and told the startled man my sad story. For some reason, whether from
shock or pity, he hired me at $1.27 an hour to be a cross-checker of foreign
currency transactions, and with two phone calls found me lodgings at a
commercial school's dormitory.

From eight to five each weekday my duty was to sit in a windowless 19
room with six impeccably dressed people, all of whom were totaling identical additions and subtractions. We were highly dignified with each other,
very professional, no *tutoyering*.[1] Monsieur Saint presided, but the formidable Mademoiselle was the true power; she oversaw each of our columns
and shook her head sadly at my American-shaped numbers.

My legacy from that summer, however, was more than an enduring pen- 20
chant for crossed 7s. After I had worked for six weeks, M. Saint asked me
during a coffee break why I didn't follow the example of other foreign students he had known and depart the office at noon in order to spend the
afternoon touring the sights of Paris with the *Alliance Française*.

"Because," I replied in my halting French, "that costs money. I depend 21
upon my full salary the same as any of you." M. Saint nodded gravely and
said no more, but then on the next Friday he presented me with a white
envelope along with my check.

"Do not open this until you have left the Société Générale," he said 22
ominously. I thought I was fired for the time I had mixed up krøners and
guilders, and, once on the sidewalk, I steeled myself to read the worst. I felt
the quiet panic of blankness.

"Dear Sir," I translated the perfectly formed script. "You are a person of 23
value. It is not correct that you should be in our beautiful city and not see
it. Therefore we have amassed a modest sum to pay the tuition for a two-
week afternoon program for you at the *Alliance Française*. Your wages will
not suffer, for it is your assignment to appear each morning in this bureau

---

[1]*tutoyer* To use the familiar personal pronoun *tu*, appropriate within family and other
close relations. [Editor's note.]

and reacquaint us with the places you have visited. We shall see them afresh through your eyes." The letter had thirty signatures, from the Director to the janitor, and stuffed inside the envelope was a sheaf of franc notes in various denominations.

I rushed back to the tiny office. M. Saint and Mademoiselle had waited,   24 and accepted my gratitude with their usual controlled smiles and precise handshakes. But they had blown their Gallic cover, and for the next ten days and then through all the days until I went home in September, our branch was awash with sightseeing paraphernalia. Everyone had advice, favorite haunts, criticisms of the *Alliance's* choices or explanations. Paris passed through the bank's granite walls as sweetly as a June breeze through a window screen, and ever afterward the lilt of overheard French, a photograph of *Sacré Coeur* or the Louvre, even a monthly bank statement, recalls to me that best of all summers.

I didn't wind up in an occupation with any obvious connection to the   25 careers I sampled during my school breaks, but I never altogether abandoned those brief professions either. They were jobs not so much to be held as to be weighed, absorbed, and incorporated, and, collectively, they carried me forward into adult life like overlapping stairs, unfolding a particular pattern at once haphazard and inevitable.

Analyzing This Section

1. **THE WRITER'S METHOD**   Dorris begins by contrasting how Native American and white culture recognize maturity. What positive and negative effects does the author see in each approach? Do you see additional pros and cons?

2. Dorris recounts some summer jobs that were futile or absurd. Are they effective rites of passage? What did Dorris gain from them? Can you find evidence of these gains in the essay's tone?

3. Explain why the dignified formality of the French bank contributed to the job's ultimate value to Dorris. Why was it "the best of all summers"?

Analyzing Connections

4. Dorris and Greeley (see "Why Do Catholics Stay in the Church? Because of the Stories," p. 213) each find their meaning in varied, contrasting, even conflicting stories, not just one. Explain which writer seems more integrated to you.

Analyzing by Writing

5. Dorris observes that cultural contexts can paradoxically make drudgery or subjugation liberating. Analyze the customary rites of passage in your social or religious group. What ordinary responsibilities and routine challenges stirred — or were supposed to stir — your sense of maturity? How has your attitude toward such activities changed?

Shelby Steele

ON BEING BLACK AND MIDDLE CLASS

SHELBY STEELE (b. 1946) grew up in an African American community in Chicago. He earned his Ph.D. in history from the University of Utah. His essays on race relations have appeared in magazines such as *Harper's*, the *New York Times Magazine, Commentary, Black World*, and the *New Republic*. His criticisms of both white and black social policies on affirmative action and other issues are collected in *The Content of Our Character: A New Vision of Race in America* (1990), which won a National Book Critics Circle Award. Steele's social criticism continues in *A Dream Deferred: The Second Betrayal of Black Freedom in America* (1998).

Not long ago a friend of mine, black like myself, said to me that the term "black middle class" was actually a contradiction in terms. Race, he insisted, blurred class distinctions among blacks. If you were black, you were just black and that was that. When I argued, he let his eyes roll at my naivete. Then he went on. For us, as black professionals, it was an exercise in self-flattery, a pathetic pretention, to give meaning to such a distinction. Worse, the very idea of class threatened the unity that was vital to the black community as a whole. After all, since when had white America taken note of anything but color when it came to blacks? He then reminded me of an old Malcolm X line that had been popular in the sixties. Question: What is a black man with a Ph.D.? Answer: A nigger.

For many years I had been on my friend's side of this argument. Much of my conscious thinking on the old conundrum of race and class was shaped during my high school and college years in the race-charged sixties, when the fact of my race took on an almost religious significance. Progressively, from the mid-sixties on, more and more aspects of my life found their explanation, their justification, and their motivation in race. My youthful concerns about career, romance, money, values, and even styles of dress became a subject [of] consultation with various oracular sources of racial wisdom. And these ranged from a figure as ennobling as Martin Luther King, Jr., to the underworld elegance of dress I found in jazz clubs on the South Side of Chicago. Everywhere there were signals, and in those days I considered myself so blessed with clarity and direction that I pitied my white classmates who found more embarrassment than guidance in the face of *their* race. In 1968, inflated by my new power, I took a mischievous delight in calling them culturally disadvantaged.

But now, hearing my friend's comment was like hearing a priest from a 3 church I'd grown disenchanted with. I understood him, but my faith was weak. What had sustained me in the sixties sounded monotonous and off the mark in the eighties. For me, race had lost much of its juju, its singular capacity to conjure meaning. And today, when I honestly look at my life and the lives of many other middle-class blacks I know, I can see that race never fully explained our situation in American society. Black though I may be, it is impossible for me to sit in my single-family house with two cars in the driveway and a swing set in the back yard and *not* see the role class has played in my life. And how can my friend, similarly raised and similarly situated, not see it?

Yet despite my certainty I felt a sharp tug of guilt as I tried to explain 4 myself over my friend's skepticism. He is a man of many comedic facial expressions and, as I spoke, his brow lifted in extreme moral alarm as if I were uttering the unspeakable. His clear implication was that I was being elitist and possibly (dare he suggest?) antiblack — crimes for which there might well be no redemption. He pretended to fear for me. I chuckled along with him, but inwardly I did wonder at myself. Though I never doubted the validity of what I was saying, I felt guilty saying it. Why?

After he left (to retrieve his daughter from a dance lesson) I realized that 5 the trap I felt myself in had a tiresome familiarity and, in a sort of slow-motion epiphany, I began to see its outline. It was like the suddenly sharp vision one has at the end of a burdensome marriage when all the long-repressed incompatibilities come undeniably to light.

What became clear to me is that people like myself, my friend, and 6 middle-class blacks generally are caught in a very specific double bind that keeps two equally powerful elements of our identity at odds with each other. The middle-class values by which we were raised — the work ethic, the importance of education, the value of property ownership, of respectability, of "getting ahead," of stable family life, of initiative, of self-reliance, etc. — are, in themselves, raceless and even assimilationist. They urge us toward participation in the American mainstream, toward integration, toward a strong identification with the society — and toward the entire constellation of qualities that are implied in the word "individualism." These values are almost rules for how to prosper in a democratic, free-enterprise society that admires and rewards individual effort. They tell us to work hard for ourselves and our families and to seek our opportunities whenever they appear, inside or outside the confines of whatever ethnic group we may belong to.

But the particular pattern of racial identification that emerged in the six- 7 ties and that still prevails today urges middle-class blacks (and all blacks) in the opposite direction. This pattern asks us to see ourselves as an embattled minority, and it urges an adversarial stance toward the mainstream, an emphasis on ethnic consciousness over individualism. It is organized around an implied separatism.

The opposing thrust of these two parts of our identity results in the double 8 bind of middle-class blacks. There is no forward movement on either plane that does not constitute backward movement on the other. This was the familiar trap I felt myself in while talking with my friend. As I spoke about class, his eyes reminded me that I was betraying race. Clearly, the two indispensable parts of my identity were a threat to each other.

Of course when you think about it, class and race are both similar in 9 some ways and also naturally opposed. They are two forms of collective identity with boundaries that intersect. But whether they clash or peacefully coexist has much to do with how they are defined. Being both black and middle class becomes a double bind when class and race are defined in sharply antagonistic terms, so that one must be repressed to appease the other.

But what is the "substance" of these two identities, and how does each 10 establish itself in an individual's overall identity? It seems to me that when we identify with any collective we are basically identifying with images that tell us what it means to be a member of that collective. Identity is not the same thing as the fact of membership in a collective; it is, rather, a form of self-definition, facilitated by images of what we wish our membership in the collective to mean. In this sense, the images we identify with may reflect the aspirations of the collective more than they reflect reality, and their content can vary with shifts in those aspirations.

But the process of identification is usually dialectical. It is just as neces- 11 sary to say what we are *not* as it is to say what we are — so that finally identification comes about by embracing a polarity of positive and negative images. To identify as middle class, for example, I must have both positive and negative images of what being middle class entails; then I will know what I should and should not be doing in order to be middle class. The same goes for racial identity.

In the racially turbulent sixties the polarity of images that came to define 12 racial identification was very antagonistic to the polarity that defined middle-class identification. One might say that the positive images of one lined up with the negative images of the other, so that to identify with both required either a contortionist's flexibility or a dangerous splitting of the self. The double bind of the black middle class was in place.

The black middle class has always defined its class identity by means of 13 positive images gleaned from middle- and upper-class white society, and by means of negative images of lower-class blacks. This habit goes back to the institution of slavery itself, when "house" slaves both mimicked the whites they served and held themselves above the "field" slaves. But in the sixties the old bourgeois impulse to dissociate from the lower classes (the "we-they" distinction) backfired when racial identity suddenly called for the celebration of this same black lower class. One of the qualities of a double bind is that one feels it more than sees it, and I distinctly remember the tension and strange sense of dishonesty I felt in those days as I moved back and forth like a bigamist between the demands of class and race.

Though my father was born poor, he achieved middle-class standing through much hard work and sacrifice (one of his favorite words) and by identifying fully with solid middle-class values — mainly hard work, family life, property ownership, and education for his children (all four of whom have advanced degrees). In his mind these were not so much values as laws of nature. People who embodied them made up the positive images in his class polarity. The negative images came largely from the blacks he had left behind because they were "going nowhere."

No one in my family remembers how it happened, but as time went on, the negative images congealed into an imaginary character named Sam, who, from the extensive service we put him to, quickly grew to mythic proportions. In our family lore he was sometimes a trickster, sometimes a boob, but always possessed a catalogue of sly faults that gave up graphic images of everything we should not be. On sacrifice: "Sam never thinks about tomorrow. He wants it now or he doesn't care about it." On work: "Sam doesn't favor it too much." On children: "Sam likes to have them but not to raise them." On money: "Sam drinks it up and pisses it out." On fidelity: "Sam has to have two or three women." On clothes: "Sam features loud clothes. He likes to see and be seen." And so on. Sam's persona amounted to a negative instruction manual in class identity.

I don't think that any of us believed Sam's faults were accurate representations of lower-class black life. He was an instrument of self-definition, not of sociological accuracy. It never occurred to us that he looked very much like the white racist stereotype of blacks, or that he might have been a manifestation of our own racial self-hatred. He simply gave us a counterpoint against which to express our aspirations. If self-hatred was a factor, it was not, for us, a matter of hating lower-class blacks but of hating what we did not want to be.

Still, hate or love aside, it is fundamentally true that my middle-class identity involved a dissociation from images of lower-class black life and a corresponding identification with values and patterns of responsibility that are common to the middle class everywhere. These values sent me a clear message: Be both an individual and a responsible citizen; understand that the quality of your life will approximately reflect the quality of effort you put into it; know that individual responsibility is the basis of freedom and that the limitations imposed by fate (whether fair or unfair) are no excuse for passivity.

Whether I live up to these values or not, I know that my acceptance of them is the result of lifelong conditioning. I know also that I share this conditioning with middle-class people of all races and that I can no more easily be free of it than I can be free of my race. Whether all this got started

14

15

16

17

18

because the black middle class modeled itself on the white middle class is no longer relevant. For the middle-class black, conditioned by these values from birth, the sense of meaning they provide is as immutable as the color of his skin.

In my junior year in college I rode to a debate tournament with three   19
white students and our faculty coach, an elderly English professor. The experience of being the lone black in a group of whites was so familiar to me that I thought nothing of it as our trip began. But then, halfway through the trip, the professor casually turned to me and, in an isn't-the-world-funny sort of tone, said that he had just refused to rent an apartment in a house he owned to a "very nice" black couple because their color would "offend" the white couple who lived downstairs. His eyebrows lifted helplessly over his hawkish nose, suggesting that he too, like me, was a victim of America's racial farce. His look assumed a kind of comradeship: He and I were above this grimy business of race, though for expediency we had occasionally to concede the world its madness.

My vulnerability in this situation came not so much from the professor's   20
blindness to his own racism as from his assumption that I would participate in it, that I would conspire with him against my own race so that he might remain comfortably blind. Why did he think I would be amenable to this? I can only guess that he assumed my middle-class identity was so complete and all-encompassing that I would see his action as nothing more than a trifling concession to the folkways of our land, that I would in fact applaud his decision not to disturb propriety. Blind to both his own racism and to me — one blindness serving the other — he could not recognize that he was asking me to betray my race in the name of my class.

His blindness made me feel vulnerable because it threatened to expose   21
my own repressed ambivalence. His comment pressured me to choose between my class identification, which had contributed to my being a college student and a member of the debating team, and my desperate desire to be "black." I could have one but not both; I was double-bound.

Because double binds are repressed there is always an element of terror   22
in them: the terror of bringing to the conscious mind the buried duplicity, self-deception, and pretense involved in serving two masters. This terror is the stuff of vulnerability, and since vulnerability is one of the least tolerable of all human feelings, we usually transform it into an emotion that seems to restore the control of which it has robbed us; most often, that emotion is anger. And so, before the professor had even finished his little story, I had become a furnace of rage. The year was 1967, and I had been primed by endless hours of nap-matching[1] to feel, at least consciously, completely at one with the victim-focused black identity. This identity gave me the license, and the impunity, to unleash upon this professor one of those vol-

[1]***Nap-matching*** Slang for measuring one's black identification. [Editor's note.]

canic eruptions of racial indignation familiar to us from the novels of Richard Wright. Like Cross Damon in *Outsider,* who kills in perfectly righteous anger, I tried to annihilate the man. I punished him not according to the measure of his crime but according to the measure of my vulnerability, a measure set by the cumulative tension of years of repressed terror. Soon I saw that terror in *his* face, as he stared hollow-eyed at the road ahead. My white friends in the back seat, knowing no conflict between their own class and race, were astonished that someone they had taken to be so much like themselves could harbor a rage that for all the world looked murderous.

Though my rage was triggered by the professor's comment, it was deep- 23 ened and sustained by a complex of need, conflict, and repression in myself of which I had been wholly unaware. Out of my racial vulnerability I had developed the strong need of an identity with which to defend myself. The only such identity available was that of me as victim, him as victimizer. Once in the grip of this paradigm, I began to do far more damage to myself than he had done.

Seeing myself as a victim meant that I clung all the harder to my racial 24 identity, which, in turn, meant that I suppressed my class identity. This cut me off from all the resources my class values might have offered me. In those values, for instance, I might have found the means to a more dispassionate response, the response less of a victim attacked by a victimizer than of an individual offended by a foolish old man. As an individual I might have reported this professor to the college dean. Or I might have calmly tried to reveal his blindness to him, and possibly won a convert. (The flagrancy of his remark suggested a hidden guilt and even self-recognition on which I might have capitalized. Doesn't confession usually signal a willingness to face oneself?) Or I might have simply chuckled and then let my silence serve as an answer to his provocation. Would not my composure, in any form it might take, deflect into his own heart the arrow he'd shot at me?

Instead, my anger, itself the hair-trigger expression of a long-repressed 25 double bind, not only cut me off from the best of my own resources, it also distorted the nature of my true racial problem. The righteousness of this anger and the easy catharsis it brought buoyed the delusion of my victimization and left me as blind as the professor himself.

Analyzing This Selection

1. In paragraph 6, Steele lists specific values that define the middle class. Would you add to or challenge any items on his list? What items would define a lower class? an upper class?

2. **THE WRITER'S METHOD** How, if at all, did the imaginary Sam differ from a racist image? From an advertising image?

3. Steele criticizes his younger reaction to an insult from his college debate coach. How do you regard his response? Do you think the alternatives he names are preferable?

4. Do you think Steele was most powerfully influenced by race, class, or family? Choose one and support your choice.

Analyzing Connections

5. Steele and Gates (see "In the Kitchen," p. 206) both grew up aware of class differences within family life. What conflicts over class did they resolve within their race and their families?

Analyzing by Writing

6. In your family or social group, what circumstances put you in conflict with another good part of yourself? What two identities or allegiances can turn into a double bind? Perhaps your religious or ethnic upbringing, your athletic ability, your family's expectations for you, or your desire to travel aimlessly for a while threatens some other value or goal you uphold. Analyze the double bind that can operate in your situation.

Camilo José Vergara

THE GHETTO CITYSCAPE

CAMILO JOSÉ VERGARA (b. 1944), photographer and writer, used a camera to document his graduate studies in sociology at Columbia University before turning to photography as a career. His illustrated essays on urban blight and ghetto cultures have been published in magazines such as the *Nation*, the *Atlantic*, and *Architectural Record*. Vergara's exhibition "The New American Ghetto" was shown in New York and other cities before its publication as a book (1995), from which the following selection was taken. His recent exhibition "El Nuevo Mundo: The Landscape of Latino Los Angeles" (2000) explores neighborhood decorations as forms of public art.

If you were among the nearly eleven thousand people who lived in two-story row houses in North Camden in the 1960s, you could walk to work at Esterbrook Pen, at Knox Gelatin, at RCA, or at J. R. Evans Leather. You could shop on Broadway, a busy three-mile-long commercial thoroughfare, nicknamed the "Street of Lights" because of its five first-run movie theaters with their bright neon signs. 1

After J. R. Evans Leather was abandoned and almost completely demolished, its smokestack stood alone in a vast field by the Delaware River, a symbol of the demise of industry in Camden. Hundreds of row houses — once counted among the best ordinary urban dwellings in America — have been scooped up by bulldozers, their debris carted to a dump in Delaware. Walking along North Camden's narrow streets, one passes entire blocks without a single structure, the empty land crisscrossed by footpaths. The scattered dwellings that remain are faced with iron bars, so that they resemble cages. 2

With nearly half of its overwhelmingly Latino population on some form of public assistance, this once thriving working-class neighborhood is now the poorest urban community in New Jersey. In 1986, former mayor Alfred Pierce called Camden a reservation for the destitute. The north section of the city has become the drug center for South Jersey, and it hosts a large state prison. 3

North Camden is not unique. Since the riots of the 1960s, American cities have experienced profound transformations, best revealed in the spatial restructuring of their ghettos and in the emergence of new urban forms. 4

231

A section of Fern Street, semi-abandoned, yet with most of its row houses still standing. North Camden, 1979.

During the past decade, however, the "underclass" and homelessness have dominated the study of urban poverty. Meanwhile, the power of the physical surroundings to shape lives, to mirror people's existence, and to symbolize social relations has been ignored. When scholars from across the political spectrum discuss the factors that account for the persistence of poverty, they fail to consider its living environments. And when prescribing solutions, they overlook the very elements that define the new ghettos: the ruins and the semi-ruins; the medical, warehousing, and behavior-modification institutions; the various NIMBYs, fortresses, and walls; and, not least, the bitterness and anger resulting from living in these places.

Dismissing the value of information received through sight, taste, and smell, or through the emotional overtones in an informant's voice, or from the sensation of moving through the spaces studied, has led to the creation of constructs without character, individuality, or a sense of place. And although the limitations of statistical data — particularly when dealing with very poor populations — are widely acknowledged, our great dependency on numbers is fiercely defended. Other approaches are dismissed as impressionistic, anecdotal, as poetry, or "windshield surveys."

Yet today's ghettos are diverse, rich in public and private responses to the environment, in expressions of cultural identity, and in reminders of history. These communities are uncharted territory; to be understood, their forms need to be identified, described, inventoried, and mapped.

An examination of scores of ghettos across the nation reveals three types: "green ghettos," characterized by depopulation, vacant land overgrown by nature, and ruins; "institutional ghettos," publicly financed places of confinement designed mainly for the native-born; and "new immigrant ghettos," deriving their character from an influx of immigrants, mainly Latino and West Indian. Some of these communities have continued to lose population; others have emerged where a quarter-century ago there were white ethnic blue-collar neighborhoods; and sections of older ghettos have remained stable, working neighborhoods or have been rebuilt.

The surviving houses have fenced porches and their rough sides have been smoothed out with a covering of cement. Weeds grow on the sidewalk in front of clusters of abandoned houses, and people and dogs walk in the middle of the street. This block of Fern Street, where less than 20 percent of the original houses remain occupied, exemplifies the dismantling of the city. North Camden, 1994.

Green ghettos, where little has been done to counter the effect of disin- 8
vestment, abandonment, depopulation, and dependency, are the leftovers
of a society. Best exemplified by North Camden, Detroit's East Side,
Chicago's Lawndale, and East St. Louis in Illinois, they are expanding outward to include poor suburbs of large cities such as Robbins, Illinois, and
are even found in small cities such as Benton Harbor, Michigan.

Residents, remembering the businesses that moved to suburban malls, 9
the closed factories, the fires, complain of living in a threatening place
bereft of jobs and stores and neglected by City Hall. In many sections of
these ghettos, pheasants and rabbits have regained the space once occupied
by humans, yet these are not wilderness retreats in the heart of the city.
"Nothing but weeds are growing there," is a frequent complaint about
vacant lots, expressing no mere distaste for the vegetation, but moral outrage at the neglect that produces these anomalies. Plants grow wildly on
and around the vestiges of the former International Harvester Component
Plant in West Pullman, Chicago. Derelict industrial buildings here and in
other ghettos have long ago been stripped of anything of value. Large
parcels of land lie unkempt or paved over, subtracted from the life of the
city. Contradicting a long-held vision of our country as a place of endless
progress, ruins, once unforeseen, are now ignored.

In New York City, Newark, and Chicago, large and expensive habitats — 10
institutional ghettos — have been created for the weakest and most vulnerable
members of our society. Institution by institution, facility by facility, these
environments have been assembled in the most drug-infested and destitute
parts of cities. They are the complex poorhouses of the twenty-first century,
places to store a growing marginal population officially certified as "not
employable." Residents are selected from the entire population of the
municipality for their lack of money or home, for their addictions, for their
diseases and other afflictions. Nonresidents come to these institutions to
pick up medications, surplus food, used clothes; to get counseling or training; or to do a stint in prison. Other visitors buy drugs and sex.

As Greg Turner, the manager of a day shelter on the Near West Side of 11
Chicago, puts it: "They say, 'Let's get them off the streets and put them
together in groups.' It is like the zoo: we are going to put the birds over
here; we are going to put the reptiles over there; we are going to put the
buffalo over here; we are going to put the seals by the pool. It is doing
nothing to work with the root of the problem, just like they do nothing to
work with the children, to teach them things so they don't grow up and
become more homeless people or substance abusers."

Although the need for individual components — for instance, a homeless 12
shelter or a waste incinerator — may be subject to public debate, the overall consequences of creating such "campuses" of institutions are dismissed.
The most important barrier to their growth is the cost to the taxpayers of
building and maintaining them.

Such sections of the city are not neighborhoods. The streets surrounding   13
Lincoln Park in south Newark, for example, an area that includes landmark
houses, grand public buildings, and a once-elegant hotel, were chosen by
two drug treatment programs because six of its large mansions would provide inexpensive housing for a residential treatment program. On the
northwest corner of the park, a shelter for battered women just opened in
another mansion, and a block north in a former garage is a men's shelter
and soup kitchen. The largest structures overlooking the park, the hotel
and a former federal office building, house the elderly, who fear going out
by themselves. No children play in the park: no parents come home from
work. This is a no-man's-land devoted to the contradictory goals of selling
drugs and getting high, on the one hand, and becoming clean and employed
on the other.

In other parts of New York and Chicago a community of recent immi-   14
grants is growing up, but this type of ghetto is most visible in South Central Los Angeles and Compton, where the built environment is more
intimate than in older ghettos, the physical structures are more adaptable,
and it is easier for newcomers to imprint their identity. Here paint goes a
long way to transform the appearance of the street.

The new immigrant ghettos are characterized by tiny offices providing   15
services such as driving instruction, insurance, and immigration assistance;
by stores that sell imported beer, produce, and canned goods; and by
restaurants offering home cooking. Notable are the businesses that reflect
the busy exchange between the local population and their native country:
money transfers, travel agencies, even funeral homes that arrange to have
bodies shipped home.

To get by, most residents are forced to resort to exploitative jobs paying   16
minimum wage or less and usually lacking health benefits. For housing
they crowd together in small, badly maintained apartments, in cinder-block
garages, or in trailers.

Not being eligible for public or city-owned housing may in the long run   17
prove to be a blessing for the newcomers. Although forced to pay high
rents, immigrants tend to concentrate in neighborhoods that are part of the
urban economy, thus avoiding the extreme social disorganization, isolation,
and violence that characterize other types of ghettos. Because of the huge
influx of young people with expectations that life will be better for their
children and grandchildren, these ghettos are more dynamic and fluid,
resembling the foreign-born communities of a century ago.

No single ghetto is completely green, institutional, or immigrant in char-   18
acter. Although the overwhelming trend is toward greater waste, abandonment, and depopulation, these three models are related, channeling people
and land to one another. Fires and demolitions in the green ghettos provide large tracts of cleared land where poverty institutions and other facilities can be built. By default, the most desperate people and neighborhoods

become wards of the government in communities where, in the words of a Brooklyn organizer, "All the social disasters of the city are located."

If nothing is done to prevent it, within a decade more working-class [19] communities are likely to belong to one of these types. Conversely, some institutional ghettos, such as the Near West Side of Chicago, are likely to be squeezed out by expanding sports and medical complexes. And the same forces of abandonment that open the way for the modern poorhouses can at other times free land for townhouses built for working families.

These are the "reclaimed ghettos." With their horror stories of violence, [20] governmental incompetence, and waste, ghettos are used to provide strong moral justification for privately managed programs of redevelopment. Under the leadership of churches, community development organizations, private developers, and recent immigrants, such ghettos have kicked out most of the dependent poor and have refused to admit the institutions that serve them. Instead, they focus on attracting working families, keeping out drug dealers, and building guarded enclaves.

These communities are on the verge of melding into mainstream soci- [21] ety. But when examining the contribution of community development corporations, we need to ask ourselves whether their efforts are leading to the elimination of ghettos, or toward the creation of mini-cities of exclusion within the larger wasteland.

For it is at the boundaries that the individual character of ghettos reveals [22] itself most clearly: around embattled clusters of dwellings where ethnic groups assert themselves, in blocks where strong buildings share a wall with dilapidated crackhouses, and along the perimeter of hospitals, universities, and other citadels. Borders where white meets black are stark, presenting a graphic contrast between a seemingly victorious white community and what appears to be a defeated minority community. Along Mack Avenue, as it crosses from Detroit's East Side into affluent Grosse Pointe, for example, and along Chicago's East Sixty-second Street, the border between Wood-lawn and Hyde Park (home of the University of Chicago), a history of race relations has been written into the landscape. Security barriers, guards, dead-end streets, well-tended lawns on one side; on the other, vacant lots, abandoned buildings, out-of-work people hanging out.

Writers for the popular press call ghettos intractable, expressing concern [23] about the public burden they impose. The system works for those who are motivated, many outsiders say, pointing to the presence of minorities in more affluent suburbs, to reclaimed ghettos, and to the economic success of recent West Indian, Latino, and Asian immigrants.

But among many ghetto dwellers, particularly native-born African Amer- [24] icans, there is growing ideological hardening and a yearning to close ranks, to reemerge from destitution and to prosper among themselves. A journalist in Gary, Indiana, a city almost completely abandoned by whites, remarked: "I don't know why people have to have white people to succeed." A Chicago construction worker called blacks who moved to the suburbs "imitation white people." A Newark woman suggested that such people have sold out, are living a lie. "They need to take a good look in the mirror," she said. Also in Newark, on the walls of the abandoned Macy's department store, graffiti by "The Natural Thebians" complains: "How can you talk about nation time and wear the underwear of your enemy!"

Echoing Malcolm X, most ghetto residents I have encountered see the devastation and violence in their communities as part of a white strategy of domination. Drugs are widely perceived as part of a monstrous plot to destroy and contain poor blacks and Latinos. A Chicago minister states: "White supremacy, a system of oppression that comes out of Western society, is the real problem." A Brooklyn artist declares: "People of color have a right to be paranoid." A national mood of desperation and resentment, expressed by words like "genocide," "concentration camps," and "apartheid," has developed to account for the conditions of our ghettos. 25

Within ghetto walls a new generation is growing along with new activities, ideologies, institutions, and drugs. Crack sells briskly across the street from drug treatment centers, and children walk past homeless shelters. An army of men strips cars, and hordes of scavengers push loaded shopping carts along the streets. Houses, turned into fortresses, stand alone, enclosed by fences. Dozens of cities are falling into ruin, and along their streets billboards plead for people to stop killing one another. 26

Today, there is renewed talk of strategies to bring jobs, to improve education, to build better housing, and to provide adequate health care for all Americans. Such developments would certainly improve the conditions in poor communities, but would not change their isolation, racial composition, and fragmentation. Ghettos would continue to expand, new ones to emerge, and the anger of their residents would remain unabated. 27

Public policy must also address the unique characteristics of our ghettos. A crucial step is to change policies and practices that concentrate in these communities the poor and the institutions that serve them. We need regional and national approaches to population redistribution, such as the building of low-income housing in wealthy suburbs and the elimination of the barriers that define ghettos. And as we once did in the 1960s, we need to convince ourselves that as a nation we have the power not just to improve the ghetto, but to abolish it. To do this we must go beyond the statistics and into the streets, alleys, and buildings. 28

In reply to those for whom dreams of a more just society have lost their power, and to those who believe that ghettos are necessary to have stronger communities elsewhere, stand the haunting, defiant, and despairing words scribbled on the stairway of an East Harlem high-rise: "Help me before I die, motherfucker!" 29

Analyzing This Selection

1. What features define each type of ghetto? Which type does the author criticize more than the others?

2. **THE WRITER'S METHOD**   According to Vergara, how does his visual approach to ghettos differ from other kinds of studies? How do the illustrations contribute to Vergara's argument?

3. In the final paragraph, how do you react to this use of obscenity? How was the obscenity intended to affect the public?

Analyzing Connections

4. Vergara and Steele (see "On Being Black and Middle Class," p. 224) each examine class differences in society. What different explanations do they offer for the persistence of an underclass?

Analyzing by Writing

5. Analyze the features of a special area on your campus. It could be the sports complex, the central quad or plaza, or recently built dormitories and cafeterias. Like Vergara, question the effects of these places.

Arthur Ashe and Arnold Rampersad

THE BURDEN OF RACE

ARTHUR ASHE (1943–1993) broke the color barrier in professional tennis. Born in Richmond, Virginia, he lived under segregation. He ascended to top world rank by winning the U.S. Open in 1968 and Wimbledon in 1975. Illness requiring heart bypass surgery forced his retirement and led to his contracting AIDS through blood transfusions. By publicizing his illness, Ashe increased public awareness of AIDS and raised funds for research. The following selection is excerpted from his memoir, *Days of Grace* (1993), which was written with assistance from Arnold Rampersad.

I had spent more than an hour talking in my office at home with a reporter for *People* magazine. Her editor had sent her to do a story about me and how I was coping with AIDS. The reporter's questions had been probing and yet respectful of my right to privacy. Now, our interview over, I was escorting her to the door. As she slipped on her coat, she fell silent. I could see that she was groping for the right words to express her sympathy for me before she left.

"Mr. Ashe, I guess this must be the heaviest burden you have ever had to bear, isn't it?" she asked finally.

I thought for a moment, but only a moment. "No, it isn't. It's a burden, all right. But AIDS isn't the heaviest burden I have had to bear."

"Is there something worse? Your heart attack?"

I didn't want to detain her, but I let the door close with both of us still inside. "You're not going to believe this," I said to her, "but being black is the greatest burden I've had to bear."

"You can't mean that."

"No question about it. Race has always been my biggest burden. Having to live as a minority in America. Even now it continues to feel like an extra weight tied around me."

I can still recall the surprise and perhaps even the hurt on her face. I may even have surprised myself, because I simply had never thought of comparing the two conditions before. However, I stand by my remark. Race is for me a more onerous burden than AIDS. My disease is the result of biological factors over which we, thus far, have had no control. Racism, however, is entirely made by people, and therefore it hurts and inconveniences infinitely more.

239

Since our interview (skillfully presented as a first-person account by me)   9
appeared in *People* in June 1992, many people have commented on my
remark. A radio station in Chicago aimed primarily at blacks conducted a
lively debate on its merits on the air. Most African Americans have little
trouble understanding and accepting my statement, but other people have
been baffled by it. Even Donald Dell, my close friend of more than thirty
years, was puzzled. In fact, he was so troubled that he telephoned me in
the middle of the night from Hamburg, Germany, to ask if I had been mis-
quoted. No, I told him, I had been quoted correctly. Some people have
asked me flatly, what could *you*, Arthur Ashe, possibly have to complain
about? Do you want more money or fame than you already have? Isn't
AIDS inevitably fatal? What can be worse than death?

The novelist Henry James suggested somewhere that it is a complex fate   10
being an American. I think it is a far more complex fate being an African
American. I also sometimes think that this indeed may be one of those fates
that are worse than death.

I do not want to be misunderstood. I do not mean to appear fatalistic,   11
self-pitying, cynical, or maudlin. Proud to be an American, I am also proud
to be an African American. I delight in the accomplishments of fellow citizens of my color. When one considers the odds against which we have
labored, we have achieved much. I believe in life and hope and love, and
I turn my back on death until I must face my end in all its finality. I am an
optimist, not a pessimist. Still, a pall of sadness hangs over my life and the
lives of almost all African Americans because of what we as a people have
experienced historically in America, and what we as individuals experience
each and every day. Whether one is a welfare recipient trapped in some
blighted "housing project" in the inner city or a former Wimbledon champion who is easily recognized on the streets and whose home is a luxurious
apartment in one of the wealthiest districts of Manhattan, the sadness is
still there.

In some respects, I am a prisoner of the past. A long time ago, I made   12
peace with the state of Virginia and the South. While I, like other blacks,
was once barred from free association with whites, I returned time and time
again, under the new rule of desegregation, to work with whites in my
hometown and across the South. But segregation had achieved by that time
what it was intended to achieve: It left me a marked man, forever aware of
a shadow of contempt that lays across my identity and my sense of self-
esteem. Subtly the shadow falls on my reputation, the way I know I am perceived; the mere memory of it darkens my most sunny days. I believe that
the same is true for almost every African American of the slightest sensitivity and intelligence. Again, I don't want to overstate the case. I think of
myself, and others think of me, as supremely self-confident. I know objec-
tively that it is almost impossible for someone to be as successful as I have
been as an athlete and to lack self-assurance. Still, I also know that the
shadow is always there; only death will free me, and blacks like me, from
its pall.

The shadow fell across me recently on one of the brightest days, literally   13
and metaphorically, of my life. On August 30, 1992, the day before the
U.S. Open, the USTA and I together hosted an afternoon of tennis at the
National Tennis Center in Flushing Meadows, New York. The event was a
benefit for the Arthur Ashe Foundation for the Defeat of AIDS. Before the
start, I was nervous. Would the invited stars (McEnroe, Graf, Navratilova,
et al.) show up? Would they cooperate with us, or be difficult to manage?
And, on the eve of a Grand Slam tournament, would fans pay to see light-
hearted tennis? The answers were all a resounding yes (just over ten thousand fans turned out). With CBS televising the event live and Aetna having
provided the air time, a profit was assured. The sun shone brightly, the
humidity was mild, and the temperature hovered in the low 80s.

What could mar such a day? The shadow of race, and the sensitivity, or   14
perhaps hypersensitivity, to its nuances. Sharing the main stadium box with
Jeanne, Camera, and me, at my invitation, were Stan Smith, his wife Mar-
jory, and their daughter Austin. The two little girls were happy to see one
another. During Wimbledon in June, they had renewed their friendship
when we all stayed near each other in London. Now Austin, seven years
old, had brought Camera a present. She had come with twin dolls, one for
herself, one for Camera. A thoughtful gesture on Austin's part, and on her
parents' part, no doubt. The Smiths are fine, religious people. Then I
noticed that Camera was playing with her doll above the railing of the box,
in full view of the attentive network television cameras. The doll was the
problem; or rather, the fact that the doll was conspicuously a blond. Camera owns dolls of all colors, nationalities, and ethnic varieties. But she was
now on national television playing with a blond doll. Suddenly I heard
voices in my head, the voices of irate listeners to a call-in show on some
"black format" radio station. I imagined insistent, clamorous callers attacking Camera, Jeanne, and me:

"*Can you believe the doll Arthur Ashe's daughter was holding up at the*   15
AIDS benefit? Wasn't that a shame?"

"*Is that brother sick or what? Somebody ought to teach that poor child*   16
about her true black self!"

"*What kind of role model is Arthur Ashe if he allows his daughter to be*   17
brainwashed that way?"

"*Doesn't the brother* understand *that he is corrupting his child's mind*   18
with notions about the superiority of the white woman? I tell you, I thought
we were long past that!"

The voices became louder in my head. Despite the low humidity, I   19
began to squirm in my seat. What should I do? Should I say, To hell with
what some people might think? I know that Camera likes her blond dolls,
black dolls, brown dolls, Asian dolls, Indian dolls just about equally; I know
that for a fact, because I have watched her closely. I have searched for signs
of racial partiality in her, indications that she may be dissatisfied with herself, with her own color. I have seen none. But I cannot dismiss the voices.
I try always to live practically, and I do not wish to hear such comments on

the radio. On the other hand, I do not want Austin's gift to be sullied by an ungracious response. Finally, I act.

"Jeanne," I whisper, "we have to do something."   20

"About what?" she whispers back.   21

"That doll. We have to get Camera to put that doll down."   22

Jeanne takes one look at Camera and the doll and she understands   23 immediately. Quietly, cleverly, she makes the dolls disappear. Neither Camera nor Austin is aware of anything unusual happening. Smoothly, Jeanne has moved them on to some other distraction.

I am unaware if Margie Smith has noticed us, but I believe I owe her an   24 explanation. I get up and go around to her seat. Softly I tell her why the dolls have disappeared. Margie is startled, dumbfounded.

"Gosh, Arthur, I never thought about that. I never *ever* thought about   25 anything like that!"

"*You* don't have to think about it," I explain. "But it happens to us, in   26 similar situations, all the time."

"All the time?" She is pensive now.   27

"All the time. It's perfectly understandable. And it certainly is not your   28 fault. You were doing what comes naturally. But for us, the dolls make for a bit of a problem. All for the wrong reasons. It shouldn't be this way, but it is."

I return to my seat, but not to the elation I had felt before I saw that   29 blond doll in Camera's hand. I feel myself becoming more and more angry. I am angry at the force that made me act, the force of racism in all its complexity, as it spreads into the world and creates defensiveness and intolerance among the very people harmed by racism. I am also angry with myself. I am angry with myself because I have just acted out of pure practicality, not out of morality. The moral act would have been to let Camera have her fun, because she was innocent of any wrongdoing. Instead, I had tampered with her innocence, her basic human right to act impulsively, to accept a gift from a friend in the same beautiful spirit in which it was given.

Deeply embarrassed now, I am ashamed at what I have done. I have   30 made Camera adjust her behavior merely because of the likelihood that some people in the African American community would react to her innocence foolishly and perhaps even maliciously. I know I am not misreading the situation. I would have had telephone calls that very evening about the unsuitability of Camera's doll. Am I being a hypocrite? Yes, definitely, up to a point. I have allowed myself to give in to those people who say we must avoid even the slightest semblance of "Eurocentric" influence. But I also know what stands behind the entire situation. Racism ultimately created the state in which defensiveness and hypocrisy are our almost instinctive responses, and innocence and generosity are invitations to trouble.

This incident almost ruined the day for me. That night, when Jeanne   31 and I talked about the excitement of the afternoon, and the money that would go to AIDS research and education because of the event, we nevertheless ended up talking mostly about the incident of the dolls. We also talked about perhaps its most ironic aspect. In 1954, when the Supreme Court ruled against school segregation in *Brown v. Board of Education,* some of the most persuasive testimony came from the psychologist Dr. Kenneth Clark concerning his research on black children and their pathetic preference for white dolls over black. In 1992, the dolls are still a problem.

Once again, the shadow of race had fallen on me.   32

Analyzing This Selection

1. **THE WRITER'S METHOD**   Clarify Ashe's statement that he is proud to be an African American, though it is a fate worse than death. Is this a contradiction?

2. How did earlier segregation affect Ashe's later character?

3. In your opinion, did Ashe act appropriately during the doll incident? Was the alternative truly better? Explain the dilemma and its effects.

Analyzing Connections

4. Read the interview in *People* magazine (June 1992), and compare both versions of the incident. What aspects are developed differently? In your opinion, why did Ashe reconsider it in this memoir?

Analyzing by Writing

5. Ashe examines the fate of being an African American, and Theodor Reik defines group identity as "the community of fate" in the Insights on pages 194–95. What sense of *fate* connects you to other people? Examine how, if at all, your identity includes a destiny in common with others.

Alice Walker

EVERYDAY USE

ALICE WALKER (b. 1944), one of America's leading contemporary writers, was raised in a Georgia sharecropper's family as the youngest of eight children. After graduating from Sarah Lawrence College, she became active in the civil rights and feminist movements. Her work as a poet, essayist, and fiction writer includes five novels, among them *The Color Purple* (1982), winner of both the Pulitzer Prize and the American Book Award. Walker's collections of essays include *The Same River Twice: Honoring the Difficult* (1996) and *Anything We Love Can Be Saved* (1997). The following short story was collected in *In Love and Trouble: Stories of Black Women* (1973).

for your grandmama

I will wait for her in the yard that Maggie and I made so clean and wavy yesterday afternoon. A yard like this is more comfortable than most people know. It is not just a yard. It is like an extended living room. When the hard clay is swept clean as a floor and the fine sand around the edges lined with tiny, irregular grooves, anyone can come and sit and look up into the elm tree and wait for the breezes that never come inside the house.

Maggie will be nervous until after her sister goes: She will stand hopelessly in corners, homely and ashamed of the burn scars down her arms and legs, eyeing her sister with a mixture of envy and awe. She thinks her sister has held life always in the palm of one hand, that "no" is a word the world never learned to say to her.

You've no doubt seen those TV shows where the child who has "made it" is confronted, as a surprise, by her own mother and father, tottering in weakly from backstage. (A pleasant surprise, of course: What would they do if parent and child came on the show only to curse out and insult each other?) On TV mother and child embrace and smile into each other's faces. Sometimes the mother and father weep, the child wraps them in her arms and leans across the table to tell how she would not have made it without their help. I have seen these programs.

Sometimes I dream a dream in which Dee and I are suddenly brought together on a TV program of this sort. Out of a dark and soft-seated limousine I am ushered into a bright room filled with many people. There I meet a smiling, gray, sporty man like Johnny Carson who shakes my hand and tells me what a fine girl I have. Then we are on the stage and Dee is embracing me with tears in her eyes. She pins on my dress a large orchid, even though she has told me once that she thinks orchids are tacky flowers.

In real life I am a large, big-boned woman with rough, man-working   5
hands. In the winter I wear flannel nightgowns to bed and overalls during the day. I can kill and clean a hog as mercilessly as a man. My fat keeps me hot in zero weather. I can work outside all day, breaking ice to get water for washing; I can eat pork liver cooked over the open fire minutes after it comes steaming from the hog. One winter I knocked a bull calf straight in the brain between the eyes with a sledge hammer and had the meat hung up to chill before nightfall. But of course all this does not show on television. I am the way my daughter would want me to be: a hundred pounds lighter, my skin like an uncooked barley pancake. My hair glistens in the hot bright lights. Johnny Carson has much to do to keep up with my quick and witty tongue.

But that is a mistake. I know even before I wake up. Who ever knew a   6
Johnson with a quick tongue? Who can even imagine me looking a strange white man in the eye? It seems to me I have talked to them always with one foot raised in flight, with my head turned in whichever way is farthest from them. Dee, though. She would always look anyone in the eye. Hesitation was no part of her nature.

"How do I look, Mama?" Maggie says, showing just enough of her thin   7
body enveloped in pink skirt and red blouse for me to know she's there, almost hidden by the door.

"Come out into the yard," I say.   8

Have you ever seen a lame animal, perhaps a dog run over by some   9
careless person rich enough to own a car, sidle up to someone who is ignorant enough to be kind to him? That is the way my Maggie walks. She has been like this, chin on chest, eyes on ground, feet in shuffle, ever since the fire that burned the other house to the ground.

Dee is lighter than Maggie, with nicer hair and a fuller figure. She's a   10
woman now, though sometimes I forget. How long ago was it that the other house burned? Ten, twelve years? Sometimes I can still hear the flames and feel Maggie's arms sticking to me, her hair smoking and her dress falling off her in little black papery flakes. Her eyes seemed stretched open, blazed open by the flames reflected in them. And Dee. I see her standing off under the sweet gum tree she used to dig gum out of; a look of concentration on her face as she watched the last dingy gray board of the house fall in toward the red-hot brick chimney. Why don't you do a dance around the ashes? I'd wanted to ask her. She had hated the house that much.

I used to think she hated Maggie, too. But that was before we raised the   11
money, the church and me, to send her to Augusta to school. She used to

read to us without pity; forcing words, lies, other folks' habits, whole lives upon us two, sitting trapped and ignorant underneath her voice. She washed us in a river of make-believe, burned us with a lot of knowledge we didn't necessarily need to know. Pressed us to her with the serious way she read, to shove us away at just the moment, like dimwits, we seemed about to understand.

Dee wanted nice things. A yellow organdy dress to wear to her gradua-   12 tion from high school; black pumps to match a green suit she'd made from an old suit somebody gave me. She was determined to stare down any disaster in her efforts. Her eyelids would not flicker for minutes at a time. Often I fought off the temptation to shake her. At sixteen she had a style of her own: and knew what style was.

I never had an education myself. After second grade the school was   13 closed down. Don't ask me why: In 1927 colored asked fewer questions than they do now. Sometimes Maggie reads to me. She stumbles along good-naturedly but can't see well. She knows she is not bright. Like good looks and money, quickness passed her by. She will marry John Thomas (who has mossy teeth in an earnest face) and then I'll be free to sit here and I guess just sing church songs to myself. Although I never was a good singer. Never could carry a tune. I was always better at a man's job. I used to love to milk till I was hooked in the side in '49. Cows are soothing and slow and don't bother you, unless you try to milk them the wrong way.

I have deliberately turned my back on the house. It is three rooms, just   14 like the one that burned, except the roof is tin; they don't make shingle roofs any more. There are no real windows, just some holes cut in the sides, like the portholes in a ship, but not round and not square, with rawhide holding the shutters up on the outside. This house is in a pasture, too, like the other one. No doubt when Dee sees it she will want to tear it down. She wrote me once that no matter where we "choose" to live, she will manage to come see us. But she will never bring her friends. Maggie and I thought about this and Maggie asked me, "Mama, when did Dee ever *have* any friends?"

She had a few. Furtive boys in pink shirts hanging about on washday   15 after school. Nervous girls who never laughed. Impressed with her they worshiped the well-turned phrase, the cute shape, the scalding humor that erupted like bubbles in lye. She read to them.

When she was courting Jimmy T she didn't have much time to pay to   16 us, but turned all her faultfinding power on him. He *flew* to marry a cheap city girl from a family of ignorant flashy people. She hardly had time to recompose herself.

When she comes I will meet — but there they are!   17

Maggie attempts to make a dash for the house, in her shuffling way, but   18 I stay her with my hand. "Come back here," I say. And she stops and tries to dig a well in the sand with her toe.

It is hard to see them clearly through the strong sun. But even the first   19
glimpse of leg out of the car tells me it is Dee. Her feet were always neat-
looking, as if God himself had shaped them with a certain style. From the
other side of the car comes a short, stocky man. Hair is all over his head a
foot long and hanging from his chin like a kinky mule tail. I hear Maggie
suck in her breath. "Uhnnnh," is what it sounds like. Like when you see
the wriggling end of a snake just in front of your foot on the road.
"Uhnnnh."

Dee next. A dress down to the ground, in this hot weather. A dress so   20
loud it hurts my eyes. There are yellows and oranges enough to throw back
the light of the sun. I feel my whole face warming from the heat waves it
throws out. Earrings gold, too, and hanging down to her shoulders.
Bracelets dangling and making noises when she moves her arm up to shake
the folds of the dress out of her armpits. The dress is loose and flows, and
as she walks closer, I like it. I hear Maggie go "Uhnnnh" again. It is her sister's hair. It stands straight up like the wool on a sheep. It is black as night
and around the edges are two long pigtails that rope about like small
lizards disappearing behind her ears.

"Wa-su-zo-Tean-o!" she says, coming on in that gliding way the dress   21
makes her move. The short stocky fellow with the hair to his navel is all
grinning and he follows up with "Asalamalakim, my mother and sister!" He
moves to hug Maggie but she falls back, right up against the back of my
chair. I feel her trembling there and when I look up I see the perspiration
falling off her chin.

"Don't get up," says Dee. Since I am stout it takes something of a push.   22
You can see me trying to move a second or two before I make it. She turns,
showing white heels through her sandals, and goes back to the car. Out she
peeks next with a Polaroid. She stoops down quickly and lines up picture
after picture of me sitting there in front of the house with Maggie cowering
behind me. She never takes a shot without making sure the house is
included. When a cow comes nibbling around the edge of the yard she
snaps it and me and Maggie *and* the house. Then she puts the Polaroid in
the back seat of the car, and comes up and kisses me on the forehead.

Meanwhile Asalamalakim is going through motions with Maggie's hand.   23
Maggie's hand is as limp as a fish, and probably as cold, despite the sweat,
and she keeps trying to pull it back. It looks like Asalamalakim wants to
shake hands but wants to do it fancy. Or maybe he don't know how people
shake hands. Anyhow, he soon gives up on Maggie.

"Well," I say. "Dee."   24

"No, Mama," she says. "Not 'Dee,' Wangero Leewanika Kemanjo!"   25

"What happened to 'Dee'?" I wanted to know.   26

"She's dead," Wangero said. "I couldn't bear it any longer, being named   27
after the people who oppress me."

"You know as well as me you was named after your aunt Dicie," I said.   28
Dicie is my sister. She named Dee. We called her "Big Dee" after Dee was
born.

"But who was *she* named after?" asked Wangero.   29

"I guess after Grandma Dee," I said.   30

"And who was she named after?" asked Wangero.   31

"Her mother," I said, and saw Wangero was getting tired. "That's about   32
as far back as I can trace it," I said. Though, in fact, I probably could have
carried it back beyond the Civil War through the branches.

"Well," said Asalamalakim, "there you are."   33

"Uhnnnh," I heard Maggie say.   34

"There I was not," I said, "before 'Dicie' cropped up in our family, so   35
why should I try to trace it that far back?"

He just stood there grinning, looking down on me like somebody   36
inspecting a Model A car. Every once in a while he and Wangero sent eye
signals over my head.

"How do you pronounce this name?" I asked.   37

"You don't have to call me by it if you don't want to," said Wangero.   38

"Why shouldn't I?" I asked. "If that's what you want us to call you, we'll   39
call you."

"I know it might sound awkward at first," said Wangero.   40

"I'll get used to it," I said. "Ream it out again."   41

Well, soon we got the name out of the way. Asalamalakim had a name   42
twice as long and three times as hard. After I tripped over it two or three
times he told me to just call him Hakim-a-barber. I wanted to ask him was
he a barber, but I didn't really think he was, so I didn't ask.

"You must belong to those beef-cattle peoples down the road," I said.   43
They said "Asalamalakim" when they met you, too, but they didn't shake
hands. Always too busy: feeding the cattle, fixing the fences, putting up salt-
lick shelters, throwing down hay. When the white folks poisoned some of
the herd the men stayed up all night with rifles in their hands. I walked a
mile and a half just to see the sight.

Hakim-a-barber said, "I accept some of their doctrines, but farming and   44
raising cattle is not my style." (They didn't tell me, and I didn't ask,
whether Wangero (Dee) had really gone and married him.)

We sat down to eat and right away he said he didn't eat collards and pork   45
was unclean. Wangero, though, went on through the chitlins and corn
bread, the greens and everything else. She talked a blue streak over the
sweet potatoes. Everything delighted her. Even the fact that we still used
the benches her daddy made for the table when we couldn't afford to buy
chairs.

"Oh, Mama!" she cried. Then turned to Hakim-a-barber. "I never knew   46
how lovely these benches are. You can feel the rump prints," she said, running her hands underneath her and along the bench. Then she gave a sigh
and her hand closed over Grandma Dee's butter dish. "That's it!" she said. "I
knew there was something I wanted to ask you if I could have." She jumped
up from the table and went over in the corner where the churn stood, the
milk in it clabber by now. She looked at the churn and looked at it.

"This churn top is what I need," she said. "Didn't Uncle Buddy whittle 47 it out of a tree you all used to have?"

"Yes," I said. 48

"Uh huh," she said happily. "And I want the dasher, too." 49

"Uncle Buddy whittle that, too?" asked the barber. 50

Dee (Wangero) looked up at me. 51

"Aunt Dee's first husband whittled the dash," said Maggie so low you 52 almost couldn't hear her. "His name was Henry, but they called him Stash."

"Maggie's brain is like an elephant's," Wangero said, laughing. "I can 53 use the churn top as a centerpiece for the alcove table," she said, sliding a plate over the churn, "and I'll think of something artistic to do with the dasher."

When she finished wrapping the dasher the handle stuck out. I took it 54 for a moment in my hands. You didn't even have to look close to see where hands pushing the dasher up and down to make butter had left a kind of sink in the wood. In fact, there were a lot of small sinks; you could see where thumbs and fingers had sunk into the wood. It was beautiful light yellow wood, from a tree that grew in the yard where Big Dee and Stash had lived.

After dinner Dee (Wangero) went to the trunk at the foot of my bed 55 and started rifling through it. Maggie hung back in the kitchen over the dishpan. Out came Wangero with two quilts. They had been pieced by Grandma Dee and then Big Dee and me had hung them on the quilt frames on the front porch and quilted them. One was in the Lone Star pattern. The other was Walk Around the Mountain. In both of them were scraps of dresses Grandma Dee had worn fifty and more years ago. Bits and pieces of Grandpa Jarrell's Paisley shirts. And one teeny faded blue piece, about the size of a penny matchbox, that was from Great Grandpa Ezra's uniform that he wore in the Civil War.

"Mama," Wangero said sweet as a bird. "Can I have these old quilts?" 56

I heard something fall in the kitchen, and a minute later the kitchen 57 door slammed.

"Why don't you take one or two of the others?" I asked. "These old 58 things was just done by me and Big Dee from some tops your grandma pieced before she died."

"No," said Wangero. "I don't want those. They are stitched around the 59 borders by machine."

"That'll make them last better," I said. 60

"That's not the point," said Wangero. "These are all pieces of dresses 61 Grandma used to wear. She did all this stitching by hand. Imagine!" She held the quilts securely in her arms, stroking them.

"Some of the pieces, like those lavender ones, come from old clothes 62 her mother handed down to her," I said, moving up to touch the quilts. Dee (Wangero) moved back just enough so that I couldn't reach the quilts. They already belonged to her.

"Imagine!" she breathed again, clutching them closely to her bosom.   63

"The truth is," I said, "I promised to give them quilts to Maggie, for   64
when she marries John Thomas."

She gasped like a bee had stung her.   65

"Maggie can't appreciate these quilts!" she said. "She'd probably be   66
backward enough to put them to everyday use."

"I reckon she would," I said. "God knows I been saving 'em for long   67
enough with nobody using 'em. I hope she will!" I didn't want to bring up
how I had offered Dee (Wangero) a quilt when she went away to college.
Then she had told me they were old-fashioned, out of style.

"But they're *priceless!*" she was saying now, furiously; for she has a tem-   68
per. "Maggie would put them on the bed and in five years they'd be in rags.
Less than that!"

"She can always make some more," I said. "Maggie knows how to quilt."   69

Dee (Wangero) looked at me with hatred. "You just will not understand.   70
The point is these quilts, *these* quilts!"

"Well," I said, stumped. "What would *you* do with them?"   71

"Hang them," she said. As if that was the only thing you *could* do with   72
quilts.

Maggie by now was standing in the door. I could almost hear the sound   73
her feet made as they scraped over each other.

"She can have them, Mama," she said, like somebody used to never win-   74
ning anything, or having anything reserved for her. "I can 'member
Grandma Dee without the quilts."

I looked at her hard. She had filled her bottom lip with checkerberry   75
snuff and it gave her face a kind of dopey, hangdog look. It was Grandma
Dee and Big Dee who taught her how to quilt herself. She stood there with
her scarred hands hidden in the folds of her skirt. She looked at her sister
with something like fear but she wasn't mad at her. This was Maggie's portion. This was the way she knew God to work.

When I looked at her like that something hit me in the top of my head   76
and ran down to the soles of my feet. Just like when I'm in church and the
spirit of God touches me and I get happy and shout. I did something I
never had done before: hugged Maggie to me, then dragged her on into the
room, snatched the quilts out of Miss Wangero's hands and dumped them
into Maggie's lap. Maggie just sat there on my bed with her mouth open.

"Take one or two of the others," I said to Dee.   77

But she turned without a word and went out to Hakim-a-barber.   78

"You just don't understand," she said, as Maggie and I came out to the   79
car.

"What don't I understand?" I wanted to know.   80

"Your heritage," she said. And then she turned to Maggie, kissed her,   81
and said, "You ought to try to make something of yourself, too, Maggie. It's
really a new day for us. But from the way you and Mama still live you'd
never know it."

She put on some sunglasses that hid everything above the tip of her nose 82 and her chin.

Maggie smiled; maybe at the sunglasses. But a real smile, not scared. 83 After we watched the car dust settle I asked Maggie to bring me a dip of snuff. And then the two of us sat there just enjoying, until it was time to go in the house and go to bed.

Analyzing This Selection

1. **THE WRITER'S METHOD**   Mama says, "I was always better at a man's job." How does her mannishness affect our sympathy with or detachment from her as the narrator?

2. How does Mama's decision about the quilts add to the meaning of the story's title?

3. Analyze the conflict of generations between Mama and Dee. How does each generation appear in the eyes of the other?

Analyzing Connections

4. Do Mama and Tillie Olsen's narrator (see "I Stand Here Ironing," p. 92) have similar or differing views of themselves as mothers?

Analyzing by Writing

5. Do young people (adolescents through twenty-somethings) need to identify with or be liberated from their group identities? What strengths and vulnerabilities draw you close to your heritage — or pull you farther away? Discuss one connection to your ethnic, racial, or religious heritage that you have embraced or rejected. Explain why you made the choice you did.

PART 5

LEARNING CURVES

INSIGHTS

Education! Which of the various me's do you propose to educate, and which do you propose to suppress?

Anyhow I defy you. I defy you, oh society, to educate me or to suppress me, according to your dummy standards....

There are other men in me, besides this patient ass who sits here in a tweed jacket. What am I doing, playing the patient ass in a tweed jacket? Who am I talking to? Who are you, at the other end of this patience?

Who are you? How many selves have you? And which of these selves do you want to be?

Is Yale College going to educate the self that is in the dark of you, or Harvard College?

—D. H. LAWRENCE

You go to a great school not for knowledge so much as for arts and habits; for the habit of attention, for the art of expression, for the art of assuming at a moment's notice a new intellectual posture, for the art of entering quickly into another person's thought, for the habit of submitting to censure and refutation, for the art of indicating assent or dissent in graduated terms, for the habit of regarding minute points of accuracy, for the habit of working out what is possible in a given time, for taste, for discrimination, for mental courage and mental soberness. Above all, you go to a great school for self-knowledge.

—WILLIAM CORY

Books are the best of things, well used; abused, among the worst. What is the right use? What is the one end which all means go to effect? They are for nothing but to inspire. I had better never see a book than to be warped by its attraction clean out of my own orbit, and made a satellite instead of a system. The one thing in the world, of value, is the active soul. This every man is entitled to; this every man contains within him, although in almost all men obstructed and as yet unborn. The soul active sees absolute truth and utters truth, or creates. In this action it is genius; not the privilege of here and there a favorite, but the sound estate of every man. In its essence it is progressive. The book, the college, the school of art, the institution of any kind, stop with some past utterance of genius. This is good, say they, — let us hold by this. They pin me down. They look backward and not forward. But genius looks forward: the eyes of man are set in his forehead, not in his hindhead: man hopes: genius creates. Whatever talents may be, if the man create not, the pure efflux of the Deity is not his; — cinders and smoke there may be, but not yet flame. There are creative manners, there are creative actions, and creative words; manners, actions, words, that is, indicative of no custom or authority, but springing spontaneous from the mind's own sense of good and fair.

— RALPH WALDO EMERSON

But it is not hard work which is dreary; it is superficial work. That is always boring in the long run, and it has always seemed strange to me that in our endless discussions about education so little stress is ever laid on the pleasure of becoming an educated person, the enormous interest it adds to life. To be able to be caught up into the world of thought — that is to be educated.

— EDITH HAMILTON

It ought to be embarrassing, in this age of celebration of America's diversity, that the schools have been so slow to move toward teaching about our nation's diverse religious traditions.... After all, if the material is well taught, many children will surely be intrigued by what will be for many their first exposure to religious traditions different than their own — or, in some instances, to any religious traditions at all.

— STEPHEN L. CARTER

M. Degas Teaches Art & Science at Durfee Intermediate School

Detroit, 1942

> He made a line on the blackboard,
> one bold stroke from right to left
> diagonally downward and stood back
> to ask, looking as always at no one
> in particular, "What have I done?"
> From the back of the room Freddie
> shouted, "You've broken a piece

of chalk." M. Degas did not smile.
"What have I done?" he repeated.
The most intellectual students
looked down to study their desks
except for Gertrude Bimmler, who raised
her hand before she spoke. "M. Degas,
you have created the hypotenuse
of an isosceles triangle." Degas mused.
Everyone knew that Gertrude could not
be incorrect. "It is possible,"
Louis Warshowsky added precisely,
"that you have begun to represent
the roof of a barn." I remember
that it was exactly twenty minutes
past eleven, and I thought at worst
this would go on another forty
minutes. It was early April,
the snow had all but melted on
the playgrounds, the elms and maples
bordering the cracked walks shivered
in the new winds, and I believed
that before I knew it I'd be
swaggering to the candy store
for a Milky Way. M. Degas
pursed his lips, and the room
stilled until the long hand
of the clock moved to twenty one
as though in complicity with Gertrude,
who added confidently, "You've begun
to separate the dark from the dark."
I looked back for help, but now
the trees bucked and quaked, and I
knew this could go on forever.
                                    —PHILIP LEVINE

   The plots and stories in the novels did not interest me so much as the
point of view revealed. I gave myself over to each novel without reserve,
without trying to criticize it; it was enough for me to see and feel something
different. And for me, everything was something different. Reading was like
a drug, a dope. The novels created moods in which I lived for days. But I
could not conquer my sense of guilt, my feeling that the white men around
me knew that I was changing, that I had begun to regard them differently.
                                    —RICHARD WRIGHT

FOCUSING BY WRITING

1. What does a school really do to develop adolescent students? impart skills and knowledge? instill values? aid in gaining self-discipline? guide social development? Establish your order of importance for two or three things that a secondary school actually does for its students.

2. Some teachers seem to be completely identified with their subjects. They appear to embody *history, math, music, science, French, art, physics,* or *English.* Explain which teacher personified a particular subject for you. What were the traits, mannerisms, attitudes, clothes, style, or other features that played a part in the role? Was the teacher aware of the symbolic role? If so, did the deliberateness make it less effective or more effective?

3. Did you get mixed messages in high school about achieving high grades? Among students and their families, how openly were grades pursued? Were teachers, students, or parents hypocritical about their value? Do grades just open doors or do they mean more? What happened when kindness, loyalty, or generosity came into conflict with achievement goals? Examine the various attitudes in and around you at the time.

4. Where and how, if at all, should religion be taught in school? Consider Carter's observation in the Insights on page 255. Should knowing about religion be part of everybody's education?

Maya Angelou

GRADUATION

Maya Angelou (b. 1928) was raised by her grandmother, who ran a small store for African Americans in the town of Stamps, Arkansas. She survived a childhood that seemed certain to defeat her, and as she once told an interviewer: "One would say of my life — born loser — had to be; from a broken family, raped at eight, unwed mother at sixteen." During her adult life, she became a dancer, an actress, a poet, a television writer and producer, and a coordinator in Martin Luther King Jr.'s Southern Christian Leadership Conference. She is most widely known for her autobiographical books, beginning with *I Know Why the Caged Bird Sings* (1970), from which this selection is taken. Her most recent memoir is *Even the Stars Look Lonesome* (1997). Angelou's latest collection of essays is *Wouldn't Take Nothing for My Journey Now* (1993).

The children in Stamps trembled visibly with anticipation. Some adults were excited too, but to be certain the whole young population had come down with graduation epidemic. Large classes were graduating from both the grammar school and the high school. Even those who were years removed from their own day of glorious release were anxious to help with preparations as a kind of dry run. The junior students who were moving into the vacating classes' chairs were tradition-bound to show their talents for leadership and management. They strutted through the school and around the campus exerting pressure on the lower grades. Their authority was so new that occasionally if they pressed a little too hard it had to be overlooked. After all, next term was coming, and it never hurt a sixth grader to have a play sister in the eighth grade, or a tenth-year student to be able to call a twelfth grader Bubba. So all was endured in a spirit of shared understanding. But the graduating classes themselves were the nobility. Like travelers with exotic destinations on their minds, the graduates were remarkably forgetful. They came to school without their books, or tablets, or even pencils. Volunteers fell over themselves to secure replacements for the missing equipment. When accepted, the willing workers might or might not be thanked, and it was of no importance to the pregraduation rites. Even teachers were respectful of the now quiet and aging seniors, and tended to speak to them, if not as equals, as beings only slightly lower than themselves. After tests were returned and grades given, the student body, which acted like an extended family, knew who did well, who excelled, and what piteous ones had failed.

Unlike the white school, Lafayette County Training School distin- 2 guished itself by having neither lawn, nor hedges, nor tennis court, nor climbing ivy. Its two buildings (main classrooms, the grade school, and home economics) were set on a dirt hill with no fence to limit either its boundaries or those of bordering farms. There was a large expanse to the left of the school which was used alternately as a baseball diamond or a basketball court. Rusty hoops on the swaying poles represented the permanent recreational equipment, although bats and balls could be borrowed from the P.E. teacher if the borrower was qualified and if the diamond wasn't occupied.

Over this rocky area relieved by a few shady tall persimmon trees the 3 graduating class walked. The girls often held hands and no longer bothered to speak to the lower students. There was a sadness about them, as if this old world was not their home and they were bound for higher ground. The boys, on the other hand, had become more friendly, more outgoing. A decided change from the closed attitude they projected while studying for finals. Now they seemed not ready to give up the old school, the familiar paths and classrooms. Only a small percentage would be continuing on to college — one of the South's A & M (agricultural and mechanical) schools, which trained Negro youths to be carpenters, farmers, handymen, masons, maids, cooks, and baby nurses. Their future rode heavily on their shoulders, and blinded them to the collective joy that had pervaded the lives of the boys and girls in the grammar school graduating class.

Parents who could afford it had ordered new shoes and ready-made 4 clothes for themselves from Sears and Roebuck or Montgomery Ward. They also engaged the best seamstresses to make the floating graduating dresses and to cut down secondhand pants which would be pressed to a military slickness for the important event.

Oh, it was important, all right. Whitefolks would attend the ceremony, 5 and two or three would speak of God and home, and the Southern way of life, and Mrs. Parsons, the principal's wife, would play the graduation march while the lower-grade graduates paraded down the aisles and took their seats below the platform. The high school seniors would wait in empty classrooms to make their dramatic entrance.

In the Store I was the person of the moment. The birthday girl. The 6 center. Bailey[1] had graduated the year before, although to do so he had had to forfeit all pleasures to make up for his time lost in Baton Rouge.

My class was wearing butter-yellow piqué dresses, and Momma launched 7 out on mine. She smocked the yoke into tiny crisscrossing puckers, then shirred the rest of the bodice. Her dark fingers ducked in and out of the

---

[1]The author's brother. The children help out in their grandmother's store. [Editor's note.]

lemony cloth as she embroidered raised daisies around the hem. Before she considered herself finished she had added a crocheted cuff on the puff sleeves, and a pointy crocheted collar.

I was going to be lovely. A walking model of all the various styles of fine hand sewing and it didn't worry me that I was only twelve years old and merely graduating from the eighth grade. Besides, many teachers in Arkansas Negro schools had only that diploma and were licensed to impart wisdom.

The days had become longer and more noticeable. The faded beige of former times had been replaced with strong and sure colors. I began to see my classmates' clothes, their skin tones, and the dust that waved off pussy willows. Clouds that lazed across the sky were objects of great concern to me. Their shiftier shapes might have held a message that in my new happiness and with a little bit of time I'd soon decipher. During that period I looked at the arch of heaven so religiously my neck kept a steady ache. I had taken to smiling more often, and my jaws hurt from the unaccustomed activity. Between the two physical sore spots, I suppose I could have been uncomfortable, but that was not the case. As a member of the winning team (the graduating class of 1940) I had outdistanced unpleasant sensations by miles. I was headed for the freedom of open fields.

Youth and social approval allied themselves with me and we trammeled memories of slights and insults. The wind of our swift passage remodeled my features. Lost tears were pounded to mud and then to dust. Years of withdrawal were brushed aside and left behind, as hanging ropes of parasitic moss.

My work alone had awarded me a top place and I was going to be one of the first called in the graduating ceremonies. On the classroom blackboard, as well as on the bulletin board in the auditorium, there were blue stars and white stars and red stars. No absences, no tardinesses, and my academic work was among the best of the year. I could say the preamble to the Constitution even faster than Bailey. We timed ourselves often: "WethepeopleoftheUnitedStatesinordertoformamoreperfectunion..." I had memorized the Presidents of the United States from Washington to Roosevelt in chronological as well as alphabetical order.

My hair pleased me too. Gradually the black mass had lengthened and thickened, so that it kept at last to its braided pattern, and I didn't have to yank my scalp off when I tried to comb it.

Louise and I had rehearsed the exercises until we tired out ourselves. Henry Reed was class valedictorian. He was a small, very black boy with hooded eyes, a long, broad nose, and an oddly shaped head. I had admired him for years because each term he and I vied for the best grades in our class. Most often he bested me, but instead of being disappointed I was pleased that we shared top places between us. Like many Southern Black children, he lived with his grandmother, who was as strict as Momma and as kind as she knew how to be. He was courteous, respectful, and soft-spoken to elders, but on the playground he chose to play the roughest games. I admired him. Anyone, I reckoned, sufficiently afraid or sufficiently dull could be polite. But to be able to operate at a top level with both adults and children was admirable.

His valedictory speech was entitled "To Be or Not to Be." The rigid   14
tenth-grade teacher had helped him to write it. He'd been working on the dramatic stresses for months.

The weeks until graduation were filled with heady activities. A group of   15
small children were to be presented in a play about buttercups and daisies and bunny rabbits. They could be heard throughout the building practicing their hops and their little songs that sounded like silver bells. The older girls (nongraduates, of course) were assigned the task of making refreshments for the night's festivities. A tangy scent of ginger, cinnamon, nutmeg, and chocolate wafted around the home economics building as the budding cooks made samples for themselves and their teachers.

In every corner of the workshop, axes and saws split fresh timber as the   16
woodshop boys made sets and stage scenery. Only the graduates were left out of the general bustle. We were free to sit in the library at the back of the building or look in quite detachedly, naturally, on the measures being taken for our event.

Even the minister preached on graduation the Sunday before. His subject   17
was, "Let your light so shine that men will see your good works and praise your Father, Who is in Heaven." Although the sermon was purported to be addressed to us, he used the occasion to speak to backsliders, gamblers, and general ne'er-do-wells. But since he had called our names at the beginning of the service we were mollified.

Among Negroes the tradition was to give presents to children going only   18
from one grade to another. How much more important this was when the person was graduating at the top of the class. Uncle Willie and Momma had sent away for a Mickey Mouse watch like Bailey's. Louise gave me four embroidered handkerchiefs. (I gave her three crocheted doilies.) Mrs. Sneed, the minister's wife, made me an underskirt to wear for graduation, and nearly every customer gave me a nickel or maybe even a dime with the instruction "Keep on moving to higher ground," or some such encouragement.

Amazingly the great day finally dawned and I was out of bed before I   19
knew it. I threw open the back door to see it more clearly, but Momma said, "Sister, come away from that door and put your robe on."

I hoped the memory of that morning would never leave me. Sunlight   20
was itself still young, and the day had none of the insistence maturity would bring it in a few hours. In my robe and barefoot in the backyard, under cover of going to see about my new beans, I gave myself up to the gentle warmth and thanked God that no matter what evil I had done in my life He had allowed me to live to see this day. Somewhere in my fatalism I had expected to die, accidentally, and never have the chance to walk up

the stairs in the auditorium and gracefully receive my hard-earned diploma.
Out of God's merciful bosom I had won reprieve.

Bailey came out in his robe and gave me a box wrapped in Christmas   21
paper. He said he had saved his money for months to pay for it. It felt like
a box of chocolates, but I knew Bailey wouldn't save money to buy candy
when we had all we could want under our noses.

He was as proud of the gift as I. It was a soft-leather-bound copy of a col-   22
lection of poems by Edgar Allan Poe, or, as Bailey and I called him, "Eap."
I turned to "Annabel Lee" and we walked up and down the garden rows,
the cool dirt between our toes, reciting the beautifully sad lines.

Momma made a Sunday breakfast although it was only Friday. After we   23
finished the blessing, I opened my eyes to find the watch on my plate. It
was a dream of a day. Everything went smoothly and to my credit. I didn't
have to be reminded or scolded for anything. Near evening I was too jittery
to attend to chores, so Bailey volunteered to do all before his bath.

Days before, we had made a sign for the Store and as we turned out the   24
lights Momma hung the cardboard over the doorknob. It read clearly:
CLOSED. GRADUATION.

My dress fitted perfectly and everyone said that I looked like a sunbeam   25
in it. On the hill, going toward the school, Bailey walked behind with
Uncle Willie, who muttered, "Go on, Ju." He wanted him to walk ahead
with us because it embarrassed him to have to walk so slowly. Bailey said
he'd let the ladies walk together, and the men would bring up the rear. We
all laughed, nicely.

Little children dashed by out of the dark like fireflies. Their crepepaper   26
dresses and butterfly wings were not made for running and we heard more
than one rip, dryly, and the regretful "uh uh" that followed.

The school blazed without gaiety. The windows seemed cold and un-   27
friendly from the lower hill. A sense of ill-fated timing crept over me, and
if Momma hadn't reached for my hand I would have drifted back to Bailey
and Uncle Willie, and possibly beyond. She made a few slow jokes about
my feet getting cold, and tugged me along to the now-strange building.

Around the front steps, assurance came back. There were my fellow   28
"greats," the graduating class. Hair brushed back, legs oiled, new dresses
and pressed pleats, fresh pocket handkerchiefs and little handbags, all
homesewn. Oh, we were up to snuff, all right. I joined my comrades and
didn't even see my family go in to find seats in the crowded auditorium.

The school band struck up a march and all classes filed in as had been   29
rehearsed. We stood in front of our seats, as assigned, and on a signal from
the choir director, we sat. No sooner had this been accomplished than the
band started to play the national anthem. We rose again and sang the song,
after which we recited the pledge of allegiance. We remained standing for a
brief minute before the choir director and the principal signaled to us, rather
desperately I thought, to take our seats. The command was so unusual that
our carefully rehearsed and smooth-running machine was thrown off. For a

full minute we fumbled for our chairs and bumped into each other awkwardly. Habits change or solidify under pressure, so in our state of nervous tension we had been ready to follow our usual assembly pattern: the American National Anthem, then the pledge of allegiance, then the song every Black person I knew called the Negro National Anthem. All done in the same key, with the same passion and most often standing on the same foot.

Finding my seat at last, I was overcome with a presentiment of worse   30 things to come. Something unrehearsed, unplanned, was going to happen, and we were going to be made to look bad. I distinctly remember being explicit in the choice of pronoun. It was "we," the graduating class, the unit, that concerned me then.

The principal welcomed "parents and friends" and asked the Baptist   31 minister to lead us in prayer. His invocation was brief and punchy, and for a second I thought we were getting back on the high road to right action. When the principal came back to the dais, however, his voice had changed. Sounds always affected me profoundly and the principal's voice was one of my favorites. During assembly it melted and lowed weakly into the audience. It had not been in my plan to listen to him, but my curiosity was piqued and I straightened up to give him my attention.

He was talking about Booker T. Washington, our "late great leader,"   32 who said we can be as close as the fingers on the hand, etc. . . . Then he said a few vague things about friendship and the friendship of kindly people to those less fortunate than themselves. With that his voice nearly faded, thin, away. Like a river diminishing to a stream and then to a trickle. But he cleared his throat and said, "Our speaker tonight, who is also our friend, came from Texarkana to deliver the commencement address, but due to the irregularity of the train schedule, he's going to, as they say, 'speak and run.'" He said that we understood and wanted the man to know that we were most grateful for the time he was able to give us and then something about how we were willing always to adjust to another's program, and without more ado — "I give you Mr. Edward Donleavy."

Not one but two white men came through the door offstage. The shorter   33 one walked to the speaker's platform, and the tall one moved over to the center seat and sat down. But that was our principal's seat, and already occupied. The dislodged gentleman bounced around for a long breath or two before the Baptist minister gave him his chair, then with more dignity than the situation deserved, the minister walked off the stage.

Donleavy looked at the audience once (on reflection, I'm sure that he   34 wanted only to reassure himself that we were really there), adjusted his glasses, and began to read from a sheaf of papers.

He was glad "to be here and to see the work going on just as it was in   35 the other schools."

At the first "Amen" from the audience I willed the offender to immedi-   36 ate death by choking on the word. But Amens and Yes, sir's began to fall around the room like rain through a ragged umbrella.

He told us of the wonderful changes we children in Stamps had in store. 37
The Central School (naturally, the white school was Central) had already
been granted improvements that would be in use in the fall. A well-known
artist was coming from Little Rock to teach art to them. They were going
to have the newest microscopes and chemistry equipment for their laboratory. Mr. Donleavy didn't leave us long in the dark over who made these
improvements available to Central High. Nor were we to be ignored in the
general betterment scheme he had in mind.

He said that he had pointed out to people at a very high level that one 38
of the first-line football tacklers at Arkansas Agricultural and Mechanical
College had graduated from good old Lafayette County Training School.
Here fewer Amens were heard. Those few that did break through lay dully
in the air with the heaviness of habit.

He went on to praise us. He went on to say how he had bragged that 39
"one of the best basketball players at Fisk sank his first ball right here at
Lafayette County Training School."

The white kids were going to have a chance to become Galileos and 40
Madame Curies and Edisons and Gauguins, and our boys (the girls weren't
even in on it) would try to be Jessie Owenses and Joe Louises.

Owens and the Brown Bomber were great heroes in our world, but what 41
school official in the white-goddom of Little Rock had the right to decide
that those two men must be our only heroes? Who decided that for Henry
Reed to become a scientist he had to work like George Washington Carver,
as a bootblack, to buy a lousy microscope? Bailey was obviously always
going to be too small to be an athlete, so which concrete angel glued to
what country seat had decided that if my brother wanted to become a
lawyer he had to first pay penance for his skin by picking cotton and hoe-
ing corn and studying correspondence books at night for twenty years?

The man's dead words fell like bricks around the auditorium and too 42
many settled in my belly. Constrained by hard-learned manners I couldn't
look behind me, but to my left and right the proud graduating class of 1940
had dropped their heads. Every girl in my row had found something new
to do with her handkerchief. Some folded the tiny squares into love knots,
some into triangles, but most were wadding them, then pressing them flat
on their yellow laps.

On the dais, the ancient tragedy was being replayed. Professor Parsons 43
sat, a sculptor's reject, rigid. His large, heavy body seemed devoid of will or
willingness, and his eyes said he was no longer with us. The other teachers
examined the flag (which was draped stage right) or their notes, or the windows which opened on our now-famous playing diamond.

Graduation, the hush-hush magic time of frills and gifts and congratula- 44
tions and diplomas, was finished for me before my name was called. The
accomplishment was nothing. The meticulous maps, drawn in three colors
of ink, learning and spelling decasyllabic words, memorizing the whole of
The Rape of Lucrece — it was nothing. Donleavy had exposed us.

We were maids and farmers, handymen and washerwomen, and any- 45
thing higher that we aspired to was farcical and presumptuous. Then I
wished that Gabriel Prosser and Nat Turner had killed all whitefolks in
their beds and that Abraham Lincoln had been assassinated before the signing of the Emancipation Proclamation, and that Harriet Tubman had been
killed by that blow on her head and Christopher Columbus had drowned
in the *Santa Maria*.

It was awful to be Negro and have no control over my life. It was brutal 46
to be young and already trained to sit quietly and listen to charges brought
against my color with no chance of defense. We should all be dead. I
thought I should like to see us all dead, one on top of the other. A pyramid
of flesh with the whitefolks on the bottom, as the broad base, then the Indians with their silly tomahawks and teepees and wigwams and treaties, the
Negroes with their mops and recipes and cotton sacks and spirituals sticking out of their mouths. The Dutch children should all stumble in their
wooden shoes and break their necks. The French should choke to death on
the Louisiana Purchase (1803) while silkworms ate all the Chinese with
their stupid pigtails. As a species, we were an abomination. All of us.

Donleavy was running for election, and assured our parents that if he 47
won we could count on having the only colored paved playing field in that
part of Arkansas. Also — he never looked up to acknowledge the grunts of
acceptance — also, we were bound to get some new equipment for the
home economics building and the workshop.

He finished, and since there was no need to give any more than the 48
most perfunctory thank-you's, he nodded to the men on the stage, and the
tall white man who was never introduced joined him at the door. They left
with the attitude that now they were off to something really important.
(The graduation ceremonies at Lafayette County Training School had been
a mere preliminary.)

The ugliness they left was palpable. An uninvited guest who wouldn't 49
leave. The choir was summoned and sang a modern arrangement of
"Onward, Christian Soldiers," with new words pertaining to graduates seeking their place in the world. But it didn't work. Elouise, the daughter of the
Baptist minister, recited "Invictus," and I could have cried at the imperti-
nence of "I am the master of my fate, I am the captain of my soul."

My name had lost its ring of familiarity and I had to be nudged to go 50
and receive my diploma. All my preparations had fled. I neither marched
up to the stage like a conquering Amazon, nor did I look in the audience
for Bailey's nod of approval. Marguerite Johnson, I heard the name again,
my honors were read, there were noises in the audience of appreciation,
and I took my place on the stage as rehearsed.

I thought about colors I hated: ecru, puce, lavender, beige, and black. 51

There was shuffling and rustling around me, then Henry Reed was giv- 52
ing his valedictory address, "To Be or Not to Be." Hadn't he heard the
whitefolks? We couldn't *be*, so the question was a waste of time. Henry's

voice came out clear and strong. I feared to look at him. Hadn't he got the message? There was no "nobler in the mind" for Negroes because the world didn't think we had minds, and they let us know it. "Outrageous fortune"? Now, that was a joke. When the ceremony was over I had to tell Henry Reed some things. That is, if I still cared. Not "rub," Henry, "erase." "Ah, there's the erase." Us.

Henry had been a good student in elocution. His voice rose on tides of 53 promise and fell on waves of warnings. The English teacher had helped him to create a sermon winging through Hamlet's soliloquy. To be a man, a doer, a builder, a leader, or to be a tool, an unfunny joke, a crusher of funky toadstools. I marveled that Henry could go through the speech as if we had a choice.

I had been listening and silently rebutting each sentence with my eyes 54 closed; then there was a hush, which in an audience warns that something unplanned is happening. I looked up and saw Henry Reed, the conservative, the proper, the A student, turn his back to the audience and turn to us (the proud graduating class of 1940) and sing, nearly speaking,

> Lift ev'ry voice and sing
> Till earth and heaven ring
> Ring with the harmonies of Liberty...

It was the poem written by James Weldon Johnson. It was the music composed by J. Rosamond Johnson. It was the Negro National Anthem. Out of habit we were singing it.

Our mothers and fathers stood in the dark hall and joined the hymn of 55 encouragement. A kindergarten teacher led the small children onto the stage and the buttercups and daisies and bunny rabbits marked time and tried to follow:

> Stony the road we trod
> Bitter the chastening rod
> Felt in the days when hope, unborn, had died.
> Yet with a steady beat
> Have not our weary feet
> Come to the place for which our fathers sighed?

Every child I knew had learned that song with his ABCs and along with 56 "Jesus Loves Me This I Know." But I personally had never heard it before. Never heard the words, despite the thousands of times I had sung them. Never thought they had anything to do with me.

On the other hand, the words of Patrick Henry had made such an 57 impression on me that I had been able to stretch myself tall and trembling and say, "I know not what course others may take, but as for me, give me liberty or give me death."

And now I heard, really for the first time: 58

> We have come over a way that with tears has been watered,
> We have come, treading our path through the blood
>   of the slaughtered.

While echoes of the song shivered in the air, Henry Reed bowed his 59
head, said "Thank you," and returned to his place in the line. The tears
that slipped down many faces were not wiped away in shame.

We were on top again. As always, again. We survived. The depths had 60
been icy and dark, but now a bright sun spoke to our souls. I was no longer
simply a member of the proud graduating class of 1940; I was a proud
member of the wonderful, beautiful Negro race.

Oh, Black known and unknown poets, how often have your auctioned 61
pains sustained us? Who will compute the lonely nights made less lonely
by your songs, or by the empty pots made less tragic by your tales?

If we were a people much given to revealing secrets, we might raise 62
monuments and sacrifice to the memories of our poets, but slavery cured
us of that weakness. It may be enough, however, to have it said that we survive in exact relationship to the dedication of our poets (include preachers,
musicians, and blues singers).

Analyzing This Selection

1. What changes come over the student body as the time for graduation
   approaches? What phrases convey a special atmosphere? What changes come
   over Angelou in particular?

2. What details indicate the involvement of the entire African American community in the student graduations? Does the selection seem to exaggerate
   the public importance of the event, or is the account entirely believable?
   Does Angelou as an eighth-grader appear too impressionable to be storing
   up accurate memories?

3. **THE WRITER'S METHOD**   What details in the narrative contribute to
   the suspense and the worry that something might go wrong? What kind of a
   calamity are we led to anticipate?

4. How do you explain Angelou's immediate response to Donleavy's speech?
   Does it seem excessive?

5. In what sense is this graduation truly a "commencement" for Angelou?
   Make your answer detailed and explicit.

Analyzing Connections

6. Angelou and Nora Ephron (see "Shaping Up Absurd," p. 16) each recapture
   the style of adolescent impulsiveness and exaggeration. Compare their uses
   of humor in dealing with serious subjects.

Analyzing by Writing

7. Traditional ceremonies are formal initiations to a new status, as in a graduation, confirmation, bar or bat mitzvah, or wedding. Analyze the customs associated with one such passage you experienced or witnessed. What meanings and ideals are suggested by the details of the ritual? If you could, what parts of the ceremony would you change? Which parts do you think are most important?

Maxine Hong Kingston

THE MISERY OF SILENCE[1]

MAXINE HONG KINGSTON (b. 1940) grew up in a Chinese immigrant community in Stockton, California, where her parents ran a laundry. Kingston graduated from the University of California at Berkeley. As a first-generation American, Kingston had to learn how to live in two distinctly contrasting societies. This was confusing and difficult for a five- to seven-year-old child, as she recalls in this selection from her autobiography, *The Woman Warrior: Memoirs of a Girlhood Among Ghosts* (1976). The immigrants regarded all non-Chinese as "ghosts"—pale, insubstantial, and threatening. *China Men* (1980) extends her story of Chinese American girlhood by describing the lives of the fathers and sons in China and America. Kingston published her first novel, *Tripmaster Monkey: His Fake Book*, in 1989.

When I went to kindergarten and had to speak English for the first time, I became silent. A dumbness — a shame — still cracks my voice in two, even when I want to say "hello" casually, or ask an easy question in front of the check-out counter, or ask directions of a bus driver. I stand frozen, or I hold up the line with the complete, grammatical sentence that comes squeaking out at impossible length. "What did you say?" says the cab driver, or "Speak up," so I have to perform again, only weaker the second time. A telephone call makes my throat bleed and takes up that day's courage. It spoils my day with self-disgust when I hear my broken voice come skittering out into the open. It makes people wince to hear it. I'm getting better, though. Recently I asked the postman for special-issue stamps; I've waited since childhood for postmen to give me some of their own accord. I am making progress, a little every day.

My silence was thickest — total — during the three years that I covered my school paintings with black paint. I painted layers of black over houses and flowers and suns, and when I drew on the blackboard, I put a layer of chalk on top. I was making a stage curtain, and it was the moment before the curtain parted or rose. The teachers called my parents to school, and I saw they had been saving my pictures, curling and cracking, all alike and black. The teachers pointed to the pictures and looked serious, talked

[1]Editor's title.

seriously too, but my parents did not understand English. ("The parents and teachers of criminals were executed," said my father.) My parents took the pictures home. I spread them out (so black and full of possibilities) and pretended the curtains were swinging open, flying up, one after another, sunlight underneath, mighty operas.

During the first silent year I spoke to no one at school, did not ask 3 before going to the lavatory, and flunked kindergarten. My sister also said nothing for three years, silent in the playground and silent at lunch. There were other quiet Chinese girls not of our family, but most of them got over it sooner than we did. I enjoyed the silence. At first it did not occur to me I was supposed to talk or to pass kindergarten. I talked at home and to one or two of the Chinese kids in class. I made motions and even made some jokes. I drank out of a toy saucer when the water spilled out of the cup, and everybody laughed, pointing at me, so I did it some more. I didn't know that Americans don't drink out of saucers.

I liked the Negro students (Black Ghosts) best because they laughed the 4 loudest and talked to me as if I were a daring talker too. One of the Negro girls had her mother coil braids over her ears Shanghai-style like mine; we were Shanghai twins except that she was covered with black like my paintings. Two Negro kids enrolled in Chinese school, and the teachers gave them Chinese names. Some Negro kids walked me to school and home, protecting me from the Japanese kids, who hit me and chased me and stuck gum in my ears. The Japanese kids were noisy and tough. They appeared one day in kindergarten, released from concentration camp, which was a tic-tac-toe mark, like barbed wire, on the map.

It was when I found out I had to talk that school became a misery, that 5 the silence became a misery. I did not speak and felt bad each time that I did not speak. I read aloud in first grade, though, and heard the barest whisper with little squeaks come out of my throat. "Louder," said the teacher, who scared the voice away again. The other Chinese girls did not talk either, so I knew the silence had to do with being a Chinese girl.

Reading out loud was easier than speaking because we did not have to 6 make up what to say, but I stopped often, and the teacher would think I'd gone quiet again. I could not understand "I." The Chinese "I" has seven strokes, intricacies. How could the American "I," assuredly wearing a hat like the Chinese, have only three strokes, the middle so straight? Was it out of politeness that this writer left off the strokes the way a Chinese has to write her own name small and crooked? No, it was not politeness; "I" is a capital and "you" is lower-case. I stared at that middle line and waited so long for its black center to resolve into tight strokes and dots that I forgot to pronounce it. The other troublesome word was "here," no strong consonant to hang on to, and so flat, when "here" is two mountainous ideographs. The teacher, who had already told me every day how to read "I" and "here," put me in the low corner under the stairs again, where the noisy boys usually sat.

When my second grade class did a play, the whole class went to the 7
auditorium except the Chinese girls. The teacher, lovely and Hawaiian,
should have understood about us, but instead left us behind in the classroom. Our voices were too soft or nonexistent, and our parents never
signed the permission slips anyway. They never signed anything unnecessary. We opened the door a crack and peeked out, but closed it again
quickly. One of us (not me) won every spelling bee, though.

I remember telling the Hawaiian teacher, "We Chinese can't sing 'land 8
where our fathers died.'" She argued with me about politics, while I meant
because of curses. But how can I have that memory when I couldn't talk?
My mother says that we, like the ghosts, have no memories.

After American school, we picked up our cigar boxes, in which we had 9
arranged books, brushes, and an inkbox neatly, and went to Chinese
school, from 5:00 to 7:30 p.m. There we chanted together, voices rising and
falling, loud and soft, some boys shouting, everybody reading together,
reciting together and not alone with one voice. When we had a memoriza-
tion test, the teacher let each of us come to his desk and say the lesson to
him privately, while the rest of the class practiced copying or tracing. Most
of the teachers were men. The boys who were so well behaved in the
American school played tricks on them and talked back to them. The girls
were not mute. They screamed and yelled during recess, when there were
no rules; they had fistfights. Nobody was afraid of children hurting themselves or of children hurting school property. The glass doors to the red and
green balconies with the gold joy symbols were left wide open so that we
could run out and climb the fire escapes. We played capture-the-flag in the
auditorium, where Sun Yat-sen and Chiang Kai-shek's pictures hung at the
back of the stage, the Chinese flag on their left and the American flag on
their right. We climbed the teak ceremonial chairs and made flying leaps
off the stage. One flag headquarters was behind the glass door and the
other on stage right. Our feet drummed on the hollow stage. During recess
the teachers locked themselves up in their office with the shelves of books,
copybooks, inks from China. They drank tea and warmed their hands at a
stove. There was no play supervision. At recess we had the school to ourselves, and also we could roam as far as we could go — downtown, China-
town stores, home — as long as we returned before the bell rang.

At exactly 7:30 the teacher again picked up the brass bell that sat on his 10
desk and swung it over our heads, while we charged down the stairs, our
cheering magnified in the stairwell. Nobody had to line up.

Not all of the children who were silent at American school found voice 11
at Chinese school. One new teacher said each of us had to get up and
recite in front of the class, who was to listen. My sister and I had memorized the lesson perfectly. We said it to each other at home, one chanting,
one listening. The teacher called on my sister to recite first. It was the first
time a teacher had called on the second-born to go first. My sister was
scared. She glanced at me and looked away; I looked down at my desk. I

hoped that she could do it because if she could, then I would have to. She opened her mouth and a voice came out that wasn't a whisper, but it wasn't a proper voice either. I hoped that she would not cry, fear breaking up her voice like twigs underfoot. She sounded as if she were trying to sing through weeping and strangling. She did not pause or stop to end the embarrassment. She kept going until she said the last word, and then she sat down. When it was my turn, the same voice came out, a crippled animal running on broken legs. You could hear splinters in my voice, bones rubbing jagged against one another. I was loud, though. I was glad I didn't whisper.

How strange that the emigrant villagers are shouters, hollering face to   12 face. My father asks, "Why is it I can hear Chinese from blocks away? Is it that I understand the language? Or is it they talk loud?" They turn the radio up full blast to hear the operas, which do not seem to hurt their ears. And they yell over the singers that wail over the drums, everybody talking at once, big arm gestures, spit flying. You can see the disgust on American faces looking at women like that. It isn't just the loudness. It is the way Chinese sounds, ching-chong ugly, to American ears, not beautiful like Japanese sayonara words with the consonants and vowels as regular as Italian. We make guttural peasant noise and have Ton Duc Thang names you can't remember. And the Chinese can't hear Americans at all; the language is too soft and western music unhearable. I've watched a Chinese audience laugh, visit, talk-story, and holler during a piano recital, as if the musician could not hear them. A Chinese-American, somebody's son, was playing Chopin, which has no punctuation, no cymbals, no gongs. Chinese piano music is five black keys. Normal Chinese women's voices are strong and bossy. We American-Chinese girls had to whisper to make ourselves American-feminine. Apparently we whispered even more softly than the Americans. Once a year the teachers referred my sister and me to speech therapy, but our voices would straighten out, unpredictably normal, for the therapists. Some of us gave up, shook our heads, and said nothing, not one word. Some of us could not even shake our heads. At times shaking my head no is more self-assertion than I can manage. Most of us eventually found some voice, however faltering. We invented an American-feminine speaking personality.

Analyzing This Selection

1. What was the connection between Kingston's silence and her paintings? What did the paintings signify to *her*?

2. Why did the English pronouns "I" and "you" strike Kingston as unnatural? How do they differ from their Chinese equivalents? What looks wrong about the word "here"?

3. Does this account reinforce a stereotype of the Asian woman? What does Kingston suggest that Chinese women are like when they are among Chinese?

4. In the concluding sentence Kingston refers to "an American-feminine speaking personality." What would that be? Can you describe or imitate the tone and manner she suggests?

Analyzing Connections

5. W. E. B. Du Bois says in the Insights on page 195 that segregation makes people inaudible but not silent. Does Kingston's silence fit Du Bois's description of inaudibility, or was she merely shy?

Analyzing by Writing

6. **THE WRITER'S METHOD**   At the beginning of this selection, Kingston says that even today she has trouble speaking up in public situations. Does her style of writing indicate any hesitation or absence of assertiveness in using English for writing to the public? Is her language easy or hard to read? What is the tone of her voice? Write about Kingston's style in relation to her childhood experience.

Helen Vendler

KNOWING POEMS[1]

HELEN VENDLER (b. 1933), a distinguished literary critic, went to parochial school in Boston, Massachusetts, as the following selection discusses. She graduated from Emmanuel College and received a Ph.D. from Harvard University, where she now teaches. She has received numerous fellowships, including a Guggenheim Fellowship, and awards, including the Lowell Prize for *On Extended Wings: Wallace Stevens' Longer Poems* (1969) and the National Book Critics Circle Award for *Part of Nature, Part of Us: Modern American Poets* (1980). "Knowing Poems" is excerpted from a longer personal essay commissioned for *Communion: Contemporary Writers Reveal the Bible in Their Lives* (1996). Because this selection mentions her early responses to Shakespeare's sonnets, students may wish to examine Vendler's *The Art of Shakespeare's Sonnets* (1997).

My days as a child invariably began with the morning Mass to which my   1
mother took us. It was almost always a requiem Mass, sung in Latin, since deaths were commemorated a month afterward and a year afterward, and, in a sizable parish, such memorials crowded the calendar. My earliest memories are of the *Dies Irae* and, for some reason, of the long mournful strophes of the preface: "*Tuis enim fidelibus, Domine, vita mutatur, non tollitur; et dissoluta huius terrestris incolatus domo, aeterna in coelo habitatio comparatur,*"[2] all sung to the plangent lifts and falls of Gregorian chant. At nine, teaching my seven-year-old brother the Latin responses to the Mass so that he could be an altar boy, I learned the Latin of the Mass more or less by heart, and this gave me the wish to learn Latin (I already knew Spanish, French, and Italian, which my father had taught us). It was in the text of the Mass that I first met the antiphonal rhythms of the Psalms: "*Introibo ad altare Dei, ad Deum qui laetificat juventutem meam.*"[3] At the same time, I was hearing the Psalms (the more amiable ones, naturally) read

---

[1]Editor's title.

[2]*Tuis...comparatur* For those who are faithful to thee, Lord, life is changed, not ended; and when their earthly dwelling place decays, an everlasting mansion stands prepared for them in heaven (from the Missal). [All notes are the editor's.]

[3]*Introibo...meam* I will go in to the altar of God: to God who giveth joy to my youth (from the Douay Bible).

to us, in the King James Version, in my public school, one a day, before we pledged allegiance to the flag. Miss Fallon's low, harmonious voice is still in my ear, reading the obscurely satisfying cadences: "I will lift up mine eyes unto the hills, from whence cometh my help." But the Psalms were then no more than ravishing turns of phrase, whether in Latin or in English. I did not yet *need* the Psalms, or didn't know I needed them.

At ten, old enough for the streetcar, I was sent to the parochial school in the next parish (our parish had not yet acquired a school). Among many ungifted teachers, there was one uncannily inspired one, a young Lebanese nun who was (in spite of my having had two piano teachers) the first musical person I had encountered. She believed that a random group of mostly lower-class children could be taught to sing the Latin liturgy in Gregorian chant, and with her expressive eyes and her even more expressive conducting hand, she took us into the Psalms, notably during the long Holy Week service (now discontinued in the Roman Catholic Church) called *Tenebrae*. The nine Psalms of Matins and the four of Lauds for the appropriate day were sung: for Good Friday, for instance, this meant (in the Douay Bible numbering), Psalms 2, 21, 26, 37, 39, 53, 58, 87, 93, 50, 142, 84, and 147. I took to spending my spare time in the seventh and eighth grade learning Latin so I could follow the texts at least approximately; and since I was steeped in friendless adolescent misery at school, and the beginnings of appalled recognition of the life at home, the Psalms became my poems of reference.

I had had poetry read to me since birth by my melancholy mother (a primary-school teacher who, by marrying, had lost her fourteen-year career, since married women were not permitted to continue to work in the Boston school system); and I had read a fair amount of verse here and there on my own; but the Psalms were, I think, the first sublime poetry I consciously took on as my own. I didn't, even then, read them as the word of God. I don't believe I read them, or sang them, chiefly in an inner atmosphere of belief. I had already begun the rude questioning of the dogma and discipline of Roman Catholicism that led to my abandoning the Church forever as soon as I left my parents' house; and I was always of a skeptical temperament, impatient of all nonevidential talk of Virgin Birth and Resurrection (taught by the church as facts, not symbols).

When I try, now, to recapture my feelings at eleven and twelve, singing the verses of the Psalms, what I recall is the fierceness with which I appropriated the Psalmist's voice as mine. *I* cried out of the depths; *I* asked my soul, "Why art thou sad, O my soul? and why doest thou trouble me? Why go I mourning, whilst my enemy afflicteth me?" I was as likely to say it to myself in the language of the Mass — "*Quare tristis es, anima mea, et quare conturbas me?*" — as I was to read it in the Bible.

What did I gain, between ten and thirteen, from the Voice of the Psalmist? Equivalents for all my stifled and inarticulate feelings. I didn't

often turn to those kinder psalms that had been read to me in public
school. What I found were the wild psalms:

> I am poured out like water; and all my bones are scattered.
> My heart is become like wax melting in the midst of my bowels.
> My strength is dried up like a potsherd, and my tongue hath cleaved to
>   my jaws: and thou hast brought me down into the dust of death.

If anyone doubts that these are the emotions of adolescence, he has forgotten his youth. The insanity of stifled feeling, in my case, could only be
stemmed by adequacy of expression, and since I had absolutely no adequate words myself for my own despair, I was abjectly grateful to the
Psalmist.

The Psalms gave me, too, my first intuition of intertextuality.[4] As I came   6
on Psalm 21 for the first time, I remember being shocked, because I had
had no idea, when I had heard the Passion read in church, that Jesus was
quoting when he cried out, "My God, my God, why hast thou forsaken
me" — the phrase that opens Psalm 21. If *he* could borrow the Psalmist's
words and say them *in propria persona*,[5] so could I. The psalm that best
expressed my feeling of being sentenced to indefinite punishment merely
by living as and where I did, in an atmosphere that permitted no personal
freedom of thought or action, was 128:

> Often have they fought against me from my youth, let Israel now say.
> Often have they fought against me from my youth; but they could not
>   prevail over me.
> The wicked have wrought upon my back: they have lengthened their
>   iniquity...
> And they that passed by have not said: The blessing of the Lord be
>   upon you: we have blessed you in the name of the Lord.

Lest it be thought that I exaggerate my feelings, let me add the fact that a
poem I wrote at fifteen began, "Pitiless with repression, / They told me I
must dwell / Within the narrow prison / They lived in." I was enraged, and
helpless, and in prison; and I knew, in my twelfth year, no words but the
Psalmist's to say my feelings for me. The Psalmist had satisfying curses, a
form not much encouraged in books for the young; the Psalms thus
became my first clandestine literature:

> May his children be fatherless, and his wife a widow.
> Let his children be carried about vagabonds, and beg; and let them be
>   cast out of their dwellings...
> May the iniquity of his fathers be remembered in the sight of the Lord:
>   and let not the sin of his mother be blotted out...
> And he put on cursing, like a garment: and it went in like water into
>   his entrails, and like oil in his bones. (108)

---

[4]*intertextuality* Allusion to another work.
[5]*in propria persona* Jesus quoted this familiar line as if it were his own.

These words were for me like plasters applied to nameless wounds. 7
Almost everything I felt the Psalmist had words for. (The other feelings
found solace three years later, when I was fifteen, in Shakespeare's sonnets.)
I don't know what I would have done with the grinding and self-abasing
and furious and lacerating feelings of my twelfth year without the Psalms.
They drew off the worst of the poison (by allowing me, among other things,
to put on cursing like a garment), and they filled my mouth with language.
A choking sensation in the heart, a smothering in the lungs, a frenzy in the
brain, an anger in the blood, tormented me every day, all day, in those
years. I had no one to confide in and no one to explain my feelings to me.
Only the Psalmist knew my soul, and I his. . . .

Because the speech of the Psalms is often choral, and because it was 8
adapted to liturgical use, it never seemed to me language written with
respect to gender. Rather, like most lyric speech, it was voiceable by anyone. I believe that poetry became for me the most natural of the genres
because of the Psalms; and later, when I came to study poetry and write
about it, I found that the web composed of biblical texts, the liturgy, and
the hymnal extended its threads deep into the English lyric. Most readers
are drawn to narrative, to the line that prolongs itself to an end; but I was
drawn to meditation, to the ripples of intensification extending out from a
center of thought. It is that concentric structure of the meditative lyric,
from the Psalms to Wallace Stevens, that still seems to me the most compelling form of writing ever invented. . . .

The Psalms were not the sort of reading given to young girls by schools 9
and public libraries in my day — nor would they be recommended to twelve-
year-old girls these days, either. Without disparaging the release of inchoate
feeling offered adolescents by the Judy Blumes of the Young Adult shelves,
I wish that our culture dealt out the wild verities of the Psalmist (and, to
supplement him, the Shakespeare of the *Sonnets*) instead. Imagine a school
system where every day a psalm and a Shakespeare sonnet were chorally
recited by every class. When the end of the Psalter was reached, Psalm I
would come round again; when the end of the *Sonnets* was reached, the
cycle would rebegin. From, say, the third grade on, the whole Psalter, every
year, and the 154 sonnets, every year: why, by Grade 12 the students would
be literate. And, as a dividend, liberated in their hearts' passions.

Analyzing This Selection

1. **THE WRITER'S METHOD**   The author's upbringing was unusual, but
   Vendler says her feelings were "the emotions of adolescence." Do you think
   they expressed what most adolescents feel? What details help generalize her
   feelings?

2. When Vendler was twelve, how did the Psalms affect her? When she was fifteen, why did she prefer other poems?

3. What is your view of Vendler's proposal for schools? How would such a requirement have affected your schooling? affected your feelings?

Analyzing Connections

4. Vendler and Angelou (see "Graduation," p. 258) were sustained in adolescence by poems. What similar and differing circumstances and feelings did they experience? Consider whether Angelou's essay supports or contradicts Vendler's statement that her feelings were "the emotions of adolescence."

Analyzing by Writing

5. Examine your reasons for reading a novel or collection of poems over and over. What satisfactions did you find in that particular book and not another? Take into account the range of relevant circumstances that may have included reading aloud, reading in solitude, imagining yourself participating, getting away, or other repetitions.

Pico Iyer

IN PRAISE OF THE HUMBLE COMMA

Pico Iyer (b. 1957) was born in England to Indian parents. Educated at Eton and Oxford University, he became a travel writer by taking notes on vacation trips and "just writing about my holidays," he said in a recent interview. In graduate school at Harvard University, Iyer held summer jobs doing field work for *Let's Go,* a series of guidebooks for students. His travel book, *Video Night in Kathmandu: And Other Reports from the Not-So-Far East* (1988), observes the effects of consumer culture on traditional societies. His most recent book is *The Global Soul: Jet Lag, Shopping Malls, and the Search for Home* (2000). Iyer contributes articles to *Harper's,* the *New York Times,* and *Time* magazine, where this essay appeared.

The gods, they say, give breath, and they take it away. But the same could be said — could it not? — of the humble comma. Add it to the present clause, and, of a sudden, the mind is, quite literally, given pause to think; take it out if you wish or forget it and the mind is deprived of a resting place. Yet still the comma gets no respect. It seems just a slip of a thing, a pedant's tick, a blip on the edge of our consciousness, a kind of printer's smudge almost. Small, we claim, is beautiful (especially in the age of the microchip). Yet what is so often used, and so rarely recalled, as the comma — unless it be breath itself?

Punctuation, one is taught, has a point: to keep up law and order. Punctuation marks are the road signs placed along the highway of our communications — to control speeds, provide directions and prevent head-on collisions. A period has the unblinking finality of a red light; the comma is a flashing yellow light that asks us only to slow down; and the semicolon is a stop sign that tells us to ease gradually to a halt, before gradually starting up again. By establishing the relations between words, punctuation establishes the relations between the people using words. That may be one reason why schoolteachers exalt it and lovers defy it ("We love each other and belong to each other let's don't ever hurt each other Nicole let's don't ever hurt each other," wrote Gary Gilmore[1] to his girlfriend). A comma, he must have known, "separates inseparables," in the clinching words of H. W. Fowler, King of English Usage.

[1]*Gary Gilmore* A serial killer executed in 1977. [Editor's note.]

Punctuation, then, is a civic prop, a pillar that holds society upright. (A   3
run-on sentence, its phrases piling up without division, is as unsightly as a
sink piled high with dirty dishes.) Small wonder, then, that punctuation
was one of the first proprieties of the Victorian age, the age of the corset,
that the modernists threw off: the sexual revolution might be said to have
begun when Joyce's Molly Bloom spilled out all her private thoughts in
thirty-six pages of unbridled, almost unperioded and officially censored
prose; and another rebellion was surely marked when E. E. Cummings first
felt free to commit "God" to the lower case.

Punctuation thus becomes the signature of cultures. The hot-blooded   4
Spaniard seems to be revealed in the passion and urgency of his doubled
exclamation points and question marks ("*¡Caramba! ¿Quien sabe?*"), while
the impassive Chinese traditionally added to his so-called inscrutability
by omitting directions from his ideograms. The anarchy and commotion of
the '60s were given voice in the exploding exclamation marks, riotous capital letters and Day-Glo italics of Tom Wolfe's spray-paint prose; and in Communist societies, where the State is absolute, the dignity — and divinity — of
capital letters is reserved for Ministries, Sub-Committees and Secretariats.

Yet punctuation is something more than a culture's birthmark; it scores   5
the music in our minds, gets our thoughts moving to the rhythm of our
hearts. Punctuation is the notation in the sheet music of our words, telling
us where to rest, or when to raise our voices; it acknowledges that the meaning of our discourse, as of any symphonic composition, lies not in the units
but in the pauses, the pacing and the phrasing. Punctuation is the way one
bats one's eyes, lowers one's voice or blushes demurely. Punctuation adjusts
the tone and color and volume till the feeling comes into perfect focus, not
disgust exactly, but distaste; not lust, or like, but love.

Punctuation, in short, gives us the human voice, and all the meanings   6
that lie between the words. "You aren't young, are you?" loses its innocence
when it loses the question mark. Every child knows the menace of a
dropped apostrophe (the parent's "Don't do that" shifting into the more
slowly enunciated "Do not do that"), and every believer, the ignominy of
having his faith reduced to "faith." Add an exclamation point to "To be or
not to be…" and the gloomy Dane has all the resolve he needs; add a
comma, and the noble sobriety of "God save the Queen" becomes a cry of
desperation bordering on double sacrilege.

Sometimes, of course, our markings may be simply a matter of aesthet-   7
ics. Popping in a comma can be like slipping on the necklace that gives an
outfit quiet elegance, or like catching the sound of running water that com-
plements, as it completes, the silence of a Japanese landscape. When V. S.
Naipaul, in his latest novel, writes, "He was a middle-aged man, with
glasses," the first comma can seem a little precious. Yet it gives the description a spin, as well as a subtlety, that it otherwise lacks, and it shows that
the glasses are not part of the middle-agedness, but something else.

Thus all these tiny scratches give us breadth and heft and depth. A world 8 that has only periods is a world without inflections. It is a world without shade. It has a music without sharps and flats. It is a martial music. It has a jackboot rhythm. Words cannot bend and curve. A comma, by comparison, catches the gentle drift of the mind in thought, turning in on itself and back on itself, reversing, redoubling and returning along the course of its own sweet river music; while the semicolon brings clauses and thoughts together with all the silent discretion of a hostess arranging guests around her dinner table.

Punctuation, then, is a matter of care. Care for words, yes, but also, and 9 more important, for what the words imply. Only a lover notices the small things: the way the afternoon light catches the nape of a neck, or how a strand of hair slips out from behind an ear, or the way a finger curls around a cup. And no one scans a letter so closely as a lover, searching for its small print, straining to hear its nuances, its gasps, its sighs and hesitations, poring over the secret messages that lie in every cadence. The difference between "Jane (whom I adore)" and "Jane, whom I adore," and the difference between them both and "Jane — whom I adore —" marks all the distance between ecstasy and heartache. "No iron can pierce the heart with such force as a period put at just the right place," in Isaac Babel's lovely words: a comma can let us hear a voice break, or a heart. Punctuation, in fact, is a labor of love. Which brings us back, in a way, to gods.

Analyzing This Selection

1. **THE WRITER'S METHOD**   In paragraph 1, how does the author make the topic humorous? What details and methods start it off?
2. What is the effect of the selection's abundant metaphors and analogies? Are there too many, overcrowding and cluttering the explanations?

Analyzing Connections

3. Examine the punctuation in paragraphs 1 and 2 of Kingston's essay ("The Misery of Silence," p. 269), and explain how the marks express her "care…for what the words imply." How do changes in punctuation alter the meaning?

Analyzing by Writing

4. Write two paragraphs using no commas but including other punctuation marks. Write fully developed sentences, and try to find varied, equivalent punctuation for nuances of meaning.

Richard Rodriguez

PUBLIC AND PRIVATE LANGUAGE

RICHARD RODRIGUEZ (b. 1944) grew up in San Francisco, where as the child of Spanish-speaking Mexican Americans he received his education in a language that was not spoken at home. His attraction to English and to English-speaking culture became his avenue to a promising future. Rodriguez graduated from Stanford University. He pursued graduate study in English at other universities until he decided to write about the conflicting aspirations that divided him between two cultures. This selection from his autobiography, *Hunger of Memory* (1982), recounts the origin of his adult views about bilingualism. Rodriguez has continued his memoir in *Days of Obligation: An Argument with My Mexican Father* (1992).

Supporters of bilingual education today imply that students like me miss a great deal by not being taught in their family's language. What they seem not to recognize is that, as a socially disadvantaged child, I considered Spanish to be a private language. What I needed to learn in school was that I had the right — and the obligation — to speak the public language of *los gringos*.[1] The odd truth is that my first-grade classmates could have become bilingual, in the conventional sense of that word, more easily than I. Had they been taught (as upper-middle-class children are often taught early) a second language like Spanish or French, they could have regarded it simply as that: another public language. In my case such bilingualism could not have been so quickly achieved. What I did not believe was that I could speak a single public language.

Without question, it would have pleased me to hear my teachers address me in Spanish when I entered the classroom. I would have felt much less afraid. I would have trusted them and responded with ease. But I would have delayed — for how long postponed? — having to learn the language of public society. I would have evaded — and for how long could I have afforded to delay? — learning the great lesson of school, that I had a public identity.

Fortunately, my teachers were unsentimental about their responsibility. What they understood was that I needed to speak a public language. So their voices would search me out, asking me questions. Each time I'd hear them,

---

[1]*los gringos* Foreigners. [All notes are the editor's.]

I'd look up in surprise to see a nun's face frowning at me. I'd mumble, not really meaning to answer. The nun would persist, "Richard, stand up. Don't look at the floor. Speak up. Speak to the entire class, not just to me!" but I couldn't believe that the English language was mine to use. (In part, I did not want to believe it.) I continued to mumble. I resisted the teacher's demands. (Did I somehow suspect that once I learned public language my pleasing family life would be changed?) Silent, waiting for the bell to sound, I remained dazed, diffident, afraid.

Because I wrongly imagined that English was intrinsically a public language and Spanish an intrinsically private one, I easily noted the difference between classroom language and the language of home. At school, words were directed to a general audience of listeners. ("Boys and girls.") Words were meaningfully ordered. And the point was not self-expression alone but to make oneself understood by many others. The teacher quizzed: "Boys and girls, why do we use that word in this sentence? Could we think of a better word to use there? Would the sentence change its meaning if the words were differently arranged? And wasn't there a better way of saying much the same thing?" (I couldn't say. I wouldn't try to say.) 4

Three months. Five. Half a year passed. Unsmiling, ever watchful, my teachers noted my silence. They began to connect my behavior with the difficult progress my older sister and brother were making. Until one Saturday morning three nuns arrived at the house to talk to our parents. Stiffly, they sat on the blue living room sofa. From the doorway of another room, spying the visitors, I noted the incongruity — the clash of two worlds, the faces and voices of school intruding upon the familiar setting of home. I overheard one voice gently wondering, "Do your children speak only Spanish at home, Mrs. Rodriguez?" While another voice added, "That Richard especially seems so timid and shy." 5

That Rich-heard! 6

With great tact the visitors continued, "Is it possible for you and your husband to encourage your children to practice their English when they are home?" Of course, my parents complied. What would they not do for their children's well-being? And how could they have questioned the Church's authority which those women represented? In an instant, they agreed to give up the language (the sounds) that had revealed and accentuated our family's closeness. The moment after the visitors left, the change was observed. "*Ahora*, speak to us *en inglés*,"[2] my father and mother united to tell us. 7

At first, it seemed a kind of game. After dinner each night, the family gathered to practice "our" English. (It was still then *inglés*, a language foreign to us, so we felt drawn as strangers to it.) Laughing, we would try to define words we could not pronounce. We played with strange English sounds, often overanglicizing our pronunciations. And we filled the smiling 8

---

[2]"*Now*, speak to us *in English.*"

gaps of our sentences with familiar Spanish sounds. But that was cheating, somebody shouted. Everyone laughed. In school, meanwhile, like my brother and sister, I was required to attend a daily tutoring session. I needed a full year of special attention. I also needed my teachers to keep my attention from straying in class by calling out, *Rich-heard* — their English voices slowly prying loose my ties to my other name, its three notes, *Ri-car-do.* Most of all I needed to hear my mother and father speak to me in a moment of seriousness in broken — suddenly heartbreaking — English. The scene was inevitable: One Saturday morning I entered the kitchen where my parents were talking in Spanish. I did not realize that they were talking in Spanish however until, at the moment they saw me, I heard their voices change to speak English. Those *gringo* sounds they uttered startled me. Pushed me away. In that moment of trivial misunderstanding and profound insight, I felt my throat twisted by unsounded grief. I turned quickly and left the room. But I had no place to escape to with Spanish. (The spell was broken.) My brother and sisters were speaking English in another part of the house.

Again and again in the days following, increasingly angry, I was obliged   9 to hear my mother and father: "Speak to us *en inglés*." (*Speak*.) Only then did I determine to learn classroom English. Weeks after, it happened: One day in school I had my hand raised to volunteer an answer. I spoke out in a loud voice. And I did not think it remarkable when the entire class understood. That day, I moved very far from the disadvantaged child I had been only days earlier. The belief, that calming assurance that I belonged in public, had at last taken hold.

Shortly after, I stopped hearing the high and loud sounds of *los gringos.*   10 A more and more confident speaker of English, I didn't trouble to listen to *how* strangers sounded, speaking to me. And there simply were too many English-speaking people in my day for me to hear American accents anymore. Conversations quickened. Listening to persons whose voices sounded eccentrically pitched, I usually noted their sounds for an initial few seconds before I concentrated on *what* they were saying. Conversations became content-full. Transparent. Hearing someone's *tone* of voice — angry or questioning or sarcastic or happy or sad — I didn't distinguish it from the words it expressed. Sound and word were thus tightly wedded. At the end of a day, I was often bemused, always relieved, to realize how "silent," though crowded with words, my day in public had been. (This public silence measured and quickened the change in my life.)

At last, seven years old, I came to believe what had been technically true   11 since my birth: I was an American citizen.

But the special feeling of closeness at home was diminished by then.   12 Gone was the desperate, urgent, intense feeling of being at home; rare was the experience of feeling myself individualized by family intimates. We remained a loving family, but one greatly changed. No longer so close; no longer bound tight by the pleasing and troubling knowledge of our public separateness. Neither my older brother nor sister rushed home after school anymore. Nor did I. When I arrived home there would often be neighborhood kids in the house. Or the house would be empty of sounds.

Following the dramatic Americanization of their children, even my parents grew more publicly confident. Especially my mother. She learned the names of all the people on our block. And she decided we needed to have a telephone installed in the house. My father continued to use the word *gringo*. But it was no longer charged with the old bitterness or distrust. (Stripped of any emotional content, the word simply became a name for those Americans not of Hispanic descent.) Hearing him, sometimes, I wasn't sure if he was pronouncing the Spanish word *gringo* or saying gringo in English.

Matching the silence I started hearing in public was a new quiet at home. The family's quiet was partly due to the fact that, as we children learned more and more English, we shared fewer and fewer words with our parents. Sentences needed to be spoken slowly when a child addressed his mother or father. (Often the parent wouldn't understand.) The child would need to repeat himself. (Still the parent misunderstood.) The young voice, frustrated, would end up saying, "Never mind" — the subject was closed. Dinners would be noisy with the clinking of knives and forks against dishes. My mother would smile softly between her remarks; my father at the other end of the table would chew and chew at his food, while he stared over the heads of his children.

My *mother!* My *father!* After English became my primary language, I no longer knew what words to use in addressing my parents. The old Spanish words (those tender accents of sound) I had used earlier — *mamá* and *papá* — I couldn't use anymore. They would have been too painful reminders of how much had changed in my life. On the other hand, the words I heard neighborhood kids call *their* parents seemed equally unsatisfactory. *Mother* and *Father; Ma, Papa, Pa, Dad, Pop* (how I hated the all-American sound of that last word especially) — all these terms I felt were unsuitable, not really terms of address for *my* parents. As a result, I never used them at home. Whenever I'd speak to my parents, I would try to get their attention with eye contact alone. In public conversations, I'd refer to "my parents" or "my mother and father."

My mother and father, for their part, responded differently, as their children spoke to them less and less. She grew restless, seemed troubled and anxious at the scarcity of words exchanged in the house. It was she who would question me about my day when I came home from school. She smiled at the small talk. She pried at the edges of my sentences to get me to say something more. (What?) She'd join conversations she overheard, but her intrusions often stopped her children's talking. By contrast, my father seemed reconciled to the new quiet. Though his English improved somewhat, he retired into silence. At dinner he spoke very little. One night his children and even his wife helplessly giggled at his garbled English pronunciation of the Catholic Grace before Meals. Thereafter he made his wife recite the prayer at the start of each meal, even on formal occasions, when there were guests in the house. Hers became the public voice of the family. On official business, it was she, not my father, one would usually hear on the phone or in stores, talking to strangers. His children grew so accustomed to his silence that, years later, they would speak routinely of his shyness. (My mother would often try to explain: Both his parents died when he was eight. He was raised by an uncle who treated him like little more than a menial servant. He was never encouraged to speak. He grew up alone. A man of few words.) But my father was not shy, I realized, when I'd watch him speaking Spanish with relatives. Using Spanish, he was quickly effusive. Especially when talking with other men, his voice would spark, flicker, flare alive with sounds. In Spanish, he expressed ideas and feelings he rarely revealed in English. With firm Spanish sounds, he conveyed confidence and authority English would never allow him.

The silence at home, however, was finally more than a literal silence. 17 Fewer words passed between parent and child, but more profound was the silence that resulted from my inattention to sounds. At about the time I no longer bothered to listen with care to the sounds of English in public, I grew careless about listening to the sounds family members made when they spoke. Most of the time I heard someone speaking at home and didn't distinguish his sounds from the words people uttered in public. I didn't even pay much attention to my parents' accented and ungrammatical speech. At least not at home. Only when I was with them in public would I grow alert to their accents. Though, even then, their sounds caused me less and less concern. For I was increasingly confident of my own public identity.

Today I hear bilingual educators say that children lose a degree of "indi- 18 viduality" by becoming assimilated into public society. (Bilingual schooling was popularized in the seventies, that decade when middle-class ethnics began to resist the process of assimilation — the American melting pot.) But the bilingualists simplistically scorn the value and necessity of assimilation. They do not seem to realize that there are *two* ways a person is individualized. So they do not realize that while one suffers a diminished sense of *private* individuality by becoming assimilated into public society, such assimilation makes possible the achievement of *public* individuality.

Analyzing This Selection

1. How does Rodriguez regard his childhood teachers? Distinguish between his childhood and his adult perspectives.
2. How does the English language change his parents' lives? How does Rodriguez respond to those changes?

3. **THE WRITER'S METHOD**   Rodriguez differentiates between private and public individuality, but he does not explicitly define either concept. Has he defined them implicitly? Explain his terms, adding your understanding of what they mean.

Analyzing Connections

4. Rodriguez and Kingston (see "The Misery of Silence," p. 269) were isolated by increased silences when the English language entered their lives. In your opinion, which writer's silences caused longer lasting solitude?

Analyzing by Writing

5. Should schools offer bilingual education to children of minority groups? Or perhaps to all children? (For instance, in Canada, all children learn both English and French.) Consider positive and negative effects of having a single public language in a multicultural society.

Howard Gardner

MULTIPLE INTELLIGENCES

HOWARD GARDNER (b. 1943) is a leading critic of traditional ideas about intelligence and IQ testing. He graduated and obtained a Ph.D. from Harvard University, where he teaches education and developmental psychology. Among his many influential works are *Frames of Mind* (1983) and *Multiple Intelligences: The Theory in Practice* (1993), from which the following selection is excerpted. Gardner has received a MacArthur Fellowship and other awards.

In a traditional view, intelligence is defined operationally as the ability 1
to answer items on tests of intelligence. The inference from the test scores
to some underlying ability is supported by statistical techniques that compare responses of subjects at different ages; the apparent correlation of these
test scores across ages and across different tests corroborates the notion
that the general faculty of intelligence, g, does not change much with age
or with training or experience. It is an inborn attribute or faculty of the
individual.

Multiple intelligences theory, on the other hand, pluralizes the tradi- 2
tional concept. An intelligence entails the ability to solve problems or
fashion products that are of consequence in a particular cultural setting
or community. The problem-solving skill allows one to approach a situation in which a goal is to be obtained and to locate the appropriate route
to that goal. The creation of a *cultural* product is crucial to such functions as capturing and transmitting knowledge or expressing one's views
or feelings. The problems to be solved range from creating an end for a
story to anticipating a mating move in chess to repairing a quilt. Products
range from scientific theories to musical compositions to successful political
campaigns.

MI theory is framed in light of the biological origins of each problem- 3
solving skill. Only those skills that are universal to the human species are
treated. Even so, the biological proclivity to participate in a particular form
of problem solving must also be coupled with the cultural nurturing of that
domain. For example, language, a universal skill, may manifest itself particularly as writing in one culture, as oratory in another culture, and as the
secret language of anagrams in a third.

Given the desire of selecting intelligences that are rooted in biology, and 4 that are valued in one or more cultural settings, how does one actually identify an "intelligence"? In coming up with our list, we consulted evidence from several different sources: knowledge about normal development and development in gifted individuals; information about the breakdown of cognitive skills under conditions of brain damage; studies of exceptional populations, including prodigies, idiots savants, and autistic children; data about the evolution of cognition over the millennia; cross-cultural accounts of cognition; psychometric studies, including examinations of correlations among tests; and psychological training studies, particularly measures of transfer and generalization across tasks. Only those candidate intelligences that satisfied all or a majority of the criteria were selected as bona fide intelligences. A more complete discussion of each of these criteria for an "intelligence" and the seven intelligences that have been proposed so far, is found in *Frames of Mind*.[1] This book also considers how the theory might be disproven and compares it to competing theories of intelligence....

An intelligence must also be susceptible to encoding in a symbol system — 5 a culturally contrived system of meaning, which captures and conveys important forms of information. Language, picturing, and mathematics are but three nearly worldwide symbol systems that are necessary for human survival and productivity. The relationship of a candidate intelligence to a human symbol system is no accident. In fact, the existence of a core computational capacity anticipates the existence of a symbol system that exploits that capacity. While it may be possible for an intelligence to proceed without an accompanying symbol system, a primary characteristic of human intelligence may well be its gravitation toward such an embodiment.

The Seven Intelligences

Having sketched the characteristics and criteria of an intelligence, we 6 turn now to a brief consideration of each of the seven intelligences. We begin each sketch with a thumbnail biography of a person who demonstrates an unusual facility with that intelligence. These biographies illustrate some of the abilities that are central to the fluent operation of a given intelligence. Although each biography illustrates a particular intelligence, we do not wish to imply that in adulthood intelligences operate in isolation. Indeed, except for abnormal individuals, intelligences always work in concert, and any sophisticated adult role will involve a melding of several of them. Following each biography we survey the various sources of data that support each candidate as an "intelligence."

---

[1]Gardner, H. (1983). *Frames of mind: The theory of multiple intelligences*. New York: Basic Books. [All notes are Gardner's.]

Musical Intelligence

When he was three years old, Yehudi Menuhin was smuggled into the San Francisco Orchestra concerts by his parents. The sound of Louis Persinger's violin so entranced the youngster that he insisted on a violin for his birthday and Louis Persinger as his teacher. He got both. By the time he was ten years old, Menuhin was an international performer.[2]

Violinist Yehudi Menuhin's musical intelligence manifested itself even   7
before he had touched a violin or received any musical training. His powerful reaction to that particular sound and his rapid progress on the instrument suggest that he was biologically prepared in some way for that endeavor. In this way evidence from child prodigies supports our claim that there is a biological link to a particular intelligence. Other special populations, such as autistic children who can play a musical instrument beautifully but who cannot speak, underscore the independence of musical intelligence.

A brief consideration of the evidence suggests that musical skill passes   8
the other tests for an intelligence. For example, certain parts of the brain play important roles in perception and production of music. These areas are characteristically located in the right hemisphere, although musical skill is not as clearly "localized," or located in a specifiable area, as language. Although the particular susceptibility of musical ability to brain damage depends on the degree of training and other individual differences, there is clear evidence for "amusia" or loss of musical ability.

Music apparently played an important unifying role in Stone Age (Pa-   9
leolithic) societies. Birdsong provides a link to other species. Evidence from various cultures supports the notion that music is a universal faculty. Studies of infant development suggest that there is a "raw" computational ability in early childhood. Finally, musical notation provides an accessible and lucid symbol system.

In short, evidence to support the interpretation of musical ability as an   10
"intelligence" comes from many different sources. Even though musical skill is not typically considered an intellectual skill like mathematics, it qualifies under our criteria. By definition it deserves consideration; and in view of the data, its inclusion is empirically justified.

Bodily-Kinesthetic Intelligence

Fifteen-year-old Babe Ruth played third base. During one game his team's pitcher was doing very poorly and Babe loudly criticized him from third base. Brother Mathias, the coach, called out, "Ruth, if you know so much about it, YOU pitch!" Babe was surprised and embarrassed because he had never pitched before, but Brother Mathias insisted. Ruth said later that at the very moment he took the pitcher's mound, he KNEW he was supposed to be a pitcher and that it was "natural" for him

[2]Menuhin, Y. (1977). *Unfinished journey*. New York: Knopf.

to strike people out. Indeed, he went on to become a great major league pitcher (and, of course, attained legendary status as a hitter).[3]

Like Menuhin, Babe Ruth was a child prodigy who recognized his 11 "instrument" immediately upon his first exposure to it. This recognition occurred in advance of formal training.

Control of bodily movement is, of course, localized in the motor cortex, 12 with each hemisphere dominant or controlling bodily movements on the contra-lateral side. In right-handers, the dominance for such movement is ordinarily found in the left hemisphere. The ability to perform movements when directed to do so can be impaired even in individuals who can perform the same movements reflexively or on a nonvoluntary basis. The existence of specific *apraxia* constitutes one line of evidence for a bodily-kinesthetic intelligence.

The evolution of specialized body movements is of obvious advantage to 13 the species, and in humans this adaptation is extended through the use of tools. Body movement undergoes a clearly defined developmental schedule in children. And there is little question of its universality across cultures. Thus it appears that bodily-kinesthetic "knowledge" satisfies many of the criteria for an intelligence.

The consideration of bodily-kinesthetic knowledge as "problem solving" 14 may be less intuitive. Certainly carrying out a mime sequence or hitting a tennis ball is not solving a mathematical equation. And yet, the ability to use one's body to express an emotion (as in a dance), to play a game (as in a sport), or to create a new product (as in devising an invention) is evidence of the cognitive features of body usage. The specific computations required to solve a particular bodily-kinesthetic *problem*, hitting a tennis ball, are summarized by Tim Gallwey:

> At the moment the ball leaves the server's racket, the brain calculates approximately where it will land and where the racket will intercept it. This calculation includes the initial velocity of the ball, combined with an input for the progressive decrease in velocity and the effect of wind and after the bounce of the ball. Simultaneously, muscle orders are given: not just once, but constantly with refined and updated information. The muscles must cooperate. A movement of the feet occurs, the racket is taken back, the face of the racket kept at a constant angle. Contact is made at a precise point that depends on whether the order was given to hit down the line or cross-court, an order not given until after a split-second analysis of the movement and balance of the opponent.
>
> To return an average serve, you have about one second to do this. To hit the ball at all is remarkable and yet not uncommon. The truth is that everyone who inhabits a human body possesses a remarkable creation.[4]

[3]Connor, A. (1982). *Voices from Cooperstown.* New York: Collier. (Based on a quotation taken from *The Babe Ruth story,* Babe Ruth & Bob Considine. New York: Dutton, 1948.)
[4]Gallwey, T. (1976). *Inner tennis.* New York: Random House.

Logical-Mathematical Intelligence

In 1983 Barbara McClintock won the Nobel Prize in medicine or phys-   15
iology for her work in microbiology. Her intellectual powers of deduction
and observation illustrate one form of logical-mathematical intelligence
that is often labeled "scientific thinking." One incident is particularly illuminating. While a researcher at Cornell in the 1920s McClintock was
faced one day with a problem: while *theory* predicted 50-percent pollen
sterility in corn, her research assistant (in the "field") was finding plants
that were only 25- to 30-percent sterile. Disturbed by this discrepancy,
McClintock left the cornfield and returned to her office where she sat for
half an hour, thinking:

> Suddenly I jumped up and ran back to the (corn) field. At the top of the
> field (the others were still at the bottom) I shouted "Eureka, I have it! I
> know what the 30% sterility is!"... They asked me to prove it. I sat down
> with a paper bag and a pencil and I started from scratch, which I had not
> done at all in my laboratory. It had all been done so fast; the answer
> came and I ran. Now I worked it out step by step — it was an intricate
> series of steps — and I came out with [the same result]. [They] looked at
> the material and it was exactly as I'd said it was; it worked out exactly as
> I had diagrammed it. Now, why did I know, without having done it on
> paper? Why was I so sure?[5]

This anecdote illustrates two essential facts of the logical-mathematical   16
intelligence. First, in the gifted individual, the process of problem solving
is often remarkably rapid — the successful scientist copes with many variables at once and creates numerous hypotheses that are each evaluated and
then accepted or rejected in turn.

The anecdote also underscores the *nonverbal* nature of the intelligence.   17
A solution to a problem can be constructed *before* it is articulated. In fact,
the solution process may be totally invisible, even to the problem solver.
This need not imply, however, that discoveries of this sort — the familiar
"Aha!" phenomenon — are mysterious, intuitive, or unpredictable. The fact
that it happens more frequently to some people (perhaps Nobel Prize winners) suggests the opposite. We interpret this as the work of theological-
mathematical intelligence.

Along with the companion skill of language, logical-mathematical rea-   18
soning provides the principal basis for IQ tests. This form of intelligence
has been heavily investigated by traditional psychologists, and it is the
archetype of "raw intelligence" or the problem-solving faculty that purport-
edly cuts across domains. It is perhaps ironic, then, that the actual mechanism by which one arrives at a solution to a logical-mathematical problem
is not as yet properly understood.

This intelligence is supported by our empirical criteria as well. Certain   19
areas of the brain are more prominent in mathematical calculation than

[5]Keller, E. (1983). *A feeling for the organism* (p. 104). Salt Lake City: W. H. Freeman.

others. There are idiots savants who perform great feats of calculation even though they remain tragically deficient in most other areas. Child prodigies in mathematics abound. The development of this intelligence in children has been carefully documented by Jean Piaget and other psychologists.

Linguistic Intelligence

At the age of ten, T. S. Eliot created a magazine called "Fireside" to which he was the sole contributor. In a three-day period during his winter vacation, he created eight complete issues. Each one included poems, adventure stories, a gossip column, and humor. Some of this material survives and it displays the talent of the poet.[6]

As with the logical intelligence, calling linguistic skill an "intelligence" 20 is consistent with the stance of traditional psychology. Linguistic intelligence also passes our empirical tests. For instance, a specific area of the brain, called "Broca's Area," is responsible for the production of grammatical sentences. A person with damage to this area can understand words and sentences quite well but has difficulty putting words together in anything other than the simplest of sentences. At the same time, other thought processes may be entirely unaffected.

The gift of language is universal, and its development in children is 21 strikingly constant across cultures. Even in deaf populations where a manual sign language is not explicitly taught, children will often "invent" their own manual language and use it surreptitiously! We thus see how an intelligence may operate independently of a specific input modality or output channel.

Spatial Intelligence

Navigation around the Caroline Islands in the South Seas is accomplished without instruments. The position of the stars, as viewed from various islands, the weather patterns, and water color are the only sign posts. Each journey is broken into a series of segments; and the navigator learns the position of the stars within each of these segments. During the actual trip the navigator must envision mentally a reference island as it passes under a particular star and from that he computes the number of segments completed, the proportion of the trip remaining, and any corrections in heading that are required. The navigator cannot *see* the islands as he sails along; instead he maps their locations in his mental "picture" of the journey.[7]

Spatial problem solving is required for navigation and in the use of the 22 notational system of maps. Other kinds of spatial problem solving are brought to bear in visualizing an object seen from a different angle and in playing chess. The visual arts also employ this intelligence in the use of space.

[6]Soldo, J. (1982). Jovial juvenilia: T. S. Eliot's first magazine. *Biography*, 5, 25–37.
[7]Gardner, H. (1983). *Frames of mind: The theory of multiple intelligences*. New York: Basic Books.

Evidence from brain research is clear and persuasive. Just as the left   23
hemisphere has, over the course of evolution, been selected as the site of
linguistic processing in right-handed persons, the right hemisphere proves
to be the site most crucial for spatial processing. Damage to the right posterior regions causes impairment of the ability to find one's way around a
site, to recognize faces or scenes, or to notice fine details.

Patients with damage specific to regions of the right hemisphere will   24
attempt to compensate for their spacial deficits with linguistic strategies.
They will try to reason aloud, to challenge the task, or even make up
answers. But such nonspatial strategies are rarely successful.

Blind populations provide an illustration of the distinction between the   25
spatial intelligence and visual perception. A blind person can recognize
shapes by an indirect method: running a hand along the object translates
into length of time of movement, which in turn is translated into the size
of the object. For the blind person, the perceptual system of the tactile
modality parallels the visual modality in the seeing person. The analogy
between the spatial reasoning of the blind and the linguistic reasoning of
the deaf is notable.

There are few child prodigies among visual artists, but there are idiots   26
savants such as Nadia.[8] Despite a condition of severe autism, this preschool
child made drawings of the most remarkable representational accuracy and
finesse.

Interpersonal Intelligence

With little formal training in special education and nearly blind herself,   27
Anne Sullivan began the intimidating task of instructing a blind and deaf
seven-year-old Helen Keller. Sullivan's efforts at communication were complicated by the child's emotional struggle with the world around her. At
their first meal together, this scene occurred:

> Annie did not allow Helen to put her hand into Annie's plate and take
> what she wanted, as she had been accustomed to do with her family. It
> became a test of wills — hand thrust into plate, hand firmly put aside.
> The family, much upset, left the dining room. Annie locked the door and
> proceeded to eat her breakfast while Helen lay on the floor kicking and
> screaming, pushing and pulling at Annie's chair. [After half an hour]
> Helen went around the table looking for her family. She discovered no
> one else was there and that bewildered her. Finally, she sat down and
> began to eat her breakfast, but with her hands. Annie gave her a spoon.
> Down on the floor it clattered, and the contest of wills began anew.[9]

Anne Sullivan sensitively responded to the child's behavior. She wrote   28
home: "The greatest problem I shall have to solve is how to discipline and

[8]Selfe, L. (1977). *Nadia: A case of extraordinary drawing in an autistic child.* New York:
Academic Press.
[9]Lash, J. (1980). *Helen and teacher: The story of Helen Keller and Anne Sullivan Macy*
(p. 52). New York: Delacorte.

control her without breaking her spirit. I shall go rather slowly at first and try to win her love."

In fact, the first "miracle" occurred two weeks later, well before the famous incident at the pumphouse. Annie had taken Helen to a small cottage near the family's house, where they could live alone. After seven days together, Helen's personality suddenly underwent a profound change — the therapy had worked:

> My heart is singing with joy this morning. A miracle has happened! The wild little creature of two weeks ago has been transformed into a gentle child.[10]

It was just two weeks after this that the first breakthrough in Helen's grasp of language occurred; and from that point on, she progressed with incredible speed. The key to the miracle of language was Anne Sullivan's insight into the *person* of Helen Keller.

Interpersonal intelligence builds on a core capacity to notice distinctions among others; in particular, contrasts in their moods, temperaments, motivations, and intentions. In more advanced forms, this intelligence permits a skilled adult to read the intentions and desires of others, even when these have been hidden. This skill appears in a highly sophisticated form in religious or political leaders, teachers, therapists, and parents. The Helen Keller–Anne Sullivan story suggests that this interpersonal intelligence does not depend on language.

All indices in brain research suggest that the frontal lobes play a prominent role in interpersonal knowledge. Damage in this area can cause profound personality changes while leaving other forms of problem solving unharmed — a person is often "not the same person" after such an injury.

Alzheimer's disease, a form of presenile dementia, appears to attack posterior brain zones with a special ferocity, leaving spatial, logical, and linguistic computations severely impaired. Yet, Alzheimer's patients will often remain well groomed, socially proper, and continually apologetic for their errors. In contrast, Pick's disease, another variety of presenile dementia that is more frontally oriented, entails a rapid loss of social graces.

Biological evidence for interpersonal intelligence encompasses two additional factors often cited as unique to humans. One factor is the prolonged childhood of primates, including the close attachment to the mother. In those cases where the mother is removed from early development, normal interpersonal development is in serious jeopardy. The second factor is the relative importance in humans of social interaction. Skills such as hunting, tracking, and killing in prehistoric societies required participation and cooperation of large numbers of people. The need for group cohesion, leadership, organization, and solidarity follows naturally from this.

[10]Lash (p. 54).

Intrapersonal Intelligence

In an essay called "A Sketch of the Past," written almost as a diary entry,   35
Virginia Woolf discusses the "cotton wool of existence" — the various mundane events of life. She contrasts this "cotton wool" with three specific and
poignant memories from her childhood: a fight with her brother, seeing a
particular flower in the garden, and hearing of the suicide of a past visitor.

> These are three instances of exceptional moments. I often tell them over,
> or rather they come to the surface unexpectedly. But now for the first
> time I have written them down, and I realize something that I have never
> realized before. Two of these moments ended in a state of despair. The
> other ended, on the contrary, in a state of satisfaction.
>
> The sense of horror (in hearing of the suicide) held me powerless. But
> in the case of the flower, I found a reason; and was thus able to deal with
> the sensation. I was not powerless.
>
> Though I still have the peculiarity that I receive these sudden shocks,
> they are now always welcome; after the first surprise, I always feel instantly
> that they are particularly valuable. And so I go on to suppose that the
> shock-receiving capacity is what makes me a writer. I hazard the expla-
> nation that a shock is at once in my case followed by the desire to explain
> it. I feel that I have had a blow; but it is not, as I thought as a child, sim-
> ply a blow from an enemy hidden behind the cotton wool of daily life; it
> is or will become a revelation of some order; it is a token of some real
> thing behind appearances; and I make it real by putting it into words.[11]

This quotation vividly illustrates the intrapersonal intelligence — knowl-   36
edge of the internal aspects of a person: access to one's own feeling life,
one's range of emotions, the capacity to effect discriminations among these
emotions and eventually to label them and to draw upon them as a means
of understanding and guiding one's own behavior. A person with good
intrapersonal intelligence has a viable and effective model of himself or
herself. Since this intelligence is the most private, it requires evidence from
language, music, or some other more expressive form of intelligence if the
observer is to detect it at work. In the above quotation, for example, linguistic intelligence is drawn upon to convey intrapersonal knowledge; it
embodies the interaction of intelligences, a common phenomenon to which
we will return later.

We see the familiar criteria at work in the intrapersonal intelligence. As   37
with the interpersonal intelligence, the frontal lobes play a central role in
personality change. Injury to the lower area of the frontal lobes is likely to
produce irritability or euphoria; while injury to the higher regions is more
likely to produce indifference, listlessness, slowness, and apathy — a kind of
depressive personality. In such "frontal-lobe" individuals, the other cognitive functions often remain preserved. In contrast, among aphasics who
have recovered sufficiently to describe their experiences, we find consistent

---

[11]Woolf, V. (1976). *Moments of being* (pp. 69–70). Sussex: The University Press.

testimony: while there may have been a diminution of general alertness and considerable depression about the condition, the individual in no way felt himself to be a different person. He recognized his own needs, wants, and desires and tried as best he could to achieve them.

The autistic child is a prototypical example of an individual with im- 38
paired intrapersonal intelligence; indeed, the child may not even be able to refer to himself. At the same time, such children often exhibit remarkable abilities in the musical, computational, spatial, or mechanical realms.

Evolutionary evidence for an intrapersonal faculty is more difficult to 39
come by, but we might speculate that the capacity to transcend the satisfaction of instinctual drives is relevant. This becomes increasingly important in a species not perennially involved in the struggle for survival.

In sum, then, both interpersonal and intrapersonal faculties pass the tests 40
of an intelligence. They both feature problem-solving endeavors with significance for the individual and the species. Interpersonal intelligence allows one to understand and work with others; intrapersonal intelligence allows one to understand and work with oneself. In the individual's sense of self, one encounters a melding of inter- and intrapersonal components. Indeed, the sense of self emerges as one of the most marvelous of human inventions — a symbol that represents all kinds of information about a person and that is at the same time an invention that all individuals construct for themselves.

Summary: The Unique Contributions of the Theory

As human beings, we all have a repertoire of skills for solving different 41
kinds of problems. Our investigation has begun, therefore, with a consideration of these problems, the contexts they are found in, and the culturally significant products that are the outcome. We have not approached "intelligence" as a reified human faculty that is brought to bear in literally any problem setting; rather, we have begun with the problems that humans *solve* and worked back to the "intelligences" that must be responsible.

Evidence from brain research, human development, evolution, and 42
cross-cultural comparisons was brought to bear in our search for the relevant human intelligences: a candidate was included only if reasonable evidence to support its membership was found across these diverse fields. Again, this tack differs from the traditional one: since no candidate faculty is *necessarily* an intelligence, we could choose on a motivated basis. In the traditional approach to "intelligence," there is no opportunity for this type of empirical decision.

We have also determined that these multiple human faculties, the intel- 43
ligences, are to a significant extent *independent*. For example, research with brain-damaged adults repeatedly demonstrates that particular faculties can be lost while others are spared. This independence of intelligence implies

that a particularly high level of ability in one intelligence, say mathematics, does not require a similarly high level in another intelligence, like language or music. This independence of intelligences contrasts sharply with traditional measures of IQ that find high correlations among test scores. We speculate that the usual correlations among subtests of IQ tests come about because all of these tasks in fact measure the ability to respond rapidly to items of a logical-mathematical or linguistic sort; we believe that these correlations would be substantially reduced if one were to survey in a contextually appropriate way the full range of human problem-solving skills.

Until now, we have supported the fiction that adult roles depend largely   44
on the flowering of a single intelligence. In fact, however, nearly every cultural role of any degree of sophistication requires a combination of intelligences. Thus, even an apparently straightforward role, like playing the violin, transcends a reliance on simple musical intelligence. To become a successful violinist requires bodily-kinesthetic dexterity and the interpersonal skills of relating to an audience and, in a different way, choosing a manager; quite possibly it involves an intrapersonal intelligence as well. Dance requires skills in bodily-kinesthetic, musical, interpersonal, and spatial intelligences in varying degrees. Politics requires an interpersonal skill, a linguistic facility, and perhaps some logical aptitude. Inasmuch as nearly every cultural role requires several intelligences, it becomes important to consider individuals as a collection of aptitudes rather than as having a singular problem-solving faculty that can be measured directly through pencil-and-paper tests. Even given a relatively small number of such intelligences, the diversity of human ability is created through the differences in these profiles. In fact, it may well be that the "total is greater than the sum of the parts." An individual may not be particularly gifted in any intelligence; and yet, because of a particular combination or blend of skills, he or she may be able to fill some niche uniquely well. Thus it is of paramount importance to assess the particular combination of skills that may earmark an individual for a certain vocational or avocational niche.

Analyzing This Selection

1. Gardner's theory includes seven independent intelligences. Do you think they are all separable even in theory? Which, if any, would you combine?

2. **THE WRITER'S METHOD** Gardner's paragraphs are usually short and he highlights topics, but along with these journalistic customs, he provides footnotes. Who is his intended audience? How does his audience differ from yours?

3. How do Gardner's criteria for selecting an intelligence guard against over-specificity or trivializing? What, if anything, rules out *osculatory* skill (good kissing) as an intelligence?

Analyzing Connections

4. What kinds of intelligence interfered with Amy Tan's test achievements? (See "Mother Tongue," p. 200).

Analyzing by Writing

5. What is your idea of intelligence? Do you give high or low value to analytical skills with words? with math? Are creative people smart or just expressive? Do athletes function mentally in their athletic abilities? Analyze your attitudes and explain what you think intelligence really is. (Stay focused on intelligence. Don't drift into what you like or dislike about personalities.)

6. **RESEARCH TOPIC** Find out about the science of phrenology that flourished in the 1830s–40s. How does MI theory reflect and expand upon phrenological theory?

Neil Postman

THE NECESSITY OF MYTHS[1]

Neil Postman (b. 1931) is a professor of communications at New York University. His writings examine the debased state of American popular culture and its impact on learning and society. His books include *Amusing Ourselves to Death: Public Discourse in the Age of Show Business* (1985), and *The End of Education* (1995), from which the following essay is excerpted.

In considering how to conduct the schooling of our young, adults have 1 two problems to solve. One is an engineering problem; the other, a metaphysical one. The engineering problem, as all such problems are, is essentially technical. It is the problem of the *means* by which the young will become learned. It addresses the issues of where and when things will be done, and, of course, how learning is supposed to occur....

But it is important to keep in mind that the engineering of learning is 2 very often puffed up, assigned an importance it does not deserve. As an old saying goes, There are one and twenty ways to sing tribal lays, and all of them are correct. So it is with learning. There is no one who can say that this or that is the best way to know things, to feel things, to see things, to remember things, to apply things, to connect things and that no other will do as well. In fact, to make such a claim is to trivialize learning, to reduce it to a mechanical skill.

Of course, there are many learnings that are little else but a mechanical 3 skill, and in such cases, there well may be a best way. But to become a different person because of something you have learned — to appropriate an insight, a concept, a vision, so that your world is altered — that is a different matter. For that to happen, you need a reason. And this is the metaphysical problem I speak of.

A reason, as I use the word here, is different from a motivation. Within 4 the context of schooling, motivation refers to a temporary psychic event in which curiosity is aroused and attention is focused. I do not mean to disparage it. But it must not be confused with a reason for being in a classroom, for listening to a teacher, for taking an examination, for doing homework, for putting up with school even if you are not motivated.

[1]Editor's title.

This kind of reason is somewhat abstract, not always present in one's consciousness, not at all easy to describe. And yet for all that, without it schooling does not work. For school to make sense, the young, their parents, and their teachers must have a god to serve, or, even better, several gods. If they have none, school is pointless. Nietzsche's famous aphorism is relevant here: "He who has a *why* to live can bear with almost any *how*." This applies as much to learning as to living.

To put it simply, there is no surer way to bring an end to schooling than for it to have no end.

By a god to serve, I do not necessarily mean *the* God, who is supposed to have created the world and whose moral injunctions as presented in sacred texts have given countless people a reason for living and, more to the point, a reason for learning.... With some reservations but mostly with conviction, I use the word *narrative* as a synonym for *god*, with a small *g*. I know it is risky to do so, not only because the word *god*, having an aura of sacredness, is not to be used lightly, but also because it calls to mind a fixed figure or image. But it is the purpose of such figures or images to direct one's mind to an idea and, more to my point, to a story — not any kind of story, but one that tells of origins and envisions a future, a story that constructs ideals, prescribes rules of conduct, provides a source of authority, and, above all, gives a sense of continuity and purpose. A god, in the sense I am using the word, is the name of a great narrative, one that has sufficient credibility, complexity, and symbolic power to enable one to organize one's life around it....

Our genius lies in our capacity to make meaning through the creation of narratives that give point to our labors, exalt our history, elucidate the present, and give direction to our future. To do their work, such narratives do not have to be "true" in a scientific sense. There are many enduring narratives whose details include things that are false to observable fact. The purpose of a narrative is to give meaning to the world, not to describe it scientifically. The measure of a narrative's "truth" or "falsity" is in its consequences: Does it provide people with a sense of personal identity, a sense of a community life, a basis for moral conduct, explanations of that which cannot be known?

You will recognize that this kind of storytelling goes by many different names. Joseph Campbell and Rollo May refer to it as "myth." Freud, who understood better than anyone the creative source and psychic need of such tales, nonetheless called them "illusions." One may even say, without much of a stretch, that Marx had something of this in mind in using the word *ideology*. But it is not my point to differentiate with scholarly nuance the subtle variations among these terms. The point is that, call them what you will, we are unceasing in creating histories and futures for ourselves through the medium of narrative. Without a narrative, life has no meaning. Without meaning, learning has no purpose. Without a purpose, schools are houses of detention, not attention....

The most comprehensive narratives are, of course, found in such texts as 10
the Old Testament, the New Testament, the Koran, the Bhagavad Gita.
But beginning in the sixteenth century, at least in the West, there began to
emerge narratives of a different sort, although with power enough to serve
as alternate gods. Among the most enduring is the great narrative known as
"inductive science." It is worth noting of this god that its first storytellers —
Descartes, Bacon, Galileo, Kepler, and Newton, for example — did not
think of their story as a replacement for the great Judeo-Christian narrative,
but as an extension of it. In fact, the point has been made more than once
that the great age of science was based on a belief in a God who was himself a scientist and technician, and who would therefore approve of a civilization committed to such an enterprise. "For all we know," Eric Hoffer
wrote, "one of the reasons that other civilizations, with all their ingenuity
and skill, did not develop a machine age is that they lacked a God whom
they could readily turn into an all-powerful engineer. For has not the
mighty Jehovah performed from the beginning of time the feats that our
machine age is even now aspiring to achieve?"[2] Galileo, Kepler, and Newton would largely agree, conceiving of God, as they did, as a great clock-
maker and mathematician. In any case, there is no doubt that from the
beginning of the age of science, its creators believed in the great narrative of
Jehovah. Their discoveries were made in the service of the Judeo-Christian
God. And could they know of Stephen Hawking's remark that the research
permitted by the (now abandoned) supercollider would give insight into
the mind of God, they would be pleased. The difference between them
and Hawking is that Hawking, as an avowed atheist, does not believe what
he said. To him, the story of Jehovah's wonders is only a dead metaphor,
perhaps a tale told by an idiot. Apparently, the great story of science, all
by itself, is enough for Hawking, as it has been for many others. It is a story
that exalts human reason, places criticism over faith, disdains revelation as
a source of knowledge, and, to put a spiritual cast upon it, postulates...that
our purpose on Earth is to discover reliable knowledge. Of course, the great
narrative of science shares with the great religious narratives the idea that
there is order to the universe, which is a fundamental assumption of all
important narratives....

Nonetheless, like all gods, it is imperfect. Its story of our origins and of 11
our end is, to say the least, unsatisfactory. To the question, How did it all
begin?, science answers, Probably by an accident. To the question, How
will it all end?, science answers, Probably by an accident. And to many
people, the accidental life is not worth living. Moreover, regarding the
question, What moral instruction do you give us?, the science-god maintains a tight-lipped silence. It places itself at the service of both the benefi-

[2]Eric Hoffer, *The Ordeal of Change* (New York: Harper & Row), p. 62. [All notes are Postman's.]

cent and the cruel, and its grand moral impartiality, if not indifference, has made it welcome the world over....

What happens to people when they have no gods to serve? Some commit suicide. There is more of this in the United States, particularly among our young, than in most other places in the world. Some envelop themselves in drugs, including alcohol. Some take whatever pleasure is to be found in random violence. Some encase themselves in an impenetrable egoism. Many, apparently, find a momentary and pitiful release from dread in commercial re-creations of once-powerful narratives of the past.   12

I have before me an account of the proliferation of "theme parks" in both the United States and Europe. As I write, one of them is about to arise in Poland, where, according to *Travel and Leisure* magazine, its staff will dress in replica uniforms of the Luftwaffe and Wehrmacht to inspire nightly dances at "Hitler's Bunker Disco." Another, an amusement park near Berlin, will take as its theme "East Germany under Communism." Its service people will pretend to be agents of the secret police, and will put those making critical remarks about the government into a fake jail. Across the ocean, near Atlanta, Georgia, an amusement park is being developed around the theme "Gone with the Wind Country." Not to be outdone, the Walt Disney Company, whose prosperity is entirely based on the timely and romantic re-creation of narratives, has drawn up plans for still another amusement park near Manassas, Virginia, with the theme "The Civil War Experience." Apparently, the exhibits are to include a dramatization of the experience of slavery — whether for it or against is not yet clear (nor indeed, as I write, is the future of this project).[3]   13

Is all of this a mere rehearsal for the mass consumption of "virtual reality," as Joy Gould Boyum suspects? Are we being readied for a time when we will not require expensive theme parks to re-create the nightmare or fantasy of our choice, but can materialize either with the press of a button? Whether we are or not, what is certainly happening here is, to use Rollo May's phrase, a "cry for myth." Nightmare or fantasy, these parks allow one to inhabit a world where some powerful narrative once held sway, a narrative that gave people a reason for living, and in whose absence a kind of psychic trauma ensues. Even if a narrative places one in hell, it is better to be there than to be nowhere. To be nowhere means to live in a barren culture, one that offers no vision of the past or future, no clear voice of authority, no organizing principles. In such a culture, what are schools for? What *can* they be for?   14

There was a time when American culture knew what schools were for because it offered fully functioning multiple narratives for its people to embrace. There was, for example, the great story of democracy, which the American artist Ben Shahn once proclaimed "the most appealing idea that the world has yet known." Alexis de Tocqueville called it "the principle of   15

[3]Gary Krist, "Tragedyland," *New York Times*, November 27, 1993, 19.

civic participation." Gunnar Myrdal encapsulated the idea in the phrase "The American Creed," which he judged to be the most explicitly articulated system of general ideals of any country in the West. The first chapter of the story opens with "In the beginning, there was a revolution." As the story unfolds, there arise sacred words such as "government of the people, by the people and for the people." Because he helped to write the story, Thomas Jefferson, the Moses of the great democracy-god, knew what schools were for — to ensure that citizens would know when and how to protect their liberty. This is a man who produced an essay that could have cost him his life, and that included the words: "We hold these truths to be self-evident; that all men are created equal; that they are endowed by their creator with certain unalienable rights; that among these are life, liberty, and the pursuit of happiness." It would not have come easily to the mind of such a man, as it does to political leaders today, that the young should be taught to read exclusively for the purpose of increasing their economic productivity. Jefferson had a more profound god to serve.

As did Emma Lazarus, whose poem celebrates another once-powerful 16 American narrative. "Give me your tired, your poor, your huddled masses yearning to breathe free," she wrote. Where else, save the great narrative of Jesus, can one find a story that so ennobles the huddled masses? Here, America is portrayed as the great melting pot. Such a story answers many profound questions, including, What are schools for? Schools are to fashion Americans out of the wretched refuse of teeming shores. Schools are to provide the lost and lonely with a common attachment to America's history and future, to America's sacred symbols, to its promise of freedom. The schools are, in a word, the affirmative answer to the question, Can a coherent, stable, unified culture be created out of people of diverse traditions, languages, and religions?...

As early as 1915, grievances were expressed against the melting-pot 17 metaphor and more particularly against its supposed reality.[4] While it was conceded that the American Creed was based predominantly on an Anglo-Saxon tradition, the argument was made that its principles were being enacted largely by immigrants, who enriched it by their own traditions and who, in any case, would not abandon their tribal identities. Thus, the idea of cultural pluralism entered the schools, mostly beginning in the 1930s. This meant that in many public schools (not mine), the history, literature, and traditions of different immigrant groups were included as part of the great tale of the American Creed. I do not know if the self-esteem and ethnic pride of the children of the huddled masses were elevated by cultural pluralism. Probably yes in some cases; maybe no, with accompanying embarrassment, in a few. Although my own schools were considerably late

---

[4]See the February 18 and 25 issues of the *Nation*. The articles were written by Horace Kallen.

in adopting cultural pluralism, I do remember an occasion when a teacher, in a rare gesture of accommodation to ethnic diversity, made a point of emphasizing the contribution of the Jew Haim Salomon to the financing of the Revolutionary War. The financing? I would have much preferred if Salomon had been Paul Revere's backup.

Whatever the gains or losses may have been in the self-esteem of the students, cultural pluralism made three positive contributions toward maintaining the vitality and usefulness of the narratives underlying the public school experience. First, it provided a fuller and more accurate picture of American culture and, especially, its history — which is to say, it revealed the dynamic nature of the great American narratives. Melting pot or not, America was shown to be a composite culture from which, in principle, none were excluded. Second, at no point was the inclusion of the immigrant narratives presented as a refutation of the American Creed. Even the horrendous stories of the massacre of "native" Americans, slavery, and the exploitation of "coolie" labor could be told without condemning the ideals of democracy, the melting pot, or the Protestant ethic. Indeed, such stories often served as an inspiration to purify the American Creed, to overcome prejudice, to redeem ourselves from the blighted parts of our history. Third, the inclusion of any immigrant narrative was not intended to promote divisiveness among different groups. The idea was to show that there were substance and richness in each tribal tale, and that we were better for knowing the gods of other people.

It would seem that certain versions of what is now called "multiculturalism" reject all three of these ideas, and this rejection, I will soon argue, seriously threatens the future of *public*, as opposed to private, schools. Here, I will say only that the idea of public education depends absolutely on the existence of shared narratives *and* the exclusion of narratives that lead to alienation and divisiveness. What makes public schools public is not so much that the schools have common goals but that the students have common gods. The reason for this is that public education does not serve a public. It *creates* a public. And in creating the right kind of public, the schools contribute toward strengthening the spiritual basis of the American Creed. That is how Jefferson understood it, how Horace Mann understood it, how John Dewey understood it. And, in fact, there is no other way to understand it. The question is not, Does or doesn't public schooling create a public? The question is, What kind of public does it create? A conglomerate of self-indulgent consumers? Angry, soulless, directionless masses? Indifferent, confused citizens? Or a public imbued with confidence, a sense of purpose, a respect for learning, and tolerance? The answer to this question has nothing whatever to do with computers, with testing, with teacher accountability, with class size, and with the other details of managing schools. The right answer depends on two things, and two things alone: the existence of shared narratives and the capacity of such narratives to provide an inspired reason for schooling.

Analyzing This Selection

1. What does inductive science share with the Judeo-Christian narrative? What did it eliminate from the story?

2. How does the author explain the popularity of theme parks? What is Postman's attitude toward each of the examples?

3. According to Postman, how does multiculturalism differ from earlier cultural pluralism?

4. In paragraph 19, do you agree or disagree with Postman's view of the chief service of public education?

5. **THE WRITER'S METHOD**   Postman's style is lively even though his subject is abstract and theoretical. Find examples of words, sentences, and paragraphs that illustrate how the author enlivens his writing.

Analyzing Connections

6. What myths competed at Angelou's graduation? (See "Graduation," p. 258.)

Analyzing by Writing

7. Analyze the great narratives that compete in your family's views of your education. Are there conflicting gods or no gods? Examine the different reasons and meanings upheld by yourself and by your parents, grandparents, siblings, or other family members.

George Steiner

BOOKS AND THE END OF
LITERATURE[1]

GEORGE STEINER (b. 1929) grew up in Paris and was brought by his family to the United States in 1940. He graduated from the University of Chicago and received a Ph.D. from Oxford University, where he now teaches comparative literature. He contributes articles and reviews to the *New Yorker,* the *Times Literary Supplement,* and *Salmagundi.* Steiner's numerous books include *In Bluebeard's Castle: Some Notes Towards the Redefinition of Culture* (1974) and essays on his pleasures in the life of the mind, *Errata: An Examined Life* (1998). The following selection, first delivered as a public lecture at Oxford, was printed in *New Perspectives Quarterly* in 1996.

I imagine many of you will already have seen it, so I apologize. The current issue of that key journal of comparative papyrology of the Romanian Academy has an enormously interesting fragment, recently deciphered. It appears to be a conversation from 5th century B.C. Corinth about the first public readings of the *Iliad* and the *Odyssey.* It is quite clear from the conversation that these are judged to have no future whatsoever. The issue is whether to waste expensive sheep skin — and a great many sheep — on transcription when the story is so manifestly too long, too repetitive, full of endless formulas, with that rosy-fingered dawn every 10 lines, so full of dull patches and with such a messy ending. Is Odysseus going to stay at home, or is he leaving? No one can really make it out. It was a very brave effort, but destined for oblivion. 1

The point is obvious. When did literature have a future? Probably never. 2 What we know as literature has had a very, very short run. Scholars say we can start with St. Augustine's famous observation of his master and teacher, St. Ambrose, in the courtyard in Milan. Augustine says: "This is the first man in the West who could read without moving his lips." A man reading in silence, having a relationship to a text which is more or less that of a modern act of reading. This sense of a private and personal relationship to the text, of remembrance and return, and of text engendering text, breaks down around 1914 — the beginning of the catastrophe of our culture in the West.

Today, we need to address these themes again for two reasons: technology and talent. Gutenberg was not a fundamental revolution. It extended the life of the written word. In the 80 years following Gutenberg, there were more illuminated manuscripts produced and commissioned than in the previous century. It was not a revolution of the kind we may now be experiencing. What will virtual reality mean for the imagination, for the habits of narrative and imagining of its practitioners? It is not only virtual reality. My colleagues in the Cambridge engineering department tell me that they are very close to a "small-scale, portable, total display" computer — meaning that you will carry with you or have on your desk or by your bed, for bedtime reading, this small and versatile screen. It will be online to the libraries of the world; the 14 million books of the Library of Congress will be at your fingertips and it will be clearer, easier to carry, infinitely more responsive to your interests and needs than any book. Then, we are truly in a new world.

But it takes two. There can be no literature without readers. Readers shape literature. Literature shapes readers and has done so since the beginning of the notion of literacy. So if readers change altogether, as they will with the new possibilities, what they are reading will change also, however ancient it is. A CD-ROM presentation of *Homer*, now available, is completely different from the papyrus version, the print version, the comic book version. They all have a metaphysic of their own in terms of narrative, pace, excitement, stimulus.

From my boyhood I remember the smell of books, immensely different, the different kinds of savor, the paper, the print. Books are complex phenomena. The way we hold them. Where we store them. The way we can return to them. The paperback is a revolution of its own, as was the folio, the quarto, the duodecimo. Books, and the libraries in which they were kept, shaped much of what we think of as literature, history and philosophy. If the book is to be replaced by electronic means, many of them as yet unimagined, if it is to become an archive of remembrance, an archaeology of dead love, then literature itself will change very profoundly.

Marxism taught us a brilliant, simple observation (the big thoughts are so simple and yet one does not have them!): that there is no chamber music before chambers. That is to say, what you and I know as chamber music — particularly the quartet, the dominant form of high music — could only occur under very specific spatial, economic and sociological conditions. If there are no more private spaces for chamber music, no new chamber music will be commissioned or written; and that vast musical literature will have to find, as it does now, an essentially museum character. It will be the historical reproduction of conditions which are no longer immediate or natural to performer and listener. This will also become true of literature and the book.

Let me move from technology to talent. We do not know why it is, but   7
in any given historical moment, the amount of creative talent is not infinite. There are phenomena here which we do not understand. Thank God
there is something for us not to understand! Why should certain periods
produce a floreat of great writers and others be barren for long periods?
Why should great literatures — Portuguese, Spanish, Italian are cases in
point — know two or three high moments of concentrated force? What
determines, on a distribution curve, the cluster of talent in a given moment
and what that talent wants to do? Very roughly — and these figures, of
course, are always open to challenge — the latest evidence we have on IQ
curves or any comparable measure (to be treated with care, of course) is that
over 80 percent of the top of the curve today are in the sciences. Less than
20 percent are doing anything we could identify as the humanities at the
top end of the curve — top in intelligence, will, energy, ambition. If I had
lived in Florence in the *quattrocento* I would, from time to time, have
begged breakfast off a painter. Instead, I have tried all my life to be among
scientists because today that is where the joy is, that is where the hope is,
the energy, the sense of world upon world opening up.

There are fewer and fewer prerequisites to studying the humanities. But   8
in today's Cambridge, in today's MIT, in today's Princeton or, until
recently still, in Moscow, the entrance exams in mathematics and physics
for the first-year student now include what was classified as post-doctoral
research only 15 years ago. That is your *accelerando.* That is the measure of
what is being asked of the young and what they are able to supply.

There is no law which says that great literature gets produced in any   9
given time or that a language will renew its poetic and creative energies.
There are periods of tiredness and exhaustion in certain great literatures.
Probably fewer people are at the top end of excellence today in the production of literary artistic works. Does this mean that less is being produced? No. We have a paradox of prodigality and plethora. More books are
being published and remaindered and pulped very rapidly. There is a huge
amount being produced; very little of it seems to be of commanding
stature. Talent is going into the competing media of television, film and
their allied arts. Again and again there will crackle off our screen a piece of
dialogue, a confrontation, a scene, where you say — "My God, that is better
than any novel I have read in a long time." It is more insightful, it is better
written, it is sharper.

Film is already in a condition where it can proudly speak of its classics,   10
of classics which have changed perception, which have changed imagining, which have altered our sense of what a narrative is — of how you tell a
story. It is not the same thing as in the novel. It can resemble the novel,
and it is fascinating to watch the interaction between classic fiction and
television.

The commissioning of a book is now often done with a view to its pro-   11
duction in other media. The calculation of the print run is almost unimportant compared to the hope of its acquisition for television or film rights

which, in turn, presses on the structure of the written text. There are masters of this form who write knowing that if the television or cinema production is a great success, people will return to the book. It is a creative boomerang of the most interesting kind. There are even cases where the book has been commissioned after the film or the television version. The book is no longer the pretext, it is the post-text of its distribution.

None of us can measure the quantum of intelligence, of imagining   12
going into the media. It is prodigious — even the quantum of intelligence that can go into a great advertising campaign. The difference between poetry and jingles is difficult to distinguish. There are advertising people who can write one-liners of which Restoration comedy would have been proud — you can compare the skill, the caricature skill of a human situation explod-ing into an unforgettable *bon mot* or *repartee*. Imagination, fun, energy, even serious political and social comment often see in the book a form that is too slow, when in other media they can get through immediately on a vast scale to a great public and to the shapers of political opinion.

But can "literature" be preserved? A very, very difficult question. Some   13
years ago, you remember, a number of young publishers began publishing film scripts. It did not work out well. That does not mean it will not. Cer-tain great television artists, Dennis Potter and others, have hoped that their works would be preserved in some literary form so that people could read with the play or film.

There is an oral dimension as well. This became clear to me on a recent   14
visit to Harvard University. *Casablanca* was being shown for the millionth time. There was a queue outside of students who had seen it 10 or 15 times. At a certain point, about 10 minutes from the end, hands shot up and they switched off the sound and the students got up, crossed their arms, and recited in chorus the last 10 minutes, which are quite complex. I was yelling with them: "Arrest the usual suspects." These are students who, if you said to them, "Would you please learn a poem by heart," would blench with dismay; but they see no difficulty whatsoever in learning the polyphonic, six or eight voices of those last 10 minutes.

This suggests a tenacity in the oral form. Poetry has an immense future —   15
limitless, I think. Russian poetry survived orally and then in readings to 10 and 20 thousand — Yevgeny Yevtushenko, Andre Voznesensky. Also Allen Ginsberg. Poetry always has behind it the probability of the oral, of being spoken together and learnt by heart if you love it. We are in a period of great poets and many, many are to come; they will work with music and drama, with choreography, forms as yet unimagined, which go back to the origins of poetry in ancient Greece so far as we can make them out.

Poetry means every form of drama, and I would like to be around for it.   16
Television drama, amateur drama, audience participation. The world of drama for children seems, at the moment, almost boundless. The theater in the largest sense — the art of the human body — is opening up. The

elimination of the human body from so much of high literature is a brief phenomenon which took place roughly between Christianity's triumph in late Hellenism and the academic, mandarin, high bourgeois cultures at the beginning of this century. It is no longer so. The body is reasserting its presence at every range of the culture. Language is, after all, a bodily function, deeply and intensely.

Hegel said it so clearly. The novel is inseparable from the triumph of the   17 middle classes, their habits of leisure, of privacy, the space for reading, the time for reading; the novel philosophically is a narrative in a large, rich, stable, social context, even if its own particular narrative is one of chaos, revolution or disorder. The way George Lukacs, the greatest of Marxist critics, put it was: "No novel ends unhappily." That is not a stupid statement. What he referred to was the fact that after you have read a novel, you can go back to it; there is always a window on the future, on the story continuing, and it is in essence a middle-class story.

It is no accident that the industrial revolution, the French revolution,   18 occurred in the great age of the novel. It is almost axiomatic that today the great novels are coming from the far rim, from India, from the Caribbean, from Latin America — from countries which are in an earlier stage of bourgeois culture, in a rougher, more problematic form.

We are getting very tired in our novel writing; that makes perfect sense,   19 there is nothing apocalyptic about it. Genres rise, genres fall, the epic, the verse epic, the formal verse tragedy, all have great moments, then they ebb. Novels will continue to be written for some time, but increasingly the search is on for hybrid forms, what we call fact/fiction. This alerts us to something important. What novel can today compete with the best of reportage, the best of immediate narrative? Not only the media, but also journalism in the high and legitimate sense, the masters of the immediate whom we can read every day.

James Joyce was certain that *Finnegans Wake* would be the end of the   20 novel. It is a very deliberate attempt, marvelously arrogant, to say: "Not after this, that is it. In *Ulysses* I had once more done the totality, once more held the world in one grasp, now *Finnegans Wake* is the chaos of the night," and when told it was unreadable he said, "Of course, that is the point, then you have understood. This is meant to be the epilogue." There are still excellent novels after *Finnegans Wake*. But my guess is that nothing at the moment is more artificial, in some ways more a gamble against reality, than a first novel, and I think many publishers know this.

We have a very exciting time ahead, when literature itself will have to re-   21 examine what literacy is. Who is literate today? There are children who are finding "beautiful" solutions to problems on their computers, on their holographic screens.

I meet one of these children; I am told he can neither read nor write, or   22 barely; he resents any attempt to pull him away from the screen and make him read. I lose my temper and shout, "You are illiterate?" and the child says, "You are illiterate" because, indeed, I cannot follow what he is doing. If you have watched some of these children, their fingers are like those of a great piano virtuoso. I cannot put this intelligently — their fingers are thinking and creating. The way the fingers move is the way a musician with a motif, or the sketch of a motif or a bar relation, comes back to it through his fingers to re-examine its possibilities, to correct it. And the child says I am illiterate. *Dialogue de sourds.*[2] We stare at each other.

And what next? Who is going to be literate? Who will define basic liter-   23
acy? It is a very frightening period. That is what makes it so exciting and rewarding. Underlying it may be a slow, glacial shift in Western culture's attitude toward death. The way we think of death, the way we experience it, imagine it; the way we turn our consciousness toward it. Literature, as we have known it, springs out of a wild and magnificent piece of arrogance, old as Pindar, Horace and Ovid. *Exegi aere perennius* — what I have written will outlive time. Stronger than bronze, less breakable than marble, this poem. Pindar was the first man on record to say that his poem will be sung when the city which commissioned it has ceased to exist. Literature's immense boast against death. Even the greatest poet, I dare venture, would be profoundly embarrassed to be quoted saying such a thing today.

Something enormous is happening, due in part to the barbarism of this   24
century, perhaps due to DNA, perhaps due to fundamental changes in longevity, in cellular biology, in the conception of what it is to have children. We cannot phrase it with any confidence, but it will profoundly affect the great classical vainglory of literature — I am stronger than death! I can speak about death in poetry, drama, the novel, because I have overcome it; I am more or less permanent.

That is no longer available. A quite different order of imagining is begin-   25
ning to arise, and it may be that when we look back on this time we will suddenly see that the very great artists, in the sense of changing our views — of what is art, what is human identity — are not the ones we usually name but rather exasperating, surrealist, jokers. Marcel Duchamp.[3] If I call this *pissoir* a great work of art and sign it, who are you to disprove that? Or, even more so, the artist Jean Tinguely, who built immense structures which he then set on fire, saying: "I want this to be ephemeral. I want it to have happened only once."

That is the contrary of literature as we have known it, literature which   26
always says: "I want to be returned to over and over and over." This does not mean that the new work will be any less exciting. It does not mean that it will be any less inventive. It just means that to be a publisher in the next century is going to be a very chancy enterprise.

---

[2]*Dialogue de sourds* A conversation in which neither hears the other. [All notes are the editor's.]

[3]*Marcel Duchamp* French artist (1887–1968) who exhibited a urinal in a Dada art show.

Analyzing This Selection

1. What indications suggest to Steiner that literature may not continue? What suggests it will? If it continues, what specific kinds of literature are most likely to change?

2. Do you agree with Steiner that technology may influence basic attitudes toward death? Form an opinion about connections, if any, between literature, technology, and permanence.

3. **THE WRITER'S METHOD**   Steiner makes speculative observations about our past, present, and future. Is his manner pompous? What tone does he maintain in the essay as a whole? How does it differ or develop from the tone in paragraph 1?

4. What are Steiner's goals in this lecture? How do you rate him as a lecturer?

Analyzing Connections

5. Steiner and Vendler (see "Knowing Poems," p. 274) anticipate different futures for literature. Which writer's anticipations are closer to your own expectations of books in your life?

Analyzing by Writing

6. Steiner suggests that films based on books create a world of their own in terms of story, viewpoint, and stimulus. Examine the differences between a book and its film version. Are the same things possible or meaningful in each?

Ha Jin

OCEAN OF WORDS

Ha Jin (b. 1956) lived his first twenty-eight years in mainland China. He served in the army from age fourteen to nineteen. For his college education the subject of English was selected by the government. When Ha Jin came to Brandeis University for a Ph.D., he began writing fiction and poetry. His work has appeared in the *Paris Review*, the *Kenyon Review*, *Ploughshares*, and the *Atlantic Monthly*. His first novel, *Waiting* (1999), won the National Book Award. His fiction collection *Ocean of Words* (1996) includes the following title story.

Zhou Wen's last year in the People's Army was not easy. All his comrades 1 pestered him, because in their eyes he was a bookworm, a scholar of sorts. Whenever they played poker, or chatted, or cracked jokes, he would sneak out to a place where he could read alone. This habit annoyed not only his fellow soldiers but also the chief of the Radio-telegram Station, Huang Peng, whose rank was equal to a platoon commander's. Chief Huang would say to his men, "This is not college. If you want to be a college student, you'd better go home first." Everybody knew he referred to Zhou.

The only thing they liked about Zhou was that he would work the shift 2 they hated most, from 1:00 A.M. to 8:00 A.M. During the small hours Zhou read novels and middle school textbooks instead of the writings by Chairman Mao, Marx, Lenin, and Stalin. Often in the early morning he watched the eastern sky turn gray, pale, pink, and bright. The dawn was driving the night away from Longmen City bit by bit until, all of a sudden, a fresh daybreak descended, shining upon thousands of red roofs.

If not for the help of Director Liang Ming of the Divisional Logistics 3 Department, Zhou's last year in the army would have been disastrous. Liang and his family lived in a grand church built by nineteenth-century Russian missionaries, which was at the southern corner of the Divisional Headquarters compound. A large red star stood atop the steeple. Within the church many walls had been knocked down to create a large auditorium, which served as the division's conference hall, movie house, and theater. All the fancy bourgeois pews had been pulled out and replaced by long proletarian benches, and Chairman Mao's majestic portrait had driven off the superstitious altarpiece.

The Liangs lived in the back of the church, as did the soldiers of the 4
Radio-telegram Station. Because the antennas needed height, the radiomen
occupied the attic, while the director's family had for themselves the three
floors underneath. Whenever there was a movie on, the men at the station
would steal into the auditorium through the rear door and sit against the
wall, watching the screen from the back stage. They never bothered to get
tickets. But except for those evenings when there were movies shown or
plays performed, the back door would be locked. Very often Zhou dreamed
of studying alone in the spacious front hall. Unable to enter it, he had to
go outside to read in the open air.

One evening in October he was reading under a road lamp near the 5
church. It was cloudy and a snow was gathering, just as the loudspeaker
had announced that morning. Zhou was so engrossed he didn't notice
somebody approaching until a deep voice startled him. "What are you
doing here, little comrade?" Director Liang stood in front of Zhou, smiling kindly. His left sleeve, without an arm inside, hung listlessly from his
shoulder, the cuff lodged in his pocket. His baggy eyes were fixed on
Zhou's face.

"Reading," Zhou managed to say, closing the book and reluctantly show- 6
ing him the title. He tried to smile but only twitched his lips, his eyes dim
with fear.

"*The Three Kingdoms!*"[1] Liang cried. He pointed at the other book under 7
Zhou's arm. "How about this one?"

"*Ocean of Words*, a dictionary." Zhou regretted having taken the big 8
book out with him.

"Can I have a look?" 9

Zhou handed it to the old man, who began flicking through the pages 10
between the green covers. "It looks like a good book," Liang said and gave
it back to Zhou. "Tell me, what's your name?"

"Zhou Wen." 11

"You're in the Radio Station upstairs, aren't you?" 12

"Yes." 13

"Do you often read old books?" 14

"Yes." Zhou was afraid the officer would confiscate the novel, which he 15
had borrowed from a friend in the Telephone Company.

"Why don't you read inside?" Liang asked. 16

"It's noisy upstairs. They won't let me read in peace." 17

"Tickle their grandmothers!" Liang shook his gray head. "Follow me." 18

Unsure what was going on, Zhou didn't follow him. Instead he watched 19
Liang's stout back moving away.

"I order you to come in," the director said loudly, opening the door to 20
his home.

[1]*The Three Kingdoms* A historical novel by Lo Kuan-Chung, popular writer of the four-
teenth century. It is comparable to *Ivanhoe* for British readers. [All notes are the editor's.]

Zhou followed Liang to the second floor. The home was so spacious that   21
the first floor alone had five or six rooms. Down the hall the red floor was
shiny under the chandelier; the brown windowsill at the stairway was large
enough to be a bed. Liang opened a door and said, "You use this room.
Whenever you want to study, come here and study inside."

"This, this —"   22

"I order you to use it. We have lots of rooms. From now on, if I see you   23
reading outside again, I will kick all of you out of this building."

"No, no, they may want me at any time. What should I say if they can't   24
find me?"

"Tell them I want you. I want you to study and work for me here." Liang   25
closed the door, and his leather boots thumped away downstairs.

Outside, snowflakes suddenly began fluttering to the ground. Through   26
the window Zhou saw the backyard of the small grocery that was run by
some officers' wives. A few naked branches were tossing, almost touching
the panes. Inside, green curtains covered the corners of the large window.
Though bright and clean, the room seemed to be used as a repository for
old furniture. On the floor was a large desk, a stool, a chair, a wooden bed
standing on its head against the wall, and a rickety sofa. But for Zhou this
was heaven. Full of joy, he read three chapters that evening.

Soon the downstairs room became Zhou's haven. In the Radio Com-   27
pany he could hardly get along with anybody; there was a lot of ill feeling
between him and his leaders and comrades. He tried forgetting all the
unhappy things by making himself study hard downstairs, but that didn't
always help. His biggest headache was his imminent discharge from the
army: not the demobilization itself so much as his non-Party status. It was
obvious that without Communist Party membership he wouldn't be assigned
a good job once he returned home. Thinking him bookish, the Party members in the Radio Company were reluctant to consider his application seriously. Chief Huang would never help him; neither would Party Secretary
Si Ma Lin. Zhou had once been on good terms with the secretary; he had
from time to time helped Si Ma write articles on current political topics
and chalked up slogans and short poems on the large blackboard in front
of the Company Headquarters. That broad piece of wood was the company's face, because it was the first thing a visitor would see and what was
on it displayed the men's sincere political attitudes and lofty aspirations.
The secretary had praised Zhou three times for the poems and calligraphy
on the blackboard, but things had gone bad between Zhou and Si Ma
because of *Ocean of Words*.

The dictionary was a rare book, which Zhou's father had bought in the   28
early 1950s. It was compiled in 1929, was seven by thirteen inches in size
and over three thousand pages thick, and had Chinese, Latin, and English
indexes. Its original price was eighty silver dollars, but Zhou's father had paid
a mere one *yuan* for it at a salvage station, where all things were sold by

weight. The book weighed almost three *jin*. Having grown up with the small *New China Dictionary*, which had only a few thousand entries, Secretary Si Ma had never imagined there was such a big book in the world. When he saw it for the first time, he browsed through the pages for two hours, pacing up and down in his office with the book in his arms as if cradling a baby. He told Zhou, "I love this book. What a treasure. It's a gold mine, an armory!"

One day at the Company Headquarters the secretary asked Zhou, "Can I have that great book, Young Zhou?"   29

"It's my family's heirloom. I can't give it to anybody." Zhou regretted having shown him the dictionary and having even told him that his father had spent only one *yuan* for it.   30

"I won't take it for free. Give me a price. I'll pay you a good sum."   31

"Secretary Si Ma, I can't sell it. It's my father's book."   32

"How about fifty *yuan*?"   33

"If it were mine I would give it to you free."   34

"A hundred?"   35

"No, I won't sell."   36

"Two hundred?"   37

"No."   38

"You are a stubborn, Young Zhou, you know." The secretary looked at Zhou with a meaningful smile.   39

From that moment on, Zhou knew that as long as Si Ma was the Party secretary in the company, there would be no hope of his joining the Party. Sometimes he did think of giving him the dictionary, but he could not bear to part with it. After he had refused Si Ma's request for the second time, his mind could no longer remain at ease; he was afraid somebody would steal the book the moment he didn't have it with him. There was no safe place to hide it at the station; his comrades might make off with it if they knew the secretary would pay a quarter of his yearly salary for it. Fortunately, Zhou had his own room now, so he kept the dictionary downstairs in a drawer of the desk.   40

One evening as Zhou was reading in the room, Director Liang came in, followed by his wife carrying two cups. "Have some tea, Little Zhou?" Liang said. He took a cup and sat down on the sofa, which began squeaking under him.   41

Zhou stood up, receiving the cup with both hands from Mrs. Liang. "Please don't do this for me."   42

"Have some tea, Little Zhou," she said with a smile. She looked very kind, her face covered with wrinkles. "We are neighbors, aren't we?"   43

"Yes, we are."   44

"Sit down, and you two talk. I have things to do downstairs." She turned and walked away.   45

"Don't be so polite. If you want tea, just take it," Liang said, blowing away the tea leaves in his cup. Zhou took a sip.   46

"Little Zhou," Liang said again, "you know I like young people who   47
study hard."

"Yes, I know."   48

"Tell me, why do you want to study?"   49

"I don't know for sure. My grandfather was a scholar, but my father   50
didn't finish middle school. He joined the Communist Army to fight
the Japanese. He always wants me to study hard and says we are a family
of scholars and must carry on the tradition. Besides, I like reading and
writing."

"Your father is a good father," Liang announced, as if they were at a   51
meeting. "I'm from a poor peasant's family. If a carrying pole stood up on
the ground, my father couldn't tell it means 'one.' But I always say the
same thing to my kids like your father says. You see, nowadays schools are
closed. Young people don't study but make revolution outside school. They
don't know a fart about the revolution. For the revolutionary cause I lost
my arm and these fingers." He raised his only hand, whose little and ring
fingers were missing. The stumps quivered in the fluorescent light.

Zhou nerved himself for the question. "Can I ask how you lost your arm?"   52

"All right, I'm going to tell you the story, so that you will study harder."   53
Liang lifted the cup and took a gulp. The tea gargled in his mouth for a
few seconds and then went down. "In the fall of 1938, I was a commander
of a machine-gun company in the Red Army, and we fought against Chiang Kai-shek's troops in a mountain area in Gansu. My company's task was
to hold a hilltop. From there you could control two roads with machine
guns. We took the hill and held it to protect our retreating army. The first
day we fought a battle with two enemy battalions that attempted to take the
hill from us. They left about three hundred bodies on the slopes, but our
Party secretary and sixteen other men were killed. Another twenty were
badly wounded. Night came, and we had no idea if all of our army had
passed and how long we had to stay on the hill. At about ten o'clock, an
orderly came from the Regimental Staff and delivered a message. It had
only two words penciled on a scrap of paper. I could tell it was Regimental
Commander Hsiao Hsiong's bold handwriting.

"I turned the paper up and down, left and right, but couldn't figure out   54
the meaning. I shouted to the whole company, 'Who can read?' Nobody
answered. In fact, only the Party secretary could read, but we had lost him.
You can imagine how outraged I was. We were all blind with good eyes! I
beat my head with my fists and couldn't stop cursing. Grabbing the messenger's throat, I yelled, 'If you don't tell me what the message is, I'll shoot
you in the eye!'

"The platoon leaders saved the boy's life. They told me it wasn't his   55
fault; he couldn't read either. And a messenger never knew the contents of
a message, because if he was caught by the enemy they could make him
tell them what he knew. Usually, he was ordered to swallow the message
before it fell into the enemy's hands.

"What should we do now? We had no idea where our army was, 56 although we had been told that if we retreated we should go to Maliang Village. That was twenty *li* away in the north. Racking our brains together, we figured there could be only two meanings in the message; one was to stay and the other to retreat, but we couldn't decide which was the one. If the message said to stay but we retreated, then the next day, when our troops passed the mountain without covering fire, there would be heavy casualties and I would be shot by the higher-ups. If the message said to retreat but we stayed, we merely took a risk. That meant to fight more battles or perhaps lose contact with our army for some time afterwards. After weighing the advantages and disadvantages, I decided to stay and told my men to sleep so we could fight the next day. Tired out, we all slept like dead pigs."

Zhou almost laughed, but he restrained himself. Liang went on, "At 57 about five in the morning, the enemy began shelling us. We hadn't expected they would use heavy artillery. The day before they had only launched some mortar shells. Within a minute, rocks, machine guns, arms and legs, branches and trunks of trees were flying everywhere. I heard bugles buzzing on all sides below. I knew the enemy had surrounded us and was charging. At least two thirds of my men were already wiped out by the artillery — there was no way to fight such a battle. I shouted, 'Run for your lives, brothers!' and led my orderly and a dozen men running away from the hilltop. The enemy was climbing all around. Machine guns were cracking. We had only a few pistols with us — no way to fight back. We were just scrambling for our lives. A shell exploded at our rear and killed seven of the men following me. My left arm was smashed. These two fingers were cut off by a piece of shrapnel from that shell." Liang raised his crippled hand to the level of his collarbone. "Our regiment was at Maliang Village when we arrived. Regimental Commander Hsiao came and slapped my face while the medical staff were preparing to saw my arm off. I didn't feel anything; I almost blacked out. Later I was told that the words in the message were 'Retreat immediately.' If I hadn't lost this arm, Commander Hsiao would've finished me off on the spot. The whole company and twenty-two heavy machine guns, half the machine guns our regiment had, were all gone. Commander Hsiao punished me by making me a groom for the Regimental Staff. I took care of horses for six years. You see, Little Zhou, just two small words, each of them cost sixty lives. Sixty lives! It's a bloody lesson, a bloody lesson!" Liang shook his gray head and drank up the tea.

"Director Liang, I will always remember this lesson." Zhou was moved. 58 "I understand now why you want us to study hard."

"Yes, you're a good young man, and you know the value of books and 59 knowledge. To carry out the revolution we must have literacy and knowledge first."

"Yes, we must." 60

"All right, it's getting late. I must go. Stay as long as you want. Remem- 61
ber, come and study every day. Never give up. A young man must have a
high aspiration and then pursue it."

From then on, Zhou spent more time studying in the room. In the 62
morning, when he was supposed to sleep, he would doze for only an hour
and then read for three hours downstairs. His comrades wondered why his
bed was empty every morning. When they asked where he had been, he
said that Director Liang had work for him to do and that if they needed
him, just give the Liangs a ring. Of course, none of them dared go down to
check or call the director's home.

Now the "study" was clean and more furnished. The floor was mopped 63
every day. On the desk sat a cup and a thermos bottle always filled with
boiled water. Liang's orderly took care of that. Occasionally, the director
would come and join Zhou in the evenings. He wanted Zhou to tell him
the stories in *The Three Kingdoms*, which in fact Liang knew quite well,
for he had heard them time and again for decades. Among the five gener-
als in the classic, he adored Guan Yu, because Guan had both bravery and
strategy. After *The Three Kingdoms*, they talked of *All Men Are Brothers*.[2]
Liang had Zhou tell him the stories of those outlaw heroes, which Liang
actually knew by heart; he was just fond of listening to them. Whenever a
battle took a sudden turn, he would give a hearty laugh. Somehow Zhou
felt the old man looked younger during these evenings — pink patches
would appear on his sallow cheeks after they had sat together for an hour.

Naturally Zhou became an enigma to his comrades, who were eager to 64
figure out what he did downstairs. One afternoon Chief Huang had a talk
with Zhou. He asked, "Why do you go to Director Liang's home so often,
Young Zhou?"

"I work for him." Zhou would never reveal that he studied downstairs, 65
because the chief could easily find a way to keep him busy at the station.

"What work exactly?" 66

"Sometimes little chores, and sometimes he wants me to read out Chair- 67
man Mao's works and newspaper to him."

"Really? He studies every day?" 68

"Yes, he studies hard." 69

"How can you make me believe you?" 70

"Chief Huang, if you don't believe me, go ask him yourself." Zhou knew 71
the chief dared not make a peep before the director. Huang had better
keep himself away from Liang, or the old man would curse his ancestors of
eight generations.

"No, it's unnecessary. Zhou Wen, you know I'm not interested in what 72
you do downstairs. It's Secretary Si Ma Lin who asked me about what's
going on. I have no idea how he came to know you often stay in Director
Liang's home."

[2]*All Men Are Brothers* Another novel by Lo.

"Thanks for telling me that, Chief Huang. Please tell Secretary Si Ma   73
that Director Liang wants me to work for him."

After that, the chief never bothered Zhou again, but Zhou's fellow com-   74
rades didn't stop showing their curiosity. They even searched through his
suitcase and turned up his mattress to see what he had hidden from them.
Zhou realized how lucky it was that he had put his *Ocean of Words* downstairs beforehand. They kept asking him questions. One would ask, "How
did you get so close to Director Liang?" Another, "Does he pay you as his
secretary?" Another would sigh and say, "What a pity Old Liang doesn't
have a daughter!"

It was true Director Liang had only three sons. The eldest son was an   75
officer in Nanjing Military Region; the second worked as an engineer at an
ordnance factory in Harbin; his youngest son, Liang Bin, was a middle
school student at home. The boy, tall and burly, was a wonderful soccer
player. One afternoon during their break from the telegraphic training,
Zhou Wen, Zhang Jun, and Gu Wan were playing soccer in the yard
behind the church when Liang Bin came by. Bin put down his satchel,
hooked up the ball with his instep, and began juggling it on his feet, then
on his head, on his shoulders, on his knees — every part of his body seemed
to have a spring. He went on doing this for a good three minutes without
letting the ball touch the ground. The soldiers were all impressed and
asked the boy why he didn't play for the Provincial Juvenile Team.

"They've asked me many times," Bin said, "but I never dare play for them."   76
"Why?" Gu asked.   77
"If I did, my dad would break my legs. He wants me to study." He   78
picked up his satchel and hurried home.

Both Zhang and Gu said Director Liang was a fool and shouldn't ruin   79
his son's future that way. Zhou understood why, but he didn't tell them,
uncertain if Director Liang would like other soldiers to know his story,
which was profound indeed but not very glorious.

Every day the boy had to return home immediately after school, to   80
study. One evening Zhou overheard Director Liang criticizing his son.
"Zhou Wen read *The Three Kingdoms* under the road lamp. You have everything here, your own lamp, your own books, your own desk, and your own
room. What you lack is your own strong will. Your mother has spoiled you.
Come on, work on the geometry problems. I'll give you a big gift at the
Spring Festival if you study hard."

"Will you allow me to join the soccer team?"   81
"No, you study."   82
A few days later, Director Liang asked Zhou to teach his son, saying that   83
Zhou was the most knowledgeable man he had ever met and that he
trusted him as a young scholar. Zhou agreed to try his best. Then Liang
pulled a dog-eared book out of his pocket. "Teach him this," he said. It was
a copy of *The Three-Character Scripture.*[3]

---

[3]***The Three-Character Scripture*** A selection of Confucian texts simplified for readers.

Zhou was surprised, not having expected the officer wanted him to 84
teach his son classical Chinese, which Zhou had merely taught himself a
little. Where did Liang get this small book? Zhou had heard of the scripture but never seen a copy. Why did a revolutionary officer like Liang want
his son to study such a feudal book? Zhou dared not ask and kept the question to himself. Neither did he ever mention the scripture to his comrades.
Instead he told them that Director Liang ordered him to teach his son
Chairman Mao's *On Practice*, a booklet Zhou knew well enough to talk
about in their political studies. Since none of his comrades understood the
Chairman's theory, they believed what Zhou told them, and they were
impressed by his comments when they studied together.

As his demobilization drew near, Zhou worried desperately and kept ask- 85
ing himself, What will you do now? Without the Party membership you
won't get a good job at home, but how can you join the Party before leaving the army? There are only five weeks left. If you can't make it by the
New Year, you'll never be able to in the future. Even if you give the dictionary to Secretary Si Ma now, it's already too late. Too late to do anything. But you can't simply sit back waiting for the end; you must do
something. There must be a way to bring him around. How?

After thinking of the matter for three days, he decided to talk to Direc- 86
tor Liang. One evening, as soon as Zhou sat down in the room, the old
man rushed in with snowflakes on his felt hat. "Little Zhou," he said in a
thick voice, "I came to you for help."

"How can I help?" Zhou stood up. 87

"Here, here is Marx's book." Liang put his fur mitten on the desk and 88
pulled a copy of *Manifesto of the Communist Party* out of it. "This winter
we divisional leaders are studying this little book. Vice Commissar Hou
gave the first lecture this afternoon. I don't understand what he said at all.
It wasn't a good lecture. Maybe he doesn't understand Marx either."

"I hope I can help." 89

"For example," Liang said, putting the book on the desk and turning a 90
few pages, "here, listen: 'An apparition — an apparition of Communism —
has wandered throughout Europe.'[4] Old Hou said an apparition is a 'spook.'
Europe was full of spooks. I wonder if it's true. What's an 'apparition,' do
you know?"

"Let's see what it means exactly." Zhou took his *Ocean of Words* out of 91
the drawer and began to turn the pages.

"This must be a treasure book, having all the rare characters in it," Liang 92
said, standing closer to watch Zhou searching for the word.

"Here it is." Zhou lifted the dictionary and read out the definition: 93
"'Apparition — specter, ghost, spiritual appearance.'"

---

[4]"***An apparition…Europe***" A specter is haunting Europe — the specter of Communism."

"See, no 'spook' at all."   94

"'Spook' may not be completely wrong for 'apparition,' but it's too low a   95
word."

"You're right. Good. Tomorrow I'll tell Old Hou to drop his 'spook.' By   96
the way, I still don't understand why Marx calls Communism 'an operation.' Isn't Communism a good ideal?"

Zhou almost laughed out loud at Liang's mispronunciation, but controlled   97
himself and said, "Marx must be ironic here, because the bourgeoisie takes
the Communists as poisonous snakes and wild beasts — something like an
apparition."

"That's right." Liang slapped his paunch, smiling and shaking his head.   98
"You see, Little Zhou, my mind always goes straight and never makes turns.
You're a smart young man. I regret I didn't meet you earlier."

Here came Zhou's chance. He said, "But we can't be together for long,   99
because I'll leave for home soon. I'm sure I will miss you and this room."

"What? You mean you'll be discharged?"   100

"Yes."   101

"Why do they want a good soldier like you to go?"   102

Zhou told the truth. "I want to leave the army myself, because my old   103
father is in poor health."

"Oh, I'm sorry you can't stay longer."   104

"I will always be grateful to you."   105

"Anything I can do for you before you leave?"   106

"One thing, though I don't know if it's right to mention."   107

"Just say it. I hate men who mince words. Speak up. Let's see if this old   108
man can be helpful." Liang sat down on the sofa.

Zhou pulled over the chair and sat on it. "I'm not a Party member yet.   109
It's shameful."

"Why? Do you know why they haven't taken you into the Party?"   110

"Yes, because my comrades think I have read too much and I am differ-   111
ent from them."

"What?" The thick eyebrows stood up on Liang's forehead. "Does Sec-   112
retary Si Ma Lin have the same opinion?"

"Yes, he said I had some stinking airs of a petty intellectual. You know I   113
didn't even finish middle school."

"The bastard, I'll talk to him right now. Come with me." Liang went out   114
to the corridor, where a telephone hung on the wall. Zhou was scared but
had to follow him. He regretted having blurted out what the secretary had
said and was afraid Director Liang would ask Si Ma what he meant by
"stinking airs of a petty intellectual."

"Give me Radio Company," Liang grunted into the phone.   115

"Hello, who's this?...I want to speak to Si Ma Lin." Liang turned to   116
Zhou. "I must teach this ass a lesson."

"Hello," he said into the phone again. "Is that you, Little Si Ma?...Sure,   117
you can tell my voice. Listen, I have a serious matter to discuss with you...."

It's about Zhou Wen's Party membership. He is a young friend of mine. I have known him for a while and he is a good soldier, a brilliant young man. For what reason haven't you accepted him as a Party member? Isn't he going to leave soon?"

He listened to the receiver. Then he said out loud, "What? The devil   118
take you! That's exactly why he can be a good Party member. What time are we in now? — the seventies of the twentieth century — and you are still so hostile to a knowledgeable man. You still have a peasant's mind. Why does he have to stand the test longer than others? Only because he's learned more? You have a problem in your brain, you know. Tell me, how did we Communists defeat Chiang Kai-shek? With guns? Didn't he have American airplanes and tanks? How come our army, with only rifles plus millet, beat his eight million troops equipped with modern weapons?"

The smart secretary was babbling his answer at the other end. Zhou   119
felt a little relieved, because the director hadn't mentioned what he had told him.

"That's rubbish!" Liang said. "We defeated him by having the Pen. Old   120
Chiang only had the Gun, but we had both the Gun and the Pen. As Chairman Mao has taught us: The Gun and the Pen, we depend on both of them to make revolution and cannot afford to lose either. Are you not a Party secretary? Can't you understand this simple truth? You have a problem here, don't you?"

The clever secretary seemed to be admitting his fault, because the old   121
man sounded less scathing now. "Listen, I don't mean to give you a hard time. I'm an older soldier, and my Party membership is longer than your age, so I know what kind of people our Party really needs. We can recruit men who carry guns by the millions, easily. What we want badly is those who carry pens. My friend Zhou Wen is one of them, don't you think?... Comrade Si Ma Lin, don't limit your field of vision to your own yard. Our revolutionary cause is a matter of the entire world. Zhou Wen may not be good in your eyes, but to our revolutionary cause, he is good and needed. Therefore, I suggest you consider his application seriously....Good, I'm pleased you understood it so quickly....Good-bye now." Liang hung up and said to Zhou, "The ass, he's so dense." Zhou was sweating, his heart thumping.

Director Liang's call cleared away all obstacles. Within two weeks Zhou   122
joined the Party. Neither Secretary Si Ma nor Chief Huang said a word alluding to the call. It seemed the secretary had not divulged to anybody the lesson he had received on the telephone. Certainly Zhou's comrades were amazed by the sudden breakthrough, and he became more mysterious in their eyes. It was rumored that Zhou wouldn't be discharged and instead would be promoted to officer's rank and do propaganda work in the Divisional Political Department. But that never materialized.

The day before he left the army, Zhou went downstairs to fetch his   123
things and say good-bye to Director Liang. No sooner had he entered the

room than the old man came in holding something in his hand. It was a small rectangular box covered with purple satin. Liang placed it on the desk and said, "Take this as a keepsake."

Zhou picked it up and opened the lid — a brown Hero pen perched in   124
the white cotton groove. On its chunky body was a vigorous inscription carved in golden color: "For Comrade Zhou Wen — May You Forever Hold Tight the Revolutionary Pen, Liang Ming Present."

"I appreciate your helping my son," the old man said.   125

Too touched to say a word, Zhou put the pen into his pocket. Though   126
he had taught the boy *The Three-Character Scripture*, Liang had helped him join the Party, which was an important event in anyone's life, like marriage or rebirth. Even without this gift, Zhou was the one who was indebted, so now he had to give something in return. But he didn't have any valuables with him. At this moment it dawned on him that his *Ocean of Words* was in the drawer. He took it out and presented it to Liang with both hands. "You may find this useful, Director Liang."

"Oh, I don't want to rob you of your inheritance. You told me it's your   127
father's book." Liang was rubbing his hand on his leg.

"Please keep it. My father will be glad if he knows it's in your hands."   128

"All right, it's a priceless treasure." Liang's three fingers were caressing   129
the solid spine of the tome. "I'll cherish it and make my son read ten pages of this good book every day."

Zhou was ready to leave. Liang held out his hand; for the first time   130
Zhou shook that crippled hand, which was ice cold.

"Good-bye," Liang said, looking him in the eye. "May you have a bright   131
future, Little Zhou. Study hard and never give up. You will be a great man, a tremendous scholar. I just know that in my heart."

"I will study hard. Take good care of yourself, Director Liang. I'll write   132
to you. Good-bye."

The old man heaved a feeble sigh and waved his hand. Zhou walked   133
out, overwhelmed by the confidence and resolution surging up in his chest. Outside, the air seemed to be gleaming, and the sky was blue and high. Up there, in the distance, two Chinese jet fighters were soaring noiselessly, ready to knock down any intruder. It was at this moment that Zhou made up his mind to become a socialist man of letters, fighting with the Revolutionary Pen for the rest of his life.

Analyzing This Selection

1. **THE WRITER'S METHOD**   In addition to Chinese names, what details indicate that the society described in this selection is different from ours? How is the story addressed to readers in China or in the United States?

2. What mistreatment and risks increase for Zhou by following his bookish interests? Does he deal with the problem as you would?

3. In the final paragraph Zhou confidently foresees "the rest of his life." Do you think his life will turn out that way? Explain reasons in the story to share or not to share his confidence.

Analyzing Connections

4. The story's political perspective raises issues about books that Steiner doesn't consider in "Books and the End of Literature" (p. 307). What possible gains or losses of freedom would result from producing literature using high technology without books? In "Ocean of Words" which is the political instrument — pen or book?

Analyzing by Writing

5. Should a book be banned? Assuming that censorship is designed to protect the interests of society, consider reasons for and against banning hate literature, hard-core pornography, or other deeply offensive material. Examine difficulties and risks in the problem; do not rush into a glib solution.

PART 6

WORK RULES

INSIGHTS

Winning is not the most important thing. It's the only thing.

—VINCE LOMBARDI

The school that pays its students to play games for it not only loses some of its integrity as a school (i.e., as a self-sufficient exchange center for academic goods and services, ideas, and values), it is also saying some very peculiar things about the nature of games themselves and their relationship to other college activities across the board.

It is saying, for instance, that playing in the band at half time is still fun (no one has ever suggested paying the band), but that throwing and catching a ball is work — and that even this depends on what kind of ball you're using. A football equals work, a volleyball is only play. Appearing on television is obviously work, but even here distinctions are made: players work, cheerleaders have fun. Shooting baskets is work, helping to clean up afterward is its own reward.

The greatest chasm of all would open up between sports and the whole outside world of student activity, including such strenuous matters as staying up all night for a month to put the yearbook to bed, rehearsing the class play till your eyes cross, or working overtime in the lab. All of these tortures are considered so much part of the college experience that you actually pay the place to let you undergo them. But basketball is different. For basketball, the college pays *you*.

—WILFRID SHEED

In sheer quantity, household labor, including child care, constitutes a huge amount of socially necessary production. Nevertheless, in a society based on commodity production, it is not usually considered as "real work" since it is outside of trade and the marketplace....In a society in which money determines value, women are a group who work outside the money economy.

—MARGARET LOWE BENSTON

The ability to take pride in your own work is one of the hallmarks of sanity. Take away the ability to both work and be proud of it and you can drive anyone insane.

—NIKKI GIOVANNI

You cannot hope to build a better world without improving the individuals. To that end each of us must work for his own improvement, and at the same time share a general responsibility for all humanity, our particular duty being to aid those to whom we think we can be most useful.

—MARIE CURIE

If you hear a voice within you saying, "You are not a painter," *then by all means paint*, boy, and that voice will be silenced, but only by working. He who goes to friends and tells his troubles when he feels like that loses part of his manliness, part of the best that's in him; your friends can only be those who themselves struggle against it, who raise your activity by their own example of action. One must undertake it with confidence, with a certain assurance that one is doing a reasonable thing, like the farmer drives his plow, or like our friend in the scratch below, who is harrowing, and even drags the harrow himself. If one hasn't a horse, one is one's own horse — many people do so here.

—VINCENT VAN GOGH

Who Burns for the Perfection of Paper

At sixteen, I worked after high school hours
at a printing plant
that manufactured legal pads:
Yellow paper
stacked seven feet high
and leaning
as I slipped cardboard
between the pages,
then brushed red glue
up and down the stack.
No gloves: fingertips required
for the perfection of paper,

smoothing the exact rectangle.
Sluggish by 9 PM, the hands
would slide along suddenly sharp paper,
and gather slits thinner than the crevices
of the skin, hidden.
Then the glue would sting,
hands oozing
till both palms burned
at the punchclock.

Ten years later, in law school,
I knew that every legal pad
was glued with the sting of hidden cuts,
that every open lawbook
was a pair of hands
upturned and burning.

—MARTÍN ESPADA

It is a truism of the new economy that the ultimate success of any enterprise lies with the quality of the people it hires. At many technology companies, employees are asked to all but live at the office, in conditions of intimacy that would have been unthinkable a generation ago. The artifacts of the prototypical Silicon Valley office — the video-games, the espresso bar, the bunk beds, the basketball hoops — are the elements of the rec room, not the workplace. And in the rec room you want to play only with your friends. But how do you find out who your friends are? Today, recruiters canvas the country for résumés. They analyze employment histories and their competitors' staff listings. They call references, and then do what I did with Nolan Myers: sit down with a perfect stranger for an hour and a half and attempt to draw conclusions about that stranger's intelligence and personality. The job interview has become one of the central conventions of the modern economy. But what, exactly, can you know about a stranger after sitting down and talking with him for an hour?

—MALCOLM GLADWELL

FOCUSING BY WRITING

1. The word *professional* is widely and often carelessly used to signify someone's attitudes and special skills. What does the concept mean to you? Clarify the standards, values, and occupations that define it for you. Include at least one illustration of a careless or misleading use of the term.

2. Are summer jobs worth your time and efforts? Months of low pay, futureless tasks, and sometimes very hard labor mean lost opportunities for travel, cultural enrichment, reading, pursuing special interests or studies, and just recharging batteries. Long summers for work are an American custom initially devised to permit schoolchildren to help with crops in an earlier agricultural society. Based on your experiences and present outlook, what are the pros and cons of keeping summertime a work season?

3. What does society owe to its members in financial trouble, such as the homeless? What portions, if any, of your campus and college services would you make available to them? Should they be permitted to sleep in sheltered areas? to congregate around the quad or plaza? expect food or money from students? If you don't think colleges should deal with the problem, explain why not.

4. Military personnel are not supposed to follow orders that violate their conscience, but what if regulations prohibit what their own conscience condones? Consider one of many recent situations involving consensual sex relations between military men and women. Examine issues of authority and freedom in this complicated matter. Should people obey rules they don't believe are valid?

Abigail Witherspoon (Pseud.)

THIS PEN FOR HIRE

ABIGAIL WITHERSPOON is a pseudonym adopted to protect the writer and her co-workers. This essay is excerpted from a longer article that appeared in *Harper's* magazine in 1995.

I am an academic call girl. I write college kids' papers for a living. Term 1
papers, book reports, senior theses, take-home exams. My "specialties": art history and sociology, international relations and comparative literature, English, psychology, "communications," Western philosophy (ancient and contemporary), structural anthropology, film history, evolutionary biology, waste management and disposal, media studies, and pre-Confederation Canadian history. I throw around allusions to Caspar Weinberger and Alger Hiss, Sacco and Vanzetti, Haldeman and Ehrlichman, Joel Steinberg and Baby M. The teaching assistants eat it up. I can do simple English or advanced jargon. Like other types of prostitutes, I am, professionally, very accommodating.

I used to tell myself I'd do this work only for a month or two, until I 2
found something else. But the official unemployment rate in this large Canadian city where I live is almost 10 percent, and even if it were easy to find a job, I'm American, and therefore legally prohibited from receiving a paycheck. So each day I walk up the stairs of a rotting old industrial building to an office with a sign on the window: TAILORMADE ESSAYS, WRITING AND RESEARCH. The owner, whom I'll call Matthew, claims that he started the business for ghostwriters, speechwriters, and closet biographers, and only gradually moved into academic work as a sideline. But even Grace, the oldest surviving writer on Tailormade's staff, can't remember anybody ever writing much other than homework for students at one university or another.

This is a good city for Tailormade. Next door is the city's university and 3
its tens of thousands of students, a school that was once somewhat better when not all of its computer-registered classes numbered in the hundreds. Orders come in from Vancouver, Calgary, Winnipeg. There are plenty of essay services in the States, of course; they advertise in campus newspapers and the back pages of music magazines. Some of the big ones have toll-free

phone numbers. They're sprinkled all over: California, Florida, New Jersey. But we still get American business too. Orders come in here from Michigan, Vermont, Pennsylvania; from Illinois, Wisconsin, upstate New York, sometimes California; from Harvard, Cornell, and Brown. They come in from teachers' colleges, from people calling themselves "gifted students" (usually teenagers at boarding schools), and, once in a while, from the snazzy places some of our customers apparently vacation with their divorced dads, like Paris.

Matthew runs the business with his wife, Sylvia. Or maybe she is his ex-wife, nobody's exactly sure. When you call Tailormade — it's now in the phone book — you hear Sylvia say that Tailormade is Canada's foremost essay service; that our very qualified writers handle most academic subjects; and that we are fast, efficient, and completely confidential. Sylvia speaks loudly and slowly and clearly, especially to Asian customers. She is convinced that everyone who phones the office will be Asian, just as she's convinced that all Asians drive white Mercedes or black BMWs with cellular phones in them. From my personal experience, I find the Asian customers at least more likely to have done the assigned reading.... 4

This afternoon, October 10, I'm here to hand in a paper and fight it out with the other writers for more assignments. Some of us are legal, some aren't. Some have mortgages and cars, some don't. All of us are hungry. The office is jammed, since it's almost time for midterms. Tailormade does a brisk business from October to May, except for January. The chairs are full of customers studiously filling out order forms. You can always tell who is a student and who is a writer. The students are dressed elegantly and with precision; the writers wear ripped concert T-shirts or stained denim jackets with white undershirts peeking out. The students wear mousse and hair gel and nail polish and Tony Lama western boots and Tourneau watches and just the right amount of makeup. They smell of Escape, Polo for men, and gum. The writers smell of sweat, house pets, and crushed cigarettes. Four of the other writers are lolling in their chairs and fidgeting; work usually isn't assigned until all the order forms have been filled out, unless somebody requests a topic difficult to fill. Then Matthew will call out like an auctioneer: "Root Causes of the Ukrainian Famine? Second year? Anyone? Grace?" or "J. S. Mill's Brand of Humane Utilitarianism? Third year? Henry, that for you?" as some customer hovers in front of the desk, eyes straight ahead. Someone else in the room might idly remark that he or she took that course back in freshman year and it was a "gut" or a "real bird." 5

I suspect that each of us in the Tailormade stable of hacks sorts out the customers differently: into liberal-arts students and business students; into those that at least do the reading and those that don't bother; into those that have trouble writing academic English and those that just don't care about school; into those that do their assignments in other subjects and 6 those that farm every last one of them out to us; into the struggling and inept versus the rich, lazy, and stupid. But for Matthew and Sylvia, the clientele are divisible, even before cash versus credit card, or paid-up versus owing, into Asian customers and non-Asian ones. There's been an influx of wealthy immigrants from Hong Kong in recent years, fleeing annexation. Matthew and Sylvia seem to resent their presence and, particularly, their money. Yet they know that it's precisely this pool of customers — who have limited written English language skills but possess education, sophistication, ambition, cash, and parents leaning hard on them for good grades — that keeps the business going....

I'm still waiting for an assignment. In fact, all the writers are still wait- 7 ing. We often wait at the bar around the corner; Tailormade has its own table there, permanently reserved. But we all have to get ourselves to the office eventually to pick up assignments. Grace, the oldest writer and by now, probably, the best, sits sorrowfully by the window, her long gray hair falling into her lap and her head jammed into her turtleneck, on her thin face a look of permanent tragedy. Grace gets up at three in the morning to work; she never forgets a name, a fact, or an assignment; she has a deep, strange love for Japanese history and in ten years here has probably hatched enough pages and research for several doctoral dissertations in that field. Elliott, another writer, reclines near the door, his little dog asleep under his chair. He uses the dog as an icebreaker with the clients, especially young women. He is six and a half feet tall and from somewhere far up in the lunar landscape of northern Ontario. He has a huge head of blond hair down to his eyes and pants as tight as a rock star's. Elliott is the business writer. He specializes in finance, investment, management, and economics. He lives out of a suitcase; he and the little dog, perhaps practicing fiscal restraint, seem to stay with one of a series of girlfriends. When the relationship comes to an end, Elliott and the little dog wind up back in the office, where they sleep in the fax room and Elliott cranks out essays on his laptop. Henry and Russell, two other writers, twist around, changing position, the way travelers do when they're trying to nap on airport lounge chairs. They both look a little like El Greco saints, although perhaps it just seems that way to me because lately I've been doing a lot of art history papers. They both have long skinny legs, long thin white nervous twiddling hands, long thin faces with two weeks' worth of unintentional beard. Henry points out how good Russell looks, and we all agree. Russell is forty. He has a new girlfriend half his age who has, he says, provided a spiritual reawakening. Before he met her, Russell drank so much and held it so badly that he had the distinction of being the only staff member to be banned from the bar around the corner for life. Henry, by contrast, looks terrible. He's always sick, emaciated, coughing, but he invariably manages to meet his deadlines, to make his page quotas, and to show up on time. We used to have another writer on staff, older even than Russell or Grace, who smoked a pipe, nodded a lot, and never said anything. He was a professor who'd been fired from some school, we were never really sure where. Eventually, he went AWOL and started an essay-writing service of his own. He's now Tailormade's main competition. The only other competitors, apparently, worked out of a hot-dog stand parked next to a campus bookstore. Nobody knows whether they're open anymore.

In general, there is a furtiveness about the way we writers talk to one another, the way we socialize. In the office, we're a little like people who know each other from A.A. meetings or rough trade bars encountering each other on a Monday morning at the photocopy machine. It's not because we're competing for work. It's not even because some of us are illegal and everyone else knows it. It is, if anything, collective embarrassment. We know a lot more than Matthew and Sylvia do. They sit dumbly as we bullshit with the clients about their subjects and assignments ("Ah, introductory psychology! The evolution of psychotherapy is a fascinating topic...ever read a guy called Russell Jacoby?") in order to impress them and get them to ask for us. This must be the equivalent of the harlots' competitive bordello promenade. But we work for Matthew and Sylvia. They have the sense to pit us against each other, and it works. We can correct their pronunciation of "Goethe" and they don't care. They know it makes no difference. I suspect they have never been farther away than Niagara Falls; neither of them may have even finished high school. It doesn't matter. The laugh's on us, of course: they own the business. 8

OCTOBER 12, 1994. A tall gangly kid comes in for a twenty-page senior history essay about the ancient local jail. It involves research among primary sources in the provincial archives, and I spend a week there, going page by page through the faded brown script of the warden's prison logbooks of the 1830s. Agitators are being executed for "high treason" or "banished from the realm," which, I assume, means being deported. Once in a while there's a seductive joy to a project. You forget that you've undertaken it for money, that it isn't yours. 9

Most of the time, though, all I think about is the number of pages done, the number to go. Tailormade charges twenty dollars Canadian a page for first- and second-year course assignments, twenty-two a page for third- and fourth-year assignments, twenty-four for "technical, scientific, and advanced" topics. "Technical, scientific, and advanced" can mean nuclear physics, as it does in September when there is no business. Or it can mean anything Matthew and Sylvia want it to, as it does in March. Most major spring-term essays are due when final exams begin, in April, and so in March kids are practically lined up in the office taking numbers and spilling out into the hall. The writers get half, in cash: ten and eleven bucks a page; twelve for the technical, scientific, and advanced. 10

There's one other charge: if the client doesn't bring in her or his own books, except in September and January, she or he is "dinged," charged an 11 extra two dollars a page for research. When the writers get an assignment, we ask if there are books. If there are, it saves us time, but we have to lug them home, and often they're the wrong books. If there are no books, we have to go to the libraries and research the paper ourselves. "Client wants twelve pages on clinical social work intervention," Matthew and Sylvia might tell us. "She has a reading list but no books. I think we can ding her." "He wants a book report on something called *Gravity's Rainbow*? Doesn't have the book, though. I'm gonna ding him."...

OCTOBER 13....It was different, though, when I was a university student   12
in the early 1980s. I wasn't aware of anyone who bought his or her home-work anywhere, although it must have happened. It was about that time that Tailormade was putting up signs on the telephone poles outside the university's main classroom buildings. It advertised just outside the huge central library as well as outside the libraries of three or four smaller schools a few minutes' drive away. This burst of entrepreneurial confidence almost led to the service's undoing. In a spectacular cooperative sting oper-ation among the security departments of the various schools, the office was raided. This event has become a sort of fearsome myth at Tailormade, dis-cussed not unlike the way Syrians might occasionally mention the Israeli raid on Entebbe. Matthew and Sylvia were hauled off to court and a dozen or so clients were thrown out of their respective universities. Matthew and Sylvia, however, must have hired the right lawyer: they were allowed to reopen, provided that they stayed away from campuses and that they stamped every page of every essay TAILORMADE ESSAY SERVICE: FOR RESEARCH PURPOSES ONLY. Now the clients take the stamped essays home, retype them, and print them out on high-end laser printers much better than ours. If the client is obnoxious, complains, or is considered a whiner, each type-written page will be stamped in the middle. If the client is steady and has good credit, each page will be stamped in the margin so that the stamp can be whited out and the pages photocopied.

By the time Tailormade reopened, I had moved back to this country   13
after some years at home in the States. I had no money and no prospects of a legal job. I came in, handed Matthew a résumé, spent a couple of weeks on probationary trial, and then began a serious career as a hack. "What are your specialties?" Matthew had asked me. I told him I'd majored in history and political science as an undergraduate. Over time, as my financial situ-ation grew worse, my "specialties" grew to include everything except math, accounting, economics, and the hard sciences.

OCTOBER 23. Three weeks ago I was assigned an essay on the establish-   14
ment and growth of political action committees among the Christian right. I am earnest about this one; I actually overprepare. I want to document, with carefully muted horror, the world of Paul Laxalt and direct mail, the

arm-twisting of members of Congress on the school prayer issue. My contempt for the client was mixed with pity: he knew not how much he was missing. Only afterward do I realize that after doing an essay I take seriously, I still expect, as in college, to get something back with a mark on it, as a reward or at least as an acknowledgment. I hear nothing, of course. I feel oddly let down. I'm certain it got the client an A. Today, the same client stops in to order something else and helpfully points out what he thinks I could have done to improve the essay I'd written for him....

NOVEMBER 8. I will not go into any of the university's libraries. I will not   15
risk running into anyone I know, anyone who might think I'm one of those perpetual graduate students who never finished their dissertations and drift pathetically around university libraries like the undead, frightening the undergraduates. It would be as bad to be thought one of these lifelong grad students as to be suspected of being what I am. So I use the public libraries, usually the one closest to my apartment, on my street corner. It's a community library, with three wonderful librarians, three daily newspapers, and remarkably few books. If I haven't been given the books already, if the client has been dinged and I have to do research on my own, I come here. I have my favorite chair. The librarians assume I am a "mature" and "continuing" community college student, and make kind chitchat with me.

Sometimes, when I can't find any of the sources listed in the library's   16
computer and don't have time to go to a real library, I use books barely appropriate for the essay: books for "young adults," which means twelve-year-olds, or books I have lying around my apartment.... Books somewhere between the classic and the old chestnut; terrific books, yet with no relation to the topic at hand. But they're good for the odd quote and name-drop, and they can pad a bibliography. Sometimes I can't get away with this, though, and then I have no choice but to go back to an actual place of research, like the archives....

NOVEMBER 18. Things are picking up for Christmas vacation; everything,   17
it seems, is due December 5 or December 15. The essay order form asks, "Subject & Level," "Topic," "No. of Pages," "Footnotes," "Bibliography," and then a couple of lines marked "Additional Information," by far the most common of which is "Simple English." As the year rolls on, we hacks will all, out of annoyance, laziness, or just boredom, start unsimplifying this simple English; by April it will approach the mega-watt vocabulary and tortured syntax of the Frankfurt School. But people hand these papers in and don't get caught, people who have difficulty speaking complete sentences in English; perhaps this is because classes and even tutorials are so big they never have to speak. But in December we're all still on pretty good behavior, simple instead of spiteful. I've just handed in an assignment in "Simple English," a paper titled "Mozart's Friendship with Joseph and

Johann Michael Haydn and Its Impact on Mozart's Chamber Music." It reads, in part:

> Mozart was undeniably original. He was never derivative. That was part of his genius. So were the Haydn brothers. All of them were totally unique.

The little library on my corner didn't have much on Mozart or the Haydn brothers. As a result, one of the items in my bibliography is a child's book with a cardboard pop-up of a doughy-looking little Mozart, in a funky pigtail and knee breeches, standing proudly beside a harpsichord.... [18]

DECEMBER 2. Occasionally there is an assignment the writers fight for. This week somebody — not me — gets to take home *Fanny Hill* and *Lady Chatterley's Lover*, and get paid for it. I guess some kids really, *really* hate to read. [19]

DECEMBER 5. A bad assignment: unnecessarily obscure, pedantic, pointless. Certain courses seem to consist of teaching kids the use of jargon as though it were a substitute for writing or thinking well. Often there is an implied pressure to agree with the assigned book. And many are simply impossible to understand; I often take home a textbook or a sheaf of photocopies for an assignment and see, next to a phrase such as "responsible acceptance of the control dimension," long strings of tiny Chinese characters in ballpoint pen. No wonder the students find the assignments incomprehensible; they are incomprehensible to me. [20]

DECEMBER 8. I hand in a paper on Machiavelli. "How'd it go?" asked the client, a boy in a leather bomber jacket reading John Grisham. I begin to go on about how great one of the books was, a revisionist biography called *Machiavelli in Hell*. I am hoping, with my scholarly enthusiasm, to make the client feel particularly stupid. "It's an amazing book," I tell him. "It makes a case for Machiavelli actually being kind of a liberal humanist instead of the cynical guy everybody always thinks he was — amazing." "That's good," the kid says. "I'm glad you're enjoying yourself on my tab. Did you answer the essay question the way you were supposed to?" [21]

DECEMBER 16. Every so often clients come in with an opinion they want us to replicate. The freshman sociology and political science essays are already starting to rain in: a deluge of "Show why immigrants are a dead weight on the economy and take jobs away from us"; "Show why most social programs will become too expensive for an aging population"; "Show why gun control can be interpreted as an infringement on civil rights"; "Show the Pacific Rim's single-handed assault on North American economies." I ignore them. I write, depending on my mood, about the INS's unequal criteria for refugee status, or the movie *Roger and Me*, or the [22]

NRA's political clout. For instance, there is today's assignment: to describe Locke's influence, as an Enlightenment figure, on our own time. I think this is baloney. I talk about how the postwar military-industrial complex proves that God really did give the world, whatever Locke thought, to the covetous and contentious instead of to the industrious and the rational. No one's ever complained about finding my opinion in a paper instead of their own. Now I realize this isn't because I've persuaded anybody of anything. It's just laziness: there are some customers who actually retype their stamped essays without bothering to read them....

JANUARY 10, 1995. School has been back in session for a week now. The   23
only work that is in are essays from the education students. I hate these assignments. I have trouble manipulating the self-encapsulated second language in which teaching students seem compelled to write. But it's after Christmas, and I'm broke. Education assignments all involve writing up our customers' encounters in their "practicum." Teaching students work several times a week as assistant teachers in grade school classrooms; instead of getting paid for this work, they pay tuition for it. Unfortunately, these expensive practice sessions don't seem to go well. My first such assignment was to write "reflections" on a "lesson plan" for a seventh-grade English class. The teaching student had given me some notes, and I had to translate these into the pedagogical jargon used in her textbooks. The idea seems to be that you have to say, as obscurely as possible, what you did with your seventh-grade kids and what you think about what you did:

> Preliminary Lesson Formulations: My objectives were to integrate lesson content with methodology to expand students' receptiveness and responsiveness to the material and to one another by teaching them how to disagree with one another in a constructive way. The class will draw up a T-chart covering "Disagreeing in an Agreeable Way," roughly in the manner of Bennett et al. Check for understanding. When the students discuss this, they are encouraged to listen to one another's language carefully and "correct" it if the wording is unhelpful, negative, or destructive. I shared my objectives with the class by asking them to read a fable and then divide into pairs and decide together what the moral was. Clearly, this is the "Think-Pair-Share" technique, as detailed in Bennett et al. The three strategies in use, then, are: 1) pair and sharing; 2) group discussion of the fable with mind-mapping; 3) group discussion of ways of disagreement. The teacher, modeling, divides the board in two with a line.

"Pair and share" seemed to mean "find a partner." I had no idea what   24
"mind-mapping" or a "T-chart" was supposed to be. And come to think of it, after reading the fable, I had no idea what the moral was.

JANUARY 18. Somebody is applying to the graduate program in family   25
therapy at some university somewhere and wants us to write the application. "She's my friend," said the young woman sitting across from Matthew

at the desk. "She wants to start her own private practice as a therapist, right? So she can buy a house, right? And if you're a psychiatrist you have to go all the way through med school, right? So she's given me some notes for you about her here — she only needs one credit for her B.A. in psychology, and she volunteered at a shelter one summer. She wants you to tell them all that. Maybe make up some other things."

"See," Matthew tells me after she leaves. "If you ever go to one of those   26 therapists, that's something you should think about."

JANUARY 20. When I first started this work, friends of mine would try to   27 comfort me by telling me it would teach me to write better. Actually, academic prostitution, just like any other kind, seems to bring with it diseases, afflictions, vices, and bad habits. There is, for instance, the art of pretending you've read a book you haven't. It's just like every speed-reading course ever offered by the Learning Annex: read the introduction, where the writer outlines what he's going to say, and the conclusion, where he repeats what he's said.

> In his book *The Technological Society*, Jacques Ellul begins by defining the technical simply as the search for efficiency. He claims, however, that technique itself is subdivided into three categories: the social, the organizational, and the economic.

This is all on the book's *first four pages*. Sometimes — often — I find   28 myself eating up as much space as possible. There are several ways to do this. One is to reproduce lengthy, paragraph-long quotes in full; another is to ramble on about your own apparently passionate opinion on something. Or you start talking about the United States and what a handbasket it's going to hell in. This is equally useful, for different reasons, on either side of the border. You can ask rhetorical questions to obsessive excess. ("Can Ellul present the technical in such a reductionist way? Can he really define technique in such a way? And is it really valid to distinguish between the social and the organizational?" etc.) And there's always the art of name-dropping as a way to fill pages and convince the teaching assistant that your client has read *something*, even if it wasn't what was on the syllabus.

> Certainly, as writers from Eduardo Galeano to Andre Gunder Frank to Noam Chomsky to Philip Agee to Allan Frankovich to Ernesto Laclau document, the CIA has long propped up the United Fruit Company.

At least you can make the client feel stupid. It's the third week of January, my apartment is cold, and I am bitter.

FEBRUARY 8. I'm learning, as the environmentalists tell us, to reuse and   29 recycle. It's easier when I adapt a paper, with minor changes, on the same topic for different classes, or when I use the same paper for the same class again the following year. I've never worried much about a recycled essay being recognized: the pay for teaching assistants is low enough, and the burnout rate high enough, that the odds are substantially against the same person reading and grading papers for the same course two years in a row. Some topics just seem to beg for recycling: freshmen are forever being asked to mull over the roles of determinism, hubris, and moral responsibility in the Oedipus cycle; sociology and philosophy majors, the ethics of abortion. There are essays on shantytowns in developing countries, export-oriented economies in developing countries, structural adjustment in developing countries, and one only has to make the obvious case that the three are interrelated to be able to extend the possibilities for parts of essays in any of those three categories to resurface magically within another. Other essays can be recycled with just a little tinkering to surmount minor differences in topic or in emphasis: for instance, "Italian Fascists in North America," to which "The Italian-Canadian Family" lends itself nicely; "Taboo-Breaking in Racine and Ford," which re-emerges, after minor cosmetic surgery, as "Master-Slave Relationships in Ford and Racine: What They Tell Us About Lust, Fate, and Obligation." And so on....

MARCH 16. There's a regular customer whose course load would be   30
appropriate for the résumé of a U.N. secretary general. She's taking several courses on developing economies, including one referred to by other clients in the same class as "Third World Women." And one on the history of black Americans from Reconstruction to the present. I wrote her a twenty-five-page history of the early years of the civil-rights movement. She was sitting in the office when I handed it in. "Interesting course, isn't it?" she asked. She requested me again. I wrote her a paper on Costa Rica, one on dowry murders in India, one on the black leader W. E. B. Du Bois. "It's a great course isn't it?" she asked me when she got the paper on dowry murders. "He seems like a fascinating guy," she said the day she collected W. E. B. Du Bois. "Somebody told me he wound up in *Ghana*." Today I take a shortcut across the university campus on my way to the essay service and see her with a group of other students. I make a direct beeline for her and I smile. I watch her blanch, look around, try to decide whether to pretend not to know me, decide that maybe that isn't a good idea. She gives me a stricken look and a big toothy grin.

MARCH 26. One day I'm given five pages on the Treaty of Versailles. Last   31
year at the same time, I was assigned a paper on the same topic. A memorable paper. Two days after I turned it in, there was a camera crew outside. It turned out to be the local cable station for kids, doing an "exposé" on cheating. We taped it when it came on. It featured kids sitting in shadow, faces obscured, *60 Minutes* style.

"There she is, the little rat," Sylvia glowered at the time. The pretty   32
young fake client handed my paper to some professor sitting behind a desk and asked, "What do you think about this? Is it better or worse than what

you would normally get? Would you assume that it was a real paper or one that had been bought?"

"Well...it's a *credible* paper," said the professor. "I mean, one wouldn't   33
think it was...*synthetic* unless one had reason to."

"What kind of grade would you give it?"   34

"Oh, I'd give it...a B minus."   35

"*Please.*" I was really offended. Elliott comforted me. "Well, he has to   36
say that. Now that he knows it's ours, he can't admit it's an A paper even if
he wants to."

We all sat tight and waited for every professor within fifty miles to call   37
us, threatening death. But professors don't watch cable shows for teenagers;
neither do ambitious young teaching assistants. Instead, the show turned
out to be a free advertising bonanza. Soon the phone rang off the hook
with kids calling up and asking, "You mean, like, you can write my term
paper for me if I pay you?"

APRIL 16. Today, working on a paper, I was reminded that there *are* good   38
professors. They're the ones who either convince the kids the course content is inherently interesting and get them to work hard on the assignments
or who figure out ways to make the assignments, at least, creative events to
enjoy. But students with shaky language skills falter at surprises, even good
ones; lazy students farm the assignments out no matter what they are. Such
assignments are oddly comforting for me: I can almost pretend the two
of us are talking over the clients' heads. When I'm alone in my room, in
front of the computer and between the headphones, it's hard not to want to
write something good for myself and maybe even for the imaginary absentee professor or appreciative T.A., something that will last. But when I'm
standing in the crowded Tailormade office, next to someone elegant and
young and in eight hundred bucks' worth of calfskin leather, someone who
not only has never heard of John Stuart Mill and never read *Othello* but
doesn't even know he hasn't, doesn't even mind that he hasn't, and doesn't
even care that he hasn't, the urge to make something that will last somehow vanishes.

APRIL 28. The semester is almost at an end. Exams have started; the   39
essays have all been handed in. Elliott and Russell begin their summer jobs
as bike couriers. Henry, like me, is illegal; but he confides to me that he's
had enough. "You can only do so much of this," he says. I know, I tell him.
I know.

Analyzing This Selection

1. What details indicate the atmosphere around the office? When Abigail is
   there, how is she affected?

2. **THE WRITER'S METHOD**   From paragraph 9 the essay continues in the form of a diary. Are Abigail's entries for herself or readers? What does the diary form contribute to her account?

3. In addition to her attitudes about students using the service, what does Abigail criticize in the educational system? Do you observe similar conditions in your college?

Analyzing Connections

4. This job and the summer jobs held by Michael Dorris (see "Life Stories," p. 218) required dishonest efforts. How did the jobs change the writers' outlook?

Analyzing by Writing

5. Examine attitudes among college students and their families toward earning high grades. How strenuously are grades pursued? How are academic achievements acknowledged? What hypocrisies are accepted by students or parents? What dishonesties are tolerated? What happens when loyalty, ambition, or sympathy comes into conflict with academic honesty? Examine attitudes closely, and suggest a remedy for problems you find.

Gary Soto

BLACK HAIR

GARY SOTO (b. 1952) writes poetry, fiction, and essays about Mexican American life. He grew up in Fresno, California, and received a B.A. from California State University (Fresno) and an M.F.A. from the University of California at Irvine. Soto teaches writing at the University of California at Riverside. His work has appeared in the *Nation*, *Ploughshares*, the *Iowa Review*, and *Poetry*. Soto's most recent collection of essays and stories is *Jesse* (1994). "Black Hair" is from his volume of autobiographical pieces, *Living up the Street* (1985).

There are two kinds of work: One uses the mind and the other uses muscle. As a kid I found out about the latter. I'm thinking of the summer of 1969 when I was a seventeen-year-old runaway who ended up in Glendale, California, to work for Valley Tire Factory. To answer an ad in the newspaper I walked miles in the afternoon sun, my stomach slowly knotting on a doughnut that was breakfast, my teeth like bright candles gone yellow.

I walked in the door sweating and feeling ugly because my hair was still stiff from a swim at the Santa Monica beach the day before. Jules, the accountant and part owner, looked droopily through his bifocals at my application and then at me. He tipped his cigar in the ashtray, asked my age as if he didn't believe I was seventeen, but finally after a moment of silence, said, "Come back tomorrow. Eight-thirty."

I thanked him, left the office, and went around to the chain link fence to watch the workers heave tires into a bin; others carted uneven stacks of tires on hand trucks. Their faces were black from tire dust and when they talked — or cussed — their mouths showed a bright pink.

From there I walked up a commercial street, past a cleaners, a motorcycle shop, and a gas station where I washed my face and hands; before leaving I took a bottle that hung on the side of the Coke machine, filled it with water, and stopped it with a scrap of paper and a rubber band.

The next morning I arrived early at work. The assistant foreman, a potbellied Hungarian, showed me a timecard and how to punch in. He showed me the Coke machine, the locker room with its slimy shower, and also pointed out the places where I shouldn't go: The ovens where the tires were recapped and the customer service area, which had a slashed couch, a coffee table with greasy magazines, and an ashtray. He introduced me to Tully, a fat man with one ear, who worked the buffers that resurfaced the white walls. I was handed an apron and a face mask and shown how to use the buffer: Lift the tire and center, inflate it with a footpedal, press the buffer against the white band until cleaned, and then deflate and blow off the tire with an air hose.

With a paint brush he stirred a can of industrial preserver. "Then slap this blue stuff on." While he was talking a co-worker came up quietly from behind him and goosed him with the air hose. Tully jumped as if he had been struck by a bullet and then turned around cussing and cupping his genitals in his hands as the other worker walked away calling out foul names. When Tully turned to me smiling his gray teeth, I lifted my mouth into a smile because I wanted to get along. He has to be on my side, I thought. He's the one who'll tell the foreman how I'm doing.

I worked carefully that day, setting the tires on the machine as if they were babies, since it was easy to catch a finger in the rim that expanded to inflate the tire. At the day's end we swept up the tire dust and emptied the trash into bins.

At five the workers scattered for their cars and motorcycles while I crossed the street to wash at a burger stand. My hair was stiff with dust and my mouth showed pink against the backdrop of my dirty face. I then ordered a hotdog and walked slowly in the direction of the abandoned house where I had stayed the night before. I lay under the trees and within minutes was asleep. When I woke my shoulders were sore and my eyes burned when I squeezed the lids together.

From the backyard I walked dully through a residential street, and as evening came on, the TV glare in the living rooms and the headlights of passing cars showed against the blue drift of dusk. I saw two children coming up the street with snow cones, their tongues darting at the packed ice. I saw a boy with a peach and wanted to stop him, but felt embarrassed by my hunger. I walked for an hour only to return and discover the house lit brightly. Behind the fence I heard voices and saw a flashlight poking at the garage door. A man on the back steps mumbled something about the refrigerator to the one with the flashlight.

I waited for them to leave, but had the feeling they wouldn't because there was the commotion of furniture being moved. Tired, even more desperate, I started walking again with a great urge to kick things and tear the day from my life. I felt weak and my mind kept drifting because of hunger. I crossed the street to a gas station where I sipped at the water fountain and searched the Coke machine for change. I started walking again, first up a commercial street, then into a residential area where I lay down on someone's lawn and replayed a scene at home — my mother crying at the kitchen table, my stepfather yelling with food in his mouth. They're cruel, I thought, and warned myself that I should never forgive them. How could they do this to me.

When I got up from the lawn it was late. I searched out a place to sleep   11
and found an unlocked car that seemed safe. In the back seat, with my
shoes off, I fell asleep but woke up startled about four in the morning when
the owner, a nurse on her way to work, opened the door. She got in and
was about to start the engine when I raised my head up from the backseat
to explain my presence. She screamed so loudly when I said "I'm sorry"
that I sprinted from the car with my shoes in hand. Her screams faded,
then stopped altogether, as I ran down the block where I hid behind a trash
bin and waited for a police siren to sound. Nothing. I crossed the street to
a church where I slept stiffly on cardboard in the balcony.

I woke up feeling tired and greasy. It was early and a few street lights   12
were still lit, the east growing pink with dawn. I washed myself from a garden hose and returned to the church to break into what looked like a
kitchen. Paper cups, plastic spoons, a coffee pot littered on a table. I found
a box of Nabisco crackers which I ate until I was full.

At work I spent the morning at the buffer, but was then told to help Iggy,   13
an old Mexican, who was responsible for choosing tires that could be
recapped without the risk of exploding at high speeds. Every morning a
truck would deliver used tires, and after I unloaded them Iggy would step
among the tires to inspect them for punctures and rips on the side walls.

With a yellow chalk he marked circles and Xs to indicate damage and   14
called out "junk." For those tires that could be recapped, he said "goody"
and I placed them on my hand truck. When I had a stack of eight I kicked
the truck at an angle and balanced them to another work area where Iggy
again inspected the tires, scratching Xs and calling out "junk."

Iggy worked only until three in the afternoon, at which time he went to   15
the locker room to wash and shave and to dress in a two-piece suit. When
he came out he glowed with a bracelet, watch, rings, and a shiny fountain
pen in his breast pocket. His shoes sounded against the asphalt. He was the
image of a banker stepping into sunlight with millions on his mind. He
said a few low words to workers with whom he was friendly and none to
people like me.

I was seventeen, stupid because I couldn't figure out the difference   16
between an F 78 14 and 750 14 at sight. Iggy shook his head when I
brought him the wrong tires, especially since I had expressed interest in
being his understudy. "Mexican, how can you be so stupid?" he would yell
at me, slapping a tire from my hands. But within weeks I learned a lot
about tires, from sizes and makes to how they are molded in iron forms to
how Valley stole from other companies. Now and then we received a truck-
load of tires, most of them new or nearly new, and they were taken to our
warehouse in the back where the serial numbers were ground off with a
sander. On those days the foreman handed out Cokes and joked with us as
we worked to get the numbers off.

Most of the workers were Mexican or black, though a few redneck   17
whites worked there. The base pay was a dollar sixty-five, but the average

was three dollars. Of the black workers, I knew Sugar Daddy the best. His body carried two hundred and fifty pounds, armfuls of scars, and a long knife that made me jump when he brought it out from his boot without warning. At one time he had been a singer, and had cut a record in 1967 called *Love's Chance*, which broke into the R and B charts. But nothing came of it. No big contract, no club dates, no tours. He made very little from the sales, only enough for an operation to pull a steering wheel from his gut when, drunk and mad at a lady friend, he slammed his Mustang into a row of parked cars.

"Touch it," he smiled at me one afternoon as he raised his shirt, his 18 black belly kinked with hair. Scared, I traced the scar that ran from his chest to the left of his belly button, and I was repelled but hid my disgust.

Among the Mexicans I had few friends because I was different, a *pocho*[1] 19 who spoke bad Spanish. At lunch they sat in tires and laughed over burritos, looking up at me to laugh even harder. I also sat in tires while nursing a Coke and felt dirty and sticky because I was still living on the street and had not had a real bath in over a week. Nevertheless, when the border patrol came to round up the nationals, I ran with them as they scrambled for the fence or hid among the tires behind the warehouse. The foreman, who thought I was an undocumented worker, yelled at me to run, to get away. I did just that. At the time it seemed fun because there was no risk, only a goodhearted feeling of hide-and-seek, and besides it meant an hour away from work on company time. When the police left we came back and some of the nationals made up stories of how they were almost caught — how they out-raced the police. Some of the stories were so convoluted and unconvincing that everyone laughed *mentiras*,[2] especially when one described how he overpowered a policeman, took his gun away, and sold the patrol car. We laughed and he laughed, happy to be there to make up a story.

If work was difficult, so were the nights. I still had not gathered enough 20 money to rent a room, so I spent the nights sleeping in parked cars or in the balcony of a church. After a week I found a newspaper ad for room for rent, phoned, and was given directions. Finished with work, I walked the five miles down Mission Road looking back into the traffic with my thumb out. No rides. After eight hours of handling tires I was frightening, I suppose, to drivers since they seldom looked at me; if they did, it was a quick glance. For the next six weeks I would try to hitchhike, but the only person to stop was a Mexican woman who gave me two dollars to take the bus. I told her it was too much and that no bus ran from Mission Road to where I lived, but she insisted that I keep the money and trotted back to her idling car. It must have hurt her to see me day after day walking in the heat and looking very much the dirty Mexican to the many minds that didn't know

---

[1]*pocho* Derogatory term for a Mexican American who is overassimilated to U.S. culture. [All notes are the editor's.]
[2]*mentiras* Liar.

what it meant to work at hard labor. That woman knew. Her eyes met mine as she opened the car door, and there was a tenderness that was surprisingly true — one for which you wait for years but when it comes it doesn't help. Nothing changes. You continue on in rags, with the sun still above you.

I rented a room from a middle-aged couple whose lives were a mess. 21 She was a school teacher and he was a fireman. A perfect set up, I thought. But during my stay there they would argue with one another for hours in their bedroom.

When I rang at the front door both Mr. and Mrs. Van Deusen answered 22 and didn't bother to disguise their shock at how awful I looked. But they let me in all the same. Mrs. Van Deusen showed me around the house, from the kitchen and bathroom to the living room with its grand piano. On her fingers she counted out the house rules as she walked me to my room. It was a girl's room with lace curtains, scenic wallpaper of a Victorian couple enjoying a stroll, canopied bed, and stuffed animals in a corner. Leaving, she turned and asked if she could do laundry for me and, feeling shy and hurt, I told her no; perhaps the next day. She left and I undressed to take a bath, exhausted as I sat on the edge of the bed probing my aches and my bruised places. With a towel around my waist I hurried down the hallway to the bathroom where Mrs. Van Deusen had set out an additional towel with a tube of shampoo. I ran the water in the tub and sat on the toilet, lid down, watching the steam curl toward the ceiling. When I lowered myself into the tub I felt my body sting. I soaped a wash cloth and scrubbed my arms until they lightened, even glowed pink, but still I looked unwashed around my neck and face no matter how hard I rubbed. Back in the room I sat in bed reading a magazine, happy and thinking of no better luxury than a girl's sheets, especially after nearly two weeks of sleeping on cardboard at the church.

I was too tired to sleep, so I sat at the window watching the neighbors 23 move about in pajamas, and, curious about the room, looked through the bureau drawers to search out personal things — snapshots, a messy diary, and a high school yearbook. I looked up the Van Deusen's daughter, Barbara, and studied her face as if I recognized her from my own school — a face that said "promise," "college," "nice clothes in the closet." She was a skater and a member of the German Club; her greatest ambition was to sing at the Hollywood Bowl.

After awhile I got into bed and as I drifted toward sleep I thought about 24 her. In my mind I played a love scene again and again and altered it slightly each time. She comes home from college and at first is indifferent to my presence in her home, but finally I overwhelm her with deep pity when I come home hurt from work, with blood on my shirt. Then there was another version: Home from college she is immediately taken with me, in spite of my work-darkened face, and invites me into the family car for a milkshake across town. Later, back at the house, we sit in the living room talking about school until we're so close I'm holding her hand. The truth of the matter was that Barbara did come home for a week, but was bitter toward her parents for taking in boarders (two others besides me). During that time she spoke to me only twice: Once, while searching the refrigerator, she asked if we had any mustard; the other time she asked if I had seen her car keys.

But it was a place to stay. Work had become more and more difficult. I   25 not only worked with Iggy, but also with the assistant foreman who was in charge of unloading trucks. After they backed in I hopped on top to pass the tires down by bouncing them on the tailgate to give them an extra spring so they would be less difficult to handle on the other end. Each truck was weighed down with more than two hundred tires, each averaging twenty pounds, so that by the time the truck was emptied and swept clean I glistened with sweat and my T-shirt stuck to my body. I blew snot threaded with tire dust onto the asphalt, indifferent to the customers who watched from the waiting room.

The days were dull. I did what there was to do from morning until the   26 bell sounded at five; I tugged, pulled, and cussed at tires until I was listless and my mind drifted and caught on small things, from cold sodas to shoes to stupid talk about what we would do with a million dollars. I remember unloading a truck with Hamp, a black man.

"What's better than a sharp lady?" he asked me as I stood sweaty on a   27 pile of junked tires. "Water. With ice," I said.

He laughed with his mouth open wide. With his fingers he pinched the   28 sweat from his chin and flicked at me. "You be too young, boy. A woman can make you a god."

As a kid I had chopped cotton and picked grapes, so I knew work. I   29 knew the fatigue and the boredom and the feeling that there was a good possibility you might have to do such work for years, if not for a lifetime. In fact, as a kid I imagined a dark fate: To marry Mexican poor, work Mexican hours, and in the end die a Mexican death, broke and in despair.

But this job at Valley Tire Company confirmed that there was some-   30 thing worse than field work, and I was doing it. We were all doing it, from foreman to the newcomers like me, and what I felt heaving tires for eight hours a day was felt by everyone — black, Mexican, redneck. We all despised those hours but didn't know what else to do. The workers were unskilled, some undocumented and fearful of deportation, and all struck with an uncertainty at what to do with their lives. Although everyone bitched about work, no one left. Some had worked there for as long as twelve years; some had sons working there. Few quit; no one was ever fired. It amazed me that no one gave up when the border patrol jumped from their vans, baton in hand, because I couldn't imagine any work that could be worse — or any life. What was out there, in the world, that made men run for the fence in fear?

Iggy was the only worker who seemed sure of himself. After five hours of   31 "junking," he brushed himself off, cleaned up in the washroom, and came out gleaming with an elegance that humbled the rest of us. Few would look him straight in the eye or talk to him in our usual stupid way because he was so much better. He carried himself as a man should — with that old world "dignity" — while the rest of us muffed our jobs and talked dully about dull things as we worked. From where he worked in his open shed he would now and then watch us with his hands on his hips. He would shake his head and click his tongue in disgust.

The rest of us lived dismally. I often wondered what the others' homes 32 were like; I couldn't imagine that they were much better than our work place. No one indicated that his outside life was interesting or intriguing. We all looked defeated and contemptible in our filth at the day's end. I imagined the average welcome at home: Rafael, a Mexican national who had worked at Valley for five years, returned to a beaten house of kids who were dressed in mismatched clothes and playing kick-the-can. As for Sugar Daddy, he returned home to a stuffy room where he would read and reread old magazines. He ate potato chips, drank beer, and watched TV. There was no grace in dipping socks into a wash basin where later he would wash his cup and plate.

There was no grace at work. It was all ridicule. The assistant foreman 33 drank Cokes in front of the newcomers as they laced tires in the afternoon sun. Knowing that I had a long walk home, Rudy, the college student, passed me waving and yelling "Hello," as I started down Mission Road on the way home to eat out of cans. Even our plump secretary got into the act by wearing short skirts and flaunting her milky legs. If there was love, it was ugly. I'm thinking of Tully and an older man whose name I can no longer recall fondling one another in the washroom. I had come in cradling a smashed finger to find them pressed together in the shower, their pants undone and partly pulled down. When they saw me they smiled their pink mouths but didn't bother to push away.

How we arrived at such a place is a mystery to me. Why anyone would 34 stay for years is even a deeper concern. You showed up, but from where? What broken life? What ugly past? The foreman showed you the Coke machine, the washroom, and the yard where you'd work. When you picked up a tire, you were amazed at the black it could give off.

Analyzing This Selection

1. **THE WRITER'S METHOD**   Soto presents abundant details about uninteresting places and routines. What makes the account itself interesting? How do the details serve the author's purpose?

2. Young Soto wasn't certain whether Iggy's "dignity" is false or genuine. What effects does Iggy have on his co-workers? Do you think Iggy should change or keep up his appearances?

3. Though it pays more, why is the tire job "worse than field work" (para. 30)?

4. The final paragraph states questions and uncertainties about the job. How do they weaken or strengthen the essay?

Analyzing Connections

5. Soto's job lasted only a summer, but he does not present the experience as a temporary summer job, like Michael Dorris's unpleasant jobs in "Life Stories" (p. 218). How do the authors indicate different involvement or entrapment by their jobs? How do they send us different signals about the work?

Analyzing by Writing

6. Analyze Soto's views about the emotional and intellectual effects of poverty. Examine how he connects it to peoples' despair, illness, lawlessness, and breakdowns of civility. How does he illustrate poverty's lasting effects? You may wish to compare his assessment with Raymond Carver's account of hard physical labor in "My Father's Life" (p. 69).

John Updike

A & P

JOHN UPDIKE (b. 1932), one of America's most recognized and prolific writers, started his career on the staff of the *New Yorker* after graduating from Harvard in 1954. His contribution to this and other major magazines — of stories, poems, essays, and reviews — continues to this day. His major novels include four about Harry "Rabbit" Angstrom: *Rabbit, Run* (1960), *Rabbit Redux* (1971), *Rabbit Is Rich* (1981), which won three major literary awards, and *Rabbit at Rest* (1990). His best-known novel may well be *The Witches of Eastwick* (1984), also adapted into a movie. As an essayist Updike often writes about painting and other visual art, his secondary interest. The following story first appeared the *New Yorker* in 1962.

In walks these three girls in nothing but bathing suits. I'm in the third 1
checkout slot, with my back to the door, so I don't see them until they're over by the bread. The one that caught my eye first was the one in the plaid green two-piece. She was a chunky kid, with a good tan and a sweet broad soft-looking can with those two crescents of white just under it, where the sun never seems to hit, at the top of the backs of her legs. I stood there with my hand on a box of HiHo crackers trying to remember if I rang it up or not. I ring it up again and the customer starts giving me hell. She's one of these cash-register-watchers, a witch about fifty with rouge on her cheekbones and no eyebrows, and I know it made her day to trip me up. She'd been watching cash registers for fifty years and probably never seen a mistake before.

By the time I got her feathers smoothed and her goodies into a bag — 2
she gives me a little snort in passing, if she'd been born at the right time they would have burned her over in Salem — by the time I get her on her way the girls had circled around the bread and were coming back, without a pushcart, back my way along the counters, in the aisle between the checkouts and the Special bins. They didn't even have shoes on. There was this chunky one, with the two-piece — it was bright green and the seams on the bra were still sharp and her belly was still pretty pale so I guessed she just got it (the suit) — there was this one, with one of those chubby berry-faces, the lips all bunched together under her nose, this one, and a tall one, with black hair that hadn't quite frizzed right, and one of these sunburns right across under the eyes, and a chin that was too long — you know,

the kind of girl other girls think is very "striking" and "attractive" but never quite makes it, as they very well know, which is why they like her so much — and then the third one, that wasn't quite so tall. She was the queen. She kind of led them, the other two peeking around and making their shoulders round. She didn't look around, not this queen, she just walked straight on slowly, on these long white prima-donna legs. She came down a little hard on her heels, as if she didn't walk in her bare feet that much, putting down her heels and then letting the weight move along to her toes as if she was testing the floor with every step, putting a little delib-erate extra action into it. You never know for sure how girls' minds work (do you really think it's a mind in there or just a little buzz like a bee in a glass jar?) but you got the idea she had talked the other two into coming in here with her, and now she was showing them how to do it, walk slow and hold yourself straight.

She had on a kind of dirty-pink — beige maybe, I don't know — bathing 3 suit with a little nubble all over it, and what got me, the straps were down. They were off her shoulders looped loose around the cool tops of her arms, and I guess as a result the suit had slipped a little on her, so all around the top of the cloth there was this shining rim. If it hadn't been there you wouldn't have known there could have been anything whiter than those shoulders. With the straps pushed off, there was nothing between the top of the suit and the top of her head except just *her*, this clean bare plane of the top of her chest down from the shoulder bones like a dented sheet of metal tilted in the light. I mean, it was more than pretty.

She had sort of oaky hair that the sun and salt had bleached, done up in 4 a bun that was unravelling, and a kind of prim face. Walking into the A & P with your straps down, I suppose it's the only kind of face you *can* have. She held her head so high her neck, coming up out of those white shoul-ders, looked kind of stretched, but I didn't mind. The longer her neck was, the more of her there was.

She must have felt in the corner of her eye me and over my shoulder 5 Stokesie in the second slot watching, but she didn't tip. Not this queen. She kept her eyes moving across the racks, and stopped, and turned so slow it made my stomach rub the inside of my apron, and buzzed to the other two, who kind of huddled against her for relief, and then they all three of them went up the cat-and-dog-food-breakfast-cereal-macaroni-rice-raisins-seasonings-spreads-spaghetti-soft-drinks-crackers-and-cookies aisle. From the third slot I look straight up this aisle to the meat counter, and I watched them all the way. The fat one with the tan sort of fumbled with the cook-ies, but on second thought she put the package back. The sheep pushing their carts down the aisle — the girls were walking against the usual traffic (not that we have one-way signs or anything) — were pretty hilarious. You could see them, when Queenie's white shoulders dawned on them, kind of jerk, or hop, or hiccup, but their eyes snapped back to their own baskets and on they pushed. I bet you could set off dynamite in an A & P and the people would by and large keep reaching and checking oatmeal off their lists and muttering "Let me see, there was a third thing, began with A, asparagus, no, ah, yes, applesauce!" or whatever it is they do mutter. But there was no doubt, this jiggled them. A few houseslaves in pin curlers even looked around after pushing their carts past to make sure what they had seen was correct.

You know, it's one thing to have a girl in a bathing suit down on the   6
beach, where what with the glare nobody can look at each other much anyway, and another thing in the cool of the A & P, under the fluorescent lights, against all those stacked packages, with her feet paddling along naked over our checkboard green-and-cream rubber-tile floor.

"Oh Daddy," Stokesie said beside me. "I feel so faint."   7

"Darling," I said. "Hold me tight." Stokesie's married, with two babies   8
chalked up on his fuselage already, but as far as I can tell that's the only difference. He's twenty-two, and I was nineteen this April.

"Is it done?" he asks, the responsible married man finding his voice. I   9
forgot to say he thinks he's going to be manager some sunny day, maybe in 1990 when it's called the Great Alexandrov and Petrooshki Tea Company or something.

What he meant was, our town is five miles from a beach, with a big   10
summer colony out on the Point, but we're right in the middle of town, and the women generally put on a shirt or shorts or something before they get out of the car into the street. And anyway these are usually women with six children and varicose veins mapping their legs and nobody, including them, could care less. As I say, we're right in the middle of town, and if you stand at our front doors you can see two banks and the Congregational church and the newspaper store and three real-estate offices and about twenty-seven old freeloaders tearing up Central Street because the sewer broke again. It's not as if we're on the Cape; we're north of Boston and there's people in this town haven't seen the ocean for twenty years.

The girls had reached the meat counter and were asking McMahon   11
something. He pointed, they pointed, and they shuffled out of sight behind a pyramid of Diet Delight peaches. All that was left for us to see was old McMahon patting his mouth and looking after them sizing up their joints. Poor kids, I began to feel sorry for them, they couldn't help it.

Now here comes the sad part of the story, at least my family says it's sad,   12
but I don't think it's so sad myself. The store's pretty empty, it being Thursday afternoon, so there was nothing much to do except lean on the register and wait for the girls to show up again. The whole store was like a pinball machine and I didn't know which tunnel they'd come out of. After a while they come around out of the far aisle, around the light bulbs, records at discount of the Caribbean Six or Tony Martin Sings or some such gunk you wonder they waste the wax on, sixpacks of candy bars, and plastic toys done up in cellophane that fall apart when a kid looks at them anyway. Around they come, Queenie still leading the way, and holding a little gray jar in

her hand. Slots Three through Seven are unmanned and I could see her wondering between Stokes and me, but Stokesie with his usual luck draws an old party in baggy gray pants who stumbles up with four giant cans of pineapple juice (what do these bums *do* with all that pineapple juice? I've often asked myself) so the girls come to me. Queenie puts down the jar and I take it into my fingers icy cold. Kingfish Fancy Herring Snacks in Pure Sour Cream: 49¢. Now her hands are empty, not a ring or a bracelet, bare as God made them, and I wonder where the money's coming from. Still with that prim look she lifts a folded dollar bill out of the hollow at the center of her nubbled pink top. The jar went heavy in my hand. Really, I thought that was so cute.

Then everybody's luck begins to run out. Lengel comes in from haggling 13 with a truck full of cabbages on the lot and is about to scuttle into that door marked MANAGER behind which he hides all day when the girls touch his eye. Lengel's pretty dreary, teaches Sunday school and the rest, but he doesn't miss that much. He comes over and says, "Girls, this isn't the beach."

Queenie blushes, though maybe it's just a brush of sunburn I was notic- 14 ing for the first time, now that she was so close. "My mother asked me to pick up a jar of herring snacks." Her voice kind of startled me, the way voices do when you see the people first, coming out so flat and dumb yet kind of tony, too, the way it ticked over "pick up" and "snacks." All of a sudden I slid right down her voice into her living room. Her father and the other men were standing around in ice-cream coats and bow ties and the women were in sandals picking up herring snacks on toothpicks off a big glass plate and they were all holding drinks the color of water with olives and sprigs of mint in them. When my parents have somebody over they get lemonade and if it's a real racy affair Schlitz in tall glasses with "They'll Do It Every Time" cartoons stencilled on.

"That's all right," Lengel said. "But this isn't the beach." His repeating 15 this struck me as funny, as if it had just occurred to him, and he had been thinking all these years the A & P was a great big sand dune and he was the head lifeguard. He didn't like my smiling — as I say he doesn't miss much — but he concentrates on giving the girls that sad Sunday-school-superintendent stare.

Queenie's blush is no sunburn now, and the plump one in plaid, that I 16 liked better from the back — a really sweet can — pipes up, "We weren't doing any shopping. We just came in for the one thing."

"That makes no difference," Lengel tells her, and I could see from the 17 way his eyes went that he hadn't noticed she was wearing a two-piece before. "We want you decently dressed when you come in here."

"We *are* decent," Queenie says suddenly, her lower lip pushing, getting 18 sore now that she remembers her place, a place from which the crowd that runs the A & P must look pretty crummy. Fancy Herring Snacks flashed in her very blue eyes.

"Girls, I don't want to argue with you. After this come in here with your   19
shoulders covered. It's our policy." He turns his back. That's policy for you.
Policy is what the kingpins want. What the others want is juvenile delin-
quency.

All this while, the customers had been showing up with their carts but,   20
you know, sheep, seeing a scene, they had all bunched up on Stokesie, who
shook open a paper bag as gently as peeling a peach, not wanting to miss a
word. I could feel in the silence everybody getting nervous, most of all
Lengel, who asks me, "Sammy, have you rung up their purchase?"

I thought and said "No" but it wasn't about that I was thinking. I go   21
through the punches, 4, 9, GROC, TOT — it's more complicated than you
think, and after you do it often enough, it begins to make a little song,
that you hear words to, in my case "Hello (*bing*) there, you (*gung*) hap-py
pee-pul (*splat*)!" — the *splat* being the drawer flying out. I uncrease the bill,
tenderly as you may imagine, it just having come from between the two
smoothest scoops of vanilla I had ever known were there, and pass a half
and a penny into her narrow pink palm, and nestle the herrings in a bag
and twist its neck and hand it over, all the time thinking.

The girls, and who'd blame them, are in a hurry to get out, so I say "I   22
quit" to Lengel enough for them to hear, hoping they'll stop and watch me,
their unsuspected hero. They keep right on going, into the electric eye; the
door flies open and they flicker across the lot to their car, Queenie and
Plaid and Big Tall Goony-Goony (not that as raw material she was so bad),
leaving me with Lengel and a kink in his eyebrow.

"Did you say something, Sammy?"   23

"I said I quit."   24

"I thought you did."   25

"You didn't have to embarrass them."   26

"It was they who were embarrassing us."   27

I started to say something that came out "Fiddle-de-doo." It's a saying of   28
my grandmother's, and I know she would have been pleased.

"I don't think you know what you're saying," Lengel said.   29

"I know you don't," I said. "But I do." I pull the bow at the back of my   30
apron and start shrugging it off my shoulders. A couple customers that had
been heading for my slot begin to knock against each other, like scared pigs
in a chute.

Lengel sighs and begins to look very patient and old and gray. He's been   31
a friend of my parents for years. "Sammy, you don't want to do this to your
Mom and Dad," he tells me. It's true, I don't. But it seems to me that once
you begin a gesture it's fatal not to go through with it. I fold the apron,
"Sammy" stitched in red on the pocket, and put it on the counter, and
drop the bow tie on top of it. The bow tie is theirs, if you've ever wondered.
"You'll feel this for the rest of your life," Lengel says, and I know that's true,
too, but remembering how he made that pretty girl blush makes me so
scrunchy inside I punch the No Sale tab and the machine whirs "pee-pul"

and the drawer splats out. One advantage to this scene taking place in summer, I can follow this up with a clean exit, there's no fumbling around getting your coat and galoshes, I just saunter into the electric eye in my white shirt that my mother ironed the night before, and the door heaves itself open, and outside the sunshine is skating around on the asphalt.

I look around for my girls, but they're gone, of course. There wasn't anybody but some young married screaming with her children about some candy they didn't get by the door of a powder-blue Falcon station wagon. Looking back in the big windows, over the bags of peat moss and aluminum lawn furniture stacked on the pavement, I could see Lengel in my place in the slot, checking the sheep through. His face was dark gray and his back stiff, as if he'd just had an injection of iron, and my stomach kind of fell as I felt how hard the world was going to be to me hereafter.   32

Analyzing This Selection

1. Compare how Sammy looked at the girls with how the other three men looked at them. How do the looks reflect their characters?

2. **THE WRITER'S METHOD**   Did the girls enter the store to buy herring snacks or for another reason? Find details to support your interpretation.

3. What has Sammy done that makes him fear the world will be hard on him? Do you think it will?

Analyzing Connections

4. Sammy and young Soto (see "Black Hair," p. 344) learn about the world from their unimportant jobs. Do they receive similar or contrasting kinds of instruction? How do the jobs affect their outlooks?

Analyzing by Writing

5. Sammy observes, "Policy is what the kingpins want." Examine the widespread use of terms such as "our policy," "company policy," "school policy." What advantages are gained by using the term? What disadvantages arise for all parties? Explain its purpose and effects in interactive situations.

Peter Schwendener

REFLECTIONS OF
A BOOKSTORE TYPE

PETER SCHWENDENER (b. 1957) graduated from Northwestern University.
He has worked as a staff writer for *Chicago Reader* and as a jazz pianist.
His essays and reviews have appeared in *TriQuarterly*, the *New Criterion*,
and the *American Scholar*, where this essay was printed in 1995.

In 1936, George Orwell wrote an essay entitled "Bookshop Memories," 1
which was a bitter account of a job he had held in a used bookstore. The
thing he seems to have disliked the most was the clientele, who he
arranged in a kind of hierarchy of loathsomeness. At the top are "unmis-
takable paranoiacs," also described as "not quite certifiable lunatics." Below
are "the decayed person smelling of old breadcrusts," customers who order
books without intending to purchase them, "the dear old lady who 'wants a
book for an invalid,'" the customer who wants a certain book but knows
nothing about it other than that it is red, and on and on, until one realizes
that what Orwell hated was waiting on people, period. Anyone who has
worked in a bookstore, new or used, large or small, will recognize the reality of what he is talking about.

I have been working for about nine months in a large bookstore in 2
Evanston, Illinois, a Barnes & Noble superstore, to be exact. Although I
have not researched the topic, I am aware that the superstore concept is
still somewhat avant-garde, at least as far as traditionally small businesses
such as bookstores are concerned. Our store is extremely large, easily as
large as a supermarket, and it intimidated me the first time I laid eyes on
it. It takes up two stories of a large building in the middle of downtown
Evanston and is probably as much a microcosm of the town as a store
could be. It is very far from the bookshop Orwell describes, yet much of
what Orwell writes fits it exactly.

According to Orwell, "a bookseller lives on his windows"; my store is 3
window-dominated, and looks like an oasis of leisure and enjoyment, especially at night. Orwell calls bookselling "a humane trade which is not
capable of being vulgarized beyond a certain point." True: my store sells
pornography, self-help books, books on how to "write that novel," stupid
and possibly even degrading children's books, and yet these books, or rather

these book-shaped objects ("things in book's clothing," as Charles Lamb calls them) do not give the store its tone. The tone is given by the unbought, rarely browsed complete set of Trollope's novels, the surprisingly large philosophy section, and other parts of the store that are bad economic risks, though perhaps less so than they would be in a non-college town. As long as only a few adult books, in the pre-1970s meaning of the word *adult*, are on the premises, the vulgarization to which Orwell refers cannot take hold.

The position I hold, along with several other people, is that of "book- 4 seller," which means "sales clerk." I walk around the store, making myself a moving target for customers with vague requests, take turns running one of the six cash registers (Orwell would be amazed at the size of our operation), station myself at the always-busy information desk, or engage in the activity known to all booksellers as "reshelve," as in (spoken by a supervisor), "There's a pile of reshelve over in Self-Help. Could you take care of it?" Easily the worst thing about the job is reshelving the books and magazines that customers have looked at and abandoned miles away from where they belong. Yet even with "reshelve" (the word is both a verb and a noun) one notices interesting things.

Savage browsing occurs in the Travel section, where customers, sick of 5 living where they live, rifle through seven or eight books on Colorado or Guam and leave them in piles. The one section I don't know much about is Children's, which is anachronistically taken care of by female booksellers, all of whom, even more anachronistically, seem to enjoy it, at least as much as anyone can enjoy a low-paying job. Some sections are never messed up by customers: Theater and Drama, consisting mostly of plays and books about acting and directing, attracts almost no one, probably because actors, in common with most performing artists, don't enjoy reading, and directing and acting are the last things one learns to do by reading books. Other sections that are chronically unvisited, kept on the premises merely to bolster our claim to have everything, are Linguistics and, I fear, Poetry, though we have a rather good poetry section.

The fact that "reshelve" is the worst thing about the job says some- 6 thing — namely, that it is far from a bad job. The conventional wisdom, in fact, is that as far as retail work goes, working in a bookstore is as good as it gets. The job depresses me, when it does, simply because it pays barely enough to live on, but I can suffer that, for now at least.

There is a bookstore type, and I am afraid I am of that type. I like being 7 around books, even crappy ones, I'm not physically threatening, and waiting on customers doesn't upset me as much as it seems to have upset Orwell. The job asks almost nothing of me other than that I be there on time. What is more, the management does not mind if one browses as one works, as long as blatant loafing is avoided. One learns the difference between improving one's product knowledge and lounging at the information desk with a cup of coffee and a huge art book.

Our store has a problem with security. There is, I am told, a fair amount   8
of theft, or attempted theft, and yet the store has its hands tied as far as
cracking down is concerned. A bookstore's primary association is with
friendliness and leisure, and the presence of armed security guards, or security guards period, does not conduce to either. A small, I thought rather
fierce-looking, man who didn't carry a gun was sent by one security agency,
but he was eventually let go because the management didn't think he
looked formidable enough. He was succeeded by two uniformed men with
huge revolvers at their sides, as if they were prepared for Scorcese-like car-
nage in the Self-Help section. They are gone now, and a large individual
without visible weaponry makes himself conspicuous among the shelves.
Books are, unfortunately for us, not a bad thing to steal: a pile of fresh best-
sellers, or new paperbacks, are apparently easy to unload. Many books are
attractive, and I can see someone with no interest in reading stealing a pile
just because of the way they look.

One thing taboo in bookselling is to let customers know what you think   9
of their purchases. The problem arises occasionally at the cash register. For
the most part, maintaining impassive features in the face of curious (or
worse) purchases is not hard. Once, someone materialized at the register
with three self-help books and a magazine. The books all had gentle titles
like *Managing Your Anger* or *Towards Serenity*, and the magazine was *Modern Handgun*. The sale went off without the hint of a grimace on my part.
A well-known Chicago painter came in one evening with a female companion and bought her a book entitled *How to Write Erotica*. An older
woman who seemed at, or near, the verge of mental collapse bought the
complete, or near-complete works of the poet John Ashbery (did she know
what she was doing?). There is a book among our stock entitled *Subway
Art* that is basically a how-to for graffiti artists. Occasionally a distracted
youth asks for it, but it is never on hand because, as soon as we order it,
it is immediately stolen. One evening a worried-looking mother and her
leather-jacketed teenage son came to the register with two or three books
on punk rock, one I believe a biography of the singer Johnny Rotten. The
weary mother, breaking out her checkbook, could not forbear to ask her
son, "Are you *sure* this was approved as a project?" "I don't care if it was or
not," the boy said with surprising hatred, or something near it. "You'll reim-
burse me when we get home," she said, handing me the check.

Books are not exactly luxuries, but neither are they necessities. They are   10
inveterately connected, as even Orwell seems to grasp, with pleasure. There
is something gratuitous about them, even the ones that look drenched in boring or forbidding practicality such as electronics manuals and used-car
price guides (we sell both). People are off their guard in a bookstore as they
are not in a clothing or a toy store, which makes it unfair, if one is the typically overeducated bookstore employee, to make fun of what they buy.

Many of our customers take an undisguised pleasure in spending   11
money, as if the fact that books are involved sanctifies the lack of prudence.

A bearded man came into the store one night and collected a huge pile of books on the theme of self-betterment: three or four oily self-help books, a couple of neo-pagan treatises from the New Age section, and (I'm not sure what his reasoning was) two or three books on how to write fiction. It was a huge tab, but he looked extremely happy, on the verge of some kind of transformation. The next evening he reappeared to return virtually all the books. Fortunately for him, our return policy is liberal in the extreme. Just buying the books had given him a lift, maybe saved him from doing something foolish.

Orwell comments on the different buying habits of men and women.   12
"Roughly speaking," he writes, "what one might call the *average* novel — the ordinary, good-bad, Galsworthy-and-water stuff which is the norm of the English novel — seems to exist only for women. Men read either the novels it is possible to respect, or detective stories." Today it can only safely be said that men buy magazines such as *Modern Handgun* and fishing magazines such as *Bassin'*, while women buy novels of all kinds. Best-sellers are all unisex in their audience. The real problem in updating Orwell's division of male and female purchases is the overwhelmingly large number of young people that increasingly seem to make up the book-buying public. The books, or in corporate terms the "product," has mutated, and is still mutating, to match the volatile tastes of the young.

There is a substantial category of books called "graphic novels," which   13
are, simply, comic books that feature Batman and Superman but cost around $12.95 apiece. Their entitlement to the honorific term "novel" is gravely in doubt, but some of them are attractive, and they are taken very seriously, and not just by adolescents. Many books in the Children's section contain, on their covers or elsewhere, buzzers, tiny music boxes, bells, and other encumbrances that make them amphibious, neither book nor toy but something indeterminate (there is a small, heavily picked over section in Children's called Classics, containing *Alice in Wonderland*, A. A. Milne, and the rest). Many of the titles in Self-Help are "workbooks," as in the *Depression Workbook*, a more or less graded series of exercises (I believe the pages tear out) designed to lead the reader, or purchaser, out of his or her despair.

According to a recent article in the *New York Times*, the physical iden-   14
tity of books is in deep flux, with publishers experimenting with various unconventional shapes: novels, for example, that are slightly larger than cigarette packs (Douglas Coupland's short-story collection *Life After God* is an example). A number of novels pitched to young people (the so-called members of Generation X, people in their twenties) are large colorful squares, eerily reminiscent of record albums. Only mysteries and detective stories are still issued in what might be called the traditional book shape, the quiet rectangle that looks as if it is made to be actually read as opposed to merely owned or looked at.

It is now obligatory for a bookstore to contain a café, and ours contains   15
a sizable one on the second floor. I have noticed that, while all kinds of

people come into the store, not all kinds linger in the café, whose prices are fairly steep. The café is given over mostly to older people, students who seem to be actually studying, and quiet couples. The store's extreme permissiveness is apparent in its café policy. Cups of foaming coffee, donuts, butter-drenched scones, and muffins can be consumed anywhere in the store, among the opulent art books, while reading unpurchased novels, or dreaming over travel books. If I rack my brains I cannot really think of anything our customers are not, in principle, allowed to do. Generally, the policy of maintaining the store as a kind of moral free zone seems to pay off. Customers do not abuse the policy except in one area, that of the magazines. They swarm over the magazine racks on the first floor and leave their contents in shocking heaps, fashion magazines sprawling in V-shapes, computer magazines gutted for the free software they often contain, copies even of rational periodicals such as the *Economist* flipped through and thrown on the floor.

16   The bookstore is haunted, and even shaped, by some of the prevailing issues of the day. Chief among these is the gap, which can be raged at or philosophized about but not wished away, between high and low culture. Anyone who thinks that this gap is frivolous should work in a bookstore. A rather accomplished artist has been retained by Barnes & Noble to furnish its stores with large caricatures of Shakespeare (the only writer with his own section, though Virginia Woolf commands something close to her own in fiction), George Bernard Shaw, and others, as well as popular deities such as John Grisham, James Michener, and Sue Grafton. From where I sit, John Grisham is the most powerfully popular writer in America, meaning that his fans seem the most intelligently devoted; the fans of other blockbuster novelists such as Tom Clancy seem to buy his huge dreary volumes out of something like duty. Grisham is regarded by the bookselling industry as a force of nature. I have been on the floor when shipments of bestsellers have arrived, and can testify to the almost numinous power that radiates from a V-cart (a rolling device used to move two or three dozen books) full of fresh copies of a Grisham novel.

17   Our store has a curiously large section entitled Literary Theory that holds the works of deconstructionists, New Historicists, Reader Response Theorists, and other academic scrutinizers of texts. I don't think that this section is there simply for prestige; it is there because these books sell, and not just to academics. An utterly unpretentious woman asked me for a book on postmodernism, and she wasn't a student (I asked). It can now be said that deconstruction, though to a limited extent, is genuinely popular. We have, I think, the complete works of Paul de Man, and multiple copies of the complete works of Jacques Derrida, not to mention much of the latest scholarship connected with these and related writers. The increasingly mainstream profile of deconstruction came to mind as a possible paranoid hypothesis when I recently tried to order a book critical (though hardly dismissive) of the movement, David Lehmann's highly readable *Signs of the*

Times, which offers a chronicle of the political misbehavior (among other things) of the late Paul de Man: it is unaccountably out of print.

As an ex-graduate student (surprise, surprise), I am both drawn to and depressed by the works of literary theory and I seek diversion in other sections. There is one book, in the section ambiguously designated Nature, that can always be counted on to brighten my mood after too much time in the theory section. It is a large collection of photographs entitled *Dangerous Aquatic Animals,* and it features not only pictures of killer whales, sharks, jellyfish, piranhas, and other bad actors of the sea, but photographs — not too gross, but gross enough — of the damage they have done to human beings (no decapitated scuba divers, just the anonymous swollen hands of someone who tried to embrace a toxic crustacean, etc.). The thing about the book is its dust jacket, which has been reduced to near tatters by, I like to think, myriads of ten-year-olds who have ritually gathered after school to gape at it ("Cool! Look at that guy!" "Come on, let me see it! Quit hogging it!"). Along with Woodworking perhaps, the Nature section is the most innocent in the store, a refuge from the rows of Tom Clancy novels and treatises of Derrida. I hope it doesn't sound like straining after paradox to observe how much Derrida and Clancy have in common: their books tend alike to strand the reader at some point infinitely removed from human thought and experience.

We have a very high turnover among the employees. I have been at the store longer than most of the other booksellers, and I have not been there that long. We hired a lot of part-timers to work over the Christmas holidays, and most of them were let go, some to their dismay, after the rush subsided. The store is fairly brusque in its hiring and, I fear, in its firing, policies. As with security, the matter of hiring and firing is interestingly complicated by the fact that books, meaning culture, meaning enlightenment, meaning humanism, are what we trade in. As a matter of fact, most of the employees do seem to have an unforced respect for books as more than saleable objects; otherwise they wouldn't work here. It is, however, a business, not a school or a church. The head office in New York recently sent out a Statement of Purpose that was posted in the employee lounges of Barnes & Noble stores around the country. It said that the company's ambition was to be the best retail store regardless of its product, but that because "our product happens to be books" we are obliged to make sure that our business practices "live up to the promise and idealism of the volumes that line our shelves."

Before one starts snickering at this, it is worth noting how indissoluble the tie between books and "idealism" (however understood) is. The Barnes & Noble CEO is, in his way, giving a bland rephrasing to the belief of Matthew Arnold, I. A. Richards, and others (here I draw triumphantly on my graduate school experience) that literature, or humanistic learning, is somehow capable of saving us. This is a belief that I do not share but nonetheless respect. Now for the snickering: our stock includes, besides

How to Write Erotica, such idealism-soaked productions as *Transactional Analysis for Toddlers*, *The Dark Side of Your Inner Child*, and my nominee for the most pathos-drenched of our titles, *Seven Weeks to a Settled Stomach*. The proper response to the CEO's mandate that we live up to the books we sell was made by one of my co-workers: "I'm willing, as long as the company accepts legal responsibility."

It goes without saying that no one at the store, with the exception of the 21 boss and one or two of the assistant managers, regards it as a real job. I fell into conversation with an erudite customer one night, a retired history professor, and, without any obvious intention of offending me, he referred to working in a bookstore such as ours as a "McJob." If one presses further, into the dark heart of the average bookstore employee, one discovers that the only thing worthy of being called a job is something in, or vaguely related to, the arts. With its staggeringly large collection of art books, its substantial section devoted to Writing and Publishing, and the huge drawings of Oscar Wilde and Virginia Woolf staring down at everyone, the store itself is a kind of massive jibe at the fundamental unseriousness of everything that is not the arts. (I forgot to mention something that didn't bother me at all for the first few months but has now become maddening, the relentless twittering of classical music over the loudspeakers.) To subject oneself to such an art-saturated atmosphere once or twice a week is blissful, but to make it one's daily haunt is risking satiety. Marxist analysts of the corruption of culture under late capitalism would enjoy directing bitter commentary at the store, though they would have to step lightly around the fact that books by Marxists bitterly denouncing enterprises such as Barnes & Noble's make up the better part of our Sociology section.

Bookselling — at least at superstores such as ours that, like the gates of 22 hell, are open almost all the time (9:00 A.M. to 11:00 P.M. every day except Christmas) and accordingly need a large staff — is the ideal job for people who don't want to sleep in the streets but find most ways of earning money not to their liking. I fear that bookselling is for people who are somewhat work-shy. Let me revise that to people who are pathologically averse to exertion of most kinds. There is serious responsibility at our store, but it is monopolized by the managers, mostly by the general manager, a woman in our case, who has to answer to the district supervisor, and by the folks in Receiving, who undoubtedly, and justly, regard the booksellers as glorified wastrels.

Below the level of management there is not much to do. Books sell 23 themselves. In this, books differ from most merchandise. Nonetheless, I have noticed that, despite the extreme unstrenuousness of my job, not everyone can do it. One has to be courteous to customers without inducing in oneself overmastering feelings of servility. To grovel is not the way to ingratiate yourself, and to blow up at a customer, even if he insults you (it happens, it happens) is the only sure way to be fired immediately. When a putative book buyer whom I have never seen before abruptly calls me by my first name (we wear name tags), I begin, dangerously, wondering if sleeping on the streets is as bad as it seems.

What one observes in many booksellers, myself very much included, is an interest in, yes, the arts combined with a disinclination to align oneself with the forces of hard-core bohemia, the wearers of black clothing who swarm in cafés and have earned from an acquaintance of mine the name "art nuns." I have known many bohemians, and, contrary to what some may think, they often work, but not at bookstores, which are incurably square places, really: they earn whatever money they need at copy stores, as waiters and waitresses, or as bartenders. Orwell calls bookselling "an unhealthy life," but, as low-paying work goes, it is far from life-threatening. I do not find it impossible to leave work and read for a few hours, hang out with friends, and, in short, live. I don't love the job, but that is because I find the idea of work itself a kind of antidote to desire. The bouts of shame I endure at having to wear a tie and a name tag are not incapacitating. I cannot suppress the hope that I will one day leave the store, and I feel sure that if this hope is realized it will not occasion loud weeping on my employer's part.

Analyzing This Selection

1. How do book superstores differ in resources and atmosphere from other bookshops? What are Schwendener's views toward the differences?

2. Why do most employees and customers consider bookselling as not "a real job" (para. 21)? How does it differ from other retail sales jobs?

3. **THE WRITER'S METHOD** Why, if at all, is Schwendener "afraid" that he is "a bookstore type" (para. 7)? What characteristics does he attribute to booksellers? Does he minimize or emphasize his typical characteristics?

Analyzing Connections

4. Schwendener doesn't worry about Nikki Giovanni's concern in the Insights on page 329. How does he keep his "sanity"? Whose view of work do you share?

Analyzing by Writing

5. You have probably held a McJob — perhaps as a McLifeguard, McCoach, or McWaiter. Write an essay of reflections or memories about your work experience. Examine matters such as the clientele, workplace, hierarchy, satisfactions, and dissatisfactions. Consider similarities and differences between you and others who work there. Write interesting reflections about matters that may or may not have been interesting at the time. In either case, as you think about them, they can gain significance.

Virginia Woolf

PROFESSIONS FOR WOMEN

Virginia Woolf (1882–1941) was an important British novelist noted for her emphasis on the subjective meaning of events rather than the outward circumstances of plot and appearance. Her novels include *Mrs. Dalloway* (1925) and *To the Lighthouse* (1927). Born into a distinguished literary family, she was educated at home and began her writing career as a book reviewer for the London *Times Literary Supplement*. With her husband she lived among a group of artists and intellectuals known as the Bloomsbury group — a group that included E. M. Forster, John Maynard Keynes, Bertrand Russell, and Lytton Strachey. She spoke out consistently for freedom and equality for women in works such as *A Room of One's Own* (1929) and the following address to the Women's Service League. Her essays are collected in four volumes of *Collected Essays* (1967).

When your secretary invited me to come here, she told me that your   1
Society is concerned with the employment of women and she suggested that I might tell you something about my own professional experiences. It is true I am a woman; it is true I am employed; but what professional experiences have I had? It is difficult to say. My profession is literature; and in that profession there are fewer experiences for women than in any other, with the exception of the stage — fewer, I mean, that are peculiar to women. For the road was cut many years ago — by Fanny Burney, by Aphra Behn, by Harriet Martineau, by Jane Austen, by George Eliot[1] — many famous women, and many more unknown and forgotten, have been before me, making the path smooth, and regulating my steps. Thus, when I came to write, there were very few material obstacles in my way. Writing was a reputable and harmless occupation. The family peace was not broken by the scratching of a pen. No demand was made upon the family purse. For ten and sixpence one can buy paper enough to write all the plays of Shakespeare — if one has a mind that way. Pianos and models, Paris, Vienna and Berlin, masters and mistresses, are not needed by a writer. The cheapness of writing paper is, of course, the reason why women have succeeded as writers before they succeeded in the other professions.

[1]*Fanny Burney...George Eliot* British women novelists of the eighteenth and nineteenth centuries. [Editor's note.]

But to tell you my story — it is a simple one. You have only got to figure 2
to yourselves a girl in a bedroom with a pen in her hand. She had only to
move that pen from left to right — from ten o'clock to one. Then it
occurred to her to do what is simple and cheap enough after all — to slip a
few of those pages into an envelope, fix a penny stamp in the corner, and
drop the envelope into the red box at the corner. It was thus that I became
a journalist; and my effort was rewarded on the first day of the following
month — a very glorious day it was for me — by a letter from an editor containing a check for one pound ten shillings and sixpence. But to show you
how little I deserve to be called a professional woman, how little I know
of the struggles and difficulties of such lives, I have to admit that instead of
spending that sum upon bread and butter, rent, shoes and stockings, or
butcher's bills, I went out and bought a cat — a beautiful cat, a Persian cat,
which very soon involved me in bitter disputes with my neighbors.

What could be easier than to write articles and to buy Persian cats with 3
the profits? But wait a moment. Articles have to be about something. Mine,
I seem to remember, was about a novel by a famous man. And while I was
writing this review I discovered that if I were going to review books I should
need to do battle with a certain phantom. And the phantom was a woman,
and when I came to know her better I called her after the heroine of a
famous poem, The Angel in the House. It was she who used to come between me and my paper when I was writing reviews. It was she who bothered me and wasted my time and so tormented me that at last I killed her.
You who come of a younger and happier generation may not have heard of
her — you may not know what I mean by the Angel in the House. I will
describe her as shortly as I can. She was intensely sympathetic. She was
immensely charming. She was utterly unselfish. She excelled in the difficult arts of family life. She sacrificed herself daily. If there was chicken,
she took the leg; if there was a draught, she sat in it — in short she was so
constituted that she never had a mind or a wish of her own, but preferred
to sympathize always with the minds and wishes of others. Above all — I
need not say it — she was pure. Her purity was supposed to be her chief
beauty — her blushes, her great grace. In those days — the last of Queen
Victoria — every house had its Angel. And when I came to write I encountered her with the very first words. The shadow of her wings fell on my
page; I heard the rustling of her skirts in the room. Directly, that is to say,
I took my pen in hand to review that novel by a famous man, she slipped
behind me and whispered: "My dear, you are a young woman. You are
writing about a book that has been written by a man. Be sympathetic; be
tender; flatter; deceive; use all the arts and wiles of our sex. Never let anybody guess that you have a mind of your own. Above all, be pure." And she
made as if to guide my pen. I now record the one act for which I take some
credit to myself, though the credit rightly belongs to some excellent ancestors of mine who left me a certain sum of money — shall we say five hundred pounds a year? — so that it was not necessary for me to depend solely

on charm for my living. I turned upon her and caught her by the throat. I did my best to kill her. My excuse, if I were to be had up in a court of law, would be that I acted in self-defense. Had I not killed her she would have killed me. She would have plucked the heart out of my writing. For, as I found, directly I put pen to paper, you cannot review even a novel without having a mind of your own, without expressing what you think to be the truth about human relations, morality, sex. And all these questions, according to the Angel in the House, cannot be dealt with freely and openly by women; they must charm, they must conciliate, they must — to put it bluntly — tell lies if they are to succeed. Thus, whenever I felt the shadow of her wing or the radiance of her halo upon my page, I took up the inkpot and flung it at her. She died hard. Her fictitious nature was of great assistance to her. It is far harder to kill a phantom than a reality. She was always creeping back when I thought I had despatched her. Though I flatter myself that I killed her in the end, the struggle was severe; it took much time that had better have been spent upon learning Greek grammar; or in roaming the world in search of adventures. But it was a real experience; it was an experience that was bound to befall all women writers at that time. Killing the Angel in the House was part of the occupation of a woman writer.

But to continue my story. The Angel was dead; what then remained? 4
You may say that what remained was a simple and common object — a young woman in a bedroom with an inkpot. In other words, now that she had rid herself of falsehood, that young woman had only to be herself. Ah, but what is "herself"? I mean, what is a woman? I assure you, I do not know. I do not believe that you know. I do not believe that anybody can know until she has expressed herself in all the arts and professions open to human skill. That indeed is one of the reasons why I have come here — out of respect for you, who are in process of showing us by your experiment what a woman is, who are in process of providing us, by your failures and successes, with that extremely important piece of information.

But to continue the story of my professional experiences. I made one 5
pound ten and six by my first review; and I bought a Persian cat with the proceeds. Then I grew ambitious. A Persian cat is all very well, I said; but a Persian cat is not enough. I must have a motor car. And it was thus that I became a novelist — for it is a very strange thing that people will give you a motor car if you will tell them a story. It is a still stranger thing that there is nothing so delightful in the world as telling stories. It is far pleasanter than writing reviews of famous novels. And yet, if I am to obey your secretary and tell you my professional experiences as a novelist, I must tell you about a very strange experience that befell me as a novelist. And to understand it you must try first to imagine a novelist's state of mind. I hope I am not giving away professional secrets if I say that a novelist's chief desire is to be as unconscious as possible. He has to induce in himself a state of perpetual lethargy. He wants life to proceed with the utmost quiet and regu-

larity. He wants to see the same faces, to read the same books, to do the same things day after day, month after month, while he is writing, so that nothing may break the illusion in which he is living — so that nothing may disturb or disquiet the mysterious nosings about, feelings round, darts, dashes, and sudden discoveries of that very shy and illusive spirit, the imagination. I suspect that this state is the same both for men and women. Be that as it may, I want you to imagine me writing a novel in a state of trance. I want you to figure to yourselves a girl sitting with a pen in her hand, which for minutes, and indeed for hours, she never dips into the inkpot. The image that comes to my mind when I think of this girl is the image of a fisherman lying sunk in dreams on the verge of a deep lake with a rod held out over the water. She was letting her imagination sweep unchecked round every rock and cranny of the world that lies submerged in the depths of our unconscious being. Now came the experience, the experience that I believe to be far commoner with women writers than with men. The line raced through the girl's fingers. Her imagination had rushed away. It had sought the pools, the depths, the dark places where the largest fish slumber. And then there was a smash. There was an explosion. There was foam and confusion. The imagination had dashed itself against something hard. The girl was roused from her dream. She was indeed in a state of the most acute and difficult distress. To speak without figure she had thought of something, something about the body, about the passions which it was unfitting for her as a woman to say. Men, her reason told her, would be shocked. The consciousness of what men will say of a woman who speaks the truth about her passions had roused her from her artist's state of unconsciousness. She could write no more. The trance was over. Her imagination could work no longer. This I believe to be a very common experience with women writers — they are impeded by the extreme conventionality of the other sex. For though men sensibly allow themselves great freedom in these respects, I doubt that they realize or can control the extreme severity with which they condemn such freedom in women.

These then were two very genuine experiences of my own. These were   6
two of the adventures of my professional life. The first — killing the Angel in the House — I think I solved. She died. But the second, telling the truth about my own experiences as a body, I do not think I solved. I doubt that any woman has solved it yet. The obstacles against her are still immensely powerful — and yet they are very difficult to define. Outwardly, what is simpler than to write books? Outwardly, what obstacles are there for a woman rather than for a man? Inwardly, I think, the case is very different; she has still many ghosts to fight, many prejudices to overcome. Indeed it will be a long time still, I think, before a woman can sit down to write a book without finding a phantom to be slain, a rock to be dashed against. And if this is so in literature, the freest of all professions for women, how is it in the new professions which you are now for the first time entering?

Those are the questions that I should like, had I time, to ask you. And   7
indeed, if I have laid stress upon these professional experiences of mine, it
is because I believe that they are, though in different forms, yours also.
Even when the path is nominally open — when there is nothing to prevent
a woman from being a doctor, a lawyer, a civil servant — there are many
phantoms and obstacles, as I believe, looming in her way. To discuss and
define them is I think of great value and importance; for thus only can the
labor be shared, the difficulties be solved. But besides this, it is necessary
also to discuss the ends and the aims for which we are fighting, for which
we are doing battle with these formidable obstacles. Those aims cannot be
taken for granted; they must be perpetually questioned and examined. The
whole position, as I see it — here in this hall surrounded by women practicing for the first time in history I know not how many different professions — is one of extraordinary interest and importance. You have won
rooms of your own in the house hitherto exclusively owned by men. You
are able, though not without great labor and effort, to pay the rent. You are
earning your five hundred pounds a year. But this freedom is only a beginning; the room is your own, but it is still bare. It has to be furnished; it has
to be decorated; it has to be shared. How are you going to furnish it, how
are you going to decorate it? With whom are you going to share it, and
upon what terms? These, I think, are questions of the utmost importance
and interest. For the first time in history you are able to ask them; for the
first time you are able to decide for yourselves what the answers should be.
Willingly would I stay and discuss those questions and answers — but not
tonight. My time is up; and I must cease.

Analyzing This Selection

1. **THE WRITER'S METHOD**   In the first two paragraphs, what relation
   does Woolf establish with her audience? What details make her appear
   ingratiating? condescending? earnest?

2. Does the Angel in the House still exist? What has changed, and what
   remains the same, in current expectations of women?

3. Does Woolf assume that men writers encounter no difficulties or conflicts in
   thinking independently and expressing themselves? Is Woolf a female sexist
   in some of her observations?

4. What relationships between men and women are implied in Woolf's many
   references to women in a house and a room? What changes in the future
   are suggested by the metaphorical use of "house" in the final paragraph?

Analyzing Connections

5. How does Woolf's purpose as a lecturer differ from George Steiner's (see
   "Books and the End of Literature," p. 307)? Whose tone do you think is
   more effective for the lecture's purpose?

Analyzing by Writing

6. Should young men and women ever be educated separately for part of their lives? At what age can it do the most good or the most harm to change or reinforce gender roles through separate schools or separate classes? Draw on any of your relevant experiences in single-sex associations such as scouting, sports, clubs, and being with just "the boys" or "the girls." Consider what it has meant to you to have these associations, and how they might have been more beneficial, or less limiting, than they were.

Francine D'Amico

WOMEN WARRIORS

Francine D'Amico received her Ph.D. from Cornell University and teaches political science at the State University of New York at Cortland. She has contributed articles to journals and to anthologies such as *Wives and Warriors: Women and the Military in the U.S. and Canada* (1997). The following essay is excerpted from her chapter in *The Women and War Reader* (1998).

War has been perceived as men's domain, a masculine endeavor for which women may serve as victim, spectator, or prize....The image of the woman warrior has been viewed as distressing, intriguing, and compelling. Antifeminists decry the image as unnatural and warn us that women's increased military participation destroys both the family and the fabric of civil society while also impairing military efficiency. Their argument assumes inherent and natural gender differences.

Radical feminists see the image of the woman warrior as representing women's potential for power, as lingering evidence of an ancient matriarchy or woman-centered and woman-governed society. They embrace the image as a symbol of solidarity and sisterhood, and argue for a separatist philosophy of empowerment. Some see military means as necessary for liberating and defending women from patriarchy. In this view, as with the antifeminists, gender differences are seen as natural and immutable, and as barriers to gender equality within any community. But while antifeminists would maintain the current gender hierarchy, radical feminists would either reverse it or disengage from it via separation.

In contrast, another group of feminists touts the image of the woman warrior as evidence of women's equality with men: "See, we can do it, too." This "me-too" variety of liberal or equal rights feminism argues that women may prove their worth, may earn equality, by assuming social roles ascribed to men. In this view, the goal of women's militarization is women's equality, which they define as sameness with men. Some liberal feminists also argue that women's entry into the military will gradually transform it into a less hierarchical, more democratic and egalitarian social institution.

A third group of feminists warns us of the dangers of the woman warrior image: it draws from a "warrior mystique," promoting martial and masculine values rather than redefining gender-based social values and hierarchical power structures. These critical feminists argue that the woman warrior image subjects women to greater manipulation by those controlling military institutions, thus allowing women to be militarized but not empowered. Thus, women's militarization provides no substantive "feminization" of the military as a social institution. Military institutions and their needs (not women's needs) determine women's role in the armed forces. Women's military participation reinforces rather than undermines the gendered structure of the military and the broader society....

Liberal feminists, on the other hand, say that the military is good for women, and argue that military service has various payoffs. They see economic benefits from women's military participation in the form of higher wages, better benefits, and more educational opportunities. In many countries, military service carries the additional benefits of land or housing grants and employment training and placement, such as the "veteran's preference" in the United States civil service system. The political benefits of the military include the end of women's "second-class citizen" status; they can achieve full civil rights by fulfilling the same civil obligations borne by men. Thus, liberal feminists encourage women to believe the "warrior mystique," founded upon the martial power and political independence of the "citizen-soldier."... 5

Critical feminists argue that the liberal feminist fascination with the warrior image is dangerous, since the military reflects the racism, sexism, and heterosexism of the larger society. Further, the military insulates these practices behind the wall of "national security," constraining incursions by civil rights activists. The military as an institution successfully resists changes in personnel practices that privilege the dominant racial-ethnic gender group unless military planners recognize that such changes benefit the military mission itself. They then use the language of "women's liberation" to meet the institution's needs and employ gender categories to control women's participation. 6

A critical feminist perspective sees the expanded military participation of women as a symptom of the militarization of society, not as evidence of women's achievement of "equality." While some women may benefit from the educational or employment opportunities the military service provides, women's increasing presence in the military does not change the institution's fundamentally gendered structure, which at its core is coercive, hierarchical, and patriarchal. In fact, the increasing presence of women helps legitimize the institution by giving it an egalitarian façade. When women accept the "warrior mystique," they soften the military's image as an agent of coercion and destruction, and help promote the myth of the military as a democratic institution, as an "equal opportunity employer" like any other, without reference to its essential purpose: organized killing for political objectives. 7

In the Gulf War context, the media advertised the "equality" of United   8
States women and men, evidenced by women's military participation, as
compared to the "inequality" of Saudi women and men, represented by the
veil, by mobility restrictions, and by women's lack of formal political rights.
Much was made of the "liberalizing effect" that uniformed United States
women would have on gender relations in Saudi Arabia; this further
obscured the unequal gender relations in the United States military and
the wider society. In the military, these include structural barriers to
women's entry and advancement, such as higher recruitment standards,
enlistment ceilings, and occupational specialty restrictions based on a rule
of "combat exclusion," as well as institutional practices that celebrate masculinity and criticize femininity.

Descriptions of the Desert Shield and Desert Storm operations by   9
United States public officials invariably referred to "our men and women
in the Gulf" or "our brave servicemen and women." Servicewomen are
thus useful to the military not only because they perform jobs necessary to
the military mission, but also because they legitimize that mission. From
military planners' perspective, servicewomen are also valuable because they
boost the morale of male troops with their "nurturant socialization" and
their availability for sexual service: they therefore make war more possible,
the killing machine more efficient.

The militarization of any society is a gendered process. The essence of   10
military training consists of the subordination of the individual to the institution, a desensitization to violence, and a dehumanization of the potential
opponent. For male recruits, it also includes a process of masculinization
where female and feminine are defined as "other" and as unworthy. The
military seeks "to make a man out of you" or "to separate the men from the
boys," and from the women. Military service constitutes a quintessentially
male activity, a confirmation of masculinity, a proof of manhood. The military as an institution is thus sustained by this gender differentiation. The
military milieu celebrates and privileges maleness. The marines are still
"looking for a few good men."

The only place for women in this environment is that defined by this   11
gender distinction: support and service in traditional female occupations
and roles. Within this context, military planners define equality as allowing
some women to do some of the important jobs men do (but not all the
important jobs — hence the policy of combat exclusion, which maintains
the male protector/female protected gender distinction) while simultaneously denying women's ability and worth. The standard to which women
must measure up is men; military equality is gendered equality.

The specific training given to men and women, and the particular tasks   12
they are assigned, reinforce gender differences. For women recruits and
draftees in most state militaries, training in feminine rather than martial
arts prevails. For example, Israeli women soldiers are taught the "regulation

way" of applying makeup and how to comport themselves as "an officer and a lady." Even in militaries where women receive weapons training, they are rarely assigned to job specialties that require them to carry and use arms. Generally, weapons and physical training are emphasized as self-defense preparation in the event the unspeakable should happen, that is, that male soldiers could fail to protect them and women might come face-to-face with the enemy.

Like their sisters in the civilian labor force in most countries, service-women predominate in clerical, administrative, and support medical specialties such as being a nurse or technician. Unlike their civilian coun-terparts, military women have not, for the most part, been able to use liti-gation to protest their exclusion from certain occupations, especially those with the highly contested designation of "combat." Recent challenges to combat exclusion policies in the United States, Canada, and Israel have redrawn rather than erased the gender boundaries separating military jobs. For example, although after the Gulf War the United States Congress rescinded those sections of the United States Code barring women from combat, United States servicewomen are still excluded from ground com-bat, submarine billets, special forces, and other assignments. While one court upheld a woman's challenge to the Israeli policy prohibiting women from serving as combat pilots, most military and political officials support continued combat exclusion. 13

The formalization of women's relation to the military, that is, the shift from auxiliary to regular service, has not secured equal rights or equal treat-ment for women in any country. Yet the formalization of women's role in the armed forces gives military officials direct control over women as personnel resources; they may use women's skills, talents, and energies as the military deems appropriate. When the boss/officer, usually a man, is one's military "superior," the potential for the abuse and sexual harassment of the employee/soldier, usually a woman, differs from that in the civilian employer-employee relation. His power over her has multiplied not only because of his gender and job title but also because of his rank. She has little immediate recourse: she cannot just quit because that would subject her to prosecution for insubordination or desertion. She may request a trans-fer but he must approve the request. And she may be frightened into silence by his threat to initiate discharge proceedings against her on the charge that she is a lesbian. If she attempts to lodge a complaint she will likely be told that she will ruin the career chances of a "fine officer" by making such a charge, and will be accused of having initiated the sexual contact. 14

In militaries where personnel policy excludes gays and lesbians, periodic witch hunts help keep military women in their places: "troublemakers," that is, those who reject male soldiers' sexual advances, who report harass-ment, who advocate changes in policies considered "women's issues," or otherwise engage in subversive solidarity and "buck the system" are targeted 15 in these roundups. Military personnel policymakers attempt to justify the exclusion of gays/lesbians on the grounds that their presence in the ranks constitutes a national security risk and has a chilling effect on morale and recruitment. These rationalizations mask the heterosexism and homophobia of the policymakers and give them a tool to determine the number and kind of women who will be permitted to serve.

Thus, whether she is straight or gay, the servicewoman's sexuality be-   16
comes a weapon the military establishment uses to control her. A military career can hardly be considered, therefore, as a vehicle for women's empowerment, as the liberal feminists have argued. Instead of expending our energies on "making women equal" within the state military apparatus, feminists must work to dismantle the structure of the military institution and the destructive foreign policy it carries out.

We must begin by publicly challenging the myth of the egalitarian mil-   17
itary and by working to provide women, especially working-class women and women of color, with real alternatives to military service as a way "up and out." The "easy victory" in the Gulf War will make these tasks more difficult, but…we can and must deconstruct the "warrior mystique" and build in its place a positive concept of citizenship and equality.

Analyzing This Selection

1. Paragraphs 1 to 4 identify four views toward women in the military. How do these views differ from each other?

2. Which feminist viewpoint initially appears most attractive to you? Which view could most benefit people in the future?

3. In the author's opinion, how does the military co-opt feminist goals?

Analyzing Connections

4. D'Amico and Woolf (see "Professions for Women," p. 366) each consider working women's needs in male-dominated society. Which feminist group's goals did Woolf pursue? Which feminist goals does she, in paragraph 7, suggest to her audience?

Analyzing by Writing

5. **THE WRITER'S METHOD** Adapting D'Amico's categories, analyze your own position supporting or opposing women in the military. Like D'Amico, develop your argument by raising issues or refuting claims of an opposing view.

6. **RESEARCH TOPIC** Using D'Amico's categories, analyze the position on women and the military taken by Virginia Woolf in *Three Guineas*, written on the eve of World War II. Did Woolf become primarily a radical or liberal or critical feminist?

FORUM: WORK AND POWER

Laura L. Nash, *The Virtual Job*
Ian Angell, *Winners and Losers in the Information Age*
Barbara Ehrenreich, *Warning: This Is a*
Rights-Free Workplace

FOCUSING ON THE FORUM: Part-time or summer jobs often introduce young people to work attitudes not condoned at home and school. Teenagers confront bosses deliberately cheating customers, co-workers stealing from the company, or falsifying their hours, and they even encounter jobs that require no work. How did your temporary employment challenge your work ethic? As a worker, did you feel empowered or entrapped? or both?

Laura L. Nash

THE VIRTUAL JOB

LAURA L. NASH is a writer and consultant on business ethics. She received her Ph.D. in classical philology from Harvard University. Nash writes textbooks and managers' handbooks on business practices and corporate culture. This selection is excerpted from an article in the *Wilson Quarterly* in 1994.

Something very odd is going on in the American corporate workplace. 1 Employees are being told to prepare for a radical new condition of permanent insecurity, a future full of sporadic layoffs, endless efforts to upgrade job skills, and perpetually recombining work teams of insiders and "outsourcers." Continuous corporate "rightsizing" will dictate a "portfolio career" strategy: Since workers will no longer spend their careers with one or two employers, accumulating a portfolio of portable skills will be essential. Yet even as the corporation encourages "hard" qualities such as self-reliance and adaptability, it is also rushing headlong toward a supposedly kinder, gentler ethos. Large firms in particular are providing a growing variety of programs and social supports for those who remain under the corporate umbrella — however long that may be. The new formula might be described as a "love the one you're with" approach.

The turmoil in the workplace is being presented as stimulating and   2
exciting, an opportunity for personal and professional growth. The modern corporation will supply precious training and experience, *Fortune* said recently in describing the "new deal" between employers and employees, and workers in turn will be expected to act like entrepreneurs (or "intrapreneurs") within the corporation: Find a way to "add value to the organization" and you get a new job. Fail and you look for a job elsewhere. But that is not so bad. "If the old arrangement sounded like binding nuptial vows," says *Fortune*, "the new one suggests a series of casual, thrilling — if often temporary — encounters."

One might almost be tempted to conclude that a new age of self-   3
actualizing individualism is dawning. Released from the paternalistic and hierarchical strictures of the old corporation, the new employee will be free to blaze his or her own professional trail while the corporation stands by to help tend to personal needs that might impair performance, from child care to treatment for alcoholism. At the same time, it is also possible to see these developments as disturbing signs of an emerging form of corporatism in which areas of life once thought to be strictly private are increasingly regulated by a supposedly beneficent corporation. Those without ties to such a large institution will be spared such intrusions, of course, but may also be forced to go without many of the benefits accompanying it. Despite its simultaneous appeal to humanism and good economic sense, this new corporatism may not be kinder and gentler at all, and it may not even be all that good for business.

Even as it downsizes and rightsizes, the large American corporation   4
is increasingly assuming the role of a nanny. In 1992, benefits accounted for 32 percent of employee pay and were the fastest-growing element of compensation. Benefits include not only the traditional health insurance and pensions but a broad array of other goodies, ranging from those of the sensible-shoes variety (job training and tuition reimbursements at $35 billion annually) to more exotic offerings. Employer-provided legal services, for example, have increased sevenfold in the last decade. The corporate reach increasingly extends into what was once considered private life. Employer-sponsored health maintenance organizations, with their sometimes intrusive in-house "wellness" programs (Stop smoking! Lose weight!) are becoming part of the corporate way of life. Child-care programs of var-

ious kinds are proliferating, and among forward-looking people in the business world there is talk of the need to transform child care into "dependent care" programs providing various benefits to employees with elderly parents.

It is not unusual for today's large corporation to offer fitness programs, 5 marriage counseling, substance-abuse detection and treatment, AIDS counseling, diversity training, creative-thinking seminars, treatment of depression, diet and nutrition oversight, yoga instruction, interpersonal-relations counseling, and personal financial planning. One well-known company, EDS, even has on-site car care.

Many of these offerings involve things that were formerly considered 6 personal or domestic responsibilities, frequently managed by a wife who held no paying job. Now, as a demonstration of its newfound concern with employees' sense of well-being — and an undisguised desire to mitigate any condition that might detract from employee performance and the corporate bottom line — the corporation offers to take care of these matters. One might call this new, kinder and gentler approach to the employer-employee contract the "feminization" of the corporation.

Accompanying the trend is a growing emphasis on "softer" management 7 skills as the key to getting ahead in the managerial world. High on the list of qualities thought necessary for executive effectiveness in the 1990s are interpersonal skills, an ability to work with others in teams, and various kinds of "soft" abilities, such as intuitive reasoning, "people skills," and "creative thinking." Physical self-improvement is also in, and mental health is a major area of focus. Company-sponsored meditation programs and wilderness experiences designed to build trust and foster team spirit are becoming the vogue in corporate America. Now there are even humor consultants to help make fun and profit work together.

Despite its soft face and seemingly benign motivations, there is a dis- 8 tinctively hard edge to the new corporate humanism. Employees who are showered with benefits may pay a price in the loss of personal choice. Formerly private decisions about lifestyle and even personality may now be restricted by the company in the name of boosting personal performance and cutting costs. Today's well-bred manager may find, for example, that the powers that be in the personnel department regard his or her high cholesterol count as an indication of selfish disregard for the corporate team or a sign of insufficient self-discipline. The employee who insists on taking time off to care for a sick child despite the first-rate day-care services offered by the company may find his or her dedication to the job questioned a little more closely....

Deep organizational changes are exacerbating instability. Business is mov- 9 ing inexorably toward a new model of operation, the "virtual corporation."

As management specialists describe it, the virtual corporation will be a legal-financial entity whose physical plant is scattered across the globe and whose people-parts are almost as interchangeable as chips in a computer motherboard. Goods and services will be produced by a movable feast of temporary global teams. Geographically limited only by the reach of a telecommunications satellite, a team of "intrapreneurs" and outsiders will be patched together for a particular project and then disbanded when their work is through. Employees will then recombine into new teams for the next venture. A new product may be funded in Hong Kong, researched in Chicago and Japan, manufactured in Singapore, and marketed throughout the world. Economic factors being what they are (rotten and uncertain), the smart corporation will reduce its capital investment by farming out to smaller independent firms many of the functions it used to support in house, from manufacturing products to billing customers.

These trends contribute to individual uncertainty and promote a new   10
individualism. In a flexible, unforgiving marketplace, people will need greater adaptive skills and self-confidence. The new training programs of the virtual corporation may offer a softer and more humane visage to its employees, but it will not offer any soft jobs. The successful future employee will be the person with transferable skills, high self-motivation — and no demands on the company pension plan. This is the "new deal."

The rise of nannyism, seemingly the antithesis of all that is implied by   11
this trend toward a sink-or-swim workplace, is often justified as a rational response to the virtual corporation. Loyalty ("some degree of commitment to company purpose and community for as long as the employee works there," as Robert Waterman describes it in a recent article with two co-authors) remains important to the virtual corporation, and indeed may be at a greater premium than before. Well-educated and well-trained employees are vital to its success, and training new employees is costlier than retraining old ones. The virtual corporation cannot offer job security, but it can offer another kind of security that comes from knowing that some of one's needs will be taken care of. This response, however, is more likely to foster *dependency* among employees than self-reliance....

Company-subsidized programs may also carry hidden costs for the rest of   12
society. As corporations put more and more money into child-care programs for their employees, what will happen to the quality of the services available to others? Will the corporate programs sop up the best labor, for example, leaving second-rate child-care workers to tend the children of those outside the charmed corporate circle? Or consider an in-house fitness center, many of whose basic costs (such as space) can be easily and nearly invisibly subsidized through balance sheet complexities. Will the private health club that serves all comers be able to compete?

Most disturbing of all is the distant specter of a society in which many   13
people receive important social benefits from their companies and thus see

no need to provide for the have-nots through publicly funded programs or voluntaristic means. Or perhaps people who have reoriented their private lives toward the corporation will find the duties and demands of citizenship in the larger community beside the point. Today's health-care debate suggests that such concerns are not completely far-fetched. Opinion polls consistently show broad but shallow support for change, in large part because those already insured (disproportionately employees of large organizations) are happy with their own arrangements. For better or worse, the expected groundswell of public support needed to push through reform has never materialized.

Discussion of such real and potential downsides of the new corporate 14 nannyism are generally considered taboo. But there are alternatives. All of the new benefits cost money — for example, money that comes directly out of salaries. Why not consider paying employees more, giving them the means (and the freedom) to decide on their own how to deal with their personal problems and challenges?

Every juncture of the new flexible work force and the new caring cor- 15 poration is a tension point of contradictory expectations. The first is the tension between job insecurity and stress relief. Many features of the new humanism in employee relations stem from a perception that stress is rising, not only among employees but in the institutions of public and private life. But a good deal of that stress is caused by the corporation itself, particularly in its inchoate vision of the temporary employee contract and its continued celebration of macho (male and female) workaholics who constantly sacrifice their personal and family lives to the demands of the job.

The ministrations of the nanny corporation can inadvertently worsen the 16 very problems they seek to address. The in-house child-care program, rationalized as a means to relieve stress, promote diversity, and retain employees, may provide an excuse to work managers even longer. After all, now there is no need to worry about the children. Meanwhile, with family life reduced to a few hours of private time a week, other forms of social stress begin to emerge. Where else but to the humane corporation would a dependent employee turn for help? Down the road, the parent of older children finds that he or she has made career decisions that require a commitment of time that leaves no room for attending to the many needs of, say, preteens who are too old for child-care but too young to drive themselves to music lessons or soccer practice. What is the corporation going to do now?

The second tension springs from the dismemberment of existing com- 17 munities inside (and outside) the corporation and the attempt to create a virtual corporation. Interchangeable gypsy job teams and portfolio careers will continue to undercut a sense of community in companies. The future corporation is said to depend on teamwork. The employer-employee contract, however, encourages self-aggrandizing career strategies. Nomadic managers, with no home in a single corporation, will have little motivation to compromise or sacrifice unless there is a negotiated, guaranteed payback in advance for Number One. Even their duties as citizens will have to be regulated by the corporation. Many communities today, for example, increasingly rely on help from public-private partnerships spearheaded by managers who "volunteer" their time for the public good only after the company guarantees in advance that their service will bring them later career benefits.

The third tension is the nearly utopian promotion of individualism, self-actualization, and empowerment at the same time that teamwork, tolerance, and communication are emphasized. This tension will only be exacerbated if boundaries between private and corporate life continue to blur. As employees' personal identity, family life, and physical habits are increasingly "commodified" into performance issues, and as growing numbers of employees are regarded as permanently impermanent in the organization, calls for a new humaneness and self-actualization will ring more and more hollow. Widespread cynicism and disloyalty are likely results — a particularly volatile combination when mixed with the hyper-individualism of the virtual corporation. 18

Ultimately, the issues raised by the emergence of the new corporatism are questions of personal and collective character. The danger is that what seems a rational response to genuine problems in our society may in the end only raise those problems to a new pitch of urgency. New management doctrines that seek to make a virtue out of constant instability and insecurity will put the cynical, self-aggrandizing, hyper-individualistic character type that afflicts us today on a new footing and promote its spread. Meanwhile, the nanny corporation's protective cocoon for the chosen can only reduce our already diminished sense of citizenship and public responsibility. Historically, democratic capitalism has promoted a sense of mutuality, trust, and self-restraint among individuals, and it relies on these qualities for its continued survival. If the corporation now adds to the forces undermining them, these virtues may not hold. 19

Analyzing This Selection

1. **THE WRITER'S METHOD**   In paragraphs 1 to 8 does the author regard this "new deal" as a good one? How does her tone suggest her attitude toward these changes?

2. How does a "virtual job" reduce or increase nannyism?

3. Nash sees three tension points between new workers and companies. As an employee, how would each tension affect you?

4. According to Nash, how do the new conditions affect society? In your opinion, what additional or contrary effects are probable?

Analyzing Connections

5. In "The Value of Families" (p. 119), Amitai Etzioni is concerned about new conditions of employment affecting family life. What changes, if any, would Etzioni recommend on behalf of family in the "virtual job"? in the "nanny corporation"? Would Nash agree or disagree?

Analyzing by Writing

6. Attempts to stimulate excellence can result in the erosion of the quality of life and work, as Nash notes. Examine the effects of intense competitiveness in an athletic, musical, or artistic activity. Analyze some mixed results for you and others around you. Assess the gains and losses from your present perspective.

Ian Angell

WINNERS AND LOSERS
IN THE INFORMATION AGE

IAN ANGELL (b. 1947) is a leading British designer of computer graphics
who writes about social issues in information technology. He earned
undergraduate and doctoral degrees in mathematics from the University
of London. He is a professor of information systems at the London
School of Economics. Angell's research stresses the harsh consequences
of advances in telecommunications. This selection is excerpted from a
longer article in the *LSE Magazine* that appeared in 1996.

... "History," said Leon Trotsky, "is the natural selection of accidents," and 1
our world today is full of accidents just waiting to happen. The very natures
of work, of institutions, of society, and even of capitalism itself are mutating.
These mutations are confronting each other in the political power vacuum
left by the fall of communism and the increasing impotence of liberal
democracy, as the utopia promised by science and technology has turned
into a nightmare for the "common man." Poverty, unemployment, pollution, overpopulation, mass migration, global plagues, and other catastrophes
have left us with a world full of frightened people. For the masses will not
win in the natural selection for dominance of an increasingly elitist world....

A new order (which many will call disorder) is being forced upon an 2
unsuspecting world by advances in telecommunications. The future is
being born on the so-called information superhighways. Very soon these
electronic telecommunication networks, covering the world via cable and
satellite, will enable everyone in the world to "talk" to everyone else. We
are entering a new elite cosmopolitan age. Global commerce will force the
construction of multimedia highways, and anyone bypassed by these highways faces ruin. Information technology, together with speedy international
travel, is changing the whole nature of political governance, its relationship
to commerce, and commerce itself.

One major consequence emerging out of the new freedoms bestowed by 3
global telecommunications is the globalization — not merely the interna-
tionalization — of organizations. Individuals and companies are setting up
large transnational networks that pay absolutely no heed to national bound-

aries and barriers. The commercial enterprise of the future will be truly global: it will relocate (physically or electronically) to where the profit is greatest and the regulation least. The umbilical cords have been cut; the global company no longer feels the need to support the national aspirations of the country of its birth. Recently this new business paradigm was expressed most forcibly by Akio Morita, who caused an uproar in Japan when he announced that Sony was a global company and not Japanese!

But, paradoxically, globalization is resulting in a trend toward localiza-   4 tion or, as Morita calls it, "global localization." Global companies are setting themselves up within virtual enterprises at the hub of loosely knit alliances of local companies, all linked together by global networks, both electronic and human. These companies assemble to take advantage of any temporary business opportunity, and then they separate, searching for the next major deal. Apart from local products, local companies also deliver local expertise and access to home markets for other products created within the wider alliance. Companies and countries outside such networks have no future.

International trading now includes new forms of barter and exchange on   5 these networks, particularly in superior scientific and technological expertise and knowledge. Money, which is merely a means of facilitating economic transactions, has itself become electronic information, and the ability to determine what constitutes money can no longer be monopolized by national governments. This inevitably lowers the transaction costs of money and makes taxation of profits and regulation of the process almost impossible — a real competitive advantage for any virtual enterprise with a movable center of gravity and for those individuals who are willing to trade their expertise in this electronic market.

Knowledge Workers Versus Service Workers

The rise of teleworking/telecommuting/televillages has led Peter Drucker   6 to a very interesting forecast. He says that humanity is polarizing into two employment categories: the intellectual, cultural, and business elite (the mobile and independent knowledge workers) and the rest (the immobile and dependent service workers). In a similar vein, Robert Reich believes that in the information age people will work in three categories: symbolic-analytic services (the knowledge workers who are problem identifiers, solvers, and brokers), in-person services, and routine production services. The latter two groups roughly correspond to Drucker's service workers.

Routine production services can either be performed by robots or   7 exported anywhere on the globe. Wages in this sector are already beginning to converge worldwide to Third-World levels. British Polythene Industries (BPI) is to close its factory at Telford, with the loss of 150 jobs, and switch to China. BPI's payroll bill will be cut by 90 percent. Even the British Home Office at one time was seriously considering subcontracting a large but straightforward data-entry job to the Philippines. Such "social dumping" is dragging down the wages of in-person service workers, a sector that is itself being increasingly automated. It is estimated that 150,000 UK bank jobs will eventually be lost because of automation. Millions of jobs will be lost if teleshopping takes off. Inevitably, the slow redistribution of wealth that has occurred over the last few centuries is being reversed, rapidly. Societies are stratifying; new elites are appearing. The future is inequality; at the very bottom of the heap, Western societies are already witnessing the emergence of a rapidly expanding underclass.

Now we can see that knowledge workers are the real generators of   8 wealth. The income of these owners of intellectual and financial wealth will increase substantially, and they will be made welcome anywhere in the world. As of October 1994, foreign "entrepreneurial investors" with £1 million at their disposal can bypass the usual entry rules into Britain. But Britain has been slow off the mark and suffers the added embarrassment that none of the migrant rich want to live there. In the United States, there is a fast-track immigration policy for businessmen and women who can offer $1 million and guarantee to employ ten people. Six hundred millionaires emigrated to the United States in 1993. It is only a matter of time before intellectual capital, such as scientific and technological expertise, will be included on the balance sheet.

On the other side of the coin, there is a growing realization that each   9 service worker is a net loss both to the state and to the company: They cost far more than they generate. Service workers will now be expected to add far more value to the company, unlike in the past, when service work meant just turning up. Companies will be reducing the wages and staffing levels of service workers, and it is no accident that most Western companies are presently instigating major downsizing programs.

This is all happening against a background of an exploding population   10 in the Third World (95 percent of the world's population increase is in developing countries). To combat the inevitable mass migrations, state barriers will be thrown up everywhere to keep out alien service workers; each state has a surplus of its own to support. This is already happening. Canada is to impose a $1,000 tax on people seeking landed immigration status, thus sending out a message that is likely to reduce applications from poor service workers but increase applications from richer knowledge workers. In California, Proposition 187 intends to bar the nearly two million illegal immigrants from schools, welfare services, and all but emergency health care. How long will it be before there are "differential rights" for "differentiated citizens," identified in a database and policed by smart cards? How long before the notion of "Human Rights" is as outdated as the "Divine Right of Kings"?...

We are rapidly approaching a situation in which, in order to attract the 11 elite who have the knowledge and money to enliven the economy, the elite group will be expected to pay less tax and not more. The great majority of governments are lowering top tax rates in line with declining global levels. Geoff Mulgan claims that "top income tax rates fell an average of 16.5% between 1975 and 1989." "The main producers and repositories of wealth — multinational companies — have increasingly been able to adjust their accounts and the prices of their internal international transactions so that their profits are declared in low tax countries, while they continue to operate in high tax ones." Very soon companies will be negotiating preferential tax deals not only for themselves but also for chosen elite employees....

All the while, the disposable income for most of society will be drasti- 12 cally reduced. The power in global economic forces means that the tax burden is irrevocably moving onto the shoulders of the immobile as well as away from income and onto expenditure. When Leona Helmsley said, "Only the little people pay taxes," she was unwittingly making a prediction. This goes counter to every notion of social justice that has been prevalent over the past two hundred years. Inevitably in the transition we can expect massive civil unrest and disorder....

A Future for Democracy?

Because of the need to employ the local masses, the major social prob- 13 lem for politicians in the coming decades is going to be how to attract global employers to partner local companies and how to keep them attracted. Governments will have no choice other than to acquiesce to the will of global enterprises. A new paradigm is upon us in which the nation-state has mutated into just another form of organization, a form of organization that will delegate market regulations — such as North American Free Trade Agreement or the European Union — to continent-wide bodies, which in turn will use their economic muscle to undermine each member state. Not only will state be pitted against state, but also area will compete against area, town against town, even suburb against suburb. Nation-states will inevitably fragment: rich areas will dump poor areas. Such shakeout trends can be interpreted as downsizing, a strategy that is being considered by most shrewd major corporations these days. As Daniel Bell so eloquently put it, "The nation-state is too small for the big things and too big for the small things." Some futurologists expect that early in the next century the number of states in the United Nations will increase from the present number of 184 to over a thousand. Each state will permit entry to holders of "UN style" company passports. Tax holidays and reduced regulation aimed at attracting employers will be the name of the game everywhere....

One inevitable consequence of global trade will be the rise of the new   14
city-state at the hub of global electronic and transport networks. The
nondemocratic model of Hong Kong is an exemplar, even though the city
itself doesn't yet realize that it has defined the future. Singapore under the
enlightened leadership of Lee Kwan Yew is another. What European city
will be the first to break ranks with the nation-state mentality holding back
progress? A number of European cities can make the leap. Liechtenstein
has already started; what about Monaco? And let us not forget Venice; perhaps it will rediscover former glories. What about Lisbon? They have the
singular example of attracting the Gulbenkian wealth earlier this century.
The Corporation of the City of London too has enormous potential and
could be revitalized, although the dead hand of the "Mother of Parlia-
ments" will make this far more difficult.

To protect their wealth, rich areas will also undertake a "rightsizing"   15
strategy, ensuring a high proportion of (wealth-generating) knowledge workers to (wealth-depleting) service workers. Rich areas have to maintain and
expand a critical mass of scientific and technological expertise and have to
use it to underpin an effective education system to regenerate the resource.
These rich areas will reject the liberal attitudes of the present century as
the expanding underclass being spawned by these liberal attitudes and the
untrained migrants they welcomed previously are increasingly seen as economic liabilities. In Nietzsche's words, "Many too many are born. The state
was devised for the superfluous ones." Mass-production methods needed an
oversupply of humanity; in a sense, the machine age spawned the nation-
state, but what is to be done with the glut as the machine age dies and we
enter the information age?

As far as global enterprises are concerned, liberal democracy is an arti-   16
fact of the machine age, an ideology from a time when the masses were
needed — but it will soon mutate into an irrelevancy. It will be merely the
means of governing the immobile and dependent service workers. That citizens elect their slave masters makes democracy slavery none the less.

Analyzing This Selection

1. The author refers to the evolutionary process of natural selection (paragraph
   1). Does natural selection apply to economics and politics? Do societies biologically evolve or change by other means? Explain your opinion.

2. Angell points out that telecommunication networks simultaneously global-
   ize and localize companies. How do these changes affect knowledge workers? How do they affect service workers?

3. Assess Angell's evidence and arguments supporting his predictions about
   future states and citizenship. What is most convincing? most disturbing?

4. **THE WRITER'S METHOD**   How do you feel at the end of the essay? Is
   that the intended effect of Angell's tone or a counterreaction to it?

Analyzing Connections

5. Angell and Nash (see "The Virtual Job," p. 377) both examine social consequences of new employment conditions. How do they agree or differ in their outlook on society?

Analyzing by Writing

6. Analyze positive and negative effects resulting from telecommunications in your work and life as a student. What evidence of winners and losers do you find in your segment of the information age? Do telecommunications place you in an elite cosmopolitan category? Examine how your access to the highway affects your relation to others who learn and teach. How does it affect your relation to those with whom you "talk" by network? Do inequities in telecommunications skills or access put deserving, intelligent people at a disadvantage?

Barbara Ehrenreich

WARNING: THIS IS A
RIGHTS-FREE WORKPLACE

BARBARA EHRENREICH (b. 1941) writes on feminist and social issues such as health care, popular culture, and class inequities. She graduated from Reed College and received a Ph.D. from Rockefeller University. Her articles and columns have appeared in magazines such as *Mother Jones*, the *Nation*, the *New Republic*, *Ms.*, *Time*, and the *New York Times Magazine*. Ehrenreich was awarded a Guggenheim Fellowship. Her book-length critiques of American society include *Fear of Falling: The Inner Life of the Middle Class* (1988) and *Blood Rites: Origins and History of the Passions of War* (1997). The following article appeared in the *New York Times Magazine* in 2000.

If the laws of economics were enforced as strictly as the laws of physics, America would be a workers' paradise. The supply of most kinds of labor is low, relative to the demand, so each worker should be treated as a cherished asset, right? But there have been only grudging gains in wages over the last few years, and in the realm of dignity and autonomy, a palpable decline.

In the latest phase of America's one-sided class war, employers have taken to monitoring employees' workplace behavior right down to a single computer keystroke or bathroom break, even probing into their personal concerns and leisure activities. Sure, there's a job out there for anyone who can get to an interview sober and standing upright. The price, though, may be one's basic civil rights and — what boils down to the same thing — self-respect.

Not that the Bill of Rights ever extended to the American workplace. In 1996, I was surprised to read about a grocery store worker in Dallas who was fired for wearing a Green Bay Packers T-shirt to work on the day before a Cowboys-Packers game. All right, this was insensitive of him, but it certainly couldn't have influenced his ability to keep the shelves stocked with Doritos. A few phone calls, though, revealed that his firing was entirely legal. Employees have the right to express their religious preferences at work, by wearing a cross or a Star of David, for example. But most other forms of "self-expression" are not protected, and strangely enough, Green Bay Packer fandom has not yet been recognized as a legitimate religion.

Freedom of assembly is another right that never found its way into the 4
workplace. On a recent journalistic foray into a series of low-wage jobs, I
was surprised to discover that management often regarded the most innocent conversation between employees as potentially seditious. A poster in
the break room at one restaurant where I worked as a waitress prohibited
"gossip," and a manager would hastily disperse any gathering of two or
more employees. At the same time, management everywhere enjoys the
right to assemble employees for lengthy anti-union harangues.

Then there is the more elemental and biological right — and surely it 5
should be one — to respond to nature's calls. Federal regulations forbid
employers to "impose unreasonable restrictions on employee use of the
facilities." But according to Marc Linder and Ingrid Nygaard, co-authors of
"Void Where Prohibited: Rest Breaks and the Right to Urinate on Company Time," this regulation is only halfheartedly enforced. Professionals
and, of course, waitresses can usually dart away and relieve themselves as
they please. Not so for many cashiers and assembly-line workers, some of
whom, Linder says, have taken to wearing adult diapers to work.

In the area of privacy rights, workers have actually lost ground in recent 6
years. Here, too, the base line is not impressive — no comprehensive right
to personal privacy on the job has ever been established. I learned this on
my first day as a waitress, when my fellow workers warned me that my
purse could be searched by management at any time. I wasn't carrying
stolen salt shakers or anything else of a compromising nature, but there's
something about the prospect of a purse search that makes a woman feel a
few buttons short of fully dressed. After work, I called around and found
that this, too, is generally legal, at least if the boss has reasonable cause and
has given prior notification of the company's search policies.

Purse searches, though, are relatively innocuous compared with the 7
sophisticated chemical and electronic forms of snooping adopted by many
companies in the '90s. The American Management Association reports
that in 1999 a record two-thirds of major American companies monitored
their employees electronically: videotaping them; reviewing their e-mail
and voice-mail messages; and, most recently, according to Lewis Maltby,
president of the Princeton-based National Workrights Institute, monitoring
any Web sites they may visit on their lunch breaks. Nor can you count on
keeping anything hidden in your genes; a growing number of employers
now use genetic testing to screen out job applicants who carry genes for
expensive ailments like Huntington's disease.

But the most ubiquitous invasion of privacy is drug testing, usually of 8
urine, more rarely of hair or blood. With 81 percent of large companies
now requiring some form of drug testing — up from 21 percent in 1987 —
job applicants take it for granted that they'll have to provide a urine sample
as well as a résumé. This is not restricted to "for cause" testing — of people
who, say, nod or space out on the job. Nor is it restricted to employees in
"safety-sensitive occupations," like airline pilots and school-bus drivers.

Workers who stack boxes of Cheerios in my local supermarkets get tested, as do the editorial employees of this magazine, although there is no evidence that a weekend joint has any more effect on Monday-morning performance than a Saturday-night beer.

Civil libertarians see drug testing as a violation of our Fourth Amendment protection from "unreasonable search," while most jobholders and applicants find it simply embarrassing. In some testing protocols, the employee has to strip to her underwear and urinate into a cup in the presence of an aide or technician, who will also want to know what prescription drugs she takes, since these can influence the test results.   9

According to a recent report from the American Civil Liberties Union, drug testing has not been proven to achieve its advertised effects, like reducing absenteeism and improving productivity. But it does reveal who's on antidepressants or suffering with an ailment that's expensive to treat, and it is undeniably effective at weeding out those potential "troublemakers" who are too independent-minded to strip and empty their bladders on command.   10

Maybe the prevailing trade-off between jobs and freedom would make sense, in the narrowest cost-benefit terms, if it contributed to a more vibrant economy. But this is hardly the case. In fact, a 1998 study of sixty-three computer-equipment and data-processing firms found that companies that performed both pre-employment and random drug testing actually "reduced rather than enhanced productivity" — by an eye-popping 29 percent, presumably because of its dampening effect on morale.   11

Why, then, do so many employers insist on treating their workers as a kind of fifth column within the firm? Certainly the government has played a role with its misguided antidrug crusade, as has the sheer availability of new technologies of snooping. But workplace repression signals a deeper shift away from the postwar social contract in which a job meant a straightforward exchange of work for wages.   12

Economists trace the change to the 1970s, when, faced with falling profits and rising foreign competition, America's capitalists launched an offensive to squeeze more out of their workers. Supervision tightened, management expanded and union-busting became a growth industry. And once in motion, the dynamic of distrust is hard to stop. Workers who are routinely treated like criminals and slackers may well bear close watching.   13

The mystery is why American workers, the political descendants of proud revolutionaries, have so meekly surrendered their rights. Sure, individual workers find ways to cheat on their drug tests, outwit the electronic surveillance and sneak in a bit of "gossip" here and there. But these petty acts of defiance seldom add up to concerted resistance, in part because of the weakness of American unions. The A.F.L.-C.I.O. is currently conducting a nationwide drive to ensure the right to organize, and the downtrodden workers of the world can only wish the union well. But what about all the other rights missing in so many American workplaces? It's not easy to   14 organize your fellow workers if you can't communicate freely with them on the job and don't dare carry union literature in your pocketbook.

In a tight labor market, workers have another option, of course. They 15 can walk. The alarming levels of turnover in low-wage jobs attest to the popularity of this tactic, and if unemployment remains low, employers may eventually decide to cut their workers some slack. Already, companies in particularly labor-starved industries like ski resorts and software are dropping drug testing rather than lose or repel employees. But in the short run, the mobility of workers, combined with the weakness of unions, means that there is little or no sustained on-site challenge to overbearing authority.

What we need is nothing less than a new civil rights movement — this 16 time, for American workers. Who will provide the leadership remains to be seen, but clearly the stakes go way beyond "labor issues," as these are conventionally defined. We can hardly call ourselves the world's pre-eminent democracy if large numbers of citizens spend half of their waking hours in what amounts, in plain terms, to a dictatorship.

Analyzing This Selection

1. The author objects to some, but not all, invasions of employee privacy. Which work conditions does Ehrenreich find objectionable and for what reasons?

2. According to Ehrenreich, how did workers lose their rights? What possible remedies does she suggest?

3. **THE WRITER'S METHOD**   Is Ehrenreich one of the "troublemakers"? What tone toward her readers does she take in this critique of the economy?

Analyzing Connections

4. Ehrenreich and Soto (see "Black Hair," p. 344) both examine exploitive working conditions. Does Soto's essay support or refute Ehrenreich's explanation of their cause?

Analyzing by Writing

5. Restrictive dress codes and name rules operate in all work situations, from casual, as in summer camp, to formal, as in the military. Analyze the purpose and effect of the rules about clothes and speech that you had to follow in a job such as restaurant worker or counselor.

FORUM: WORK AND POWER

Nash, Angell, and Ehrenreich consider new kinds of work conditions that deeply affect self-image and social attitudes. In the work world you expect to enter, which issues of individual power and vulnerability will be important to you? Examine your assumptions and outlooks on such matters as:

- flexible hours
- Internet privacy
- health insurance benefits and confidentiality about medical details
- union membership
- maternity leave
- child care
- corporation home country
- work sites

Assess job demands and competitive economic forces that threaten your priorities. As you look ahead, try to foresee issues that will probably remain unimportant, and explain why you think they won't matter. Develop your own agenda of powers and cautions for a twenty-first–century working life.

PART 7

POSSESSIONS

Harry Crews, *The Car*
E. M. Forster, *My Wood*
James B. Twitchell, *Two Cheers for Materialism*
Holly Brubach, *Mail-Order America*
Lars Eighner, *On Dumpster Diving*
William Ian Miller, *Gifts and Honor: An Exchange*
Toni Cade Bambara, *The Lesson* (fiction)
Maguelonne Toussaint-Samat, *Chocolate and Divinity*

INSIGHTS

It is easier for a camel to go through the eye of a needle, than for a rich man to enter into the kingdom of God.

—MATTHEW 19:24

A man is rich in proportion to the number of things which he can afford to let alone.

—HENRY DAVID THOREAU

There is something about holding on to things that I find therapeutic.

—EDNA O'BRIEN

I call people rich when they're able to meet the requirements of their imagination.

—HENRY JAMES

I instinctively like to acquire and store up what promises to outlast me.

—COLETTE

In thinking of clothes as passing fashions, we repeat less than a half-truth. Bodies come and go; the clothes that have received those bodies survive. They circulate through secondhand shops, through rummage sales, through the Salvation Army; or they are transmitted from parent to child, from sister to sister, from brother to brother, from sister to brother, from lover to lover, from friend to friend.

Clothes receive the human imprint. Jewelry lasts longer, and can also move us. But, even though it has a history, it resists the history of our bodies. Enduring, it rebukes our mortality, which it imitates only in the occasional scratch. On the other hand, food, which, like jewelry, is a gift that joins us to each other, rapidly *becomes* us and disappears. Like food, cloth can be shaped by our touch; like jewelry, it endures beyond the immediate moment of consumption. It endures, but it is mortal. As Lear says disgustedly of his own hand, "it smels of mortalitie." It is a smell that I love.

It is the smell that attaches a child to its comforter. A piece of cloth, a teddy bear, whatever. Cloth that can be put in the mouth, chewed upon, anything but washed. Cloth that bears the teeth marks, the grime, the bodily presence of the child. Cloth that decays: the teddy bear's arm falls off, the edge of the cloth frays. Cloth that endures and comforts. Cloth that, as any child knows, is *specific*. Once, looking after a friend's child, I couldn't find her comforter and attempted to "replace" it with a piece of cloth that looked exactly like it. She, of course, knew immediately that it was a fraudulent imitation, and I still remember her look of distrust and disgust at my betrayal. The comforter, however much it stands in for absences and loss, remains irrevocably its material self even as it is transformed by touch and lips and teeth.

—PETER STALLYBRASS

It is ironic that the very kind of thinking which produces all our riches also renders them unable to satisfy us. Our restless desire for more and more has been a major dynamic for economic growth, but it has made the achievement of that growth largely a hollow victory. Our sense of contentment and satisfaction is not a simple result of any absolute level of what we acquire or achieve. It depends upon our frame of reference, on how what we attain compares to what we expected. If we get farther than we expected we tend to feel good. If we expected to go farther than we have then even a rather high level of success can be experienced as disappointing. In America, we keep upping the ante. Our expectations keep accommodating to what we have attained. "Enough" is always just over the horizon, and like the horizon it recedes as we approach it.

We do not tend to think in terms of a particular set of conditions and amenities that we regard as sufficient and appropriate for a good life. Our calculations tend to be relative. It is not what we have that determines whether we think we are doing well; it is whether we have *more* — more than our parents, more than we had ten years ago, perhaps more than our neighbors. This latter source of relativity, keeping up with (or ahead of) the Joneses, is the most frequently commented upon. But it is probably less important, and less destructive, than our comparisons with our own previous levels and with the new expectations they generate. Wanting more remains a constant, regardless of what we have.

— PAUL WACHTEL

Private Property, the Law of Accumulation of Wealth, and the Law of Competition...these are the highest results of human experience, the soil in which society so far has produced the best fruit.

— ANDREW CARNEGIE

People who have lived for centuries in poverty in the relative isolation of the rural village have come to terms with this existence. It would be astonishing were it otherwise. People do not strive, generation after generation, century after century, against circumstances that are so constituted as to defeat them. They accept. Nor is such acceptance a sign of weakness of character. Rather, it is a profoundly rational response. Given the formidable hold of the...poverty within which they live, accommodation is the optimal solution. Poverty is cruel. A continuing struggle to escape that is continuously frustrated is more cruel. It is more civilized, more intelligent, as well as more plausible, that people, out of the experience of centuries, should reconcile themselves to what has for so long been the inevitable.

The deeply rational character of accommodation lies back, at least in part, of the central instruction of the principal world religions. All, without exception, urge acquiescence, some in remarkably specific form. The blessedness that Christianity accords to the meek is categorical. The pain of poverty is not denied, but its compensatory spiritual reward is very high. The poor pass through the eye of the needle into Paradise; the rich remain outside with the camels. Acquiescence is equally urged, or as in the case of Hinduism compelled, by the other ancient faiths. There has long been a suspicion, notably enhanced by Marx, that the contentment urged by religion is a design for diverting attention from the realities of class and exploitation — it is the opiate of the people. It is, more specifically, a formula for making the best of a usually hopeless situation.

— JOHN KENNETH GALBRAITH

A Summer Morning

Her young employers, having got in late
From seeing friends in town
And scraped the right front fender on the gate,
Will not, the cook expects, be coming down.

She makes a quiet breakfast for herself.
The coffee-pot is bright,
The jelly where it should be on the shelf.
She breaks an egg into the morning light,

Then, with the bread-knife lifted stands and hears
The sweet efficient sounds
Of thrush and catbird, and the snip of shears
Where, in the terraced backward of the grounds,

A gardener works before the heat of day.
He straightens for a view
Of the big house ascending stony-gray
Out of his beds mosaic with the dew.

His young employers having got in late,
He and the cook alone
Receive the morning on their old estate,
Possessing what the owners can but own.

—RICHARD WILBUR

FOCUSING BY WRITING

1. Our possessions can possess us, and they frequently do — sometimes delightfully, sometimes harmfully. Nearly everyone has felt that the essence of life was summed up for the moment by having a dog, an electronic toy or game, a pair of skis, or shoes or sneakers, or special jeans. In a brief essay, define your past or present obsession with a special personal belonging that affects your life.

2. Do you prefer shopping at a department store, specialty boutique, discount store, superstore, or manufacturer's outlet? Or do you prefer Internet shopping? Examine the attractions of the ambience that make shopping more pleasurable in one kind of store, including the sales personnel, the sense of abundance, or the advantages of avoiding stores altogether.

3. In many households there is some treasured object that is associated with earlier generations or with an important period in the recent family past. Perhaps it is a vase or lamp, a Bible or jewelry, a piece of furniture or a rug. The object comes to be treated as something precious and irreplaceable — even though it may be fairly common — because it embodies certain ideals or meanings. Select any single object that holds special status in your household; explain its meanings and how they are kept alive by customs and habits.

4. Sometimes money is given as a gift, instead of a present selected by the giver. Do you think this is a good way to avoid disappointments, or is it disappointing? On important occasions such as graduation, Christmas, a bar or bat mitzvah, or a wedding, significant amounts of money can accumulate instead of numerous presents. How, if at all, does the money increase or diminish the value of the traditional occasion?

Harry Crews

THE CAR

HARRY CREWS (b. 1935), who was raised in Georgia, joined the Marine Corps after high school and became a sergeant before he left the corps to go to college. He was educated at the University of Florida, where he later taught writing. His novels include CAR (1972), A *Feast of Snakes* (1976), and *Celebration* (1998). He often writes for magazines such as *Playboy* and *Esquire*, in the latter of which this essay first appeared.

The other day, there arrived in the mail a clipping sent by a friend of mine. It had been cut from a Long Beach, California, newspaper and dealt with a young man who had eluded police for fifty-five minutes while he raced over freeways and through city streets at speeds up to 130 miles per hour. During the entire time, he ripped his clothes off and threw them out the window bit by bit. It finally took twenty-five patrol cars and a helicopter to catch him. When they did, he said that God had given him the car, and that he had "found God." 1

I don't want to hit too hard on a young man who obviously has his own troubles, maybe even is a little sick with it all, but when I read that he had found God in the car, my response was: *So say we all.* We have found God in cars, or if not the true God, one so satisfying, so powerful, and awe-inspiring that the distinction is too fine to matter. Except perhaps ultimately, but pray we must not think too much on that. 2

The operative word in all this is *we.* It will not do for me to maintain that I have been above it all, that somehow I've managed to remain aloof from the national love affair with cars. It is true that I got a late start. I did not learn to drive until I was twenty-one; my brother was twenty-five before he learned. The reason is simple enough. In Bacon County, Georgia, where I grew up, many families had nothing with a motor in it. Ours was one such family. But starting as late as I did, I still had my share, and I've remembered them all, the cars I've owned. I remember them in just the concrete specific way you remember anything that changed your life. Especially I remember the early ones. 3

The first car I ever owned was a 1938 Ford coupe. It had no low gear and the door on the passenger side wouldn't open. I eventually put a low gear in it, but I never did get the door to work. One hot summer night on 4 a clay road a young lady whom I'll never forget had herself braced and ready with one foot on the rearview mirror and the other foot on the wind vent. In the first few lovely frantic moments, she pushed out the wing vent, broke off the rearview mirror, and left her little footprints all over the ceiling. The memory of it was so affecting that I could never bring myself to repair the vent or replace the headliner she had walked all over upside down.

Eight months later I lost the car on a rain-slick road between Folkston, 5 Georgia, and Waycross. I'd just stopped to buy a stalk of bananas (to a boy raised in the hookworm and rickets belt of the South, bananas will always remain an incredibly exotic fruit, causing him to buy whole stalks at a time), and back on the road again I was only going about fifty in a misting rain when I looked over to say something to my buddy, whose nickname was Bonehead and who was half drunk in the seat beside me. For some reason I'll never understand, I felt the back end of the car get loose and start to come up on us in the other lane. Not having driven very long, I overcorrected and stepped on the brake. We turned over four times. Bonehead flew out of the car and shot down a muddy ditch about forty yards before he stopped, sober and unhurt. I ended up under the front seat, thinking I was covered with gouts of blood. As it turned out, I didn't have much wrong with me and what I was covered with was gouts of mashed banana.

The second car I had was a 1940 Buick, square, impossibly heavy, built 6 like a Sherman tank, but it had a '52 engine in it. Even though it took about ten miles to get her open full bore, she'd do over a hundred miles an hour on flat ground. It was so big inside that in an emergency it could sleep six. I tended to live in that Buick for almost a year and no telling how long I would have kept it if a boy who was not a friend of mine and who owned an International Harvester pickup truck hadn't said in mixed company that he could make the run from New Lacy in Coffee County, Georgia, to Jacksonville, Florida, quicker than I could. He lost the bet, but I wrung the speedometer off the Buick, and also — since the run was made on a blistering day in July — melted four inner tubes, causing them to fuse with the tires, which were already slick when the run started. Four new tires and tubes cost more than I had or expected to have anytime soon, so I sadly put that old honey up on blocks until I could sell it to a boy who lived up toward Macon.

After the Buick, I owned a 1953 Mercury with three-inch lowering 7 blocks, fender skirts, twin aerials, and custom upholstering made of rolled Naugahyde. Staring into the bathroom mirror for long periods of time I practiced expressions to drive it with. It was that kind of car. It looked mean, and it was mean. Consequently, it had to be handled with a certain style. One-handing it through a ninety-degree turn on city streets in a power slide where you were in danger of losing your ass as well as the car, you were obligated to have your left arm hanging half out the window and a very *bored* expression on your face. That kind of thing.

Those were the sweetest cars I was ever to know because they were my   8
first. I remember them like people — like long-ago lovers — their idiosyn-
crasies, what they liked and what they didn't. With my hands deep in
crankcases, I was initiated into their warm greasy mysteries. Nothing in the
world was more satisfying than winching the front end up under the shade
of a chinaberry tree and sliding down the chassis on a burlap sack with a
few tools to see if the car would not yield to me and my expert ways.

The only thing that approached working on a car was talking about one.   9
We'd stand about for hours, hustling our balls and spitting, telling stories
about how it had been somewhere, sometime, with the car we were driving. It gave our lies a little focus and our talk a little credibility, if only
because we could point to the evidence.

"But, hell, don't it rain in with that wing vent broke out like that?"   10

"Don't mean nothing to me. Soon's Shirley kicked it out, I known I was   11
in love. I ain't about to put it back."

Usually we met to talk at night behind the A&W Root Beer stand, with   12
the air heavy with the smell of grease and just a hint of burned French fries
and burned hamburgers and burned hot dogs. It remains one of the most
sensuous, erotic smells in my memory because through it, their tight little
asses ticking like clocks, walked the sweetest softest short-skirted carhops in
the world. I knew what it was to stand for hours with my buddies, leaning
nonchalant as hell on a fender, pretending not to look at the carhops, and
saying things like: "This little baby don't look like much, but she'll git rubber in three gears." And when I said it, it was somehow my own body I was
talking about. It was *my* speed and *my* strength that got rubber in three
gears. In the mystery of that love affair, the car and I merged.

But, like many another love affair, it has soured considerably. Maybe it   13
would have been different if I had known cars sooner. I was already out of
the Marine Corps and twenty-two years old before I could stand behind the
A&W Root Beer and lean on the fender of a 1938 coupe. That seems
pretty old to me to be talking about getting rubber in three gears, and I'm
certain it is *very* old to feel your own muscle tingle and flush with blood
when you say it. As is obvious, I was what used to be charitably called a late
bloomer. But at some point I did become just perceptive enough to recognize bullshit when I was neck deep in it.

The 1953 Mercury was responsible for my ultimate disenchantment   14
with cars. I had already bored and stroked the engine and contrived to
place a six-speaker sound system in it when I finally started to paint it. I
spent the better half of a year painting that car. A friend of mine owned a
body shop and he let me use the shop on weekends. I sanded the Mercury
down to raw metal, primed it, and painted it. Then I painted it again. And
again. And then again. I went a little nuts, as I am prone to do, because I'm
the kind of guy who if he can't have too much of a thing doesn't want any
at all. So one day I came out of the house (I was in college then) and saw
it, the '53 Mercury, the car upon which I had heaped more attention and

time and love than I had ever given a human being. It sat at the curb, its black surface a shimmering of the air, like hundreds of mirrors turned to catch the sun. It had twenty-seven coats of paint, each coat laboriously hand-rubbed. It seemed to glow, not with reflected light, but with some internal light of its own.

I stood staring, and it turned into one of those great scary rare moments   15
when you are privileged to see into your own predicament. Clearly, there were two ways I could go. I could sell the car, or I could keep on painting it for the rest of my life. If twenty-seven coats of paint, why not a hundred and twenty-seven? The moment was brief and I understand it better now than I did then, but I did realize, if imperfectly, that something was dreadfully wrong, that the car owned me much more than I would ever own the car, no matter how long I kept it. The next day I drove to Jacksonville and left the Mercury on a used-car lot. It was an easy thing to do.

Since that day, I've never confused myself with a car, a confusion com-   16
mon everywhere about us — or so it seems to me. I have a car now, but I use it like a beast, the way I've used all cars since the Mercury, like a beast unlovely and unlikable but necessary. True as all that is, though, God knows I'm in the car's debt for that blistering winning July run to Jacksonville, and the pushed-out wing vent, and finally for that greasy air heavy with the odor of burned meat and potatoes there behind the A&W Root Beer. I'll never smell anything that good again.

Analyzing This Selection

1. What does Crews mean in saying, "We have found God in cars"? Why does the thought lead him to say, in almost the same breath, "pray we must not think too much on that"?

2. **THE WRITER'S METHOD** Crews seems to be exaggerating some details in his descriptions of his cars and in his accounts of his experiences. What kinds of exaggerations does he lard into his essay, and what effects do they have on our response to him as a writer? What qualities of his might be objectionable? What qualities might be thought of as attractive?

3. At what point did Crews begin to realize that he was identifying himself too closely with his cars? What other realization is this one linked with?

4. In the final paragraph, Crews says that people around him seem to be confusing themselves with their cars. In what way do they do this? What features of common American life is he alluding to in that observation?

5. The tone of the essay includes some nostalgia. Over what does Crews feel nostalgic? What broader theme is included in his treatment of the main topic?

Analyzing Connections

6. Compare the ways that Crews and Thomas Simmons (see "Motorcycle Talk," p. 65) were changed by their vehicles. What aspects of themselves did they come to possess through their possessions?

Analyzing by Writing

7. Do young Americans currently idolize cars? What are contemporary teenage attitudes and expectations about cars? Discuss the role of the car in male or female rites of passage, new freedoms, and social relations, and consider its other symbolic and practical roles. If you think the thrill of cars has diminished for American youth (since Crews's generation), try to explain reasons for the decline.

E. M. Forster

MY WOOD

E. M. FORSTER (1879–1970) was a British novelist and essayist who was educated at Cambridge University. Except for periods of travel to India and the Mediterranean, where he was deeply affected by his contacts with ancient cultures, he continued to live at his college through most of his adulthood. His fiction is often about conventionally educated young English people discovering something unconventional in themselves in response to symbolic places, such as other countries or old houses. Even the titles of his novels suggest traveling to take up a fresh perspective on things: *Where Angels Fear to Tread* (1905), *The Longest Journey* (1907), *A Room with a View* (1908), *Howards End* (1910), and *A Passage to India* (1924), which is the book Forster mentions in the first sentence of this selection from his collection of essays *Abinger Harvest* (1936).

A few years ago I wrote a book which dealt in part with the difficulties 1 of the English in India. Feeling that they would have had no difficulties in India themselves, the Americans read the book freely. The more they read it the better it made them feel, and a check to the author was the result. I bought a wood with the check. It is not a large wood — it contains scarcely any trees, and it is intersected, blast it, by a public footpath. Still, it is the first property that I have owned, so it is right that other people should participate in my shame, and should ask themselves, in accents that will vary in horror, this very important question: What is the effect of property upon the character? Don't let's touch economics; the effect of private ownership upon the community as a whole is another question — a more important question, perhaps, but another one. Let's keep to psychology. If you own things, what's their effect on you? What's the effect on me of my wood?

In the first place, it makes me feel heavy. Property does have this effect. 2 Property produces men of weight, and it was a man of weight who failed to get into the Kingdom of Heaven. He was not wicked, that unfortunate millionaire in the parable, he was only stout; he stuck out in front, not to mention behind, and as he wedged himself this way and that in the crystalline entrance and bruised his well-fed flanks, he saw beneath him a comparatively slim camel passing through the eye of a needle and being woven into

406

the robe of God. The Gospels all through couple stoutness and slowness. They point out what is perfectly obvious, yet seldom realized: that if you have a lot of things you cannot move about a lot, that furniture requires dusting, dusters require servants, servants require insurance stamps, and the whole tangle of them makes you think twice before you accept an invitation to dinner or go for a bathe in the Jordan. Sometimes the Gospels proceed further and say with Tolstoy that property is sinful; they approach the difficult ground of asceticism here, where I cannot follow them. But as to the immediate effects of property on people, they just show straightforward logic. It produces men of weight. Men of weight cannot, by definition, move like the lightning from the East unto the West, and the ascent of a fourteen-stone bishop into a pulpit is thus the exact antithesis of the coming of the Son of Man. My wood makes me feel heavy.

In the second place, it makes me feel it ought to be larger.   3

The other day I heard a twig snap in it. I was annoyed at first, for I   4 thought that someone was blackberrying, and depreciating the value of the undergrowth. On coming nearer, I saw it was not a man who had trodden on the twig and snapped it, but a bird, and I felt pleased. My bird. The bird was not equally pleased. Ignoring the relation between us, it took fright as soon as it saw the shape of my face, and flew straight over the boundary hedge into a field, the property of Mrs. Henessy, where it sat down with a loud squawk. It had become Mrs. Henessy's bird. Something seemed grossly amiss here, something that would not have occurred had the wood been larger. I could not afford to buy Mrs. Henessy out, I dared not murder her, and limitations of this sort beset me on every side. . . .

In the third place, property makes its owner feel that he ought to do   5 something to it. Yet he isn't sure what. A restlessness comes over him, a vague sense that he has a personality to express — the same sense which, without any vagueness, leads the artist to an act of creation. Sometimes I think I will cut down such trees as remain in the wood, at other times I want to fill up the gaps between them with new trees. Both impulses are pretentious and empty. They are not honest movements toward money-making or beauty. They sprang from a foolish desire to express myself and from an inability to enjoy what I have got. Creation, property, enjoyment form a sinister trinity in the human mind. Creation and enjoyment are both very, very good, yet they are often unattainable without a material basis, and at such moments property pushes itself in as a substitute, saying, "Accept me instead — I'm good enough for all three." It is not enough. It is, as Shakespeare said of lust, "The expense of spirit in a waste of shame": it is "Before, a joy proposed; behind, a dream." Yet we don't know how to shun it. It is forced on us by our economic system as the alternative to starvation. It is also forced on us by an internal defect in the soul, by the feeling that in property may lie the germs of self-development and of exquisite or heroic deeds. Our life on earth is, and ought to be, material and carnal. But we have not yet learned to manage our materialism and carnality properly; they are still entangled with the desire for ownership, where (in the words of Dante) "Possession is one with loss."

And this brings us to our fourth and final point: the blackberries.   6

Blackberries are not plentiful in this meager grove, but they are easily   7 seen from the public footpath which traverses it, and all too easily gathered. Foxgloves, too — people will pull up the foxgloves, and ladies of an educational tendency even grub for toadstools to show them on the Monday in class. Other ladies, less educated, roll down the bracken in the arms of their gentlemen friends. There is paper, there are tins. Pray, does my wood belong to me or doesn't it? And, if it does, should I not own it best by allowing no one else to walk there? There is a wood near Lyme Regis, also cursed by a public footpath, where the owner has not hesitated on this point. He had built high stone walls each side of the path, and has spanned it by bridges, so that the public circulate like termites while he gorges on the blackberries unseen. He really does own his wood, this able chap. And perhaps I shall come to this in time. I shall wall in and fence out until I really taste the sweets of property. Enormously stout, endlessly avaricious, pseudo-creative, intensely selfish, I shall weave upon my forehead the quadruple crown of possession until those nasty Bolshies[1] come and take it off again and thrust me aside into the outer darkness.

[1]*Bolshies* Bolsheviks. [Editor's note.]

Analyzing This Selection

1. In the second paragraph, the terms "heavy" and "weight" include nonliteral meanings. Give a literal explanation of this first effect of property on Forster's character. What is added by Forster's figurative presentation?

2. In paragraph 4, explain the effect of the short sentence "My bird."

3. Explain Forster's somewhat difficult point about property becoming a substitute for creativity and enjoyment. From his viewpoint, how is that to be avoided?

4. **THE WRITER'S METHOD**   The essay includes an abundance of references to history, literature, and religion, and they occur without much introduction or clarification. What is their purpose? And what is the effect of their suddenness?

Analyzing Connections

5. Forster and Crews (see "The Car," p. 401) both discover a "defect in the soul" through their possessions. But their defect gave them pleasure. Which writer is more ambivalent about his weakness? Which writer is more critical of similar weaknesses in his society?

Analyzing by Writing

6. If you were designing a better society, what would you allow individuals to own privately? Conversely, what should be owned publicly? Would you change the status of utilities, transportation systems, communication networks, hospitals, schools, shorelines, family housing, or any other major components of present society? Explain why your plan for ownership would be good for people.

James B. Twitchell

TWO CHEERS FOR MATERIALISM

JAMES B. TWITCHELL (b. 1943) writes criticism of popular culture and commercial society. He graduated from the University of Vermont and received a Ph.D. from the University of North Carolina. Twitchell teaches at the University of Florida. His books include *Adcult USA: The Triumph of Advertising in America* (1995) and *Dumbing Down: Essays in the Strip Mining of American Culture* (1996). This selection is excerpted from a longer essay in the *Wilson Quarterly* (1999).

Of all the strange beasts that have come slouching into the 20th century, none has been more misunderstood, more criticized, and more important than materialism. Who but fools, toadies, hacks, and occasional loopy libertarians have ever risen to its defense? Yet the fact remains that while materialism may be the most shallow of the 20th century's various -isms, it has been the one that has ultimately triumphed. The world of commodities appears so antithetical to the world of ideas that it seems almost heresy to point out the obvious: most of the world most of the time spends most of its energy producing and consuming more and more stuff. The really interesting question may be not why we are so materialistic, but why we are so unwilling to acknowledge and explore what seems the central characteristic of modern life.

When the French wished to disparage the English in the 19th century, they called them a nation of shopkeepers. When the rest of the world now wishes to disparage Americans, they call us a nation of consumers. And they are right. We are developing and rapidly exporting a new material culture, a mallcondo culture. To the rest of the world we do indeed seem not just born to shop, but alive to shop. Americans spend more time tooling around the mallcondo — three to four times as many hours as our European counterparts — and we have more stuff to show for it. According to some estimates, we have about four times as many things as Middle Europeans, and who knows how much more than people in the less developed parts of the world. The quantity and disparity are increasing daily, even though, as we see in Russia and China, the "emerging nations" are playing a frantic game of catch-up.

410

This burst of mallcondo commercialism has happened recently — in my ₃
lifetime — and it is spreading around the world at the speed of television.
The average American consumes twice as many goods and services as in
1950; in fact, the poorest fifth of the current population buys more than the
average fifth did in 1955. Little wonder that the average new home of today
is twice as large as the average house built in the early years after World
War II. We have to put that stuff somewhere — quick! — before it turns to
junk.

Sooner or later we are going to have to acknowledge the uncomfortable ₄
fact that this amoral consumerama has proved potent because human
beings *love* things. In fact, to a considerable degree we live for things. In all
cultures we buy things, steal things, exchange things, and horde things.
From time to time, some of us collect vast amounts of things, from tulip
bulbs to paint drippings on canvasses to matchbook covers. Often these
objects have no observable use.

We live through things. We create ourselves through things. And we ₅
change ourselves by changing our things. In the West, we have even developed the elaborate algebra of commercial law to decide how things are exchanged, divested, and recaptured. Remember, we call these things "goods,"
as in "goods and services." We don't — unless we are academic critics — call
them "bads." This sounds simplistic, but it is crucial to understanding the
powerful allure of materialism....

Karl Marx understood the magnetism of things better than anyone else. ₆
In *The Communist Manifesto* (1848), he wrote:

> The bourgeoisie, by the rapid improvement of all instruments of produc-
> tion, by the immensely facilitated means of communication, draws all,
> even the most barbarian nations into civilization. The cheap prices of its
> commodities are the heavy artillery with which it batters down all Chi-
> nese walls.... It compels all nations, on pain of extinction, to adopt the
> bourgeois mode of production; it compels them to introduce what it calls
> civilization into their midst, i.e. to become bourgeois themselves. In one
> word, it creates a world after its own image.

Marx used this insight to motivate the heroic struggle against capitalism.
But the struggle should not be to deter capitalism and its mad consumptive
ways, but to appreciate how it works so its furious energy may be understood and exploited....

If you want to understand the potency of American consumer culture, ₇
ask any group of teenagers what democracy means to them. You will hear
an extraordinary response. Democracy is the right to buy anything you
want. Freedom's just another word for lots of things to buy. Appalling perhaps, but there is something to their answer. Being able to buy what you
want when and where you want it was, after all, the right that made 1989 a
watershed year in Eastern Europe.

Recall as well that freedom to shop was another way to describe the right   8
to be served in a restaurant that provided one focus for the early civil rights
movement. Go back further. It was the right to consume freely which
sparked the fires of separation of this country from England. The freedom
to buy what you want (even if you can't pay for it) is what most foreigners
immediately spot as what they like about our culture, even though in the
next breath they will understandably criticize it....

The grandfather of today's academic scolds is Thorstein Veblen (1857–   9
1929), the eccentric Minnesotan who coined the phrase "conspicuous consumption" and has become almost a cult figure among critics of consumption. All of his books (save for his translation of the *Lexdaela Saga*) are still
in print. His most famous, *The Theory of the Leisure Class*, has never been
out of print since it was first published in 1899.

Veblen claimed that the leisure class set the standards for conspicuous   10
consumption. Without sumptuary laws to protect their markers of distinction, the rest of us could soon make their styles into our own — the Industrial Revolution saw to that. But since objects lose their status distinctions
when consumed by the hoi polloi, the leisure class must eternally be finding newer and more wasteful markers. Waste is not just inevitable, it is
always increasing as the foolish hounds chase the wily fox.

Veblen lumped conspicuous consumption with sports and games,   11
"devout observances," and aesthetic display. They were all reducible, he
insisted, to "pecuniary emulation," his characteristically inflated term for
getting in with the in-crowd. Veblen fancied himself a socialist looking forward to the day when "the discipline of the machine" would be turned
around to promote stringent rationality among the entire population instead of wasted dispersion. If only we had fewer choices we would be happier, there would be less waste, and we would accept each other as equals.

The key to Veblen's argumentative power is that like Hercules cleaning   12
the Augean stables, he felt no responsibility to explain what happens next.
True, if we all purchased the same toothpaste things would be more efficient and less wasteful. Logically we should all read *Consumer Reports*, find
out the best brand, and then all be happy using the same product. But we
aren't. Procter & Gamble markets 36 sizes and shapes of Crest. There are
41 versions of Tylenol. Is this because we are dolts afflicted with "pecuniary
emulation," obsessed with making invidious distinctions, or is the answer
more complex? Veblen never considered that consumers might have other
reasons for exercising choice in the marketplace. He never considered, for
example, that along with "keeping up with the Joneses" runs "keeping away
from the Joneses."...

The process of consumption is creative and even emancipating. In an   13
open market, we consume the real and the imaginary meanings, fusing
objects, symbols, and images together to end up with "a little world made
cunningly." Rather than lives, individuals since midcentury have had

lifestyles. For better or worse, lifestyles are secular religions, coherent patterns of valued things. Your lifestyle is not related to what you do for a living but to what you buy. One of the chief aims of the way we live now is the enjoyment of affiliating with those who share the same clusters of objects as we do.

Mallcondo culture is so powerful in part because it frees us from the 14
strictures of social class. The outcome of material life is no longer preordained by coat of arms, pew seat, or trust fund. Instead, it evolves from a never-ending shifting of individual choice. No one wants to be middle class, for instance. You want to be cool, hip, with it, with the "in" crowd, instead.

One of the reasons terms like Yuppie, Baby Boomer, and GenX have 15
elbowed aside such older designations as "upper middle class" is that we no longer understand social class as well as we do lifestyle, or what marketing firms call "consumption communities." Observing stuff is the way we understand each other. Even if no one knows exactly how much money it takes to be a yuppie, or how young you have to be, or how upwardly aspiring, everybody knows where yuppies gather, how they dress, what they play, what they drive, what they eat, and why they hate to be called yuppies.

For better or worse, American culture is well on its way to becoming 16
world culture. The Soviets have fallen. Only quixotic French intellectuals and anxious Islamic fundamentalists are trying to stand up to it. By no means am I sanguine about such a material culture. It has many problems that I have glossed over. Consumerism is wasteful, it is devoid of otherworldly concerns, it lives for today and celebrates the body, and it overindulges and spoils the young with impossible promises.

"Getting and spending" has eclipsed family, ethnicity, even religion as a 17
defining matrix. That doesn't mean that those other defining systems have disappeared, but that an increasing number of young people around the world will give more of their loyalty to Nike than to creeds of blood, race, or belief. This is not entirely a bad thing, since a lust for upscale branding isn't likely to drive many people to war, but it is, to say the least, far from inspiring.

It would be nice to think that materialism could be heroic, self-abnegating, 18
and redemptive. It would be nice to think that greater material comforts will release us from racism, sexism, and ethnocentrism, and that the apocalypse will come as it did at the end of romanticism in Shelley's *Prometheus Unbound*, leaving us "Scepterless, free, uncircumscribed...Equal, unclassed, tribeless, and nationless."

But it is more likely that the globalization of capitalism will result in the 19
banalities of an ever-increasing worldwide consumerist culture. The French don't stand a chance. The untranscendent, repetitive, sensational, democratic, immediate, tribalizing and unifying force of what Irving Kristol calls the American Imperium need not necessarily result in a Bronze Age of culture. But it certainly will not produce what Shelley had in mind.

We have not been led into this world of material closeness against our 20
better judgment. For many of us, especially when young, consumerism *is*
our better judgment. We have not just asked to go this way, we have
demanded. Now most of the world is lining up, pushing and shoving, eager
to elbow into the mall. Getting and spending has become the most passionate, and often the most imaginative, endeavor of modern life. While
this is dreary and depressing to some, as doubtless it should be, it is liberating and democratic to many more.

Analyzing This Selection

1. What evidence of the triumph of mallcondo commercialism does Twitchell
   present? Examine the diverse range of evidence, and identify what is convincing to you.

2. What does a *lifestyle* produce? How does it, if at all, liberate us?

3. How did Marx and Veblen criticize the effects of capitalism? According to
   Twitchell, in what ways were they mistaken? In what ways were they correct?

4. **THE WRITER'S METHOD**   Reconsider the essay's title. What would
   prompt Twitchell to give the third cheer? How does he convey this attitude
   in the essay?

Analyzing Connections

5. Twitchell and Forster (see "My Wood," p. 406) both examine the effects of
   possessions on character. Does Twitchell answer or avoid Forster's objections?

Analyzing by Writing

6. Analyze the issues involved when consumerism *was* your better judgment.
   Consider a conflict over buying, wearing, or using possessions. Examine the
   issues of equality, justice, power, loyalty, or autonomy in your choice. Be
   specific about your gains and losses in making the choice. Do you think, in
   retrospect, that you had other means to bring about change at the time?

Holly Brubach

MAIL-ORDER AMERICA

HOLLY BRUBACH (b. 1953) graduated from Duke University. In New York she wrote fashion articles for *Vogue* magazine and contributed dance criticism to the *Atlantic Monthly*. Joining the *New Yorker* as a fashion columnist, Brubach continued to write about dance, scripting television programs for *Dance in America*. Presently, she is the style editor of the *New York Times Magazine*, where this essay appeared in 1993.

Growing up in Pittsburgh, I had an uncle who never obtained a passport because he had made up his mind that he was never going to need one: he had no intention of ever leaving the country. For that matter, he had never left the state of Pennsylvania, except for one brief foray into Ohio, which, he realized in retrospect, had been a mistake. For a soul so utterly lacking in wanderlust, however, he was full of curiosity. In the pages of *National Geographic*, he visited the steppes of Russia and the Pyramids and the Great Wall, and on those rare occasions when bona fide travelers happened to cross his path, he could converse with them about the average rainfall in the month of August or the mathematical basis of the architecture or the worsening condition of the mortar, as if he'd not only gone on a tour but guided it. I remember regarding this knowledge as somehow illegitimate, acquired rather than earned. And with all the superiority of youth, I viewed him as lazy and complacent for not having gone out and seen the world for himself.

Now, however, I confess that the older I get, the more I'm inclined to follow his example, in my way. Late at night, when the stores are closed, or on a Saturday afternoon, while weary women with swollen feet and cranky children are competing for an overworked salesman's attention, I'm at home with a stack of mail-order catalogues, redecorating my apartment and browsing for Christmas presents and planning what I'll wear next season. With time, I find, the best catalogues come to seem familiar: you recognize their tone of voice, their quirks, the faces that appear over and over again in their pages. Leafing through one recent arrival, a friend shook his head at the sight of so many models who for years now have been turning up in his mailbox on a regular basis. "I feel like I know these people better than the people I know," he said.

For those of us who feel that our lives have been inundated with cata- 3
logues, there is corroboration in statistics: last year, according to the Direct
Marketing Association, more than 10,000 mail-order companies sent out
13.5 billion catalogues and some 55 percent of the adult population
bought $51.5 billion worth of goods by mail. These figures have been
steadily on the rise, climbing steeply during the '80s, when mail-order businesses grew at triple the rate of most retailers. Industry analysts say that this
boom has come about for a variety of reasons, including the introduction of
ZIP codes and toll-free telephone numbers, the spread of credit cards, the
use of computer networks that cross-check information about individual
spending habits and the sizable contingent of women in the work force.
Women no longer have the time for recreational shopping, it seems, and
men, who never had the time to shop, can no longer expect women to do
their shopping for them.

Somehow, over the course of the past fifteen years or so, our collective 4
attitude toward shopping — or at least toward the idea of it — seems to have
shifted from delight to loathing. Those who once relished the chase, tracking down the perfect raincoat or duffel bag or fly-fishing rod or coffee
maker or scented candle, can no longer be bothered. The audience for the
department-store-as-theater has pretty much disappeared. In 1978, shoppers
flocked to Bloomingdale's India promotion, buying souvenirs and saving
themselves the trip (an idea that would have appealed to my uncle); now
they can save themselves the trip across town. Although (or maybe because) we still look on the things with which people surround themselves
as indicative of something deeply personal — as a form of self-expression —
the act of furnishing our lives now strikes us as a chore. Perhaps it's our
conscience, which we misplaced during the '80s, that is telling us not to
set foot in the temples of consumerism. Perhaps it's our sense of decorum:
we haven't stopped spending our money, but we're more reluctant to spend
it in public. Most likely, mail-order catalogues are about sheer convenience: the catalogues have done for stores what videos have done for movie
theaters.

Possibly due to the mistaken assumption that people who can afford 5
expensive clothes have more time to shop or that luxury goods would be
tainted by the stigma of catalogue shopping, the top of the retail market
has yet to be colonized by the mail-order business. Despite the occasional
exception..., mail order in many people's minds retains the down-market
connotations of the "wish books" that peddled dinette sets to the children
of immigrants. Within the past few years, however, fashion designers have
begun to view the success of catalogues like J. Crew with increasing envy,
and some — among them Calvin Klein and Carolyne Roehm — have
begun to make inroads into the field.

What industry analysts leave unsaid, but what millions of mail-order cus- 6
tomers know firsthand, is that the catalogues are beating not only the stores

but also the fashion magazines at their own game. Fashion magazines now find themselves preaching almost exclusively to the converted, reporting designers' runway proclamations as if they mattered (which they do, in a way). Mail-order catalogues, however, insinuate themselves into the homes of the indifferent and the disaffected, who couldn't care less what Karl Lagerfeld has to say. Where magazines have come to look more and more like catalogues, offering a little something for everyone (the advertisers, the designers, the multitudes of readers), catalogues have come to look more and more like magazines, with a distinct editorial point of view. While magazines have waxed prosaic, catalogues have turned poetic, portraying a world that, for all its resemblance to the one in which we live, is of their own creation — a place with its own landscape, its indigenous population, its native customs, its dialect. If our forays into this world are increasingly frequent, perhaps it's because they confirm a number of things we like to believe: that life is happy, harmonious and just and that people get what they deserve, which in our case is the best.

The territory staked out by J. Crew in the pages of its catalogue was, until recently, easy to locate — just down the road from where the people in Ralph Lauren's ads lived. The real estate was a little more affordable, the local inhabitants — attractive, unfailingly stylish men and women — weren't quite so stuck-up and self-conscious. Clearly, we were somewhere in America, but in an America that was scenic and vaguely nostalgic, where there were no strip malls or nuclear power plants or fast-food restaurants. In this place, Coca-Cola still came in the old green glass bottles — no garish aluminum cans. The people who lived there drove Land Rovers and convertible two-seaters. They packed their picnics in antique wicker hampers. They painted an old table they bought at a yard sale and got the paint all over themselves. Shucking corn, eating watermelon, drinking iced tea and homemade lemonade, they were caught in the act by the camera, in pictures that could have been snapshots taken by a friend. These people's sailboats and their golden retrievers and their Alumni Day visit to a university that looked to be either Princeton or Yale situated them squarely in the upper middle class. The men were well groomed, clean shaven, with short hair and high cheekbones. The women wore little or no makeup, and an inordinate number of them were pale and blue-eyed and blond; one, a regular, bore a remarkable resemblance to Glenn Close. (The portfolio of dressier women's clothes modeled by Lauren Hutton, a regular feature every season, has always looked more like a fashion story from Mirabella than a weekday extension of the life depicted in the rest of the catalogue.)

Lately, however, there's been an influx of ethnicity into J. Crew's pages (it's happening in Ralph Lauren's neighborhood, too). This fall, there are not one but four different editions of the J. Crew catalogue — one set in downtown Manhattan, the others in the usual picturesque country retreat, with small inset photographs from the urban version. Our old acquaintances have been moved aside to make room for an aspiring rock band and its assorted hangers-on. The split-rail fences, the stands of trees, the path along the crest of the dunes give way, in the downtown edition, to corrugated fencing, cracked windows held together with duct tape and graffiti. A pick-up basketball game in a city schoolyard includes three blacks, one Asian and a couple of white guys. There are men with long, unruly hair and women who appear to be of Mediterranean extraction, or part-Hispanic, or part-black. Blondes are rare.

But in one sense the demographics are still surprisingly narrow: there   9
are no old people. Here, as in the mythical place where J. Crew's catalogue used to reside, the population ranges in age from late teens to mid-30's, with a handful of children — none of them old enough to wear braces or need advice about birth control.

At first glance, the multiculturalism that has found its way into J. Crew's   10
catalogue looks like an injection of reality into what had been an airtight fantasy, but closer inspection reveals that only the trappings have changed; the fantasy remains the same. This is a world whose affable inhabitants live in harmony. Camaraderie prevails. No one is ever alone, unless it's to read a book, and even then we feel sure that there are friends somewhere close at hand, sleeping late or poring over the Sunday paper or planning dinner. All dark thoughts, all solitary bouts of melancholy and despair, have been banished. On page after page, the good times unfold. Life is a party to which we wish we'd been invited. The only difference is that this season, there are some new people on the guest list.

The voice in the copy that accompanies the photographs remains cor-   11
dial and sensible-sounding — no flowery odes to a shirt, no wheedling sales pitches about the role it will play in your wardrobe. No full sentences, either. The machine-gun rhythm gets to be a little irritating: "Buttons. Collar. Placket. Seams. A hefty cotton jersey." Every once in a while the polite reserve falls away and then J. Crew gives in to snobbery and name-dropping. "We can't say for sure, but we seem to remember old photos of Jackson Pollock in East Hampton wearing pants like these," one caption claims.

Nearly everything J. Crew sells — new editions of standard sportswear   12
that's in the public domain — seems calculated to be instantly familiar, to take its place beside those favorite items in our wardrobes that have earned the status of old friends. The "barn jackets" are "pre-aged" and appear slightly battered; the twill work shirts are dyed to look as if they've faded over the course of long years. Many of the items are just like something we already own, except for some small detail, some slight improvement that makes us suddenly feel that the version we have is inferior: the phys. ed. shorts are in vivid colors they never came in at school; the rope-soled espadrilles are gingham-checked; the denim jackets have a tartan lining. The appeal of these clothes is based on novelty rather than fashion....

The guys in the J. Crew catalogue are the "new men" we've heard so   13
much about: they throw their arms around each other's shoulders; they

know their way around a kitchen; they feed their baby children. Although in the past the men wearing wedding bands outnumbered the women who wore them, there was never the slightest suspicion that the men might be married to somebody else who wasn't pictured — that they'd left their wives at home and run off for an illicit weekend in the catalogue's pages. In fact, it seemed to go without saying that these women *were* the wives and that, while the new men may have relished a wedding ring as a token of commitment, the women were so secure and independent that they didn't need one.

This fall, however, there are fewer men and women wearing wedding   14 bands. What this means for marriage is anybody's guess. Maybe it's still going strong, but the signs of it aren't fashionable anymore. Maybe this crowd is younger and they're still waiting to meet their mates. Or maybe people who live in lofts in New York don't get married as much as people who live in places where Coke still comes in bottles. The old cast of characters had about it an air of satisfaction, of being settled; this new crowd projects a sense of possibilities.

Unlike J. Crew — the name of no one in particular, which conjures up   15 images of oarsmen on the Charles — L. L. Bean was a real person: Leon Leonwood Bean who, as faithful readers of his catalogues have learned over the years, loved to go fishing, hunting and camping, lived to be 94, sent his favorite dog tins of biscuits when he went away on trips and gave each newly married L. L. Bean employee a Hudson's Bay blanket as a wedding present. Though he is no longer the company's animating presence, there's a distinct personality that survives in the tone of the catalogue copy. Plain-spoken, chatty and respectful, the corporate voice of L. L. Bean keeps up a fairly steady monologue in a mature-sounding first-person plural, taking full responsibility for the products for sale, offering bits of arcane information (it takes thirty to fifty gallons of maple-sugar sap to produce a single gallon of syrup), creating the impression that on the other side of the image and the "800" number there's somebody home. "Our product testers found these versatile boots ideal for mountain biking and day hiking," the catalogue announces. At Christmas, L. L. Bean greets its customers with the fond good wishes of an old friend: "We hope to hear from you and hope you have a safe and memorable holiday season."

The people pictured in L. L. Bean's pages look like attractive customers   16 or friends of the employees or teachers at the local elementary school in Freeport, Me., the company's headquarters; they're simply too ordinary to qualify as models. All fantasy, all glamour, all aspirations to a better life than the one in which the readers might find themselves are absent here. The appeal rests entirely on reality — or, rather, on some approximation of reality, since the majority of L. L. Bean's customers probably don't live in log cabins or houses with stone hearths. Where several other, glossier catalogues with pretensions to elegance routinely offer certain items at discreet "marked-down" prices in order to avoid the stigma of discount retailing (in the Victoria's Secret catalogue, the Chancery Lace Bra has been on sale for at least four years now), L. L. Bean makes no bones about appealing to the reader's desire to save a dollar here, a dollar there; thrift is a Yankee virtue. A shirt is advertised as "priced at an exceptional value — $4 less than last year."

The houses are modest. The landscape is strictly local, off the circuit that the power brokers travel. The Christmas trees that appear in the background in the holiday edition are hung not with precious, glittering gold and cut-crystal ornaments, as they are in the Victoria's Secret catalogue, but with pretzels and cranberry strands and strung popcorn. If L. L. Bean is guilty of romanticizing anything, it's the continuous present of the American home, cozy and unbroken, as it exists for most people only in the imagination. Microwave ovens, Nintendo, 12-step programs — the world as we now know it has been held at bay, with no more than a few recent developments like step aerobics selectively admitted. The TV, VCR, stereo and CD player are housed in a cabinet designed to look like an old-fashioned icebox. Though the loving hands that stitch Bean's sampler quilts and crewel-embroidered sweaters are anonymous, their products are suffused with intimations of mythical grandmothers.   17

The people L. L. Bean depicts, one gathers, are mostly married, with car pools and mortgages and aging parents — the full weight of adult responsibility on their shoulders. They are pictured fetching a few logs from the woodpile, teaching their tow-headed children to read or curled up in their flannel pajamas, book in hand. Personality, 10. Sex appeal, 0. It's not so much the clothes they wear that make them look so dowdy, since many of the items aren't significantly different from their trendier counterparts (J. Crew's Barn Jacket is nearly indistinguishable from Bean's Canvas Field Coat). It's the way the clothes are worn — their tidy fit, their matching colors, their utter lack of any sense of adventure (paradoxical in people who profess to love exploring the outdoors). The cut is prudish at times: the caption for one cotton shirt assures the reader that the V-neck is "not too low." The catalogue repeatedly draws the line between "roomy" and "relaxed" (both desirable traits) and "oversized" (taboo in this context). Fashion is suspect, to be avoided at all costs. The people at L. L. Bean refer consistently to their "apparel designers," in a locution as quaint as a Norman Rockwell illustration. The free and loose style that dominates the pages of J. Crew would surely dismay these adherents to the rule book of convention. Shirts and turtleneck jerseys are worn close to the body and tucked in. Sweaters are ribbed at the cuffs and at the waistband. The effect is Republican.   18

In the world evoked by the L. L. Bean catalogue, there is no room for the confusion about sex roles that currently besets the rest of our society. Androgyny is prohibited. Those garments that the Bean people countenance for both men and women are designated outright "For Men and   19

Women," with separate sizes or, in a few cases, men's sizes followed by a list of women's equivalents; the word "unisex" is never spoken. Likewise, the people at L. L. Bean have their minds made up on the subject of color palettes and gender. Mock turtlenecks are available in, among other colors: "Maroon (Men's only). Honey (Women's only). Blue (Men's only)." When it comes to the Blanket Plaid Flannel Shirts, the men get brown; the women, red. There is, of course, nothing to prevent a woman from ordering the same shirt in brown, in a men's size, for a fit that's slightly funkier, but the distinctions here are so firmly drawn that so brash an act would be tantamount to cross-dressing.

This catalogue sure is talkative, with a lengthy caption for every item, 20 listing its attributes in scrupulous detail. "Buttons along left side for easy on/off," the catalogue says of a jumper. A jersey dress is "fun to wear — needs no special care." The longstanding Yankee suspicion of fashion is coupled here with the conviction that clothes are a lot of bother.

Ironically, plaid flannel shirts, along with Birkenstocks and several other 21 items L. L. Bean sells, are "hot" right now — a fact of which the Bean people seem oblivious. Where J. Crew takes essentially standard items and presents them in a manner that's glamorous and up to the minute — shirts tied around the waist, shorts two sizes too big, worn low on the hips of young models — L. L. Bean's approach is stolid and plain. The appeal of this is probably lost on people who buy into the heat of the moment, but for those who have opted out of the rat race, including (paradoxically) many full-time fashion types, L. L. Bean is a relief, a refuge from the onslaughts of trendiness.

Bean's style might be called New England provincial, and like all 22 provincial esthetics, it is ultimately corrupted by sentimentality. Ankle socks "patterned with cows and pigs grazing amid tulip rows." The "Warm Feelings Blanket." J. Crew has found a harmless enough outlet for its elegiac impulses in the names of colors, which ramble from the botanical (weed, thistle, yucca, aloe, glade, balsam) to the oceanographic (Pacific, surf, kelp, lake, lagoon) to the culinary (Dijon, cola, chili). But L. L. Bean refuses to get carried away in this respect: "yellow, orange, magenta, dark purple, white, turquoise, royal, navy," the catalogue states flatly. This penchant for simplicity is every so often overcome by some lyric impulse and then the hardheaded Yankee is revealed to be a sap, particularly when it comes to the local landscape: a sweater captures "the soft tones of a Maine seaside garden muted by fog" or a quilt evokes a wave of memories, including "the cry of loons in early morning." But these outbursts, rare and always brief, were outdone in the catalogue this spring by the emotionalism of one C. H. Gray, a customer from Hillsboro, Ore. His paean to his Maine Hunting Shoes, received in 1945 as a gift from his father, is written in iambic septameter, and the penultimate couplet reads: "These boots have kept my feet warm, comfortable and dry,/And the thought of simply discarding them can almost make me cry."

In the end, what saves L. L. Bean from bathos is the sense that the   23
people behind the catalogue actually live the life depicted in its pages. The
outdoorsy, sports-loving attitude is not a pose. Though L. L. Bean's fishing
vest may be worn by photographers and other people in need of lots of
pockets, it is designed for someone who actually fishes. The context in
which the clothes are presented confirms their authenticity. The Fly Fishing catalogue (a separate edition) is packed with fascinating lore, as well
as flies called "Mickey Finn," "Fruit Cocktail" and — wonderful finds
for the collector of affectionate nicknames — "Rat Face Irresistible" and
"Gerbubble Bug." J. Crew may sell all the makings of an outfit that one
could wear to go kayaking, but L. L. Bean sells the outfit *and* the kayak.

It is not at all clear whether the Victoria's Secret catalogue is intended   24
for the women who would wear the clothes featured in it or for the men
who would like the women in their lives to wear the clothes featured in
it — particularly the lingerie. In what is tantamount to an admission that
the catalogue has acquired a considerable following among the kind of
guys who maintain a small archive of *Sports Illustrated*'s swimsuit issues,
the copy goes back and forth, addressing first the women, who are buying
for themselves ("a great choice when dinner's at 8 and you're leaving
straight from the office") and then the men, who are buying for the women
("a sumptuous gift so wonderful, you might let her have it just a little bit
early"). The tone Victoria's Secret takes with men is hushed and conspira-
torial, as if this were their girlfriend's best friend talking — steering them
clear of all the pitfalls they would otherwise encounter in their search for
the perfect gift. Even so, this catalogue is unquestionably a female enclave,
like a beauty salon or a harem — a place to which women retreat to make
themselves more attractive. And though men are seldom admitted, their
presence and power in the world beyond its confines are implied in the
women's diligent efforts to please them.

The Victoria's Secret cast revolves around a handful of recognizable   25
stars — "supermodels" who inhabit the pages of *Vogue*, ads for designer
clothes and the runways of Europe. Linda Evangelista, Stephanie Seymour
and Karen Mulder bring to the catalogue an aura of international glamour,
or anyway that seems to be the intent. The truth is that it's always something of a shock to come upon them here, like finding movie stars playing
the dinner theater on a cruise ship. Nearly all the women have long hair
(long hair and sexy lingerie evidently go together). When it comes to clothing, models always wear the smallest size; when it comes to bras, the
women in the Victoria's Secret catalogue look as if they take a medium at
the very least.

To my mind, the better part of this catalogue's entertainment value   26
resides in watching the Victoria's Secret people walk the fine line between
sexy and trashy. The trappings are endlessly amusing, intended to set a tone
of thoroughbred elegance and high propriety by evoking the life of the

English aristocracy. But a bona fide Mayfair drawing room would run the risk of being too subtle and musty to trigger in American readers the desired intimidation at the thought of a nation full of people supposedly more civilized than we are. Instead, the Victoria's Secret masterminds have constructed what is essentially a cartoon furnished with hoity-toity, English clichés: silver salvers, Battersea boxes, leather library sofas, paintings of horses. The models — clad in scant, lace-trimmed underwear, their bra straps slipping off their shoulders — look soulfully into the eye of the camera while lying on an Oriental rug or posing next to a tea table.

The catalogue copy is likewise strewn with Britishisms: "centre," "jew- 27 ellery," "colour," "favourite," "splendour."...An ongoing series of bathrobes has identified itself with a distinguished university (the Cambridge Robe), a country house open to tourists (the Chatsworth Robe), a legendary heroine harking back to the days of chivalry (the Guinevere Robe).

The merchandise itself, ranging from suits and dresses to sports clothes 28 and what the English call "frocks" for evening, isn't bad, despite a propensity for shiny synthetic fibers that give an impression of simulated satin with an almost adhesive cling. There's a good selection of bras and underpants: demi-cup underwires, halter-neck bras, strapless bustiers, merry widows, garter belts, flutter bikinis, high-cut briefs, G-strings. But over all, the clothing is strictly middle of the road — mall fashion that steers a safe and steady course, with an occasional detour to take in some recent trend. The catalogue would have us believe that its constituency is made up mostly of successful career women; an outfit is touted for its "executive finesse." But the only executives who dress like this are the ones in television miniseries. The colors are a little too bright for the corporate life; the cut calls too much attention to the shape of the body. Five years after fashion designers finally succeeded in abolishing shoulder pads, the people at Victoria's Secret seem either not to know or not to care; nor have they heard about the demotion of the "power suit," which has been discarded by the women it was intended for and taken up by the women who work for them. In fact, the likeliest candidate for the Victoria's Secret customer would appear to be not the *Business Week* subscriber but That Cosmopolitan Girl.

The catalogue speaks the language of romance novels, fraught with 29 histrionic verbs and overwrought adjectives. Bikinis "sizzle," skirts "sweep" and "cascade," necklines "plunge," dresses "bedazzle." The clothes are routinely described as "opulent," "lavish," "sophisticated." Why use a plain word when a fancy one will do? Some of the fabrics are "launderable."

Significantly, the famous models who might have been the obvious 30 choices — buxom blondes like Claudia Schiffer and Anna Nicole Smith, the Brigitte Bardot and Marilyn Monroe look-alikes — are absent here. Victoria's Secret features good girls, well brought up, slightly nymphomaniacal, but only behind closed doors and only when they're in love. Seymour — head back, back arched — writhes with longing. Mulder projects a certain reserve, even when she's reclining on a chaise longue, wearing a push-up bra and bikini briefs. The sex appeal is of the smoldering, read-my-mind variety, not kittenish or playful. Page after page, these contemporary odalisques offer themselves, like Manet's "Olympia," in repose: passive women, waiting for a man to come along and fulfill them — not just any man but the man of their dreams.

A generation that gleaned some of its earliest information about sex by 31 scrutinizing the pages of prosthetic-looking bras and briefs in the Sears catalogue (straightforward, almost clinical — like looking up dirty words in the dictionary) has finally come of age and now studies Victoria's Secret instead. The pleasure this experience holds for men is obvious. But what women get out of it — apart from the convenience of mail-order shopping — has been largely overlooked. There is perhaps an unspoken consensus that the subject is too loaded, that the less said these days about the pleasure women may take in projecting themselves into the role of a sex object, the better. But the fact remains that for many women, looking at pictures of other women is an incitement to fantasy — not because they want to know those women but because they want in some vague way to *be* those women, to evoke in men the feelings they imagine the women in the pictures do.

Lust, however, is only part of the equation. The eroticism is always sub- 32 ordinate to a higher goal: romance. Readers of novels about American girls adrift in international society or about 18th-century virgins ravished by pirates or about small-town daughters who conquer the hearts of lonesome millionaires will recognize in Victoria's Secret's lingerie pages a kindred sensibility. The hot-blooded lover rips the heroine's bodice and discovers... the lace-edged, demi-cup, underwire bra on page 14. I have an idea for a new marketing venture: a made-for-television movie subtitled with information about the clothes the characters are wearing (fabric content, sizes, price), along with a toll-free number the viewer can call to order them.

Year in and year out, this hunger for romance and passion — the sight of 33 all these women in heat — is like an obsessive drone so that, finally, what seems most remarkable about Victoria's Secret is a certain self-referential monotony....Victoria's Secret recommends its Tapestry Keepsake Box as the perfect place to store love letters.

The heroine of the Victoria's Secret catalogue is, in many respects, the 34 ideal mail-order customer. House-bound in her lace-trimmed satin teddy, she lounges decoratively, leafing through the catalogues that get delivered to her door while she awaits the man who will transform her life. Every day brings a new harvest of things she never knew she needed: reproduction gargoyles (Design Toscano); copies of baseball uniforms from such historic teams as the Mexican Southwest League Tabasco Bananas and the Toledo Mud Hens (Ebbets Field Flannels); a lease on a lobster trap (Rent Mother Nature); and healing crystals and new-age cards dispensing sage advice: "Live Juicy....Marry Yourself....Be who you truly are and the money will follow" (Red Rose Collection). From "The Best Catalogues in the World" she orders other catalogues. In her Tapestry Keepsake Box she stashes a snack — a chocolate bar in the shape of a topographical map of Israel (The Source for Everything Jewish)....

The truth might ruin her illusion. She switches on the television, but 35 the Home Shopping Club, a cross between an auction and a telethon, strikes her as raucous and intrusive, to say nothing of the clinical way the merchandise is displayed, as if it were on exhibit in a courtroom. When information about...J. Crew's expanding retail empire makes its way into the papers, she instinctively avoids it. Too many facts would expose the stagecraft.

This is an alternative world she's living in, in which every catalogue 36 seizes on some facet of life and celebrates the hell out of it. J. Crew would have us believe that belonging to a community would fill the empty spaces in our souls. The people at L. L. Bean would turn our enthusiasm for the outdoors into a religion.... In Victoria's Secret, it's love. These are not misrepresentations, only exaggerations, and in many respects they are more comfortable than the ambiguities and compromises that permeate our everyday lives. If mail-order shopping is sweeping America, perhaps it's because we're such a willing audience for the fantasies that catalogues present: we've been led to believe that our circumstances can change overnight, that any day now we can get discovered, find true love, hit the jackpot.

So the woman reads the catalogues in solitude, in silence or while lis- 37 tening to "Classics by Request," Victoria's Secret's two-volume tape collection of classical music by Mozart, Vivaldi, Handel and others. In page after page, the catalogues lay out their merchandise for her perusal. They speak to her directly, flattering her vanity, courting her interest. "This is all for you," they say. "You are the only customer in the world."

Analyzing This Selection

1. **THE WRITER'S METHOD**   How do paragraphs 1 and 2 contribute to the rest of the essay? Since Brubach doesn't return to these personal details, do they continue to be relevant? Should paragraphs 1 and 2 be deleted?

2. Does the author condemn or enjoy each catalogue fantasy? What is the purpose of Brubach's analysis?

3. Examine Brubach's summaries of the pictorial content of each catalogue. How does her language describe the evocative pictures?

4. What does the author say about real, not mail-order, America?

Analyzing Connection

5. What is each catalogue's unspoken definition of middle class? Is the definition realistic, or is it a fantasy? Do the values resemble or differ from the middle-class values that are defined by Shelby Steele (see "On Being Black and Middle Class," p. 224)?

Analyzing by Writing

6. Examine connections between words and pictures in a catalogue or brochure. (You may still have a brochure you received as a prospective college student.) What elements of reality are missing? What attractive fantasy is suggested? Analyze the world it creates.

Lars Eighner

ON DUMPSTER DIVING

Lars Eighner (b. 1948) attended college in Texas and held various jobs before he found himself homeless. This essay about his methods of survival brought him acclaim as a writer. Eighner continues his account in *Travels with Lizbeth: Three Years on the Round and on the Streets* (1993). His most recent book is *Wank: The Tapes* (1998).

Long before I began Dumpster diving I was impressed with Dumpsters, 1 enough so that I wrote the Merriam-Webster research service to discover what I could about the word "Dumpster." I learned from them that "Dumpster" is a proprietary word belonging to the Dempster Dumpster company.

Since then I have dutifully capitalized the word although it was lower- 2 cased in almost all of the citations Merriam-Webster photocopied for me. Dempster's word is too apt. I have never heard these things called anything but Dumpsters. I do not know anyone who knows the generic name for these objects. From time to time, however, I hear a wino or hobo give some corrupted credit to the original and call them Dipsy Dumpsters.

I began Dumpster diving about a year before I became homeless. 3

I prefer the term "scavenging" and use the word "scrounging" when I 4 mean to be obscure. I have heard people, evidently meaning to be polite, using the word "foraging," but I prefer to reserve that word for gathering nuts and berries and such which I do also according to the season and the opportunity. "Dumpster diving" seems to me to be a little too cute and, in my case, inaccurate because I lack the athletic ability to lower myself into the Dumpsters as the true divers do, much to their increased profit.

I like the frankness of the word "scavenging," which I can hardly think 5 of without picturing a big black snail on an aquarium wall. I live from the refuse of others. I am a scavenger. I think it a sound and honorable niche, although if I could I would naturally prefer to live the comfortable consumer life, perhaps — and only perhaps — as a slightly less wasteful consumer owing to what I have learned as a scavenger.

While my dog Lizbeth and I were still living in the house on Avenue B 6 in Austin, as my savings ran out, I put almost all my sporadic income into rent. The necessities of daily life I began to extract from Dumpsters. Yes, we ate from Dumpsters. Except for jeans, all my clothes came from Dumpsters.

…es, candles, bedding, toilet paper, medicine, books, a typewriter,
…male love doll, change sometimes amounting to many dollars: I
…d many things from the Dumpsters.

…ve learned much as a scavenger. I mean to put some of what I have   7
learned down here, beginning with the practical art of Dumpster diving
and proceeding to the abstract.

What is safe to eat?   8

After all, the finding of objects is becoming something of an urban art.   9
Even respectable employed people will sometimes find something tempting sticking out of a Dumpster or standing beside one. Quite a number of
people, not all of them of the bohemian type, are willing to brag that they
found this or that piece in the trash. But eating from Dumpsters is the
thing that separates the dilettanti from the professionals.

Eating safely from the Dumpsters involves three principles: using the   10
senses and common sense to evaluate the condition of the found materials,
knowing the Dumpsters of a given area and checking them regularly, and
seeking always to answer the question "Why was this discarded?"

Perhaps everyone who has a kitchen and a regular supply of groceries   11
has, at one time or another, made a sandwich and eaten half of it before
discovering mold on the bread or got a mouthful of milk before realizing
the milk had turned. Nothing of the sort is likely to happen to a Dumpster
diver because he is constantly reminded that most food is discarded for a
reason. Yet a lot of perfectly good food can be found in Dumpsters.

Canned goods, for example, turn up fairly often in the Dumpsters I fre-   12
quent. All except the most phobic people would be willing to eat from a
can even if it came from a Dumpster. Canned goods are among the safest
of foods to be found in Dumpsters, but are not utterly foolproof.

Although very rare with modern canning methods, botulism is a possi-   13
bility. Most other forms of food poisoning seldom do lasting harm to a
healthy person. But botulism is almost certainly fatal and often the first
symptom is death. Except for carbonated beverages, all canned goods
should contain a slight vacuum and suck air when first punctured.
Bulging, rusty, dented cans and cans that spew when punctured should be
avoided, especially when the contents are not very acidic or syrupy.

Heat can break down the botulin, but this requires much more cooking   14
than most people do to canned goods. To the extent that botulism occurs
at all, of course, it can occur in cans on pantry shelves as well as in cans
from Dumpsters. Need I say that home-canned goods found in Dumpsters
are simply too risky to be recommended.

From time to time one of my companions, aware of the source of my   15
provisions, will ask, "Do you think these crackers are really safe to eat?" For
some reason it is most often the crackers they ask about.

This question always makes me angry. Of course I would not offer my   16
companion anything I had doubts about. But more than that I wonder why
he cannot evaluate the condition of the crackers for himself. I have no spe-

cial knowledge and I have been wrong before. Since he knows where the food comes from, it seems to me he ought to assume some of the responsibility for deciding what he will put in his mouth.

For myself I have few qualms about dry foods such as crackers, cookies, 17 cereal, chips, and pasta if they are free of visible contaminates and still dry and crisp. Most often such things are found in the original packaging, which is not so much a positive sign as it is the absence of a negative one.

Raw fruits and vegetables with intact skins seem perfectly safe to me, 18 excluding of course the obviously rotten. Many are discarded for minor imperfections which can be pared away. Leafy vegetables, grapes, cauliflower, broccoli, and similar things may be contaminated by liquids and may be impractical to wash.

Candy, especially hard candy, is usually safe if it has not drawn ants. 19 Chocolate is often discarded only because it has become discolored as the cocoa butter de-emulsified. Candying after all is one method of food preservation because pathogens do not like very sugary substances.

All of these foods might be found in any Dumpster and can be evalu- 20 ated with some confidence largely on the basis of appearance. Beyond these are foods which cannot be correctly evaluated without additional information.

I began scavenging by pulling pizzas out of the Dumpster behind a 21 pizza delivery shop. In general prepared food requires caution, but in this case I knew when the shop closed and went to the Dumpster as soon as the last of the help left.

Such shops often get prank orders, called "bogus." Because help seldom 22 stays long at these places pizzas are often made with the wrong topping, refused on delivery for being cold, or baked incorrectly. The products to be discarded are boxed up because inventory is kept by counting boxes: A boxed pizza can be written off; an unboxed pizza does not exist.

I never placed a bogus order to increase the supply of pizzas and I 23 believe no one else was scavenging in this Dumpster. But the people in the shop became suspicious and began to retain their garbage in the shop overnight.

While it lasted I had a steady supply of fresh, sometimes warm pizza. 24 Because I knew the Dumpster I knew the source of the pizza, and because I visited the Dumpster regularly I knew what was fresh and what was yesterday's.

The area I frequent is inhabited by many affluent college students. I am 25 not here by chance; the Dumpsters in this area are very rich. Students throw out many good things, including food. In particular they tend to throw everything out when they move at the end of a semester, before and after breaks, and around midterm when many of them despair of college. So I find it advantageous to keep an eye on the academic calendar.

The students throw food away around the breaks because they do not 26 know whether it has spoiled or will spoil before they return. A typical discard is a half jar of peanut butter. In fact nonorganic peanut butter does not require refrigeration and is unlikely to spoil in any reasonable time. The student does not know that, and since it is Daddy's money, the student decides not to take a chance.

Opened containers require caution and some attention to the question 27 "Why was this discarded?" But in the case of discards from student apartments, the answer may be that the item was discarded through carelessness, ignorance, or wastefulness. This can sometimes be deduced when the item is found with many others, including some that are obviously perfectly good.

Some students, and others, approach defrosting a freezer by chucking 28 out the whole lot. Not only do the circumstances of such a find tell the story, but also the mass of frozen goods stays cold for a long time and items may be found still frozen or freshly thawed.

Yogurt, cheese, and sour cream are items that are often thrown out while 29 they are still good. Occasionally I find a cheese with a spot of mold, which of course I just pare off, and because it is obvious why such a cheese was discarded, I treat it with less suspicion than an apparently perfect cheese found in similar circumstances. Yogurt is often discarded, still sealed, only because the expiration date on the carton had passed. This is one of my favorite finds because yogurt will keep for several days, even in warm weather.

Students throw out canned goods and staples at the end of semesters and 30 when they give up college at midterm. Drugs, pornography, spirits, and the like are often discarded when parents are expected — Dad's day, for example. And spirits also turn up after big party weekends, presumably discarded by the newly reformed. Wine and spirits, of course, keep perfectly well even once opened.

My test for carbonated soft drinks is whether they still fizz vigorously. 31 Many juices or other beverages are too acid or too syrupy to cause much concern provided they are not visibly contaminated. Liquids, however, require some care.

One hot day I found a large jug of Pat O'Brien's Hurricane mix. The jug 32 had been opened, but it was still ice cold. I drank three large glasses before it became apparent to me that someone had added the rum to the mix, and not a little rum. I never tasted the rum and by the time I began to feel the effects I had already ingested a very large quantity of the beverage. Some divers would have considered this a boon, but being suddenly and thoroughly intoxicated in a public place in the early afternoon is not my idea of a good time.

I have heard of people maliciously contaminating discarded food and 33 even handouts, but mostly I have heard of this from people with vivid imaginations who have had no experience with the Dumpsters themselves. Just before the pizza shop stopped discarding its garbage at night, jalapeños began showing up on most of the discarded pizzas. If indeed this was meant to discourage me it was a wasted effort because I am native Texan.

For myself, I avoid game, poultry, pork, and egg-based foods whether I 34
find them raw or cooked. I seldom have the means to cook what I find, but
when I do I avail myself of plentiful supplies of beef which is often in very
good condition. I suppose fish becomes disagreeable before it becomes
dangerous. The dog is happy to have any such thing that is past its prime
and, in fact, does not recognize fish as food until it is quite strong.

Home leftovers, as opposed to surpluses from restaurants, are very often 35
bad. Evidently, especially among students, there is a common type of personality that carefully wraps up even the smallest leftover and shoves it into
the back of the refrigerator for six months or so before discarding it. Characteristic of this type are the reused jars and margarine tubs which house
the remains.

I avoid ethnic foods I am unfamiliar with. If I do not know what it is sup- 36
posed to look like when it is good, I cannot be certain I will be able to tell
if it is bad.

No matter how careful I am I still get dysentery at least once a month, 37
oftener in warm weather. I do not want to paint too romantic a picture.
Dumpster diving has serious drawbacks as a way of life.

I learned to scavenge gradually, on my own. Since then I have initiated 38
several companions into the trade. I have learned that there is a predictable
series of stages a person goes through in learning to scavenge.

At first the new scavenger is filled with disgust and self-loathing. He is 39
ashamed of being seen and may lurk around, trying to duck behind things,
or he may try to dive at night.

(In fact, most people instinctively look away from a scavenger. By skulk- 40
ing around, the novice calls attention to himself and arouses suspicion.
Diving at night is ineffective and needlessly messy.)

Every grain of rice seems to be a maggot. Everything seems to stink. He 41
can wipe the egg yolk off the found can, but he cannot erase the stigma of
eating garbage out of his mind.

That stage passes with experience. The scavenger finds a pair of running 42
shoes that fit and look and smell brand new. He finds a pocket calculator
in perfect working order. He finds pristine ice cream, still frozen, more
than he can eat or keep. He begins to understand: People do throw away
perfectly good stuff, a lot of perfectly good stuff.

At this stage, Dumpster shyness begins to dissipate. The diver, after all, 43
has the last laugh. He is finding all manner of good things which are his for
the taking. Those who disparage his profession are the fools, not he.

He may begin to hang onto some perfectly good things for which he has 44
neither a use nor a market. Then he begins to take note of the things
which are not perfectly good but are nearly so. He mates a Walkman with
broken earphones and one that is missing a battery cover. He picks up
things which he can repair.

At this stage he may become lost and never recover. Dumpsters are full 45
of things of some potential value to someone and also of things which

never have much intrinsic value but are interesting. All the Dumpster divers I have known come to the point of trying to acquire everything they touch. Why not take it, they reason, since it is all free.

This is, of course, hopeless. Most divers come to realize that they must 46 restrict themselves to items of relatively immediate utility. But in some cases the diver simply cannot control himself. I have met several of these pack-rat types. Their ideas of the values of various pieces of junk verge on the psychotic. Every bit of glass may be a diamond, they think, and all that glistens, gold.

I tend to gain weight when I am scavenging. Partly this is because I 47 always find far more pizza and doughnuts than water-packed tuna, nonfat yogurt, and fresh vegetables. Also I have not developed much faith in the reliability of Dumpsters as a food source, although it has been proven to me many times. I tend to eat as if I have no idea where my next meal is coming from. But mostly I just hate to see food go to waste and so I eat much more than I should. Something like this drives the obsession to collect junk.

As for collecting objects, I usually restrict myself to collecting one kind 48 of small object at a time, such as pocket calculators, sunglasses, or campaign buttons. To live on the street I must anticipate my needs to a certain extent: I must pick up and save warm bedding I find in August because it will not be found in Dumpsters in November. But even if I had a home with extensive storage space I could not save everything that might be valuable in some contingency.

I have proprietary feelings about my Dumpsters. As I have suggested, it 49 is no accident that I scavenge from Dumpsters where good finds are common. But my limited experience with Dumpsters in other areas suggests to me that it is the population of competitors rather than the affluence of the dumpers that most affects the feasibility of survival by scavenging. The large number of competitors is what puts me off the idea of trying to scavenge in places like Los Angeles.

Curiously, I do not mind my direct competition, other scavengers, so 50 much as I hate the can scroungers.

People scrounge cans because they have to have a little cash. I have 51 tried scrounging cans with an able-bodied companion. Afoot a can scrounger simply cannot make more than a few dollars a day. One can extract the necessities of life from the Dumpsters directly with far less effort than would be required to accumulate the equivalent value in cans.

Can scroungers, then, are people who *must* have small amounts of cash. 52 These are drug addicts and winos, mostly the latter because the amounts of cash are so small.

Spirits and drugs do, like all other commodities, turn up in Dumpsters 53 and the scavenger will from time to time have a half bottle of a rather good wine with his dinner. But the wino cannot survive on these occasional finds; he must have his daily dose to stave off the DTs. All the cans he can carry will buy about three bottles of Wild Irish Rose.

I do not begrudge them the cans, but can scroungers tend to tear up the   54
Dumpsters, mixing the contents and littering the area. They become so
specialized that they can see only cans. They earn my contempt by passing
up change, canned goods, and readily hockable items.

There are precious few courtesies among scavengers. But it is a common   55
practice to set aside surplus items: pairs of shoes, clothing, canned goods,
and such. A true scavenger hates to see good stuff go to waste and what he
cannot use he leaves in good condition in plain sight.

Can scroungers lay waste to everything in their path and will stir one of   56
a pair of good shoes to the bottom of a Dumpster, to be lost or ruined in
the muck. Can scroungers will even go through individual garbage cans,
something I have never seen a scavenger do.

Individual garbage cans are set out on the public easement only on   57
garbage days. On other days going through them requires trespassing close
to a dwelling. Going through individual garbage cans without scattering litter is almost impossible. Litter is likely to reduce the public's tolerance of
scavenging. Individual garbage cans are simply not as productive as Dumpsters; people in houses and duplexes do not move as often and for some
reason do not tend to discard as much useful material. Moreover, the time
required to go through one garbage can that serves one household is not
much less than the time required to go through a Dumpster that contains
the refuse of twenty apartments.

But my strongest reservation about going through individual garbage   58
cans is that this seems to me a very personal kind of invasion to which I
would object if I were a householder. Although many things in Dumpsters
are obviously meant never to come to light, a Dumpster is somehow less
personal.

I avoid trying to draw conclusions about the people who dump in the   59
Dumpsters I frequent. I think it would be unethical to do so, although I
know many people will find the idea of scavenger ethics too funny for
words.

Dumpsters contain bank statements, bills, correspondence, and other   60
documents, just as anyone might expect. But there are also less obvious
sources of information. Pill bottles, for example. The labels on pill bottles
contain the name of the patient, the name of the doctor, and the name of
the drug. AIDS drugs and antipsychotic medicines, to name but two groups,
are specific and are seldom prescribed for any other disorders. The plastic
compacts for birth control pills usually have complete label information.

Despite all of this sensitive information, I have had only one apartment   61
resident object to my going through the Dumpster. In that case it turned
out the resident was a university athlete who was taking bets and who was
afraid I would turn up his wager slips.

Occasionally a find tells a story. I once found a small paper bag con-   62
taining some unused condoms, several partial tubes of flavored sexual lubri-
cant, a partially used compact of birth control pills, and the torn pieces of

a picture of a young man. Clearly she was through with him and planning to give up sex altogether.

Dumpster things are often sad — abandoned teddy bears, shredded wedding books, despaired-of sales kits. I find many pets lying in state in Dumpsters. Although I hope to get off the streets so that Lizbeth can have a long and comfortable old age, I know this hope is not very realistic. So I suppose when her time comes she too will go into a Dumpster. I will have no better place for her. And after all, for most of her life her livelihood has come from the Dumpster. When she finds something I think is safe that has been spilled from the Dumpster I let her have it. She already knows the route around the best Dumpsters. I like to think that if she survives me she will have a chance of evading the dog catcher and of finding her sustenance on the route.

Silly vanities also come to rest in the Dumpsters. I am a rather accomplished needleworker. I get a lot of materials from the Dumpsters. Evidently sorority girls, hoping to impress someone, perhaps themselves, with their mastery of a womanly art, buy a lot of embroider-by-number kits, work a few stitches horribly, and eventually discard the whole mess. I pull out their stitches, turn the canvas over, and work an original design. Do not think I refrain from chuckling as I make original gifts from these kits.

I find diaries and journals. I have often thought of compiling a book of literary found objects. And perhaps I will one day. But what I find is hopelessly commonplace and bad without being, even unconsciously, camp. College students also discard their papers. I am horrified to discover the kind of paper which now merits an A in an undergraduate course. I am grateful, however, for the number of good books and magazines the students throw out.

In the area I know best I have never discovered vermin in the Dumpsters, but there are two kinds of kitty surprise. One is alley cats which I meet as they leap, claws first, out of Dumpsters. This is especially thrilling when I have Lizbeth in tow. The other kind of kitty surprise is a plastic garbage bag filled with some ponderous, amorphous mass. This always proves to be used cat litter.

City bees harvest doughnut glaze and this makes the Dumpster at the doughnut shop more interesting. My faith in the instinctive wisdom of animals is always shaken whenever I see Lizbeth attempt to catch a bee in her mouth, which she does whenever bees are present. Evidently some birds find Dumpsters profitable, for birdie surprise is almost as common as kitty surprise of the first kind. In hunting season all kinds of small game turn up in Dumpsters, some of it, sadly, not entirely dead. Curiously, summer and winter, maggots are uncommon.

The worst of the living and near-living hazards of the Dumpsters are the fire ants. The food that they claim is not much of a loss, but they are vicious and aggressive. It is very easy to brush against some surface of the Dumpster and pick up half a dozen or more fire ants, usually in some sensitive area such as the underarm. One advantage of bringing Lizbeth along as I make Dumpster rounds is that, for obvious reasons, she is very alert to ground-based fire ants. When Lizbeth recognizes the signs of fire ant infestation around our feet she does the Dance of the Zillion Fire Ants. I have learned not to ignore this warning from Lizbeth, whether I perceive the tiny ants or not, but to remove ourselves at Lizbeth's first pas de bourrée.[1] All the more so because the ants are the worst in the months I wear flip-flops, if I have them.

(Perhaps someone will misunderstand the above. Lizbeth does the   69 Dance of the Zillion Fire Ants when she recognizes more fire ants than she cares to eat, not when she is being bitten. Since I have learned to react promptly, she does not get bitten at all. It is the isolated patrol of fire ants that falls in Lizbeth's range that deserves pity. Lizbeth finds them quite tasty.)

By far the best way to go through a Dumpster is to lower yourself into it.   70 Most of the good stuff tends to settle at the bottom because it is usually weightier than the rubbish. My more athletic companions have often demonstrated to me that they can extract much good material from a Dumpster I have already been over.

To those psychologically or physically unprepared to enter a Dumpster,   71 I recommend a stout stick, preferably with some barb or hook at one end. The hook can be used to grab plastic garbage bags. When I find canned goods or other objects loose at the bottom of a Dumpster I usually can roll them into a small bag that I can then hoist up. Much Dumpster diving is a matter of experience for which nothing will do except practice.

Dumpster diving is outdoor work, often surprisingly pleasant. It is not   72 entirely predictable; things of interest turn up every day and some days there are finds of great value. I am always very pleased when I can turn up exactly the thing I most wanted to find. Yet in spite of the element of change, scavenging more than most other pursuits tends to yield returns in some proportion to the effort and intelligence brought to bear. It is very sweet to turn up a few dollars in change from a Dumpster that has just been gone over by a wino.

The land is now covered with cities. The cities are full of Dumpsters. I   73 think of scavenging as a modern form of self-reliance. In any event, after ten years of government service, where everything is geared to the lowest common denominator, I find work that rewards initiative and effort refreshing. Certainly I would be happy to have a sinecure again, but I am not heartbroken not to have one anymore.

I find from the experience of scavenging two rather deep lessons. The   74 first is to take what I can use and let the rest go by. I have come to think that there is no value in the abstract. A thing I cannot use or make useful, perhaps by trading, has no value however fine or rare it may be. I mean

---

[1]*pas de bourrée* A ballet step. [Editor's note.]

useful in a broad sense — so, for example, some art I would think useful and valuable, but other art might be otherwise for me.

I was shocked to realize that some things are not worth acquiring, but now I think it is so. Some material things are white elephants that eat up the possessor's substance. 75

The second lesson is of the transience of material being. This has not quite converted me to a dualist, but it has made some headway in that direction. I do not suppose that ideas are immortal, but certainly mental things are longer-lived than other material things. 76

Once I was the sort of person who invests material objects with sentimental value. Now I no longer have those things, but I have the sentiments yet. 77

Many times in my travels I have lost everything but the clothes I was wearing and Lizbeth. The things I find in Dumpsters, the love letters and ragdolls of so many lives, remind me of this lesson. Now I hardly pick up a thing without envisioning the time I will cast it away. This I think is a healthy state of mind. Almost everything I have now has already been cast out at least once, proving that what I own is valueless to someone. 78

Anyway, I find my desire to grab for the gaudy bauble has been largely sated. I think this is an attitude I share with the very wealthy — we both know there is plenty more where what we have came from. Between us are the rat-race millions who have confounded their selves with the objects they grasp and who nightly scavenge the cable channels looking for they know not what. 79

I am sorry for them. 80

Analyzing This Selection

1. Eighner provides practical advice about being a scavenger. What makes this advice interesting to his nonscavenger readers? What, if anything, did you learn?

2. **THE WRITER'S METHOD** In paragraphs 1 to 5 Eighner examines words and usages. How does this regard for preciseness continue in the essay? Are there sections you find excessive? sections that are amusing?

3. The only other individual in the essay is a dog. How does Eighner humanize their relationship?

4. In scavenging, hard work and intelligence are justly rewarded, according to the author (para. 72). Is this attitude bourgeois? What would you consider bourgeois, if anything, in Eighner's manner, pursuits, and responses?

Analyzing Connections

5. Eighner and Twitchell (see "Two Cheers for Materialism," p. 410) both assess material things. How do they regard consumerism? For what reasons, if any, would Twitchell express sympathy as in Eighner's final paragraph?

Analyzing by Writing

6. Analyze the abstract lessons Eighner learned, and test his outlook by your outlook toward specific possessions. Be honest about what you value and identify with—and what you look forward to. Consider whether Eighner's outlook resembles someone else's, perhaps that of someone in your family, more closely than your own.

William Ian Miller

GIFTS AND HONOR:
AN EXCHANGE[1]

WILLIAM IAN MILLER (b. 1946) is a professor of law at the University of Michigan. He earned a Ph.D. in English at Yale University before turning to scholarship on ancient and modern law. His books include *Blood-taking and Peacemaking: Feud, Law, and Society in Saga Iceland* (1990) and *Humiliation and Other Essays on Honor, Social Discomfort, and Violence* (1993), from which the following selection is excerpted. Miller's book *The Anatomy of Disgust* (1997) continues his analyses of acute discomfort. His most recent book is *The Mystery of Courage* (2000).

One Valentine's Day the doorbell rang around six in the evening. At the door were the four-year-old boy who lived around the corner and his mother. My wife answered the door, and seeing that they had a valentine for Bess, my three-year-old daughter, got the valentine she had had Bess make for the boy that afternoon. I marveled at my wife's skill in handling this. How in the world did she know to be ready for this exchange? The boy, a year older than our daughter, was not a very frequent playmate of Bess's and we were only on cordial but standoffishly neighborly terms with his parents. What luck, I thought, that she had thought to have something ready for the boy. Then the glitch occurred. What Bobby handed over to Bess was an expensive doll, some twenty dollars' worth, clearly bought for this occasion. What Bess handed Bobby was some scribbling, representing an attempt to draw a heart, and a cookie that my wife, with Bess's indispensable assistance, had baked that afternoon. The visit broke up quickly after the exchange. We had been fixing dinner when they appeared, and Bobby and his mother only got far enough beyond the threshold so that we could close the storm door on the cold air outside. There was an undeniable look of disappointment on the boy's face when he left, and Bess, though hardly disappointed, was mildly bewildered at having gotten such a nice gift out of the blue. As soon as the door closed my wife expressed her embarrassment and acute discomfort. What could we do? How could we repay them? How could we rectify the situation? I too felt embarrassed

[1]Editor's title.

although not quite to the same extent as Kathy; for it was not me who was going to have to have future dealings with Bobby and his mother. It is also true that Kathy and I felt some amusement with our embarrassment. Discomfitures of this sort are funny even at the cost of your own pain. And of course, academic that I am, I started immediately wondering why we felt acutely embarrassed and maybe even shamed and Bobby's mother did not, because she did not manifest any sense that something had not been quite right in the exchange.

The structure of the valentine exchange can be described as a simple 2 game. The players each have one move and each must make that move (in this instance the move is giving a gift to the other) without knowledge of what the other has given. The object of the game is to match the value of the other's move. Both players lose if there is great discrepancy between their moves. Both win if there is a small increment between their moves. Normal social interaction presents various versions of this game fairly frequently. Christmas-gift exchanges and choosing how to dress for a party or other social function in which it is not totally clear that there is one correct way of attiring oneself follow this pattern. (Birthday-gift exchanges, however, follow a different structure unless the players celebrate their birthdays on the same day.) This game requires certain broad skills no matter what its particular setting may be. Adept players must understand the norms that govern the situation; they must also have the ability to judge the other party's understanding of those norms and his or her willingness to adhere to them even if understood, and they must make reasonably accurate assessments of the other party's assessments of themselves in these same matters.

Winning in the gift exchange does not mean getting the best present. 3 That is what Kathy and I understood to be a loss. Winning is guessing what the other will give and giving a gift adequate to requite it. Social norms do the work of coordinating people's behavior so that most of the time these interactions pass without glitch. We know what to give and how much to spend and we reasonably expect that others know what we know and that they will act accordingly. Small variations can be tolerated; they are even desired to some extent. If, for instance, you want to dress at a level of formality that will accord with that of everyone else, you might still want to wear something more tasteful or nicer than what others have on. If I give you a gift costing twelve dollars and you give me one costing ten dollars, no one is embarrassed, and I might even exact a very small amount of greater gratitude than the gratitude I have to give you to make up the difference. But when my gift to you cost a dime and your gift to me cost twenty dollars we should, if we are properly socialized, feel awkward and embarrassed. The embarrassment, however, will not be equally distributed. The person who spent the most will feel the least embarrassed, generally speaking. Why? We can even make the question a little harder by referring back to Bess's valentine. Why was it that my wife and I felt greater unpleasant feelings, when we followed the norms governing the situation, than I am supposing Bobby's mother did, who clearly broke the rules by vastly exceeding the appropriate amount of expenditure for little kids on Valentine's Day?

Just what are the sources of embarrassment, shame, humiliation, and [4] even guilt (perhaps) that were provoked by this situation? The lowrollers cannot feel embarrassed that they broke the rules of the Valentine game, because they did not. By one account the highrollers, if embarrassed, are embarrassed more because they caused the lowroller's embarrassment than because they exceeded the norms of propriety governing the game. No doubt there is a causal connection between the highrollers' embarrassment and their failure to adhere to the norms of the Valentine game inasmuch as that was what caused the lowrollers' embarrassment, but that would be getting the psychology of it wrong. Their experience is one of second-order embarrassment, the embarrassment of witnessing another's embarrassment, not the primary embarrassment of having done something embarrassing. It seems that what is going on here is that there is more than one game being played and that there are more than one set of norms governing the transaction. The true source of the lowrollers' embarrassment is that they have also been shamed by being bested in the much more primitive game of gift exchange....The simple fact remains that a gift demands an adequate return even if that gift, by its size, breaks the rules governing the particular exchange. The norms of adequate reciprocity trumped the norms of Valentine's Day. Yet there is a cost here borne by the highrollers. Because the highrollers defied the normal expectation they do not acquire honor to the extent that they caused shame. Their action, in effect, has made the whole transaction less than zero-sum.

A somewhat difficult account also suggests itself. I have been supposing [5] the giver's lack of primary embarrassment. But it might be that Bobby's mother was more than embarrassed by embarrassing us, she might have felt humiliated, not by breaking the rules of the Valentine's Day game but by having to realize how much more greatly she valued us than we valued her. Her pain then, if pain she felt, was not really a function of misplaying the Valentine game in the same way ours was. To be sure, the game provided the setting for her humiliation but it needn't have. Her pain, in other words, was not caused because she violated the norms of Valentine's Day, but because she overvalued us. In contrast, our pain was solely a function of the Valentine's Day glitch. Yet I suspect that she felt no humiliation whatsoever, for the situation provided her with an adequate nondemeaning explanation for the smallness of our gift. Our gift, she would know, was exactly what the situation called for. The normal expectations of the situation thus shielded her from more painful knowledge.

The peculiar facts of Bess's gift show us also that who ends up bearing [6] the costs of norm transgression will depend on the makeup of the opposing sides. The discussion above assumed highroller and lowroller to be individual actors in a one-on-one game, but in our Valentine situation there were mother and son on one side and mother and daughter on the other. If we look now only at the emotions engendered by the exchange, Bobby's mother felt no shame and only a little embarrassment. Bess's mother felt much embarrassment. Bess felt quite pleased. But Bobby, alas poor Bobby. Here was the true bearer of the cost of his mother's indiscretion. Bobby, one can reasonably suppose, was deeply envious of the gift Bess was to receive and had been sick with desire for a similar gift. Recall, when you were little, the painful experience of being the guest watching the birthday child open the presents. But Bobby can console himself that this Valentine gift will lead to an immediate return and not be miserably deferred as with birthday gifts. And what has Bobby's mother led him to believe he will be receiving? I would guess it was a little more exciting than Bess's scribblings and one chocolate chip cookie (made according to a health-food recipe no less).

Our discomfort was utterly unassuaged by the knowledge that our gifts 7 involved our own efforts (or at least Bess's and Kathy's). Our personalized efforts did not match the larger money expenditure of the other party. The issue wasn't just the money, because if Bobby had handed Bess a twenty-dollar bill we would have refused the gift without much anxiety. Here a breach of norms governing the form of the gift (e.g., no money unless under very certain conditions) is not as capable of embarrassing the receiver, if at all, as are breaches of norms governing the value of the gift. But we need to be more specific. The failure to abide by the norms governing the value of a gift only embarrasses the receiver if it exceeds the value of a normal gift; embarrassment is the lot of the giver if the gift's value is less than the norm. It seems in the end that our judgments are also quite particularized, taking into account not only the money spent but time and energy expended, the uniqueness of the gift, the seriousness of it, how individualized it is, how much such things mean to the giver, how much they mean to the receiver, the state of relations between the parties, and so on. Our cookie and Bess's scribbling were not going to balance the money and the time Bobby's mother took in picking out a gift for Bess. Our cookies were promiscuous, meant to be eaten by us and by anyone who stumbled by when we were eating them. When it is not clear that the personalized effort of one party was significant, when the labors engaged in could also be interpreted as an attempt to avoid spending money or were not engaged in specifically for the recipient, then monetary value will probably trump mere expenditures of effort. Obviously these rankings can undergo readjustment. If Bess were a recognized art prodigy, if Kathy were a professional cook, then our gifts would carry other meanings, as they would, too, if Bobby were the Cookie Monster.

One of the immediate moves that the embarrassed recipient makes is 8 desperately to try to reconstruct a plausible account for the breach, to attempt to interpret it away by supposing legitimizing or justifying states of mind for the giver. Perhaps she was playing a different game. Could the value of the gift be partially excused because Bobby was a year older than

Bess, or because Bobby was a boy, or because his mother had a warm spot for Kathy or a warm spot for Bess? Was this really a gift initiating a youthful courtship in which gifts do not demand returns in the same specie? Was it simply that Bobby's mother never stinted in buying Bobby anything and that the toy she bought Bess had a much lower value to her than it did to us? Was she known to be inept in these kinds of things and hence each subsequent ineptitude bore a diminishing power to humiliate and embarrass? Or was the embarrassment that we thought she might be making a pitiable attempt to buy our friendship, in which case our very palpable embarrassment at our own failings would be compounded with our embarrassment for her as well. Whatever, no amount of such explanation for her action made us feel any less embarrassed. And we had played by the rules! But, as it turns out, only by the rules of the Valentine game. This game, as we discovered, was nested within a larger game of honor that demanded that each gift be requited with an adequate return, and that game we had lost.

The cost of our losing was our minor humiliation and shame and our great embarrassment. In our culture in that particular setting it was a cost we could bear. In other settings we may have had to suffer the sanction of being reputed cheap and even ostracized on account of it. In other cultures humiliation and shame exact a greater toll. Reuters recently published the following story picked up by papers as column filler:

> *Monday June 10, 1991:* **Scorn over gift leads to double suicide.** Beijing: A couple from northern China committed suicide on their nephew's wedding day after relatives scoffed at the value of their gift to him, a Shanghai newspaper said.
>
> Following custom, the couple from the province of Shanxi wrote in a gift book that they were giving a total of $3.70 as a wedding gift, less than half the $8.50 other relatives gave, said the Xinmin Evening News.
>
> Unable to bear their relatives' scorn and worried about future wedding gifts for their other nephews and nieces, husband Yang Baosheng hanged himself after his wife, Qu Junmei, drowned herself in a vat, the newspaper said.

For Reuters and the newspapers that printed it, the story was clearly intended to be comical in a black way, an example of the strange behavior of people with strange names (note that giving the names of the suicides is part of the process of ridicule). The story is told as one of silly people who kill themselves for trifles. Any possibility of tragedy is skillfully prevented by several devices. There are the strange names already mentioned. There is the detail of drowning in a vat, which carries with it all the indignities of pure farce. Above all, there are the money amounts involved: these people committed suicide because of $4.80. And therein lies the real comedy of the presentation. Such levels of poverty and economic underdevelopment are so unthinkable for us to be a source of amusement and wonder. But anyone...should be able to discern the unfathomable shame and the desperate reassertion of dignity which these people tried to accomplish with their suicides. Suicide proved them anything but shameless and hence showed them to be people of honor. Reuters got their genre wrong. This is not comedy, but the stuff of epic and tragedy.

Analyzing This Selection

1. Explain the rules of gift exchange. Why did both parties lose in the Valentine episode? What constitutes "winning"?

2. **THE WRITER'S METHOD**   What is the author's use or purpose for the exhaustive abstract analysis of the episode? How does he win our patience for it?

3. Does the author approve of the suicide of the Chinese couple? What does their story illustrate to him? How does it affect you?

Analyzing Connections

4. Did the parting gifts between Zhou and Liang follow or break the rules of gift exchange (see Ha Jin's "Ocean of Words," p. 314)? How does Miller's essay change our response to Zhou's loss?

Analyzing by Writing

5. Writing as an observer of the customs of high school seniors, explain the system of gift exchange that operated among your friends during your final year in high school. At Christmas, at graduation, or on birthdays, did you pay more than usual attention to expecting and giving gifts? How did you deal with problems involving esteem, embarrassment, and shame? Did some people receive gifts only because they were part of a group including other, more valued friends? How did you negotiate exchanges of adequate reciprocity among all your friends?

Toni Cade Bambara

THE LESSON

Toni Cade Bambara (1939–1995) grew up in the black districts of New York City, where she experienced racism and poverty set in sharp contrast to the opulence of white Manhattan, as the following story reflects. After graduating from Queens College, she studied dance and acting in Italy and France before returning to New York, where she took an M.A. degree at City College. Bambara worked as a welfare investigator and youth counselor as well as a college teacher of English while writing short stories. Her selected short fiction, essays, and interviews are collected in *Deep Sightings and Rescue Missions* (1996).

Back in the days when everyone was old and stupid or young and fool- 1
ish and me and Sugar were the only ones just right, this lady moved on our block with nappy hair and proper speech and no makeup. And quite naturally we laughed at her, laughed the way we did at the junk man who went about his business like he was some big-time president and his sorry-ass horse his secretary. And we kinda hated her too, hated the way we did the winos who cluttered up our parks and pissed on our handball walls and stank up our hallways and stairs so you couldn't halfway play hide-and-seek without a goddamn gas mask. Miss Moore was her name. The only woman on the block with no first name. And she was black as hell, cept for her feet, which were fish-white and spooky. And she was always planning these boring-ass things for us to do, us being my cousin, mostly, who lived on the block cause we all moved North the same time and to the same apartment then spread out gradual to breathe. And our parents would yank our heads into some kinda shape and crisp up our clothes so we'd be presentable for travel with Miss Moore, who always looked like she was going to church, though she never did. Which is just one of the things the grown-ups talked about when they talked behind her back like a dog. But when she came calling with some sachet she'd sewed up or some gingerbread she'd made or some book, why then they'd all be too embarrassed to turn her down and we'd get handed over all spruced up. She'd been to college and said it was only right that she should take responsibility for the young ones' education, and she not even related by marriage or blood. So they'd go for it. Specially Aunt Gretchen. She was the main gofer in the family. You got some ole

dumb shit foolishness you want somebody to go for, you send for Aunt Gretchen. She been screwed into the go-along for so long, it's a blood-deep natural thing with her. Which is how she got saddled with me and Sugar and Junior in the first place while our mothers were in a la-de-da apartment up the block having a good ole time.

So this one day Miss Moore rounds us all up at the mailbox and it's puredee hot and she's knockin herself out about arithmetic. And school suppose to let up in the summer I heard, but she don't never let up. And the starch in my pinafore scratching the shit outta me and I'm really hating this nappy-head bitch and her goddamn college degree. I'd much rather go to the pool or to the show where it's cool. So me and Sugar leaning on the mailbox being surly, which is a Miss Moore word. And Flyboy checking out what everybody brought for lunch. And Fat Butt already wasting his peanut-butter-and-jelly sandwich like the pig he is. And Junebug punchin on Q.T.'s arm for potato chips. And Rosie Giraffe shifting from one hip to the other waiting for somebody to step on her foot or ask if she from Georgia so she can kick ass, preferably Mercedes'. And Miss Moore asking us do we know what money is, like we a bunch of retards. I mean real money, she say, like it's only poker chips or monopoly papers we lay on the grocer. So right away I'm tired of this and say so. And would much rather snatch Sugar and go to the Sunset and terrorize the West Indian kids and take their hair ribbons and their money too. And Miss Moore files that remark away for next week's lesson on brotherhood, I can tell. And finally I say we oughta get to the subway cause it's cooler and besides we might meet some cute boys. Sugar done swiped her mama's lipstick, so we ready.

So we heading down the street and she's boring us silly about what things cost and what our parents make and how much goes for rent and how money ain't divided up right in this country. And then she gets to the part about we all poor and live in the slums, which I don't feature. And I'm ready to speak on that, but she steps out in the street and hails two cabs just like that. Then she hustles half the crew in with her and hands me a five-dollar bill and tells me to calculate 10 percent tip for the driver. And we're off. Me and Sugar and Junebug and Flyboy hanging out the window and hollering to everybody, putting lipstick on each other cause Flyboy a faggot anyway, and making farts with our sweaty armpits. But I'm mostly trying to figure how to spend this money. But they all fascinated with the meter ticking and Junebug starts laying bets as to how much it'll read when Flyboy can't hold his breath no more. Then Sugar lay bets as to how much it'll be when we get there. So I'm stuck. Don't nobody want to go for my plan, which is to jump out at the next light and run off to the first bar-b-que we can find. Then the driver tells us to get the hell out cause we there already. And the meter reads eight-five cents. And I'm stalling to figure out the tip and Sugar say give him a dime. And I decide he don't need it bad as I do, so later for him. But then he tries to take off with Junebug foot still in the door so we talk about his mama something ferocious. Then we check out that we on Fifth Avenue and everybody dressed up in stockings. One lady in a fur coat, hot as it is. White folks crazy.

"This is the place," Miss Moore say, presenting it to us in the voice she uses at the museum. "Let's look in the windows before we go in." 4

"Can we steal?" Sugar asks very serious like she's getting the ground rules squared away before she plays. "I beg your pardon," say Miss Moore, and we fall out. So she leads us around the windows of the toy store and me and Sugar screamin, "This is mine, that's mine, I gotta have that, that was made me, I was born for that," till Big Butt drowns us out. 5

"Hey, I'm goin to buy that there." 6

"That there? You don't even know what it is, stupid." 7

"I do so," he say punchin on Rosie Giraffe. "It's a microscope." 8

"Whatcha gonna do with a microscope, fool?" 9

"Look at things." 10

"Like what, Ronald?" ask Miss Moore. And Big Butt ain't got the first notion. So here go Miss Moore gabbing about the thousands of bacteria in a drop of water and the somethinorother in a speck of blood and the million and one living things in the air around us is invisible to the naked eye. And what she say that for? Junebug go to town on that "naked" and we rolling. Then Miss Moore ask what it cost. So we all jam into the window smudgin it up and the price tag say $300. So then she ask how long'd take for Big Butt and Junebug to save up their allowances. "Too long," I say. "Yeh," adds Sugar, "outgrown it by that time." And Miss Moore say no, you never outgrow learning instruments. "Why, even medical students and interns and," blah, blah, blah. And we ready to choke Big Butt for bringing it up in the first damn place. 11

"This here costs four hundred eighty dollars," say Rosie Giraffe. So we pile up all over her to see what she pointin out. My eyes tell me it's a chunk of glass cracked with something heavy, and different-color inks dripped into the splits, then the whole thing put into a oven or something. But for $480 it don't make sense. 12

"That's a paperweight made of semi-precious stones fused together under tremendous pressure," she explains slowly, with her hands doing the mining and all the factory work. 13

"So what's a paperweight?" asks Rosie Giraffe. 14

"To weigh paper with, dumbbell," say Flyboy, the wise man from the East. 15

"Not exactly," say Miss Moore, which is what she say when you warm or way off too. "It's to weigh paper down so it won't scatter and make your desk untidy." So right away me and Sugar curtsy to each other and then to Mercedes who is more the tidy type. 16

"We don't keep paper on top of the desk in my class," say Junebug, figuring Miss Moore crazy or lyin one. 17

"At home, then," she say. "Don't you have a calendar and a pencil case and a blotter and a letter-opener on your desk at home where you do your 18 homework?" And she know damn well what our homes look like cause she nosys around in them every chance she gets.

"I don't even have a desk," say Junebug. "Do we?"   19

"No. And I don't get no homework neither," says Big Butt.   20

"And I don't even have a home," say Flyboy like he do at school to keep   21
the white folks off his back and sorry for him. Send this poor kid to camp posters, is his specialty.

"I do," says Mercedes. "I have a box of stationery on my desk and a pic-   22
ture of my cat. My godmother bought the stationery and the desk. There's a big rose on each sheet and the envelopes smell like roses."

"Who wants to know about your smelly-ass stationery," say Rosie Giraffe   23
fore I can get my two cents in.

"It's important to have a work area all your own so that..."   24

"Will you look at this sailboat, please," say Flyboy, cuttin her off and   25
pointin to the thing like it was his. So once again we tumble all over each other to gaze at this magnificent thing in the toy store which is just big enough to maybe sail two kittens across the pond if you strap them to the posts tight. We all start reciting the price tag like we in assembly. "Handcrafted sailboat of fiberglass at one thousand one hundred ninety-five dollars."

"Unbelievable," I hear myself say and am really stunned. I read it again   26
for myself just in case the group recitation put me in a trance. Same thing. For some reason this pisses me off. We look at Miss Moore and she lookin at us, waiting for I dunno what.

"Who'd pay all that when you can buy a sailboat set for a quarter at   27
Pop's, a tube of glue for a dime, and a ball of string for eight cents? It must have a motor and a whole lot besides," I say. "My sailboat cost me about fifty cents."

"But will it take water?" say Mercedes with her smart ass.   28

"Took mine to Alley Pond Park once," say Flyboy. "String broke. Lost it.   29
Pity."

"Sailed mine in Central Park and it keeled over and sank. Had to ask my   30
father for another dollar."

"And you got the strap," laugh Big Butt. "The jerk didn't even have a   31
string on it. My old man wailed on his behind."

Little Q.T. was staring hard at the sailboat and you could see he wanted   32
it bad. But he too little and somebody'd just take it from him. So what the hell. "This boat for kids, Miss Moore?"

"Parents silly to buy something like that just to get all broke up," say   33
Rosie Giraffe.

"That much money it should last forever," I figure.   34

"My father'd buy it for me if I wanted it."   35

"Your father, my ass," say Rosie Giraffe getting a chance to finally push   36
Mercedes.

"Must be rich people shop here," say Q.T.   37

"You are a very bright boy," say Flyboy. "What was your first clue?" And 38
he rap him on the head with the back of his knuckles, since Q.T. the only
one he could get away with. Though Q.T. liable to come up behind you
years later and get his licks in when you half expect it.

"What I want to know is," I says to Miss Moore though I never talk to 39
her, I wouldn't give the bitch that satisfaction, "is how much a real boat
costs? I figure a thousand'd get you a yacht any day?"

"Why don't you check that out," she says, "and report back to the 40
group?" Which really pains my ass. If you gonna mess up a perfectly good
swim day least you could do is have some answers. "Let's go in," she say
like she got something up her sleeve. Only she don't lead the way. So me
and Sugar turn the corner to where the entrance is, but when we get there
I kinda hang back. Not that I'm scared, what's there to be afraid of, just a
toy store. But I feel funny, shame. But what I got to be shamed about? Got
as much right to go in as anybody. But somehow I can't seem to get hold
of the door, so I step away for Sugar to lead. But she hangs back too. And
I look at her and she looks at me and this is ridiculous. I mean, damn, I
have never ever been shy about doing nothing or going nowhere. But then
Mercedes steps up and then Rosie Giraffe and Big Butt crowd in behind
and shove, and next thing we all stuffed into the doorway with only Mercedes squeezing past us, smoothing out her jumper and walking right down
the aisle. Then the rest of us tumble in like a glued-together jigsaw done all
wrong. And people lookin at us. And it's like the time me and Sugar
crashed into the Catholic church on a dare. But once we got in there and
everything so hushed and holy and the candles and the bowin and the
handkerchiefs on all the drooping heads, I just couldn't go through with
the plan. Which was for me to run up to the altar and do a tap dance while
Sugar played the nose flute and messed around in the holy waters. And
Sugar kept givin me the elbow. Then later teased me so bad I tied her up
in the shower and turned it on and locked her in. And she'd be there till
this day if Aunt Gretchen hadn't finally figured I was lyin about the boarder
takin a shower.

Same thing in the store. We all walkin on tiptoe and hardly touchin the 41
games and puzzles and things. And I watched Miss Moore who is steady
watchin us like she waiting for a sign. Like Mama Drewery watches the sky
and sniffs the air and takes note of just how much slant is in the bird formation. Then me and Sugar bump smack into each other, so busy gazing
at the toys, 'specially the sailboat. But we don't laugh and go into our fat-
lady bump-stomach routine. We just stare at that price tag. Then Sugar run
a finger over the whole boat. And I'm jealous and want to hit her. Maybe
not her, but I sure want to punch somebody in the mouth.

"Watcha bring us here for, Miss Moore?"   42

"You sound angry, Sylvia. Are you mad about something?" Givin me 43
one of them grins like she tellin a grown-up joke that never turns out to be
funny. And she's lookin very closely at me like maybe she plannin to do my

portrait from memory. I'm mad, but I won't give her that satisfaction. So I slouch around the store bein very bored and say, "Let's go."

Me and Sugar at the back of the train watchin the tracks whizzin by 44 large then small then gettin gobbled up in the dark. I'm thinkin about this tricky toy I saw in the store. A clown that somersaults on a bar then does chin-ups just cause you yank lightly at his leg. Cost $35. I could see me askin my mother for a $35 birthday clown. "You wanna who that costs what?" she'd say, cocking her head to the side to get a better view of the hole in my head. Thirty-five dollars and the whole household could go visit Grandaddy Nelson in the country. Thirty-five dollars would pay for the rent and the piano bill too. Who are these people that spend that much for performing clowns and $1000 for toy sailboats? What kinda work they do and how they live and how come we ain't in on it? Where we are is who we are, Miss Moore always pointin out. But it don't necessarily have to be that way, she always adds then waits for somebody to say that poor people have to wake up and demand their share of the pie and don't none of us know what kind of pie she talkin about in the first damn place. But she ain't so smart cause I still got her four dollars from the taxi and she sure ain't gettin it. Messin up my day with this shit. Sugar nudges me in my pocket and winks.

Miss Moore lines us up in front of the mailbox where we started from, 45 seem like years ago, and I got a headache for thinkin so hard. And we lean all over each other so we can hold up under the draggy-ass lecture she always finishes us off with at the end before we thank her for borin us to tears. But she just looks at us like she readin tea leaves. Finally she say, "Well, what did you think of F.A.O. Schwartz?"

Rosie Giraffe mumbles, "White folks crazy."   46

"I'd like to go there again when I get my birthday money," says Mer- 47 cedes, and we shove her out the pack so she has to lean on the mailbox by herself.

"I'd like a shower. Tiring day," say Flyboy.   48

Then Sugar surprises me by saying, "You know, Miss Moore, I don't 49 think all of us here put together eat in a year what that sailboat costs." And Miss Moore lights up like something goosed her. "And?" she say, urging Sugar on. Only I'm standin on her foot so she don't continue.

"Imagine for a minute what kind of society it is in which some people 50 can spend on a toy what it would cost to feed a family of six or seven. What do you think?"

"I think," say Sugar pushing me off her feet like she never done before, 51 cause I whip her ass in a minute, "that this is not much of a democracy if you ask me. Equal chance to pursue happiness means an equal crack at the dough, don't it?" Miss Moore is besides herself and I am disgusted with Sugar's treachery. So I stand on her foot one more time to see if she'll shove me. She shuts up, and Miss Moore looks at me, sorrowfully I'm thinkin. And somethin weird is goin on. I can feel it in my chest.

"Anybody else learn anything today?" lookin dead at me. I walk away   52
and Sugar has to run to catch up and don't even seem to notice when I
shrug her arm off my shoulder.

"Well, we got four dollars anyway," she says.   53

"Uh hunh."   54

"We could go to Hascombs and get half a chocolate layer and then to   55
the Sunset and still have plenty of money for potato chips and ice cream
sodas."

"Uh hunh."   56

"Race you to Hascombs," she say.   57

We start down the block and she gets ahead which is O.K. by me cause   58
I'm goin to the West End and then over to the Drive to think this day
through. She can run if she want to and even run faster. But ain't nobody
gonna beat me at nuthin.

Analyzing This Selection

1. Based on details in the first paragraph, about how old is the narrator? What
   particular characteristics lead you to this informed guess?

2. Why does Sylvia continue to resist Miss Moore's efforts to teach the children?

3. **THE WRITER'S METHOD**   What tone do the slang and obscenities add
   to the story? What attitudes do you think the author has toward the kids?

Analyzing Connections

4. Bambara and John Updike (see "A & P," p. 352) both use young, naive
   speakers to tell the story. How do the authors get us to grasp more than the
   narrators do?

Analyzing by Writing

5. Going to look at the trappings of great wealth — for instance, the elegant
   houses of the very rich, royalty's crown jewels, or a magnificent yacht — can
   be sometimes enjoyable and sometimes disturbing. Think of an example of
   evidence of wealth that you admired or criticized. What lesson, if any, did
   you take from your exposure? Do you feel differently about it today?

Maguelonne Toussaint-Samat

CHOCOLATE AND DIVINITY

MAGUELONNE TOUSSAINT-SAMAT is a French journalist and writer. She has published many books on the history of food and French regional culture. This essay is from her book titled *A History of Food* (1992), translated by Anthea Bell.

That witty letter-writer the Marquise de Sévigné had strong feelings 1 about the exotic foodstuff chocolate. On 11 February 1671 she was obviously madly in love with it. She writes to her daughter, Mme de Grignan: "If you are not feeling well, if you have not slept, chocolate will revive you. But you have no chocolate pot! I think of that again and again. How will you manage?" By 15th April disillusion has set in: "I can tell you, my dear child, chocolate is not what it was to me. I was carried away by the fashion, as usual. All who used to praise chocolate to me now condemn it. It is scorned. It is accused of causing every evil under the sun." On 13th May she is in a state of great anxiety, for her daughter is pregnant. "My dear, my beautiful child, I do beg you not to drink chocolate. In your present condition it would prove fatal to you." By 23rd October she is quite paranoid on the subject: "The Marquise de Coëtlogon drank so much chocolate when she was expecting last year that she was brought to bed of a little boy as black as the devil, who died." (There were rumors at court that, the year before that birth, Mme de Coëtlogon's chocolate had been brought to her every morning and evening by a young and very affectionate African slave.)

At the end of the nineteenth century a chocolate maker of Royat who 2 had literary leanings took the outspoken Marquise as the emblem of his brand, and made a fortune.

But long before the good lady ever raised a cup of chocolate to her lips 3 cocoa had existed — or rather *cacahuaquchtl*, a tree four to ten meters tall growing in the virgin forests of Yucatan and Guatemala. *Cacahuaquchtl* means not only cocoa tree but simply, and principally, just "tree." It was *the* Tree, the tree of the Mayan gods.

The gods, whoever they are and wherever they come from, do not eat 4 the food of ordinary mortals. In Greece, they fed on ambrosia. In Mexico and Guatemala they favored a decoction of the seeds of the fruit of the

Tree, and it was not made like any ordinary tisane. You took the seeds (later described by the unimaginative Spanish as "beans") of the cocoa pods, called *cabosses* in French, from Spanish *cabeza*, "head," a word perhaps suggested by the long, narrow heads of the Amerindians. You roasted them in an earthenware pot. You crushed them between two stones. You then mixed the powder you had obtained with boiling water and whisked it with little twigs — chac-chac, choc-choc, went the twigs as they whisked up little bubbles. You could add other things to this boiling liquid (*tchacahoua*, as it was called in Mayan, or *tchocoatl*, in Aztec): either chilli, musk and honey, or ground maize when you were going to war and needed additional calories. Then you drank it.

You drank it because the gods were good and in certain very specific cir-   5
cumstances allowed mortals to taste their sacred food. This is one of the usual features of a sacrifice; there can be no question of the actual physical matter of the foods involved being lost to human consumption, it is the religious intention that counts. The Mayas, like other peoples, took that attitude.

Who exactly were the Mayas? Towards the beginning of the fourth cen-   6
tury A.D. the Maya people, who had come down from Alaska in the course of the millennia, occupied Yucatan, an enormous peninsula situated between Mexico and Guatemala. Around the year 900 their remarkable but bloodthirsty civilization was suddenly extinguished. We still do not know why. Their cities, some still being built, were abandoned, with temples, pyramids, paved roads and all. The Mayas went into the all-concealing virgin forest and never came out again. It was in this forest that the Tree grew. When the Spanish penetrated Central America for the first time in 1523 there was nothing left of the Mayas but a few primitive tribes, as if they had forgotten everything they once knew.

Meanwhile first the Toltecs and then the Aztecs of Mexico, who had   7
come down from North America in their turn, had occupied the territory, sending expeditions not always of a peaceful nature into the forest to get various provisions which included stocks of the beans of the Tree. The Aztecs loved *tchocoatl* as much as the Mayas had liked *tchacahoua*.

Now Quetzalcoatl, the great bearded god of the forest, was also the gar-   8
dener of Paradise. It was to him that mankind owed the Tree, *cacahua-quchtl*, giving both fortune and strength, for he even allowed the seeds of his tree to be used as money. However, in time the Aztecs found themselves in great and lasting distress, and it was all his fault.

One day, no one knew just when — perhaps at the time of the decline of   9
the Mayas? — the god had boarded a raft and gone east across the ocean, towards the rising of the sun. Ever since then his people had been impatiently awaiting his return. It would be a day of great rejoicing. Everyone would whisk *tchocoatl* to a froth and drink it till they could drink no more.

Accordingly when the conquistador Cortez, bearded and clad in iron,   10
arrived on a strange creature which was also iron-clad, coming from the

east across the sea, the Emperor Moctezuma and his subjects, delirious with joy, hailed him as the god. Cortez took advantage of this warm welcome to ask at once where the treasures were kept. The treasures? "Come, great god!" was the reply — as if the god did not know! Still, they led him to the royal plantation of Maniapeltec where the Tree had been greatly improved over the years, and offered him mountains of cocoa. After a fit of rather discourteous mirth, the bearded newcomer managed to explain that he had come for gold, not cocoa beans. He wanted mountains of gold. Eventually, he realized that possession of the cocoa was the way to get possession of the precious yellow metal.

The ceremonial attending the growing and harvesting of cocoa impressed the visitors, who were less world-weary than they liked to appear: it included human sacrifice, masked dancing, propitiatory rites (13 days of abstinence by the workers, followed by orgiastic erotic games on the day of the harvest itself). This final ritual particularly interested the soldiers, and they no longer felt like laughing during the community cocoa-parties when the Emperor, behind a screen, and the court dressed in their best and seated on the palace esplanade, religiously enjoyed the frothing drink served in two thousand fine golden cups by delightfully unclad virgins. 11

When the Emperor explained, therefore, that he never entered his harem without drinking this dark brown brew first, the Spanish held out their cups with one accord. Whether because of the chilli, ambergris and musk added to it or not, no one liked his first mouthful of chocolate. Then they became used to the drink, either for its aphrodisiac virtues or as a substitute for the wine they missed. After Cortez had gone home in 1527 he always kept a full chocolate-pot on his desk. 12

The first concern of the missionary nuns in Central America was to use their culinary gifts to convert chocolate to Christianity. They thought, correctly, that it was diabolical only because of the spices and flavorings added to it. They replaced them with vanilla, sugar and cream, and the result was delicious. 13

In 1585 the fame of Moctezuma's brew had spread so far through Europe that the first cargo to reach land from Vera Cruz was snapped up at once, despite the high price. 14

Although he had been among the first to be informed of the discovery, Pope Clement VII, formerly Giulio de Medici, could not actually drink chocolate at his coronation in 1523, for all he had was the enthusiastic description in Latin of Father Petrus de Angleria, who said it made the mouth water and soothed the soul: "It is not only a delicious drink, but a useful form of money which permits no speculation, since it cannot be kept very long." 15

Pope Clement VIII did drink a cup of cocoa in 1594; it was given him by the Florentine Father Francesco Carlati, just back from America, but he was the eleventh Pope in line from Giulio de Medici, and it was his task to resolve the grave question of whether or not drinking chocolate broke the 16 fast. Not only did Spanish ladies of both the colonies and the mother country have such a passion for cocoa flavored with cinnamon that they drank it all day long, they even had it served to them in church. The Jesuit Father Escobar, renowned for his casuistry, and Cardinal François-Marie Brancacio could hardly suppress the fashion unless they wanted to see the Communion table deserted, so they appeared to go along with it and reiterated, on behalf of their lady penitents, the old adage *liquidum non frangit jejunum*, "liquid does not break the fast" — in this case chocolate made with water. The Sorbonne fulminated; Pius V, who had not drunk chocolate any more than Clement VII, expressed his own doubts and let it be known that he differed from the cardinal and the reverend father.

In the year 1636 the problem loomed large. A priest of Madrid discussed 17 it at length in a quarto entitled *Question moral si el chocolate quebrante el ayuno ecclesiastico*. Was it mortal sin for a priest to drink chocolate before celebrating Mass? Mme de Sévigné, still an enthusiast at this point, wrote to her daughter that she drank chocolate before going to bed to nourish her at night, and on getting up in the morning so that she could fast better. "The agreeable part of it all is that what counts is the intention." (She was referring to the opinion held by such priests as Escobar that purity of intention justifies otherwise immoral actions.)

A certain Bachot, in a medical thesis published on 20 March 1685, 18 maintained that cocoa and not ambrosia must have been the food of the gods. This opinion aroused a certain amount of interest, and fifty years later, when Carl von Linné published his *Systema Naturae* in 1737, he classed the cocoa tree in "the eighteenth polyadelphy of Candire" as the genus *Theobroma*, meaning "divine food." Theobromine, a medicament extracted from cocoa, is an alkaloid similar to caffeine, and its diuretic qualities also make it a cardiovascular analeptic.

During the first half of the seventeenth century exorbitant taxes pre- 19 vented ordinary mortals from serving the drink of the gods on their own tables. The scientist Johann Georg Volkmer brought it from Naples to Germany in 1641 and then to the Netherlands, where it was a huge success in high society. England, perhaps for economic or political (anti-Spanish) reasons, politely turned its nose up at cocoa in 1657. It is true that the Londoners tried making it with Madeira.

France had received chocolate in two stages, with the successive mar- 20 riages of two of its kings to Spanish Infantas: Louis XIII to Anne of Austria, Louis XIV to Maria Theresa of Spain. The maid who brewed Maria Theresa's chocolate must have been better at it than her mother-in-law's maid, for "the Queen's one passion" ("after the King," the modest wife used to remind people, eyes cast down) soon spread spontaneously to the whole court. However, Fagon, the Queen's doctor, was accused of making a brew of it which hastened her demise at the eleventh hour, much to the satisfaction of Mme de Maintenon.

Louis XIV, with his habitual distrust, did not develop a taste for choco- 21
late until he developed one for Mme de Maintenon, another enthusiastic
lover of chocolate who made her favorite drink for herself. It was the safer
course. However, in 1682 the *Mercure de France* published an account of
a party at Versailles where the popular drink of cocoa was served.

A former page of the queen mother Anne of Austria, one David Chail- 22
lon (or possibly Chalion), obtained from the Sun King, who still preferred
Burgundy wine to the Aztec brew, the "sole privilege for twenty-three years
of making, retailing and selling in all towns of the Kingdom a certain composition known as chocolate, in liquid form or as pastilles or in any other
form that he may please." By now a way of evaporating the liquid chocolate
and moulding it into solid shapes had been discovered.

David Chaillon (or Chalion) therefore set up shop at the sign of "La 23
Croix du Tiroir" (or "Trahoir") at the corner of the rue Saint-Honoré and
the rue de l'Arbre-Sec, in the confectioners' quarter. His establishment was
opened on 20 May 1659. In 1690 chocolate reached the Left Bank when
the Sieur Rère and the Sieur Renaud, new license-holders, both occupied
premises in the rue Dauphine. Then the great grocer François Dumaine
extended his catalogue, which already listed coffee beans at four francs the
pound and tea at one hundred francs, to include cocoa at four francs and
chocolate at six francs the pound.

You could drink a cup of cocoa for eight sous, expensive in view of the 24
fact that even in the most fashionable establishments tea or coffee cost
three sous six deniers at the most. But the cocoa prices were of the black
market variety, because of the license held by Chaillon and his successors.
Finally, in 1693, the sale of cocoa and chocolate was thrown open to all,
much to the annoyance of the religious communities, who had been
dreaming for years of obtaining a monopoly of the drink of the gods.

In 1770 the first industrial chocolate-manufacturing firm was set up: 25
Chocolats et Thés Pelletier & Compagnie. Van Houten & Bvloker opened
in Amsterdam in 1815. Cailler was set up at Vevey in Switzerland in 1819,
and Suchard occupied Neuchâtel. The first true chocolate factories, however, were those of Menier in the Paris region, first opened in 1824.

In 1826, Brillat-Savarin, the pundit of gastronomy, was still advocating 26
"ambered chocolate," which he described as "the chocolate of the afflicted."
He recommended it to "any man who has drunk too deeply of the cup of
pleasure...who finds his wit temporarily losing its edge, the atmosphere
humid, time dragging...or who is tortured by a fixed idea." Alexandre
Dumas mentions Brillat-Savarin's endorsement of "chocolate with ambergris as a sovereign remedy for those fatigued by any sort of labour," which
obviously means a great many people.

Le confiseur royal ou art du confiseur, published in Paris in 1818, how- 27
ever, mentions only confectionery or chocolate such as pistachios with
chocolat de santé, diablotins au chocolat, and a pastille or dragée stuffed

with chocolate paste "identical to that so greatly liked by the unfortunate Queen Marie-Antoinette."

Finally, in 1875, a Swiss from Vevey called Daniel Peter had the dis-   28
tinction of inventing milk chocolate. He then went into partnership with
his competitors Cailler and Kohler. The three brands merged with Nestlé
in 1929, and thereafter Switzerland was one of the world's great shrines to
chocolate.

Analyzing This Selection

1. **THE WRITER'S METHOD**   This selection is a chapter in A *History of Food*. Is the essay written principally for historians or eaters?

2. New information can change your view of something familiar. How, if at all, did this expository essay serve that purpose?

Analyzing Connections

3. This essay and Forster's "My Wood" (see p. 406) contain many allusions to knowledge not every reader has. Examine how the authors give informative contexts to knowledge they seem to take for granted. Which selection is written for a wider audience?

Analyzing by Writing

4. The tomato and potato have had colorful histories since their discovery by European colonizers. Using research sources, write a brief history of either one or a similar New World edible. Synthesize the available information, and come to a unified point about the food's effects on society.

PART 8

MEDIA IMAGES

INSIGHTS

Everybody watches it, but no one really likes it. This is the open secret of TV today. Its only champions are its own executives, the advertisers who exploit it, and a compromised network of academic boosters. Otherwise, TV has no spontaneous defenders, because there is almost nothing in it to defend. In many ways at once, TV negates the very "choices" that it now promotes with rising desperation. It promises an unimpeded vision of the whole known universe, and yet it shows us nothing but the laughable reflection of our own unhappy faces. It seems to offer us a fresh, "irreverent" view of the oppressive past, and yet that very gesture of rebelliousness turns out to be a ploy by those in power. Night after night, TV displays a bright infinitude of goods, employs a multitude of shocks and teases; and the only purpose of that spectacle is to promote the habit of spectatorship. It celebrates unending "choice" while trying to keep a jeering audience all strung out. TV begins by offering us a beautiful hallucination of diversity, but it is finally like a drug whose high is only the conviction that its user is too cool to be addicted.

—MARK CRISPIN MILLER

It should not be surprising that all sorts of Americans — not only the bed- and house-ridden — find solace in the mythically stable communities of soap operas. Some soap communities, after all, have lasted over thirty years. All potential viewers are members of a society that has been in constant transformation through geographic mobility and the loss of extended fami- lies. Loneliness, we are repeatedly told, has become pandemic in America, and the longing for community is a palpable need. Whether through reli- gion, clubs, associations, or support groups — or through daily immersion in a favorite soap — many Americans search for some kind of communal life to counter varying degrees of social isolation and alienation.

—RUTH ROSEN

The Miss America pageant is the worst sort of "Americanism," the soft smile of sex and the hard sell of toothpaste and hair dye ads wrapped in the dreamy ideological gauze of "making it through one's own effort." In a per-

458

verse way, I like the show; it is the only live television left other than sports, news broadcasts, performing arts awards programs, and speeches by the president. I miss live TV. It was the closest thing to theater for the masses. And the Miss America contest is, as it has been for some time, the most perfectly rendered theater in our culture, for it so perfectly captures what we yearn for: a low-class ritual, a polished restatement of vulgarity, that wants to open the door to high-class respectability by way of plain middle-class anxiety and ambition. "Am I doing all right?" the contestants seem to ask in a kind of reassuring, if numbed, way. The contest brings together all the American classes in a show-biz spectacle of classlessness and tastelessness.

—GERALD EARLY

The movies are an encyclopedia of gestures. They fix indelibly the look of things — a woman throwing her drink in a man's face, someone being shot through the head, a swimmer wrestling a crocodile, a police car flying off the side of the road and executing a slow half twist before landing on its roof — that, if you are halfway lucky, you can pass a lifetime without seeing anywhere except in the movies. But the movies make these things familiar. They can even, through endless repetition, make them boring. If you have seen a swimmer wrestling a crocodile twice, you may choose the third occasion to go out for popcorn.

Some movie-made gestures never become boring, of course. They're returned to again and again, and are even incorporated into your own repertoire. One of the important social services the movies have performed over the years, for example, is the instruction of generations of interested pre-adolescents in the mechanics of kissing — from the early-movie manner, in which the man rather suddenly and violently mashes his face onto the woman's and grinds slowly against it (are both mouths wide open, or only his?), to more recent representations, in which sheer face-swallowing is less emphasized and a good deal of nibbling and tongue work are indicated. It's not that you would never have figured out how to kiss (or to perform related activities, since kissing in the movies is usually a synecdoche for intimacies that cannot be shown: as above, so below) if you hadn't had Gary Cooper or Ellen Barkin to help you out. It's that it is impossible to say what in your knowledge of kissing comes from kissing and what comes from movies of people kissing.

—LOUIS MENAND

Dear John Wayne

August and the drive-in picture is packed.
We lounge on the hood of the Pontiac

surrounded by the slow-burning spirals they sell
at the window, to vanquish the hordes of mosquitoes.
Nothing works. They break through the smoke-screen for blood.

Always the look-out spots the Indians first,
spread north to south, barring progress.
The Sioux, or Cheyenne, or some bunch
in spectacular columns, arranged like SAC missiles,
their feathers bristling in the meaningful sunset.

The drum breaks. There will be no parlance.
Only the arrows whining, a death-cloud of nerves
swarming down on the settlers
who die beautifully, tumbling like dust weeds
into the history that brought us all here
together: this wide screen beneath the sign of the bear.

The sky fills, acres of blue squint and eye
that the crowd cheers. His face moves over us,
a thick cloud of vengeance, pitted
like the land that was once flesh. Each rut,
each scar makes a promise: *It is
not over, this fight, not as long as you resist.*

Everything we see belongs to us.
A few laughing Indians fall over the hood
slipping in the hot spilled butter.
*The eye sees a lot, John, but the heart is so blind.
How will you know what you own?*

He smiles, a horizon of teeth
the credits reel over, and then the white fields
again blowing in the true-to-life dark.
The dark films over everything.
We get into the car
scratching our mosquito bites, speechless and small
as people are when the movie is done.
We are back in ourselves.

How can we help but keep hearing his voice,
the flip side of the sound-track, still playing:
*Come on, boys, we've got them
where we want them, drunk, running.
They will give us what we want, what we need:
The heart is a strange wood inside of everything
we see, burning, doubling, splitting out of its skin.*
                                        —LOUISE ERDRICH

FOCUSING BY WRITING

1. Talk shows on television and radio offer a public forum for discussing controversial personal and national issues. They air diverse opinions from hosts, studio guests, and call-in listeners, and sometimes heated discussions get out of control. Are talk shows valuable as democratic forums of debate, or do they trivialize opinions into statements that shock but have no social or moral consequences? Consider a recent talk show that you have seen or heard. How did the program affect you? Did you become more or less concerned to form an opinion on the issues that were discussed?

2. What was the dominant impression you received during your visit to a Disney park or other entertainment park? Consider what details of the place created the atmosphere. (It is possible that the atmosphere you felt was not the one intended by the park.) Is your present memory of the park significantly different from your response to it at the time?

3. Examine the effects of telephone technology on your life. Consider the positive and negative ways that answering machines, cordless phones, cell phones, or other telecommunication devices play a part in your social and family relations. Consider your gains and losses in matters affecting your freedom, vulnerability to others, and social status.

4. Explain the appeal of two dissimilar television or radio celebrities. Mix your selection among entertainers, advertising images, and news reporters, and possibly include a cartoon or puppet personality. What personal qualities appear in their aura? What, if any, similarities underlie their different appeal?

Anthony Lane

A REVIEW OF *TITANIC*[1]

ANTHONY LANE is a British film critic who also writes frequently for the *New Yorker*. He was educated at Cambridge University. Lane's book reviews and film critiques have appeared in periodicals such as *The Independent*, the *Spectator*, and the *Sunday Telegraph*. The following film review was printed in the *New Yorker*.

After all the hullabaloo, James Cameron's *Titanic* will finally set sail on   1
December 19th. Already, however, the film has moved away from the quay-side, with a première in Tokyo and a public screening in London. The latter was attended by the Prince of Wales, and if any of us wondered whether His Royal Highness was well advised to lend his gracious presence to the tragedy of a sinking ship we were too polite to say. It was altogether a polite occasion; there is always something absurd about going to the movies in a tuxedo, even more so when the movie in question wastes no opportunity to laugh at stuffed shirts. If he really wanted to show solidarity with *Titanic*, Prince Charles should have rolled up in corduroy and old boots.

The hero of the tale is Jack Dawson (Leonardo DiCaprio), a freewheel-   2
ing scruff — a skinny kindred spirit, perhaps, of his namesake Jack London — who wins a couple of steerage tickets in a poker game. Armed with little more than a sketchbook and an insolent grin, he leaps aboard the *Titanic* as she is about to cast off from Southampton on her maiden — and, as it turns out, her funeral — voyage. Jack thus joins the hundreds of other happy fools who believe that they are heading for a nice time; among them are the nervy and elegant Ruth DeWitt Bukater (Frances Fisher), the suspiciously moneyed Molly Brown (Kathy Bates), and Smith (Bernard Hill), the captain of the ship. The only glum face on view is that of Ruth's daughter Rose (Kate Winslet), a young first-class Philadelphian who has already foreseen her own demise — not in the form of a large lump of ice in the North Atlantic but, far more scarily, at the hands of her fiancé, Cal Hockley (Billy Zane), the man with a heart of absolute zero. Unless something happens, she will marry him, live comfortably, and suffer the long, slow

[1]Editor's title.

462

death of the soul. The something is Jack, of course, who rescues a despairing Rose as she stands at the stern, red silk shoes on the railing, and prepares to jump. He hauls her back, they fall in love, he draws her nude, they make out in the cargo hold, and then the ship, in a touching display of erotic sympathy, rears up on end and goes down.

You might ask how such a simple story can take almost three and a half   3
hours to tell — and by what miracle, moreover, *Titanic* should feel like the least boring movie of the year. The answer to both questions lies in the assiduous grace with which Cameron has framed, decorated, and wrapped the love affair. The film has been hailed as a fresh departure for him — as a flight from the panting mayhem of his *Terminator* films — but both of those pictures were obsessed by the bending and shaping of time. It is only in retrospect, appropriately, that we can see how serious that obsession was, how swiftly it went beyond a technical trick, and how thoroughly it has crept into every cranny of *Titanic*. If you've heard nothing about the movie, it's a shock to see it open in a modern-day setting, with a deep-sea expedition to the wreck of the ship. Like the spacemen who cut into Ripley's lost craft in Cameron's *Aliens*, a bunch of scientists descend to the gray ghost of the *Titanic*, send robots through the fish-filled rooms, and retrieve a safe. Back on the surface, they pry it open, expecting jewels; instead, they find a drawing of a naked girl. A lady of a hundred and one sees the image on TV and phones the explorers. "Oh yes," she says calmly, "the woman in the picture is me."

This is the aged but still blooming Rose (Gloria Stuart), a survivor in   4
every sense — "Wasn't I a dish?" she says, looking at the drawing. From here the story unfurls in flashback, as she recounts her distant experience. Cameron's great achievement is to shrink that distance: as Rose peers into the video monitor that displays the wreck, you see her face reflected in the screen until past and present are no more than a breath apart. Even finer are those sequences where the *Titanic* is resurrected; rather than simply cut to the spring of 1912, Cameron sends his camera gliding along the decks and gangways of the encrusted vessel until, as if in fulfillment of a wish, she *melts* into life. This may be the most beautiful special effect ever seen; in its peculiar magic, at once decorous and delirious, it feels closer to the Cocteau of *Beauty and the Beast*, say, than to the tedious wizardry of recent blockbusters. Many moviegoers, and almost all critics, inveigh against special effects, but what rankles is the abuse of effects; Cameron has repeatedly shown that in the right hands they are as fertile and provocative as any other artistic resource. At best, indeed, they answer to our hopes and terrors of transfiguration: the metallic morphing of the T-1000 in *Terminator 2* offered the most succulent image of self-replenishing evil since *Dracula*, and, at the other extreme, the way in which sunshine imperceptibly breaks upon the drowned corpse of the *Titanic*, and in which passengers start to stroll again upon its gleaming decks, is as bracing a prospect of rebirth as you could hope to imagine.

No wonder Leonardo DiCaprio looks so chipper. His performance is 5 indeed that of a youth who has been given a new lease, or even the freehold, on life. Some of Jack's lines are straight out of the Hobo's Handbook — "I've got ten bucks in my pocket, I've got nothing to offer you" — but he manages to conjure an age when both he and the twentieth century were still in their teens and it was not entirely fanciful to be fancy-free. There's an extraordinary moment, near the end, when Jack and Rose cling once more to the stern where they first met; now, however, they are right at the summit of the ship, which is vertical and poised to plunge. As it begins to slide like a sword into the waves, Jack shouts "This is it!" and you realize that, even in the face of death — or especially there, when their hearts are on overload — these two are having fun. Kate Winslet is in her element, and that element is water; given her bright, bedraggled Rose and her Ophelia in Kenneth Branagh's *Hamlet,* not to mention the bathtub scene in *Heavenly Creatures,* you could plausibly argue that Winslet is emerging, like a shell-borne Venus, as the Esther Williams *de nos jours.* Winslet's talent, however, extends beyond her gills, and from the opening scene, when the camera curves down to seek out Rose's proudly pale face beneath the brim of her hat, you catch the same air of principled unpredictability — more Jeanne Moreau than bathing beauty — that lit up Winslet's fiery, cigarette-waving heroine in last year's *Jude.* Isn't she a dish?

It took guts, and a certain generosity, for Cameron to cast his two leads 6 like this. The movie is blissfully free of the middle-aged A-list that you would expect from a project of this magnitude, not to mention the B-minus list that used to bedevil disaster flicks; I like both Mel Gibson and Harrison Ford, for instance, but imagine how ponderous and straightforward *Titanic* would have seemed under their influence. As for Shelley Winters, there would have been no need for the iceberg. The best performance in *Titanic* comes from Victor Garber, who plays Andrews, the Irish builder of the ship. It would have been easy to nudge the role toward hysteria as his beloved creation breaks up beneath him, but Andrews is never more civilized and kindly than when he is overseeing the progress of doom. "She is made of iron, and she will sink," he says firmly. Garber offers a wonderful portrait of a man who is stricken, but not by panic; as the *Titanic* tilts and sinks, Andrews stands by a mantelpiece with a drink and adjusts the clock by the time on his fob watch. Not only is he a model of conduct to the other passengers; he corrects and refines the movie's automatic satire. For much of the time, we are invited to scoff at the snobs as they bicker and dine, and to relax in the unbuttoned company of Jack and his ilk. At one postprandial point, the camera whirls around with Rose as she dances a Celtic reel belowdecks — a shot borrowed from *Whiskey Galore* — and then cuts hard to Cal and his cronies talking politics through a fug of cigar. Later, amid the chaos, Rose tells him that half the people on the boat are going to die. "Not the better half," says Cal. Boo! Hiss!

I didn't object to the presence of this stage villain — he could walk into 7 a one-reel melodrama from 1912, no questions asked — because he reinforced the growing sense that *Titanic* is, for all its narrative dexterity and the formidable modernity of its methods, an old-fashioned picture. The most radical thing about it is the version of the *Demoiselles d'Avignon* which Rose appears to have bought in Paris, and is presumably lost forever, together with the fifteen hundred dead. In both its emotional thrust and its social judgment, *Titanic* pursues a clear and often obvious route. Like *The English Patient*, it could be described as a long historical romance, and yet it boasts none of the intricate byways that darkened Minghella's movie. At the close of the century, Cameron is pushing at cinema much as D. W. Griffith did at the start — raising the stakes of the spectacular, outwitting the intellect, and heading straight for the guts. He piles on the astonishment as if he owed it to the nature of his medium; there are sights here that no other director would have the nerve to design and stage — an old couple embracing on their double bed while the water flows beneath it like Lethe, or the ice-whitened bodies of passengers bobbing in the endless darkness, as if on a battlefield of water.

Some viewers have confessed themselves disappointed by the computer- 8 generated images of the *Titanic*; the daytime shots, in particular, are lightened by a strange haze, and there are times when this unrusting palace resembles not so much an actual ship as one of those splendid, stylized liners from travel posters of the nineteen-twenties. Yet even that, I found, was no shortcoming, for it drove home the *Titanic* as a dream — a fatal vision of efficient loveliness for those who sailed in her, and a kind of unreal, awesome trip for those of us watching her now. She went down, according to this movie, as a direct result of Rose and Jack, because the men in the crow's nest were too busy spying on the smooching couple to notice what was looming ahead. So now you know: the *Titanic* was lost for love. James Cameron's film is grand and wrenching rather than clever or subtle, and it floods your eyes; if you are going to spend two hundred million dollars on a movie, this is the way to do it.

Analyzing This Selection

1. How does Lane's review differ from your own response to *Titanic*? What did you most enjoy? How does Lane assess what you liked?

2. How does Lane explain the appeal of the movie's special effects? Does he overstate their relevance to you? How has the review changed your interest, if it has, in special effects?

3. **THE WRITER'S METHOD**   How does Lane indicate his negative reactions? Find sentences that illustrate his judgments. What tone does he take toward the film's shortcomings?

Analyzing Connections

4. Lane and Neil Postman (see "The Necessity of Myths," p. 300) both analyze narratives that entertain us. What "myth" does Lane discover in *Titanic*? How would Postman review the film?

Analyzing by Writing

5. Review a film that you liked as much as or better than *Titanic*. Assess elements such as characters and acting, story and dialogue, visual effects, and the coherence of a director's purpose. Avoid retelling events. As a reviewer you are writing for readers who haven't yet seen the movie; consider what they want and don't want to know.

Gregg Easterbrook

WATCH AND LEARN

GREGG EASTERBROOK (b. 1953) graduated from Colorado College. He contributes articles to magazines such as the *Atlantic, Newsweek, Washington Monthly,* and the *New Republic,* where the following essay appeared. Easterbrook's book *A Moment on the Earth: The Coming Age of Environmental Optimism* (1995) explores ways that human industry can develop in ecological harmony with nature.

Defenders of bloodshed in film, television, and writing often argue that depictions of killing don't incite real violence because no one is really affected by what they see or read; it's all just water off a duck's back. At heart, this is an argument against free expression. The whole reason to have a First Amendment is that people *are* influenced by what they see and hear: words and images do change minds, so there must be free competition among them. If what we say, write, or show has no consequences, why bother to have free speech? 1

Defenders of Hollywood bloodshed also employ the argument that, since millions of people watch screen mayhem and shrug, feigned violence has no causal relation to actual violence.... For those on the psychological borderline, the calculus is different. There have, for example, been at least two instances of real-world shootings in which the guilty imitated scenes in *Natural Born Killers....* 2

Except for the unbalanced, exposure to violence in video "is not so important for adults; adults can watch anything they want," Eron says.[1] Younger minds are a different story. Children who don't yet understand the difference between illusion and reality may be highly affected by video violence. Between the ages of two and eight, hours of viewing violent TV programs and movies correlates closely to felonies later in life; the child comes to see hitting, stabbing, and shooting as normative acts. The link between watching violence and engaging in violence continues up to about the age of nineteen, Eron finds, after which most people's characters have been formed, and video mayhem no longer correlates to destructive behavior. 3

---

[1] Leonard Eron, a research psychologist, studies correlations of video and actual violence. [Editor's note.]

Trends in gun availability do not appear to explain the murder rise that 4
has coincided with television and violent films. Research by John Lott Jr.,
of the University of Chicago Law School, shows that the percentage of
homes with guns has changed little throughout the postwar era. What
appears to have changed is the willingness of people to fire their guns at
one another. Are adolescents now willing to use guns because violent
images make killing seem acceptable or even cool? Following the Colorado
slaughter, the *New York Times* ran a recounting of other postwar mass murders staged by the young, such as the 1966 Texas tower killings, and noted
that they all happened before the advent of the Internet or shock rock,
which seemed to the *Times* to absolve the modern media. But all the mass
killings by the young occurred after 1950 — after it became common to
watch violence on television.

When horrific murders occur, the film and television industries routinely 5
attempt to transfer criticism to the weapons used. Just after the Colorado
shootings, for instance, TV talk-show host Rosie O'Donnell called for a
constitutional amendment banning all firearms. How strange that O'Donnell didn't call instead for a boycott of Sony or its production company,
Columbia Tristar — a film studio from which she has received generous
paychecks and whose current offerings include *8MM*, which glamorizes
the sexual murder of young women, and *The Replacement Killers*, whose
hero is a hit man and which depicts dozens of gun murders. Handguns
should be licensed, but that hardly excuses the convenient sanctimony of
blaming the crime on the weapon, rather than on what resides in the
human mind.

And, when it comes to promoting adoration of guns, Hollywood might 6
as well be the NRA's marketing arm. An ever-increasing share of film and
television depicts the firearm as something the virile must have and use, if
not an outright sexual aid. Check the theater section of any newspaper, and
you will find an ever-higher percentage of movie ads in which the stars are
prominently holding guns. Keanu Reeves, Uma Thurman, Laurence Fish-
burne, Geena Davis, Woody Harrelson, and Mark Wahlberg are just a few
of the hip stars who have posed with guns for movie advertising. Hollywood
endlessly congratulates itself for reducing the depiction of cigarettes in
movies and movie ads. Cigarettes had to go, the film industry admitted,
because glamorizing them gives the wrong idea to kids. But the glamoriza-
tion of firearms, which is far more dangerous, continues. Today, even female stars who otherwise consider themselves politically aware will model
in sexualized poses with guns. Ads for the new movie *Goodbye Lover* show
star Patricia Arquette nearly nude, with very little between her and the
viewer but her handgun.

But doesn't video violence merely depict a stark reality against which 7
the young need be warned? American society is far too violent, yet the
forms of brutality highlighted in the movies and on television — predomi-

nantly "thrill" killings and serial murders — are pure distortion. Nearly 99 percent of real murders result from robberies, drug deals, and domestic disputes; figures from research affiliated with the FBI's behavioral sciences division show an average of only about thirty serial or "thrill" murders nationally per year. Thirty is plenty horrifying enough, but, at this point, each of the major networks and movie studios alone depicts more "thrill" and serial murders annually than that. By endlessly exploiting the notion of the "thrill" murder, Hollywood and television present to the young an entirely imaginary image of a society in which killing for pleasure is a common event. The publishing industry, including some TNR advertisers, also distorts for profit the frequency of "thrill" murders.

The profitability of violent cinema is broadly dependent on the "down-rating" of films — movies containing extreme violence being rated only R instead of NC-17 (the new name for X) — and the lax enforcement of age restrictions regarding movies. Teens are the best market segment for Hollywood: when moviemakers claim their violent movies are not meant to appeal to teens, they are simply lying. The millionaire status of actors, directors, and studio heads — and the returns of the mutual funds that invest in movie companies — depends on not restricting teen access to theaters or film rentals. Studios in effect control the movie ratings board and endlessly lobby it not to label extreme violence with an NC-17, the only form of rating that is actually enforced. *Natural Born Killers*, for example, received an R following Time-Warner lobbying, despite its repeated close-up murders and one charming scene in which the stars kidnap a high school girl and argue about whether it would be more fun to kill her before or after raping her. Since its inception, the movie ratings board has put its most restrictive rating on any realistic representation of lovemaking, while sanctioning ever-more-graphic depictions of murder and torture. In economic terms, the board's pro-violence bias gives studios an incentive to present more death and mayhem, confident that ratings officials will smile with approval.

When R-and-X battles were first fought, intellectual sentiment regarded the ratings system as a way of blocking the young from seeing films with political content, such as *Easy Rider*, or discouraging depictions of sexuality; ratings were perceived as the rubes' counterattack against cinematic sophistication. But, in the 1960s, murder after murder after murder was not standard cinema fare. The most controversial violent film of that era, *A Clockwork Orange*, depicted a total of one killing, which was heard but not on-camera. (*Clockwork Orange* also had genuine political content, unlike most of today's big-studio movies.) In an era of runaway screen violence, the '60s ideal that the young should be allowed to see what they want has been corrupted. In this, trends in video mirror the misuse of liberal ideals generally.

Anti-censorship battles of this century were fought on firm ground, advocating the right of films to tackle social and sexual issues (the 1930s Hays office forbid among other things cinematic mention of cohabitation) and free access to works of literature such as *Ulysses, Story of O,* and the original version of Norman Mailer's *The Naked and the Dead.* Struggles against censors established that suppression of film or writing is wrong.

But to say that nothing should be censored is very different from saying   11
that everything should be shown. Today, Hollywood and television have twisted the First Amendment concept that occasional repulsive or worthless expression must be protected, so as to guarantee freedom for works of genuine political content or artistic merit, into a new standard in which constitutional freedoms are employed mainly to safeguard works that make no pretense of merit. In the new standard, the bulk of what's being protected is repulsive or worthless, with the meritorious work the rare exception.

Not only is there profit for the performers, producers, management, and   12
shareholders of films that glorify violence, so, too, is there profit for politicians. Many conservative or Republican politicians who denounce Hollywood eagerly accept its lucre. Bob Dole's 1995 anti-Hollywood speech was not followed up by any anti-Hollywood legislation or campaign-funds strategy. After the Colorado murders, President Clinton declared, "Parents should take this moment to ask what else they can do to shield children from violent images and experiences that warp young perceptions." But Clinton was careful to avoid criticizing Hollywood, one of the top sources of public backing and campaign contributions for him and his would-be successor, Vice President Al Gore. The president had nothing specific to propose on film violence — only that parents should try to figure out what to do.

When television producers say it is the parents' obligation to keep chil-   13
dren away from the tube, they reach the self-satire point of warning that their own product is unsuitable for consumption. The situation will improve somewhat beginning in 2000, by which time all new TVs must be sold with the "V chip" — supported by Clinton and Gore — which will allow parents to block violent shows. But it will be at least a decade before the majority of the nation's sets include the chip, and who knows how adept young minds will prove at defeating it? Rather than relying on a technical fix that will take many years to achieve an effect, TV producers could simply stop churning out the gratuitous violence. Television could dramatically reduce its output of scenes of killing and still depict violence in news broadcasts, documentaries, and the occasional show in which the horrible is genuinely relevant. Reduction in violence is not censorship; it is placing social responsibility before profit.

The movie industry could practice the same kind of restraint without   14
sacrificing profitability. In this regard, the big Hollywood studios, including Disney, look craven and exploitative compared to, of all things, the porn-video industry. Repulsive material occurs in underground porn, but, in the products sold by the mainstream triple-X distributors such as Vivid

Video (the MGM of the erotica business), violence is never, ever, ever depicted — because that would be irresponsible. Women and men perform every conceivable explicit act in today's mainstream porn, but what is shown is always consensual and almost sunnily friendly. Scenes of rape or sexual menace never occur, and scenes of sexual murder are an absolute taboo.

It is beyond irony that today Sony and Time-Warner eagerly market 15 explicit depictions of women being raped, sexually assaulted, and sexually murdered, while the mainstream porn industry would never dream of doing so. But, if money is all that matters, the point here is that mainstream porn is violence-free and yet risqué and highly profitable. Surely this shows that Hollywood could voluntarily step back from the abyss of glorifying violence and still retain its edge and its income....

Analyzing This Selection

1. How does Easterbrook refute arguments supporting screen violence? How does he support his own argument?

2. How do films and television distort violence in American society? What would a truer view show?

3. **THE WRITER'S METHOD** What is the author's attitude toward government and industry acceptance (if not approval) of screen violence? Find sentences that illustrate his tone.

Analyzing Connections

4. Does Lane's view of special effects (see "A Review of *Titanic*," p. 462) change your outlook on screen violence? Does Easterbrook's argument adequately acknowledge the unreality of sensational violence?

Analyzing by Writing

5. Propose a remedy for one part of the complex problem of screen violence as recreation and entertainment. What measures can, and should, be taken? Respond to the kind of opposition your measure will probably encounter. Try to foresee who might support your plan.

Kurt Andersen

ANIMATION NATION

KURT ANDERSEN (b. 1954) graduated from Harvard University and began writing for magazines as a reporter for *Time*. His articles have appeared also in *Rolling Stone, Vanity Fair,* and *New York,* where Andersen became the editor-in-chief. His first novel, *Turn of the Century,* was published in 1999. He is currently a staff columnist for the *New Yorker,* where this commentary appeared in 1997.

Are you by any chance hoping that the millennium will usher in some 1 sort of cleansing cultural flood tide — a next big thing that's not just a half-ironic recycling of a previous big thing, like miniskirts or Corinthian columns? Well, it may have happened already. The new era, which is about to ripen into its golden age, was born eight and a half years ago. It was then, over a brief period in 1988 and 1989, that *Who Framed Roger Rabbit?* posited a world cohabited by human beings and cartoon characters, *The Little Mermaid* inaugurated a new Disney animation hegemony, and — the key event — *The Simpsons* went on the air.

What will be the big musical of 1997? *Hercules,* the Disney cartoon that 2 opens in New York this weekend. What is the only successful new television series of the year so far? *King of the Hill,* a cartoon. What is the only genre of TV program to which Steven Spielberg attaches his name? Cartoon shows — four of them, including *Freakazoid* and *Pinky and the Brain.* Which is the most successful new cable channel? The Cartoon Network. What cable network is insanely profitable? Nickelodeon, thanks partly to its cartoon shows *Ren & Stimpy* and *Rugrats.* Who are the most deeply resonant, compellingly humane people on the tube? Cartoon characters.

There are now entire genres and character types that audiences will 3 wholeheartedly embrace only in cartoon form. The live-action movie musical has been a fading form since the time of *Mary Poppins,* but put old-fashioned tunes and drippy sentiment in the mouths of animated lions and princesses and toy cowboys, and audiences will buy them (plus all licensed gewgaws). Even small children aren't innocent enough nowadays to put up with actual human beings who profess love, perform heroic deeds, and then break into song about it. But animated characters can still plausibly portray purity and nobility. Cartoons — and, pretty much, only cartoons — allow us our corn.

Satire, too, has been rather suddenly yet thoroughly colonized by the cartoons. There's *Duckman* (USA Network), *Dr. Katz, Professional Therapist* (Comedy Central), and *Beavis and Butt-head* and *Daria* (MTV). Not only is *The Simpsons* smarter, sharper, and more allusive than any other show on television; it's also TV's oasis of commedia dell'arte (a flesh-and-blood Homer Simpson would be bathetically repellent), and of believable warmth as well.

If cartoons on TV have become the form in which we permit ourselves to enjoy poignancy and sass and human weirdness, in movies the distinction between cartoons and live action is blurry, on the way to moot. Digitally animated special effects transmute reality into cartoons and cartoons into reality. In Spielberg's new megahit, *The Lost World: Jurassic Park*, the animated dinosaurs seem in every way more genuine and less mechanical than the people. In *The Fifth Element*, Bruce Willis zooms through a real-looking twenty-third-century New York designed by the legendary French cartoonist Jean (Moebius) Giraud. The fourth in the current series of Batman movies will open against *Hercules* next week. A live-action *George of the Jungle* is to come out next month; two different Casper movies are on the way; and Philip Kaufman, who made *The Unbearable Lightness of Being*, is developing a movie about the Marvel Comics character Sub-Mariner.

It cannot be coincidental that millions of people now achieve their most intimate and satisfying human connections electronically, by going on-line behind cartoony noms de net and exchanging pixels with other, uh, characters. Flirting with someone in an Internet chat room, making love to Jessica Rabbit — what's the difference? The plot of *Roger Rabbit*, remember, concerned a development scheme by a money-mad evil genius to destroy the cartoon characters and their funky L.A. quarter, and replace them with human beings: justice triumphs, Toontown survives. We are now living in a sequel, *Toontown Strikes Back*, in which the animated creatures (thanks to certain money-mad L.A. geniuses) have left their old ghetto and moved en masse into our human neighborhoods.

Welcome, Toons! A recent *Simpsons* episode lampooned, with perfect contempt, various live-action TV genres. Its parody of a sitcom included, of course, plenty of robotically hysterical canned laughter. It was a joke that only an animated show could do perfectly, and it highlighted another virtue of *The Simpsons*: almost alone among TV comedies, it doesn't have a laugh track. *King of the Hill*, which follows it on Sunday nights, doesn't have one, either. If we find these shows funny, we have the luxury of grinning or chuckling or guffawing without electronic encouragement — by ourselves, at home, in real life. Thanks to cartoons, we can respond like human beings.

Analyzing This Selection

1. **THE WRITER'S METHOD**   In paragraphs 1 to 2, how do the rhetorical questions change? What is their cumulative effect? What risks does the author take in using this tactic?

2. How does Andersen imply regrets and reservations along with his endorsement of cartoons?

Analyzing Connections

3. Cartoons such as *The Simpsons* can acquire the acceptance of cultural "myths" (see Neil Postman, "The Necessity of Myths," p. 300). How, if at all, does the cartoon medium affect the story's relevance? How would Postman evaluate the *Simpsons* myth?

Analyzing by Writing

4. Review a cartoon show Andersen mentions, and analyze its popular appeal. How does it differ from nonanimated situation comedies? Do cartoons broaden or narrow our range of empathy? If you select one of the satires, clarify its type of wit. Do cartoons strengthen or weaken the power of ridicule?

Ellen Ullman

GETTING CLOSE
TO THE MACHINE

ELLEN ULLMAN (b. 1948) is a software engineer who writes about her profession. She graduated from Cornell University. This essay appeared in *Harper's* magazine in 1995.

People imagine that computer programming is logical, a process like fix- 1
ing a clock. Nothing could be further from the truth. Programming is more like an illness, a fever, an obsession. It's like riding a train and never being able to get off.

The problem with programming is not that the computer is illogical — 2
the computer is terribly logical, relentlessly literal. It demands that the programmer explain the world on its terms; that is, as an algorithm that must be written down in order, in a specific syntax, in a strange language that is only partially readable by regular human beings. To program is to translate between the chaos of human life and the rational, line-by-line world of computer language.

When you program, reality presents itself as thousands of details, millions 3
of bits of knowledge. This knowledge comes at you from one perspective and then another, then comes a random thought, then you remember something else important, then you reconsider that idea with a what-if attached. For example, try to think of everything you know about something as simple as an invoice. Now try to tell an idiot how to prepare one. That is programming.

I used to have dreams in which I was overhearing conversations I had 4
to program. Once I dreamed I had to program two people making love. In my dream they sweated and tumbled while I sat looking for the algorithm. The couple went from gentle caresses to ever-deepening passion, and I tried desperately to find a way to express the act of love in the C computer language.

When you are programming, you must not let your mind wander. As the 5
human-world knowledge tumbles about in your head, you must keep typing, typing. You must not be interrupted. Any break in your concentration

causes you to lose a line here or there. Some bit comes, then — oh no, it's leaving, please come back. But it may not come back. You may lose it. You will create a bug and there's nothing you can do about it.

People imagine that programmers don't like to talk because they prefer 6
machines to people. This is not completely true. Programmers don't talk because they must not be interrupted.

This need to be uninterrupted leads to a life that is strangely asynchro- 7
nous to the one lived by other human beings. It's better to send e-mail to a programmer than to call. It's better to leave a note on the chair than to expect the programmer to come to a meeting. This is because the pro-grammer must work in mind time while the phone rings and the meetings happen in real time. It's not just ego that prevents programmers from work-ing in groups — it's the synchronicity problem. Synchronizing with other people (or their representations in telephones, buzzers, and doorbells) can only mean interrupting the thought train. Interruptions mean bugs. You must not get off the train.

I once had a job in which I didn't talk to anyone for two years. Here was 8
the arrangement: I was the first engineer to be hired by a start-up software company. In exchange for large quantities of stock that might be worth something someday, I was supposed to give up my life.

I sat in a large room with two other engineers and three workstations. 9
The fans in the machines whirred, the keys on the keyboards clicked. Occasionally one of us would grunt or mutter. Otherwise we did not speak. Now and then I would have an outburst in which I pounded the keyboard with my fists, setting off a barrage of beeps. My colleagues might have looked up, but they never said anything.

Real time was no longer compelling to me. Days, weeks, months, and 10
years came and went without much change in my surroundings. Surely I was aging. My hair must have grown, I must have cut it, it must have slowly become grayer. Gravity must have been working on my late-thirties body, but I didn't pay attention.

What was compelling was the software. I was making something out of 11
nothing, I thought, and I admit that the software had more life for me dur-ing those years than a brief love affair, my friends, my cat, my house, or my neighbor who was stabbed and nearly killed by her husband. One day I sat in a room by myself, surrounded by computer monitors. I remember look-ing at the screens and saying, "Speak to me."

I was creating something called a device-independent interface library. 12
("Creating" — that is the word we used, each of us a genius in the attic.) I completed the library in two years and left the company. Five years later, the company's stock went public, and the original arrangement was made good: the engineers who stayed — the ones who had given seven years of their lives to the machine — became very, very wealthy.

If you want money and prestige, you need to write code that only 13
machines or other programmers understand. Such code is called "low." In
regular life, "low" usually signifies something bad. In programming, "low"
is good. Low means that you are close to the machine.

If the code creates programs that do useful work for regular human 14
beings, it is called "high." Higher-level programs are called "applications."
Applications are things that people use. Although it would seem that usefulness is a good thing, direct people-use is bad from a programmer's point
of view. If regular people, called "users," can understand the task accomplished by your program, you will be paid less and held in lower esteem.

A real programmer wants to stay close to the machine. The machine 15
means midnight dinners of Diet Coke. It means unwashed clothes and
bare feet on the desk. It means anxious rides through mind time that have
nothing to do with the clock. To work on things used only by machines or
other programmers — that's the key. Programmers and machines don't care
how you live. They don't care when you live. You can stay, come, go,
sleep — or not. At the end of the project looms a deadline, the terrible
place where you must get off the train. But in between, for years at a
stretch, you are free: free from the obligations of time.

I once designed a graphical user interface with a man who wouldn't 16
speak to me. My boss hired him without letting anyone else sit in on the
interview. My boss lived to regret it.

I was asked to brief my new colleague with the help of the third mem- 17
ber of our team. We went into a conference room, where my co-worker
and I filled two white boards with lines, boxes, circles, and arrows while the
new hire watched. After about a half hour, I noticed that he had become
very agitated.

"Are we going too fast?" I asked him.   18

"Too much for the first day?" asked my colleague.   19

"No," said our new man, "I just can't do it like this."   20

"Do what?" I asked. "Like what?"   21

His hands were deep in his pockets. He gestured with his elbows. "Like 22
this," he said.

"You mean design?" I asked.   23

"You mean in a meeting?" asked my colleague.   24

No answer from the new guy. A shrug. Another elbow motion.   25

Something terrible was beginning to occur to me. "You mean talking?"   26
I asked.

"Yeah, talking," he said. "I can't do it by talking."   27

By this time in my career, I had met many strange software engineers.   28
But here was the first one who wouldn't talk at all. We had a lot of design
work to do. No talking was certainly going to make things difficult.

"So how *can* you do it?" I asked.   29

"Mail," he said. "Send me e-mail."   30

Given no choice, we designed a graphical user interface by e-mail.   31
Corporations across North America and Europe are still using a system
designed by three people in the same office who communicated via computer, one of whom barely spoke at all.

Pretty graphical interfaces are commonly called "user-friendly." But they   32
are not really your friends. Underlying every user-friendly interface is terrific contempt for the humans who will use it.

The basic idea of a graphical interface is that it will not allow anything   33
alarming to happen. You can pound on the mouse button, your cat can run
across it, your baby can punch it, but the system should not crash.

To build a crash-proof system, the designer must be able to imagine —   34
and disallow — the dumbest action possible. He or she has to think of every
single stupid thing a human being could do. Gradually, over months and
years, the designer's mind creates a construct of the user as an imbecile.
This image is necessary. No crash-proof system can be built unless it is
made for an idiot.

The designer's contempt for your intelligence is mostly hidden deep in   35
the code. But now and then the disdain surfaces. Here's a small example:
You're trying to do something simple such as copying files onto a diskette
on your Mac. The program proceeds for a while, then encounters an error.
Your disk is defective, says a message, and below the message is a single
button. You absolutely must click this button. If you don't click it, the program will hang there indefinitely. Your disk is defective, your files may be
bollixed up, but the designer leaves you only one possible reply. You must
say, "OK."

The prettier the user interface, and the fewer replies the system allows   36
you to make, the dumber you once appeared in the mind of the designer.
Soon, everywhere we look, we will see pretty, idiot-proof interfaces designed
to make us say, "OK." Telephones, televisions, sales kiosks will all be wired
for "interactive," on-demand services. What power — demand! See a movie,
order seats to a basketball game, make hotel reservations, send a card to
mother — all of these services will be waiting for us on our televisions or
computers whenever we want them, midnight, dawn, or day. Sleep or order
a pizza: it no longer matters exactly what we do when. We don't need to
involve anyone else in the satisfaction of our needs. We don't even have to
talk. We get our services when we want them, free from the obligations of
regularly scheduled time. We can all live, like programmers, close to the
machine. "Interactivity" is misnamed. It should be called "asynchrony": the
engineering culture come to everyday life.

The very word "interactivity" implies something good and wonderful.   37
Surely a response, a reply, an answer is a positive thing. Surely it signifies
an advance over something else, something bad, something that doesn't
respond. There is only one problem: what we will be interacting with is
a machine. We will be "talking" to programs that are beginning to look sur-

prisingly alike; each has little animated pictures we are supposed to choose from, like push buttons on a toddler's toy. The toy is meant to please us. Somehow it is supposed to replace the rewards of fumbling for meaning with a mature human being, in the confusion of a natural language, together, in a room, within touching distance.

As the computer's pretty, helpful face (and contemptuous underlying code) penetrates deeper into daily life, the cult of the engineer comes with it. The engineer's assumptions and presumptions are in the code. That's the purpose of the program, after all: to sum up the intelligence and intentions of all the engineers who worked on the system over time — tens and hundreds of people who have learned an odd and highly specific way of doing things. The system reproduces and re-enacts life as engineers know it: alone, out of time, disdainful of anyone far from the machine.

Analyzing This Selection

1. What did Ullman like and dislike in her work? What do you think led her to be a specialist at programming?

2. **THE WRITER'S METHOD** How is the term "interactive" misleading? Why is the "OK" reply demeaning? Do you agree or disagree with Ullman's assessments?

Analyzing Connections

3. How do programming and military service (see Francine D'Amico's "Women Warriors," p. 372) affect normal thoughts and feelings? Explain why you would prefer either kind of work.

Analyzing by Writing

4. Examine the attractions and distresses of using personal computer and network terminals. How do they enhance or distort mental functions? Why do users get lost in cyberspace? Should users and society be concerned about how computers may cause the deterioration of certain ways of thinking and living?

Wendy Lesser

THE CONVERSION

WENDY LESSER (b. 1952) writes about painting and literature in relation to society. She graduated from Harvard University and received a Ph.D. in English from the University of California at Berkeley. Her essays have appeared in the *New Republic,* the *Yale Review,* the *Hudson Review,* and *Southwest Review,* and she is the founding editor of a similar magazine, *The Threepenny Review.* Lesser's books include *His Other Half: Men Looking at Women Through Art* (1991) and *Pictures at an Execution: An Inquiry into the Subject of Murder* (1994), which examines the moral issues surrounding a televised gas chamber execution. Her most recent book of essays is *The Amateur: An Independent Life of Letters* (1999). Lesser has received a Guggenheim Fellowship and other major awards. The following essay appeared in *Greywolf Forum* in an issue devoted to technology and the arts.

I resisted e-mail for at least two or three years. Many of my Berkeley 1 friends are academics, so they got it automatically as part of their jobs and then annoyingly sang its praises. "It replaces long-distance phone calls!" "You can dig up old recipes from libraries across the Midwest!" "It allows you to communicate instantaneously with colleagues from South Africa!" None of these seemed like things I particularly wanted to do. Moreover, I had strong if somewhat irrational reasons for resisting. I did not want my computer talking on the phone to anyone else's computer, because who knew what could happen once you opened up those lines? I wasn't just worried about viruses, though those were indeed a concern; but how could you be sure that someone wouldn't sneak through the e-mail door and thereby penetrate your hard disk, stealing or at any rate messing up your closely held documents? I preferred to keep my computer chaste and self-contained, aloof from all potential communicants. And then, I didn't see the point of getting those unreadable little messages that seemed to go on forever, with little or no punctuation. To judge by the e-mail I had read in newspapers and magazines (the kind that was always reproduced to show how fun and liberating this new mode of communication was), these emissions were somewhere below the level of the worst unsolicited manuscripts I habitually receive in the course of editing a literary magazine. Why should I want to read *more* of the stuff, especially on a barely legible computer screen? What was the good of a technological form that erased the boundary between intimate friends and total strangers, reducing everyone to a digital printout? Where was *handwriting* in all this? Where was *personal style?*

I should interrupt my screed to say that I am not a complete antitech- 2 nologist. I watch more television than just about anyone I know, and believe that *Hill Street Blues* and *NYPD Blue* are among the major artistic achievements of late twentieth-century America. I use the latest (well, the second-latest) desktop publishing equipment to put out my magazine, and rely on a rather complex database software to organize its subscriber list. I adore the fax machine and have long considered it the single greatest invention since the telephone — the fax machine, after all, respects and transmits handwriting, just as the telephone conveys the nuances of the individual voice. I am not, that is, a hermit. I constantly employ and enjoy electronic transmissions of all sorts, and I do not feel that they in any way sap my capacity to be an Emersonian individual. On the contrary, they enhance it: without all my little machines, I could not make a living as a self-employed, self-designated arbiter of cultural taste. In Emerson's time, you had to inherit a comfortable income if you wished to subsist as a man of letters; in our day, technology can substitute for and even generate the freeing effects of wealth.

But for some reason this dashing perspective, this resolutely cheerful opti- 3 mism about mechanical progress, did not make a dent in my fear of e-mail. From the perspective of one who has now crossed the great divide, I can see that my phobia stemmed in part from a category error. That is, I thought that "e-mail" and "the Internet" were identical: I believed that in order to communicate with my friends and colleagues, I would have to place myself squarely in front of all the oncoming lanes of traffic in the Information Superhighway. Worse: I was persuaded that those snippets of generic e-mail clipped from the bulletin boards of the Internet represented what my own friends would sound like if I had to talk to them by computer. I wrongly supposed that the machine controlled its own content, that the medium (as we used to say, *pace* McLuhan, in the '60s) would be the message.

Why I should have believed Marshall McLuhan in this respect when I 4 had long since discarded his views on television is a question that perhaps requires a cultural psychotherapist to answer. (I don't know that there *is* such a thing as a cultural psychotherapist, but since I have recently learned of something called "ecopsychology" — which is designed to help us bond with Mother Earth — I assume there are no limits.) For some reason, fear makes us believe in false prophets, the more apocalyptic the better. Clinging to the printed pages of my old-fashioned literary quarterly and my beloved cloth- and paperbound books, I thought that e-mail spelt the end of reading as I knew it. After all, you couldn't do it in the bathtub.

Well, there are lots of things you can't do in the bathtub and even I have 5 to admit that doesn't make them useless or unacceptable. I wouldn't want to read a novel or even a ten-page story on e-mail, and faced with that little message screen, I probably couldn't compose an essay worth printing. But for daily correspondence, electronic mail has become my essential instrument. And like all tools, it is more than just a simple replacement of the previous technology — it acts on you as well as you on it, and it acts in ways you can't always predict. In effect, e-mail has restored the personal letter to my life.

If you are like me, you went through a phase when personal letters occu-   6
pied a central place in your existence. You were probably in your late teens or early twenties. Possibly you were living away from home for the first time, or perhaps you had just embarked on your first long-term (and long-distance) love affair, or maybe you were traveling alone through Europe, or all of the above. The mail became your lifeline, and you honored it accordingly. You poured everything into your letters — the engaging details of daily existence, the special sights, the serious emotions, the witty observations — to such an extent that even journal-keeping, by comparison, seemed onerous and redundant. You tailored each letter to the personality of the recipient, delightedly imagining the eventual response to the in-jokes of a shared history. You received as good as you gave, and each day's mail delivery marked an emotional high or low point. And then, at some point, you grew out of all this, and household bills, business letters, magazines, and fund-raising pleas came to fill your mailbox instead.

Just as personal letters define a phase in an individual's life, so do they   7
also define a period in Western history. I didn't realize this until I read P. N. Furbank's review of the *Oxford Book of Letters*, wherein he remarks

> ...how deprived the ancient world was, not having discovered the secret of personal letters — long, spontaneous, chatty letters, as funny as they can be made but not always just funny, and coming nice and often — the sort of letters you might have got if you had known Henry James or Bernard Shaw or Philip Larkin. You would have been expected to answer them, and that would have been marvelous too, at least for oneself. It would be like enjoying a second life.

Exactly. And, as Furbank goes on to say, "The ancients knew nothing of this. With what leaden spirits one would have received a letter from Cicero! One may hazard that this best kind of letter-writing began in the eighteenth century and really came into its own in the nineteenth." Not coincidentally, this was just when the postal system was reaching a pinnacle of service, in terms of frequency and reliability.

For one of the keys to the pleasure of letters lies in that half-buried little   8
phrase, "and coming nice and often." In London, where P. N. Furbank lives, mail is still delivered twice a day, and a letter posted first-class will reach its destination anywhere in the United Kingdom by the next day. It is still possible to keep up a satisfying personal correspondence under such circumstances. For the rest of the world, however, mail is generally too

slow to gratify the needs of the moment. You might choose to rely on the stamp and envelope on special occasions, or for particularly delicate communications, or if (like a young person in her teens or twenties) you live on a very limited budget; but when you have something important to say, you're much more likely to pick up the telephone.

The crisis in my attitude toward e-mail occurred when I realized that I   9
would no longer be able to afford the telephone. I was about to leave America for four months, and to indulge in long-distance calling from Europe would be ruinously expensive. Nor could I tolerate waiting the two weeks it would take for the round-trip communication by post. It was e-mail or nothing.

One problem with e-mail, though, is that it takes two actively willing   10
participants. Anyone in the modern world can receive a postal letter, but only those with an e-mail hookup can receive e-mail. So I had to get my near and dear to join up at the same time I did. Among those I had to persuade was a writer in New York, a friend of twenty years' standing on whom I normally lavish at least one long-distance phone call a day. As he is even more of a Luddite than I am, this was no easy task.

"I feel very resistant to the idea," he explained.   11

"I know, I know," I said. "I've already been resistant for three years, so   12
can't we take it as done?"

Finally, I just cheated. I ordered *his* CompuServe introductory package   13
when I ordered my own, knowing that when the user-friendly software slipped through his mail slot, he would be unable to resist trying it on. (Or, to put it more truthfully: I planned to make life miserable for him via telephone until he got around to applying his e-mail diskettes.)

It was slow to catch on. At first my friend and I used e-mail mainly as a   14
toy, in between the more substantial communication of our transcontinental phone calls, and most of our electronic conversation was metaconversation, in that it dealt with the ins and outs of using e-mail. But when I left California on a Wednesday night, arrived in London on a Thursday morning, hooked up my computer, received my New York friend's welcoming message, and instantly e-mailed back — well, that was a revelation for both of us. Soon we were up to three or even four exchanges a day. The five-hour time difference meant nothing: he could post a note before he went to sleep, and I would receive it when I woke up the next day. And what I discovered, to my enormous pleasure, was that the electronic mode did not wash out his characteristic tones. On the contrary, he sounded in his virtual incarnation exactly as he did in real life: wry, observant, dryly affectionate, subtle, and sharp. Personal style, it turned out, did not get blotted out by the machine. In some ways it was even enhanced, with new opportunities for humorous self-expression and literary allusion afforded by the title spaces in our messages. "Internettled," his title bar announced when he had been fiddling all day to make the machine do something new. "Later the Same Day," I called one of my frequent messages, echoing Grace

Paley.[1] And it was inevitable, given the technology, that we would soon feel inspired to use E. M. Forster's "Only connect."[2]

Even in our differing responses to the availability of e-mail, my friend 15 and I were faithful to our respective personalities. Something of a self-styled loner, he built up a tiny, highly selective list of e-mail addresses and mailed only to those two or three people. (His willful resistance to technological self-education may have had something to do with this. "How do you communicate with those outside our parish?" he once complained, stumped by the difficulty of crossing over from CompuServe to America Online or Prodigy.)

I, on the other hand, verged on epistolary promiscuity. Within my first 16 week on-line, I had mailed to a number of my Berkeley pals, a long-lost classmate in Tasmania, three Londoners, my husband at his work address, my stepson at college, my father, my sister, a good friend who had temporarily moved to St. Louis, and my exercise teacher. I became an e-mail maniac, checking in every hour or so and collapsing with disappointment if I got the empty-mailbox beep. I found myself waxing expansive on-screen, chatting on about virtually nothing. I was responding, I now think, to the special enticements of the form's mixed nature — at once private and public, solitary and communal, so that it seems to combine the two oldest types of American writing, the diary and the sermon. With e-mail, you begin with the former, alone at your desk, and end (if you use your "multiple send" button) with the latter, broadcasting to the whole congregation.

One of the first responses I got from old e-mail hands, when I contacted 17 them with my newly acquired address, was scorn at the impersonal nature of my mailing moniker. Everybody else, it appeared, had managed to craft idiosyncratic, sometimes poetic, always memorable labels for themselves. Using the loose conventions set up by most e-mail providers, they had come up with word combinations that were nearly as distinctive as their own names (and that often incorporated those names into the address). But CompuServe allowed for no such creativity: we were simply allocated a number. "Your address sounds like something from the Planet Zog," one of my correspondents wrote. Another mocked me for my long resistance to e-mail. "This is just the kind of address I would expect a confirmed Luddite to get," he noted. "Those who resist the machine are doomed to be punished by it."

Whatever form it takes, your e-mail address becomes a part of your per- 18 manent identity in a way that no mere phone number can. For one thing, you can't hide it. You can make an obscene phone call from an anonymous number or mail a poison pen letter without giving a return address, but your e-mail message carries its provenance in its heading. This necessary mutuality is both e-mail's virtue and its curse. That is, you have to consider before engaging in any communication whether you want to hear *from* someone as well as speak *to* him, because he will thereafter possess

[1] ***Grace Paley*** An American fiction writer. [All notes are the editor's.]
[2] **"Only connect"** The epigraph to Forster's novel *Howards End*.

your address. There are no one-way assaults in the world of e-mail: if you launch a missive, you automatically open yourself up to a counterattack.

And unlike a phone number, which can be as temporary as your present   19 whereabouts, your e-mail address travels with you. I had exactly the same CompuServe number during my European stay as during my normal Berkeley life. People seeking to contact me didn't have to know I was out of the country or even out of the office. Sometimes I would amuse myself by trying to imagine where my virtual mailbox was located. Did it float somewhere in the fourth dimension, rushing into my computer only when it was actually consulted? Or did it hover somewhere over the Atlantic, relaying messages between my temporarily European self and my North American correspondents? I had been told it was in cyberspace — but what kind of space *was* that, exactly? Thinking such thoughts is a bit like trying to imagine how one's voice gets through those little telephone wires into the other person's receiver, only more so. You regress to your childhood self, for whom all such concepts are made concrete and miniature: the little person inside the telephone receiver, the tiny mailbox inside the computer. And the fact that my computer was itself a laptop (a ridiculously compact mechanism which, the dealer told me, was more powerful than the huge computer that had flown the first man to the moon) made the miniaturization imagery even more credible.

I discovered just how portable my e-mail was when a thief crept into my   20 house and walked off with my computer. One day I had been happily communicating with the entire world, the next I was reduced to virtual silence. My anxiety at the loss of my equipment was exacerbated by my sense of all the messages I was missing. I had become dependent on my daily fix, and the burglar, as if guessing at this aspect of my psychology, had even cut the phone wire that led into the computer — a symbolic act, easily remedied by the purchase of a new wire, but one that drove home for me my feeling of violent interruption. "I feel as if I'm hemorrhaging information," I told my husband. But information was only the half of it. All the little pieces of *me* that I had been feeding into cyberspace were loosed into the world, never to return.

Yet when I got a new computer, hooked myself back up to CompuServe,   21 and checked my old mailbox, there it still was, just as if no interruption had ever occurred. My e-mail had been patiently waiting for me out there in Nowhere Land, the messages accumulating until I was once again able to pick them up. The beauty of the system, it turns out, is precisely that it's *not* connected to any physical object. They can steal the transmitting device from you, but the mail service continues unabated in its ideal Platonic form — temporarily inaccessible, maybe, but always ready to be picked up. I had my answer to Bishop Berkeley's question:[3] if the tree had

---

[3]**Bishop Berkeley's question** "If a tree falls where no creature hears it, does it make a sound?" The English philosopher's attempt to answer this question led him to a philosophical proof of God's existence.

fallen in cyberspace, the sound could simply have waited decades or generations or millennia until someone came along to hear it, and *then* it would have existed. In this respect, as in so much else, e-mail's qualities are strangely mixed. It is both speedy to the point of instantaneousness, and arrested in a state of timelessness.

So have I lost my soul to e-mail? I think not. Of course, proper use of it   22 requires some mastery, and particularly self-mastery. One's initial subservience to the medium's surprising delights is inevitably a bit enslaving. (But this must have been true of all new media, even the cave paint at Lascaux.) Still, once it has been brought under control and made to function in the life you have already constructed for yourself, e-mail can be a great gift. If you keep all those strangers and business connections and mass-directory people off your screen, it can be, as Furbank put it, "like enjoying a second life." You will be rewarded with all the old-fashioned pleasures of the intimate personal letter. You will be offered, in other words, the chance to *gain* a soul rather than lose one. As an agnostic, I'm not even sure I believe in the very idea of a soul; but if I had to say where it resides, I would point to the thing in us that allows us to be and have intimate friends. And e-mail, by bringing back personal correspondence, reintroduces us to the form of writing that best enables us to know and acknowledge friendship.

Analyzing This Selection

1. What role did letters once have for the author? What, if anything, plays this role in your life?
2. **THE WRITER'S METHOD** In paragraph 22, does Lesser mock or believe in the significance of her conversion? What details throughout the essay indicate her attitude toward e-mail's effects?

Analyzing Connections

3. Lesser and Meghan Daum (see "On the Fringes of the Physical World," p. 143) both examine the effects of e-mail on intimate friendships. Are the contrasting effects explainable as personal, mainly situational, or social?

Analyzing by Writing

4. Compare the telephone, letters, and e-mail for personal communication. Teenagers, many of whom appear to talk on the phone endlessly and tirelessly, may be dealing with important interactive situations. Letters, as Lesser points out, are "like enjoying a second life." What are the positive and negative effects of e-mail on personal life?

Francine Prose

A WASTELAND OF ONE'S OWN

FRANCINE PROSE (b. 1947) is an essayist and fiction writer. She graduated and obtained a master's degree from Harvard University. Prose has contributed fiction and articles to magazines such as the *Atlantic, Redbook, Commentary, Glamour, Harper's Bazaar,* and the *New York Times Magazine,* where the following essay appeared (2000). Her volume *A Peaceable Kingdom* (1993) includes stories about modern family life. Prose's recent novel is *Blue Angel* (2000).

The TV ads for iVillage.com, one of the rising stars in the ever-expanding galaxy of women's Web sites, suggests that, for the modern woman, logging on to the Internet provides all the comfort Mom found in the long hot bath combined with the fun and fellowship of an evening out with the girls. The animation of the actresses playing ordinary women intensely engaged with their computers implies that the after-hours "cybervisit" is the perfect antidote to an exhausting day of work or child care, or both. It promises relaxation and distraction, solitude and community, the I and the Village, all during a few precious moments stolen — just for us! — from our families and jobs.

How dispiriting, then, to discover that what we've stolen is the chance to read an online women's magazine, far below whatever standard still prevails in the most dumbed-down print magazines, and with far less attractive graphics than *Martha Stewart Living.* The articles are short, vapid, carelessly written; the tone is Valley Girl friendly, relentlessly chipper and upbeat. Did you know that chocolate may be good for your heart? "Take some time to make yourself look good!" suggests an advice column on Making the Transition From Housewife to Employee. "Not interested in football?" asks a winter-weekend feature. "Cook up a 'Souper' Bowl and other tasty snacks for your favorite football fans!" The challenge is to absorb all this useful information while ignoring the flashing full-color advertisements tempting us to go shopping, the real cure for women's problems. Buy yourself a sexy new dress and shoes to match!

iVillage is only a symptom of the virulent cultural separatism currently generating a profusion of products and services created specifically for women. This new "women's culture" embraces not only Web sites and online magazines but also books, films, television series and entertainment networks that circumscribe, and then pander to, so-called women's interests — an admittedly narrow range that runs the entire gamut from cosmetics to child care, from personal grooming to personal relationships.

Underneath this otherwise inexplicable new eagerness to give women 4 what they want are surveys proving that an exponentially growing number of traditional and e-commerce consumers are female. (Even more excitingly, reports the marketing consultant Ellen Reid Smith, "women move from browsing to shopping much faster than men shop.") A Jupiter Communications study predicts that by 2003, women will be spending a cool $53 billion per year on Internet purchases. Were it not for the promise of money to be made, women's culture would be arousing about as much attention as, say, Uzbek culture. This may explain why marketers tend to adopt an anthropological tone, implying that women are an alien species, mystifying yet tractable if approached correctly. What's truly mystifying, however, is that it's so often women — and not clueless male executives — staging these expensive inquests into the natures and buying patterns of their newly affluent sisters. Much of the theorizing and sloganeering is being done by women like Candice Carpenter, a co-founder of iVillage.com; Geraldine Laybourne, chairman of Oxygen Media; and a newly visible group of female C.E.O.'s and marketing consultants.

What everyone appears to agree on is that women's off- and online 5 needs are determined by the "fact" that females value human relationships more than do their male counterparts. Faith Popcorn, the trend spotter and corporate consultant whose book on marketing to women, "EVEolution," will appear this June, counsels: "Marketing to women requires not just learning, but unlearning. Marketers will need to create a rich series of connections and bonds rather than episodic consumer collisions." This re-education will, it seems, come naturally to women, thanks to what MLM Talk Online calls "their advanced social and people skills. The current rage of 'Relationship Marketing' just puts a new label on the tools that women have always used to build their business."

If the notion of female entrepreneurs forging mutually gratifying bonds 6 with suppliers and clients is new, the basic idea has been floating through the culture for some time. For isn't this what certain psychologists — Carol Gilligan, et al. — have been claiming for years: that women are by nature more feeling, more nurturing, more relationship-oriented? Gilligan's landmark book, *In a Different Voice*, argues that women make moral decisions based on issues of human relationship; her influential studies of adolescent girls suggest that females see themselves as existing in relationship with others. The prodigiously popular work of the linguist Deborah Tannen (*You Just Don't Understand*) has helped persuade us that men and women speak differently, hear differently, respond differently — that the area of the brain governing communication comes in His and Hers models. "Difference feminism" helped make the concept of the emotive, relationship-oriented woman seem like a biological fact; "relationship marketing" and "women's culture" are its intellectual progeny.

In theory, "women's culture" sounds like a good idea; women doing and   7 buying what they want, no longer having to get dressed up and go out and pretend to be enthralled by some guy's pontifications. Surely that's the sentiment behind the current ads for Women.com. In the TV spot, a computer cursor types "Women can't resist powerful men," then deletes "powerful" and in its place types "gingerbread." The apparently subversive subtext running beneath this — and beneath so much of the new women's culture — suggests that women, tired of being denied power in a man's world, have decided to take their toys and play elsewhere.

On the surface, it's a feminist's dream: women earning more and using   8 the clout that only hard cash can command. Women designing products and services to meet the needs of women. Why shouldn't we be gladdened by this evidence of what some feminists have long suspected: that our voices would be heard when we had enough money to guarantee that someone would listen?

Why? Because the culture being sold to women not only reinforces retro   9 clichés and stereotypical notions of male and female behavior but also is the cultural equivalent of the slightly out-of-date baby formula that, through some regrettable corporate error, gets shipped to third-world countries. Because only the most starry-eyed difference feminist could seriously have imagined that "women's culture" would be any more noble, intelligent, high-minded or less blatantly meretricious than the "male culture" peddled by *Maxim* magazine and Comedy Central's *Man Show*. And because so much of what is flashing across our television, movie and computer screens suggests that what women are being offered is not just separate but sequestered, not challenging or provocative but intellect-numbing and reactionary — an expensive, seductive, glossy mass invitation to disappear into Cyberpurdah.

Perhaps the most insidious paradox of the new women's culture — from   10 the Oxygen network to *Bridget Jones's Diary* to *Judging Amy* — is that its purveyors can make lots of money from women and simultaneously claim to be doing it all for women's own good, to give women what they want and need and deserve. It is like having a best friend with her hand in your pocket.

Why else — except to help women like you and me — would Oprah   11 Winfrey take precious time from her busy life to star in a new 12-part series, *Oprah Goes Online*? This program is among the initial offerings of the new Oxygen network, which made its debut earlier this month. Masterminded by Geraldine Laybourne, the former president of Disney/ABC Cable Networks (in cooperation with powerful partners including Oprah Winfrey's Harpo Entertainment Group, America Online and the television producers Marcy Carsey, Tom Werner and Caryn Mandabach), Oxygen

Media combines a cable TV and Internet network into an entertainment and marketing conglomerate intended predominantly for women.

Billing itself as "the first and only network to combine advocacy, tech- 12 nology and creativity for a single purpose: releasing the energy of women to do great things," the Oxygen cable channel includes such features as the unfortunately titled sports program *We Sweat*; a comedy series, *Ripe Tomatoes*, "for anyone who agrees that women's lives sometimes border on the absurd and can be a laughing matter"; an animated cartoon called *X-Chromosome*; a talk show with Candice Bergen as its host; and, for those dateless Friday nights, *Pajama Party*: "New millennium 'It Girl' Katie Puckrick hosts a weekly pajama party with her best friend, Lisa Kushell. Sharp, funny and frank, this talk-variety show subverts the classic sleepover ingredients — taboo topics, mind-bending trends and far-out music — into grown-up friskiness with the help of an audience of 20- and 30-something women and visiting celebrities, all hanging out in their PJ's in Katie's living room." To brighten the grim, penitential weekend mornings that follow such PJ-clad carousings, we have *SheCommerce*, a program planned to comple-ment its eponymous Web site: "Whether one shops to live, lives to shop, clicks to shop or bricks to shop, our shopping guides will take viewers on a more informed, economical, time-efficient and entertaining virtual shop-ping trip that helps them be better consumers, smarter shoppers and satis-fied customers both on- and offline."

To ready themselves for this brave new world, Oprah and her best 13 friend, Gayle King, will learn, in front of our eyes, how to access the Inter-net. This protracted (12 sessions!) course will owe its inordinate length not, as one might suppose, to lots of Oprah tears and hugs (though there is a box of tissues placed conveniently near the monitor) but to scads of hard information: "From e-mail to chats to search engines to home pages, the two women will explore their options and experience firsthand how the Web will change the way women look at money, shopping, education, community, technology and themselves." Guided by an immensely hand-some and unthreatening young computer expert named Omar, Oprah and Gayle learn the basics ("A mouse pad is not a coaster!"), ask essential ques-tions ("Is there an 'on' button?") and step by difficult step, find their way around the Internet so that Oprah can pay her very first visit to her very own Web site.

Conceivably, it could be argued that the show is a public service for hap- 14 less, technologically challenged women who are intimidated to tears by the Web, who couldn't find the "on" button without Oprah's guidance and who feel more comfortable Net surfing if a friend and her friend are there to hold their hands. And if we women use this new knowledge to do a little shopping? Oxygen will understand. Oxygen wants women to do whatever makes them feel good about themselves.

The question of whether gender difference is innate or conditioned 15
has been thoroughly raked over and will be of continuing interest only to
someone who has never met a male or female year-old baby. Of course
there are gender differences, but probably not as many as there would be if
this were a society in which men and women could casually decide which
gender wants to be president this term, and which one wants to take care
of the kids and Great-Grandma. Humans are adaptive creatures, and the
people who are responsible for the family tend to get interested in family
relationships.

For some reason, it's less often pointed out that men also exist in relation- 16
ship to other human beings, and that much of what we think of as Culture —
the work of Sophocles, Shakespeare, Tolstoy — is about relationships. Despite
the spattered blood and brains punctuating its weekly episodes, HBO's
"Sopranos" is basically about domestic, community and personal relationships, and is watched with pleasure by both men and women. Despite how
much action transpires in the kitchen and around the dinner table, no one
would dream of calling *The Sopranos* a "women's" series.

NBC's *Providence* is, however, a women's series. And how does *The Sopra-* 17
nos differ from *Providence? The Sopranos* is well written, original, funny,
smart, peopled with lively, gritty characters so multilayered, recognizably
and mysteriously human that their audience gossips about them as they
would about mutual friends. The snappy dialogue, the details ("the Ba-Da-
Bing Club") all feel painfully and exhilaratingly real. The nutty, heartbreaking lives of Tony Soprano and his family and friends are interesting to
adults, partly because of the show's commitment, like that of art, to getting
everything (from the jokes to the home décor) right. And *Providence?*

If *The Sopranos* seems like more reality than we're used to seeing on TV, 18
Providence is pure fantasy — and not mine, I should say. Melina Kanakare-
des plays a female doctor and a babe, a caring family physician, evidently
with a subspecialty in sustained, tearful eye contact. Dr. Syd Hansen's
dance card is awfully full, but luckily she has a supportive family, a veterinarian dad (the most caring of professions!), a good-hearted sister, who
oddly seems to belong to a different social class than her siblings, and an
affable brother hopelessly in love with Dad's endearingly daffy receptionist.
Even the lovable Dead Mother hangs about to give her daughters otherworldly support and approval. Some of us might have concerns about a
physician who sees Mom's ghost, but then none of this is supposed to be
real. Dr. Hansen is not the *Sopranos* therapist, Dr. Melfi.

There's not one funny line in the script, though everything is broad and 19
cartoonish, nor is there one surprising moment, anything you can't see
coming miles ahead, except the sort of plot twist in which the single
mother falsely accused of suffering from Munchausen syndrome by proxy
(there is a long lecture on this, disguised as dialogue) and poisoning her
daughter in order to get attention, turns out to have been (this transpires in

the last few minutes, so pay attention) raped on her honeymoon in Europe. Which means that the little girl is not really all Irish but half-Italian, which explains why she has a rare Mediterranean blood disorder and is *not* being slowly murdered by Psycho Mom. Of course, our heroine figures this out, standing up (gracefully, and with consummate tact) to the older, authoritarian male doctor whose false diagnosis resulted partly from his not listening to the mother and daughter.

The trouble with this idea of women's culture is that, in this case, 20 "women's" is a euphemism for Bad, or at least Low-to-Middlebrow. Though it concerns relationships, *Anna Karenina* is not a women's novel. Anna Quindlen's novels are. To attach the word "women's" to a cultural product is to devalue it; in the view of the larger culture, "women's" is only a step above "young adult." Though no one will admit it, the prevailing wisdom is that women are stupid and narcissistic and desire childish, mindless entertainment.

To claim that the popularity of these Web sites, TV shows and films 21 proves that they're what women truly want is rather like saying that supermarket shoppers want those hard, pink, tasteless tomatoes; it's less a question of preference than of choice (or lack of choice) and availability. At the same time, the fact that droves of women are hungrily consuming this substandard culture raises the heartbreaking possibility that contemporary women's lives are so painful that what they desire is a good cry and some brainless, narcotizing amusement — a fantasy in which the stresses and irreconcilable conflicts of family and work are magically resolved by the closing credits or the final commercial, a chance to assuage their grief and worries with the bright optimistic promise of buying a brand-new lipstick.

And the SmartGirl-turned-Oxygen-woman will be able to do all the 22 shopping she wants, thanks to female-friendly Web sites that dispense financial advice and help women reconcile consumer fantasy with bank-account reality. Thus iVillage counsels us on Making Money Work in Your Relationship ("Perhaps you make financial decisions easily, quickly and sometimes impulsively, and he has analysis paralysis and can't bring himself to make a decision until forced to do so.") and on Dating and Dollars. ("If you go out six times and decide it's over, you won't feel bad because the guy's spent his life's savings buying you dinner.")

And yet despite this barrage of queries, the chatty interrogation designed 23 to make us feel that iVillage and Oxygen.com are interested in us — Are fitness videos part of your regime? Are you and your mate a match made in heaven? What do men think of women as breadwinners? — no one is asking, or prompting women to ask, the unresolved questions that the more levelheaded feminists have been posing for decades, queries that might actually affect women's lives. How can you get him to help change the baby's diapers? Why aren't you making as much as the guys in the office — the guys who do exactly what you do? What do you do if you're pregnant and poor and have to drive 500 miles to the nearest abortion clinic? Why does everyone assume you're incapable of thinking about anything more profound than nail polish and preschool jitters? Why are our lives so dreary and stressful that watching *Providence* offers a welcome minivacation?

There's plenty of advice on how to change ourselves — woman by 24 woman, pound by pound, wrinkle by wrinkle — but not a shred of guidance on how to change our situation. Nor is there any suggestion that we might want, or need, to rethink basic issues of power, equity and economics, or that our interest and passions should expand to acknowledge the world beyond the narrow confines of the kitchen, the nursery, the beauty salon and the office.

Quite the contrary, really. *A Dating Story*, *A Wedding Story* and *A Baby* 25 *Story* convince us that anatomy is indeed destiny. *Providence* and *Judging Amy* promulgate a new brand of fantasy: professional women who really do have it all — rewarding careers, supportive families and really fabulous hair. The new Web sites advertise themselves as solace and escape, consolation at the end of our impossibly stressful days of full-time work and full-time child care: the pause that refreshes, that revivifying — and pacifying — break that enables us to get up the next morning and endure another impossible day. Geraldine Laybourne's credo for Oxygen — that women "are pushed and pressured in such amazing ways that they deserve to have a place where they can take a deep breath" — falls far short of suggesting that we examine the source of that pressure, or that we begin to push back, or that we face the problems that no amount of shopping can solve.

And finally, there's the ultimate deception: the marketing-research-driven 26 con, the appalling bait-and-switch practiced on the woman who is being promised relationship, being sold on community, and who is in fact buying into a progressively deeper isolation and seclusion. For what is this new culture offering us, exactly, except the chance to work (at least) two jobs, eight hours in the workplace, another eight in the home, followed by the marvelous reward, the invitation to watch "reality" on television or to read a barely literate online magazine, alone in Cyberpurdah, satisfied and at peace, with nothing to disturb our blessed, hard-won tranquillity except the brief, spiky thrill of a purchase and the gentle click of the mouse?

Analyzing This Selection

1. What assumption about gender underlies women's marketing theory and practices? In what ways does the author dispute that assumption?

2. Have you enjoyed the kind of programs that Prose considers bad? Explain what you liked at the time. How, if at all, has the essay changed your view?

3. What concerns would the author like to see develop in women's media?

Analyzing Connections

4. **THE WRITER'S METHOD**   Prose and Easterbrook (see "Watch and Learn," p. 467) each condemn matters that are widely accepted or even highly popular. What stance do they take toward readers? For you, which writer's tone and methods are more effective?

Analyzing by Writing

5. Analyze one episode of a weekly drama or comedy series to determine its targeted audience. Identify details and issues intended to evoke familiar recognition. What signs of the larger world have been reduced or eliminated? What is good and what is bad in the episode? Explain how the program illuminates or trivializes the social significance of its intended audience.

Robert Goodman

THE LUCK BUSINESS[1]

ROBERT GOODMAN (b. 1936) is an urban planner and economic development consultant. He currently teaches at Hampshire College and is the executive director of the United States Gambling Research Institute in Northampton, Massachusetts. His books include *After the Planners* (1971) and *The Last Entrepreneurs* (1979). This selection is excerpted from *The Luck Business* (1995).

This could be your ticket out.

—AN ILLINOIS STATE LOTTERY BILLBOARD
IN A LOW-INCOME CHICAGO NEIGHBORHOOD[2]

The proliferation of legalized gambling in America is probably the only example of a situation where government is not simply legalizing a potentially harmful activity, but is actually promoting it.... Governments did not decide to allow new gambling ventures in response to rising popular demands for more gambling. This is not, for example, like the repeal of Prohibition, where government found itself responding to a popular political movement to legalize the business of producing and selling liquor.

In the case of gambling, it is the government which is explicitly trying to get people to participate more, through advertisements, media promotions, and public relations campaigns. It is the government which is expanding the availability of more addictive forms of gambling like electronic gambling machines. The result is a dangerous shift in the fundamental role of government — from regulator of gambling to promoter of gambling. Governments are gutting regulations designed to protect the public, spending millions on promotions and advertisements, and in some cases even subsidizing private gambling enterprises. In the process, they are also recruiting millions of people into gambling who have never gambled before.

This stands in stark contrast to the role of government, especially since the 1930s, as a protector of citizens through a host of laws and regulations

---

[1]Editor's title.

[2]Taylor Branch, "What's Wrong with the Lottery," *New England Monthly* January 1990: 41. [All notes are Goodman's.]

designed to protect workplace conditions, health and safety, environment, civil rights, and so forth. In sponsoring more gambling, governments do not even require accurate social and economic impact statements about their expansion plans, the way they do in the case of potential environmental impacts of an expanding industry or the construction of a new highway.

In this new promotional role, government finds itself in a strange and   4 contradictory position which makes it difficult to carry out its role of protecting the public. While it once regulated gambling in order to guard against gambling operators who might take advantage of its citizens, the government's own growing dependence on gambling revenues puts pressure on state officials to increase advertising and relax regulations. A 1988 New Jersey Governor's Advisory Commission observing what happened in Atlantic City put it simply: "The more entrenched is gambling in the budget process, then the more successful the industry may be in causing the relaxation of regulatory policies and procedures with which they do not agree."[3]

As far back as the 1950s, politicians argued that by legalizing gambling,   5 governments would capture money that was already being bet illegally, eliminate the role of organized crime, and ensure that players weren't being cheated.[4] Yet criminals never promoted their gambling operations the way governments now do with multi-million dollar advertising campaigns, public relations efforts, focus group research, and penetration studies. "No matter what you do for a living," says a Massachusetts Lottery advertisement, "there's an easier way to make money."[5] And in contrast to the ventures of organized crime, government-supported gambling is given extensive free publicity through newspaper and TV stories about incredible jackpots, happy winners, and transformed lives.

From a psychological perspective, people's ability to dream and to hope   6 for a better life can be a very healthy and useful human attribute. It helps them persevere under difficult circumstances, and it can motivate people to change and improve their lives. But by enticing people to spend their money on fantasies, governments are preying on people's ability to dream and hope. Rather than providing real hope for economic improvement, public officials are promoting the illusion of economic improvement — becoming deeply involved in finding new ways of manipulating people's desire for a more secure future. They are enticing people into taking part in what should properly be called the "pathology of hope." When a gov-

[3]*Report and Recommendations of the Governor's Advisory Commission on Gambling*, Trenton, N.J. June 30, 1988: 12.

[4]See, for example, "Communication by Mayor William O'Dwyer to the New York State Legislature, January 10, 1950," in "Gambling," *Annals of the American Academy of Political and Social Science* 266 (1950): 35, 36.

[5]Paul Della Valle and Scott Farmelant, "A Bad Bet: Who Really Pays for the Massachusetts Lottery's Success?" *Worcester Magazine* January 27, 1993: 16.

ernment agency, like the New York State Lottery, says its players' "whimsical fantasies" are being given "the hope of fulfillment" or that its gambling products offer people a chance to dream of paying off their debts or to dream about paying for their children's education, then governments have gotten themselves into playing a new and very dangerous role.[6]

By 1994, state lotteries were spending over $350 million a year to advertise their products.[7] In 1991, the California Lottery had become the largest purchaser of advertising in Los Angeles County.[8] Gregory Ziemak, Director of the Kansas Lottery and the former director of the Connecticut State Lottery, reflected on government's schizophrenia of trying to both regulate and promote gambling. In his Connecticut job, Ziemak says, he was criticized by some legislators and community leaders for his advertisements. "They said just the fact that you're advertising the lottery is wrong." But the bottom line of keeping his job ultimately depended on pleasing politicians who were judging him by the revenues he generated. "My success or failure," he said "was how sales were. Were sales better than last year, or were they worse?"[9]

One of the most effective publicity techniques to promote more lottery play, according to Ziemak, was getting the media to produce stories about the winners. "People see a picture of a Lotto winner in the paper," said Ziemak. "You know he's a guy like you; he works in the shop, he has kids, he's going to use the money to put the kids through college. You say, 'You know maybe I could win'." When some winners shun this publicity, lottery officials find ways of persuading them. According to Ziemak:

> What we tell the winners is, look you won $5 million, that's news. It's public information whether you agree to talk to the press, or allow us to release it to the press, we're still going to have to release your name, your town, and the amount won. And if we do that the press might call you because you're not saying anything. Sometimes they get more interested. What we suggest you do, is go downstairs and talk to them.[10]

Government promotion of its gambling products not only persuades people to gamble at legal operations, but, according to William Jahoda, a former gambling operator for organized crime in Chicago, also benefits illegal ventures. "[Public] agency marketing and media advertising blitzes promoting

[6]See New York State Lottery, *Annual Report 1988–89.*

[7]Information provided by Bill Hennessey, Media and Advertising Specialist, State of Connecticut, Department of Revenue Services, Division of Special Revenue. See Robert Goodman, "Legalized Gambling...," *Strategy for Economic Development* (Northampton, Mass.: United States Gambling Study, 1994).

[8]"Lottery Leads List of L.A. Radio Advertisers," *L.A. Business Journal* (June 4, 1990). Cited in I. Nelson Rose, "Gambling and the Law: Update 1993," *COMM/ENT,* Hastings Communications and Entertainment Law Journal, Hastings College of Law, University of California (fall 1992).

[9]Personal Interview with Gregory A. Ziemak (July 8, 1992).

[10]Ibid.

gambling," he told the Chicago Gaming Commission, give people the perception that gambling is "healthy entertainment." Jahoda characterized the public officials involved in promoting government gambling ventures as "our unwitting front men and silent partner."[11]

In finding new ways to stimulate more demand for their gambling products, government officials have become increasingly adept at manipulating player behavior through the use of sophisticated market research analysis, consumer surveys, penetration studies, and focus groups.[12] They continuously monitor player attitudes and behaviors in order to design new sales pitches which are closely attuned to people's psychological needs and fears. One Massachusetts Lottery television ad focused on a real fear of many hard-core players — that they won't play their number on the day that it finally comes up. In the staged commercial, a newsman attempts to interview a number of distraught players who would have won on the day they forgot to play. Lance Dodes, the operator of a Massachusetts treatment center for problem gamblers, described such government-promoted ads as ones which lead to more problem gambling. "[Players] are terrified not to play their number," he explained, "and the Lottery preys on those fears."[13]   9

Despite this obvious manipulation, in 1991 Jim Hosker, Kentucky's lottery director, said that lottery players tend to absolve government of responsibility for their losses. Since people know they are playing against enormous odds, he said, they tend to blame themselves and not the state when they lose. Their psychological reaction, according to Hosker, is "I didn't pick the right numbers."[14]   10

The goal of lottery advertising is not only to increase the amount of money that people gamble, but also to increase the number of people who gamble — what those who market gambling call "expanding the player base." To accomplish this, lottery managers are constantly trying to find new ways of getting people to shift their spending away from other consumer products and services and into gambling at lotteries. As the marketing director of a Canadian lottery said, "We believe any promotion that can alter the regular purchasing habits of the consumer is viewed as significantly benefiting our long-term success."[15]   11

According to Jim Davey, a former Oregon State Lottery director, "We're a market-driven organization and I mean we're going to go out and expand   12

[11]Better Government Association, *Staff White Paper: Casino Gambling in Chicago*, Chicago (October 1992).

[12]Erik Calonius, "The Big Payoff from Lotteries," *Fortune* March 25, 1991; Jeffrey L. Katz, "Waking Up the Lottery," *Governing* September 1991.

[13]Mitchell Zuckoff, "State-Run Games Flout Ad Standards," *Boston Globe* September 27, 1993: 9.

[14]Katz, "Waking Up the Lottery."

[15]According to J. Jourdain, Marketing Director of the Western Canada Lottery, in "Quote of the Month," *Gaming and Wagering Business* July 15–August 14, 1992: 4.

this business."[16] The way to increase sales, according to Davey and other lottery managers, is to constantly change games. "Offer something that looks new," said Davey, who later became president of Automated Wagering International, an electronic gambling machine manufacturer. "At Christmas we do Holiday Cash. With Lucky Stars we play on people's astrological signs. We find that if you run two or three, four or five games at the same time, you'll sell more tickets."[17]...

To gain public support, gambling revenues are often used for highly vis- 13
ible and popular social programs — what one gambling executive called "the three big E's — education, environment and economic development."[18] He could have added a fourth "E," for the elderly. The arts have sometimes also received similar treatment. But when a specific program or a city's budget gets tied to gambling proceeds, it is relying on an unstable source of funds, since it is dependent on how much people can be persuaded to gamble. This gambling-for-good-things approach also hampers the ability of those who receive the revenues to lobby state legislators and voters for any additional funds they might need for their programs.

Most often, revenues from gambling simply replace, rather than supple- 14
ment, the funds for programs whose budgets get tied to gambling revenues. By 1991, thirteen states, including rural ones, like Idaho and Montana, and urban ones, like New York and California, had earmarked all or part of their lottery proceeds for education.[19] According to Bill Honig, California's Public School Superintendent, "For every $5 the lottery gives to the schools, the state takes away $4."[20] Honig complained that lottery funds earmarked for education made it difficult to raise educational funds from other places. "The public is more reluctant to pass education bond issues because they think we're floating in lottery money."[21] In California, lottery funds for education depended on the fortunes of the state's lottery, which declined from about $1 billion in 1988 to $500 million in 1991.[22]...

While the actual chance of winning a big lottery jackpot is virtually 15
zero, people play on the fantastic chance that their lives will somehow be dramatically transformed. Lottery advertising campaigns capitalize on such remote hope. Impossible dreams have been substituted for ones that once seemed real.

[16]Interview with Jim Davey (September 17, 1992).

[17]James Cook, "Lottomania," *Forbes* March 6, 1989: 94.

[18]Bruce W. Wentforth, General Manager of Dubuque Greyhound Park, in Edward Walsh, "Despite Revenue Drop, States Continue to Bet on Gambling to Cure Economies," *Washington Post* October 3, 1991.

[19]Chris Pipho, "Watching the Legislatures," *Phi Delta Kappan* January 1990: 342.

[20]Peter Passell, "Lotto Is Financed by the Poor and Won by the States," *New York Times* May 21, 1989: E6.

[21]Erik Calonius, "The Big Pay-Off from Lotteries," *Fortune* March 25, 1991.

[22]Laurel Shaper Walters, "Taking a Chance on Education," *Christian Science Monitor* August 16, 1993: 9.

In May 1994, Peter Lynch, Director of the New York State Lottery, 16 appeared before an international gathering of lottery directors at the exhibition hall at the Louvre in Paris to illustrate the methods his state agency used to get people to gamble more money. Of primary importance, said Lynch, was conducting ongoing research to constantly monitor "what's going on in the minds of your customer." This included gathering information not only about their attitudes toward lottery games, but also about "their lives and their general outlook." This is done with the help of a yearly "Attitude and Usage Benchmark Study."

Such information allowed his agency to continually revise games in 17 order not only to entice its steady players to gamble more, but also to encourage those nonplayers who, Lynch said, demonstrated "apathy" to the state's games to begin to play. Although the lottery has sometimes been enormously successful in persuading state residents to increase their gambling, it has had difficulty maintaining a constant high level of play. Lynch complained of "lapsed players," those who became "disenchanted" and "jaded," and of people who suffered from "high-odds burnout."

According to Lynch, the government's "all you need is a dollar and a 18 dream campaign" was aimed at getting infrequent players to gamble more through what he called "anticipatory dreaming."

> We had to make Lotto a more socially acceptable thing to do....we needed to remind occasional customers of the fun of anticipation and that it's okay to enjoy the experience because lots of people just like them share these emotions. We needed, therefore, to have our occasional players empathize with both the dream and dreamer....the most critical move we made was to shift from advertising focused on winners to the anticipation of winning....the theory was while only one person wins, everyone who plays enjoys the anticipatory dreaming.[23]

Describing the psychological backdrop to the success of its games, the 19 Lottery agency's 1988–1989 Annual Report explained, "from the moment of a ticket's purchase to the conclusion of the drawing, the 'dream' that is impossible when seen in the cold, hard light of reality has the means of coming true — moments to be savored and enjoyed no matter what the ultimate outcome."[24] In planning their "dream" ads, the lottery relied on using real people instead of actors. According to Lynch, this involved the "casting of warm, lively, regular people." The goal, he said, was to create "a genuine empathy between the target audience and infrequent players with encouragement of infrequent players to play more frequently."[25]...

---

[23]Peter Lynch, "Matching Advertising to Products," Talk at the Twentieth Congress of l'Association Internationale des Loteries d'État (AILE), Paris (May 1994), reprinted in *Gaming and Wagering Business* August 5, 1994: 45.

[24]New York State Lottery, *Annual Report 1988–89*.

[25]Lynch.

While people have always dreamed of a lucky break in a card game or 20
perhaps picking a winning number, never before have they been so blatantly
urged by their political leaders to risk their money in order to transform the
declining situation of their lives. What began perhaps as a reasonable effort
to capture, for the public coffers, dollars already being bet illegally has
mushroomed into an enterprise that is radically transforming the role of
government. In their attempt to solve economic problems with gambling,
government leaders are further undermining their already precarious credibility with their constituents. They are encouraging a public perception
that governments can do little to support a healthier economic climate for
all citizens, and that the best they can do is to provide enormous windfalls
for gambling companies and the limited possibility of jobs for those fortunate enough to work for these companies. That we have also arrived at a
point in time where state government agencies are studying demographics
and psychological behavior of state residents in order to encourage them to
gamble more, not only raises serious moral questions, but calls for a more
fundamental reassessment of the nature of government's role in the business of gambling.

Analyzing This Selection

1. What draws state governments into the gambling business? What are Goodman's criticisms of the purposes?

2. According to the author, why is gambling not good for people? Why are
   lotteries not good for governments? Which effect do you think is more
   harmful?

3. **THE WRITER'S METHOD**   Find examples of Goodman's tactfulness.
   In opposing a popular activity, is his approach persuasive or weak?

Analyzing Connections

4. Fantasizing is an intended effect of all contemporary advertising, as Holly
   Brubach observes about catalogues (see "Mail-Order America," p. 415). What
   differences, if any, make lottery ads more harmful than other sales pitches?

Analyzing by Writing

5. Analyze one government-sponsored media campaign such as advertising
   against drunk or reckless driving, against smoking, against forest fires,
   against pollution, or favoring health measures such as testing for cancer,
   reducing cholesterol, or other public policies. Examine the tactics used to
   scare and lure people into changing their behavior. Assess the ads by comparing their effectiveness with other media campaigns, including commer-
   cials and government ads for lotteries.

Oscar Hijuelos

THE MAMBO KINGS
PLAY SONGS OF LOVE

OSCAR HIJUELOS (b. 1951) was born of Cuban parents in New York City. He graduated from City College, where he also earned a master's degree. He has won several fiction awards, including a National Endowment for the Arts fellowship and a Pulitzer Prize for his second novel, *The Mambo Kings Play Songs of Love* (1989), from which this story was excerpted. His most recent novel is *Empress of the Splendid Season* (1999).

It was a Saturday afternoon on La Salle Street, years and years ago when 1 I was a little kid, and around three o'clock Mrs. Shannon, the heavy Irish woman in her perpetually soup-stained dress, opened her back window and shouted out into the courtyard, "Hey, Cesar, yoo-hoo, I think you're on television, I swear it's you!" When I heard the opening strains of the *I Love Lucy* show I got excited because I knew she was referring to an item of eternity, that episode in which my dead father and my Uncle Cesar had appeared, playing Ricky Ricardo's singing cousins fresh off the farm in Oriente Province, Cuba, and north in New York for an engagement at Ricky's nightclub, the Tropicana.

This was close enough to the truth about their real lives — they were 2 musicians and songwriters who had left Havana for New York in 1949, the year they formed the Mambo Kings, an orchestra that packed clubs, dance halls, and theaters around the East Coast — and, excitement of excitements, they even made a fabled journey in a flamingo-pink bus out to Sweet's Ballroom in San Francisco, playing on an all-star mambo night, a beautiful night of glory, beyond death, beyond pain, beyond all stillness.

Desi Arnaz had caught their act one night in a supper club on the West 3 Side, and because they had perhaps already known each other from Havana or Oriente Province, where Arnaz, like the brothers, was born, it was natural that he ask them to sing on his show. He liked one of their songs in particular, a romantic bolero written by them, "Beautiful María of My Soul."

Some months later (I don't know how many, I wasn't five years old yet) 4 they began to rehearse for the immortal appearance of my father on this show. For me, my father's gentle rapping on Ricky Ricardo's door has always been a call from the beyond, as in Dracula films, or films of the walking dead, in which spirits ooze out from behind tombstones and through the cracked windows and rotted floors of gloomy antique halls: Lucille Ball, the lovely red-headed actress and comedienne who played Ricky's wife, was housecleaning when she heard the rapping of my father's knuckles against that door.

"I'm commmmmming," in her singsong voice. 5

Standing in her entrance, two men in white silk suits and butterfly-looking 6 lace bow ties, black instrument cases by their side and black-brimmed white hats in their hands — my father, Nestor Castillo, thin and broad-shouldered, and Uncle Cesar, thickset and immense.

My uncle: "Mrs. Ricardo? My name is Alfonso and this is my brother 7 Manny..."

And her face lights up and she says, "Oh, yes, the fellows from Cuba. 8 Ricky told me all about you."

Then, just like that, they're sitting on the couch when Ricky Ricardo 9 walks in and says something like, "Manny, Alfonso! Gee, it's really swell that you fellas could make it up here from Havana for the show."

That's when my father smiled. The first time I saw a rerun of this, I 10 could remember other things about him — his lifting me up, his smell of cologne, his patting my head, his handing me a dime, his touching my face, his whistling, his taking me and my little sister, Leticia, for a walk in the park, and so many other moments happening in my thoughts simultaneously that it was like watching something momentous, say the Resurrection, as if Christ had stepped out of his sepulcher, flooding the world with light — what we were taught in the local church with the big red doors — because my father was now newly alive and could take off his hat and sit down on the couch in Ricky's living room, resting his black instrument case on his lap. He could play the trumpet, move his head, blink his eyes, nod, walk across the room, and say "Thank you" when offered a cup of coffee. For me, the room was suddenly bursting with a silvery radiance. And now I knew that we could see it again. Mrs. Shannon had called out into the courtyard alerting my uncle: I was already in his apartment.

With my heart racing, I turned on the big black-and-white television set 11 in his living room and tried to wake him. My uncle had fallen asleep in the kitchen — having worked really late the night before, some job in a Bronx social club, singing and playing the horn with a pickup group of musicians. He was snoring, his shirt was open, a few buttons had popped out on his belly. Between the delicate-looking index and forefingers of his right hand, a Chesterfield cigarette burning down to the filter, that hand still holding a half glass of rye whiskey, which he used to drink like crazy because in recent years he had been suffering from bad dreams, saw apparitions, felt cursed, and, despite all the women he took to bed, found his life of bachelorhood solitary and wearisome. But I didn't know this at the time, I thought he was sleeping because he had worked so hard the night before, singing and playing the trumpet for seven or eight hours. I'm talking about a wedding party in a crowded, smoke-filled room (with bolted-shut fire doors), lasting from nine at night to four, five o'clock in the morning, the band playing one-, two-hour sets. I thought he just needed the rest. How could I have known that he would come home and, in the name of unwinding, throw back a glass of rye, then a second, and then a third, and so on, until he'd plant his elbow on the table and use it to steady his chin, as he couldn't hold his head up otherwise. But that day I ran into the kitchen to wake him up so that he could see the episode, too, shaking him gently and tugging at his elbow, which was a mistake, because it was as if I had pulled loose the support columns of a five-hundred-year-old church: He simply fell over and crashed to the floor.

A commercial was running on the television, and so, as I knew I 12 wouldn't have much time, I began to slap his face, pull on his burning red-hot ears, tugging on them until he finally opened one eye. In the act of focusing he apparently did not recognize me, because he asked, "Nestor, what are you doing here?"

"It's me, Uncle, it's Eugenio." 13

I said this in a really earnest tone of voice, just like the kid who hangs 14 out with Spencer Tracy in the movie of *The Old Man and the Sea*, really believing in my uncle and clinging on to his every word in life, his every touch like nourishment from a realm of great beauty, far beyond me, his heart. I tugged at him again, and he opened his eyes. This time he recognized me.

He said, "You?" 15

"Yes, Uncle, get up! Please get up! You're on television again. Come on." 16

One thing I have to say about my Uncle Cesar, there was very little he 17 wouldn't do for me in those days, and so he nodded, tried to push himself off the floor, got to his knees, had trouble balancing, and then fell backwards. His head must have hurt: His face was a wince of pain. Then he seemed to be sleeping again. From the living room came the voice of Ricky's wife, plotting as usual with her neighbor Ethel Mertz about how to get a part on Ricky's show at the Tropicana, and I knew that the brothers had already been to the apartment — that's when Mrs. Shannon had called out into the courtyard — that in about five more minutes my father and uncle would be standing on the stage of the Tropicana, ready to perform that song again. Ricky would take hold of the microphone and say, "Well, folks, now I have a real treat for you. Ladies and gentlemen, Alfonso and Manny Reyes, let's hear it!" And soon my father and uncle would be standing side by side, living, breathing beings, for all the world to see, harmonizing in a duet of that *canción*.

As I shook my uncle, he opened his eyes and gave me his hand, hard 18 and callused from his other job in those days, as superintendent, and he said, "Eugenio, help me. Help me."

I tugged with all my strength, but it was hopeless. Still he tried: With 19 great effort he made it to one knee, and then, with his hand braced on the floor, he started to push himself up again. As I gave him another tug, he began miraculously to rise. Then he pushed my hand away and said, "I'll be okay, kid."

With one hand on the table and the other on the steam pipe, he pulled himself to his feet. For a moment he towered over me, wobbling as if powerful winds were rushing through the apartment. Happily I led him down the hallway and into the living room, but he fell over again by the door — not fell over, but rushed forward as if the floor had abruptly tilted, as if he had been shot out of a cannon, and, wham, he hit the bookcase in the hall. He kept piles of records there, among them a number of the black and brittle 78s he had recorded with my father and their group, the Mambo Kings. These came crashing down, the bookcase's glass doors jerking open, the records shooting out and spinning like flying saucers in the movies and splintering into pieces. Then the bookcase followed, slamming into the floor beside him: The songs "Bésame Mucho," "Acérate Más," "Juventud," "Twilight in Havana," "Mambo Nine," "Mambo Number Eight," "Mambo for a Hot Night," and their fine version of "Beautiful María of My Soul" — all these were smashed up. This crash had a sobering effect on my uncle. Suddenly he got to one knee by himself, and then the other, stood, leaned against the wall, and shook his head. 20

"Bueno," he said. 21

He followed me into the living room and plopped down on the couch behind me. I sat on a big stuffed chair that we'd hauled up out of the basement. He squinted at the screen, watching himself and his younger brother, whom, despite their troubles, he loved very much. He seemed to be dreaming. 22

"Well, folks," Ricky Ricardo said, "and now I have a real treat for you..." 23

The two musicians in white silk suits and big butterfly-looking lace bow ties, marching toward the microphone, my uncle holding a guitar, my father a trumpet. 24

"Thank you, thank you. And now a little number that we composed..." And Cesar started to strum the guitar and my father lifted his trumpet to his lips, playing the opening of "Beautiful María of My Soul," a lovely, soaring melody line filling the room. 25

They were singing the song as it had been written — in Spanish. With the Ricky Ricardo Orchestra behind them, they came into a turnaround and began harmonizing a line that translates roughly into English as: "What delicious pain love has brought to me in the form of a woman." 26

My father...He looked so alive! 27

"Uncle!" 28

Uncle Cesar had lit a cigarette and fallen asleep. His cigarette had slid out of his fingers and now was burning into the starched cuff of his white shirt. I put the cigarette out, and then my uncle, opening his eyes again, smiled. "Eugenio, do me a favor. Get me a drink." 29

"But, Uncle, don't you want to watch the show?" 30

He tried really hard to pay attention, to focus on it. 31

"Look, it's you and Poppy."   32

"Coño, si…"   33

My father's face with his horsey grin, arching eyebrows, big fleshy ears —   34
a family trait — that slight look of pain, his quivering vocal cords, how
beautiful it all seemed to me then…

And so I rushed into the kitchen and came back with a glass of rye   35
whiskey, charging as fast as I could without spilling it. Ricky had joined the
brothers onstage. He was definitely pleased with their performance and
showed it, because as the last note sounded he whipped up his hand and
shouted "Olé!" a big lock of his thick black hair falling over his brows.
Then they bowed and the audience applauded.

The show continued on its course. A few gags followed: A costumed bull   36
with flowers wrapped around its horns came out dancing an Irish jig, its
horns poking into Ricky's bottom and so exasperating him that his eyes
bugged out, he slapped his forehead and started speaking a-thousand-
words-a-second Spanish. But at that point it made no difference to me, the
miracle had passed, the resurrection of a man, Our Lord's promise which I
then believed, with its release from pain, release from the troubles of this
world.

Analyzing This Selection

1. Based on your impression of the story as a whole, what sort of boy is Eugenio? Find details in the first four paragraphs that support your view of his
   personality. What did these details first lead you to expect from the character and the story?

2. **THE WRITER'S METHOD**   What is the significance of the falling bookcase? Explain the uncle's reaction. What tone of voice would you give his
   remark?

3. For the boy, what is the connection between television and his religion?
   What attitude does the story express about this connection? Find details that
   support your interpretation.

Analyzing Connections

4. Compare the influence of movies and television in Eugenio's life and in
   Erdrich's (see "Dear John Wayne" in the Insights on p. 459). What truths
   and illusions conflict in their responses to films?

Analyzing by Writing

5. Much of our sense of history comes from movie and television dramas. For
   instance, the Civil War, World War II, and the Holocaust are imprinted in
   public memory by films and miniseries. Consequently, our beliefs about
   their substance comes from the entertainment industry. By contrast, in
   school, our knowledge of history comes for the most part from reading and

lectures, not screening. What is contributed by each medium of presentation? Choose one historical topic (you are not limited to the examples given), and consider its presentation in both books and film. How have film versions enhanced or distorted the views of the past that you formed through reading? How did your reading knowledge affect your response to the screen version?

Andrea Dworkin

LETTER FROM A WAR ZONE

ANDREA DWORKIN (b. 1946) was raised in Camden, New Jersey, and attended Bennington College. Dworkin worked as a free-lance writer in New York and began her career of activism against pornography. Her first feminist book, *Woman Hating* (1974), won her a nationwide audience. In 1978 Dworkin participated in the first Take Back the Night March to protest urban districts that harbor prostitution and pornography. In *Intercourse* (1987), Dworkin attacks possessive and contemptuous attitudes in the way ordinary men write and speak about sexual intercourse. She has also published two novels, *Ice and Fire* (1987) and *Mercy* (1991). Dworkin's essays and speeches have been collected in *Letters from a War Zone* (1989). Her most recent book is *Scapegoat: The Jews, Israel and Women's Liberation* (2000).

It is late 1986 now, and we are losing. The war is men against women; the country is the United States. Here, a woman is beaten every eighteen seconds: by her husband or the man she lives with, not by a psychotic stranger in an alley. Understand: Women are also beaten by strangers in alleys but that is counted in a different category — gender-neutral assault, crime in the streets, big-city violence. Woman-beating, the intimate kind, is the most commonly committed violent crime in the country, according to the FBI, not feminists. A woman is raped every three minutes, nearly half the rapes committed by someone the woman knows. Forty-four percent of the adult women in the United States have been raped at least once. Forty-one percent (in some studies seventy-one percent) of all rapes are committed by two or more men; so the question is not how many rapes there are, but how many rapists. There are an estimated 16,000 new cases of father-daughter incest each year; and in the current generation of children, thirty-eight percent of girls are sexually molested. Here, now, less than eight percent of women have not had some form of unwanted sex (from assault to obscene harassment) forced on them. 1

We keep calling this war normal life. Everyone's ignorant; no one knows; the men don't mean it. In this war, the pimps who make pornography are the SS, an élite, sadistic, military, organized vanguard. They run an efficient and expanding system of exploitation and abuse in which women and children, as lower life forms, are brutalized. This year they will gross $10 billion. 2

We have been slow to understand. For fun they gag us and tie us up as ³ if we were dead meat and hang us from trees and ceilings and door frames and meat hooks; but many say the lynched women probably like it and we don't have any right to interfere with them (the women) having a good time. For fun they rape us or have other men, or sometimes animals, rape us and film the rapes and show the rapes in movie theaters or publish them in magazines, and the normal men who are not pimps (who don't know, don't mean it) pay money to watch; and we are told that the pimps and the normal men are free citizens in a free society exercising rights and that we are prudes because this is sex and real women don't mind a little force and the women get paid anyway so what's the big deal? The pimps and the normal men have a constitution that says the filmed rapes are "protected speech" or "free speech." Well, it doesn't actually *say* that — cameras, after all, hadn't been invented yet; but they interpret their constitution to protect their fun. They have laws and judges that call the women hanging from the trees "free speech." There are films in which women are urinated on, defecated on, cut, maimed, and scholars and politicians call them "free speech." The politicians, of course, deplore them. There are photographs in which women's breasts are slammed in rat traps — in which things (including knives, guns, glass) are stuffed in our vaginas — in which we are gang-banged, beaten, tortured — and journalists and intellectuals say: Well, there is a lot of violence against women *but*…But what, prick? But we run this country, cunt.

If you are going to hurt a woman in the United States, be sure to take a ⁴ photograph. This will confirm that the injury you did to her expressed a point-of-view, sacrosanct in a free society. Hey, you have a right not to like women in a democracy, man. In the very unlikely event that the victim can nail you for committing a crime of violence against her, your photograph is still constitutionally protected, since it communicates so eloquently. The woman, her brutalization, the pain, the humiliation, her smile — because you did force her to smile, didn't you?— can be sold forever to millions of normal men (them again) who — so the happy theory goes — are having a "cathartic" experience all over her. It's the same with snuff films, by the way. You can torture and disembowel a woman, ejaculate on her dismembered uterus, and even if they do put you away someday for murder (a rather simple-minded euphemism), the film is legally *speech. Speech.*

In the early days, feminism was primitive. If something hurt women, ⁵ feminists were against it, not for it. In 1970, radical feminists forcibly occupied the offices of the ostensibly radical Grove Press because Grove published pornography marketed as sexual liberation and exploited its female employees. Grove's publisher, an eminent boy-revolutionary, considered the hostile demonstration CIA-inspired. His pristine radicalism did not stop him from calling the very brutal New York City police and having the women physically dragged out and locked up for trespassing on his private property. Also in 1970, radical feminists seized *Rat,* an underground rag that devoted itself, in the name of revolution, to pornography and male chauvinism equally, the only attention gender got on the radical left. The pornographers, who think strategically, and actually do know what they are doing, were quick to react. "These chicks are our natural enemy," wrote Hugh Hefner in a secret memo leaked to feminists by secretaries at *Playboy*. "It is time we do battle with them....What I want is a devastating piece that takes the militant feminists apart." What he got were huge, raucous demonstrations at Playboy Clubs in big cities.

Activism against pornography continued, organized locally, ignored by   6
the media but an intrinsic part of the feminist resistance to rape. Groups called Women Against Violence Against Women formed independently in many cities. Pornography was understood by feminists (without any known exception) as woman-hating, violent, rapist. Robin Morgan pinpointed pornography as the theory, rape as the practice. Susan Brownmiller, later a founder of the immensely influential Women Against Pornography, saw pornography as woman-hating propaganda that promoted rape. These insights were not banal to feminists who were beginning to comprehend the gynocidal and terrorist implications of rape for all women. These were *emerging* political insights, not learned-by-rote slogans.

Sometime in 1975, newspapers in Chicago and New York City revealed   7
the existence of snuff films. Police detectives, trying to track down distribution networks, said that prostitutes, probably in Central America, were being tortured, slowly dismembered, then killed, for the camera. Prints of the films were being sold by organized crime to private pornography collectors in the United States.

In February 1976, a day or two before Susan B. Anthony's birthday, a   8
snazzy, first-run movie house in Times Square showed what purported to be a real snuff film. The marquee towered above the vast Times Square area, the word *Snuff* several feet high in neon, next to the title the words "made in South America where life is cheap." In the ads that blanketed the subways, a woman's body was cut in half.

We felt despair, rage, pain, grief. We picketed every night. It rained every   9
night. We marched round and round in small circles. We watched men take women in on dates. We watched the women come out, physically sick, and still go home with the men. We leafleted. We screamed out of control on street corners. There was some vandalism: not enough to close it down. We tried to get the police to close it down. We tried to get the District Attorney to close it down. You have no idea what respect those guys have for free speech.

The pimp who distributed the film would come to watch the picket line   10
and laugh at us. Men who went in laughed at us. Men who walked by laughed at us. Columnists in newspapers laughed at us. The American Civil Liberties Union ridiculed us through various spokesmen (in those days, they used men). The police did more than laugh at us. They formed a barricade with their bodies, guns, and nightsticks — to protect the film

from women. One threw me in front of an oncoming car. Three protestors were arrested and *locked up* for using obscene language to the theater manager. Under the United States Constitution, obscene language is not speech. Understand: It is not that obscene language is unprotected speech; it is not considered speech at all. The protestors, talking, used obscene language that was not speech; the maiming in the snuff film, the knife eviscerating the woman, was speech. All this we had to learn.

We learned a lot, of course. Life may be cheap, but knowledge never is.   11 We learned that the police protect property and that pornography is property. We learned that the civil liberties people didn't give a damn, my dear: A woman's murder, filmed to bring on orgasm, was speech, and they didn't even *mind* (these were the days before they learned that they had to say it was bad to hurt women). The ACLU did not have a crisis of conscience. The District Attorney went so far as to find a woman he claimed was "the actress" in the film to show she was alive. He held a press conference. He said that the only law the film broke was the law against fraud. He virtually challenged us to try to get the pimps on fraud, while making clear that if the film had been real, no United States law would have been broken because the murder would have occurred elsewhere. So we learned that. During the time *Snuff* showed in New York City, the bodies of several women, hacked to pieces, were found in the East River and several prostitutes were decapitated. We also learned that.

When we started protesting *Snuff*, so-called feminist lawyers, many still   12 leftists at heart, were on our side: No woman could sit this one out. We watched the radical boy lawyers pressure, threaten, ridicule, insult, and intimidate them; and they did abandon us. They went home. They never came back. We saw them learn to love free speech above women. Having hardened their radical little hearts to *Snuff*, what could ever make them put women first again?

There were great events. In November 1978, the first feminist conference on pornography was held in San Francisco. It culminated in the   13 country's first Take Back the Night March: Well over 3,000 women shut down San Francisco's pornography district for one night. In October 1978, over 5,000 women and men marched on Times Square. One documentary of the march shows a man who had come to Times Square to buy sex looking at the sea of women extending twenty city blocks and saying, bewildered and dismayed: "I can't find one fucking woman." In 1980, Linda Marchiano published *Ordeal*. World-famous as Linda Lovelace, the pornqueen extraordinaire of *Deep Throat*, Marchiano revealed that she had been forced into prostitution and pornography by brute terrorism. Gangraped, beaten, kept in sexual slavery by her pimp/husband (who had legal rights over her as her husband), forced to have intercourse with a dog for a film, subjected to sustained sadism rarely found by Amnesty International with regard to political prisoners, she dared to survive, escape, and expose the men who had sexually used her (including *Playboy*'s Hugh Hefner and

Screw's Al Goldstein). The world of normal men (the consumers) did not believe her; they believed *Deep Throat*. Feminists did believe her. Today Marchiano is a strong feminist fighting pornography.

In 1980, when I read *Ordeal*, I understood from it that every civil right   14
protected by law in this country had been broken on Linda's prosti-tuted body. I began to see gang rape, marital rape and battery, prostitution, and other forms of sexual abuse as civil rights violations which, in pornog-raphy, were systemic and intrinsic (the pornography could not exist without them). The pornographers, it was clear, violated the civil rights of women much as the Ku Klux Klan in this country had violated the civil rights of blacks. The pornographers were domestic terrorists determined to enforce, through violence, an inferior status on people born female. The second-class status of women itself was constructed through sexual abuse; and the name of the whole system of female subordination was *pornography* — men's orgasm and sexual pleasure synonymous with women's sexually explicit inequality. Either we were human, equal, citizens, in which case the pornographers could do to us what they did with impunity and, frankly, constitutional protection; or we were inferior, not protected as equal per-sons by law, and so the pimps could brutalize us, the normal men could have a good time, the pimps and their lawyers and the normal men could call it free speech, and we could live in hell. Either the pornographers and the pornography did violate the civil rights of women, or women had no rights of equality.

I asked Catharine A. MacKinnon, who had pioneered sexual harassment   15
litigation, if we could mount a civil rights suit in Linda's behalf. Kitty worked with me, Gloria Steinem (an early and brave champion of Linda), and several lawyers for well over a year to construct a civil rights suit. It could not, finally, be brought, because the statute of limitations on every atrocity committed against Linda had expired; and there was no law against showing or profiting from the films she was coerced into making. Kitty and I were despondent; Gloria said our day would come. It did — in Min-neapolis on December 30, 1983, when the City Council passed the first human rights legislation ever to recognize pornography as a violation of the civil rights of all women. In Minneapolis, a politically progressive city, pornography had been attacked as a *class* issue for many years. Politicians cynically zoned adult bookstores into poor and black areas of the city. Vio-lence against the already disenfranchised women and children increased massively; and the neighborhoods experienced economic devastation as legitimate businesses moved elsewhere. The civil rights legislation was passed in Minneapolis because poor people, people of color (especially Native Americans and blacks), and feminists demanded justice.

But first, understand this. Since 1970, but especially after *Snuff*, feminist   16
confrontations with pornographers had been head-on: militant, aggressive, dangerous, defiant. We had thousands of demonstrations. Some were inside theaters where, for instance, feminists in the audience would scream like

hell when a woman was being hurt on the screen. Feminists were physically dragged from the theaters by police who found the celluloid screams to be *speech* and the feminist screams to be *disturbing the peace*. Banners were unfurled in front of ongoing films. Blood was poured on magazines and sex paraphernalia designed to hurt women. Civil disobedience, sit-ins, destruction of magazines and property, photographing consumers, as well as picketing, leafleting, letter-writing, and debating in public forums, have all been engaged in over all these years without respite. Women have been arrested repeatedly: the police protecting, always, the pornographers. In one jury trial, three women, charged with two felonies and one misdemeanor for pouring blood over pornography, said that they were acting to prevent a greater harm — rape; they also said that the blood was already there, they were just making it visible. They were acquitted when the jury heard testimony about the actual use of pornography in rape and incest *from the victims*: a raped woman; an incestuously abused teenager.

So understand this too: *Feminism works*; at least primitive feminism   17 works. We used militant activism to defy and to try to destroy the men who exist to hurt women, that is, the pimps who make pornography. We wanted to destroy — not just put some polite limits on but *destroy* — their power to hurt us; and millions of women, each alone at first, one at a time, began to remember, or understand, or find words for how she herself had been hurt by pornography, what had happened to her because of it. Before feminists took on the pornographers, each woman, as always, had thought that only she had been abused in, with, or because of pornography. Each woman lived in isolation, fear, shame. Terror creates silence. Each woman had lived in unbreachable silence. Each woman had been deeply hurt by rape, the incest, the battery; but something more had happened too, and there was no name for it and no description of it. Once the role of pornography in *creating* sexual abuse was exposed — rape by rape, beating by beating, victim by victim — our understanding of the nature of sexual abuse itself changed. To talk about rape alone, or battery alone, or incest alone, was not to talk about the totality of how the women had been violated. Rape or wife-beating or prostitution or incest were not discrete or free-standing phenomena. We had thought: Some men rape; some men batter; some men fuck little girls. We had accepted an inert model of male sexuality: Men have fetishes; the women must always be blond, for instance; the act that brings on orgasm must always be the same. But abuse created by pornography was different: The abuse was multifaceted, complex, the violations of each individual woman were many and interconnected; the sadism was exceptionally dynamic. We found that when pornography created sexual abuse, men learned any new tricks the pornographers had to teach. We learned that anything that hurt or humiliated women could be sex for men who used pornography; and male sexual practice would change dramatically to accommodate violations and degradations promoted by pornography. We found that sexual abuses in a woman's life were intricately and complexly connected when pornography was a factor: Pornography was used to accomplish incest and then the child would be used to make pornography; the pornography-consuming husband would not just beat his wife but would tie her, hang her, torture her, force her into prostitution, and film her for pornography; pornography used in gang rape meant that the gang rape was enacted according to an already existing script, the sadism of the gang rape enhanced by the contributions of the pornographers. The forced filming of forced sex became a new sexual violation of women. In sexual terms, pornography created for women and children concentration camp conditions. This is not hyperbole.

One psychologist told the Minneapolis City Council about three cases 18 involving pornography used as "recipe books": "Presently or recently I have worked with clients who have been sodomized by broom handles, forced to have sex with over twenty dogs in the back seat of their car, tied up and then electrocuted on their genitals. These are children [all] in the ages of fourteen to eighteen...where the perpetrator has read the manuals and manuscripts at night and used these as recipe books by day or had the pornography present at the time of the sexual violence."

A social worker who works exclusively with adolescent female prostitutes 19 testified: "I can say almost categorically never have I had a client who has not been exposed to prostitution through pornography....For some young women that means that they are shown pornography, either films, videotapes, or pictures as this is how you do it, almost as a training manual in how to perform acts of prostitution....In addition, out on the street when a young woman is [working], many of her tricks or customers will come up to her with little pieces of paper, pictures that were torn from a magazine and say, I want this...it is like a mail order catalogue of sex acts, and that is what she is expected to perform....Another aspect that plays a bit part in my work...is that on many occasions my clients are multi, many rape victims. These rapes are often either taped or have photographs taken of the event. The young woman when she tries to escape [is blackmailed]."

A former prostitute, testifying on behalf of a group of former prostitutes 20 afraid of exposure, confirmed: "[W]e were all introduced to prostitution through pornography, there were no exceptions in our group, and we were all under eighteen." Everything done to women in pornography was done to these young prostitutes by the normal men. To them the prostitutes were synonymous with the pornography but so were all women, including wives and daughters. The abuses of prostitutes were not qualitatively different from the abuses of other women. Out of a compendium of pain, this is one incident: "[A] woman met a man in a hotel room in the 5th Ward. When he got there she was tied up while sitting on a chair nude. She was gagged and left alone in the dark for what she believed to be an hour. The man returned with two other men. They burned her with cigarettes and attached nipple clips to her breasts. They had many S and M magazines with them and showed her many pictures of women appearing to consent, enjoy, and encourage this abuse. She was held for twelve hours, continuously raped and beaten. She was paid $50 or about $2.33 per hour."

Racist violation is actively promoted in pornography; and the abuse has   21
pornography's distinctive dynamic — an annihilating sadism, the brutality and concept taken wholesale from the pornography itself. The pornographic video game "Custer's Revenge" generated many gang rapes of Native American women. In the game, men try to capture a "squaw," tie her to a tree, and rape her. In the sexually explicit game, the penis goes in and out, in and out. One victim of the "game" said: "When I was first asked to testify I resisted some because the memories are so painful and so recent. I am here because of my four-year-old daughter and other Indian children....I was attacked by two white men and from the beginning they let me know they hated my people....And they let me know that the rape of a 'squaw' by white men was practically honored by white society. In fact, it had been made into a video game called 'Custer's Last Stand' [*sic*]. They held me down and as one was running the tip of his knife across my face and throat he said, 'Do you want to play Custer's Last Stand? It's great, you lose but you don't care, do you? You like a little pain, don't you, squaw?' They both laughed and then he said, 'There is a lot of cock in Custer's Last Stand. You should be grateful, squaw, that all-American boys like us want you. Maybe we will tie you to a tree and start a fire around you.'"

The same sadistic intensity and arrogance is evident in this pornography-   22
generated gang rape of a thirteen-year-old girl. Three deer hunters, in the woods, looking at pornography magazines, looked up and saw the blond child. "There's a live one," one said. The three hunters chased the child, gang-raped her, pistol-whipped her breasts, all the while calling her names from the pornography magazines scattered at their campsite — Golden Girl, Little Godiva, and so on. "All three of them had hunting rifles. They, two men held their guns at my head and the first man hit my breast with his rifle and they continued to laugh. And then the first man raped me and when he was finished they started making jokes about how I was a virgin....The second man then raped me....The third man forced his penis into my mouth and told me to do it and I didn't know how to do it. I did not know what I was supposed to be doing...one of the men pulled the trigger on his gun so I tried harder. Then when he had an erection, he raped me. They continued to make jokes about how lucky they were to have found me when they did and they made jokes about being a virgin. They started...kicking me and told me that if I wanted more, I could come back the next day....I didn't tell anyone that I was raped until I was twenty years old." These men, like the men who gang-raped the Native American woman, had fun; they were playing a game.

I am quoting from some representative but still relatively *simple* cases.   23
Once the role of pornography in the abuse is exposed, we no longer have just rape or gang rape or child abuse or prostitution. We have, instead, sustained an intricate sadism with no inherent or predictable limits on the

kinds of degrees of brutality that will be used on women or girls. We have torture; we have killer-hostility.

Pornography-saturated abuse is specific and recognizable because it is 24 Nazism on women's bodies: The hostility and sadism it generates are carnivorous. Interviewing 200 working prostitutes in San Francisco, Mimi H. Silbert and Ayala M. Pines discovered astonishing patterns of hostility related to pornography. No questions were asked about pornography. But so much information was given casually by the women about the role of pornography in assaults on them that Silbert and Pines published the data they had stumbled on. Of the 200 women, 193 had been raped as adults and 178 had been sexually assaulted as children. That is 371 cases of sexual assault on a population of 200 women. Twenty-four percent of those who had been raped mentioned that the rapist made specific references to pornography during the rape: "The assailant referred to pornographic materials he had seen or read and then insisted that the victims not only enjoyed the rape but also the extreme violence." When a victim, in some cases, told the rapist that she was a prostitute and would perform whatever sex act he wanted (to dissuade him from using violence), *in all cases* the rapists responded in these ways: "(1) their language became more abusive, (2) they became significantly more violent, beating and punching the women excessively, often using weapons they had shown the women, (3) they mentioned having seen prostitutes in pornographic films, the majority of them mentioning specific pornographic literature, and (4) after completing the forced vaginal penetration, they continued to assault the women sexually in ways they claimed they had seen prostitutes enjoy in the pornographic literature they cited." Examples include forced and anal penetration with a gun, beatings all over the body with a gun, breaking bones, holding a loaded pistol at the woman's vagina "insisting this was the way she had died in the film he had seen."

Studies show that between sixty-five and seventy-five percent of women 25 in pornography were sexually abused as children, often incestuously, many put into pornography as children. One woman, for instance, endured this: "I'm an incest survivor, ex-pornography model, and ex-prostitute. My incest story begins before pre-school and ends many years later — this was with my father. I was also molested by an uncle and a minister...my father forced me to perform sexual acts with men at a stag party when I was a teenager. I am from a 'nice' middle-class family....My father is an $80,000 a year corporate executive, lay minister, and alcoholic....My father was my pimp in pornography. There were three occasions from ages nine to sixteen when he forced me to be a pornography model...in Nebraska, so, yes, it does happen here." This woman is now a feminist fighting pornography. She listens to men mostly debate whether or not there is any social harm connected to pornography. People want experts. We have experts. Society says we have to prove harm. We have proved harm. What we have to prove is that women are human enough for harm to matter. As one liberal so-called feminist said recently: "What's the harm of pornography? A paper cut?" This woman was a Commissioner on the so-called Meese commission.[1] She had spent a year of her life looking at the brutalization of women in pornography and hearing the life-stories of pornography-abused women. Women were not very human to her.

In pain and in privacy, women began to face, then to tell, the truth, first 26 to themselves, then to others. Now, women have testified before governmental bodies, in public meetings, on radio, on television, in workshops at conventions of liberal feminists who find all this so messy, so déclassé, *so unfortunate.* Especially, the liberal feminists hate it that this mess of pornography — having to do something about these abuses of women — might interfere with their quite comfortable political alliances with all those normal men, the consumers — who also happen to be, well, friends. They don't want the stink of this kind of sexual abuse — the down-and-dirty kind for fun and profit — to rub off on them. Feminism to them means getting success, not fighting oppression.

Here we are: Weep for us. Society, with the acquiescence of too many 27 liberal-left feminists, says that pornographers must *not* be stopped because the freedom of everyone depends on the freedom of the pornographers to exercise speech. The woman gagged and hanging remains the speech they exercise. In liberal-left lingo, stopping them is called *censorship.*

The civil rights law — a modest approach, since it is not the barrel of a 28 gun — was passed twice in Minneapolis, vetoed twice there by the mayor. In Indianapolis, a more conservative city (where even liberal feminists are registered Republicans), a narrower version was adopted: *Narrower* means that only very violent pornography was covered by the law. In Indianapolis, pornography was defined as the graphic, sexually explicit subordination of women in pictures and/or words that also included rape, humiliation, penetration by objects or animals, or dismemberment. Men, children, and transsexuals used in these ways could also use this law. The law made pornographers legally and economically responsible for the harm they did to women. Makers of pornography, exhibitors, sellers, and distributors could be sued for trafficking in pornography. Anyone coerced into pornography could hold the makers, sellers, distributors, or exhibitors liable for profiting from the coercion and could have the coerced product removed from the marketplace. Anyone forced to watch pornography in their home, place of work or education, or in public, could sue whoever forces them and any institution that sanctions the force (for instance, a university or an employer). Anyone physically assaulted or injured because of a specific piece of pornography could sue the pornographer for money damages and get the pornography off the shelves. Under this law, pornography is correctly

---

[1]Named by the pornographers and their friends after their very right-wing Edwin Meese, the Commission was actually set up by the moderate former Attorney General William French Smith. [Dworkin's note.]

understood and recognized as a practice of sex discrimination. Pornography's impact on the status of women is to keep all women second-class: targets of aggression and civilly inferior.

The United States courts have declared the Indianapolis civil rights law   29
unconstitutional. A Federal Appeals Court said that pornography did all the harm to women we said it did — causing us both physical injury and civil inferiority — but its success in hurting us only proved its power as speech. Therefore, it is protected speech. Compared with the pimps, women have no rights.

The good news is that the pornographers are in real trouble and that   30
we made the trouble. *Playboy* and *Penthouse* are both in deep financial trouble. *Playboy* has been losing subscribers, and thus its advertising base, for years; both *Playboy* and *Penthouse* have lost thousands of retail outlets for their wares in the last few years. We have cost them their legitimacy.

The bad news is that we are in trouble. There is much violence against   31
us, pornography-inspired. They make us, our bodies, pornography in their magazines and tell the normal men to get us good. We are followed, attacked, threatened. Bullets were shot into one feminist antipornography center. Feminists have been harassed out of their homes, forced to move. And the pornographers have found a bunch of girls (as the women call themselves) to work for them: not the chickenshit liberals, but real collaborators who have organized specifically to oppose the civil rights legislation and to protect the pornographers from our political activism — pornography should not be a feminist issue, these so-called feminists say. They say: Pornography is misogynist *but*... The *but* in this case is that it derepresses us. The victims of pornography can testify, and have, that when men get derepressed, women get hurt. These women say they are feminists. Some have worked for the defeated Equal Rights Amendment or for abortion rights or for equal pay or for lesbian and gay rights. But these days, they organize to stop us from stopping the pornographers.

Most of the women who say they are feminists but work to protect   32
pornography are lawyers or academics: lawyers like the ones who walked away from *Snuff*; academics who think prostitution is romantic, an unrepressed female sexuality. But whoever they are, whatever they think they are doing, the outstanding fact about them is that they are ignoring the women who have been hurt in order to help the pimps who do the hurting. They are collaborators, not feminists.

The pornographers may well destroy us. The violence against us — in   33
the pornography, in the general media, among men — is escalating rapidly and dangerously. Sometimes our despair is horrible. We haven't given in yet. There is a resistance here, a real one. I can't tell you how brave and brilliant the resisters are. Or how powerless and hurt. Surely it is clear: The most powerless women, the most exploited women, are the women fighting the pornographers. Our more privileged sisters prefer not to take sides. It's a nasty fight, all right. Feminism is dying here because so many women

who say they are feminists are collaborators or cowards. Feminism is magnificent and militant here because the most powerless women are putting their lives on the line to confront the most powerful men for the sake of all women. Be proud of us for fighting. Be proud of us for getting so far. Help us if you can. The pornographers will have to stop us. We will not give in. They know that and now so do you.

> Love,
> Andrea Dworkin

Analyzing This Selection

1. Describe the tone and explain the effect on you of Dworkin's letter. What did you find disturbing?

2. What is the effect of the statistics cited in the first paragraph? According to the author, why aren't these facts better known?

3. **THE WRITER'S METHOD**   In the essay as a whole, how does Dworkin show that reading and viewing pornography affect men's actual behavior? Which kinds of evidence are more convincing, and why?

4. What does Dworkin imply by the terms "radical" and "liberal"? What do these terms mean to you? Does either term apply to you?

5. What is the author's recommendation for dealing legally with pornography? What has frustrated such attempts?

Analyzing Connections

6. Dworkin and Goodman (see "The Luck Business," p. 495) strongly oppose accepted practices and legal businesses, but they address audiences differently. How is the sense of an audience reflected in each writer's approach? Compare their tones and methods of persuasion. Keep in mind the difference in issues.

Analyzing by Writing

7. Examine mixed attitudes about sex in a recent issue of *Playboy* or *Cosmopolitan* magazine (or another glossy magazine that has an erotic but socially acceptable appeal). Take into consideration not only the articles and the photographs but also the advertising. Analyze the tone and other connotations as well as what is explicitly said and pictured. You will probably find a wide range of attitudes, from pleasing to offensive and from exalting to degrading, that will require careful differentiation. Try to identify and define different kinds and levels of erotic appeal to the audience.

PART 9

DILEMMAS

INSIGHTS

If I had to choose between betraying my country and betraying my friend, I hope I should have the guts to betray my country.

—E. M. FORSTER

Americans profess to love loyalty, even as they design institutions that actively discourage it. Corporations, professional sports teams, and universities bestow the biggest rewards on those most willing to move elsewhere. Young people are encouraged to serve their country with promises of benefits to be obtained when their tours of duty are over. Term limits leave politicians with no strong reasons to be loyal to the electorate — and vice versa. Whatever the theory, the practice could not be clearer: the loyal, when they are not the losers, are the suckers.

—ALAN WOLFE

In our age there is no such thing as "keeping out of politics." All issues are political issues, and politics itself is a mass of lies, evasions, folly, hatred, and schizophrenia. When the general atmosphere is bad, language must suffer....Political language — and with variations this is true of all political parties, from Conservatives to Anarchists — is designed to make lies sound truthful and murder respectable, and to give an appearance of solidity to pure wind.

—GEORGE ORWELL

It is hard for a free fish to understand what is happening to a hooked one.

—KARL MENNINGER

Our treatment of both older people and children reflects the value we place on independence and autonomy. We do our best to make our children independent from birth. We leave them all alone in rooms with the lights out and tell them, "Go to sleep by yourselves." And the old people we respect most are the ones who will fight for their independence, who would sooner starve to death than ask for help.

—MARGARET MEAD

The Road Not Taken

Two roads diverged in a yellow wood,
And sorry I could not travel both
And be one traveller, long I stood
And looked down one as far as I could
To where it bent in the undergrowth;

Then took the other, as just as fair,
And having perhaps the better claim,
Because it was grassy and wanted wear;
Though as for that the passing there
Had worn them really about the same,

And both that morning equally lay
In leaves no step had trodden black.
Oh, I kept the first for another day!
Yet knowing how way leads on to way,
I doubted if I should ever come back.

I shall be telling this with a sigh
Somewhere ages and ages hence:
Two roads diverged in a wood, and I —
I took the one less travelled by,
And that has made all the difference.

—ROBERT FROST

No trumpets sound when the important decisions of our life are made. Destiny is made known silently.

—AGNES DE MILLE

FOCUSING BY WRITING

1. Consider the pros and cons of offering payment for body parts to increase their supply. As medical technology develops better ways to transplant organs and tissues, their monetary value to sellers as well as buyers could soar. Legal commerce and illegal markets could swell the supply to meet demands. We offer payment for human blood, why not for skin? for an eye, a kidney, a lung, a liver, or a heart? Argue for the principle of prohibiting or regulating payment for body parts.

2. Where did you go right or wrong in life? Develop your second thoughts about a choice, a direction, or an action you once took that you now see from a different perspective. What was the strongest factor in your decision at the time? What other factor would gain importance now? As you look back on the decision or action, do you now feel mainly regret, pride, embarrassment, relief, resentment, nostalgia, resignation, or some other emotion?

3. We are asked to support, endorse, or contribute to many more good causes than we actually join in. How do you usually decide? Does your response depend mainly on the issue involved, the people involved, or the possible misinterpretations of your support or refusal? Examine all the elements that entered your recent decision to participate or not to participate in a cause.

4. Should restrictions on alcohol advertisements be removed from television? Or should restrictions be broadened to include beer? Consider that among college students drinking is often connected to accidental deaths, serious injuries, and sexual assaults. What, if anything, should be done to increase, modify, or deregulate the advertising of alcohol?

Sallie Tisdale

WE DO ABORTIONS HERE

SALLIE TISDALE (b. 1957) received her degree in nursing at the University of Portland in Oregon. She has written two books about health care and the nursing profession: *The Sorcerer's Apprentice* (1986) and *Harvest Moon* (1987). Her writings about the impact of nature on history, and the impact of humanity on nature, include *Lot's Wife: Salt and the Human Condition* (1988) and *Stepping Westward: The Long Search for Home in the Pacific Northwest* (1991). Her most recent book is *Talk Dirty to Me: An Intimate Philosophy of Sex* (1994). Her column, "Second Thoughts," appears regularly in *Salon Magazine* (www.salon.com). Tisdale was a registered nurse in an abortion clinic when she wrote the following reflections about the tasks, the suffering, and the moral issues involved in that work.

We do abortions here; that is all we do. There are weary, grim moments 1 when I think I cannot bear another basin of bloody remains, utter another kind phrase of reassurance. So I leave the procedure room in the back and reach for a new chart. Soon I am talking to an eighteen-year-old woman pregnant for the fourth time. I push up her sleeve to check her blood pressure and find row upon row of needle marks, neat and parallel and discolored. She has been so hungry for her drug for so long that she has taken to using the loose skin of her upper arms; her elbows are already a permanent ruin of bruises. She is surprised to find herself nearly four months pregnant. I suspect she is often surprised, in a mild way, by the blows she is dealt. I prepare myself for another basin, another brief and chafing loss.

"How can you stand it?" Even the clients ask. They see the machine, 2 the strange instruments, the blood, the final stroke that wipes away the promise of pregnancy. Sometimes I see that too: I watch a woman's swollen abdomen sink to softness in a few stuttering moments and my own belly flip-flops with sorrow. But all it takes for me to catch my breath is another interview, one more story that sounds so much like the last one. There is a numbing sameness lurking in this job: the same questions, the same answers, even the same trembling tone in the voices. The worst is the sameness of human failure, of inadequacy in the face of each day's dull demands.

In describing this work, I find it difficult to explain how much I enjoy it 3 most of the time. We laugh a lot here, as friends and as professional peers.

It's nice to be with women all day. I like the sudden, transient bonds I forge with some clients: moments when I am in my strength, remembering weakness, and a woman in weakness reaches out for my strength. What I offer is not power, but solidness, offered almost eagerly. Certain clients waken in me every tender urge I have — others make me wince and bite my tongue. Both challenge me to find a balance. It is a sweet brutality we practice here, a stark and loving dispassion.

I look at abortion as if I am standing on a cliff with a telescope, gazing 4 at some great vista. I can sweep the horizon with both eyes, survey the scene in all its distance and size. Or I can put my eye to the lens and focus on the small details, suddenly so close. In abortion the absolute must always be tempered by the contextual, because both are real, both valid, both hard. How can we do this? How can we refuse? Each abortion is a measure of our failure to protect, to nourish our own. Each basin I empty is a promise — but a promise broken a long time ago.

I grew up on the great promise of birth control. Like many women my 5 age, I took the pill as soon as I was sexually active. To risk pregnancy when it was so easy to avoid seemed stupid, and my contraceptive success, as it were, was part of the promise of social enlightenment. But birth control fails, far more frequently than laboratory trials predict. Many of our clients take the pill; its failure to protect them is a shocking realization. We have clients who have been sterilized, whose husbands have had vasectomies; each one is a statistical misfit, fine print come to life. The anger and shame of these women I hold in one hand, and the basin in the other. The distance between the two, the length I pace and try to measure, is the size of an abortion.

The procedure is disarmingly simple. Women are surprised, as though 6 the mystery of conception, a dark and hidden genesis, requires an elaborate finale. In the first trimester of pregnancy, it's a mere few minutes of vacuuming, a neat tidying up. I give a woman a small yellow Valium, and when it has begun to relax her, I lead her into the back, into bareness, the stirrups. The doctor reaches in her, opening the narrow tunnel to the uterus with a succession of slim, smooth bars of steel. He inserts a plastic tube and hooks it to a hose on the machine. The woman is framed against white paper that crackles as she moves, the light bright in her eyes. Then the machine rumbles low and loud in the small windowless room; the doctor moves the tube back and forth with an efficient rhythm, and the long tail of it fills with blood that spurts and stumbles along into a jar. He is usually finished in a few minutes. They are long minutes for the woman; her uterus frequently reacts to its abrupt emptying with a powerful, unceasing cramp, which cuts off the blood vessels and enfolds the irritated, bleeding tissue.

I am learning to recognize the shadows that cross the faces of the 7 women I hold. While the doctor works between her spread legs, the paper drape hiding his intent expression, I stand beside the table. I hold the woman's hands in mine, resting them just below her ribs. I watch her eyes, finger her necklace, stroke her hair. I ask about her job, her family; in a haze she answers me; we chatter, faces close, eyes meeting and sliding apart.

I watch the shadows that creep up unnoticed and suddenly darken her   8
face as she screws up her features and pushes a tear out each side to slide down her cheeks. I have learned to anticipate the quiver of chin, the rapid intake of breath, and the surprising sobs that rise soon after the machine starts to drum. I know this is when the cramp deepens, and the tears are partly the tears that follow pain — the sharp, childish crying when one bumps one's head on a cabinet door. But a well of woe seems to open beneath many women when they hear that thumping sound. The anticipation of the moment has finally come to fruit; the moment has arrived when the loss is no longer an imagined one. It has come true.

I am struck by the sameness and I am struck every day by the variety   9
here — how this commonplace dilemma can so display the differences of women. A twenty-one-year-old woman, unemployed, uneducated, without family, in the fifth month of her pregnancy. A forty-two-year-old mother of teenagers, shocked by her condition, refusing to tell her husband. A twenty-three-year-old mother of two having her seventh abortion, and many women in their thirties having their first. Some are stoic, some hysterical, a few giggle uncontrollably, many cry.

I talk to a sixteen-year-old uneducated girl who was raped. She has gon-   10
orrhea. She describes blinding headaches, attacks of breathlessness, nausea. "Sometimes I feel like two different people," she tells me with a calm smile, "and I talk to myself."

I pull out my plastic models. She listens patiently for a time, and then   11
holds out her hands wide in front of her stomach.

"When's the baby going to go up into my stomach?" she asks.   12

I blink. "What do you mean?"   13

"Well," she says, still smiling, "when women get so big, isn't the baby in   14
your stomach? Doesn't it hatch out of an egg there?"

My first question in an interview is always the same. As I walk down the   15
hall with the woman, as we get settled in chairs and I glance through her files, I am trying to gauge her, to get a sense of the words, and the tone, I should use. With some I joke, and others I chat, sometimes I fall into a brisk, business-like patter. But I ask every woman, "Are you sure you want to have an abortion?" Most nod with grim knowing smiles. "Oh, yes," they sigh. Some seek forgiveness, offer excuses. Occasionally a woman will flinch and say, "Please don't use that word."

Later I describe the procedure to come, using care with my language. I   16
don't say "pain" any more than I would say "baby." So many are afraid to ask how much it will hurt. "My sister told me —" I hear. "A friend of mine said —" and the dire expectations unravel. I prick the index finger of a woman for a drop of blood to test, and as the tiny lancet approaches the

skin she averts her eyes, holding her trembling hand out to me and jumping at my touch.

It is when I am holding a plastic uterus in one hand, a suction tube in 17 the other, moving them together in imitation of the scrubbing to come, that women ask the most secret question. I am speaking in a matter-of-fact voice about "the tissue" and "the contents" when the woman suddenly catches my eye and asks, "How big is the baby now?" These words suggest a quiet need for a definition of the boundaries being drawn. It isn't so odd, after all, that she feels relief when I describe the growing bud's bulbous shape, its miniature nature. Again I gauge, and sometimes lie a little, weaseling around its infantile features until its clinging power slackens.

But when I look in the basin, among the curdlike blood clots, I see an 18 elfin thorax, attenuated, its pencilline ribs all in parallel rows with tiny knobs of spine rounding upwards. A translucent arm and hand swim beside.

A sleepy-eyed girl, just fourteen, watched me with a slight and goofy 19 smile all through her abortion. "Does it have little feet and little fingers and all?" she'd asked earlier. When the suction was over she sat up woozily at the end of the table and murmured, "Can I see it?" I shook my head firmly.

"It's not allowed," I told her sternly, because I knew she didn't really 20 want to see what was left. She accepted this statement of authority, and a shadow of confused relief crossed her plain, pale face.

Privately, even grudgingly, my colleagues might admit the power of 21 abortion to provoke emotion. But they seem to prefer the broad view and disdain the telescope. Abortion is a matter of choice, privacy, control. Its uncertainty lies in specific cases: retarded women and girls too young to give consent for surgery, women who are ill or hostile or psychotic. Such common dilemmas are met with both compassion and impatience; they slow things down. We are too busy to chew over ethics. One person might discuss certain concerns, behind closed doors, or describe a particularly disturbing dream. But generally there is to be no ambivalence.

Every day I take calls from women who are annoyed that we cannot see 22 them, cannot do their abortion today, this morning, now. They argue the price, demand that we stay after hours to accommodate their job or class schedule. Abortion is so routine that one expects it to be like a manicure; quick, cheap, and painless.

Still, I've cultivated a certain disregard. It isn't negligence, but I don't 23 always pay attention. I couldn't be here if I tried to judge each case on its merits; after all, we do over a hundred abortions a week. At some point each individual in this line of work draws a boundary and adheres to it. For one physician the boundary is a particular week of gestation; for another, it is a certain number of repeated abortions. But these boundaries can be fluid too: One physician overruled his own limit to abort a mature but severely malformed fetus. For me, the limit is allowing my clients to carry their own burden, shoulder the responsibility themselves. I shoulder the burden of trying not to judge them.

This city has several "crisis pregnancy centers" advertised in the Yellow 24 Pages. They are small offices staffed by volunteers, and they offer free pregnancy testing, glossy photos of dead fetuses, and movies. I had a client recently whose mother is active in the antiabortion movement. The young woman went to the local crisis center and was told that the doctor would make her touch her dismembered baby, that the pain would be the most horrible she could imagine, and that she might, after an abortion, never be able to have children. All lies. They called her at home and at work, over and over and over, but she had been wise enough to give a false name. She came to us a fugitive. We who do abortions are marked, by some, as impure. It's dirty work.

When a deliveryman comes to the sliding glass window by the reception 25 desk and tilts a box toward me, I hesitate. I read the packing slips, assess the shape and weight of the box in the light of its supposed contents. We request familiar faces. The doors are carefully locked; I have learned to half glance around at bags and boxes, looking for a telltale sign. I register with security when I arrive, and I am careful not to bang a door. We are a little on edge here.

Concern about size and shape seem to be natural, and so is the relief 26 that follows. We make the powerful assumption that the fetus is different from us, and even when we admit the similarities, it is too simplistic to be seduced by form alone. But the form is enormously potent—humanoid, powerless, palm-sized, and pure, it evokes an almost fierce tenderness when viewed simply as what it appears to be. But appearance, and even potential, aren't enough. The fetus, in becoming itself, can ruin others; its utter dependence has a sinister side. When I am struck in the moment by the contents in the basin, I am careful to remember the context, to note the tearful teenager and the woman sighing with something more than relief. One kind of question, though, I find considerably trickier.

"Can you tell what it is?" I am asked, and this means gender. This ques- 27 tion is asked by couples, not women alone. Always couples would abort a girl and keep a boy. I have been asked about twins, and even if I could tell what race the father was.

An eighteen-year-old woman with three daughters brought her husband 28 to the interview. He glared first at me, then at his wife, as he sank lower and lower in the chair, picking his teeth with a toothpick. He interrupted a conversation with his wife to ask if I could tell whether the baby would be a boy or a girl. I told him I could not.

"Good," he replied in a slow and strangely malevolent voice, "'cause if 29 it was a boy I'd wring her neck."

In a literal sense, abortion exists because we are able to ask such 30 questions, able to assign a value to the fetus which can shift with changing circumstances. If the human bond to a child were as primitive and un-flinchingly narrow as that of other animals, there would be no abortion. There would be no abortion because there would be nothing more important than caring for the young and perpetuating the species, no reason for sex but to make babies. I sense this sometimes, this wordless organic duty, when I do ultrasounds.

We do ultrasound, a sound-wave test that paints a faint, gray picture of 31 the fetus, whenever we're uncertain of gestation. Age is measured by the width of the skull and confirmed by the length of the femur or thighbone; we speak of a pregnancy as being a certain "femur length" in weeks. The usual concern is whether a pregnancy is within the legal limit for an abortion. Women this far along have bellies which swell out round and tight like trim muscles. When they lie flat, the mound rises softly above the hips, pressing the umbilicus upward.

It takes practice to read an ultrasound picture, which is grainy and 32 etched as though in strokes of charcoal. But suddenly a rapid rhythmic motion appears — the beating heart. Nearby is a soft oval, scratched with lines — the skull. The leg is harder to find, and then suddenly the fetus moves, bobbing in the surf. The skull turns away, an arm slides across the screen, the torso rolls. I know the weight of a baby's head on my shoulder, the whisper of lips on ears, the delicate curve of a fragile spine in my hand. I know how heavy and correct a newborn cradled feels. The creature I watch in secret requires nothing from me but to be left alone, and that is precisely what won't be done.

These inadvertently made beings are caught in a twisting web of motive 33 and desire. They are at least inconvenient, sometimes quite literally dangerous in the womb, but most often they fall somewhere in between — consequences never quite believed in come to roost. Their virtue rises and falls outside their own nature: They become only what we make them. A fetus created by accident is the most absolute kind of surprise. Whether the blame lies in a failed IUD, a slipped condom, or a false impression of safety, that fetus is a thing whose creation has been actively worked against. Its existence is an error. I think this is why so few women, even late in a pregnancy, will consider giving a baby up for adoption. To do so means making the fetus real — imagining it as something whole and outside oneself. The decision to terminate a pregnancy is sometimes so difficult and confounding that it creates an enormous demand for immediate action. The decision is a rejection; the pregnancy has become something to be rid of, a condition to be ended. It is a burden, a weight, a thing separate.

Women have abortions because they are too old, and too young, too 34 poor, and too rich, too stupid, and too smart. I see women who berate themselves with violent emotions for their first and only abortion, and others who return three times, five times, hauling two or three children, who cannot remember to take a pill or where they put the diaphragm. We talk glibly about choice. But the choice for what? I see all the broken promises in lives lived like a series of impromptu obstacles. There are the sweet, light promises of love and intimacy, the glittering promise of education and progress, the warm promise of safe families, long years of innocence and community. And there is the promise of freedom: freedom from failure, from faithlessness. Freedom from biology. The early feminist defense of abortion asked many questions, but the one I remember is this: Is biology destiny? And the answer is yes, sometimes it is. Women who have the fewest choices of all exercise their right to abortion the most.

Oh, the ignorance. I take a woman to the back room and ask her to 35 undress; a few minutes later I return and find her positioned discreetly behind a drape, still wearing underpants. "Do I have to take these off too?" she asks, a little shocked. Some swear they have not had sex, many do not know what a uterus is, how sperm and egg meet, how sex makes babies. Some late seekers do not believe themselves pregnant; they believe themselves *impregnable.* I was chastised when I began this job for referring to some clients as girls: It is a feminist heresy. They come so young, snapping gum, sockless and sneakered, and their shakily applied eyeliner smears when they cry. I call them girls with maternal benignity. I cannot imagine them as mothers.

The doctor seats himself between the woman's thighs and reaches into 36 the dilated opening of a five-month pregnant uterus. Quickly he grabs and crushes the fetus in several places, and the room is filled with a low clatter and snap of forceps, the click of the tanaculum, and a pulling, sucking sound. The paper crinkles as the drugged and sleepy woman shifts, the nurse's low, honey-brown voice explains each step in delicate words.

I have fetus dreams, we all do here: dreams of abortions one after the 37 other; of buckets of blood splashed on the walls; trees full of crawling fetuses. I dreamed that two men grabbed me and began to drag me away: "Let's do an abortion," they said with a sickening leer, and I began to scream, plunged into a vision of sucking, scraping pain, of being spread and torn by impartial instruments that do only what they are bidden. I woke from this dream barely able to breathe and thought of kitchen tables and coat hangers, knitting needles striped with blood, and women all alone clutching a pillow in their teeth to keep the screams from piercing the apartment-house walls. Abortion is the narrowest edge between kindness and cruelty. Done as well as it can be, it is still violence — merciful violence, like putting a suffering animal to death.

Maggie, one of the nurses, received a call at midnight not long ago. 38 It was a woman in her twentieth week of pregnancy; the necessarily gradual process of cervical dilation begun the day before had stimulated labor, as it sometimes does. Maggie and one of the doctors met the woman at the office in the night. Maggie helped her onto the table, and as she lay down the fetus was delivered into Maggie's hands. When Maggie told me about it the next day, she cupped her hands into a small bowl — "It was just like a small kitten," she said softly, wonderingly. "Everything was still attached."

At the end of the day I clean out the suction jars, pouring blood into the   39 sink, splashing the sides with flecks of tissue. From the sink rises a rich and humid smell, hot, earthy, and moldering; it is the smell of something recently alive beginning to decay. I take care of the plastic tub on the floor, filled with pieces too big to be trusted to the trash. The law defines the contents of the bucket I hold protectively against my chest as "tissue." Some would say my complicity in filling that bucket gives me no right to call it anything else. I slip the tissue gently into a bag and place it in the freezer, to be burned at another time. Abortion requires of me an entirely new set of assumptions. It requires a willingness to live with conflict, fearlessness, and grief. As I close the freezer door, I imagine a world where this won't be necessary, and then return to the world where it is.

Analyzing This Selection

1. **THE WRITER'S METHOD**   In the detailed description of an abortion, what does the author want the reader to recognize? How does her description affect you?

2. What attitude toward her clients does Tisdale reject? What attitude does she uphold? What problems does she have in controlling her attitudes? How do your responses to her clients differ from hers?

3. Explain Tisdale's stance on the public controversy over abortion. What is her attitude toward antiabortionists?

4. What is the author's outlook on humanity? What generalizations does Tisdale assert or imply about the human race?

Analyzing Connections

5. Should Tisdale quit her job? Compare her work problems with Ellen Ullman's reasons to quit programming (see "Getting Close to the Machine," p. 475). Whose job would you find more distressing?

Analyzing by Writing

6. Examine a controversy over abortion within a community, group, or family you know. What issues became important? How were disagreements handled? Present views on both sides fairly. If possible, include details from Tisdale's essay to illustrate how she regards these issues. Explain your own perspective.

K. C. Cole

CALCULATED RISKS

K. C. COLE (b. 1946), a journalist and essayist, writes mainly about science for the general public. After graduating from Columbia University, she began a career as a reporter on Eastern European affairs. Cole's science articles and essays have appeared in *Newsday*, the *Washington Post*, and the *New York Times*. This essay is excerpted from her most recent book, *The Universe and the Teacup: The Mathematics of Truth and Beauty* (1998).

Newsweek magazine plunged American women into a state of near panic 1 some years ago when it announced that the chances of a college-educated thirty-five-year-old woman finding a husband was less than her chance of being killed by a terrorist. Although Susan Faludi made mincemeat of this so-called statistic in her book *Backlash*, the notion that we can precisely quantify risk has a strong hold on the Western psyche. Scientists, statisticians, and policy makers attach numbers to the risk of getting breast cancer or AIDS, to flying and food additives, to getting hit by lightning or falling in the bathtub.

Yet despite (or perhaps because of) all the numbers floating around, most 2 people are quite properly confused about risk. I know people who live happily on the San Andreas Fault and yet are afraid to ride the New York subways (and vice versa). I've known smokers who can't stand to be in the same room with a fatty steak, and women afraid of the side effects of birth control pills who have unprotected sex with strangers. Risk assessment is rarely based on purely rational considerations — even if people could agree on what those considerations were. We worry about negligible quantities of Alar in apples, yet shrug off the much higher probability of dying from smoking. We worry about flying, but not driving. We worry about getting brain cancer from cellular phones, although the link is quite tenuous. In fact, it's easy to make a statistical argument — albeit a fallacious one — that cellular phones prevent cancer, because the proportion of people with brain tumors is smaller among cell phone users than among the general population.[1]

[1] John Allen Paulos was the first person I know of to make this calculation; it is probably related to the fact that people who use cellular phones are on average richer, and therefore healthier, than people who don't. [Cole's note.]

Even simple pleasures such as eating and breathing have become 3
suspect. Love has always been risky, and AIDS has made intimacy more
perilous than ever. On the other hand, not having relationships may be
riskier still. According to at least one study, the average male faces three
times the threat of early death associated with not being married as he does
from cancer.

Of course, risk isn't all bad. Without knowingly taking risks, no one 4
would ever walk out the door, much less go to school, drive a car, have a
baby, submit a proposal for a research grant, fall in love, or swim in the
ocean. It's hard to have any fun, accomplish anything productive, or experience life without taking on risks — sometimes substantial ones. Life, after
all, is a fatal disease, and the mortality rate for humans, at the end of the
day, is 100 percent.

Yet, people are notoriously bad at risk assessment. I couldn't get over this 5
feeling watching the aftermath of the crash of TWA Flight 800 and the horror it spread about flying, with the long lines at airports, the increased security measures, the stories about grieving families day after day in the
newspaper, the ongoing attempt to figure out why and who and what could
be done to prevent such a tragedy from happening again.

Meanwhile, tens of thousands of children die every day around the 6
world from common causes such as malnutrition and disease. That's
roughly the same as a hundred exploding jumbo jets full of children every
single day. People who care more about the victims of Flight 800 aren't callous or ignorant. It's just the way our minds work. Certain kinds of tragedies
make an impact; others don't. Our perceptual apparatus is geared toward
threats that are exotic, personal, erratic, and dramatic. This doesn't mean
we're ignorant; just human.

This skewed perception of risk has serious social consequences, however. 7
We aim our resources at phantoms, while real hazards are ignored. Parents,
for example, tend to rate drug abuse and abduction by strangers as the
greatest threats to their children. Yet hundreds of times more children die
each year from choking, burns, falls, drowning, and other accidents that
public safety efforts generally ignore....

Even in terms of simple dollars, our policies don't make any sense. It's 8
well known, for example, that prenatal care for pregnant women saves enormous amounts of money — in terms of care infants need in the first year of
life — and costs a pittance. Yet millions of low-income women don't get it.

Numbers are clearly not enough to make sense of risk assessment. Con- 9
text counts, too. Take cancer statistics. It's always frightening to hear that
cancer is on the rise. However, at least one reason for the increase is simply that people are living longer — long enough to get the disease.

What you consider risky, after all, depends somewhat on the circum- 10
stances of your life and lifestyle. People who don't have enough to eat don't
worry about apples contaminated with Alar. People who face daily violence

at their front door don't worry about hijackings on flights to the Bahamas. Attitudes toward risk evolve in cultural contexts and are influenced by everything from psychology to ethics to beliefs about personal responsibility.

In addition to context, another factor needed to see through the maze of 11 conflicting messages about risk is human psychology. For example, imminent risks strike much more fear in our hearts than distant ones; it's much harder to get a teenager than an older person to take long-term dangers like smoking seriously.

Smoking is also a habit people believe they can control, which makes 12 the risk far more acceptable. (People seem to get more upset about the effects of passive smoking than smoking itself — at least in part because smokers get to choose, and breathers don't.)

As a general principle, people tend to grossly exaggerate the risk of any 13 danger perceived to be beyond their control, while shrugging off risks they think they can manage. Thus, we go skiing and skydiving, but fear asbestos. We resent and fear the idea that anonymous chemical companies are putting additives into our food; yet the additives we load onto our own food — salt, sugar, butter — are millions of times more dangerous.

This is one reason that airline accidents seem so unacceptable — because 14 strapped into our seats in the cabin, what happens is completely beyond our control. In a poll taken soon after the TWA Flight 800 crash, an overwhelming majority of people said they'd be willing to pay up to fifty dollars more for a round-trip ticket if it increased airline safety. Yet the same people resist moves to improve automobile safety, for example, especially if it costs money.

The idea that we can control what happens also influences who we 15 blame when things go wrong. Most people don't like to pay the costs for treating people injured by cigarettes or riding motorcycles because we think they brought these things on themselves. Some people also hold these attitudes toward victims of AIDS, or mental illness, because they think the illness results from lack of character or personal morals.

In another curious perceptual twist, risks associated with losing some- 16 thing and gaining something appear to be calculated in our minds according to quite different scales. In a now-classic series of studies, Stanford psychologist Amos Tversky and colleague Daniel Kahneman concluded that most people will bend over backward to avoid small risks, even if that means sacrificing great potential rewards. "The threat of a loss has a greater impact on a decision than the possibility of an equivalent gain," they concluded.

In one of their tests, Tversky and Kahneman asked physicians to choose 17 between two strategies for combating a rare disease, expected to kill 600 people. Strategy A promised to save 200 people (the rest would die), while Strategy B offered a one-third probability that everyone would be saved, and a two-thirds probability that no one would be saved. Betting on a sure thing, the physicians choose A. But presented with the identical choice, stated differently, they choose B. The difference in language was simply this: Instead of stating that Strategy A would guarantee 200 out of 600 saved lives, it stated that Strategy A would mean 400 sure deaths.

People will risk a lot to prevent a loss, in other words, but risk very little 18 for possible gain. Running into a burning house to save a pet or fighting back when a mugger asks for your wallet are both high-risk gambles that people take repeatedly in order to hang on to something they care about. The same people might not risk the hassle of, say, fastening a seat belt in a car even though the potential gain might be much higher.

The bird in the hand always seems more attractive than the two in the 19 bush. Even if holding on to the one in your hand comes at a higher risk and the two in the bush are gold-plated.

The reverse situation comes into play when we judge risks of commis- 20 sion versus risks of omission. A risk that you assume by actually doing something seems far more risky than a risk you take by not doing something, even though the risk of doing nothing may be greater.

Death from natural causes, like cancer, are more readily acceptable than 21 deaths from accidents or murder. That's probably one reason it's so much easier to accept thousands of starving children than the death of one in a drive-by shooting. The former is an act of omission — a failure to step in and help, send food or medicine. The latter is the commission of a crime — somebody pulled the trigger.

In the same way, the Food and Drug Administration is far more likely to 22 withhold a drug that might help a great number of people if it threatens to harm a few; better to hurt a lot of people by failing to do something than act with the deliberate knowledge that some people will be hurt. Or as the doctors' credo puts it: First do no harm.

For obvious reasons, dramatic or exotic risks seem far more dangerous 23 than more familiar ones. Plane crashes and AIDS are risks associated with ambulances and flashing lights, sex and drugs. While red dye #2 strikes terror in our hearts, that great glob of butter melting into our baked potato is accepted as an old friend. "A woman drives down the street with her child romping around in the front seat," says John Allen Paulos. "Then they arrive at the shopping mall, and she grabs the child's hand so hard it hurts, because she's afraid he'll be kidnapped."

Children who are kidnapped are far more likely to be whisked away by 24 relatives than strangers, just as most people are murdered by people they know.

Familiar risks creep up on us like age and are often difficult to see until 25 it's too late to take action. Mathematician Sam C. Saunders of Washington State University reminds us that a frog placed in hot water will struggle to escape, but the same frog placed in cool water that's slowly warmed up will sit peacefully until it's cooked. "One cannot anticipate what one does not perceive," he says, which is why gradual accumulations of risk due to lifestyle choices (like smoking or eating) are so often ignored. We're in hot water, but it's gotten hot so slowly that no one notices.

To bring home his point, Saunders asks us to imagine that cigarettes are 26 not harmful — with the exception of an occasional one that has been packed with explosives instead of tobacco. These dynamite-stuffed cigarettes look just like normal ones. There's only one hidden away in every 18,250 packs — not a grave risk, you might say. The only catch is, if you smoke one of those explosive cigarettes, it might blow your head off.

The mathematician speculates, I think correctly, that given such a situa- 27 tion, cigarettes would surely be banned outright. After all, if 30 million packs of cigarettes are sold each day, an average of 1,600 people a day would die in gruesome explosions. Yet the number of deaths is the same to be expected from normal smoking. "The total expected loss of life or health to smokers using dynamite-loaded (but otherwise harmless) cigarettes over forty years would not be as great as with ordinary filtered cigarettes," says Saunders.

We can accept getting cooked like a frog, in other words, but not getting 28 blown up like a firecracker.

It won't come as a great surprise to anyone that ego also plays a role in 29 the way we assess risks. Psychological self-protection leads us to draw consistently wrong conclusions. In general, we overestimate the risks of bad things happening to others, while vastly underrating the possibility that they will happen to ourselves. Indeed, the lengths people go to minimize their own perceived risks can be downright "ingenious," according to Rutgers psychologist Neil Weinstein. For example, people asked about the risk of finding radon in their houses always rate their risk as "low" or "average," never "high." "If you ask them why," says Weinstein, "they take anything and twist it around in a way that reassures them. Some say their risk is low because the house is new; others, because the house is old. Some will say their risk is low because their house is at the top of a hill; others, because it's at the bottom of a hill."

Whatever the evidence to the contrary, we think: "It won't happen to 30 me." Weinstein and others speculate that this has something to do with preservation of self-esteem. We don't like to see ourselves as vulnerable. We like to think we've got some magical edge over the others. Ego gets involved especially in cases where being vulnerable to risk implies personal failure — for example, the risk of depression, suicide, alcoholism, drug addiction. "If you admit you're at risk," says Weinstein, "you're admitting that you can't handle stress. You're not as strong as the next person."

Average people, studies have shown, believe that they will enjoy longer 31 lives, healthier lives, and longer marriages than the "average" person. Despite the obvious fact that they themselves are, well, average people, too. According to a recent poll, 3 out of 4 baby boomers (those born between 1946 and 1964) think they look younger than their peers, and 4 out of 5 say they have fewer wrinkles than other people their age — a statistical impossibility.

Kahneman and Tversky studied this phenomenon as well and found that 32 people think they'll beat the odds because they're special. This is no doubt a necessary psychological defense mechanism, or no one would ever get married again without thinking seriously about the potential for divorce. A clear view of personal vulnerability, however, could go a long way toward preventing activities like drunken driving. But then again, most people think they are better than average drivers — even when intoxicated.

We also seem to believe it won't happen to us if it hasn't happened yet. 33 That is, we extrapolate from the past to the future. "I've been taking that highway at eighty miles per hour for ten years and I haven't crashed yet," we tell ourselves. This is rather like reasoning that flipping a coin ten times that comes up heads guarantees that heads will continue to come up indefinitely.

Curiously, one advertising campaign against drunken driving that was 34 quite successful featured the faces of children killed by drunken drivers. These children looked real to us. We could identify with them. In the same way as we could identify with the people on TWA Flight 800. It's much easier to empathize with someone who has a name and a face than a statistic.

That explains in part why we go to great expense to rescue children who 35 fall down mine shafts, but not children dying from preventable diseases. Economists call this the "rule of rescue." If you know that someone is in danger and you know that you can help, you have a moral obligation to do so. If you don't know about it, however, you have no obligation. Columnist Roger Simon speculates that's one reason the National Rifle Association lobbied successfully to eliminate the program at the Centers for Disease Control that keeps track of gun deaths. If we don't have to face what's happening, we won't feel obligated to do anything about it.

Even without the complication of all these psychological factors, how- 36 ever, calculating risks can be tricky because not everything is known about every situation. "We have to concede that a single neglected or unrecognized risk can invalidate all the reliability calculations, which are based on known risk," writes Ivar Ekeland. There is always a risk, in other words, that the risk assessment itself is wrong.

Genetic screening, like tests for HIV infection, has a certain probability 37 of being wrong. If your results come back positive, how much should you worry? If they come back negative, how safe should you feel?

The more factors involved, the more complicated the risk assessment 38 becomes. When you get to truly complex systems like nationwide telephone networks and power grids, worldwide computer networks and hugely complex machines like space shuttles, the risk of disaster becomes infinitely harder to pin down. No one knows when a minor glitch will set off a chain reaction of events that will culminate in disaster. Potential risk in complex systems, in other words, are subject to...exponential amplification....

Needless to say, the way a society assesses risk is very different from the 39
way an individual views the same choices. Whether or not you wish to ride
a motorcycle is your own business. Whether society pays the bills for the
thousands of people maimed by cycle accidents, however, is everybody's
business. Any one of us might view our own survival on a transatlantic
flight as more important than the needs of the nation's children. Governments, one presumes, ought to have a somewhat different agenda.

But how far does society want to go in strictly numerical accounting? It 40
certainly hasn't helped much in the all-important issue of health care,
where an ounce of prevention has been proven again and again to be worth
many pounds of cures. Most experts agree that we should be spending
much more money preventing common diseases and accidents, especially
in children. But no one wants to take health dollars away from precarious
newborns or the elderly — where most of it goes. These are decisions that
ultimately will not be made by numbers alone. Calculating risk only helps
us to see more clearly what exactly is going on.

According to anthropologist Melvin Konner, author of *Why the Reckless* 41
Survive, our poor judgment about potential risks may well be the legacy of
evolution. Early peoples lived at constant risk from predators, disease, accidents. They died young. And in evolutionary terms, "winning" means not
longevity, but merely sticking around long enough to pass on your genes to
the next generation. Taking risk was therefore a "winning" strategy, especially if it meant a chance to mate before dying. Besides, decisions had to
be made quickly. If going for a meal of ripe berries meant risking an attack
from a saber-toothed tiger, you dove for the berries. For a half-starved cave
dweller, this was a relatively simple choice. Perhaps our brains are simply
not wired, speculates Konner, for the careful calculations presented by the
risks of modern life....

Analyzing This Selection

1. What kinds of avoidable risks do people tend to ignore? Do the author's
   observations hold true in your experience?
2. How does the loss/gain factor affect behavior and social policy?
3. What conditions of modern life especially complicate risk assessment?
4. **THE WRITER'S METHOD** How does Cole make statistics interesting
   instead of boring? Examine the way in which she presents data and academic studies.

Analyzing Connections

5. Cole and Robert Goodman (see "The Luck Business," p. 495) are amazed
   that people believe they can beat the odds. According to Goodman, why
   doesn't risk assessment function in the lottery? Does Cole add other reasons?

Analyzing by Writing

6. Analyze your risk assessment in deciding where to apply to colleges. How did you use, or assume as true, statistics such as scores and percentages? What psychological, family, and social factors affected your choices? Would you follow similar calculations if you had to do it all over again?

Jonathan Swift

A MODEST PROPOSAL

JONATHAN SWIFT (1667–1745) has been called "the greatest satirist in the English language." Born in Ireland to English parents, he was educated at Kilkenny School and Trinity College, Dublin, and later spent much of his time in England. An active participant in the political and literary life of London, Swift became a brilliant political pamphleteer. In 1713, he obtained the deanery of St. Patrick's Cathedral in Dublin and later published several books, including his masterpiece, *Gulliver's Travels* (1726). "A Modest Proposal," published in 1729, was Swift's response to extreme poverty in Ireland, brought on by drought and exploitation by the English, who controlled a large proportion of Irish farmland.

It is a melancholy object to those who walk through this great town or travel in the country, when they see the streets, the roads, and cabin doors, crowded with beggars of the female sex, followed by three, four, or six children, all in rags and importuning every passenger for an alms. These mothers, instead of being able to work for their honest livelihood, are forced to employ all their time in strolling to beg sustenance for their helpless infants, who, as they grow up, either turn thieves for want of work, or leave their dear native country to fight for the Pretender[1] in Spain, or sell themselves to the Barbados.[2]

I think it is agreed by all parties that this prodigious number of children in the arms, or on the backs, or at the heels of their mothers, and frequently of their fathers, is in the present deplorable state of the kingdom a very great additional grievance; and therefore whoever could find out a fair, cheap, or easy method of making these children sound, useful members of the commonwealth would deserve so well of the public as to have his statue set up for a preserver of the nation.

But my intention is very far from being confined to provide only for the children of professed beggars; it is of a much greater extent, and shall take

---

[1]*Pretender* James Edward Stuart (1688–1766), "the Old Pretender," a Catholic who claimed the British throne from exile in France. [All notes are the editor's.]

[2]*Barbados* In Swift's time, many Irish sailed to Barbados, exchanging labor there for their passage.

in the whole number of infants at a certain age who are born of parents in effect as little able to support them as those who demand our charity in the streets.

As to my own part, having turned my thoughts for many years upon this important subject, and maturely weighed the several schemes of other projectors, I have always found them grossly mistaken in their computation. It is true, a child just dropped from its dam may be supported by her milk for a solar year, with little other nourishment; at most not above the value of two shillings, which the mother may certainly get, or the value in scraps, by her lawful occupation of begging; and it is exactly at one year that I propose to provide for them in such a manner as instead of being a charge upon their parents or the parish, or wanting food and raiment for the rest of their lives, they shall on the contrary contribute to the feeding, and partly to the clothing, of many thousands.

There is likewise another great advantage in my scheme, that it will prevent those voluntary abortions, and that horrid practice of women murdering their bastard children, alas, too frequent among us, sacrificing the poor innocent babes, I doubt, more to avoid the expense than the shame, which would move tears and pity in the most savage and inhuman breast.

The number of souls in this kingdom being usually reckoned one million and a half, of these I calculate there may be about two hundred thousand couples whose wives are breeders; from which number I subtract thirty thousand couples who are able to maintain their own children, although I apprehend there cannot be so many under the present distress of the kingdom; but this being granted, there will remain an hundred and seventy thousand breeders. I again subtract fifty thousand of those women who miscarry, or whose children die by accident or disease within the year. There only remain an hundred and twenty thousand children of poor parents annually born. The question therefore is, how this number shall be reared and provided for, which, as I have already said, under the present situation of affairs, is utterly impossible by all the methods hitherto proposed. For we can neither employ them in handicraft or agriculture; we neither build houses (I mean in the country) nor cultivate land. They can very seldom pick up a livelihood by stealing till they arrive at six years old, except where they are of towardly parts; although I confess they learn the rudiments much earlier, during which time they can however be looked upon only as probationers, as I have been informed by a principal gentleman in the country of Cavan, who protested to me that he never knew above one or two instances under the age of six, even in a part of the kingdom so renowned for the quickest proficiency in that art.

I am assured by our merchants that a boy or a girl before twelve years old is no salable commodity; and even when they come to this age they will not yield above three pounds; or three pounds and half a crown at most on the Exchange; which cannot turn to account either to the parents or the kingdom, the charge of nutriment and rags having been at least four times that value.

I shall now therefore humbly propose my own thoughts, which I hope 8 will not be liable to the least objection.

I have been assured by a very knowing American of my acquaintance in 9 London, that a young healthy child well nursed is at a year old a most delicious, nourishing, and wholesome food, whether stewed, roasted, baked, or boiled; and I make no doubt that it will equally serve in a fricasee or a ragout.

I do therefore humbly offer it to public consideration that of the hun- 10 dred and twenty thousand children, already computed, twenty thousand may be reserved for breed, whereof only one fourth part to be males, which is more than we allow to sheep, black cattle, or swine; and my reason is that these children are seldom the fruits of marriage, a circumstance not much regarded by our savages, therefore one male will be sufficient to serve four females. That the remaining hundred thousand may at a year old be offered in sale to the persons of quality and fortune through the kingdom, always advising the mother to let them suck plentifully in the last month, so as to render them plump and fat for a good table. The child will make two dishes at an entertainment for friends; and when the family dines alone, the fore or hind quarter will make a reasonable dish, and seasoned with a little pepper or salt will be very good boiled on the fourth day, especially in winter.

I have reckoned upon a medium that a child just born will weigh twelve 11 pounds, and in a solar year if tolerably nursed increaseth to twenty-eight pounds.

I grant this food will be somewhat dear, and therefore very proper for 12 landlords, who, as they have already devoured most of the parents, seem to have the best title to the children.

Infant's flesh will be in season throughout the year, but more plentiful 13 in March, and a little before and after. For we are told by a grave author, an eminent French physician, that fish being a prolific diet, there are more children born in Roman Catholic countries about nine months after Lent than at any other season; therefore, reckoning a year after Lent, the market will be more glutted than usual, because the number of popish infants is at least three to one in this kingdom; and therefore it will have one other collateral advantage, by lessening the number of Papists among us.

I have already computed the charge of nursing a beggar's child (in 14 which list I reckon all cottagers, laborers, and four-fifths of the farmers) to be about two shillings per annum, rags included; and I believe no gentleman would repine to give ten shillings for the carcass of a good fat child, which, as I have said, will make four dishes of excellent nutritive meat, when he hath only some particular friend or his own family to dine with him. Thus the squire will learn to be a good landlord, and grow popular among the tenants; the mother will have eight shillings net profit, and be fit for work till she produces another child.

Those who are more thrifty (as I must confess the times require) may flay the carcass; the skin of which artificially dressed will make admirable gloves for ladies, and summer boots for fine gentlemen.   15

As to our city of Dublin, shambles[3] may be appointed for this purpose in the most convenient parts of it, and butchers we may be assured will not be wanting; although I rather recommend buying the children live, and dressing them hot from the knife as we do roasting pigs.   16

A very worthy person, a true lover of his country, and whose virtues I highly esteem, was lately pleased in discoursing on this matter to offer a refinement upon my scheme. He said that many gentlemen of his kingdom, having of late destroyed their deer, he conceived that the want of venison might well be supplied by the bodies of young lads and maidens, not exceeding fourteen years of age nor under twelve, so great a number of both sexes in every county being now ready to starve for want of work and service; and these to be disposed of by their parents, if alive, or otherwise by their nearest relations. But with due deference to so excellent a friend and so deserving a patriot, I cannot be altogether in his sentiments; for as to the males, my American acquaintance assured me from frequent experience that their flesh was generally tough and lean, like that of our schoolboys, by continual exercise, and their taste disagreeable; and to fatten them would not answer the charge. Then as to the females, it would, I think with humble submission, be a loss to the public, because they soon would become breeders themselves; and besides, it is not improbable that some scrupulous people might be apt to censure such a practice (although indeed very unjustly) as a little bordering upon cruelty; which, I confess, hath always been with me the strongest objection against any project, how well soever intended.   17

But in order to justify my friend, he confessed that this expedient was put into his head by the famous Psalmanazar, a native of the island of Formosa, who came from thence to London above twenty years ago, and in conversation told my friend that in his country when any young person happened to be put to death, the executioner sold the carcass to persons of quality as a prime dainty; and that in his time the body of a plump girl of fifteen, who was crucified for an attempt to poison the emperor, was sold to his Imperial Majesty's prime minister of state, and other great mandarins of the court, in joints from the gibbet, at four hundred crowns. Neither indeed can I deny that if the same use were made of several plump young girls in this town, who without one single groat to their fortunes cannot stir abroad without a chair,[4] and appear at the playhouse and assemblies in foreign fineries which they never will pay for, the kingdom would not be the worse.   18

---

[3]*shambles* Slaughterhouses.
[4]*chair* A portable chair in which the passenger is carried by two people on foot.

Some persons of a desponding spirit are in great concern about the vast 19
number of poor people who are aged, diseased, or maimed, and I have
been desired to employ my thoughts what course may be taken to ease the
nation of so grievous an encumbrance. But I am not in the least pain upon
the matter, because it is very well known that they are every day dying and
rotting by cold and famine, and filth and vermin, as fast as can be reasonably expected. And as to the younger laborers, they are now in almost as
hopeful a condition. They cannot get work, and consequently pine away for
want of nourishment to a degree that if any time they are accidentally
hired to common labor, they have not strength to perform it; and thus the
country and themselves are happily delivered from the evils to come.

I have too long digressed, and therefore shall return to my subject. I 20
think the advantages by the proposal which I have made are obvious and
many, as well as of the highest importance.

For first, as I have already observed, it would greatly lessen the number 21
of Papists, with whom we are yearly overrun, being the principal breeders
of the nation as well as our most dangerous enemies; and who stay at home
on purpose to deliver the kingdom to the Pretender, hoping to take their
advantage by the absence of so many good Protestants, who have chosen
rather to leave their country than to stay at home and pay tithes against
their conscience to an Episcopal curate.

Secondly, the poorer tenants will have something valuable of their own, 22
which by law may be made liable to distress, and help to pay their landlord's
rent, their corn and cattle being already seized and money a thing unknown.

Thirdly, whereas the maintenance of an hundred thousand children, 23
from two years old and upwards, cannot be computed at less than ten
shillings per annum, the nation's stock will be thereby increased fifty thousand pounds per annum, besides the profit of a new dish introduced to the
tables of all gentlemen of fortune in the kingdom who have any refinement
in taste. And the money will circulate among ourselves, the goods being
entirely of our own growth and manufacture.

Fourthly, the constant breeders, besides the gain of eight shillings ster- 24
ling per annum by the sale of their children, will be rid of the charge of
maintaining them after the first year.

Fifthly, this food would likewise bring great custom to taverns, where the 25
vintners will certainly be so prudent as to procure the best receipts for
dressing it to perfection, and consequently have their houses frequented by
all the fine gentlemen, who justly value themselves upon their knowledge
in good eating; and a skillful cook, who understands how to oblige his
guests, will contrive to make it as expensive as they please.

Sixthly, this would be a great inducement to marriage, which all wise 26
nations have either encouraged by rewards or enforced by laws and penal-
ties. It would increase the care and tenderness of mothers toward their
children, when they were sure of a settlement for life to the poor babes,
provided in some sort by the public, to their annual profit instead of

expense. We should see an honest emulation among the married women, which of them could bring the fattest child to the market. Men would become as fond of their wives during the time of their pregnancy as they are now of their mares in foal, their cows in calf, or sows when they are ready to farrow; nor offer to beat or kick them (as is too frequent a practice) for fear of a miscarriage.

Many other advantages might be enumerated. For instance, the addition 27 of some thousand carcasses in our exportation of barreled beef, the propagation of swine's flesh, and improvements in the art of making good bacon, so much wanted among us by the great destruction of pigs, too frequent at our tables, which are no way comparable in taste or magnificence to a well-grown, fat, yearling child, which roasted whole will make a considerable figure at a lord mayor's feast or any other public entertainment. But this and many others I omit, being studious of brevity.

Supposing that one thousand families in this city would be constant cus- 28 tomers for infants' flesh, besides others who might have it at merry meetings, particularly weddings and christenings, I compute that Dublin would take off annually about twenty thousand carcasses, and the rest of the kingdom (where probably they will be sold somewhat cheaper) the remaining eighty thousand.

I can think of no one objection that will possibly be raised against this 29 proposal, unless it should be urged that the number of people will be thereby much lessened in the kingdom. This I freely own, and it was indeed one principal design in offering it to the world. I desire the reader will observe, that I calculate my remedy for this one individual kingdom of Ireland and for no other that ever was, is, or I think ever can be upon earth. Therefore let no man talk to me of other expedients: of taxing our absentees at five shillings a pound: of using neither clothes nor household furniture except what is of our own growth and manufacture: of utterly rejecting the materials and instruments that promote foreign luxury: of curing the expensiveness of pride, vanity, idleness, and gaming in our women: of introducing a vein of parsimony, prudence, and temperance: of learning to love our country, in the want of which we differ even from Laplanders and the inhabitants of Topinamboo: of quitting our animosities and factions, nor acting any longer like Jews, who were murdering one another at the very moment their city was taken: of being a little cautious not to sell our country and conscience for nothing: of teaching landlords to have at least one degree of mercy toward their tenants: lastly, of putting a spirit of honesty, industry, and skill into our shopkeepers; who, if a resolution could not be taken to buy only our native goods, would immediately unite to cheat and exact upon us in the price, the measure, and the goodness, nor could ever yet be brought to make one fair proposal of just dealing, though often and earnestly invited to it.

Therefore I repeat, let no man talk to me of these and the like expedi- 30 ents, till he hath at least some glimpse of hope that there will be some hearty and sincere attempt to put them in practice.

But as to myself, having been wearied out for many years with offering 31
vain, idle, visionary thoughts, and at length utterly despairing of success, I
fortunately fell upon this proposal, which, as it is wholly new, so it hath
something solid and real, and of expense and little trouble, full in our own
power, and whereby we can incur no danger in disobliging England. For
this kind of commodity will not bear exportation, the flesh being of too tender a consistence to admit a long continuance in salt, although perhaps I
could name a country which would be glad to eat up our whole nation
without it.

After all, I am not so violently bent upon my own opinion as to reject 32
any offer proposed by wise men, which shall be found equally innocent,
cheap, easy, and effectual. But before something of that kind shall be
advanced in contradiction to my scheme, and offering a better, I desire the
author or authors will be pleased maturely to consider two points. First, as
things now stand, how they will be able to find food and raiment for an
hundred thousand useless mouths and backs. And secondly, there being a
round million of creatures in human figure throughout this kingdom,
whose sole subsistence put into a common stock would leave them in debt
two millions of pounds sterling, adding those who are beggars by profession
to the bulk of farmers, cottagers, and laborers, with their wives and children
who are beggars in effect; I desire those politicians who dislike my overture,
and may perhaps be so bold to attempt an answer, that they will first ask
the parents of these mortals whether they would not at this day think it a
great happiness to have been sold for food at a year old in this manner I
prescribe, and thereby have avoided such a perpetual scene of misfortunes
as they have since gone through by the oppression of landlords, the impossibility of paying rent without money or trade, the want of common sustenance, with neither house nor clothes to cover them from the inclemencies
of the weather, and the most inevitable prospect of entailing the like or
greater miseries upon their breed forever.

I profess, in the sincerity of my heart, that I have not the least personal 33
interest in endeavoring to promote this necessary work, having no other
motive than the public good of my country, by advancing our trade, providing for infants, relieving the poor, and giving some pleasure to the rich.
I have no children by which I can propose to get a single penny; the
youngest being nine years old, and my wife past childbearing.

Analyzing This Selection

1. **THE WRITER'S METHOD**   The first three paragraphs straightforwardly
   express concern for the poor. What details in paragraph 4 begin to raise our
   suspicions about the speaker's concern for poor people?

2. What abilities and traits comprise the speaker's view of himself? What is
   your view of him? At what point in the essay are you fully shocked by his
   discussion of the problem?

3. Why is the idea of cannibalism first suggested to him by an American? Why would his references to Americans be amusing to Swift's contemporaries?

4. What are the causes of poverty in Swift's Ireland?

Analyzing Connections

5. Swift and Lars Eighner (see "On Dumpster Diving," p. 427) both rouse concern over the destitute people in their countries. What reaction to the problem does each writer stimulate? Without his ironic mask, how would Swift view scavenging in the United States?

Analyzing by Writing

6. In addition to attacking the problem of poverty, Swift satirizes the kind of reasoning that is rational without being moral, and logical without being ethical. Point out some absurdities of the so-called objective reasonableness that you find in current controversy over a public issue such as pornography (see Andrea Dworkin's "Letter from a War Zone," p. 508), gun control (see "Guns and Aims" Forum, p. 580), welfare reform, capital punishment, drug legalization, doctor-assisted suicide, or perhaps a campus issue. (You may wish to take an ironic stance as an advocate of a "reasonable" position that you find absurd.)

Joy Williams

OUR BRUTALITY TO ANIMALS[1]

JOY WILLIAMS (b. 1944), essayist and fiction writer, graduated from the
University of Iowa, where she also obtained an M.F.A. in the Writers'
Workshop. Her stories are often collected in anthologies citing the "best"
of current fiction. Williams was awarded a Guggenheim Fellowship and
a National Endowment for the Arts grant. Her latest novel is *The Quick
and the Dead* (2000). The following selection is excerpted from an essay
in *Harper's Magazine* (1997).

St. Francis once converted a wolf to reason. The wolf of Gubbio 1
promised to stop terrorizing an Italian town; he made pledges and assurances and pacts, and he kept his part of the bargains. But St. Francis only
performed this miracle once, and as miracles go, it didn't seem to capture
the public's fancy. Humans don't want to enter into a pact with animals.
They don't want animals to reason. It would be an unnerving experience.
It would bring about all manner of awkwardness and guilt. It would make
our treatment of them seem, well, unreasonable. The fact that animals are
voiceless is a relief to us, it frees us from feeling much empathy or sorrow.
If animals did have voices, if they could speak with the tongues of angels —
at the very least with the tongues of angels — it is unlikely that they could
save themselves from mankind. Their mysterious otherness has not saved
them, nor have their beautiful songs and coats and skins and shells, nor
have their strengths, their skills, their swiftness, the beauty of their flights.
We discover the remarkable intelligence of the whale, the wolf, the elephant — it does not save them, nor does our awareness of the complexity of
their lives. It matters not, it seems, whether they nurse their young or brood
patiently on eggs. If they eat meat, we decry their viciousness; if they eat
grasses and seeds, we dismiss them as weak. We know that they care for
their young and teach them, that they play and grieve, that they have memories and a sense of the future for which they sometimes plan. We know
about their habits, their migrations, that they have a sense of home, of finding, seeking, returning to home. We know that when they face death, they
fear it. We know all these things and it has not saved them from us.

[1]Editor's title.

Anything that is animal, that is not *us*, can be slaughtered as a pest or 2
sucked dry as a memento or reduced to a trophy or eaten, eaten, eaten. For
reasons of need or preference or availability. Or it's culture, it's a way to
feed the poor, it's different, it's plentiful, it's not plentiful, which makes it
more intriguing, it arouses the palate, it amuses the palate, it makes your
dick bigger, it's healthy, it's somebody's way of life, it's somebody's livelihood, it's somebody's business.

Agriculture has become agribusiness, after all. So the creatures that have 3
been under our "stewardship" the longest, that have been codified by habit
for our use, that have always suffered a special place in our regard — the
farm animals — have never been as cruelly kept or confined or slaughtered
in such numbers in all of history....Animals are no more than machines —
milk machines, piglet machines, egg machines — production units convert-
ing themselves into profits. They are explicitly excluded from any protection offered by the federal Animal Welfare Act, an act that is casually and
lightly enforced, if at all, by the Department of Agriculture: "Normal agricultural operation" precludes "humane" treatment, and anti-cruelty laws do
not apply to that which is raised for food.

The factory farm today is a crowded, stinking bedlam, filled with suffer- 4
ing animals that are quite literally insane, sprayed with pesticides and fat-
tened on a diet of growth stimulants, antibiotics, and drugs. Two hundred
and fifty thousand laying hens are confined within a single building. (The
high mortality rate caused by overcrowding is economically acceptable;
nothing is more worthless than an individual chicken.) Pigs are raised in
bare concrete cages in windowless metal buildings or tightly restrained in
foul pens and gestation boxes. Cows are kept pregnant to produce an
abnormal amount of milk, which is further artificially increased with hormone injections. The by-products of the dairy industry, calves, are chained
in crates twenty-two inches wide and no longer than their bodies, and
raised on a diet of drug-laced liquid feed for a few months until they're
slaughtered for the "delicacy" veal. (Yet some people say, *Well, apparently
they're raised in the darkness, in crates or something, but the taste is creamy,
sort of refined, a very nice taste...*) People will stop eating veal only if they
think they will get a killer disease if they don't. In England, the beef industry had a setback when a link was found between bovine spongiform
encephalopathy [BSE], a fatal disease of cattle, and Creutzfeldt-Jakob disease, a fatal neurological virus in humans. The cows became ill because
they were fed the rendered remains of sick sheep. Of course, in this country we are assured that our cows aren't being fed sick sheep and that no
BSE-infected cattle have been found here. We do have many "downer" animals, though, about 100,000 of them a year, that collapse from stress or
something, heaven knows, and end up dead prior to the slaughtering
process. They are rendered and ground up and become pet food and animal feed. Cattle do eat cattle here. They are fed the ground offal of those

that have succumbed to unknown causes, and this has been the practice for many years. If BSE were ever confirmed in this country, which is not at all unlikely, people would stop eating meat for a while for the same reasons the English did. Not because they'd had a sudden telepathic vision of the horrors of the abattoir, or because they'd all been subjected to a reading of James Agee's remarkable fable about a Christlike steer, "A Mother's Tale," but because they thought that eating steak would make their brains go funny. Once assured by the government that there was no need for alarm, they would be back in the spotless supermarkets, making their selections among the sliced, cubed, and shrink-wrapped remains, which have borne no resemblance to living things in our minds for some time now. They are merely some things, in a different department from the toilet-bowl cleanser. The supermarket has never been a place where one thinks — Animal.

Now genetic manipulation is becoming a commonplace as well. One 5 of the problems in poultry production is that bacteria-laden feces fly all over the carcasses in the slaughtering process. It's just always been a problem. Awaiting government approval is a proposed product called Rectite, a sort of superglue that seals the rectal cavities of poultry so all that salmonella contamination can be avoided. But Rectite already sounds a little oldfashioned. Genetic engineers might want to create a turkey, say, that had no vent at all, possibly no feet, and even a smaller head to save space. This would likely be hailed as quite an advantage over the traditionally constructed bird. Researchers probably dream about this nightly (when they're not dreaming about genetically identical sheep). Researchers are, in fact, creating entire new orders of creatures — specifically designed, transgenic, xenograph-ready. Around the world in labs with names such as Genpharm International Inc., Genzyme Corporation, and Pharmaceutical Proteins, biotechnocrats are inserting human genes in livestock to form animals that can produce human proteins and hormones: drugstores on the hoof. Pigs, long attractive to the farmer, not because of any Babe- or Miss Piggy–like charm but because they have short pregnancies and big litters, have become a favorite of researchers who are altering them to make the perfect organ donors. Doctors, awaiting the eventual blessing of the FDA, are eagerly anticipating placing genetically altered pig livers in just about everybody. (The drunks will probably get them to start.) Humans are requiring and demanding fresh new organs all the time (employing animals in this way seems so much more sophisticated than merely eating them), and the ethics of raising or breeding animals for body parts to replace our own failing ones seem to give people pause only when combined with warnings of dangers to human health. A person might not want that little monkey's heart, not because he wanted the monkey to keep it but because he'd worry that he might contract the Ebola virus and that his skin would get pulpy, he'd vomit black blood, and his eyeballs would burst.

We distance ourselves more and more from animals as we use them in   6
increasingly bizarre ways. Animals are being subsumed in a weird unnatu-
ralness. Indeed, technology, which is forever pressing to remove animals
from nature, to muddy and morph the remaining integrity of the animal
kingdom, has rendered the word "natural" obsolete. A side benefit of the
new and developing technologies is that soon we won't have to feel guilty
about the suffering and denigration of the animals because we will have
made them up. (That's not an animal, it's a donor...) Any sentience they
possess will have been invented by man or eliminated altogether. An animal will have no more real "life" than a lightbulb.

In the laboratory, animals have already been reclassified. They are tools,   7
they're part of the scientific apparatus, they undergo transformations, they
are metamorphosed into data. Rats and mice are already excluded from the
very definition of "animal" by the Department of Agriculture. The offspring
of these un-animals are then genetically reinvented. There are countless
variations of mutant "knock-out" mice, creatures whose genetic code has
been grotesquely altered, who lack particular genes crucial to learning or to
instinctual behavior and self-destruct in novel ways, or who develop terrible
diseases or deformities. As for the cats and dogs and rabbits and primates
other than man in the laboratory, although not deemed un-animals, they
are transformed semantically into "research animals." These animals, like
"food" animals, qualify for very little protection under the Animal Welfare
Act. At present this act does not prohibit any experiment or procedure that
might be performed on animals in labs, and makes clear that the government cannot interfere with the conduct or design of any experiment. Blinding has long been a popular procedure in the lab, as are any and all
"deprivology" studies. Of endless interest is the study of an animal's reaction to unrelieved, inescapable pain. The procedures, of course, are never
cruelty but science — they may result in data that might be of some use to
us sometime. So dogs are decerebrated or mutilated or poisoned or burned
to provide grist for a learned thesis; other dogs are tormented into states of
trauma, into states of "learned helplessness," into "psychological death," to
see if their observed decline can give any insights into human depression....

But dogs and cats and rabbits are as nothing to the researcher when   8
compared with what can be extrapolated from the most desirable lab animal of them all — the chimpanzee. The chimpanzee, humankind's closest
relative, has been infected and maimed and killed for over fifty years now,
for us, for the possible advantage to us, because they're so much like us;
they possess 98 percent of the same DNA, the same genetic material, as
humans. That missing 2 percent allows them to be vivisected on our
behalf. If it weren't for that lucky-for-us 2, they wouldn't be able to be used
as experimental surrogates because they'd be *just* like us, and medical
advancement would come to a standstill. Or at best it would, in the words
of a doctor writing in *The New Physician,* slow to a "snail's pace."

So in our country's finest universities (as well as in some of our just so-so   9
ones), researchers, not to be likened to snails, are still making chimpanzees
"hot" with deadly diseases and screwing bolts into their heads. They're still
removing infants from their mothers and "containerizing" them in solitary
so that their psychological and emotional suffering and decline can be
observed. They're still performing cataract surgery on healthy chimps, then
giving them different rehabilitative treatments, then killing them and dis-
secting their brains to see which treatment produced the best result within
the visual cortex. And they're still trying to give chimps AIDS. Scientists
have been frustrated because chimps just won't get this disease, though
their own simian immune systems can be destroyed in the lab. Over 100
chimps have been dosed with the human AIDS virus, but none have developed human AIDS. In 1995, researchers from the Yerkes Regional Primate
Research Center at Emory University in Atlanta were able to announce
that one chimp, infected with the virus ten years earlier, had come down
with AIDS, or, rather, had come down with the opportunistic diseases associated with AIDS. Managing to give one chimp the symptoms of AIDS was
certainly not science's finest hour.

In any case, what is all this "research" for? Artificially induced diseases   10
in animals practically never result in a cure that can be applicable to
humans. Even scientists have begun to recognize the ambiguity of their
work to the extent that it is common now, after the announcement of any
discovery wrung from animal research, for the researchers to caution publicly against using the findings to draw conclusions about human disease or
behavior. Still, researchers work hard at public relations. Parents' terrors of
the mysterious sudden infant death syndrome were manipulated shame-
lessly with the *cure dependent upon animal research* mantra — until the pre-
cipitous recent drop in infant deaths was attributed to the simple act of
putting babies to bed on their backs instead of their stomachs. (Prevention
may be worth a pound of cure, but it's not something the drug companies
are interested in.) Misleading monkey experiments delayed an effective
polio vaccine for decades. (As for insight into the cancer problem, 46 percent of substances deemed carcinogenic in mice are found not to be carcinogenic in rats.) Successes in human kidney transplants, blood transfusions,
and heart-bypass surgery all resulted only when doctors ignored the baleful
results of experiments on dogs and used human material. Animal tests, in
fact, do not predict side effects in humans up to 52 percent of the time.
Guinea pigs die when injected with penicillin. Thalidomide was found safe
for rodents; so was Opren, an arthritis drug that caused fatal liver toxicity in
a number of human patients before it was taken off the market. Animals
are sacrificed in laboratories to show the safety of products too; they are not
all employed to test the dangerous side effects. The tobacco industry was
able to deny a link between cigarette smoking and lung cancer for decades
because many thousands of dogs, monkeys, rabbits, and rats, fitted with
masks and placed in "smoking chambers," or immobilized in stereotaxic

chairs with tubes blowing smoke down their windpipes, could not be encouraged to develop carcinomas.

There are thousands of animal-advocacy organizations in the United   11
States, with millions of members....Only the animal people struggle to address this problem, and there is no limit to the horrible things they can worry about or the disappointments they must endure. Public awareness and revulsion at our treatment of animals is often raised only to fade or be circumvented. Two successes for the movement involved the fur and cosmetics industries. The wearing of fur was discredited for a time through the tactic of howling insult. "Corpse Coat!" activists would scream at any opportunity, or they would solicitously ask of some fur wearer, "How did you get the blood off that?" Then they'd go out and paint "Shame" and "Death" all over furriers' windows. Most cosmetics companies eliminated animal testing after the word got out to the kids (*Mommy, is it true that they blinded hundreds of white bunnies to make this pretty soap?*) and consumers were organized to boycott. But the fur industry is still around, hoping for government subsidies to boost export sales and counting on a new wave of designers — there's always a new wave — who believe the trend gurus' predictions of a "fur renaissance fueled by a growing interest in luxury investments" and are churning out the beaver capes, the burgundy pony-skin jackets, and the acid-green sable barn jackets. And some of the big names in the beauty industry — Helene Curtis, Cheseborough Pond's — continue to test on animals. Overall, the use of animals in research could very well be increasing — who knows? Corporate monoliths such as Procter & Gamble and Bausch & Lomb never stopped animal testing; the Department of Defense could still be cutting the vocal cords of beagles and testing nerve gas on them. The DOD doesn't have to release any figures at all, and research facilities in general enjoy institutionalized secrecy and seldom have to provide real numbers to the public.

No, there's little cause for real happiness among the animal people and   12
scant opportunity for self-congratulation. Commercial whaling has never really been outlawed, trade in exotic species is brisk, trophy hunting is back. Whenever a victory is claimed for the animals, it doesn't stay a victory for long: it's either not definitive or it's superseded by something worse. Cases continue to be won only to be lost on appeal, and the cases that remain won involve animal cruelty or welfare, never the rights of an animal to an equal consideration of interests, for an animal has no standing in a court of law. Injuries to a person's "aesthetic interests" can be judicially recognized (*I am offended by seeing spotted owls mounted on the hoods of logging trucks*), but an animal's interest in continuing to exist cannot.

The animal people need their day in court on the rights issue, and   13
groups such as the Animal Legal Defense Fund are seeking to find, try, and win the perfect case — the case that will take animals out of the realm of property and grant them legal status of their own. The plaintiff will un-

doubtedly be a chimp. The chimpanzees' ability to be trained in sign language, and their further ability to use that language to express their fears and needs, could provide the scientific basis for the argument that they deserve the same freedom from enslavement that humans now enjoy. Peter Singer's latest philosophical effort is the Great Ape Project, a rhetorical demand for the extension of the "community of equals" to include all the great apes: human beings and "our disquieting doubles" — chimpanzees, gorillas, and orangutans. The rights of life and freedom from torture and imprisonment would be granted to these animals, and then, possibly, would trickle down to those that are less our disquieting doubles.

Sometimes a number of the animal people gather together, as they did 14 last year for a "World Congress" at the cavernous USAir Arena in Landover, Maryland, just outside Washington, D.C. The arena can hold 18,000 people and it was far from full. There were no lovely animals there, of course. Animals can never be called upon to do a star turn on the movement's behalf — that would be using the animals. So only people were there, and only about 3,000 of them. The arena itself, so vast and impersonal, so disconcertingly inert, seemed to emphasize the gargantuan task the little group had taken on, and the gaunt specter of hopeless helplessness appeared more than once. Unspeakably wretched images were projected on immense screens: gruesome videos of steel leg-hold traps going off and nailing a remarkable array of creatures, videos of moribund lab animals and terrified stockyard animals, videos of berserk zoo and circus animals being shot. The animal people sat silently watching, watching simian horror, avian and equine horror, hunting and puppy-mill and pound horror — witnessing things a normal person would never want to know about. There were three days of speeches. The speakers were impassioned but calm, well-spoken, well-dressed, well-prepared; they politely restricted themselves to the time allotted. Nobody screamed, "We've got to stop dressing up as carrots!" or, "Whose idea was it to petition the town of Fishkill to change its name. It made us look like morons!" The importance of unity was stressed, the importance of being perceived as a single-interest political group that could effect change. Between speeches, people would wander out to the encircling satellite area and line up for the beyond-veggie, no-dairy vegan food that the arena's concessionaires were serving up with a certain amount of puzzlement. The Franks A Lot stand was sensibly shuttered. On the fourth day there was a March for Animals, from the Ellipse up Constitution Avenue to the Capitol. It was a nice march, orderly. Bystanders seemed a little baffled by it. Perhaps because there were no animals.

After the march, the animal people went home — to continue to work, 15 work, work for the animals so that they might be saved from our barbarism. Has any primarily middle-class group in this country ever had such an extremist agenda, based utterly on non-self-fulfillment and non-self-interest? The animal people are calling for a moral attitude toward a great and mysterious and mute nation, which can't, by our stem reckoning, act morally back. Their quest is quixotic; their reasoning, assailable; their intentions, almost inarticulate. The implementation of their vision would seem madness. But the future world is not this one. Our treatment of animals and our attitude toward them is crucial not only to any pretensions we have to ethical behavior but to humankind's intellectual and moral evolution. Which *is* how the human animal is meant to evolve, isn't it?

Analyzing This Selection

1. What sensitivities and responses in animals does this essay make you freshly aware of?

2. According to the author, how will genetic manipulation affect research and agribusiness?

3. Does Williams believe animals have rights? On what basis or principle does she advocate changing our practices? Do you think animals have rights?

Analyzing Connections

4. **THE WRITER'S METHOD**   Williams and Tisdale (see "We Do Abortions Here," p. 525) both present details that are disturbing. How does each writer avoid sounding sensational?

Analyzing by Writing

5. Analyze the moral differences, if any, between using humans and using other mammals for food production. Mother's milk, for instance, could be produced in quantities sufficient for business profit, and it would benefit health in every country. Considering the malnutrition and even starvation that prevail in much of the world, perhaps we should supply this food. Explain how your view pertains to human and nonhuman animals.

George Orwell

SHOOTING AN ELEPHANT

GEORGE ORWELL (1903–1950) was the pen name of Eric Blair, who was born in India and sent by his English parents to England for his education at Eton. He returned to India as an officer in the Imperial Police, but he became bitterly disenchanted with service to the empire, and he soon abandoned his career in the government. His first book, *Down and Out in Paris and London* (1933), recounts his struggles to support himself while he learned to write. His lifelong subject, however, is not bohemian life as a writer but his personal encounters with totalitarianism, which he addressed in his novel *Burmese Days* (1935) and his book *Homage to Catalonia* (1938), a chronicle of his developing despair over all political parties after he participated in the Spanish Civil War. His feelings toward politics and government are also expressed in his fiction, *Animal Farm* (1945) and *1984* (1949). The following essay is a memoir of his early period of conflicting loyalties as a British magistrate in Burma.

In Moulmein, in lower Burma, I was hated by large numbers of 1 people — the only time in my life that I have been important enough for this to happen to me. I was subdivisional police officer of the town, and in an aimless, petty kind of way anti-European feeling was very bitter. No one had the guts to raise a riot, but if a European woman went through the bazaars alone somebody would probably spit betel juice over her dress. As a police officer I was an obvious target and was baited whenever it seemed safe to do so. When a nimble Burman tripped me up on the football field and the referee (another Burman) looked the other way, the crowd yelled with hideous laughter. This happened more than once. In the end the sneering yellow faces of young men that met me everywhere, the insults hooted after me when I was at a safe distance, got badly on my nerves. The young Buddhist priests were the worst of all. There were several thousands of them in the town and none of them seemed to have anything to do except stand on street corners and jeer at Europeans.

All this was perplexing and upsetting. For at that time I had already 2 made up my mind that imperialism was an evil thing and the sooner I chucked up my job and got out of it the better. Theoretically — and secretly, of course — I was all for the Burmese and all against their oppressors, the British. As for the job I was doing, I hated it more bitterly than I can perhaps make clear. In a job like that you see the dirty work of Empire at close quarters. The wretched prisoners huddling in the stinking cages of the lock-ups, the grey, cowed faces of the long-term convicts, the scarred buttocks of the men who had been flogged with bamboos — all these oppressed me with an intolerable sense of guilt. But I could get nothing into perspective. I was young and ill-educated and I had had to think out my problems in the utter silence that is imposed on every English-man in the East. I did not even know that the British Empire is dying, still less did I know that it is a great deal better than the younger empires that are going to supplant it. All I knew was that I was stuck between my hatred of the empire I served and my rage against the evil-spirited little beasts who tried to make my job impossible. With one part of my mind I thought of the British Raj as an unbreakable tyranny, as something clamped down, in *saecula saeculorum*, upon the will of prostrate peoples; with another part I thought that the greatest joy in the world would be to drive a bayonet into a Buddhist priest's guts. Feelings like these are the nor-mal byproducts of imperialism; ask any Anglo-Indian official, if you can catch him off duty.

One day something happened which in a roundabout way was enlight-ening. It was a tiny incident in itself, but it gave me a better glimpse than I had had before of the real nature of imperialism — the real motives for which despotic governments act. Early one morning the subinspector at a police station the other end of the town rang me up on the phone and said that an elephant was ravaging the bazaar. Would I please come and do something about it? I did not know what I could do, but I wanted to see what was happening and I got on to a pony and started out. I took my rifle, an old .44 Winchester and much too small to kill an elephant, but I thought the noise might be useful *in terrorem*. Various Burmans stopped me on the way and told me about the elephant's doings. It was not, of course, a wild elephant, but a tame one which had gone "must." It had been chained up, as tame elephants always are when their attack of "must" is due, but on the previous night it had broken its chain and escaped. Its mahout, the only person who could manage it when it was in that state, had set out in pursuit, but had taken the wrong direction and was now twelve hours' journey away, and in the morning the elephant had suddenly reappeared in the town. The Burmese population had no weapons and were quite helpless against it. It had already destroyed somebody's bamboo hut, killed a cow, and raided some fruit-stalls and devoured the stock; also it had met the municipal rubbish van and, when the driver jumped out and took to his heels, had turned the van over and inflicted violences upon it. 3

The Burmese subinspector and some Indian constables were waiting for me in the quarter where the elephant had been seen. It was a very poor quarter, a labyrinth of squalid bamboo huts, thatched with palm-leaf, wind-ing all over a steep hillside. I remember that it was a cloudy, stuffy morn-ing at the beginning of the rains. We began questioning the people as to 4 where the elephant had gone and, as usual, failed to get any definite information. That is invariably the case in the East; a story always sounds clear enough at a distance, but the nearer you get to the scene of events the vaguer it becomes. Some of the people said that the elephant had gone in one direction, some said that he had gone in another, some professed not even to have heard of any elephant. I had almost made up my mind that the whole story was a pack of lies, when we heard yells a little distance away. There was a loud, scandalized cry of "Go away, child! Go away this instant!" and an old woman with a switch in her hand came round the corner of a hut, violently shooing away a crowd of naked children. Some more women followed, clicking their tongues and exclaiming; evidently there was something that the children ought not to have seen. I rounded the hut and saw a man's dead body sprawling in the mud. He was an Indian, a black Dravidian coolie, almost naked, and he could not have been dead many minutes. The people said that the elephant had come suddenly upon him round the corner of the hut, caught him with its trunk, put its foot on his back, and ground him into the earth. This was the rainy season and the ground was soft, and his face had scored a trench a foot deep and a couple of yards long. He was lying on his belly with arms crucified and head sharply twisted to one side. His face was coated with mud, the eyes wide open, the teeth bared and grinning with an expression of unendurable agony. (Never tell me, by the way, that the dead look peaceful. Most of the corpses I have seen looked devilish.) The friction of the great beast's foot had stripped the skin from his back as neatly as one skins a rabbit. As soon as I saw the dead man I sent an orderly to a friend's house nearby to borrow an elephant rifle. I had already sent back the pony, not wanting it to go mad with fright and throw me if it smelt the elephant.

The orderly came back in a few minutes with a rifle and five cartridges, 5 and meanwhile some Burmans had arrived and told us that the elephant was in the paddy fields below, only a few hundred yards away. As I started forward practically the whole population of the quarter flocked out of the houses and followed me. They had seen the rifle and were all shouting excitedly that I was going to shoot the elephant. They had not shown much interest in the elephant when he was merely ravaging their homes, but it was different now that he was going to be shot. It was a bit of fun to them, as it would be to an English crowd; besides they wanted the meat. It made me vaguely uneasy. I had no intention of shooting the elephant — I had merely sent for the rifle to defend myself if necessary — and it is always unnerving to have a crowd following you. I marched down the hill, looking and feeling a fool, with the rifle over my shoulder and an ever-growing army of people jostling at my heels. At the bottom, when you got away from the huts, there was a metalled road and beyond that a miry waste of paddy fields a thousand yards across, not yet ploughed but soggy from the first rains and dotted with coarse grass. The elephant was standing eight yards from the road, his left side towards us. He took not the slightest notice of the crowd's approach. He was tearing up bunches of grass, beating them against his knees to clean them and stuffing them into his mouth.

I had halted on the road. As soon as I saw the elephant I knew with per- 6 fect certainty that I ought not to shoot him. It is a serious matter to shoot a working elephant — it is comparable to destroying a huge and costly piece of machinery — and obviously one ought not to do it if it can possibly be avoided. And at that distance, peacefully eating, the elephant looked no more dangerous than a cow. I thought then and I think now that his attack of "must" was already passing off; in which case he would merely wander harmlessly about until the mahout came back and caught him. Moreover, I did not in the least want to shoot him. I decided that I would watch him for a little while to make sure that he did not turn savage again, and then go home.

But at that moment I glanced round at the crowd that had followed me. 7 It was an immense crowd, two thousand at the least and growing every minute. It blocked the road for a long distance on either side. I looked at the sea of yellow faces above the garish clothes — faces all happy and excited over this bit of fun, all certain that the elephant was going to be shot. They were watching me as they would watch a conjurer about to perform a trick. They did not like me, but with the magical rifle in my hands I was momentarily worth watching. And suddenly I realized that I should have to shoot the elephant after all. The people expected it of me and I had got to do it; I could feel their two thousand wills pressing me forward, irresistibly. And it was at this moment, as I stood there with the rifle in my hands, that I first grasped the hollowness, the futility of the white man's dominion in the East. Here was I, the white man with his gun, standing in front of the unarmed native crowd — seemingly the leading actor of the piece; but in reality I was only an absurd puppet pushed to and fro by the will of those yellow faces behind. I perceived in this moment that when the white man turns tyrant it is his own freedom that he destroys. He becomes a sort of hollow, posing dummy, the conventionalized figure of a sahib. For it is the condition of his rule that he shall spend his life in trying to impress the "natives," and so in every crisis he has got to do what the "natives" expect of him. He wears a mask, and his face grows to fit in. I had got to shoot the elephant. I had committed myself to doing it when I sent for the rifle. A sahib has got to act like a sahib; he has got to appear resolute, to know his own mind and do definite things. To come all that way, rifle in hand, with two thousand people marching at my heels, and then to trail feebly away, having done nothing — no, that was impossible. The crowd would laugh at me. And my whole life, every white man's life in the East, was one long struggle not to be laughed at.

But I did not want to shoot the elephant. I watched him beating his 8 bunch of grass against his knees, with that preoccupied grandmotherly air that elephants have. It seemed to me that it would be murder to shoot him.

At that age I was not squeamish about killing animals, but I had never shot an elephant and never wanted to. (Somehow it always seems worse to kill a *large* animal.) Besides, there was the beast's owner to be considered. Alive, the elephant was worth at least a hundred pounds; dead, he would only be worth the value of his tusks, five pounds, possibly. But I had got to act quickly. I turned to some experienced-looking Burmans who had been there when we arrived, and asked them how the elephant had been behaving. They all said the same thing: He took no notice of you if you left him alone, but he might charge if you went too close to him.

It was perfectly clear to me what I ought to do. I ought to walk up to within, say, twenty-five yards of the elephant and test his behavior. If he charged, I could shoot; if he took no notice of me, it would be safe to leave him until the mahout came back. But also I knew that I was going to do no such thing. I was a poor shot with a rifle and the ground was soft mud into which one would sink at every step. If the elephant charged and I missed him, I should have about as much chance as a toad under a steam-roller. But even then I was not thinking particularly of my own skin, only of the watchful yellow faces behind. For at that moment, with the crowd watching me, I was not afraid in the ordinary sense, as I would have been if I had been alone. A white man mustn't be frightened in front of "natives"; and so, in general, he isn't frightened. The sole thought in my mind was that if anything went wrong those two thousand Burmans would see me pursued, caught, trampled on, and reduced to a grinning corpse like that Indian up the hill. And if that happened it was quite probable that some of them would laugh. That would never do. There was only one alternative. I shoved the cartridges into the magazine and lay down on the road to get a better aim. 9

The crowd grew very still, and a deep, low, happy sigh, as of people who see the theater curtain go up at last, breathed from innumerable throats. They were going to have their bit of fun after all. The rifle was a beautiful German thing with cross-hair sights. I did not then know that in shooting an elephant one would shoot to cut an imaginary bar running from ear-hole to ear-hole. I ought, therefore, as the elephant was sideways on, to have aimed straight at his ear-hole; actually I aimed several inches in front of this, thinking the brain would be further forward. 10

When I pulled the trigger I did not hear the bang or feel the kick — one never does when a shot goes home — but I heard the devilish roar of glee that went up from the crowd. In that instant, in too short a time, one would have thought, even for the bullet to get there, a mysterious, terrible change had come over the elephant. He neither stirred nor fell, but every line of his body had altered. He looked suddenly stricken, shrunken, immensely old, as though the frightful impact of the bullet had paralysed him without knocking him down. At last, after what seemed a long time — it might have been five seconds, I dare say — he sagged flabbily to his knees. His mouth 11 slobbered. An enormous senility seemed to have settled upon him. One could have imagined him thousands of years old. I fired again into the same spot. At the second shot he did not collapse but climbed with desperate slowness to his feet and stood weakly upright, with legs sagging and head drooping. I fired a third time. That was the shot that did for him. You could see the agony of it jolt his whole body and knock the last remnant of strength from his legs. But in falling he seemed for a moment to rise, for as his hind legs collapsed beneath him he seemed to tower upward like a huge rock toppling, his trunk reaching skywards like a tree. He trumpeted, for the first and only time. And then down he came, his belly towards me, with a crash that seemed to shake the ground even where I lay.

I got up. The Burmans were already racing past me across the mud. It   12
was obvious that the elephant would never rise again, but he was not dead. He was breathing very rhythmically with long rattling gasps, his great mound of a side painfully rising and falling. His mouth was wide open — I could see far down into caverns of pale pink throat. I waited a long time for him to die, but his breathing did not weaken. Finally I fired my two remaining shots into the spot where I thought his heart must be. The thick blood welled out of him like red velvet, but still he did not die. His body did not even jerk when the shots hit him, the tortured breathing continued without a pause. He was dying, very slowly and in great agony, but in some world remote from me where not even a bullet could damage him further. I felt that I had got to put an end to that dreadful noise. It seemed dreadful to see the great beast lying there, powerless to move and yet powerless to die, and not even to be able to finish him. I sent back for my small rifle and poured shot after shot into his heart and down his throat. They seemed to make no impression. The tortured gasps continued as steadily as the ticking of a clock.

In the end I could not stand it any longer and went away. I heard later   13
that it took him half an hour to die. Burmans were bringing dahs[1] and baskets even before I left, and I was told they had stripped his body almost to the bones by the afternoon.

Afterwards, of course, there were endless discussions about the shooting   14
of the elephant. The owner was furious, but he was only an Indian and could do nothing. Besides, legally I had done the right thing, for a mad elephant has to be killed, like a mad dog, if its owner fails to control it. Among the Europeans opinion was divided. The older men said I was right, the younger men said it was a damn shame to shoot an elephant for killing a coolie, because an elephant was worth more than any damn Coringhee coolie. And afterwards I was very glad that the coolie had been killed; it put me legally in the right and it gave me a sufficient pretext for shooting the elephant. I often wondered whether any of the others grasped that I had done it solely to avoid looking a fool.

---

[1] *dahs* Large knives. [Editor's note.]

Analyzing This Selection

1. Why did Orwell hate his job even before this incident occurred? What effect was the job having on his feelings and attitudes? How would you describe his state of mind at the time?

2. **THE WRITER'S METHOD**   What details in the descriptions of the elephant connect it with human life? What details in the descriptions of the Burmans connect them with animals? What evokes Orwell's humane, sympathetic responses?

3. Orwell says that he acted "solely to avoid looking a fool." If he had believed in the goals and values of British imperialism, would his actions have had more integrity?

Analyzing Connections

4. In the Insights on page 522, Orwell says that "all issues are political." In this essay are there issues that are nonpolitical? any that go beyond the political? For what reasons, political or otherwise, are issues in this essay important to *you*?

Analyzing by Writing

5. You have probably openly or privately opposed something on the grounds of justice, power, equality, or rights. Perhaps it involved your parents or your school. Analyze your role as a participant in or observer of a politicized confrontation. Be specific about the stages of your engagement with the issues, and be clear about your response to the outcome. How have your views changed or developed since that confrontation?

Bel Kaufman

SUNDAY IN THE PARK

BEL KAUFMAN, granddaughter of the Yiddish humorist Sholem Alei-
chem, was born in Berlin, and she spent her childhood in Russia before
coming to the United States at the age of twelve. She graduated magna
cum laude from Hunter College and earned a master's degree from
Columbia University. From 1949 Kaufman taught English in New York
City high schools, an experience that led to her best-selling novel, *Up the
Down Staircase* (1964), which was later made into a popular film. Kaufman has written another novel, *Love, etc.* (1979), and many essays and
short stories. She has taught writing at the City University of New York.

It was still warm in the late-afternoon sun, and the city noises came 1
muffled through the trees in the park. She put her book down on the
bench, removed her sunglasses, and sighed contentedly. Morton was reading the *Times Magazine* section, one arm flung around her shoulder; their
three-year-old son, Larry, was playing in the sandbox: A faint breeze fanned
her hair softly against her cheek. It was five-thirty on a Sunday afternoon,
and the small playground, tucked away in a corner of the park, was all but
deserted. The swings and seesaws stood motionless and abandoned, the
slides were empty, and only in the sandbox two little boys squatted diligently side by side. *How good this is*, she thought, and almost smiled at her
sense of well-being. They must go out in the sun more often; Morton was
so city-pale, cooped up all week inside the gray factorylike university. She
squeezed his arm affectionately and glanced at Larry, delighting in the
pointed little face frowning in concentration over the tunnel he was digging. The other boy suddenly stood up and with a quick, deliberate swing
of his chubby arm threw a spadeful of sand at Larry. It just missed his head.
Larry continued digging; the boy remained standing, shovel raised, stolid
and impassive.

"No, no, little boy." She shook her finger at him, her eyes searching for 2
the child's mother or nurse. "We mustn't throw sand. It may get in someone's eyes and hurt. We must play nicely in the nice sandbox." The boy
looked at her in unblinking expectancy. He was about Larry's age but perhaps ten pounds heavier, a husky little boy with none of Larry's quickness
and sensitivity in his face. Where was his mother? The only other people
left in the playground were two women and a little girl on roller skates leav-

564

ing now through the gate, and a man on a bench a few feet away. He was a big man, and he seemed to be taking up the whole bench as he held the Sunday comics close to his face. She supposed he was the child's father. He did not look up from his comics, but spat once deftly out of the corner of his mouth. She turned her eyes away.

At that moment, as swiftly as before, the fat little boy threw another 3 spadeful of sand at Larry. This time some of it landed on his hair and forehead. Larry looked up at his mother, his mouth tentative; her expression would tell him whether to cry or not.

Her first instinct was to rush to her son, brush the sand out of his hair, 4 and punish the other child, but she controlled it. She always said that she wanted Larry to learn to fight his own battles.

"Don't *do* that, little boy," she said sharply, leaning forward on the 5 bench. "You mustn't throw sand!"

The man on the bench moved his mouth as if to spit again, but instead 6 he spoke. He did not look at her, but at the boy only.

"You go right ahead, Joe," he said loudly. "Throw all you want. This 7 here is a *public* sandbox."

She felt a sudden weakness in her knees as she glanced at Morton. 8 He had become aware of what was happening. He put his *Times* down carefully on his lap and turned his fine, lean face toward the man, smiling the shy, apologetic smile he might have offered a student in pointing out an error in his thinking. When he spoke to the man, it was with his usual reasonableness.

"You're quite right," he said pleasantly, "but just because this is a public 9 place...."

The man lowered his funnies and looked at Morton. He looked at him 10 from head to foot, slowly and deliberately. "Yeah?" His insolent voice was edged with menace. "My kid's got just as good a right here as yours, and if he feels like throwing sand, he'll throw it, and if you don't like it, you can take your kid the hell out of here."

The children were listening, their eyes and mouths wide open, their 11 spades forgotten in small fists. She noticed the muscle in Morton's jaw tighten. He was rarely angry; he seldom lost his temper. She was suffused with a tenderness for her husband and an impotent rage against the man for involving him in a situation so alien and so distasteful to him.

"Now, just a minute," Morton said courteously, "you must realize..." 12

"Aw, shut up," said the man. 13

Her heart began to pound. Morton half rose; the *Times* slid to the 14 ground. Slowly the other man stood up. He took a couple of steps toward Morton, then stopped. He flexed his great arms, waiting. She pressed her trembling knees together. Would there be violence, fighting? How dreadful, how incredible....She must do something, stop them, call for help. She wanted to put her hand on her husband's sleeve, to pull him down, but for some reason she didn't.

Morton adjusted his glasses. He was very pale. "This is ridiculous," he 15
said unevenly. "I must ask you..."

"Oh, yeah?" said the man. He stood with his legs spread apart, rocking a 16
little, looking at Morton with utter scorn. "You and who else?"

For a moment the two men looked at each other nakedly. Then Morton 17
turned his back on the man and said quietly, "Come on, let's get out of
here." He walked awkwardly, almost limping with self-consciousness, to the
sandbox. He stooped and lifted Larry and his shovel out.

At once Larry came to life, his face lost its rapt expression and he began 18
to kick and cry. "I don't *want* to go home, I want to play better, I don't *want*
any supper, I don't *like* supper...." It became a chant as they walked,
pulling their child between them, his feet dragging on the ground. In order
to get to the exit gate they had to pass the bench where the man sat sprawling again. She was careful not to look at him. With all the dignity she
could summon, she pulled Larry's sandy, perspiring little hand, while Morton pulled the other. Slowly and with head high she walked with her husband and child out of the playground.

Her first feeling was one of relief that a fight had been avoided, that no 19
one was hurt. Yet beneath it there was a layer of something else, something
heavy and inescapable. She sensed that it was more than just an unpleasant incident, more than defeat of reason by force. She felt dimly it had
something to do with her and Morton, something acutely personal, familiar, and important.

Suddenly Morton spoke. "It wouldn't have proved anything."   20

"What?" she asked.   21

"A fight. It wouldn't have proved anything beyond the fact that he's big- 22
ger than I am."

"Of course," she said.   23

"The only possible outcome," he continued reasonably, "would have 24
been — what? My glasses broken, perhaps a tooth or two replaced, a couple
of days' work missed — and for what? For justice? For truth?"

"Of course," she repeated. She quickened her step. She wanted only to 25
get home and to busy herself with her familiar tasks; perhaps then the feeling, glued like heavy plaster on her heart, would be gone. *Of all the stupid,
despicable bullies*, she thought, pulling harder on Larry's hand. The child
was still crying. Always before she had felt a tender pity for his defenseless
little body, the frail arms, the narrow shoulders with sharp, winglike shoulder blades, the thin and unsure legs, but now her mouth tightened in
resentment.

"Stop crying," she said sharply. "I'm ashamed of you!" She felt as if all 26
three of them were tracking mud along the street. The child cried louder.

If there had been an issue involved, she thought, *if there had been some- 27
thing to fight for....But what else could he possibly have done? Allow himself to be beaten? Attempt to educate the man? Call a policeman? "Officer,
there's a man in the park who won't stop his child from throwing sand on*

mine...." The whole thing was as silly as that, and not worth thinking about.

"Can't you keep him quiet, for Pete's sake?" Morton asked irritably.   28

"What do you suppose I've been trying to do?" she said.   29

Larry pulled back, dragging his feet.   30

"If you can't discipline this child, I will," Morton snapped, making a   31
move toward the boy.

But her voice stopped him. She was shocked to hear it, thin and cold   32
and penetrating with contempt. "Indeed?" she heard herself say. "You and
who else?"

Analyzing This Selection

1. Before the bully speaks, what are the positive and negative aspects of the woman's frame of mind?

2. Toward the end the woman wonders what there was to fight over. In your opinion, was anything really at stake?

3. **THE WRITER'S METHOD**   At the end, what is your attitude toward Morton? toward the woman? What do you think is the author's viewpoint?

Analyzing Connections

4. Like Morton, Orwell (see "Shooting an Elephant," p. 557) avoids potential embarrassment. How does each man cover up his sense of weakness? What do you think Morton might have done in Orwell's shoes?

Analyzing by Writing

5. Violent force is widely accepted if the violence is used to preserve "the nation's honor" or a person's "manly honor." Also, violence confers honor in film and video entertainment. Less acceptable but equally pervasive uses of violence are linked with honor among members of neighborhood gangs and organized crime families. What, if any, positive human attributes are contained in the link between violence and honor? What honorable goals and ideals might be separable from the violence? Try to define a concept of honor that does not depend on violence for confirmation. For details to illustrate your points, use "Sunday in the Park," news stories, videos, or just your imagination.

John Hoberman

STEROIDS AND SPORTS[1]

JOHN HOBERMAN (b. 1944), a professor of German at the University of
Texas, writes about the cultural significance of sports. His books include
The Dehumanization of Sport: Sport and Political Ideology (1984), *Mortal Engines: The Science of Performance* (1992), and most recently *Darwin's Athletes: How Sport Has Damaged Black America and Preserved the
Myth of Race* (1997). Hoberman has published widely on the doping
issue, and this selection on that topic is excerpted from a longer essay
that appeared in the *Wilson Quarterly* in 1995.

The existence of powerful drugs forces us to think about human nature 1
itself and how it can or should be transformed. As modern science
increases our power to transform minds and bodies, we will have to make
momentous decisions about how the human beings of the future will look
and function, how fast they will run, and (perhaps) how fast they will think.
To what extent do we want to preserve — and to what extent do we want to
alter — human traits? It is already clear that in an age of genetic engineering advocates of the medical transformation of human beings sound reasonable, while the proponents of preserving human traits (and, therefore,
human limitations) are likely to sound naive and opposed to progress in
principle. The unequal contest between those who favor experimentation
upon human beings and those who oppose it will be the most profound
drama of 21st-century postindustrial society. Yet few people are aware that
its essential acts have already been rehearsed during the past century of scientific sport.

Drugs have been used to enhance sexual, military, intellectual, and work 2
performances as well as sportive ones. Yet sport is somehow different. Its
exceptional status as a realm of inviolable performances becomes clear if
we compare it with some other vocations. Consider, for example, another
group of performers for whom mental and physical stress is a way of life.
Their life expectancy is 22 percent below the national average. They suffer
from tendinitis, muscle cramps, pinched nerves, a high incidence of mental health problems and heart attacks, and anxiety levels that threaten to

[1]Editor's title.

cripple their performance as professionals. These people are not fire fighters or police officers or athletes; they are orchestral musicians, and many
use "beta-blocker" drugs to control their stage fright and thereby improve
their performances. The use of these same anti-anxiety drugs has been
banned by the Medical Commission of the International Olympic Committee as a form of doping.

What accounts for this discrepancy? What makes sport the one type of   3
performance that can be "corrupted" by pharmacological intervention?
One might argue that an orchestral performance, unlike a sporting event, is
not a contest. Since the performers are not competing against one another,
deceit is not an issue. Yet even if we leave aside the prominent international music competitions, this argument overlooks the fact that an entire
field of equally doped runners who knew exactly which drugs their competitors had taken would still violate the ethics of sport, which require both
fair competition and the integrity of the performance itself — an untainted,
and therefore accurate, measure of human potential. But why is the same
requirement not imposed on the orchestral musician? Indeed, one would
expect "high" cultural performances to carry greater ethical and anthropological significance than sportive ones. Sport's role as a special index of
human capacity makes drug use by athletes uniquely problematic.

The "doping" issue within pharmacology thus originates in a tension   4
between the licit and the illicit, a conflict that is inevitable in a society that
both legitimizes and distrusts pharmacological solutions to human problems.
The enormous market for substances that are supposed to boost the human
organism in various ways benefits from the universal presumption that
almost any attempt to expand human capacities is worth trying. Technological civilization always tends to turn productive activities into measurable
performances, catalyzing an endless search for performance-enhancing
technologies, from psychotherapy to caffeine tablets.

The modern obsession with performance enhancement is reflected in   5
the wide range of substances and techniques enlisted on behalf of improving the human organism and its capacities. Commercial "brain gyms" employ stress-reduction devices such as flotation tanks, biofeedback machines,
and somatrons (which bombard the body with musical vibrations) in an
attempt to affect the brain waves and thereby increase intelligence, boost
memory, strengthen the immune system, and combat phobias. So-called
"smart drugs," none of which have been proven effective in scientifically
valid trials, are sold to promote "cognitive enhancement."

The never-ending contest between the performance principle and the   6
cultural restraints that work against it blurs the line separating the licit
and the illicit. Consider, for example, the response in 1993 to charges of
steroid doping among Chinese swimmers. A Chinese newspaper responded
that the swimmers' world-class performances had been made possible by a

"multifunctional muscle-building machine" that sends electronically controlled bursts of electricity through the muscles. That is to say, an accusation of illicit performance boosting of one kind was met with earnest assurances that Chinese athletes had succeeded by employing an equally artificial (but still legal) procedure. Few anecdotes could better illustrate the prevailing opportunism in the field.

Doping in sport has been banned for the past twenty-five years, yet less   7
than a century ago European scientists were discussing pharmacological aids to athletic performance without any qualms. The physiologists of that time understood that the pharmacologically active substances they worked with displayed a range of effects: they could be medicines, stimulants, depressants, intoxicants, antiseptics, narcotics, poisons, or antagonists of other drugs. But during this phase, physicians and others had little interest in using drugs to improve athletic performance. Sports simply did not have the social and political importance they have today. At the same time, the athletic world did not yet recognize drugs as a threat to the integrity of sport. The distinction between performance-enhancing and therapeutic medications — a prerequisite of the doping concept — was not yet established.

Condemnation of doping on ethical grounds appeared during the 1920s   8
as sport became a genuine mass-cultural phenomenon. The growth of international sporting events after the first modern Olympics, held in Athens in 1896, created a new arena for nationalistic competition that served the interests of various governments. Larger financial investments and the prominence of sport in the emerging mass media gave elite athletes a new social and political significance, which helped foster new suspicions about the competitive practices of others. Having left its age of innocence behind, sports medicine was now embarked upon a new experimental phase involving the collaboration of athletes, trainers, physicians, and the pharmaceutical industry. At the same time, a new international sports establishment arose championing an ideal of sportsmanship that was threatened by the use of drugs.

Lacking a systematic definition of doping, biomedical conservatives   9
adopted a position based on a kind of moral intuition. Dr. Otto Riesser, director of the Pharmacological Institute at the University of Breslau, was one of the few who understood the biochemical complexities of doping and its uncertain effects. In an address to the German Swimming Federation in 1933, he deplored widespread doping in German sport and blamed physicians for their collusion in these unethical practices. Riesser's response to the problem of defining doping was to say that in difficult cases "common sense and conscience must be the final judges." Such homespun wisdom, though it could not always prevail over the temptation to cheat, was an important statement of principle.... "All of us feel a healthy inner resistance to such experiments in artificially boosting athletic performance,

and, perhaps, a not unjustified fear that any pharmacological intervention, no matter how small, may cause a disturbance in the healthy organism."

The history of doping tells us that our "healthy inner resistance" to such 10 temptations is constantly being subverted by the problem of distinguishing between licit and illicit techniques....The culturally conservative response to performance-enhancing drugs, in society at large as well as in sport, is today under siege as it has never been before. In *Listening to Prozac*, Peter Kramer makes a point of undermining what he calls "pharmacological Calvinism," defined as "a general distrust of drugs used for nontherapeutic purposes." Pharmacological Calvinism, he suggests, "may be flimsy protection against the allure of medication. Do we feel secure in counting on our irrationality — our antiscientific prejudice — to save us from the ubiquitous cultural pressures for enhancement?" As Kramer (and his critics) well know, we do not. Indeed, the transformation of Otto Riesser's "healthy inner resistance" into "antiscientific prejudice" is one more sign that..."cosmetic psychopharmacology" has benefited from (and strengthened) an increasingly activist view of therapeutic intervention....

Therapy aims at human improvement, not necessarily the curing of a 11 specific malady. Precisely because we now treat the legitimacy of "therapy" as self-evident, we overlook its expanded role in modern life. Drugs in particular have a vast range of applications that extend far beyond the treatment of organic diseases. Drugs now in wide use help people cope with such "normal" challenges of daily life as work performance and mood control. The elastic concept of therapy easily accommodates the physiological conditions and psychological stresses experienced by high-performance athletes, and the fusion of everyday stress and extreme athletic exertion makes it difficult to condemn doping in sport on a priori grounds. We simply do not...distinguish...on a deep enough level between the pressures of everyday life and sportive stress. The modern English (and now internationalized) word "stress" homogenizes an entire spectrum of experiences and simultaneously implies the need for "therapies" to restore the organism to its original healthy state.

The power of this therapeutic ideal is already transforming the status of 12 the male hormone testosterone and its anabolic-androgenic steroid derivatives. These hormonal substances have been leading a double life as (legitimate) medications and (illegitimate) doping agents for almost half a century. Over the past three decades, steroid use by male and, more recently, female elite athletes has become epidemic, covertly supported by a prosteroid lobby among sports physicians that has received almost no media coverage outside Germany.

The advent of mass testosterone therapy would represent a dramatic cul- 13 tural change. The use of sex hormones as a "popular nutritional supplement" (as one German expert has put it) to strengthen aging muscles would be a major step toward equating therapy with performance enhancement. And if testosterone products proved to have a restorative effect on sexual functioning in the elderly, this would surely foster a new ideal of "normal" sexual capacity that many people would regard as a "health" entitlement. The certification of low doses as medically safe would transform the image of these drugs, "gentrifying" testosterone products and paving the way for wider use by athletes and body builders....

The use of doping substances is driven by the ambiguous status of   14
drugs that have (or may have) legitimate medical applications as well as performance-boosting value for elite athletes. The "dual-uses" of such drugs make it difficult to argue that they should be banned from sport as medically hazardous....

The gradual "gentrification" of such drugs will have diverse effects.   15
Testosterone products will be more available to the elderly and thus more acceptable to everyone, creating a market much larger than the estimated one million American males who now buy these drugs on the black market. Gentrification will also undermine the campaign against doping in sport. At the same time, destigmatizing these drugs will enable physicians to treat large groups of patients in new ways. Ironically, the criminalization of steroids has been an obstacle to their use for legitimate purposes. At the Ninth International Conference on AIDS, held in Berlin in 1993, physicians urged that anabolic steroids become a standard treatment for AIDS patients and people who are HIV-positive. The potential market represented by these patients already numbers in the tens of millions around the world....

While drug use has been epidemic among elite athletes since the late   16
1960s, the new respectability of testosterone products will put international sports officials in an unprecedented bind. How will the Medical Commission of the International Olympic Committee maintain the official notoriety of steroids once these drugs have become a standard medical therapy for millions of ordinary people? In a word, the hard line against doping is not likely to survive the gentrification process. This outcome of the contest between our "healthy inner resistance" to doping and ambitions to "improve" the human organism will have fateful consequences. New roles for drugs will promote the medicalization of everyday life at the expense of our sense of human independence from scientific domination. It will certainly affect our thinking about licit and illicit applications of genetic engineering....

The elastic concept of therapy will help to legitimize hormonal manip-   17
ulation as a mass therapy of the future. It is interesting to speculate about how the advertising experts will promote these products. It is hard to imagine that they will not turn to elite athletes, portraying them as pharma-

cologically improved examples of supercharged health. One can see the athletes now, lined up at the start of an Olympic final early in the next century, their drug-company logos gleaming in the sun.

Analyzing This Selection

1. How does drug use for improved athletic performance differ from other pursuits of excellence? Do you agree with the author that difficult issues arise only in sports?

2. **THE WRITER'S METHOD**   What is the purpose of Hoberman's historical review of medical attitudes? What does he suggest about the past and future?

3. How do steroids raise social problems beyond their use in sports?

Analyzing Connections

4. Howard Gardner asserts that athletic ability is a form of intelligence (see "Multiple Intelligences," p. 288). What would intelligence testers say about drugs? How would drug enhancement affect measures of human potential?

Analyzing by Writing

5. Explain the cultural significance of a specific sport, and consider the possible national effects of drug enhancement. Select a sport popular for ordinary players and spectators that embodies values people want confirmed by their entertainment, such as baseball, football, basketball, hockey, or golf. Perhaps the sport expresses ideals of physical perfection, team cooperation, control of power, or similar qualities people may not find in their work or home life. Perhaps the sport includes impulses that are malign or destructive. How is the cultural meaning of that sport affected by legal or illegal drugs?

Leon R. Kass

THE MORAL REPUGNANCE
OF CLONING

Leon R. Kass (b. 1939) writes about biomedical ethics. He graduated
from the University of Chicago, where he earned an M.D. degree, and
then completed a Ph.D. in biochemistry at Harvard University. His books
include *Toward a More Natural Science: Biology and Human Affairs*
(1985) and *The Hungry Soul: Eating and the Perfecting of Our Nature*
(1994). This selection is excerpted from a longer article in the *New
Republic* in 1997.

Our habit of delighting in news of scientific and technological break- 1
throughs has been sorely challenged by the birth announcement of a sheep
named Dolly. Though Dolly shares with previous sheep the "softest clothing, woolly, bright," William Blake's question, "Little Lamb, who made
thee?" has for her a radically different answer: Dolly was, quite literally,
made. She is the work not of nature or nature's God but of man, an En-
glishman, Ian Wilmut, and his fellow scientists. What's more, Dolly came
into being not only asexually — ironically, just like "He [who] calls Himself
a Lamb" — but also as the genetically identical copy (and the perfect incarnation of the form or blueprint) of a mature ewe, of whom she is a clone.
This long-awaited yet not quite expected success in cloning a mammal
raised immediately the prospect — and the specter — of cloning human
beings: "I a child and Thou a lamb," despite our differences, have always
been equal candidates for creative making, only now, by means of cloning,
we may both spring from the hand of man playing at being God.

Cloning turns out to be the perfect embodiment of the ruling opinions 2
of our new age. Thanks to the sexual revolution, we are able to deny in
practice, and increasingly in thought, the inherent procreative teleology of
sexuality itself. But, if sex has no intrinsic connection to generating babies,
babies need have no necessary connection to sex. Thanks to feminism and
the gay rights movement, we are increasingly encouraged to treat the natural heterosexual difference and its preeminence as a matter of "cultural
construction." But if male and female are not normatively complementary
and generatively significant, babies need not come from male and female
complementarity. Thanks to the prominence and the acceptability of

divorce and out-of-wedlock births, stable, monogamous marriage as the ideal home for procreation is no longer the agreed-upon cultural norm. For this new dispensation, the clone is the ideal emblem: the ultimate "single-parent child."

People are repelled by many aspects of human cloning. They recoil 3 from the prospect of mass production of human beings, with large clones of look-alikes, compromised in their individuality; the idea of father-son or mother-daughter twins; the bizarre prospects of a woman giving birth to and rearing a genetic copy of herself, her spouse or even her deceased father or mother; the grotesqueness of conceiving a child as an exact replacement for another who has died; the utilitarian creation of embryonic genetic duplicates of oneself, to be frozen away or created when necessary, in case of need for homologous tissues or organs for transplantation; the narcissism of those who would clone themselves and the arrogance of others who think they know who deserves to be cloned or which genotype any child-to-be should be thrilled to receive; the Frankensteinian hubris to create human life and increasingly to control its destiny; man playing God. Almost no one finds any of the suggested reasons for human cloning compelling; almost everyone anticipates its possible misuses and abuses. Moreover, many people feel oppressed by the sense that there is probably nothing we can do to prevent it from happening. This makes the prospect all the more revolting....

We are repelled by the prospect of cloning human beings not because of 4 the strangeness or novelty of the undertaking, but because we intuit and feel, immediately and without argument, the violation of things that we rightfully hold dear. Repugnance, here as elsewhere, revolts against the excesses of human willfulness, warning us not to transgress what is unspeakably profound. Indeed, in this age in which everything is held to be permissible so long as it is freely done, in which our given human nature no longer commands respect, in which our bodies are regarded as mere instruments of our autonomous rational wills, repugnance may be the only voice left that speaks up to defend the central core of our humanity. Shallow are the souls that have forgotten how to shudder.

The goods protected by repugnance are generally overlooked by our customary ways of approaching all new biomedical technologies. The way we 5 evaluate cloning ethically will in fact be shaped by how we characterize it descriptively, by the context into which we place it, and by the perspective from which we view it. The first task for ethics is proper description. And here is where our failure begins.

Typically, cloning is discussed in one or more of three familiar contexts, 6 which one might call the technological, the liberal and the meliorist. Under the first, cloning will be seen as an extension of existing techniques for assisting reproduction and determining the genetic makeup of children. Like them, cloning is to be regarded as a neutral technique, with no inherent meaning or goodness, but subject to multiple uses, some good, some bad. The morality of cloning thus depends absolutely on the goodness or badness of the motives and intentions of the cloners: as one bioethicist defender of cloning puts it, "the ethics must be judged [only] by the way the parents nurture and rear their resulting child and whether they bestow the same love and affection on a child brought into existence by a technique of assisted reproduction as they would on a child born in the usual way."

The liberal (or libertarian or liberationist) perspective sets cloning in the 7 context of rights, freedoms and personal empowerment. Cloning is just a new option for exercising an individual's right to reproduce or to have the kind of child that he or she wants. Alternatively, cloning enhances our liberation (especially women's liberation) from the confines of nature, the vagaries of chance, or the necessity for sexual mating. Indeed, it liberates women from the need for men altogether, for the process requires only eggs, nuclei and (for the time being) uteri — plus, of course, a healthy dose of our (allegedly "masculine") manipulative science that likes to do all these things to mother nature and nature's mothers. For those who hold this outlook, the only moral restraints on cloning are adequately informed consent and the avoidance of bodily harm. If no one is cloned without her consent, and if the clonant is not physically damaged, then the liberal conditions for licit, hence moral, conduct are met. Worries that go beyond violating the will or maiming the body are dismissed as "symbolic" — which is to say, unreal.

The meliorist perspective…see[s] in cloning a new prospect for improv- 8 ing human beings — minimally, by ensuring the perpetuation of healthy individuals by avoiding the risks of genetic disease inherent in the lottery of sex, and maximally, by producing "optimum babies," preserving outstanding genetic material, and (with the help of soon-to-come techniques for precise genetic engineering) enhancing inborn human capacities on many fronts. Here the morality of cloning as a means is justified solely by the excellence of the end, that is, by the outstanding traits or individuals cloned — beauty, or brawn, or brains.

These three approaches, all quintessentially American and all perfectly 9 fine in their places, are sorely wanting as approaches to human procreation. It is, to say the least, grossly distorting to view the wondrous mysteries of birth, renewal and individuality, and the deep meaning of parent-child relations, largely through the lens of our reductive science and its potent technologies. Similarly, considering reproduction (and the intimate relations of family life!) primarily under the political-legal, adversarial and individualistic notion of rights can only undermine the private yet fundamentally social, cooperative and duty-laden character of child-bearing, child-rearing and their bond to the covenant of marriage. Seeking to escape entirely from nature (in order to satisfy a natural desire or a natural right to reproduce!) is self-contradictory in theory and self-alienating in practice. For we are erotic beings only because we are embodied beings, and not merely intellects and wills unfortunately imprisoned in our bodies. And, though health and fitness are clearly great goods, there is something deeply disquieting in looking on our prospective children as artful products perfectible by genetic engineering, increasingly held to our willfully imposed designs, specifications and margins of tolerable error.

The technical, liberal and meliorist approaches all ignore the deeper 10 anthropological, social and, indeed, ontological meanings of bringing forth new life. To this more fitting and profound point of view, cloning shows itself to be a major alteration, indeed, a major violation, of our given nature as embodied, gendered and engendering beings — and of the social relations built on this natural ground. Once this perspective is recognized, the ethical judgment on cloning can no longer be reduced to a matter of motives and intentions, rights and freedoms, benefits and harms, or even means and ends. It must be regarded primarily as a matter of meaning: Is cloning a fulfillment of human begetting and belonging? Or is cloning rather, as I contend, their pollution and perversion? To pollution and perversion, the fitting response can only be horror and revulsion; and conversely, generalized horror and revulsion are prima facie evidence of foulness and violation. The burden of moral argument must fall entirely on those who want to declare the widespread repugnances of humankind to be mere timidity or superstition.

Asexual reproduction, which produces "single-parent" offspring, is a rad- 11 ical departure from the natural human way, confounding all normal understandings of father, mother, sibling, grandparent, etc., and all moral relations tied thereto. It becomes even more of a radical departure when the resulting offspring is a clone derived not from an embryo, but from a mature adult to whom the clone would be an identical twin; and when the process occurs not by natural accident (as in natural twinning), but by deliberate human design and manipulation; and when the child's (or children's) genetic constitution is preselected by the parent(s) (or scientists). Accordingly, as we will see, cloning is vulnerable to three kinds of concerns and objections, related to these three points: cloning threatens confusion of identity and individuality, even in small-scale cloning; cloning represents a giant step (though not the first one) toward transforming procreation into manufacture, that is, toward the increasing depersonalization of the process of generation and, increasingly, toward the "production" of human children as artifacts, products of human will and design (what others have called the problem of "commodification" of new life); and cloning — like other forms of eugenic engineering of the next generation — represents a form of despotism of the cloners over the cloned, and thus (even in benevolent cases) represents a blatant violation of the inner meaning of parent-child relations, of what it means to have a child, of what it means to say "yes" to our own demise and "replacement."

Much harm is already done by parents who try to live vicariously 12
through their children. Children are sometimes compelled to fulfill the
broken dreams of unhappy parents; John Doe Jr. or the III is under the burden of having to live up to his forebear's name. Still, if most parents have
hopes for their children, cloning parents will have expectations. In cloning,
such overbearing parents take at the start a decisive step which contradicts
the entire meaning of the open and forward-looking nature of parent-child
relations. The child is given a genotype that has already lived, with full
expectation that this blueprint of a past life ought to be controlling of the
life that is to come. Cloning is inherently despotic, for it seeks to make
one's children (or someone else's children) after one's own image (or an
image of one's choosing) and their future according to one's will. In some
cases, the despotism may be mild and benevolent. In other cases, it will be
mischievous and downright tyrannical. But despotism — the control of
another through one's will — it inevitably will be....

The defenders of cloning, of course, are not wittingly friends of despo- 13
tism. Indeed, they regard themselves mainly as friends of freedom: the freedom of individuals to reproduce, the freedom of scientists and inventors to
discover and devise and to foster "progress" in genetic knowledge and technique. They want large-scale cloning only for animals, but they wish to preserve cloning as a human option for exercising our "right to reproduce" —
our right to have children, and children with "desirable genes." As law professor John Robertson points out, under our "right to reproduce" we already
practice early forms of unnatural, artificial and extramarital reproduction,
and we already practice early forms of eugenic choice. For this reason, he
argues, cloning is no big deal.

We do indeed already practice negative eugenic selection, through 14
genetic screening and prenatal diagnosis. Yet our practices are governed by
a norm of health. We seek to prevent the birth of children who suffer from
known (serious) genetic diseases. When and if gene therapy becomes possible, such diseases could then be treated, in utero or even before implan-
tation — I have no ethical objection in principle to such a practice (though
I have some practical worries), precisely because it serves the medical goal
of healing existing individuals. But therapy, to be therapy, implies not only
an existing "patient." It also implies a norm of health. In this respect, even
germline gene "therapy," though practiced not on a human being but on
egg and sperm, is less radical than cloning, which is in no way therapeutic.
But once one blurs the distinction between health promotion and genetic
enhancement, between so-called negative and positive eugenics, one opens
the door to all future eugenic designs. "To make sure that a child will be
healthy and have good chances in life": this is Robertson's principle, and
owing to its latter clause it is an utterly elastic principle, with no boundaries. Being over eight feet tall will likely produce some very good chances
in life, and so will having the looks of Marilyn Monroe, and so will a
genius-level intelligence.

Proponents want us to believe that there are legitimate uses of cloning that can be distinguished from illegitimate uses, but by their own principles no such limits can be found. (Nor could any such limits be enforced in practice.) Reproductive freedom, as they understand it, is governed solely by the subjective wishes of the parents-to-be (plus the avoidance of bodily harm to the child). The sentimentally appealing case of the childless married couple is, on these grounds, indistinguishable from the case of an individual (married or not) who would like to clone someone famous or talented, living or dead. Further, the principle here endorsed justifies not only cloning but, indeed, all future artificial attempts to create (manufacture) "perfect" babies.

The "perfect baby," of course, is the project not of the infertility doctors, but of the eugenic scientists and their supporters. For them, the paramount right is not the so-called right to reproduce but what biologist Bentley Glass called, a quarter of a century ago, "the right of every child to be born with a sound physical and mental constitution, based on a sound genotype... the inalienable right to a sound heritage." But to secure this right, and to achieve the requisite quality control over new human life, human conception and gestation will need to be brought fully into the bright light of the laboratory, beneath which it can be fertilized, nourished, pruned, weeded, watched, inspected, prodded, pinched, cajoled, injected, tested, rated, graded, approved, stamped, wrapped, sealed and delivered. There is no other way to produce the perfect baby.

Analyzing This Selection

1. **THE WRITER'S METHOD**   Explain the conflicting attitudes that the cloned lamb and poetic lamb symbolize in paragraphs 1 to 2. Does the use of symbols contribute to Kass's continuing point, or do you think his opening technique is merely a clever introduction?

2. In paragraphs 9 to 10 Kass opposes the three perspectives favoring cloning. Does the full essay persuade you against all three points, some, or none?

Analyzing Connections

3. Kass and Hoberman (see "Steroids and Sports," p. 568) both resist engineering human perfection. Which author indicates more concern about social problems? about moral problems? Which author sounds more insistent about averting bad consequences?

Analyzing by Writing

4. In your opinion, which perspective favoring human cloning offers the best reasons to develop further technology? Take up that argument, and respond to Kass's objections. Even if you personally oppose cloning, the perspectives raise issues that can be partially supported. Develop your best case, and clarify your own position.

FORUM: GUNS AND AIMS

Steve Salerno, *"Leave Him Alone"*
Benjamin Spock, *Should Children Play with Guns?*
Daniel Lazare, *Your Constitution Is Killing You*

FOCUSING ON THE FORUM: How did you initially react to media coverage of recent school shootings such as at Columbine? Along with condemnation, what other emotions and attitudes were part of the intense attention? Were people in some ways fascinated? By what? How did responses of adults, both at school and at home, differ from student reactions? Examine the variety of responses that were part of your experience at that time. Try to uncover how they differed, if at all, from your later or current views about the event.

Steve Salerno

"LEAVE HIM ALONE"

STEVE SALERNO (b. 1950) writes for magazines and teaches magazine journalism at Indiana University. He graduated from Brooklyn College. His articles have appeared in numerous publications, including *Harper's*, the *New Republic*, *Nation's Business*, *Sports Illustrated*, the *Wall Street Journal*, *New York*, and the *New York Times Magazine*, where this selection appeared (2000).

I am just shy of my 25th birthday the night I might kill, or be killed by, two New York cops. It is February 1975. An arctic blast has emptied the streets of uptown Manhattan.

I sell door-to-door for one of the city's larger home-improvement firms. Because midtown customers tend to be too savvy for my employer's bait-

and-switch tactics, we prefer to mine the poorer neighborhoods. There, unconstrained by the limits of conscience, we find we can charge pretty much what we want. I am assigned to Harlem and the South Bronx, where I am often the lone Caucasian on the streets after dark.

Lately, I've adopted the practice of bringing my gun to work, a full-size 3 Sako 30-06 bolt-action rifle with enough fire-power to drop a rhino at half a mile. Somehow, ferrying around such a cumbersome weapon does not yet seem as ridiculous to me as it will some years later.

This particular night finds me driving south from an appointment in 4 Washington Heights. Rounding a corner on one of the back streets, I notice an empty squad car at the mouth of a small alley. It seems less parked than abandoned: front wheels closer to the curb, both doors ajar, headlights off.

Feeling a twinge of unease, I roll up and scan the unlighted alley, where 5 I make out three forms: two white cops scuffling with a black man. In recent years, a group calling itself the Black Liberation Army has been killing cops, two deaths right in this neighborhood. Propelled forward partly by a sense of civic duty — and partly, I suppose, by the same mindless voyeurism that causes people to slow near traffic accidents — I park and begin tiptoeing into the alley. I take the rifle.

As my eyes adjust, I see that the black man is defenseless. His shirt 6 seems to have been torn off during the struggle. He crouches to protect himself from the steady barrage of blows from nightsticks and fists. Suddenly my concern for the cops is replaced by a knee-jerk outrage. I have no idea what crime or crisis might have brought these men to this forbidding place, but whatever it is seems irrelevant now. This is overkill.

Within 10 yards of the fray, I raise the Sako to shoulder level and draw 7 a deep breath.

"Leave him alone," I say. 8

Everything stops cold — much, I later muse, like a videotape on pause. I 9 can see the moonlight glinting off the end of my two-foot barrel, and assume they can see it as well.

"Now throw down your guns." 10

The startled cops comply, and I tell the battered black man he's free to 11 go. After glancing at his tormentors — as if to ask permission — he bolts past me. Mimicking the wooden dialogue from some second-rate gangster flick, I instruct the cops to "count to 20, slowly," before they return to their car. Then I back out of the alley.

Their clattering footsteps echo after me as I toss the rifle into my Audi 12 and jump in behind it. Screeching away, I make a wild left at the next corner, then take a crazy-quilt escape route toward the Bronx. On the other side of the 145th Street Bridge, I pull over to collect my thoughts. Despite the heat pouring from the car's vents, my hands are ice-cold and palsied. I feel certain the cops gave chase, but the situation must have made it awkward for them to call for backup. In any case, the flashing lights I keep expecting, along with the shouted commands and the frigid steel barrel in the back of my neck — none of it materializes. I head for the Throgs Neck Bridge and the tranquil Long Island suburbs beyond.

Weeks pass. No one comes for me. I realize: they didn't get my plate 13 number. (Still, I sell the Audi.) I am home free.

Over the years, those two or three minutes in that alley have never been 14 far from my thoughts. I have replayed them countless times, trying to make sense of them. Usually I think of them as a scene from a long-ago movie or a nightmare I once had. I can think that way until present circumstances intrude: my first glimpse of the Rodney King video. The night James Byrd Jr. was dragged to his death. And now the Diallo verdict. Then the reality of that night comes as a dull ache in the gut.

I wonder about the cops: what they made of me, what words passed be- 15 tween them afterward. They're probably retired now, though I prefer to conceive them as victims of the department's periodic housecleanings. Maybe they're reading this today and can finally attach a name to a mysterious stranger. I wonder about the black man — if all I did was give him a temporary reprieve. Finally, I wonder about myself — why I escaped with my life intact, why I did it in the first place. I like to think I was motivated by a sense of racial justice, but I can't avoid the reality of how I made money in those days. And I ask myself where my black-and-white drama falls in the grand gray drama of situational ethics: a single hapless black man, his ordeal cut short by a white man who robbed scores of other blacks for a living.

Analyzing This Selection

1. **THE WRITER'S METHOD**   How is the author able to look at two separate events in the present tense? Find sentences and paragraphs in which both time frames operate.

2. Do you think Salerno might have done the same for a white victim of a police beating? Does the author think so?

Analyzing Connections

3. A gun would have been an "equalizer" for Morton (see "Sunday in the Park," p. 564). Would he have been right to brandish one? Considering that Salerno didn't know the full facts or issues, did he act rightly or wrongly?

Analyzing by Writing

4. Analyze the ethics of keeping a concealed handgun in your house, car, purse, or pocket for protection in daily life. Consider the potential complications of impulsive rage, misunderstood situations, accidental firing, victimized bystanders, or other results. How do you assess the risks of potential harm that outweigh probable benefits? Explain your supporting or opposing ethical view.

Benjamin Spock

SHOULD CHILDREN PLAY
WITH GUNS?

BENJAMIN SPOCK (1903–1998) became America's best-known pediatrician after the publication of *The Common Sense Book of Baby and Child Care*. His popular book, which went through six revisions in his lifetime, offered parents relatively relaxed advice. When Spock's view on a matter changed between editions, he led readers through his change of mind, as in the following selection.

Is gun play good or bad for children? For many years I emphasized its harmlessness. When thoughtful parents expressed doubt about letting their children have pistols and other warlike toys, because they didn't want to encourage them in the slightest degree to become delinquents or militarists, I would explain how little connection there was. In the course of growing up, children have a natural tendency to bring their aggressiveness more and more under control provided their parents encourage this. One- to two-year-olds, when they're angry with another child, may bite the child's arm without hesitation. But by 3 or 4 they have already learned that crude aggression is not right. However, they like to pretend to shoot a pretend bad guy. They may pretend to shoot their mother or father, but grinning to assure them that the gun and the hostility aren't to be taken seriously. 1

In the 6- to 12-year-old period, children will play an earnest game of war, but it has lots of rules. There may be arguments and roughhousing, but real fights are relatively infrequent. At this age children don't shoot at their mother or father, even in fun. It's not that the parents have turned stricter; the children's own conscience has. They say, "Step on a crack; break your mother's back," which means that even the thought of wishing harm to their parents now makes them uncomfortable. In adolescence, aggressive feelings become much stronger, but well-brought-up children sublimate them into athletics and other competition or into kidding their pals. 2

In other words, I'd explain that playing at war is a natural step in the disciplining of the aggression of young children; that most clergymen and pacifists probably did the same thing; that an idealistic parent doesn't really 3 need to worry about producing a scoundrel; that the aggressive delinquent was not distorted in personality by being allowed to play bandit at 5 or 10, he was neglected and abused in his first couple of years, when his character was beginning to take shape; that he was doomed before he had any toys worthy of the name.

But nowadays I'd give parents much more encouragement in their inclination to guide their child away from violence. A number of occurrences have convinced me of the importance of this.

One of the first things that made me change my mind, several years ago, was an observation that an experienced nursery school teacher told me about. Her children were crudely bopping each other much more than previously, without provocation. When she remonstrated with them, they would protest, "But that's what the Three Stooges do." (This was a children's TV program full of violence and buffoonery which had recently been introduced and which immediately became very popular.) This attitude of the children showed me that watching violence can lower a child's standards of behavior. Recent psychological experiments have shown that being shown brutality on film stimulates cruelty in adults, too.

What further shocked me into reconsidering my point of view was the assassination of President Kennedy, and the fact that some schoolchildren cheered about this. (I didn't so much blame the children as I blamed the kind of parents who will say about a president they dislike, "I'd shoot him if I got the chance!")

These incidents made me think of other evidences that Americans have often been tolerant of harshness, lawlessness, and violence. We were ruthless in dealing with the Indians. In some frontier areas we slipped into the tradition of vigilante justice. We were hard on the later waves of immigrants. At times we've denied justice to groups with different religions or political views. We have crime rates way above those of other, comparable nations. A great proportion of our adult as well as our child population has been endlessly fascinated with dramas of Western violence and with brutal crime stories, in movies and on television. We have had a shameful history of racist lynchings and murders, as well as regular abuse and humiliation. In recent years it has been realized that infants and small children are being brought to hospitals with severe injuries caused by gross parental brutality.

Of course, some of these phenomena are characteristic of only a small percentage of the population. Even the others that apply to a majority of people don't necessarily mean that we Americans on the average have more aggressiveness inside us than the people of other nations. I think rather that the aggressiveness we have is less controlled, from childhood on.

To me it seems very clear that in order to have a more stable and civilized national life we should bring up the next generation of Americans with a greater respect for law and for other people's rights and sensibilities than in the past. There are many ways in which we could and should teach these attitudes. One simple opportunity we could utilize in the first half of childhood is to show our disapproval of lawlessness and violence in television programs and in children's gun play.

I also believe that the survival of the world now depends on a much 10
greater awareness of the need to avoid war and to actively seek peaceful agreements. There are enough nuclear arms to utterly destroy all civilization. One international incident in which belligerence or brinkmanship was carried a small step too far could escalate into annihilation within a few hours. This terrifying situation demands a much greater stability and self-restraint on the part of national leaders and citizens than they have ever shown in the past. We owe it to our children to prepare them very deliberately for this awesome responsibility. I see little evidence that this is being done now.

When we let people grow up feeling that cruelty is all right provided 11
they know it is make-believe, or provided they sufficiently disapprove of certain individuals or groups, or provided the cruelty is in the service of their country (whether the country is right or wrong), we make it easier for them to go berserk when the provocation comes.

But can we imagine actually depriving American children of their guns 12
or of watching their favorite Western or crime programs? I think we should consider it — to at least a partial degree.

I believe that parents should firmly stop children's war play or any other 13
kind of play that degenerates into deliberate cruelty or meanness. (By this I don't mean they should interfere in every little quarrel or tussle.)

If I had a 3- or 4-year-old son who asked me to buy him a gun, I'd tell 14
him — with a friendly smile, not a scowl — that I don't want to give him a gun for even pretend shooting because there is too much meanness and killing in the world, that we must all learn how to get along in a friendly way together. I'd ask him if he didn't want some other present instead.

If I saw him, soon afterward, using a stick for a pistol in order to join a 15
gang that was merrily going "bang-bang" at each other, I wouldn't rush out to remind him of my views. I'd let him have the fun of participating as long as there was no cruelty. If his uncle gave him a pistol or a soldier's helmet for his birthday, I myself wouldn't have the nerve to take it away from him. If when he was 7 or 8 he decided he wanted to spend his own money for battle equipment, I wouldn't forbid him. I'd remind him that I myself don't want to buy war toys or give them as presents; but from now on he will be playing more and more away from home and making more of his own decisions; he can make this decision for himself. I wouldn't give this talk in such a disapproving manner that he wouldn't dare decide against my policy. I would feel I'd made my point and that he had been inwardly influenced by my viewpoint as much as I could influence him. Even if he should buy weapons then, he would be likely to end up — in adolescence and adulthood — as thoughtful about the problems of peace as if I'd prohibited his buying them, perhaps more so.

One reason I keep backing away from a flat prohibition is that it would   16
have its heaviest effect on the individuals who need it least. If all the parents of America became convinced and agreed on a toy-weapons ban on the first of next month, this would be ideal from my point of view. But this isn't going to happen for a long time, unless one nuclear missile goes off by accident and shocks the world into a banning of all weapons, real and pretend. A small percentage of parents — those most thoughtful and conscientious — will be the first ones who will want to dissuade their children from war toys; but their children will be most apt to be the sensitive, responsible children anyway. So I think it's carrying the issue unnecessarily far for those of us who are particularly concerned about peace and kindliness to insist that our young children demonstrate a total commitment to our cause while all their friends are gun toters. (It might be practical in a neighborhood where a majority of parents had the same conviction.) The main ideal is that children should grow up with a fond attitude toward all humanity. That will come about basically from the general atmosphere of our families. It will be strengthened by the attitude that we teach specifically toward other nations and groups. The elimination of war play would have some additional influence, but not as much as the two previous factors.

I feel less inclined to compromise on brutality on television and in   17
movies. The sight of a real human face being apparently smashed by a fist has a lot more impact on children than what they imagine when they are making up their own stories. I believe that parents should flatly forbid programs that go in for violence. I don't think they are good for adults either. Young children can only partly distinguish between dramas and reality. Parents can explain, "It isn't right for people to hurt each other or kill each other and I don't want you to watch them do it."

Even if children cheat and watch such a program in secret, they'll know   18
very well that their parents disapprove, and this will protect them to a degree from the coarsening effect of the scenes.

Analyzing This Selection

1. **THE WRITER'S METHOD**   Readers may find Spock's earlier opinions more persuasive than his current views. Do you think his argument is weakened or strengthened by his conflicting positions?

2. How does Spock explain the violence in American society? As a pediatrician, what child-rearing suggestions does he offer?

Analyzing Connections

3. Spock and Gregg Easterbrook (see "Watch and Learn," p. 467) criticize the influence of films and video. How does Spock's outlook as a pediatrician add to the argument?

Analyzing by Writing

4. Should children and adolescents have guns for play, sport, and recreational uses? Explain your well-reasoned advice to people of your generation who may become parents. Take into account relevant changes and events since 1976, when Spock wrote.

Daniel Lazare

YOUR CONSTITUTION IS KILLING YOU

Daniel Lazare (b. 1950), a free-lance writer, graduated from the University of Wisconsin and earned an M.A. from Columbia University. He authored *The Frozen Republic: How the Constitution Is Paralyzing Democracy* (1996). The following selection is excerpted from an essay in *Harper's Magazine* (1999).

A well regulated Militia, being necessary to the security of a free State, the right of the people to keep and bear Arms, shall not be infringed.
—SECOND AMENDMENT TO THE CONSTITUTION
OF THE UNITED STATES

For decades liberal constitutional scholars have maintained that, contrary to the NRA, the Second Amendment does not guarantee an individual's right to own guns, merely a right to participate in an official state militia. The key phrase, they have argued, is "[a] well regulated Militia," which the introductory clause describes as nothing less than essential to "the security of a free State." A well-regulated militia is not just a goal, consequently, but *the* goal, the amendment's raison d'être. Everything else is subordinate. The right "to keep and bear Arms" is valid only to the degree that it serves this all-important end. There is therefore no *individual* right to bear arms in and of itself, only a *collective* right on the part of the citizens of the states to do so as members of the various official state militias. The right to own the assault weapon of one's choice exists only in the fevered imagination of the National Rifle Association. Its constitutional basis is nil....

This is the cheerful, anodyne version of the Second Amendment we're used to from the American Civil Liberties Union and other liberal groups. But as the gun issue has heated up since the Sixties and Seventies, constitutional scholars have taken a second look. The result has been both a renaissance in Second Amendment studies and a remarkable about-face in how it is interpreted. The purely "collectivist" interpretation has been rejected across the board by liberals and conservatives as ahistorical and overly pat. The individualist interpretation, the one that holds that Americans have a right to bear arms whether they're serving in an official state militia or not, has been more or less vindicated....

No less strikingly, the Second Amendment renaissance has also led to a renewed appreciation for the amendment's ideological importance. Previously, scholars were inclined to view the Second Amendment as little more than a historical curiosity, not unlike the Third Amendment, which, as almost no one remembers, prohibits the peacetime quartering of troops in private homes without the owners' consent. Harvard's Laurence Tribe gave the Second Amendment no more than a footnote in the 1988 edition of his famous textbook *American Constitutional Law*, but a new edition, published this August, treats the subject much more extensively. It is now apparent that the amendment, despite its brevity, encapsulates an entire worldview concerning the nature of political power, the rights and duties of citizenship, and the relationship between the individual and the state. It is virtually a constitution-within-the-Constitution, which is undoubtedly why it fuels such fierce passions.

With crazed day traders and resentful adolescents mowing down large numbers of their fellow citizens every few weeks, the implications of this new, toughened-up version of the Second Amendment would seem to be profound. Politically, there's no doubt that it has already had an effect by encouraging the gun lobby to dig in its heels after Littleton, Conyers, the Mark Barton rampage in Atlanta, and the earlier shootings in Kentucky, Arkansas, and elsewhere....

We have long been in the habit of seeing in the Constitution whatever it is we want to see. Because liberals want a society that is neat and orderly, they tell themselves that this is what the Constitution "wants" as well. This is a little like a nineteenth-century country vicar arguing that the Bible stands for moderation, reform, and other such Victorian virtues when in fact, as anyone who actually reads the text can see, it is filled with murder, mayhem, and the arbitrary vengeance of a savage god. By the same token, the increasingly sophisticated scholarship surrounding the Second Amendment has led to renewed respect for the constitutional text as it is rather than as we would like it to be. The Constitution, it turns out, is not neat and orderly but messy and unruly. It is not modern but pre-modern. It is not the product of a time very much like our own but reflects the unresolved contradictions of a time very different from our own.

Could it be that the Constitution is not the greatest plan on earth, that it contains notions that are repugnant to the modern sensibility?... Because we have chained ourselves to a premodern Constitution, we are unable to deal with the modern problem of a runaway gun culture in a modern way. Rather than binding society together, the effort to force society to conform to the dictates of an outmoded plan of government is tearing it apart. Each new crazed gunman is a symptom of our collective — one might say our constitutional — helplessness. Someday soon, we will have to emancipate ourselves from our eighteenth-century Constitution. The only question is how.

William Safire rather naively suggested in his *New York Times* column 7 that the solution to the problem of "the Murky Second" was to use the constitutional amending process to clarify its meaning. Did Americans have an unqualified right to bear arms or merely a right to enlist in the National Guard? Since the Founders had "botched" the wording, the solution was simply to fix it. This is indeed logical, but the problem is that the amending process is entirely useless in this instance. Because Article V stipulates that two thirds of each house, plus three fourths of the states, are required to change so much as a comma, as few as thirteen states — representing, by the way, as little as 4.5 percent of the total U.S. population — would be sufficient to block any change. Since no one would have any trouble coming up with a list of thirteen states in the South or the West for whom repealing the sacred Second Amendment would be akin to repealing the four Gospels, the issue is moot....

This is the flip side of the unbounded faith of a Zoe Lofgren or a Barbara Jordan,[1] who famously declared during Watergate, "My faith in the Constitution is whole, it is complete, it is total..." If one's faith in the Constitution is total, then one's faith in the Second Amendment is total as well, which means that one places obedience to ancient law above the needs of modern society. Once all the back-and-forth over the meaning of the Second Amendment is finished, the question we're left with is: So what? No one is suggesting that the Founders' thinking on the gun issue is irrelevant, but because they settled on a certain balance between freedom and order, are we obliged to follow suit? Or are we free to strike a different balance? Times change. From a string of coastal settlements, the United States has grown into a republic of 270 million people stretching across the entire North American continent. It is a congested, polluted society filled with traffic jams, shopping malls, and anomic suburbs in which an eighteenth-century right to bear arms is as out of place as silk knee britches and tri-cornered hats. So why must we subordinate ourselves to a 208-year-old law that, if the latest scholarship is correct, is contrary to what the democratic majority believes is in its best interest? Why can't *we* create the kind of society we want as opposed to living with laws meant to create the kind of society *they* wanted? They are dead and buried and will not be around to suffer the consequences. We the living will.

There is simply no solution to the gun problem within the confines of 9 the U.S. Constitution. As the well-known Yale law professor Akhil Reed Amar put it recently, the Constitution serves to "structure the conversation of ordinary Americans as they ponder the most fundamental and sometimes divisive issues in our republic." In other words, the Constitution's

---

[1]Members of Congress. Their statements referred to presidential impeachments. [Editor's note.]

hold on our society is so complete that it controls the way we discuss and debate, even the way we think. Americans are unable to conceive of an alternative framework, to think "outside the box," as the corporate strategists put it. Other countries are free to change their constitutions when it becomes necessary. In fact, with the exception of Luxembourg, Norway, and Great Britain, there is not one advanced industrial nation that has not thoroughly revamped its constitution since 1900. If they can do it, why can't we? Why must Americans remain slaves to the past?

Analyzing This Selection

1. How has interpretation of the Second Amendment changed in recent decades? Which view is closest to your outlook and wishes?

2. According to Lazare, why is the amending process useless? Do you think the process might work for another controversial issue?

3. **THE WRITER'S METHOD**   How does the author deal with his readers' reverence for the Constitution? How does his tone affect you?

Analyzing Connections

4. Consider Salerno's perspective (see "'Leave Him Alone,'" p. 580) on American gun culture in light of Lazare's essay. What other problems or cautions arise? How, if at all, are they addressed by the Second Amendment?

Analyzing by Writing

5. As a delegate to a constitutional convention, you can revise the amendment or propose a new measure that will be decided by a referendum — that is, direct majority vote. Explain your proposal for consideration by the convention. Don't get tripped up by legalistic or constitutional phrasing: use standard English.

FORUM: GUNS AND AIMS

Salerno, Spock, and Lazare each consider guns in relation to a different problem they consider more fundamental in American society. How do their differing contexts and issues hit or miss what is urgently important to you about gun uses? Identify the writer who comes closest to your own top priority, and explain how. Develop your own thesis about guns. Refer to studies, news articles, or other essays to support your view.

APPENDIX

USING AND DOCUMENTING SOURCES

It is important to know how to use and document sources in your writing. Quoting, summarizing, or paraphrasing the work of an established author or expert can strengthen your argument, thus persuading your readers to consider your point of view. Consult this appendix to learn how to quote, summarize, and paraphrase; to avoid plagiarism; and to develop a list of Works Cited to follow your documented paper.

Quoting

Quotes can be especially useful when you want to convince your readers with an author's statistic or unique viewpoint. When you quote a source, use the author's exact words and enclose them in quotation marks. Follow the end quote with a parenthetical reference to the original source:

```
As Amitai Etzioni states, "The millions of latchkey
children, who are left alone for long stretches of
time, are but the most visible result of the parenting
deficit" (119).
```

If your quote is longer than four typewritten lines, set your quote off from the text by double-returning after the last line of text and indenting the entire quote ten spaces from the left. Do not use quotation marks around this set-off extract.

```
To this day, scholars do not know what happened to the
Mayan culture:

          Towards the beginning of the fourth century A.D.
          the Maya people, who had come down from Alaska
          in the course of the millennia, occupied Yuca-
          tan, an enormous peninsula situated between
          Mexico and Guatemala. Around the year 900 their
          remarkable but bloodthirsty civilization was sud-
          denly extinguished. We still do not know why.
          (Toussaint-Samat 452)
```

Do not let direct quotes dominate your paper. Your thoughts and the way you organize them are the most important aspects of your essay; quotes should merely emphasize your points.

Paraphrasing

Paraphrase an author's words when you want to present the details of an original passage in your own words.

Here is a passage from Michael Dorris's "Life Stories," which appears in Part 4 of this book:

> Though he had never before traveled alone outside his
> village, the Plains Indian male was expected at puberty
> to venture solo into the wilderness. There he had to
> fend for and sustain himself while avoiding the menace
> of unknown dangers, and there he had absolutely to
> remain until something happened that would transform
> him. Every human being, these tribes believed, was
> entitled to at least one moment of personal, enabling
> insight.

Here is a paraphrase:

> According to Michael Dorris, the Plains Indian male took
> a symbolic journey alone into the wilderness, a journey
> that worked as a rite of passage and a challenge to the
> young man's sense of self.

Summarizing

Summarize when you want to present an author's ideas in a shorter version, and in your own words.

The following is a summary of "The Burden of Race," by Arthur Ashe and Arnold Rampersad, which appears in Part 4 of this book:

> In "The Burden of Race," Arthur Ashe writes that being
> an African American is a greater burden to him than
> living with AIDS. While he is proud to be an African
> American and embraces his cultural heritage, he feels
> that he is a "marked man," always aware of racism in
> our society. In this essay he cites a recent example of
> the way in which race can cast a pall over an otherwise
> happy event.

Plagiarism

When you write a paper, you enter a dialogue with every author who has written before you about the subject. Accordingly, you must cite those authors whose work you have learned from. If the facts you use are common knowledge, then you do not need to cite a source. When you try to present the facts or ideas of a published author as if they were your own, however, you are committing plagiarism. Remember to always document original quotations and ideas.

Here is an example in which the source is correctly cited:

```
People tend to pay more attention to their instincts
than to statistics. As K. C. Cole has noted, "Children
who are kidnapped are far more likely to be whisked
away by relatives than strangers, just as most people
are murdered by people they know" (536).
```

In this passage, the writer has enclosed Cole's words in quotations and added a parenthetical citation after the quote. In the following passage, the writer plagiarizes because she does not quote or cite her source:

```
People tend to pay more attention to their instincts
than to statistics. For example, children who are kid-
napped are far more likely to be whisked away by rela-
tives than strangers, just as most people are murdered
by people they know.
```

Works Cited Page

When you refer to sources in your paper, include citations in parentheses following the quote you've borrowed or the idea you've summarized. At the end of your essay, include a separate "Works Cited" page, in which you list alphabetically by author the sources you have cited in parentheses. Your Works Cited page should include full publishing information about each source in case your reader wants to investigate those sources.

In most composition courses, writers use the Modern Language Association (MLA) documentation style. Below you will find examples of commonly used types of sources. For documenting other sources, consult a writing handbook or Joseph Gibaldi's *MLA Handbook for Writers of Research Papers*, 5th ed. (New York: MLA, 1999).

Books

BOOK BY ONE AUTHOR

```
Goodwin, Doris Kearns. No Ordinary Time: Franklin and
     Eleanor Roosevelt: The Home Front in World War II.
     New York: Simon, 1994.
```

BOOK BY TWO OR MORE AUTHORS

Alderman, Ellen, and Caroline Kennedy. *Right to Privacy.*
New York: Vintage, 1995. [Note that the second
author's name is not in reverse order.]

TWO OR MORE WORKS BY THE SAME AUTHOR

Gould, Stephen Jay. *Bully for Brontosaurus: Reflections
in Natural History.* New York: Norton, 1992.

---. *The Mismeasure of Man.* New York: Norton, 1996.

EDITORS

Eschholz, Paul, Alfred Rosa, and Virginia Clark, eds.
Language Awareness. 8th ed. Boston: Bedford/St.
Martin's, 2001.

WORK IN AN ANTHOLOGY

Early, Gerald. "Performance and Reality: Race, Sport,
and the Modern World." *The Writer's Presence: A
Pool of Essays.* 3rd ed. Ed. Donald McQuade and
Robert Atwan. Boston: Bedford/St. Martin's, 2000.

ENCYCLOPEDIA OR DICTIONARY

"Muscle." *Oxford English Dictionary.* 2nd ed. 1989.

TRANSLATION

García Márquez, Gabriel. *One Hundred Years of Solitude.*
Trans. Gregory Rabassa. New York: HarperPerennial,
1998.

Periodicals

ARTICLE IN AN DAILY NEWSPAPER

Pianin, Eric. "D.C. Politics: The Floor's the Limit."
Washington Post 14 July 1985: B1-2.

ARTICLE IN A WEEKLY MAGAZINE

Terry, Don. "Getting Under My Skin." *New York Times Magazine* 16 July 2000, 32+. [Use a plus sign when you
want to indicate that there is a break between some
pages.]

ARTICLE IN A MONTHLY MAGAZINE

Vulliamy, Ed. "A New Day for Romania." *National
    Geographic* Sept. 1998: 34-59.

ARTICLE IN A JOURNAL

Grundy, Scott. "Early Detection of High Cholesterol
    Levels in Young Adults." *Journal of the American
    Medical Association* 284 (2000): 365-67.

FILM OR BOOK REVIEW

Cowan, David. "Big-Top Tragedy." Rev. of *The Circus
    Fire,* by Stewart O'Nan. *Chicago Tribune* 25 June
    2000: D4-1.

Internet Sources

E-MAIL

Reblando, Jason. "Re: Lactose Intolerance." E-mail to
    the author. 30 December 1999.

ONLINE REFERENCE BOOK OR DATABASE

"Alaska." *Columbia Encyclopedia,* 6th ed. New York:
    Columbia UP, 2000. Bartleby.com. 1 June 2000.
    <http://www.bartleby.com/65/al/Alaska.html>.

ONLINE BOOK

Voltaire, François Marie Arouet de. *Candide.* Paris,
    1759. *literature.org: An Online Library of Liter-
    ature.* Ed. Peter Galbavy. 29 June 1999 <http://
    www.literature.org/authorsvoltaire/candide/>.

ARTICLE IN AN ONLINE PERIODICAL

Plotz, David. "Barak's Hard Place." *Slate* 15 July 1999.
    25 July 2000 <http://slate.msn.com/StrangeBedfellow/
    99-07-16/StrangeBedfellow.asp>.

WORK FROM AN ONLINE SUBSCRIPTION SERVICE

Pennisi, Elizabeth. "Human Genome: Finally, the Book of
    Life and Instructions for Navigating It." *Science*
    30 June 2000. Electric Lib. Tisch Lib., Tufts U.,
    Medford, MA. 24 July 2000 <http://www.elibrary.com>.

ONLINE POEM

Clifton, Lucille. "wishes for sons." *Blessing the Boats:
     New and Selected Poems 1988-2000.* Rochester: BOA,
     2000. *Poetry Daily.* Ed. Don Selby and Diane Boller.
     5 May 2000. 24 July 2000 <http://www.poems.com/
     wishecli.htm>.

PROFESSIONAL WEB SITE

American Psychological Association. Washington, DC.
     24 July 2000 <http://www.apa.org/>.

PERSONAL HOME PAGE

Charnick, Jason. Home page. 14 April 1998 <http://
     www.mindspring.com/~jason-charnick/jason.html>.

ONLINE SCHOLARLY PROJECT

The Perseus Project. Ed. Gregory Crane. Sept. 1997.
     Tufts U. July 2000 <http://www.perseus.tufts.edu/
     PerseusInfo.html>.

ONLINE POSTING

White, Lamar. "Social Security Reform." Online posting.
     10 May 2000. NPR Online. 24 July 2000 <http://
     yourturn.npr.org/cgi-bin/WebX?13@^78360@.ee709e5>.

Other Nonprint Sources

FILM OR VIDEOTAPE

The Lady with the Dog. Dir. Yosef Heifitz. Perf. Iya
     Savvina, Alexei Batalov, and Alla Chostakova.
     Tapeworm Video, 1960.

TELEVISION PROGRAM

ER. Perf. Anthony Edwards, Eriq La Salle, Noah Wyle, Alex
     Kingston. NBC. Burbank and Chicago. 10 Feb. 2000.

SOUND RECORDING

Puccini, Giacomo. *Tosca.* Orch. Mexico City Palacio de
     Bellas Artes. Perf. Maria Callas, Piero Campolonghi,
     and Giuseppe di Stefano. Cond. Guido Picco. Opera
     D'Oro, 1998.

Interviews

PERSONAL INTERVIEW

Knable, Bobbie. Personal interview. 4 Apr. 1994.

PUBLISHED INTERVIEW

Hamill, Pete. "A Thinking Life: A Conversation with Pete
　　Hamill." *Poets & Writers Magazine* 27.5 (1999):
　　30-33.

RADIO OR TELEVISION INTERVIEW

Rongji, Zhu. Interview. *News Hour with Jim Lehrer.* PBS.
　　WGBH, Boston. 9 Apr. 1999.

Acknowledgments *(continued from page iv)*

Maya Angelou, "Graduation." From *I Know Why the Caged Bird Sings* by Maya Angelou. Copyright © 1969 and renewed 1997 by Maya Angelou. Reprinted by permission of Random House, Inc.

Arthur Ashe and Arnold Rampersad, "The Burden of Race." From *Days of Grace* by Arthur Ashe and Arnold Rampersad. Copyright © 1993 by Jeanne Moutoussamy-Ashe and Arnold Rampersad. Reprinted by permission of Alfred A. Knopf, a Division of Random House, Inc.

Toni Cade Bambara, "The Lesson." From *Gorilla, My Love* by Toni Cade Bambara. Copyright © 1972 by Toni Cade Bambara. Reprinted by permission of Random House, Inc.

Holly Brubach, "Mail-Order America." Copyright ©1993, Holly Brubach, first published in *The New York Times Magazine*, reprinted with the permission of the Wylie Agency, Inc.

Raymond Carver, "My Father's Life." Copyright © 1984 by Raymond Carver. First published in *Esquire*. Reprinted by permission. "What We Talk About When We Talk About Love." From *What We Talk About When We Talk About Love* by Raymond Carver. Copyright © 1981 by Raymond Carver. Reprinted by permission of Alfred A. Knopf, a Division of Random House, Inc.

K. C. Cole, "Calculated Risks." From *The Universe and the Teacup, the Mathematics of Truth and Beauty*, copyright © 1998 by K. C. Cole, reprinted by permission of Harcourt, Inc.

Bernard Cooper, "The Fine Art of Sighing." From *Truth Serum*. Copyright © 1996 by Bernard Cooper. Reprinted by permission of Houghton Mifflin Company. All rights reserved.

Harry Crews, "The Car." Copyright © 1975 by Harry Crews. Reprinted by permission of John Hawkins and Associates. First published in *Esquire*, December 1975.

Francine D'Amico, adaptation of "Feminist Perspectives on Women Warriors." *Peace Review*, Volume 8, Number 3, September 1966. Reprinted by permission of Carfax Publishing.

Meghan Daum, "On the Fringes of the Physical World." Reprinted by permission of International Creative Management, Inc. Copyright © 1998 by Megham Daum. This article originally appeared in *The New Yorker*.

Michael Dorris, "Life Stories." Copyright ©1995 by Michael Dorris, reprinted with permission of The Wylie Agency, Inc.

Stephen Dunn, "Locker Room Talk." Copyright © 1996 by Stephen Dunn. First published in Judith Kitchen and Mary Paumier Jones, eds., *In Short*. Reprinted by permission of the author.

Andrea Dworkin, "Letter from a War Zone." Reprinted by permission of Andrea Dworkin from *Letters from a War Zone* (Lawrence Hill Books, 1993). Copyright © 1986, 1994 by Andrea Dworkin. All rights reserved.

Gregg Easterbrook, "Watch and Learn." From *The New Republic*, May 17, 1999. Reprinted by permission of *The New Republic*, © 1999, The New Republic, Inc.

Barbara Ehrenreich, "Warning: This Is a Rights-Free Workplace." Reprinted by permission of International Creative Management, Inc. Copyright 2000 by Barbara Ehrenreich.

Lars Eighner, "On Dumpster Diving." Copyright © 1993 by Lars Eighner. From *Travels with Lizbeth* by Lars Eighner. Reprinted with permission of St. Martin's Press, LLC.

Nora Ephron. "Shaping Up Absurd." From *Crazy Salad: Some Things About Women* by Nora Ephron. Copyright ©1972 by Nora Ephron. Reprinted by permission of International Creative Management, Inc.

Peter Schwendener, "Reflections of a Bookstore Type," *The American Scholar*, Autumn 1995. Copyright © 1995 by Peter Schwendener. Reprinted by permission of the author.

Thomas Simmons, "Motorcycle Talk." From *The Unseen Shore* by Thomas Simmons. Copyright © 1991 by Thomas Simmons. Reprinted by permission of Beacon Press, Boston.

Gary Soto, "Black Hair." From *Living Up the Street* (Dell, 1992). Copyright © 1985 by Gary Soto. Used by permission of the author.

Debra Spark, "Last Things." Permission is granted by the author.

Benjamin Spock, "Should Children Play with Guns?" Reprinted with the permission of Simon & Schuster from *Baby and Child Care* by Dr. Benjamin Spock. Copyright 1945, 1946, 1957, 1968, 1976 by Benjamin Spock, M.D.

Brent Staples, "Black Men and Public Space." Copyright ©1986 by Brent Staples. Reprinted by permission of the author.

Shelby Steele, "On Being Black and Middle Class," *Commentary*, January 1988. Copyright © 1988 by Shelby Steele. Reprinted by permission of the author.

George Steiner, "Books and the End of Literature" from *New Perspectives Quarterly*, Fall 1996. Reprinted by permission of the Center for the Study of Democratic Institutions.

Andrew Sullivan, "What Is a Homosexual?" From *Virtually Normal* by Andrew Sullivan. Copyright © 1995 by Andrew Sullivan. Reprinted by permission of Alfred A. Knopf, a Division of Random House, Inc.

Amy Tan, "Mother Tongue." First appeared in *The Threepenny Review*. Copyright ©1989 by Amy Tan. Reprinted by permission of the author and the Sandra Dijkstra Literary Agency.

Steve Tesich, "Focusing on Friends." Reprinted by permission of International Creative Management, Inc. Copyright © 1983 Steve Tesich.

Sallie Tisdale, "We Do Abortions Here," first published in *Harper's Magazine*, October 1987. Reprinted by permission of the author.

Alexis de Tocqueville, excerpt from *Democracy in America*. Edited by J. P. Mayer and Max Lerner. Translated by George Lawrence. English translation copyright © 1965 by Harper & Row, Publishers, Inc. Copyright Renewed. Reprinted by permission of HarperCollins Publishers, Inc.

Susan Allen Toth, "Boyfriends." From *Blooming: A Small-Town Girlhood* by Susan Allen Toth. Copyright ©1978, 1981 by Susan Allen Toth. Reprinted by permission of The Aaron M. Priest Literary Agency, Inc.

Maguelonne Toussaint-Samat, "Chocolate and Divinity." From *A History of Food* by Maguelonne Toussaint-Samat, translated by Anthea Bell. English translation © Blackwell Publishers Ltd., 1992, 1994. Reprinted by permission of the publisher.

Calvin Trillin, "It's Just Too Late." Copyright © 1979, 1984 by Calvin Trillin. From *Killings* by Calvin Trillin. Published by Ticknor & Fields. (Originally appeared in *The New Yorker*.) This usage granted by permission of Lescher & Lescher, Ltd.

Garry Trudeau, "My Inner Shrimp." *New York Times Magazine*, March 31, 1996. Copyright © 1996 by the New York Times Company. Reprinted by permission.

James B. Twitchell, "Two Cheers for Materialism." From *Wilson Quarterly*, Spring 1999. Copyright © 1999 by James B. Twitchell. Reprinted by permission of the author.

Ellen Ullman, "Getting Close to the Machine," *Harper's Magazine*, June 1995. Copyright © 1995 by Ellen Ullman. Reprinted by permission of the author.

John Updike, "A & P." From *Pigeon Feathers and Other Stories* by John Updike. Copyright © 1962 by John Updike. Reprinted by permission of Alfred A. Knopf, a Division of Random House, Inc.

Helen Vendler, "Knowing Poems." Excerpted from "Psalms and John" by Helen Vendler in David Rosenberg, ed., *Communion: Contemporary Writers Reveal the Bible in Their Lives.* Copyright © 1996 by Helen Vendler. Reprinted by permission of the author.

Camilo José Vergara, "The Ghetto Cityscape." Camilo José Vergara, *The New American Ghetto,* copyright © 1995 by Camilo José Vergara. Reprinted by permission of Rutgers University Press. Photographs accompanying "The Ghetto Cityscape" reprinted by permission of Camilo José Vergara.

Alice Walker, "Everyday Use." From *In Love and Trouble: Stories of Black Women,* copyright © 1973 by Alice Walker, reprinted by permission of Harcourt, Inc.

Anthony Walton, "Hamburger," copyright 1998 by Anthony Walton. Reprinted from *Graywolf Forum Two, Body Language: Writers on Sport,* edited by Gerald Early, with the permission of Graywolf Press, Saint Paul, Minnesota.

Barbara Dafoe Whitehead, "Women and the Future of Fatherhood," *Wilson Quarterly,* Spring 1996. Copyright ©1996 by Barbara Dafoe Whitehead. Reprinted by permission of the author.

Richard Wilbur, "A Summer Morning." From *Advice to a Prophet and Other Poems,* copyright © 1960 and renewed 1988 by Richard Wilbur, reprinted by permission of Harcourt, Inc.

Joy Williams, "Our Brutality to Animals." Adaptation of "The Animal People." Reprinted by permission of International Creative Management, Inc. Copyright © 1997 by Joy Williams.

Patricia J. Williams, "My Best White Friend: Cinderella Revisited." Originally appeared in *The New Yorker,* February 26/March 4, 1996. Copyright © 1996 by Patricia J. Williams. Reprinted by permission of Brandt & Brandt Literary Agents, Inc.

Abigail Witherspoon, "This Pen for Hire." Copyright © 1995 by *Harper's Magazine.* All rights reserved. Reproduced from the June issue by special permission.

Virginia Woolf, "Professions for Women." From *The Death of the Moth and Other Essays* by Virginia Woolf, copyright 1942 by Harcourt, Inc., and renewed 1970 by Marjorie T. Parsons, Executrix, reprinted by permission of the publisher.

RHETORICAL INDEX

Analogy

Argument and Persuasion

Cause and Effect

Comparison and Contrast

*Fiction

Definition

Description

*Fiction

Division and Classification

Example

Narration

Process Analysis

*Fiction

INDEX OF
AUTHORS AND TITLES

Research and Writing Online

Whether you want to investigate the ideas behind a thought-provoking essay or conduct in-depth research for a paper, the Web resources for *Life Studies* can help you find what you need on the Web — and then use it once you find it.

The English Research Room for Navigating the Web

www.bedfordstmartins.com/english_research

The Web brings a flood of information to your screen, but it still takes skill to track down the best sources. Not only does *The English Research Room* point you to some reliable starting places for Web investigations, it also lets you tune up your skills with interactive tutorials.

- Do you want to improve your skill at searching electronic databases, online catalogs, and the Web? Try the *Interactive Tutorials* for some hands-on practice.

- Do you need quick access to online search engines, reference sources, and research sites? Explore *Research Links* for some good starting places.

- Do you have questions on evaluating the sources you find, navigating the Web, or conducting research in general? Consult one of our *Reference Units* for authoritative advice.

Research and Documentation Online for Including Sources in Your Writing

www.bedfordstmartins.com/resdoc

Including sources correctly in a paper is often a challenge, and the Web has made it even more complex. This online version of the popular booklet *Research and Documentation in the Electronic Age*, by Diana Hacker, provides clear advice for the humanities, social sciences, history, and the sciences on —

- Which Web and library sources are relevant to your topic (with links to Web sources)

- How to integrate outside material into your paper

- How to cite sources correctly, using the appropriate documentation style

- What the format for the final paper should be